CASUALTY ROLL
FOR THE CRIMEA

CASUALTY ROLL FOR THE CRIMEA

The Casualty Rolls for the Siege of Sebastopol and

other Major Actions during the Crimean War

1854–1856

Compiled by Frank and Andrea Cook
Edited and arranged by John B. Hayward
With a foreword by
Vivian Stuart

Published by:

J. B. Hayward and Son, *Medal Specialists*
17 Piccadilly Arcade, London SW1

© J. B. Hayward & Son 1976

ISBN 0 903754 10 X

Printed by
Eyre & Spottiswoode Ltd
Her Majesty's Printers
London

CONTENTS

	Page
List of Plates	v
Maps and Plans	v
Editor's Notes	vii
Compiler's Notes	vii
Foreword	ix

The Army

The Battle of the Alma, *20th September 1854*	1
The First Bombardment of Sebastopol, *17th October 1854*, First Battle of Inkermann, *26th October 1854* and Minor Actions	22
The Action at Balaklava, *25th October 1854*	34
The Battle of Inkermann, *5th November 1854*	42
The Assault on the Quarries, *7th June 1855*	68
The First Attack on the Redan, *18th June 1855*	85
The Final Attack on the Redan, *8th September 1855*	103
The Second, Third, Fourth, Fifth and Final Bombardment of Sebastopol and Minor Actions, *5th November 1854 – 8th September 1855*	127
The Magazine Explosion at the French Siege Train, *15th November 1855*	215

The Royal Navy and Royal Marines

The Bombardment of Sebastopol by the Naval Squadron, *17th October 1854*	221
The Naval Brigade, *1854 – 1855*	228

Appendices

I Complete Analysis of the Casualties in the Crimea; Regimental or Corps Strength etc. Returns of the Name, Rank and Regiment of all Officers who Died or Fell in Action etc., etc.	243
II Chronological Précis of the Events of the War	249

Index

The Army	268
The Royal Navy and Royal Marines	269

LIST OF PLATES

Pages

Sebastopol.	Title Page
Departure of the Grenadier Guards to the East.	xviii
Her Majesty taking leave of the Fusilier Guards on their departure to the East.	xix
Lord Raglan.	xx
The Highlanders at the Battle of the Alma.	20
Battlefield of the Alma the night after the Battle.	21
The Guards working in the trenches before Sebastopol.	33
Charge of the Heavy Cavalry at Balaklava.	39
British Light Cavalry attacking the Russian Guns at Balaklava.	40
The Earl of Cardigan.	41
The Battle of Inkermann. 1.	66
The Battle of Inkermann. 2.	67
The Redan – view of a portion of the interior.	102
General Windham in the Redan.	126
Night attack in the Trenches, before Sebastopol.	211
Retreat of the Russians from Sebastopol.	212
Miss Nightingale in the Hospital at Scutari.	213
The Queen receiving the Guards at Buckingham Palace on their return from the Crimea.	214
Admiral Sir Edmund Lyons.	226
The Agamemnon attacking Fort Constantine.	227
Her Majesty distributing the Crimean Medals at the Horse Guards.	240

MAPS AND PLANS

Page

Map of the Crimea.	xxi
Plan of Attack and Defences of the South and North Sides of the Harbour and Town of Sebastopol.	210

EDITOR'S NOTES

CASUALTY ABBREVIATIONS:

W/Sv. — *Severely Wounded.*
W/Sl. — *Slightly Wounded.*
W/D. — *Dangerously Wounded.*
W/M. — *Mortally Wounded.*
D.O.W. — *Died of Wounds.*
P.O.W. — *Prisoner of War.*

Some casualties listed as wounded in one degree or another may well have died from their wounds at some later stage, this fact in some cases was not shown in the London Gazette. However, to the medal specialist, the initial date of casualty is the most important, as this will substantiate the location, therefore proving a man as being present at a well-known battle, action or one of the little known engagements or bombardments in which the Crimean War abounds.

From handwritten rolls made on the field of battle to their subsequent publication in the London Gazette, mistakes are sure to have been made. Therefore a space has been made available on each page of casualties within this work for collectors notes and possible corrections.

I would like to take this opportunity of thanking Frank and Andrea Cook for all their perseverance and hard work in compiling this casualty roll, which I am quite sure will prove to be one of the most sought after works of reference amongst the medal collecting fraternity. My thanks also to Barbara Wilson for her untiring help, advice and corrections through all stages of this publication.

Finally I would like to thank Vivian Stuart, the well known author of historic novels, for the excellent foreword, to which I was tempted to add a separate index as it turned out to be such an interesting and lengthy work of reference.

John B. Hayward.

COMPILERS' NOTES

The casualties listed in this volume have been compiled from despatches published in the London Gazette of 1854 and 1855. Although research by specialists of muster rolls and other documents may reveal occasional differences to those printed within, it must be emphasised that these are the details contained in the hand-written despatches from the field.

A great deal has been written by historians about the Crimean War, the battles of Alma and Inkermann, the confusion that became Balaklava, the appalling conditions the soldiers had to bear and, subsequently, the many deaths from sickness. This publication is for the benefit of collectors, particularly those who have never had access to medal or muster rolls, or been able to study the relevant copies of the London Gazette. To many the Crimea simply means, at best, a four clasp medal to the Light Brigade or for the non-specialist or general collector a single clasp Sebastopol, which fills the gap against Crimea. To those possessing a single clasp Sebastopol medal it is hoped that these casualty lists may arouse a great deal more interest.

Although Alma, Balaklava and Inkermann have long been the more publicised, casualties in the attack on "The Quarries" and the first and final assaults on the "Redan" equalled the three recognised battles. Minor engagements and enemy shelling also cost the British Army some four thousand additional casualties. Although nearly twenty regiments are entitled to the single clasp Sebastopol medal, their contribution was no less than that of the earlier arrivals, and it was with their help that the siege was finally raised, which subsequently led to the termination of the war. A study of these lists for a particular regiment may, therefore, produce some information not previously available. Casualties are listed regimentally, with casualty and London Gazette dates. For the naval collector, the ships taking part in the bombardment of Sebastopol are shown separately from the Naval Brigade serving ashore.

Frank and Andrea Cook.

FOREWORD
By Vivian Stuart

Author of : THE BELOVED LITTLE ADMIRAL (a biography of Admiral of the Fleet the Hon. Sir Henry Keppel, G.C.B., O.M): LIKE VICTORS AND LORDS: THE VALIANT SAILORS: THE BRAVE CAPTAINS: BLACK SEA FRIGATE: HAZARD OF HUNTRESS: HAZARD IN CIRCASSIA: VICTORY AT SEBASTOPOL.

The incident which led to the outbreak of the War with Russia — known to posterity as the Crimean War — was a priestly dispute in June, 1853, concerning keys to the Church of the Holy Sepulchre in Jerusalem. Jerusalem, like the rest of Palestine, had been part of the Ottoman Empire since 1516 and when the festering rivalry between the Roman Catholic priests — under French patronage — and those of the Orthodox Church resulted in the murder of a number of the latter, their patron, the Russian Tsar, Nicholas I, held the Turks responsible. Lord Clarendon, the British Foreign Secretary, described it at the time as *"rival Churches contending for mastery in the very place where Christ died for mankind."*

It did not seem a strong enough pretext for war but the Tsar seized upon it nevertheless. Aware that the vast, unwieldy Ottoman Empire was starting to disintegrate, he was determined to secure for Russia a major share of such territorial prizes as might become available when "the sick man of Asia" was compelled to relinquish them. Accordingly, with a fine show of crusading indignation, the Russian ruler proposed a treaty, by means of which the Orthodox Church's privileges would be extended to a Russian protectorate over all Christians in the Turkish Empire, and backed up his proposal by moving two army corps to the borders of the Danubian principalities of Moldavia and Wallachia.

Britain and France had long been alarmed by the growing strength of the Russian Black Sea Fleet and its powerful naval base at Sebastopol, on the Crimean coast, and the Tsar's action was seen as a threat to Constantinople and their hitherto unchallenged maritime supremacy in the Mediterranean — the "gateway to the East." With the Turks in control of Constantinople and the Bosphorus, the Russian ships could be kept bottled up in the Black Sea and a favourable balance of power maintained but it would be a very different story were Russia to seize the Turkish capital. A strong British fleet was sent from Malta to the Dardanelles, in order to bolster Turkish resistance; Louis Napoleon, recently proclaimed Emperor of France, prepared to send his own fleet eastward in support and, encouraged by promises of aid from the ambassadors of both countries, the Sultan rejected the Tsar's demands.

Notes were exchanged and there was a furious flurry of diplomatic activity, aimed at averting war but on 2nd. July, 1853, Russian troops crossed the border formed by the River Prut and occupied the two Danubian provinces. Turkey sent an army to stem their advance; the diplomatic activity continued with a meeting in Vienna of the Powers involved, to which Russia was invited to send a representative but Turkey was not. On 23rd. October, negotiations broke down with the rejection by Russia of what became known as the Vienna Note, and Turkey declared war, in the belief that her two powerful allies would follow suit. Neither did so, however, and both fleets remained in the Sea of Marmora until, on 30th. November, an incident occurred which rendered further neutrality impossible.

A small frigate squadron of the Turkish Navy, overtaken by a severe storm, put into the Bay of Sinope for shelter. Sinope was a small town, situated midway between Constantinople and Trebizond and 150 miles south of Sebastopol, which had been in Turkish hands since 1471. Despite the declaration of war, the Turkish commander, Vice-Admiral Osman Pasha, anticipated no danger to his small fleet, since both Tsar and Sultan had announced to the world that, although reluctantly compelled to settle their differences by force of arms, each intended to confine himself to the defensive. In callous disregard of the unofficial truce which, until then, had existed between the two opposing navies, six Russian line-of-battle ships, each mounting 80 to 100 guns, stole into the harbour under cover of fog and attacked the Turkish ships at their anchorage. Within an hour, all these had been sunk or set on fire. Having destroyed the frigates, the Russian gunners directed a murderous fire on the few survivors attempting to swim ashore and their Admiral, Nachimoff, did not call a halt to the slaughter until close on 4,000 Turkish seamen had perished, after which he turned his guns on the town.

News of the disaster reached England, via Berlin, on 12th. December, and it aroused a storm of public feeling, culminating in demands for the British fleet to be sent into the Black Sea in order to protect Turkey from further unprovoked attack. These demands were eventually answered on 3rd. January, 1854, when the British and French Fleets, numbering eighteen sail-of-the-line with escorting frigates and steamers, proceeded from the Bosphorus into the Black Sea. Based on Sebastopol were an estimated fifteen Russian sail-of-line, seven large frigates — 60's and 54's — seventeen smaller frigates and upwards of sixty steamers of various kinds, with a further twenty or thirty gunboats on the Danube. The clouds of war grew darker and more threatening and the world waited expectantly for vengeance to be taken on the perpetrators of the Sinope massacre, but the Russians kept prudently to their own territorial waters, avoiding any chance encounter with the Allied fleets, which were thus left in virtual command of the Black Sea.

Such fighting as there was took place on land, between Turk and Russian and during the spring of 1854 — apart from some spasmodic fighting in Asia Minor — the main theatre of war was the Danube basin. There the Turkish Commander-in-Chief — a shrewd, battle-hardened Croat, who had adopted the Turkish name of Omar Pasha — established his headquarters at the mountain stronghold of Shumla and, supplied through the Black Sea port of Varna, prepared to meet Prince Gortschakoff's expected attempt to cross the Danube and march on Constantinople. The key to the Turkish general's defensive strategy was the fortress of Silistria, the most vital as well as the most strongly held of his chain of fortified towns on the Bulgarian bank of the Danube, 60 miles north of Shumla.

Queen Victoria opened the British Parliament on 31st. January, 1854. In her speech from the Throne, she emphasised that — although her endeavours, in cordial co-operation with the Emperor of the French, to restore the peace between Russia and Turkey had been unremitting — she believed it necessary to make a further augmentation of Britain's naval and military forces. During February, battalions of the Guards and the 1st. Royal Fusiliers entrained for Portsmouth, where troop-transports were waiting to take them to Gallipoli and Constantinople. The British people, clamouring for war, cheered them enthusiastically as they marched through the streets.

It was announced that Lord Raglan, Master-General of the Ordnance, was to command an Expeditionary Force of 30,000 of the finest troops ever to leave England — a force which, in the event of war, would be sent to Turkey for the purpose of relieving Silistria. As it happened, Britain did not declare war until 28th. March; news of the declaration reached the British Black Sea Fleet, commanded by Vice-Admiral James Whitley Deans Dundas, officially on 9th April, the French receiving it two days later. Since only a small part of the British and French troops had, as yet, reached Constantinople, it fell to the Allied fleets to take the first active step in the prosecution of the war. An attack was successfully made on the port of Odessa by the steam frigate squadrons on Friday, 21st. April, and a blockade of the Russian Black Sea ports established. By mid-May, Allied troops were starting to reach Varna, on the Bulgarian coast but before they could march to the relief of Silistria, the Turks themselves raised the siege and, amidst scenes of terrible carnage, drove the Russians back across the river, leaving 30,000 dead behind them.

The threat to Constantinople had been removed without the British and French armies having been called upon to meet the enemy in action and on 16th. July, Lord Raglan received a despatch from the Duke of Newcastle, the Secretary of State for War, urging him to undertake an invasion of the Crimea in conjunction with his French allies. As *The Times* put it: *"The broad policy of the war consists in striking at the very heart of the Russian power in the East... and that heart is Sebastopol."* Although both expeditionary forces were experiencing the terrible ravages of cholera, two days later a conference was held at the headquarters of the French Commander-in-Chief, Marshal St. Arnaud, to consider and plan a landing on the Crimean coast and an attack on Sebastopol. Besides Raglan and St. Arnaud, the French Admiral Hamelin and his second-in-command, Admiral Bruat, and Admiral Dundas, with his second-in-command, Rear-Admiral Sir Edmund Lyons, attended the conference. All agreed in principle to the proposed invasion but the meeting was adjourned to enable a reconnaissance to be made of the Crimean coast and a suitable landing place chosen.

Admiral Lyons, to whom was entrusted responsibility for transporting the British land forces from Varna to the Crimea, had gathered an impressive armada a little over a month after the reconnaissance was completed, chartered merchant ships and specially constructed gun platforms augmenting the ships of war. Embarkation was started on 24th. August and the invasion force finally sailed on 7th. September, landing at the Old Fort, Kalamita Bay, 30 miles to the north of their objective on 14th.

The British force consisted of 26,800 men, of whom 1,100 were cavalry, 3,100 artillery and engineers and the remaining 22,600 infantry. Together with some 2,000 horses and 60 guns, they were ferried across the Black Sea in 27 steam and 55 sailing transports, each of the steam vessels taking a pair of sailing ships in tow. The French landed 28,000 men and 68 guns and the Turks, who were heavily engaged in fighting the common enemy on other fronts, contributed about 7,000 infantrymen. The landing was unopposed, in heavy rain and, with cholera taking toll of them, the Allied armies began their advance on Sebastopol, crossing the Bulgnak River on the afternoon of 19th. September. They made a brave and memorable spectacle when they set out in their ordered ranks and brilliant uniforms, with bands playing and the men singing, the French, with drums rolling, marching on the right of the line in their traditional diamond formation. After a while, however, the singing ceased and the bands were silent. Men collapsed, writhing in the agony of a cholera attack; others started to discard the heavier items of their equipment and, as the sun rose higher and the pangs of thirst grew more acute, they plodded grimly on, leaving a trail of dead and dying comrades behind them, to be given whatever attention the small, overtaxed band of stretcher bearers in the rear could provide.

Contact was made with the fleets at the river mouth and the sick transferred to the ships. From the ships came also the news that a Russian army from Sebastopol was established on the heights above the River Alma, evidently prepared to dispute the invaders' march south.

Prince Menschikoff, the Russian Commander-in-Chief, had positioned his army along a line of hills which, starting as a sheer cliff at the mouth of the river, ran precipitously for three and a half miles to a high point known, from the unfinished telegraph station at its summit, as Telegraph Hill. From here the Heights curved into a ravine-indented natural amphitheatre, about a mile across and half a mile in depth, with the post road from Eupatoria (now occupied by the Allies) to Sebastopol running through it. On the other side stood Kourgané Hill, 450 feet high and rising from the river in a series of steep plateaux, which afforded excellent concealment for heavy gun batteries among which, half way up the hill was a well entrenched battery of twelve guns, which became known as the Great Redoubt.

The plan of attack had been drawn up by Marshal St. Arnaud. General Bosquet's Division of Zouaves and Turks was to begin the battle by attacking the sparsely held cliffs close to the shore, supported by the guns of the two fleets. When Bosquet had attained his objective, the French were to cross the river at the village of Almatamak and attack from the right, striking the Russians on their left flank and rolling it up towards the centre. While this operation was in progress, the British were to attack the centre and right flank — mounting their attack from the village of Bourliouk, where they would cross the river, with Kourgané Hill as their objective — and catch the enemy in a pincer movement. The French Divisions each of 10,000 men (twice the size of the British) were commanded by Generals Canrobert, Bosquet, Prince Jerome Napoleon and Forey. The British consisted of:-

1st. Division – HRH the Duke of Cambridge. (Lt. Gen.)
Guards Brigade (Brigadier H. Bentinck)
3rd. Grenadiers: 1st. Coldstream: 1st. Scots Fusilier Guards.
Highland Brigade (Sir Colin Campbell, ranking as Brigadier–Gen.)
42nd; 79th.; 93rd Highlanders. 2 Field Batteries.

2nd. Division – Maj. Gen. Sir George de Lacy Evans.
1st. Brigade (Brigadier H. W. Adams.)
41st; 47th; 49th. Regts.
2nd. Brigade (Brigadier J. Pennefather.)
30th; 55th; 95th. 2 Field Batteries.

3rd. Division – Maj. Gen. Sir Robert England.
1st. Brigade (Brigadier Sir John Campbell)
1st.; 38th; 50th Regts.
2nd. Brigade (Brigadier Sir W. Eyre)
4th; 28th; 44th. Regts. 2 Field Batteries.

4th. Division – Maj. Gen. Sir George Cathcart.
1st. Brigade (Brigadier Torrens)
20th; 21st; 57th. Regts.
2nd. Brigade (Brigadier Goldie)
46th. (2 coys); 63rd; 68th Regts. 1st. Rifle Bde. 2 Field Batteries.

Light Division – Maj-Gen. Sir George Brown.
1st. Brigade (Brigadier Sir W. Codrington.)
7th; 23rd; 33rd. Regts.
2nd. Brigade (Brigadier G. Buller)
19th; 77th; 88th. 2nd. Rifle Brigade.
One Field Battery. One Troop Horse Artillery.

Cavalry Division – Lt. Gen. the Earl of Lucan.
Light Brigade (Maj. Gen. the Earl of Cardigan)
4th. Lt.Dgns.; 13th. Lt.Dgns.; 8th Hussars; 11th. Hussars;
17th. Lancers. One Troop Horse Artillery.
Heavy Brigade (Brigadier the Hon. J. Scarlet.)
1st Dgns (Royals); 2nd Dgns (Greys); 6th Dgns (Inniskillings)
4th. Dgn. Gds; 5th. Dgn. Gds. One Troop Horse Artillery.
(The Heavy Cavalry Brigade was still at Varna, awaiting transport
to the Crimea; so also were the ambulance waggons and transport
animals.)

Commander-in-Chief: General Lord Raglan.
Quartermaster-General: Lord de Ros. (Succeeded by Gen. Airey)
Adjutant-General: Brigadier J. B. Estcourt.
Chief Engineer: Gen. Sir John Burgoyne.
Commanding Royal Artillery: (Brigadier T. F. Strangways.)

(A number of other Regiments, as will be seen from the casualty lists were sent out as reinforcements, later in 1854 and 1855.)

The British attack began at a little after 3 p.m., after the two leading Divisions — the 2nd. on the right, flanked by the French, and the Light facing Kourgané Hill, with the 1st. to its rear — had been compelled to lie down, under heavy fire, for over an hour to await news of Bosquet's assault on the cliffs. On receiving this, Canrobert's and Prince Napoleon's Divisions moved forward to attack the Russian left. Shortly afterwards, an urgent request for help reached Lord Raglan. The Prince's Division was being massacred, the message stated, Canrobert's had crossed the river but was pinned down and Bosquet was now under heavy pressure and would be compelled to retreat unless the British launched an immediate counter-attack on the enemy's right. Lord Raglan ordered the British line to advance and not to halt until the Alma was crossed.

Under continuous fire, they were meticulously dressed into line, two deep and thus, in splendid alignment two miles in width, the Light and 2nd. Divisions began their advance, preceded by skirmishers of the Rifle Brigade in extended order. As they did so, the village of Bourliouk, which stood in the path of the 2nd. Division, was set on fire and, partly due to the dense pall of smoke which rose from its blazing houses and partly because of the uneven nature of the ground — which was broken by walls enclosing vineyards — the line of advance became broken. The leading brigades were compelled to separate and pass on either side of the blazing village, but both reached and forded the river, to begin the ascent to the lower slopes under a withering fire from the Russian guns above them.

The men of the Light Division crossed the river as best they could, further to the left, some wading up to their necks in water, rifles and ammunition pouches held above their heads. A murderous fire of grape and cannister took heavy toll and many were swept off their feet by the swift-flowing river and drowned. By the time they reached the steep bank on the opposite side, they had become completely disorganised — regiments were mixed, officers had lost sight of their men and small groups, cut off from the sight of others, found themselves isolated. Here and there an officer appeared to take command of any group, irrespective of formation, that he could rally round him. General Codrington ordered the remnant of his brigade to fix bayonets and advance to the attack and they obeyed him with splendid gallantry. Colonel Lacy Yea, of the 7th. Royal Fusiliers, and Colonel Blake of the 33rd., led another spirited up-hill charge; General Buller, with the 77th. and 88th., halted on the far side of the river, apparently expecting a cavalry attack, but the rest went on. On his left, the 19th joined with Codrington and some of the 95th., and the 23rd. Royal Welsh Fusiliers, contriving somehow to keep together under their own officers, drove back the first wave of Russian infantry, aided by the 7th. under Yea.

The British line, ragged and nowhere more than two deep, continued the advance, now pausing to fire into the grey mass of the Russians, reloading to fire a second volley and then attacking with the bayonet. Great gaps were torn in the scarlet-clad ranks but they were filled; men fell under the hail of exploding shells and were mown down by grape and cannister and round-shot . . . yet always there were others to take their places.

They came on, spent and breathless, too courageous and too well disciplined to fall back when their orders had been to advance, with Yea's Fusiliers in the van, close on their colonel's heels, cheering as they stumbled after him, straight into the mouths of the guns. Then, to their stunned astonishment, the Russian gunners wavered and took flight, hitching their guns to cavalry horses and galloping off at full speed. An ensign of the 23rd., first to reach the Great Redoubt, died as he planted the Queen's Colour of his regiment on the parapet but his men swarmed in to take possession of it, only to find themselves under heavy fire from gun emplacements higher up the hill. Despite support from two British batteries, their position became desperate when strong reserves of Russian infantry started to pour in volleys of musketry from above, whilst others launched a counter-attack. Sir George Brown, despairing of support for his shattered Division, ordered them to retire.

Support was, at that moment, on its way to them from the 1st Division but had been delayed by undue caution on the part of the Duke of Cambridge. He had advanced to the vineyards on the south bank of the Alma but here halted and ordered his men to take cover. Able to see little of what was going on through the smoke of battle, he hesitated to risk the lives of his "splendid Guards" in what appeared to be the rout of the Light Division, but he risked his own in going forward to seek the advice of General Buller and, on receiving an order to advance from General Airey, he at once obeyed it. The Guards Brigade made for the river, advancing with parade-ground steadiness, as the Highland Brigade, under Sir Colin Campbell, moved off in echelon to their left. A mistaken order for the

Fusiliers to retire — intended for Lacy Yea's gallant 7th — caused some confusion when a number of the Scots Fusilier Guards obeyed it, but this was corrected and the Scots re-formed and toiled up the hill once more to rejoin those of their comrades who had stood firm with their Colour, borne by Ensign Robert Lindsay (afterwards awarded the V.C.)

In the face of a fierce hail of cannon and musketry fire and heavily outnumbered, the two magnificently disciplined brigades fought off a series of attacks by the main body of the Russian infantry reserves and, supported by two batteries of Horse Artillery, gained the summit of Kourgané Hill in a spirited bayonet charge. The Russians were routed and in full retreat, with the 3rd. Division in pursuit, and the French had also achieved their objective . . . the way to Sebastopol was open, or so it seemed to the weary, triumphant British soldiers. Their casualties were approaching 400 killed and 1,600 wounded, but the Russians had lost three times this number, and the French, comparatively unscathed, fewer than 500.

It was the French, however, who insisted on delay. Marshal St. Arnaud, dying from an attack of cholera, handed over his command to General Canrobert. On Canrobert's obstinate insistence, instead of marching into Sebastopol which was then virtually defenceless, the Allied armies struck inland and marched in a semi-circle round the city, to establish bases ten miles to the south-east at Balaclava (British) and Kamiesch and Kazatch Bays (French.)

Lord Raglan had been eager to follow up the victory at the Alma by an immediate assault, but an assault without siege-guns would, Canrobert stated emphatically, be suicidal; in the French view, Sebastopol was impregnable from the north so — again on the French Commander-in-Chief's insistence — the siege-trains were landed. It took the better part of three weeks to haul the heavy guns into position on the Kheronese Upland Overlooking Sebastopol and to establish army camps and supply depots there. Guns landed from the British fleet during the first six days included six 68-pounder Lancaster guns, fifty 32-pounders and eighteen howitzers. Each had to be landed with sheers and, in the absence of enough horses to undertake the task, most were dragged up to the plateau by seamen, 50 men to each gun. The 68-pounders weighed 95 cwt. and were mounted on artillery gun carriages, but the 32's had to be hauled uphill for nearly six miles on the wooden trucks used for working them at sea. Small wonder, therefore, that it required three weeks of herculean effort before the Allies were ready to commence their bombardment of the city.

During those three unexpected weeks of grace, Colonel Franz Ivanovitch Todleben, a 37-year-old Prussian, born in one of Russia's Baltic provinces, set to work to render the city impregnable to the threatened attack. He was a military engineer of genius and, under his direction, the inhabitants of Sebastopol slaved day and night to repair crumbling fortifications and to construct a four-mile-long system of earthworks and batteries, in which he sited his guns. On Prince Menschikoff's orders, seven line-of-battle ships were sunk across the harbour mouth and the scuttled vessels, in line with the formidable stone forts of Constantine (100 guns) Alexander (50 guns) and the Quarantine Battery (50 guns) effectively barred its approaches to the Allied fleets. Behind this barrier, eight other sail-of-the-line were moored from east to west, three of them heeled over to give their guns sufficient elevation to sweep over the land to the north, whilst the remainder of the Russian fleet lay at anchor inside the harbour, their guns trained on its entrance.

Menschikoff had been prepared to surrender Sebastopol following his defeat at the Alma and had withdrawn all save a token garrison of seamen and gunners to the north, establishing his headquarters at Simpheropol, from which a post road ran into the city, guarded by the Star Fort, with 50 heavy guns. But when, instead of making an immediate assault, the Allied armies had made their flank march to the south-east, he began to pour reinforcements and supplies into the city he had believed indefensible and, by 9th. October — while the British and French were still struggling to site their siege guns — he had sent over 30,000 troops along the Simpheropol road to reinforce the garrison. Throughout the year-long siege, this road remained open, since lack of sufficient troops prevented the Allies from completely investing the city and Menschikoff and his successor, Prince Gortschakoff, in addition to maintaining a large and mobile army in the Valley of the Tchernaya to the north-east to pose a constant threat to the besiegers, were able to reinforce Sebastopol virtually at will.

The story of the siege and the battles fought to bring Sebastopol's stubborn resistance to an end is too well known to British medal collectors to require a detailed description. I have dealt with the Battle of the Alma in some detail because it was, seen in hindsight, the decisive battle. The Allies could, as General Sir George Cathcart claimed when he reached the Balbec, have "walked into the city, with scarcely the loss of a man." Cathcart, indeed, is on record as having volunteered to take it with his 4th. Division alone — an offer made when standing looking down into the heart of Sebastopol's then crumbling defences, which he likened to "a low park wall, not in good repair." Informed by Lord Raglan on 28th. September that it had been decided to land the siege-trains in order to bombard Sebastopol into submission, Cathcart is reported to have replied incredulously, "Land the siege-trains! But, my dear Lord Raglan, what the devil is there to knock down?"

But Canrobert — soon to be given the contemptuous nickname of "Robert Can't" by the British troops — would have none of it and Lord Raglan, whose casualties at the Alma had been so much higher than those of the French, dared not take the gamble alone, when advised by Sir John Burgoyne that to do so would almost certainly cost five hundred more British lives. He could not foresee that the bitter, long drawn out struggle would cost his country almost 20,000 lives and that close on two thirds of these would be lost from disease, cold and exposure, with cholera the major killer.

The first Allied bombardment, intended as a prelude to the long-awaited assault on Sebastopol by the land-based forces, opened on 17th October. The Royal Navy had put ashore a Naval Brigade of 3,000 seamen and Marines, who manned 29 of the 56 guns supplied by the ships of the British Fleet. In addition, both the French and British Admirals were ordered to attack the seaward defences in support of the land-based assault and this they most gallantly did, pitting their wooden ships against the stone-walled forts at the mouth of the harbour, with little effect, in an engagement which lasted from noon to dusk. When they finally hauled off, with many ships damaged or on fire and over 500 men killed and wounded, it was to learn that the land-based assault had not been launched, due to an eleventh hour decision by General Canrobert.

Thereafter the role of the Allied fleets in the prosecution of the siege became a secondary one. The blockade of the Russian Black Sea ports was enforced and ships-of-war — mainly the steam frigates — kept the armies supplied with reinforcements and the materials of war. The port of Balaklava was small and quite inadequate as a base, but it was the life-line on which the British Army on the Upland depended and therefore, at all costs, it had to be held. The flower of the British cavalry — the famous Light Brigade — perished in a desperate battle to prevent a breakthrough by the Russians from the Tchernaya Valley on 25th. October, 1854. Out of a total of 675, 247 were casualties, of whom 113 were killed, but their supremely gallant Charge against the Russian guns and cavalry at the end of the mile long North Valley — although due to a tragic misunderstanding of a written order from Lord Raglan — has become a legend in the annals of British military history. As such, it overshadows the equally gallant and brilliantly successful Charge of the Heavy Cavalry Brigade, in which General Scarlet, aged 61, led three hundred dragoons in an uphill charge and, followed by the rest of his Brigade — eight hundred men in all — cut through and routed the main body of the enemy's cavalry, numbering 3,000, for a loss in killed and wounded of 81.

Sir Colin Campbell, whose "thin red line" of 93rd. Highlanders, 550 men, drawn up not in square but in line two deep, had earlier repulsed an attempt by part of the enemy cavalry to break through to Balaklava Harbour, described the Heavy Brigade Charge as "one of the greatest feats performed by cavalry against cavalry." These actions and the disciplined courage of the ordinary British soldier saved the congested little port of Balaklava from capture but, two days later, the over-extended British perimeter was again under attack by a force of 4,000 of the enemy, this time on the northern ridge of the Upland. Supported by field guns and some squadrons of Cossacks, the Russian infantry, divided into eight separate columns, advanced under the cover of the numerous deep ravines with which it was indented and ascended the 600-foot high plateau known as Mount Inkermann. The pickets put up a valiant resistance but were driven in, until three British nine-pounder field guns were sent to their support.

In the 2nd. Division camp, a quarter of a mile south, bugles sounded the alarm and the startled troops, many of them in their shirtsleeves enjoying a Sunday rest, hurriedly stood to arms. A spirited counter-attack was launched, led by the 1st. Bn. Rifle Brigade and the Russians were driven off, with the loss of some 300 of their number and 80 prisoners, with 80 of the 2nd. Division killed or wounded. Known later as "Little Inkermann," this attack was in the nature of a probe, to test the strength of the British defences and it was followed, on 5th. November, by the Battle of Inkermann — for which, like the battles of the Alma and Balaklava, a clasp was afterwards awarded to those who took part.

It was fought and won in dense fog, a scant 8,000 British infantrymen — including the Brigade of Guards — having held off a dawn attack on the Heights of Inkermann by some 60,000 of the enemy. The confused and bloody engagement was half over before French aid, for which Lord Raglan had appealed, reached him in the form of Bosquet's Division. Canrobert now had 40,000 troops to the British 25,000 but he had waited to ascertain the outcome of two feint attacks on his own position before sending Bosquet's Zouaves to his allies' assistance. Lord Raglan's report of the battle described its opening thus:-

"The morning was extremely dark, with a drizzling rain, rendering it almost impossible to discover anything beyond the flash and smoke of artillery and heavy musketry fire. It, however, soon became evident that the enemy, under a vast cloud of skirmishers, supported by dense columns of infantry, had advanced numerous batteries of large calibre to the high ground to the left and front of the Second Division, while powerful columns of infantry attacked the Brigade of Guards.

"Strong columns of the enemy came upon the advanced pickets covering the right of the position. These pickets behaved with admirable gallantry, defending the ground foot by foot against overwhelming numbers . . . until the Second Division, under Major-General Pennefather, with its field guns, which had immediately been got under arms, was placed in position. The

Light Division, under Lieutenant-General Sir George Brown, was also brought to the front without loss of time; the 1st. Brigade, under Major-General Codrington, occupying the long slopes to the left towards Sebastopol . . . guarding against attack on that side; and the 2nd. Brigade, under Brigadier-General Buller, forming on the left of the Second Division, with the 88th. Regiment, under Lieutenant-Colonel Jeffreys, thrown in advance.

"The Brigade of Guards, under H.R.H. the Duke of Cambridge and Major-General Bentinck, proceeded likewise to the front and took up most important ground to the extreme right on the alignment of the Second Division but separated from it by a deep and precipitous ravine, and posting its guns with those of the Second Division.

"The Fourth Division, under Lieutenant-General Sir George Cathcart, having been brought from their encampment, advanced to the front and right of the attack; the 1st. Brigade, under Brigadier-General Goldie, proceeded to the left of the Inkermann road; the 2nd. Brigade, under Brigadier-General Torrens, to the right of it, and on the ridge overhanging the Valley of the Tchernaya. The Third Division, under Lieutenant-General Sir Richard England, occupied in part the ground vacated by the Fourth Division and supported the Light Division with two regiments, under Brigadier-General Sir John Campbell, while Brigadier-General Eyre held the command of the troops in the trenches . . . (Sir Colin Campbell's Highland Brigade was guarding Balaclava.)

When the day ended with the repulse of the enemy, they left an estimated 15,000 casualties behind them, 5,000 of these dead. British losses amounted to 2,575 and the list of killed included the names of Sir George Cathcart, Brigadier Strangways and Brigadier Goldie. Among the wounded were Bentinck, Codrington, Adams, Torrens, Buller and Sir John Campbell.

Casualties in the day-to-day fighting from the trenches and the gun batteries were also severe, the Naval Brigade suffering particularly badly; and the two fleets sustained disastrous losses in men and ships when a storm of hurricane force struck the Crimean coast on 14th. November. Damage was done to the tents of the men on shore by the high wind and, with the advance of winter – coupled with the sinking of the ship laden with their supply of winter clothing – mortality was high, especially among the sick and wounded. Even those who managed to survive the voyage to Florence Nightingale's Barrack Hospital at Scutari fell frequent victims to cholera and wound infections and hundreds died, following the amputation of shattered or broken limbs.

Conditions in Sebastopol could not have been very much better but the Russian defenders at least possessed adequate shelter from the intense cold and the heavy snow. Their losses as a result of the Allied bombardment – estimated at an average of 150 a day – were more easily replaced than those of Britain and France, whose reinforcements could only come by sea and whose supplies of everything from food to the munitions of war had still to be manhandled to the Upland. The congestion and chaos of the port of Balaklava made even the landing of supplies difficult; a single track railway line was planned but, until this materialised – which could not be until the snow and ice melted – men, exhausted and chilled after doing duty in the trenches, had to tramp wearily down to fetch whatever supplies happened to be available. Fodder was in short supply; cavalry horses, as well as transport animals, starved and the soldiers – infected with lice, cholera, dysentery and rheumatism and fed on a diet of salt pork and beef, which was often putrid – were in almost as bad a state as their beasts of burden.

The Naval Brigade were a good deal better off; they were fed by the fleet and their commander, Captain Stephen Lushington, maintained rigid standards of hygiene and saw to it that men going on trench or battery duty were given hot cocoa or coffee, in addition to regular issues of lime juice and quinine. Hot soup was served to those returning from duty; a drying room for wet clothes was provided and the Navy had its own field hospital.

Throughout the long, harsh winter, Sebastopol continued to hold out. Supplies of grain and other essentials from depots on the eastern shores of the Sea of Azoff reached the beleaguered garrison in substantial quantities, even in winter, via a second post road which crossed the Putrid Sea by means of a bridge from Arabat and then linked up with the road from the north. Convinced that only by depriving the garrison of its supplies could the city be forced to surrender, Admiral Sir Edmund Lyons – who had succeeded Admiral Dundas (nicknamed "D-d Ass" by the British troops) as Commander-in-Chief of the British Fleet – urged that a flotilla of light draught steam frigates should be sent into the Sea of Azoff for this purpose, as soon as the ice cleared. In order to gain entry, the fortified towns of Kertch and Yenikale, whose batteries guarded the narrow strait, would have to be taken and occupied, and the Admiral asked for a comparatively small number of troops to be made available for 10 to 14 days.

Lord Raglan firmly supported the proposed expedition, as a means of shortening the siege; so, too, did Lyons' French colleague, Admiral Bruat. The British Army, however, had been so severely depleted during the winter that only 2,500 men could be spared. Canrobert – who had recently been sent 25,000 fresh troops – agreed with reluctance to supply 7,000 but, as a result of telegraphic instructions from the Emperor, Louis Napoleon, he ordered the recall of the French ships and troops within a few hours of their arrival in the Kertch Strait. The British unable to proceed alone against an estimated 10,000 Russians, were compelled to return with their allies to Sebastopol on 6th May.

Canrobert resigned the French command and, on 19th. May was succeeded by General Pélissier (who later became known as *"l'homme brutal"* for his seeming indifference to casualties.) Within three days of his appointment, the second expedition to Kertch was under way, the British troops under the command of Sir George Brown, the Azoff squadron under that of the Admiral's son, Captain Edmund Mowbray (Jack) Lyons. Its success played a material part in the Allies' eventual victory.

By June, the situation had significantly improved for the Allies; 15,000 Sardinian troops, under General Della Marmora, had joined them and on 6th. 544 Allied guns opened a heavy bombardment on the Russian defences. The Mamelon was put out of action and the Malakoff (the principal objective of the French) severely damaged. On 7th. the French made a fierce assault on the Mamelon, captured and held it; the British 2nd. and Light Divisions, after an equally desperate struggle, occupied the position known as the Quarries (to the left of their principal objective, the Redan) for the loss of 700 men. The French lost over 5,000, but Pélissier — driven to desperation by constant and contradictory telegraphed orders from the Emperor in Paris — was determined to celebrate the anniversary of Waterloo with an Allied victory. He telegraphed, in reply: "In the situation, the complete execution of your orders is impossible. It is to place me, Sire, between insubordination and discredit." He offered his resignation but, receiving no answer from Louis Napoleon, telegraphed on 17th. June: "Tomorrow, at daybreak, in concert with the English, I attack the Redan, the Malakoff and their dependant batteries. I have firm hope."

Pélissier's hopes, however, were not to be realised. 25,000 Allied troops mustered for the assault on 18th. June and Pelissier — for once in the Canrobert tradition — cancelled the agreed plan for a preliminary bombardment. The first French column of 6,000 men launched its attack prematurely and came under fire from both sides; the second — the centre — column was delayed in going to its support and both generals, Mayran and Brunet, were killed. The third column, under D'Autemare, advanced into a withering fire of musketry and cannon and all three, after fighting heroically in the Malakoff and in the streets and houses of Sebastopol's suburbs, were being driven back with terrible slaughter. With reluctance but feeling "in honour bound" to support his allies, Lord Raglan ordered an attack by two columns on the Redan. Sir John Campbell led the left with 500 of the 1st. Division and a reserve of 800 under Lord West; Colonel Lacy Yea led the right, with a similar force from the Light Division, and parties of seamen (60) and soldiers (110) formed up, with bags of wool to fill the ditch in front of their objective and ladders with which to mount its 30-foot high escarpment.

It was a failure as disastrous as that of the French attack; Campbell and Lacy Yea were both killed, the 7th. cut to pieces and the 18th. Royal Irish, who penetrated the Russian line near Dockyard Creek, were driven back with appalling losses, and the storming parties "assailed with a most murderous fire of grape and musketry" — in Lord Raglan's own words — from the Redan.

The British casualties numbered 1,554 — including 100 officers — and the French 3,550; the Russians lost over 5,000. Lord Raglan, broken in spirit by this failure, died of cholera on 26th. June. He was succeeded by General Sir James Simpson, under whose command the bombardment continued, whilst plans were made for a final assault. Cut off from their supply route from the Sea of Azoff, the Russians launched a desperate attack on the French right from the Valley of the Tchernaya on 16th. August, with a force of 60,000. It was beaten off by the French and the Sardinians, who lost 1,700 killed and wounded (out of 27,000) but Prince Gortschakoff was defeated and compelled to withdraw, leaving 9,000 dead and wounded behind him.

Sebastopol's defenders had at last been beaten to their knees; the war with Turkey and her Allies had cost Russia more than 240,000 casualties and, in defence of Sebastopol, 81,000 had died since March, 1855. The French were sapping nearer and nearer to the Malakoff and, on 5th. September, the Allied guns began the heaviest bombardment of the whole war, which lasted three days. On 8th., the final assault was ordered. The plan was for the French to take the Malakoff; the signal for the British to attack the Redan was to be the Tricolour flying from the top of the Malakoff.

The British attack was made by the two Divisions which had defended the batteries and the approaches to the Redan, to whom the Commander-in-Chief had accorded "the honour of the assault." But General Codrington's Light Division had been bled white and both had had their losses made up by intakes of "raw boys, who had never seen action and whose experience of war had been in the trenches, learning to keep their heads down..." Simpson's choice was a strange one and, for no explicable reason, he kept Sir Colin Campbell's splendid Highland veterans in reserve, together with the Third Division, which was virtually unimpaired.

The Redan, despite the pounding to which it had been subjected by the siege-guns, was still a formidable obstacle. It had two faces, each 70 yards long, which met at an angle of 65°, and its base was a fortified line of earthworks, in front of which lay a ditch, 20 feet wide and 14 deep. It was defended by over 50 guns in two tiers, sited behind well constructed embrasures, with traverses to the rear, by means of which reserves could be brought up. To reach it, the assault troops had to cross 200 yards of uphill ground, exposed to fire from batteries to right and left, and then negotiate an *abattis* of felled trees, 50 yards in front of the ditch... a daunting prospect, even for seasoned troops, and still more so for half-trained replacements and "raw boys." And they were met by an inferno of shot and shell as they clambered out of their saps and parallels, the narrowness of which prevented them from doing so in any sort of ordered line. The ranks of the attackers were decimated, long before the skirmishers of the Rifle Brigade, with their newly issued Lee-Enfields, reached the *abattis*, and only about six of the Light Division's scaling ladders were carried as far as the ditch. A party of Royal Engineers, commanded by Lieutenant Ranken, had contrived to build a ramp across it but those who managed to cross were pinned down, forced to fling themselves flat in any cover they could find by the withering hail of musketry pouring down on them from above.

Colonel Unett was killed early in the attack and command of the Light Division's stormers devolved on Colonel Hancock of the 97th., who fell mortally wounded soon after, whereupon Colonel Bunbury of the 23rd. Royal Welsh Fusiliers took over. His regiment, acting as reserve under the command of Major Daniel Lysons, was the only one to advance in line, with bayonets fixed. Scorning the narrow saps from which the stormers had been ordered to start their advance, they came from the fifth parallel in splendid, disciplined deployment but they, too, had to run the same terrible gauntlet of fire as their predecessors and their ranks were thinned before they could gain the salient. Of the officers commanding detachments, only four entered the Redan unhurt — Colonel Windham (later to be honoured as "Windham of the Redan") Captain Fyers and Captains Lewis and Maude of the 3rd. Windham, who had tossed up with Unett for the honour of "being first into the Redan" and lost was, in fact, leading the second wave of stormers and, finding himself without support, sent back three officers in succession to request reinforcements. When none were forthcoming, he went himself and got back safely — but Codrington could send him no more troops and, by the time he obtained the promise of a single battalion from the 3rd. Division, the few who were in the Redan were killed or driven out.

The rest of the "raw boys," their ammunition expended and with no officer above the rank of captain to lead them, began to retreat in disorder but once again they were mown down by the enemy riflemen and gunners and few regained the forward parallel unwounded. Casualties were appalling. In two hours of fighting, 385 were killed, 1,914 wounded and 176 missing — the killed and wounded including 156 officers. The French who, although they took and held the Malakoff, failed to take the Central Bastion, lost over 7,000 (some authorities give this figure as 10,000) and the Russian losses were officially given as 11,328.

But Sebastopol's resistance was over. During the night, the city was evacuated and set on fire, the remaining ships in the harbour burnt or scuttled, the arsenal and main magazines blown up. Waiting to renew the attack with his Highlanders the following morning, Sir Colin Campbell was informed that the Redan had been abandoned. A burial party entered it soon after dawn, to find only the dead and dying and Sebastopol itself when the Allied troops at last marched in, was a city of the dead.

DEPARTURE OF THE GRENADIER GUARDS
FROM TRAFALGAR SQUARE, FEBY 22, 1854.
ON THEIR ROUTE TO THE EAST.

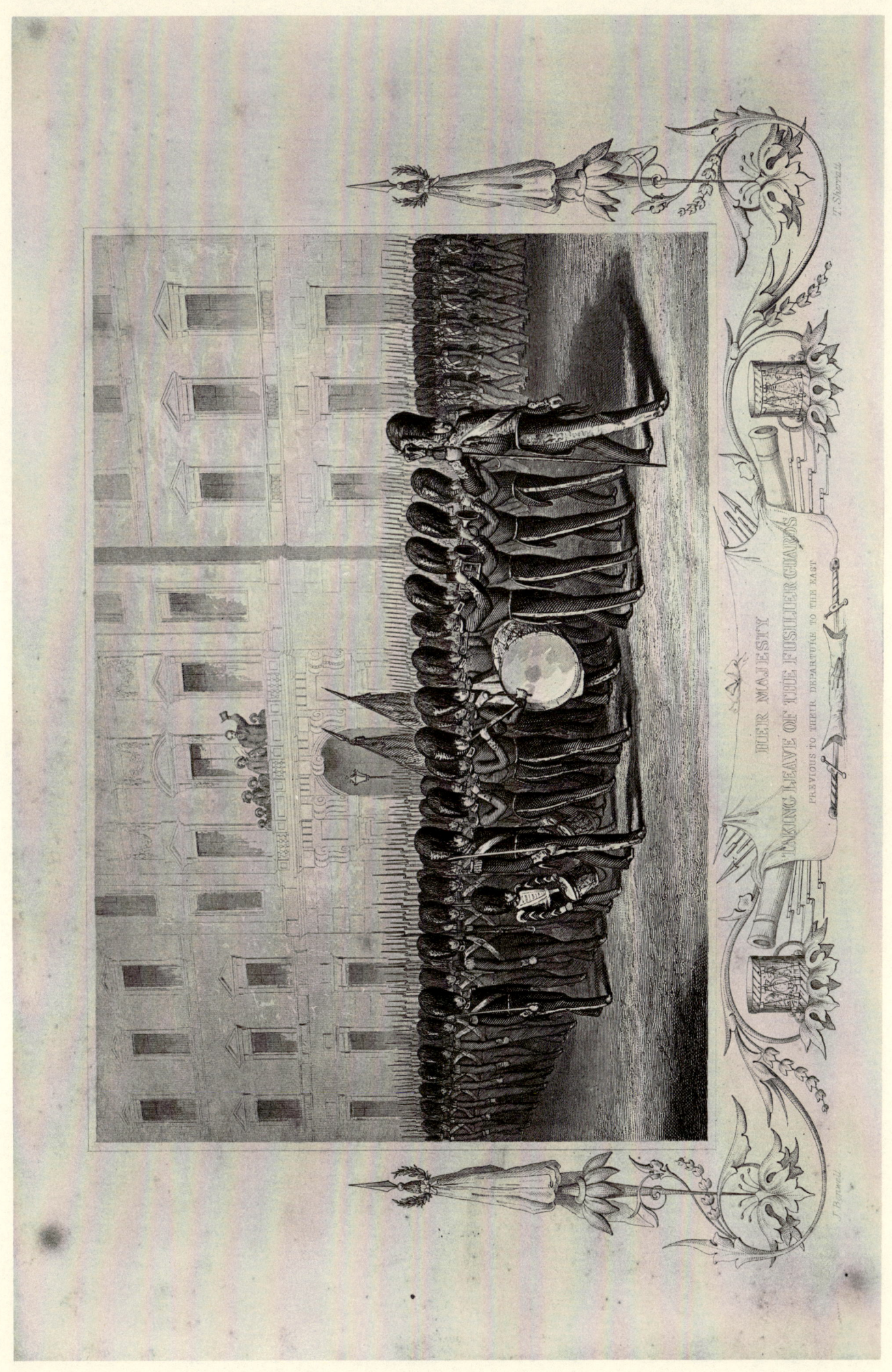

HER MAJESTY
TAKING LEAVE OF THE FUSILIER GUARDS
PREVIOUS TO THEIR DEPARTURE TO THE EAST

LORD RAGLAN,
LATE COMMANDER IN CHIEF OF
THE BRITISH ARMY IN THE EAST.
O.B. JUNE 28, 1855.

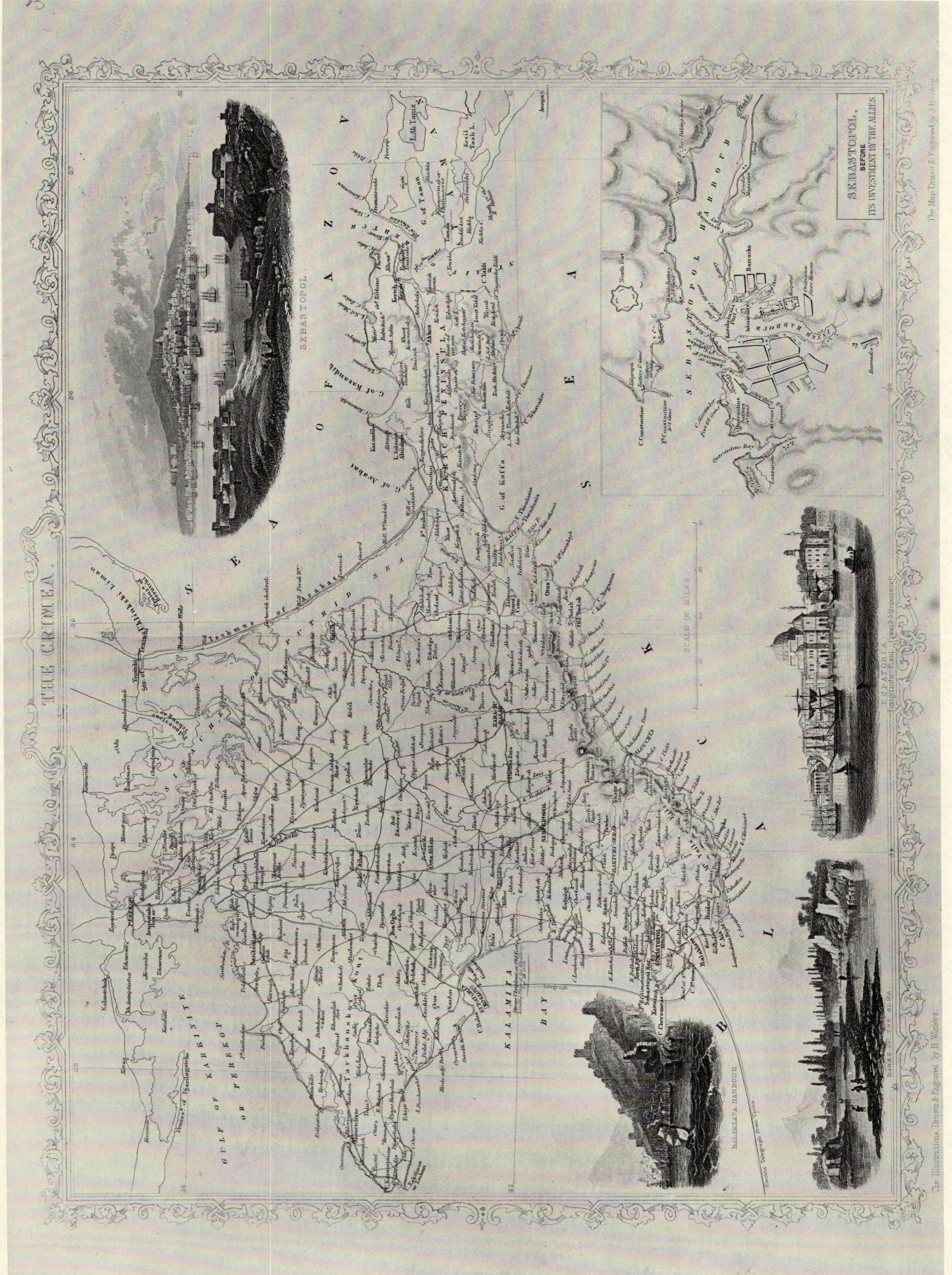

THE ARMY

THE BATTLE OF THE ALMA

The following casualties occurred among the Officers, Non-Commissioned Officers and Men of the Army during the Battle of the River Alma, 20th September, 1854.
Compiled from the London Gazette (Officers) 8th October, 1854 (Other Ranks) 17th October, 1854.

GENERAL STAFF

NAME	RANK		CASUALTY
Weare H. E.	Captain D.A.A.G.	50th Regiment	W/Sv
Leslie T.	Lieutenant Ord. Officer to Lord Raglan	Royal Horse Gds.	W/Sv

STAFF

NAME	RANK		CASUALTY
1st Division			
Cust H. W.	Captain A.D.C.	Coldstream Guards	Killed
2nd Division			
Evans Sir de Lacy	Lieut/general		W/Sv
Herbert Hon. P. E.	Lieut/Colonel A.Q.M.G.	43rd Regiment	W/Sv
McDonald A.M.	Captain A.D.C.	92nd Regiment	W/Sv
Thompson J. W.	Captain D.A.Q.M.G.		W/Sl
StClair A. B.	Ensign Act/Intpr	21st Regiment	W/Sl

ROYAL ARTILLERY

NAME	RANK	CASUALTY	TROOP	BATTALION
Dew A.	Capt.	Killed		
Cockerell R. H.	Lieut.	Killed		
Walsham A.	Lieut.	Killed		
Mortlock William	Corpl.	Killed	E	3rd
Beck Samuel	Shoeing Smith	Killed	E	3rd
Beech George	Gnr. & Drvr.	Killed	B	3rd
Crew William	Gnr. & Drvr.	Killed	W	11th
Denny Ezekiel	Gnr. & Drvr.	Killed	H	11th
Greatrix John	Gnr. & Drvr.	Killed	B	3rd
Hamilton John	Gnr. & Drvr.	Killed	B	3rd
Laing Alexander	Wheeler	Killed	G	11th
Perkins Joseph	Driver	Killed	C	R.H.A.
Martin Samuel	Sergt.	Wounded	A	8th
Wass J.	Sergt.	Wounded	A	8th
Reid James	Corpl.	Wounded	B	3rd
Jones J.	Bombardier	Wounded	G	11th

NOTES

The Battle of the Alma

ROYAL ARTILLERY

NAME	RANK	CASUALTY	TROOP	BATTALION
Bradley Henry	Gnr. & Drvr.	Wounded	E	3rd
Brennan Patrick	Gnr. & Drvr.	Wounded	E	3rd
Copeland George	Gnr. & Drvr.	Wounded	W	11th
Griller, James	Gnr. & Drvr.	Wounded	B	3rd
Harris Henry	Gnr. & Drvr.	Wounded	E	3rd
Holland John	Gnr. & Drvr.	Wounded	W	11th
McCann J. B.	Gnr. & Drvr.	Wounded	B	3rd
Paisley James	Gnr. & Drvr.	Wounded	A	8th
Poole G.	Gnr. & Drvr.	Wounded	G	11th
Radcliffe George	Gnr. & Drvr.	Wounded	E	3rd
Rea G.	Gnr. & Drvr.	Wounded	G	11th
Robinson Andrew	Gnr. & Drvr.	Wounded	B	3rd
Wadsworth Edward	Gnr. & Drvr.	Wounded	B	3rd
Wallis John	Gnr. & Drvr.	Wounded	B	3rd

ROYAL ENGINEERS

NAME	RANK	CASUALTY
Teesdale H.	Lieut.	Wounded

3rd BATTALION GRENADIER GUARDS

NAME	RANK	CASUALTY	NAME	RANK	CASUALTY
Baker James	Pte.	Killed	Cropley Jeremiah	Pte.	Wounded
Broad James	Pte.	Killed	Cunliffe Thomas	Pte.	Wounded
Champion John	Pte.	Killed	Curzons Henry	Pte.	Wounded
Firman Henry	Pte.	Killed	Drew Robert	Pte.	Wounded
Fishlock Noah	Pte.	Killed	Durber John	Pte.	Wounded
Gillard Charles	Pte.	Killed	Dury William	Pte.	Wounded
Gorton William	Pte.	Killed	Entwistle John	Pte.	Wounded
Gosling Noah	Pte.	Killed	Farmer Robert	Pte.	Wounded
Palmer Daniel	Pte.	Killed	Farmer William	Pte.	Wounded
Rowe William	Pte.	Killed	Fellowes William	Pte.	Wounded
Smith Nehemiah	Pte.	Killed	Felsham George	Pte.	Wounded
Percy Hon. H.	Lt/Col.	Wounded	George Joseph	Pte.	Wounded
Burgoyne J. M.	Lieut.	Wounded	Gerrett Robert	Pte.	Wounded
Hamilton R.	Lieut.	Wounded	Gibling Joseph	Pte.	Wounded
Coles Joseph	Sergt.	Wounded	Goodenham Charles	Pte.	Wounded
Cranfield John	Sergt.	Wounded	Griffiths Edward	Pte.	Wounded
Russell Henry	Sergt.	Wounded	Hall Launcelot	Pte.	Wounded
Edmundson Thomas	Corpl.	Wounded	Harrison John	Pte.	Wounded
Burrow Thomas	Corpl.	Wounded	Harter Thomas	Pte.	Wounded
Martin Henry	Corpl.	Wounded	Hatter Charles	Pte.	Wounded
Massey Benjamin	Corpl.	Wounded	Hawkins Isaiah	Pte.	Wounded
Rodger William	Corpl.	Wounded	Hett George	Pte.	Wounded
Alexander John	Pte.	Wounded	Hill Joseph	Pte.	Wounded
Alling William	Pte.	Wounded	Hilton James	Pte.	Wounded
Badcock Henry	Pte.	Wounded	Hope Henry	Pte.	Wounded
Baker Robert	Pte.	Wounded	James Frederick	Pte.	Wounded
Banting Thomas	Pte.	Wounded	Kelly James	Pte.	Wounded
Barrett Samuel	Pte.	Wounded	Lamb Henry	Pte.	Wounded
Beatson William	Pte.	Wounded	Leary Thomas	Pte.	Wounded
Bevers John	Pte.	Wounded	Leat William	Pte.	Wounded
Brettan George	Pte.	Wounded	Lewis Giles	Pte.	Wounded
Buck George	Pte.	Wounded	Limgeson James	Pte.	Wounded
Buck James	Pte.	Wounded	Little Samuel	Pte.	Wounded
Bull Elias	Pte.	Wounded	Margetts Richard	Pte.	Wounded
Burrow Thomas	Pte.	Wounded	Marshall George	Pte.	Wounded
Butler John	Pte.	Wounded	Martin James	Pte.	Wounded
Carter William	Pte.	Wounded	Martin John	Pte.	Wounded
Coles Henry	Pte.	Wounded	Martin Robert	Pte.	Wounded

NOTES

The Battle of the Alma

3rd BATTALION GRENADIER GUARDS

NAME	RANK	CASUALTY	NAME	RANK	CASUALTY
Maskall George	Pte.	Wounded	Salter Henry	Pte.	Wounded
Men William	Pte.	Wounded	Shaw Charles	Pte.	Wounded
Miller Samuel	Pte.	Wounded	Shergold Thomas	Pte.	Wounded
Minter William	Pte.	Wounded	Skinner William P.	Pte.	Wounded
Mitchell William	Pte.	Wounded	Smith George	Pte.	Wounded
Moodey William	Pte.	Wounded	Smith James (1st)	Pte.	Wounded
Moore William	Pte.	Wounded	Smith James	Pte.	Wounded
Moulden James	Pte.	Wounded	Smith Robert	Pte.	Wounded
Muffit William	Pte.	Wounded	Smith Thomas	Pte.	Wounded
Naginton James	Pte.	Wounded	Spencer George	Pte.	Wounded
Nichols Samuel	Pte.	Wounded	Steel William	Pte.	Wounded
Oates George	Pte.	Wounded	Stone William	Pte.	Wounded
Palmer William	Pte.	Wounded	Stone Thomas	Pte.	Wounded
Panting Edward	Pte.	Wounded	Stur James	Pte.	Wounded
Pearce James	Pte.	Wounded	Talbot James	Pte.	Wounded
Pitcher Robert	Pte.	Wounded	Tomlinson Joseph	Pte.	Wounded
Pithouse Thomas	Pte.	Wounded	Varney James	Pte.	Wounded
Powell John	Pte.	Wounded	West John	Pte.	Wounded
Poynter William	Pte.	Wounded	Wheeler George	Pte.	Wounded
Rawlinson James	Pte.	Wounded	Wilmott Abraham	Pte.	Wounded
Reading Thomas	Pte.	Wounded	Wirdman Robert	Pte.	Wounded
Reeves Henry	Pte.	Wounded	Wood John	Pte.	Wounded
Rickets John	Pte.	Wounded	Woodman Austin	Pte.	Wounded
Riley Thomas	Pte.	Wounded	Woodward John	Pte.	Wounded
Robey Elijah	Pte.	Wounded	Wright Francis	Pte.	Wounded
Robins William	Pte.	Wounded	Young Jacob	Pte.	Wounded
Rolfe Thomas	Pte.	Wounded	Young John	Pte.	Wounded

1st BATTALION COLDSTREAM GUARDS

NAME	RANK	CASUALTY	NAME	RANK	CASUALTY
Baring C.	Lieut.	Wounded	Lilley James	Pte.	Wounded
Bess George	Pte.	Wounded	Milburn Robert	Pte.	Wounded
Butcher Charles	Pte.	Wounded	Newell William	Pte.	Wounded
Clatworthy William	Pte.	Wounded	Nicholas William	Pte.	Wounded
Clow David	Pte.	Wounded	Rutter John	Pte.	Wounded
Creagh Edward M.	Pte.	Wounded	Scrutton William	Pte.	Wounded
Farrant William	Pte.	Wounded	Smith William	Pte.	Wounded
Flint Jonathan	Pte.	Wounded	Southcott Frederick	Pte.	Wounded
Groom John	Pte.	Wounded	Spark William	Pte.	Wounded
Hatton John	Pte.	Wounded	Sproat William	Pte.	Wounded
Holland George	Pte.	Wounded	Warman William	Pte.	Wounded
Hopkins Joseph	Pte.	Wounded	Winter Robert	Pte.	Wounded
Jenkinson Edmund	Pte.	Wounded	Woods Charles	Pte.	Wounded
Jeffries Nebr.	Pte.	Wounded	Yeo John	Pte.	Wounded

1st BATTALION SCOTS FUSILIER GUARDS

NAME	RANK	CASUALTY	NAME	RANK	CASUALTY
Lane Joseph	Sergt.	Killed	Miln William	Pte.	Killed
Lane Nicholas	Sergt.	Killed	Payne George	Pte.	Killed
Robbie Francis	Sergt.	Killed	Richardson John	Pte.	Killed
Blythe John	Corpl.	Killed	Satchwell George	Pte.	Killed
Dickson Alexander	Corpl.	Killed	Bailey William	Corpl.	D.O.W.
Seaton James	Corpl.	Killed	Bond Isaac	Corpl.	Killed
Aird Alexander	Pte.	Killed	Cobden Henry	Pte.	Killed
Blake Frederick	Pte.	Killed	Cole Francis	Pte.	Killed
Davis George (3665)	Pte.	Killed	Duff George	Pte.	Killed
Forbes Robert	Pte.	Killed	Martin William (3429)	Pte.	Killed
Hogg Thomas W.	Pte.	Killed	Moore Frederick	Pte.	Killed
Main John	Pte.	Killed	Ogilvie J. S.	Pte.	Killed

NOTES

The Battle of the Alma
1st BATTALION SCOTS FUSILIER GUARDS

NAME	RANK	CASUALTY	NAME	RANK	CASUALTY
Pelham Edward	Pte.	Killed	Don Robert	Pte.	Wounded
Phillips Thomas	Pte.	Killed	Douglas William	Pte.	Wounded
Stanley John	Pte.	Killed	Duncan George	Pte.	Wounded
Stokes William	Pte.	Killed	Eskins Warin	Pte.	Wounded
Smith Archibald	Pte.	Killed	Ester George	Pte.	Wounded
Berkeley C. A.	Lt/Col.	Wounded	Ferguson Hugh	Pte.	Wounded
Dalrymple J. H.	Lt/Col.	Wounded	Findlay James	Pte.	Wounded
Haygarth F.	Lt/Col.	Wounded	Flint John	Pte.	Wounded
Hepburn H. P.	Lt/Col.	Wounded	Fripp Brice	Pte.	Wounded
Astley J. D.	Capt.	Wounded	Gatehouse John	Pte.	Wounded
Buckley D. F.	Capt.	Wounded	Geddes Robert	Pte.	Wounded
Bulwer W. G.	Capt.	Wounded	Gibson James	Pte.	Wounded
Chewton Lord	Capt.	Wounded	Gordon Thomas	Pte.	Wounded
Gipps R.	Capt.	Wounded	Hannah Alexander	Pte.	Wounded
Annesley Hon. H.	Lieut.	Wounded	Harris David	Pte.	Wounded
Ennismore Lord	Lieut.	Wounded	Henry James	Pte.	Wounded
Bye Richard	Sergt.	Wounded	Hill William	Pte.	Wounded
Chalmers Peter	Sergt.	Wounded	Hiscock John	Pte.	Wounded
Charleston James	Sergt.	Wounded	Hobbs John	Pte.	Wounded
Frost William	Sergt.	Wounded	Holloway Robert	Pte.	Wounded
Gair Andrew	Sergt.	Wounded	Johnstone John	Pte.	Wounded
Jones Morgan	Sergt.	Wounded	Johnstone Robert	Pte.	Wounded
McGregor William	Sergt.	Wounded	Jones Richard	Pte.	Wounded
McKeckine James	Sergt.	Wounded	Joy William	Pte.	Wounded
McLeod George	Sergt.	Wounded	Lawrence Henry (Jnr)	Pte.	Wounded
Seers James	Sergt.	Wounded	Lawrence William	Pte.	Wounded
Stewart George	Sergt.	Wounded	Leslie George	Pte.	Wounded
Stratton John	Sergt.	Wounded	Lindores George	Pte.	Wounded
Vatter John	Sergt.	Wounded	Lindsay Daniel	Pte.	Wounded
Adams James	Corpl.	Wounded	Little Edward	Pte.	Wounded
Cameron Daniel	Corpl.	Wounded	Loader Francis	Pte.	Wounded
Craw John	Corpl.	Wounded	McChire William	Pte.	Wounded
Fall Joseph	Corpl.	Wounded	McGhee James	Pte.	Wounded
Gilchrist Colin	Corpl.	Wounded	McKerro Patrick	Pte.	Wounded
Millard James	Corpl.	Wounded	McLagan William	Pte.	Wounded
Poynty Joseph	Corpl.	Wounded	McLeary Thomas	Pte.	Wounded
Smith George	Corpl.	Wounded	McLeod George	Pte.	Wounded
Stewart William	Corpl.	Wounded	McNeil William	Pte.	Wounded
Anderson Alexander	Drummer	Wounded	McPherson William	Pte.	Wounded
Adkins Joseph	Pte.	Wounded	McRoberts Thomas	Pte.	Wounded
Alexander James	Pte.	Wounded	Mesher James	Pte.	Wounded
Anderson David	Pte.	Wounded	Mitchell John	Pte.	Wounded
Austins John	Pte.	Wounded	Moore John R.	Pte.	Wounded
Ayling Stephen	Pte.	Wounded	Morris John	Pte.	Wounded
Balcanquhal Thomas	Pte.	Wounded	Morton Andrew	Pte.	Wounded
Biddlecombe George	Pte.	Wounded	Munsie James	Pte.	Wounded
Black Alexander	Pte.	Wounded	Oak James	Pte.	Wounded
Bordon Robert	Pte.	Wounded	Organ Henry	Pte.	Wounded
Bowley Charles	Pte.	Wounded	Owen Thomas	Pte.	Wounded
Boyd William	Pte.	Wounded	Owler George	Pte.	Wounded
Brenner Andrew	Pte.	Wounded	Page Joseph	Pte.	Wounded
Brodie Andrew	Pte.	Wounded	Paine Thomas	Pte.	Wounded
Brown George	Pte.	Wounded	Parker John	Pte.	Wounded
Bruce Sinclair	Pte.	Wounded	Parry Thomas	Pte.	Wounded
Burns John	Pte.	Wounded	Payne James	Pte.	Wounded
Bywater Thomas	Pte.	Wounded	Phillips Thomas (5 Coy)	Pte.	Wounded
Cameron John	Pte.	Wounded	Presdie Thomas	Pte.	Wounded
Cameron John (3rd Coy)	Pte.	Wounded	Pulley George	Pte.	Wounded
Carpenter Alfred	Pte.	Wounded	Raffil Peter	Pte.	Wounded
Clinton George	Pte.	Wounded	Richens Elijah	Pte.	Wounded
Corben John	Pte.	Wounded	Rogers Frederick W.	Pte.	Wounded
Coulter Joseph	Pte.	Wounded	Ross Alexander	Pte.	Wounded
Craigie Peter	Pte.	Wounded	Ross Charles	Pte.	Wounded
Cross George	Pte.	Wounded	Saywell George	Pte.	Wounded
Dare Daniel	Pte.	Wounded	Scott James	Pte.	Wounded

NOTES

The Battle of the Alma

1st BATTALION SCOTS FUSILIER GUARDS

NAME	RANK	CASUALTY	NAME	RANK	CASUALTY
Scott William	Pte.	Wounded	Watts George	Pte.	Wounded
Shaw Alexander	Pte.	Wounded	Weller Charles	Pte.	Wounded
Sked George	Pte.	Wounded	Whitton Robert	Pte.	Wounded
Slow John	Pte.	Wounded	Willson Thomas	Pte.	Wounded
Smith Richard	Pte.	Wounded	Wilson James	Pte.	Wounded
Smith Robert	Pte.	Wounded	Wood Thomas	Pte.	Wounded
Walker James	Pte.	Wounded	Workman Joseph	Pte.	Wounded
Walters Thomas	Pte.	Wounded	Wylie James	Pte.	Wounded
Ward John	Pte.	Wounded	Young James	Pte.	Wounded
Wariner George	Pte.	Wounded	Young John	Pte.	Wounded
Warren James	Pte.	Wounded			

4th REGIMENT OF FOOT

NAME	RANK	CASUALTY	NAME	RANK	CASUALTY
Cobbe H. C.	Lt/Col.	Wounded	Silverthorn John	Pte.	Wounded
Thompson G. L.	Capt.	Wounded	Warden Leonard	Pte.	Wounded
Bright James	Pte.	Wounded	Williams John	Pte.	Wounded
Corry Michael	Pte.	Wounded	Cordon Garret	Pte.	Missing
Hubison Robert	Pte.	Wounded	Curley Michael	Pte.	Missing
Meakle Michael	Pte.	Wounded	Kennedy William	Pte.	Missing
Saunders Thomas	Pte.	Wounded			

7th REGIMENT OF FOOT

NAME	RANK	CASUALTY	NAME	RANK	CASUALTY
Monck Hon. W.	Capt.	Killed	Thompson Abraham	Pte.	Killed
Purcell Joshua	Col/Sgt.	Killed	Tyrrell Michael	Pte.	Killed
Everett Eli	Sergt	Killed	Wilson Henry	Pte.	Killed
Elliott Charles	Corpl.	Killed	Woolford Henry	Pte.	Killed
Wickfield Robert	Corpl.	Killed	Fitzgerald W. H. D.	Capt.	Wounded
Ambler Hugh	Pte.	Killed	Hare G. L.	Capt.	Wounded
Ball William	Pte.	Killed	Watson C. E.	Capt.	Wounded
Bates Robert	Pte.	Killed	Appleyard F. E.	Lieut.	Wounded
Barnett William	Pte.	Killed	Carpenter G. W. W.	Lieut.	Wounded
Barstow John	Pte.	Killed	Coney P. G.	Lieut.	Wounded
Bisgrove John	Pte.	Killed	Crofton Hon. A. C. H.	Lieut.	Wounded
Bowman James	Pte.	Killed	Jones H. M.	Lieut.	Wounded
Bridges Alexander	Pte.	Killed	Persse D.	Lieut.	Wounded
Brown William	Pte.	Killed	Barry Christopher	Sergt.	Wounded
Calverley Christopher	Pte.	Killed	Buckley Joseph	Sergt.	Wounded
Chappel Joseph	Pte.	Killed	Charter Arthur S.	Sergt.	Wounded
Clinton George	Pte.	Killed	Connolly Owen	Sergt.	Wounded
Cooper Robert	Pte.	Killed	Coulter John	Sergt.	Wounded
Crook William	Pte.	Killed	Donnolly John	Sergt.	Wounded
Dance John	Pte.	Killed	Duggan John	Sergt.	Wounded
Dennett William	Pte.	Killed	George Lemuel	Sergt.	Wounded
Green Richard	Pte.	Killed	Hainsworth William	Sergt.	Wounded
Guest Richard	Pte.	Killed	Kirby John	Sergt.	Wounded
Harris John	Pte.	Killed	Latimer William	Sergt.	Wounded
Ilott Richard	Pte.	Killed	Maud Simeon	Sergt.	Wounded
Irwin Joseph	Pte.	Killed	Melia John	Sergt.	Wounded
Jackson John	Pte.	Killed	Newcombe Richard	Sergt.	Wounded
Jones Jesse	Pte.	Killed	Potham John	Sergt.	Wounded
McCloy William	Pte.	Killed	Rowe Frederick	Sergt.	Wounded
McDonald James	Pte.	Killed	Vincent George	Sergt.	Wounded
McKearnon James	Pte.	Killed	Whitaker James	Sergt.	Wounded
Parke James	Pte.	Killed	Burrowes George	Corpl.	Wounded
Robinson John	Pte.	Killed	Creighton John C	Corpl.	Wounded
Swailes James	Pte.	Killed	Downes James	Corpl.	Wounded
Todd William	Pte.	Killed	Fawcett John	Corpl.	Wounded

NOTES

The Battle of the Alma
7th REGIMENT OF FOOT

NAME	RANK	CASUALTY	NAME	RANK	CASUALTY
Frost Philip	Corpl.	Wounded	Hardman John	Pte.	Wounded
Maitland William	Corpl.	Wounded	Hargadden Andrew	Pte.	Wounded
Senior William	Corpl.	Wounded	Harris Thomas	Pte.	Wounded
Severs Christopher	Corpl.	Wounded	Harrison John	Pte.	Wounded
Whittle George	Corpl.	Wounded	Hart John	Pte.	Wounded
Williams Daniel	Corpl.	Wounded	Herd John	Pte.	Wounded
Bamford Daniel	Pte.	Wounded	Hicks Thomas	Pte.	Wounded
Bannon Patrick	Pte.	Wounded	Higgins James	Pte.	Wounded
Bartley James	Pte.	Wounded	Hill William	Pte.	Wounded
Bath John	Pte.	Wounded	Hinchcliffe Mark	Pte.	Wounded
Battison George	Pte.	Wounded	Hodson Joseph	Pte.	Wounded
Bowles Goodyair	Pte.	Wounded	Holmes Thomas	Pte.	Wounded
Boyle Charles	Pte.	Wounded	Howard Richard	Pte.	Wounded
Boyle Patrick	Pte.	Wounded	Huggon Joshua	Pte.	Wounded
Bramwell Luke	Pte.	Wounded	Hurling Charles	Pte.	Wounded
Breett Whitfield	Pte.	Wounded	Jackson Henry	Pte.	Wounded
Britton William	Pte.	Wounded	Jenkins Henry	Pte.	Wounded
Brook Elliott	Pte.	Wounded	Johnson Joseph	Pte.	Wounded
Broughton George	Pte.	Wounded	Kerr William	Pte.	Wounded
Burgess Robert	Pte.	Wounded	Knight David	Pte.	Wounded
Burke Thomas	Pte.	Wounded	Lang James	Pte.	Wounded
Carroll John	Pte.	Wounded	Lawrence John	Pte.	Wounded
Carter Joseph	Pte.	Wounded	Lawrence Edward	Pte.	Wounded
Carver James	Pte.	Wounded	Leat George	Pte.	Wounded
Clarke Peter	Pte.	Wounded	Lees John	Pte.	Wounded
Clarkson John	Pte.	Wounded	Lindsay John	Pte.	Wounded
Cleary Denis	Pte.	Wounded	Lovall Thomas	Pte.	Wounded
Clements Robert	Pte.	Wounded	Luce Robert	Pte.	Wounded
Coleman Ambrose	Pte.	Wounded	Lynch William	Pte.	Wounded
Court Thomas	Pte.	Wounded	McHugh Patrick	Pte.	Wounded
Coussell James	Pte.	Wounded	McNamara Patrick	Pte.	Wounded
Cowe Robert	Pte.	Wounded	McVity William	Pte.	Wounded
Crawley John	Pte.	Wounded	McCarthy Michael	Pte.	Wounded
Cumming James	Pte.	Wounded	McGrath Thomas	Pte.	Wounded
Curry Owen	Pte.	Wounded	Manham William	Pte.	Wounded
Dawson William	Pte.	Wounded	Martin Henry	Pte.	Wounded
Day George	Pte.	Wounded	Martin Patrick	Pte.	Wounded
Dean Michael	Pte.	Wounded	Mason John	Pte.	Wounded
Degnan John	Pte.	Wounded	Mawson George	Pte.	Wounded
Dempsey James	Pte.	Wounded	Mead Thomas	Pte.	Wounded
Dennison Manasseh	Pte.	Wounded	Meleady Michael	Pte.	Wounded
Dowling Francis	Pte.	Wounded	Moan James	Pte.	Wounded
Driscoll John	Pte.	Wounded	Mole James	Pte.	Wounded
Duffy Walter	Pte.	Wounded	Mullin John	Pte.	Wounded
Faron Paul	Pte.	Wounded	Nicholson Thomas	Pte.	Wounded
Ferns William	Pte.	Wounded	O'Connor John	Pte.	Wounded
Field William	Pte.	Wounded	Paice Isaac	Pte.	Wounded
Frewin Charles	Pte.	Wounded	Painter John	Pte.	Wounded
Fry John Y.	Pte.	Wounded	Peake J. W. G.	Pte.	Wounded
Gale Thomas	Pte.	Wounded	Phillips George	Pte.	Wounded
Gardiner Henry	Pte.	Wounded	Porter Francis	Pte.	Wounded
Garmley James	Pte.	Wounded	Pye Henry	Pte.	Wounded
Garvin Archibald	Pte.	Wounded	Redman James	Pte.	Wounded
Gaynor William	Pte.	Wounded	Richardson Thomas	Pte.	Wounded
Giles James	Pte.	Wounded	Roach George	Pte.	Wounded
Goding William	Pte.	Wounded	Ryans John	Pte.	Wounded
Goldsmith Thomas	Pte.	Wounded	Sage Samuel	Pte.	Wounded
Goodhall John	Pte.	Wounded	Sergeant Richard	Pte.	Wounded
Gouge George	Pte.	Wounded	Sheppard William	Pte.	Wounded
Green Charles	Pte.	Wounded	Sheridan John	Pte.	Wounded
Gunter Thomas	Pte.	Wounded	Sheridan Patrick	Pte.	Wounded
Hammand Charles	Pte.	Wounded	Sherlock Henry	Pte.	Wounded
Hanley Thomas	Pte.	Wounded	Skeith William	Pte.	Wounded
Hardacre Andrew	Pte.	Wounded	Small William	Pte.	Wounded
Harden John	Pte.	Wounded	Smith Charles	Pte.	Wounded

NOTES

The Battle of the Alma

7th REGIMENT OF FOOT

NAME	RANK	CASUALTY	NAME	RANK	CASUALTY
Smith Owen	Pte.	Wounded	Williams Charles	Pte.	Wounded
Spofforth George	Pte.	Wounded	Williamson Robert	Pte.	Wounded
Staddon Richard	Pte.	Wounded	Wilson Adam	Pte.	Wounded
Tattersall James	Pte.	Wounded	Winters Charles	Pte.	Wounded
Timms Joseph	Pte.	Wounded	Withers James	Pte.	Wounded
Trainor William	Pte.	Wounded	Wood William Henry	Pte.	Wounded
Tyson Charles	Pte.	Wounded	Huston Michael	Drummer	Missing
Walladge Robert	Pte.	Wounded	Askwith David	Pte.	Missing
Ward Benjamin	Pte.	Wounded	Field James	Pte.	Missing

19th REGIMENT OF FOOT

NAME	RANK	CASUALTY	NAME	RANK	CASUALTY
Cardew A.	Lt. & Adj.	Killed	Hardgrave George	Sergt.	Wounded
Stockwell G. D.	Ensign	Killed	Lee Frederick	Sergt.	Wounded
Hines Robert	Corpl.	Killed	Price Charles	Sergt.	Wounded
Calkin Joseph	Drummer	Killed	Rawding James	Sergt.	Wounded
Allen Henry	Pte.	Killed	Smith John	Sergt.	Wounded
Avery Richard	Pte.	Killed	Annon John	Corpl.	Wounded
Baker Thomas	Pte.	Killed	Adkinson Richard	Corpl.	Wounded
Bastion George	Pte.	Killed	Alwell John	Corpl.	Wounded
Blackburn John	Pte.	Killed	Barlow Patrick	Corpl.	Wounded
Brown William	Pte.	Killed	Brombley William	Corpl.	Wounded
Conway Charles	Pte.	Killed	Brown John	Corpl.	Wounded
Dobbins John	Pte.	Killed	Buchanan Andrew	Corpl.	Wounded
Doherty John	Pte.	Killed	Connors Michael	Corpl.	Wounded
Downes Terrence	Pte.	Killed	Cox Thomas	Corpl.	Wounded
Doyle Thomas	Pte.	Killed	Dodds James	Corpl.	Wounded
Eatell Aaron	Pte.	Killed	Fagg John	Corpl.	Wounded
Fitzpatrick William	Pte.	Killed	Fain John	Corpl.	Wounded
Furnival Thomas	Pte.	Killed	Farrar Thomas	Corpl.	Wounded
Gaynor Patrick	Pte.	Killed	Lloyan John	Corpl.	Wounded
Giles Frederick	Pte.	Killed	Maddigan Thomas	Corpl.	Wounded
Griffin Lawrence	Pte.	Killed	Murray Francis	Corpl.	Wounded
Hanlon James	Pte.	Killed	Pope William	Corpl.	Wounded
Hitchcock John	Pte.	Killed	Voisey William	Corpl.	Wounded
Jones Reese	Pte.	Killed	Young Matthew	Corpl.	Wounded
Keicher Michael	Pte.	Killed	McCarthy Thomas	Drummer	Wounded
Leara John	Pte.	Killed	Aistin Charles	Pte.	Wounded
Luttrell George	Pte.	Killed	Allerdice John	Pte.	Wounded
Lynam Peter	Pte.	Killed	Andrews William	Pte.	Wounded
McNicholl Thomas	Pte.	Killed	Armstrong Francis	Pte.	Wounded
Pye Thomas	Pte.	Killed	Bailey William	Pte.	Wounded
Quinn Daniel	Pte.	Killed	Bailey Thomas	Pte.	Wounded
Reeves Samuel	Pte.	Killed	Barret William	Pte.	Wounded
Scanlan Edward	Pte.	Killed	Battison William	Pte.	Wounded
Scullen Joseph	Pte.	Killed	Biggins Patrick	Pte.	Wounded
Spencer Luke	Pte.	Killed	Blythe John	Pte.	Wounded
Stillwell William	Pte.	Killed	Brennan John	Pte.	Wounded
Thomas William	Pte.	Killed	Brophy James	Pte.	Wounded
Walsh William	Pte.	Killed	Butler John	Pte.	Wounded
Ward Walter	Pte.	Killed	Burke Michael	Pte	Wounded
Young Alexander	Pte.	Killed	Burke William	Pte.	Wounded
Saunders R.	Lt/Col.	Wounded	Byrne Patrick	Pte.	Wounded
McGee H. E.	Major	Wounded	Camion John	Pte.	Wounded
Warden R.	Capt.	Wounded	Campbell Patrick	Pte.	Wounded
Currie L. D.	Lieut.	Wounded	Campbell Robert	Pte.	Wounded
Wardlaw R.	Lieut.	Wounded	Candling Henry	Pte.	Wounded
Rawding William	Col/Sgt.	Wounded	Carroll Charles	Pte.	Wounded
Arthur F.	Sergt.	Wounded	Carroll James (1)	Pte.	Wounded
Bergin Finlan	Sergt.	Wounded	Carroll James (2)	Pte.	Wounded
Carville John	Sergt.	Wounded	Carse Patrick	Pte.	Wounded
Daly Patrick	Sergt.	Wounded	Chadwick Thomas	Pte.	Wounded

NOTES

The Battle of the Alma

19th REGIMENT OF FOOT

NAME	RANK	CASUALTY	NAME	RANK	CASUALTY
Clare John	Pte.	Wounded	Martin Thomas	Pte.	Wounded
Clarke Joseph	Pte.	Wounded	Moloney Patrick	Pte.	Wounded
Collett William	Pte.	Wounded	Morgan Richard	Pte.	Wounded
Connolly J.	Pte.	Wounded	Morris Michael	Pte.	Wounded
Connolly Michael	Pte.	Wounded	Mullins John	Pte.	Wounded
Cowan Patrick	Pte.	Wounded	Murdagh T.	Pte.	Wounded
Cresswell Michael	Pte.	Wounded	Munell Edward	Pte.	Wounded
Darsey James	Pte.	Wounded	Murphy Andrew	Pte.	Wounded
Davis Daniel	Pte.	Wounded	Murphy J.	Pte.	Wounded
Donohoe Maurice	Pte.	Wounded	Murphy T.	Pte.	Wounded
Donohoe Thomas	Pte.	Wounded	Neale Michael	Pte.	Wounded
Doolan Martin	Pte.	Wounded	Newcom R.	Pte.	Wounded
Doran William	Pte.	Wounded	Nicholson John	Pte.	Wounded
Doulan Martin	Pte.	Wounded	Noonan Michael	Pte.	Wounded
Downes T.	Pte.	Wounded	O'Brien Michael	Pte.	Wounded
Dubage William	Pte.	Wounded	O'Hare William	Pte.	Wounded
Eade William	Pte.	Wounded	Parker John	Pte.	Wounded
Edwards Edward	Pte.	Wounded	Peacocke Henry	Pte.	Wounded
Farise Stephen	Pte.	Wounded	Peel Paul	Pte.	Wounded
Fenaher Elijah	Pte.	Wounded	Pittman Richard	Pte.	Wounded
Foley Michael	Pte.	Wounded	Purcell P.	Pte.	Wounded
Gaffney Phillip	Pte.	Wounded	Quigley Peter	Pte.	Wounded
Gooch William	Pte.	Wounded	Rafarley Edward	Pte.	Wounded
Goulding James	Pte.	Wounded	Raffles B.	Pte.	Wounded
Grant George	Pte.	Wounded	Rawson W.	Pte.	Wounded
Hanlon John	Pte.	Wounded	Richards G.	Pte.	Wounded
Harris William	Pte.	Wounded	Rogers John	Pte.	Wounded
Harriss James	Pte.	Wounded	Roberts R.	Pte.	Wounded
Harrison W.	Pte.	Wounded	Salan John	Pte.	Wounded
Hayes Patrick	Pte.	Wounded	Sault James	Pte.	Wounded
Hearon Richard	Pte.	Wounded	Scanlon Thomas	Pte.	Wounded
Herrity James	Pte.	Wounded	Shannon Michael	Pte.	Wounded
Hickey Lawrence	Pte.	Wounded	Shepphard John	Pte.	Wounded
Higgins Thomas	Pte.	Wounded	Smith Aaron	Pte.	Wounded
Horrigan Michael	Pte.	Wounded	Smith William (1st)	Pte.	Wounded
Houraghan Jeremiah	Pte.	Wounded	Smith William	Pte.	Wounded
Hurley James	Pte.	Wounded	Soloman Jacob	Pte.	Wounded
Hurst Michael	Pte.	Wounded	Sullivan J.	Pte.	Wounded
Jarvis John	Pte.	Wounded	Sweeny John	Pte.	Wounded
Jeffries George	Pte.	Wounded	Taite William	Pte.	Wounded
Jolly John	Pte.	Wounded	Taylor John	Pte.	Wounded
Jones William	Pte.	Wounded	Turner Thomas	Pte.	Wounded
Jones Thomas	Pte.	Wounded	Turner William	Pte.	Wounded
Keating John	Pte.	Wounded	Twomey William	Pte.	Wounded
Kehoe Patrick	Pte.	Wounded	Vines John	Pte.	Wounded
Kelly William	Pte.	Wounded	Walker John	Pte.	Wounded
Lacey Thomas	Pte.	Wounded	Wall James	Pte.	Wounded
Leonard James	Pte.	Wounded	Walsh William	Pte.	Wounded
Liddle William	Pte.	Wounded	Watson James	Pte.	Wounded
Logan Peter	Pte.	Wounded	Wheatley Thomas	Pte.	Wounded
Lyons Denis	Pte.	Wounded	White Thomas	Pte.	Wounded
Lyons Francis	Pte.	Wounded	Williams John	Pte.	Wounded
McCall Michael	Pte.	Wounded	Williams Thomas	Pte.	Wounded
McElroy Thomas	Pte.	Wounded	Young Peter	Pte.	Wounded
McGuiggan William	Pte.	Wounded	Boland John	Pte.	Missing
McGuire Thomas	Pte.	Wounded	Hennesy John	Pte.	Missing
McNamara Hugh	Pte.	Wounded	Lawler Patrick	Pte.	Missing
McNamara Patrick	Pte.	Wounded	Richards George	Pte.	Missing
McNearney John	Pte.	Wounded	Rourke Bernard	Pte.	Missing
Maroney Michael	Pte.	Wounded	Stephens James	Pte.	Missing

NOTES

The Battle of the Alma

21st REGIMENT OF FOOT

NAME	RANK	CASUALTY
Dorrick Thomas	Pte.	Killed

23rd ROYAL WELSH FUSILIERS

NAME	RANK	CASUALTY	NAME	RANK	CASUALTY
Chester H. G.	Lt/Col.	Killed	Balfour C.	Sergt.	Wounded
Conolly J. C.	Capt.	Killed	Burke J.	Sergt.	Wounded
Evans F. E.	Capt.	Killed	Hill J.	Sergt.	Wounded
Wynn A. W. W.	Capt.	Killed	Kerr J.	Sergt.	Wounded
Radcliffe F. P.	Lieut.	Killed	Lloyd T.	Sergt.	Wounded
Young Sir W.	Lieut.	Killed	Norris P.	Sergt.	Wounded
Anstruther H.	2/Lieut.	Killed	O'Connor L.	Sergt.	Wounded
Butler J. H.	2/Lieut.	Killed	Smith E.	Sergt.	Wounded
Jones H.	Sgt/Mjr.	Killed	Walsh J.	Sergt.	Wounded
Hitchcock R.	Col/Sgt.	Killed	Clack W.	Corpl.	Wounded
Edwards F.	Sergt.	Killed	Devonshire H.	Corpl.	Wounded
Collins J.	Drummer	Killed	Hall W.	Corpl.	Wounded
Badcock J.	Pte.	Killed	Horner S.	Corpl.	Wounded
Barnett C.	Pte.	Killed	Jones J.	Corpl.	Wounded
Clack M.	Pte.	Killed	Ludgate J.	Corpl.	Wounded
Conroy T.	Pte.	Killed	Mason J.	Corpl.	Wounded
Dobson G.	Pte.	Killed	Payne D.	Corpl.	Wounded
Draper S.	Pte.	Killed	Powell J.	Corpl.	Wounded
Evans G.	Pte.	Killed	Williams D.	Corpl.	Wounded
Fry James	Pte.	Killed	Windsor S.	Corpl.	Wounded
Fry John	Pte.	Killed	Bampton C.	Drummer	Wounded
Goddard H.	Pte.	Killed	Cleville E.	Drummer	Wounded
Grooms J.	Pte.	Killed	Royal J.	Drummer	Wounded
Hanrahan J.	Pte.	Killed	Wooley J.	Drummer	Wounded
Hall J.	Pte.	Killed	Allen J.	Pte.	Wounded
Harrington J.	Pte.	Killed	Allen W.	Pte.	Wounded
Hine H.	Pte.	Killed	Anderson W.	Pte.	Wounded
Husband H.	Pte.	Killed	Andrews W.	Pte.	Wounded
Jones E.	Pte.	Killed	Archer T.	Pte.	Wounded
Kelly L.	Pte.	Killed	Back P.	Pte.	Wounded
Knightley J.	Pte.	Killed	Baggs R.	Pte.	Wounded
Lines W.	Pte.	Killed	Baker C.	Pte.	Wounded
Lowman G.	Pte.	Killed	Baker J.	Pte.	Wounded
Lynch J.	Pte.	Killed	Batts W.	Pte.	Wounded
Lynch T.	Pte.	Killed	Beechey J.	Pte.	Wounded
Maloney T.	Pte.	Killed	Bennett R.	Pte.	Wounded
Marsh H.	Pte.	Killed	Birch D.	Pte.	Wounded
Martin W.	Pte.	Killed	Blaney R.	Pte.	Wounded
Owens T.	Pte.	Killed	Bowles J.	Pte.	Wounded
Peterson P.	Pte.	Killed	Braden W.	Pte.	Wounded
Powell J.	Pte.	Killed	Brady J.	Pte.	Wounded
Povey D.	Pte.	Killed	Brookland G.	Pte.	Wounded
Randall T.	Pte.	Killed	Buntler T.	Pte.	Wounded
Seymour T.	Pte.	Killed	Burrows J.	Pte.	Wounded
Spiller T.	Pte.	Killed	Burrows W.	Pte.	Wounded
Stevens J.	Pte.	Killed	Chalk H.	Pte.	Wounded
Walters R.	Pte.	Killed	Clarey J.	Pte.	Wounded
Wells J.	Pte.	Killed	Clarke M. W.	Pte.	Wounded
Williams E.	Pte.	Killed	Clulee T.	Pte.	Wounded
Williams J.	Pte.	Killed	Collett H.	Pte.	Wounded
Campbell W. P.	Capt.	Wounded	Collins J.	Pte.	Wounded
Hopton E. C.	Capt.	Wounded	Conolly T.	Pte.	Wounded
Applewhaite A.	Lieut & Act/Adj.	Wounded	Cross W.	Pte.	Wounded
			Cruize W.	Pte.	Wounded
Bathurst H.	Lieut.	Wounded	Curley L.	Pte.	Wounded
Sayer F.	Lieut.	Wounded	Davies C.	Pte.	Wounded

NOTES

The Battle of the Alma

23rd ROYAL WELSH FUSILIERS

NAME	RANK	CASUALTY	NAME	RANK	CASUALTY
Davis O.	Pte.	Wounded	Mitchell J.	Pte.	Wounded
Didcote J. G.	Pte.	Wounded	Moody T.	Pte.	Wounded
Dunnecliffe W.	Pte.	Wounded	Moore W.	Pte.	Wounded
Edwards T.	Pte.	Wounded	Mullins T.	Pte.	Wounded
Egan J.	Pte.	Wounded	Murray T.	Pte.	Wounded
Elliott T.	Pte.	Wounded	Murray W.	Pte.	Wounded
English J.	Pte.	Wounded	Neal W.	Pte.	Wounded
Evans D.	Pte.	Wounded	Newman W.	Pte.	Wounded
Evans W.	Pte.	Wounded	Nicholls G.	Pte.	Wounded
Fletcher W.	Pte.	Wounded	O' Gormond T.	Pte.	Wounded
Floyd W. H.	Pte.	Wounded	Owens T.	Pte.	Wounded
Gammon W.	Pte.	Wounded	Page C.	Pte.	Wounded
Geary J.	Pte.	Wounded	Patience W.	Pte.	Wounded
Ghent E.	Pte.	Wounded	Pavey W.	Pte.	Wounded
Gibbs S.	Pte.	Wounded	Porter J.	Pte.	Wounded
Gibson J.	Pte.	Wounded	Poulton J.	Pte.	Wounded
Gittins T.	Pte.	Wounded	Price H.	Pte.	Wounded
Glass J.	Pte.	Wounded	Pudwell M.	Pte.	Wounded
Goslin G.	Pte.	Wounded	Railly J.	Pte.	Wounded
Gullock J.	Pte.	Wounded	Rielly J.	Pte.	Wounded
Hall T.	Pte.	Wounded	Rolf G.	Pte.	Wounded
Harris E.	Pte.	Wounded	Rooney J.	Pte.	Wounded
Harris J.	Pte.	Wounded	Ryan C.	Pte.	Wounded
Harrison T.	Pte.	Wounded	Sackett J.	Pte.	Wounded
Hill W.	Pte.	Wounded	Shawe J. J.	Pte.	Wounded
Hodgetts —	Pte.	Wounded	Shields J.	Pte.	Wounded
Horn W.	Pte.	Wounded	Simpson W.	Pte.	Wounded
Howarth G.	Pte.	Wounded	Smith J. (1)	Pte.	Wounded
Hughes J.	Pte.	Wounded	Smith J. (2)	Pte.	Wounded
Hunt W.	Pte.	Wounded	Smith T.	Pte.	Wounded
Hurlstone H.	Pte.	Wounded	Squires W.	Pte.	Wounded
Ingham J.	Pte.	Wounded	Stone W.	Pte.	Wounded
James A.	Pte.	Wounded	Swadling R.	Pte.	Wounded
Johnstone R.	Pte.	Wounded	Taylor T.	Pte.	Wounded
Jones S.	Pte.	Wounded	Tee G.	Pte.	Wounded
Jordan W.	Pte.	Wounded	Thrupp C.	Pte.	Wounded
Keogh J.	Pte.	Wounded	Tuite T.	Pte.	Wounded
Keycroft T.	Pte.	Wounded	Twinning D.	Pte.	Wounded
Kinchen T.	Pte.	Wounded	Walden A.	Pte.	Wounded
Lampey W.	Pte.	Wounded	Walker J.	Pte.	Wounded
Lillnord D.	Pte.	Wounded	Wall H.	Pte.	Wounded
Lush G.	Pte.	Wounded	Walls J.	Pte.	Wounded
McKeen A.	Pte.	Wounded	Webb T.	Pte.	Wounded
McDonald A.	Pte.	Wounded	Wilkinson J.	Pte.	Wounded
Maityard M.	Pte.	Wounded	Wilton H.	Pte.	Wounded
Major E.	Pte.	Wounded	Wotton C.	Pte.	Wounded
Martin A.	Pte.	Wounded	Thompson T.	Pte.	Wounded
Milden W.	Pte.	Wounded	Warburton J.	Pte.	Wounded
Millington T.	Pte.	Wounded			

30th REGIMENT OF FOOT

NAME	RANK	CASUALTY	NAME	RANK	CASUALTY
Luxmore F.	Lieut.	Killed	Mitchie George	Pte.	Killed
Emery Robert	Corpl.	Killed	Vokes John	Pte.	Killed
Beattie Alexander	Pte.	Killed	Conolly A. W.	Capt.	Wounded
Bell Robert	Pte.	Killed	Dickson G.	Capt.	Wounded
Chivers Henry	Pte.	Killed	Pakenham T. H.	Capt.	Wounded
Gaffney Michael	Pte.	Killed	Walker M.	Lieut. & Adj.	Wounded
Henshaw Joseph	Pte.	Killed			
Jackson Robert	Pte.	Killed	Day Nicholas	Sergt.	Wounded
McInness Donald	Pte.	Killed	Lydon Dominick	Sergt.	Wounded
McNally Thomas	Pte.	Killed	McFadden Samuel	Corpl.	Wounded

NOTES

The Battle of the Alma

30th REGIMENT OF FOOT

NAME	RANK	CASUALTY	NAME	RANK	CASUALTY
Page John	Corpl.	Wounded	Hartney Martin	Pte.	Wounded
Sweeney James	Corpl.	Wounded	Healy Thomas	Pte.	Wounded
Bolds John	Drummer	Wounded	Higgins Patrick	Pte.	Wounded
Anderson Hugh	Pte.	Wounded	Hodson Daniel	Pte.	Wounded
Barker George	Pte.	Wounded	Hogan Daniel	Pte.	Wounded
Bookey Thomas	Pte.	Wounded	Isherwood Thomas	Pte.	Wounded
Britt James	Pte.	Wounded	Judd Thomas	Pte.	Wounded
Burley John	Pte.	Wounded	Kershaw John	Pte.	Wounded
Byrne Martin	Pte.	Wounded	Laing David	Pte.	Wounded
Chamberlain John	Pte.	Wounded	Lockrey Charles	Pte.	Wounded
Clancy John	Pte.	Wounded	Luton William	Pte.	Wounded
Clarke Thomas (1st)	Pte.	Wounded	McCabe David	Pte.	Wounded
Conolly John	Pte.	Wounded	Miller Francis	Pte.	Wounded
Connor John (2nd)	Pte.	Wounded	Moriarty William	Pte.	Wounded
Cook Walter	Pte.	Wounded	Murphy Edmond	Pte.	Wounded
Corcoran Patrick	Pte.	Wounded	Needham Thomas	Pte.	Wounded
Davis Thomas (1st)	Pte.	Wounded	Newton James	Pte.	Wounded
Dean William	Pte.	Wounded	Oxenham James	Pte.	Wounded
Denton Elijah	Pte.	Wounded	Pairson Wm John	Pte.	Wounded
Devlin Thomas	Pte.	Wounded	Payne James	Pte.	Wounded
Dyer Peter	Pte.	Wounded	Ready Francis	Pte.	Wounded
Elliott Samuel	Pte.	Wounded	Rooke James	Pte.	Wounded
Ferrier David	Pte.	Wounded	Smith Alexander	Pte.	Wounded
Foley Michael	Pte.	Wounded	Smith John (14th)	Pte.	Wounded
Garrahan Michael	Pte.	Wounded	Stratton Samuel	Pte.	Wounded
Goddard Henry	Pte.	Wounded	Tindall Thomas	Pte.	Wounded
Grady Patrick	Pte.	Wounded	Venn Robert	Pte.	Wounded
Hale William	Pte.	Wounded	Walker Robert	Pte.	Wounded
Hardy Harry	Pte.	Wounded	Walsh Richard	Pte.	Wounded
Hardy John (2nd)	Pte.	Wounded	Wilson George	Pte.	Wounded

33rd REGIMENT OF FOOT

NAME	RANK	CASUALTY	NAME	RANK	CASUALTY
Montagu F Du Pre	Lieut	Killed	Hogan Thomas	Pte.	Killed
Byrne Charles	Col/Sgt.	Killed	Hopkins Thomas	Pte.	Killed
Feather Phaoroh	Sergt.	Killed	Horey Peter	Pte.	Killed
Ryan William	Sergt.	Killed	Hoyle James	Pte.	Killed
Bates William	Corpl.	Killed	Hunt George	Pte.	Killed
Bennett William	Corpl.	Killed	Lacy James	Pte.	Killed
Crossley Henry	Corpl.	Killed	Masters Charles	Pte.	Killed
Haines Alexander	Corpl.	Killed	Monaghan Robert	Pte.	Killed
Lee John G.	Corpl.	Killed	Mulkerrin Martin	Pte.	Killed
Ward Maurice	Corpl.	Killed	Mullen William	Pte.	Killed
Websdell William	Corpl.	Killed	Osborne George	Pte.	Killed
Allune Robert	Pte.	Killed	Quin James	Pte.	Killed
Anderson George	Pte.	Killed	Riddle John	Pte.	Killed
Ball Francis	Pte.	Killed	Shackleton William	Pte.	Killed
Barber Mark	Pte.	Killed	Shepherd Joshua	Pte.	Killed
Barnes Samuel	Pte.	Killed	Skeggs George	Pte.	Killed
Bassett William	Pte.	Killed	Smith William	Pte.	Killed
Beete Charles	Pte.	Killed	Smith William (2)	Pte.	Killed
Bettle George	Pte.	Killed	Spencer John	Pte.	Killed
Brown Thomas	Pte.	Killed	Stebbings John	Pte.	Killed
Butcher James	Pte.	Killed	Stott Joseph	Pte.	Killed
Calnan John	Pte.	Killed	Sullivan James	Pte.	Killed
Carty Martin	Pte.	Killed	Suttie Thomas	Pte.	Killed
Corrigan Edward	Pte.	Killed	Whitty James	Pte.	Killed
Crabtree George	Pte.	Killed	Woodward John	Pte.	Killed
Dare James	Pte.	Killed	Woolhouse Frederick	Pte.	Killed
Doyle James	Pte.	Killed	Gough T. B.	Major	Wounded
Futters Henry	Pte.	Killed	Fitzgerald H. C.	Capt.	Wounded
Grady Patrick	Pte.	Killed	Wallis A. B.	Lieut.	Wounded
Higgins Martin	Pte.	Killed	Worthington W. S.	Lieut.	Wounded

NOTES

The Battle of the Alma

33rd REGIMENT OF FOOT

NAME	RANK	CASUALTY	NAME	RANK	CASUALTY
Greenwood J. J.	Ensign	Wounded	Deerey James	Pte.	Wounded
Siree C. M.	Ensign	Wounded	Delamuty Michael	Pte.	Wounded
Bairstow Thomas	Col/Sgt.	Wounded	Denson William	Pte.	Wounded
Mason William	Col/Sgt.	Wounded	Dermody Thomas	Pte.	Wounded
Spense George	Col/Sgt.	Wounded	Dunn Joseph	Pte.	Wounded
Sugden William	Col/Sgt.	Wounded	Edmonds Sidney	Pte.	Wounded
Checkley Thomas	Sergt.	Wounded	Fahey Michael	Pte.	Wounded
Cockroft James	Sergt.	Wounded	Finn Patrick	Pte.	Wounded
Felningham Robert	Sergt.	Wounded	Fisher Patrick	Pte.	Wounded
Forsyth Robert	Sergt.	Wounded	Fitzgerald James	Pte.	Wounded
Hancock Elisha	Sergt.	Wounded	Fitzharris Thomas	Pte.	Wounded
Hoare Patrick	Sergt.	Wounded	Fitzpatrick Daniel	Pte	Wounded
Keane William	Sergt.	Wounded	Flahavan John	Pte.	Wounded
Morton Edward	Sergt.	Wounded	Foley Patrick	Pte.	Wounded
Townsend George	Sergt.	Wounded	Foster John	Pte.	Wounded
Vince Robert	Sergt.	Wounded	Gaffney James	Pte.	Wounded
Blake James	Corpl.	Wounded	Gardiner Michael	Pte.	Wounded
Caffray James	Corpl.	Wounded	Gascoign Joseph	Pte.	Wounded
Dagley John	Corpl.	Wounded	Gilbert Herbert	Pte.	Wounded
Lawder Charles	Corpl.	Wounded	Giles John	Pte.	Wounded
Little Alexander S.	Corpl.	Wounded	Giles Richard	Pte.	Wounded
Newcombe George	Corpl.	Wounded	Gillespie John	Pte.	Wounded
Stewart William	Corpl.	Wounded	Gilmartin James	Pte.	Wounded
Sutton William	Corpl.	Wounded	Glover John	Pte.	Wounded
Webb John	Corpl.	Wounded	Goode Michael	Pte.	Wounded
Weir William	Corpl.	Wounded	Graham Richard	Pte.	Wounded
Wood Richard	Corpl.	Wounded	Green John	Pte.	Wounded
Cassidy John	Drummer	Wounded	Green James	Pte.	Wounded
McHugh John	Drummer	Wounded	Griffin James	Pte.	Wounded
Aldred William	Pte.	Wounded	Hackett Patrick	Pte.	Wounded
Anderson James	Pte.	Wounded	Handslip William	Pte.	Wounded
Austen William	Pte.	Wounded	Henderson Thomas	Pte.	Wounded
Banyards Thomas	Pte.	Wounded	Herson John	Pte.	Wounded
Barrett John	Pte.	Wounded	Hilton John	Pte.	Wounded
Beebee Henry	Pte.	Wounded	Hoey Martin	Pte.	Wounded
Beazley Thomas	Pte.	Wounded	Hogan Patrick	Pte.	Wounded
Biddle Charles	Pte.	Wounded	Hogan Patrick (1st)	Pte.	Wounded
Bond Patrick	Pte.	Wounded	Hogan Patrick (2nd)	Pte.	Wounded
Bradley Henry	Pte.	Wounded	Holloran Matthew	Pte.	Wounded
Branagan Arthur	Pte.	Wounded	Hoolahan Michael	Pte.	Wounded
Brazzel Patrick	Pte.	Wounded	Howarth William	Pte.	Wounded
Briggs Jonas	Pte.	Wounded	Hughes John	Pte.	Wounded
Broome William	Pte.	Wounded	Iredale Henry	Pte.	Wounded
Brown William	Pte.	Wounded	Jackson Charles	Pte.	Wounded
Bryan James	Pte.	Wounded	Jackson John	Pte.	Wounded
Burns Jeremiah	Pte.	Wounded	James John	Pte.	Wounded
Burton William	Pte.	Wounded	Johnson Robert	Pte.	Wounded
Cairns James	Pte.	Wounded	Jones Henry	Pte.	Wounded
Caple Thomas	Pte.	Wounded	Keenan William	Pte.	Wounded
Carrol Thomas	Pte.	Wounded	Keilly Patrick	Pte.	Wounded
Carty Michael	Pte.	Wounded	Kelly John	Pte.	Wounded
Cassidy Henry	Pte.	Wounded	Killick George	Pte.	Wounded
Cassidy Peter	Pte.	Wounded	Kirk Robert	Pte.	Wounded
Clarke William	Pte.	Wounded	Kneale Thomas	Pte.	Wounded
Clarke Patrick	Pte.	Wounded	Knight William	Pte.	Wounded
Connell Thomas	Pte.	Wounded	Lamb George	Pte.	Wounded
Conry Patrick	Pte.	Wounded	Lindsay William	Pte.	Wounded
Cotton Charles	Pte.	Wounded	Longstaff Simeon	Pte.	Wounded
Craig Thomas	Pte.	Wounded	Lyons Thomas	Pte.	Wounded
Cranley Patrick	Pte.	Wounded	McCombish Bernard	Pte.	Wounded
Crowley Jeremiah	Pte.	Wounded	McGaw William	Pte.	Wounded
Daly James	Pte.	Wounded	McLaren John	Pte.	Wounded
Davis Andrew	Pte.	Wounded	McLaughlin Patrick	Pte.	Wounded
Davis John	Pte.	Wounded	McMahon John	Pte.	Wounded
Deaton Frederick	Pte.	Wounded	MacDermott John	Pte.	Wounded

NOTES

The Battle of the Alma

33rd REGIMENT OF FOOT

NAME	RANK	CASUALTY	NAME	RANK	CASUALTY
Mara Michael	Pte.	Wounded	Riley Thomas	Pte.	Wounded
Marshall George	Pte.	Wounded	Roberts David	Pte.	Wounded
Mayer Job	Pte.	Wounded	Robins James	Pte.	Wounded
Mayes John	Pte.	Wounded	Rogers Joseph	Pte.	Wounded
Merriot Alfred	Pte.	Wounded	Rohan Stephan	Pte.	Wounded
Merriot Joseph	Pte.	Wounded	Rowell George	Pte.	Wounded
Miller Henry	Pte.	Wounded	Rushworth William	Pte.	Wounded
Moran Michael	Pte.	Wounded	Russell James	Pte.	Wounded
Moriarty Michael	Pte.	Wounded	Seery Andrew	Pte.	Wounded
Morris Mark	Pte.	Wounded	Shaw Allen	Pte.	Wounded
Morrisay Thomas	Pte.	Wounded	Shea James	Pte.	Wounded
Nutall Isaac	Pte.	Wounded	Smith Henry	Pte.	Wounded
O'Brien John	Pte.	Wounded	Spraggins Thomas	Pte.	Wounded
O'Brien Patrick	Pte.	Wounded	Stainley George	Pte.	Wounded
Ogden John	Pte.	Wounded	Stanton Edward	Pte.	Wounded
Parker Robinson	Pte.	Wounded	Sunters Herbert	Pte.	Wounded
Parnell Thomas	Pte.	Wounded	Taylor Robert	Pte.	Wounded
Peard Henry	Pte.	Wounded	Thompson William	Pte.	Wounded
Pearman John	Pte.	Wounded	Tracey James	Pte.	Wounded
Pennefeather William	Pte.	Wounded	Walkley William	Pte.	Wounded
Penniston George	Pte.	Wounded	Walsh Michael	Pte.	Wounded
Phillips William	Pte.	Wounded	Ward William	Pte.	Wounded
Porter Edward	Pte.	Wounded	Whelan Michael	Pte.	Wounded
Power James	Pte.	Wounded	Whitehad Thomas	Pte.	Wounded
Purvis Alexander	Pte.	Wounded	Whittaker Roger	Pte.	Wounded
Quinlan Joseph	Pte.	Wounded	Whitworth Robert	Pte.	Wounded
Quinn John	Pte.	Wounded	Woodhouse Thomas	Pte.	Wounded
Quinn John	Pte.	Wounded	Woodward Charles	Pte.	Wounded
Reader Thomas	Pte.	Wounded	Allen James	Pte.	Wounded
Richards Aaron	Pte.	Wounded	Pelling Thomas	Pte.	D.O.W.
Riedy Martin	Pte.	Wounded	Minneagh J.	Pte.	Missing

41st REGIMENT OF FOOT

NAME	RANK	CASUALTY	NAME	RANK	CASUALTY
Holmes John	Pte.	Killed	Flanigan Michael	Pte.	Wounded
Hughes Michael	Pte.	Killed	Fowler James	Pte.	Wounded
Lefevre Joseph	Pte.	Killed	Hannon Thomas	Pte.	Wounded
Putland Samuel	Pte.	Killed	Johnston James	Pte	Wounded
Rees Philip	Sergt.	Wounded	Jones David	Pte.	Wounded
Jones David	Corpl.	Wounded	Kelly Andrew	Pte.	Wounded
Bradley Stephen	Pte.	Wounded	Kennedy John	Pte.	Wounded
Brown George	Pte.	Wounded	Lamb William	Pte.	Wounded
Burtonshall Jesse	Pte.	Wounded	Lawler Patrick	Pte.	Wounded
			M'Goldrick William	Pte.	Wounded
Byrnes James	Pte.	Wounded	Naughton Denis	Pte.	Wounded
Cox George	Pte.	Wounded	Pender John	Pte.	Wounded
Cullman Michael	Pte.	Wounded	Skinner John	Pte.	Wounded
Ewins Walter	Pte.	Wounded	Walton William I.	Pte.	Wounded

42nd REGIMENT OF FOOT

NAME	RANK	CASUALTY	NAME	RANK	CASUALTY
Campbell Neil	Pte.	Killed	Stewart James	Sergt.	Wounded
Fadden Richard	Pte.	Killed	Barber William	Pte.	Wounded
Hart David	Pte.	Killed	Buchannan John	Pte.	Wounded
McKenzie William	Pte.	Killed	Butler George	Pte.	Wounded
MacLeod John	Pte.	Killed	Cruickshanks William	Pte.	Wounded
Elliot Thomas	Pte.	D.O.W.	Duncan Alexander	Pte.	Wounded
McDonald Donald	Pte.	D.O.W.	Forbes Alexander	Pte.	Wounded
Lounden James	Col/Sgt.	Wounded	Forrester William	Pte.	Wounded

NOTES

The Battle of the Alma

42nd REGIMENT OF FOOT

NAME	RANK	CASUALTY	NAME	RANK	CASUALTY
Fraser Peter	Pte.	Wounded	Lynch Timothy	Pte.	Wounded
Fraser William	Pte.	Wounded	M'Alpin Archibald	Pte.	Wounded
Graham John	Pte.	Wounded	M'Donald James	Pte.	Wounded
Hamilton Henry	Pte.	Wounded	M'Math William	Pte.	Wounded
Higgie John	Pte.	Wounded	M'Nish John	Pte.	Wounded
Howinson George	Pte.	Wounded	Michie Robert	Pte.	Wounded
Hunter William	Pte.	Wounded	Muir David	Pte.	Wounded
Johnstone George	Pte.	Wounded	Norfolk Benjamin	Pte.	Wounded
King William	Pte.	Wounded	Park John	Pte.	Wounded
Laidlaw Adam	Pte.	Wounded	Roberson Alexander	Pte.	Wounded
Leitch Thomas	Pte.	Wounded	Skene James	Pte.	Wounded
Lyall Thomas	Pte.	Wounded	Taylor William	Pte.	Wounded
Lyon Andrew	Pte.	Wounded			

44th REGIMENT OF FOOT

NAME	RANK	CASUALTY	NAME	RANK	CASUALTY
Horsfall Thomas	Pte.	Killed	Hoey James	Pte.	Wounded
Walsh John	Corpl.	Wounded	Hogan Thomas	Pte.	Wounded
Crook Robert	Pte.	Wounded	Mitchell Thomas	Pte.	Wounded
Deigan Thomas	Pte.	Wounded	Suddy Henry	Pte.	Wounded

47th REGIMENT OF FOOT

NAME	RANK	CASUALTY	NAME	RANK	CASUALTY
Lomax John	Sergt.	Killed	Holland William	Pte.	Wounded
Barber Daniel	Corpl.	Killed	Ivers Daniel	Pte.	Wounded
Crowe Henry	Corpl.	Killed	Jones George	Pte.	Wounded
Huddy Samuel	Pte.	Killed	Kettle James	Pte.	Wounded
Wollocombe T.	Lieut.	Wounded	King Samuel	Pte.	Wounded
Maycock J. G.	Lieut.	Wounded	Kirwan Christopher	Pte.	Wounded
Philips N. G.	Lieut.	Wounded	Lacey James	Pte.	Wounded
Young —	Sgt/Mjr.	Wounded	Langtree Charles	Pte.	Wounded
Court Robert	Sergt.	Wounded	Lee George	Pte.	Wounded
Newport —	Sergt.	Wounded	Lohan Andrew	Pte.	Wounded
O' Neill	Sergt.	Wounded	Luff Joseph	Pte.	Wounded
Haney John	Corpl.	Wounded	McCarthy Edward	Pte.	Wounded
Lyons —	Corpl.	Wounded	McDermond John	Pte.	Wounded
Twomey —	Corpl.	Wounded	McGuire John	Pte.	Wounded
Bygroves Edward	Drummer	Wounded	McKay Joseph	Pte.	Wounded
Akers William	Pte.	Wounded	McLean Daniel	Pte.	Wounded
Allen John	Pte.	Wounded	McNamara John	Pte.	Wounded
Badman Samuel	Pte.	Wounded	McNamara Timothy	Pte.	Wounded
Barrett Daniel	Pte.	Wounded	Mackay Michael	Pte.	Wounded
Boam Edward	Pte.	Wounded	Magee Patrick	Pte.	Wounded
Burke Patrick	Pte.	Wounded	Maher Michael	Pte.	Wounded
Byng Henry	Pte.	Wounded	Mahon Michael	Pte.	Wounded
Clutlow Thomas	Pte.	Wounded	Mallet Joseph	Pte.	Wounded
Court Isaac	Pte.	Wounded	Mannion John	Pte.	Wounded
Cowey David	Pte.	Wounded	Mara James	Pte.	Wounded
Dennis Henry	Pte.	Wounded	Mathews Varner	Pte.	Wounded
Dogherty Mathew	Pte.	Wounded	O'Connor Cornelius	Pte.	Wounded
Egan John	Pte.	Wounded	O' Neill John	Pte.	Wounded
Evans George	Pte.	Wounded	Paget William	Pte.	Wounded
Gough Thomas	Pte.	Wounded	Power John	Pte.	Wounded
Harris Charles	Pte.	Wounded	Reddy William	Pte.	Wounded
Haverty Michael	Pte.	Wounded	Sainsbury —	Pte.	Wounded
Hayes George	Pte.	Wounded	Savage John	Pte.	Wounded
Hayre Patrick	Pte.	Wounded	Williams Charles	Pte.	Wounded

NOTES

The Battle of the Alma

49th REGIMENT OF FOOT

NAME	RANK	CASUALTY	NAME	RANK	CASUALTY
Hayes John	Sergt.	Killed	Livock William	Pte.	Wounded
Fraser Charles	Pte.	Killed	Longford Isaac	Pte.	Wounded
Holman William	Q/M/Sergt.	Wounded	McGrath Edward	Pte.	Wounded
French Benjamin	Sergt.	Wounded	McKinlay Joseph	Pte.	Wounded
Flannery Michael	Corpl.	Wounded	Roenan Daniel	Pte.	Wounded
Blaney John	Drummer	Wounded	Smith John	Pte.	Wounded
Ashby Joseph	Pte.	Wounded	Willis Thomas	Pte.	Wounded
Livock James	Pte.	Wounded			

55th REGIMENT OF FOOT

NAME	RANK	CASUALTY	NAME	RANK	CASUALTY
Rose J. B.	Brv/Mjr.	Killed	Fisher William	Pte.	Wounded
Schaw J. G.	Capt.	Killed	Flood John	Pte.	Wounded
Walsh Michael	Sergt.	Killed	Galway John	Pte.	Wounded
Steltzer Lewis	Corpl.	Killed	Givins John	Pte.	Wounded
Berry John	Pte.	Killed	Glasgow James	Pte.	Wounded
Byrnes Michael	Pte.	Killed	Godfrey Henry	Pte.	Wounded
Carty Thomas	Pte.	Killed	Grail Patrick	Pte.	Wounded
Corr Edward	Pte.	Killed	Guerin James	Pte.	Wounded
Darcy Richard	Pte.	Killed	Hamilton John	Pte.	Wounded
Foley Michael	Pte.	Killed	Hare John C.	Pte.	Wounded
McKay William	Pte.	Killed	Harman Henry	Pte.	Wounded
Reves Richard	Pte.	Killed	Harris Charles	Pte.	Wounded
Russell Thomas	Pte.	Killed	Heny Thomas	Pte.	Wounded
Whimper F. A.	Major	Wounded	Hill James	Pte.	Wounded
Coats J.	Brv/Mjr.	Wounded	Hill Joseph	Pte.	Wounded
Armstrong E.	Lieut.	Wounded	Hill Walter	Pte.	Wounded
Bissett G. E.	Lieut.	Wounded	Hillier Daniel	Pte.	Wounded
Warren J.	Lt/Adj.	Wounded	Holman Lawrence	Pte.	Wounded
Flanagan John	Col/Sgt.	Wounded	Hughes Edward	Pte.	Wounded
Keeshan Michael	Col/Sgt.	Wounded	Hutchinson Edward	Pte.	Wounded
Parsons William	Col/Sgt.	Wounded	Kenny William	Pte.	Wounded
Glynn John	Sergt.	Wounded	Kingham Phillip	Pte.	Wounded
Elms Robert	Corpl.	Wounded	Knopp Jonathan	Pte.	Wounded
Holohan Thomas	Corpl.	Wounded	Lawrence James	Pte.	Wounded
Ayleward Thomas	Pte.	Wounded	McAlpin John	Pte.	Wounded
Baker James	Pte.	Wounded	McDonald Norman	Pte.	Wounded
Barrow John	Pte.	Wounded	McGarity James	Pte.	Wounded
Barry John	Pte.	Wounded	McGregor William	Pte.	Wounded
Berry Thomas	Pte.	Wounded	McLeod Donald	Pte.	Wounded
Berry William	Pte.	Wounded	McMahon Thomas	Pte.	Wounded
Blair Archibald	Pte.	Wounded	McNally George	Pte.	Wounded
Boag Thomas	Pte.	Wounded	McNally James	Pte.	Wounded
Brag Michael	Pte.	Wounded	McNicol Archibald	Pte.	Wounded
Brinkworth William	Pte.	Wounded	McVean Peter	Pte.	Wounded
Brodcrick Denis	Pte.	Wounded	Marr James	Pte.	Wounded
Butler Philip	Pte.	Wounded	Meara Andrew	Pte.	Wounded
Carty Owen	Pte.	Wounded	Mera John	Pte.	Wounded
Colclough Robert	Pte.	Wounded	Minoge Edward	Pte.	Wounded
Connell John	Pte.	Wounded	Miller Samuel	Pte.	Wounded
Conway Michael	Pte.	Wounded	Murphy John	Pte.	Wounded
Cooney John	Pte.	Wounded	Nixon John	Pte.	Wounded
Craig William	Pte.	Wounded	Oakley James	Pte.	Wounded
Cross Enoch	Pte.	Wounded	O'Donnell John	Pte.	Wounded
Dally James	Pte.	Wounded	Pothcary Semer	Pte.	Wounded
Daniell John	Pte.	Wounded	Pugh Enoch	Pte.	Wounded
Dann Harold	Pte.	Wounded	Ramage Andrew	Pte.	Wounded
Doyle John	Pte.	Wounded	Rodway William	Pte.	Wounded
Edwards Robert	Pte.	Wounded	Ryan Andrew	Pte.	Wounded
Evans John	Pte.	Wounded	Sales George	Pte.	Wounded

NOTES

The Battle of the Alma

55th REGIMENT OF FOOT

NAME	RANK	CASUALTY	NAME	RANK	CASUALTY
Sedgwick William	Pte.	Wounded	Vanson John	Pte.	Wounded
Sheavor William	Pte.	Wounded	White James	Pte.	Wounded
Smith Thomas	Pte.	Wounded	Whitehead John	Pte.	Wounded
Tindall John	Pte.	Wounded	Wood Daniel	Pte.	Wounded
Townsend William	Pte.	Wounded	Young John	Pte.	Wounded
Trimmings John	Pte.	Wounded			

77th REGIMENT OF FOOT

NAME	RANK	CASUALTY	NAME	RANK	CASUALTY
Bright John	Pte.	Killed	Hundlehy George	Pte.	Wounded
Connors John	Pte.	Killed	Large Thomas	Pte.	Wounded
Kennedy Thomas	Pte.	Killed	Lyons William	Pte.	Wounded
Perry William	Corpl.	Wounded	Masterton James	Pte.	Wounded
Richards Charles	Corpl.	Wounded	Padden Thomas	Pte.	Wounded
Clarke Henry	Pte.	Wounded	Pitt Edward	Pte.	Wounded
Emery Richard	Pte.	Wounded	Sauce James	Pte.	Wounded
Harris John	Pte.	Wounded	Thompson James	Pte.	Wounded
Hicks Albert	Pte.	Wounded	Wallace John	Pte.	Wounded
Hughes Michael	Pte.	Wounded	Williams Henry J.	Pte.	Wounded

79th HIGHLANDERS

NAME	RANK	CASUALTY	NAME	RANK	CASUALTY
Baird John	Pte.	Killed	Chapman Thomas	Pte.	Wounded
Watson James	Pte.	Killed	Dunbar James	Pte.	Wounded
Thom William	Corpl.	Wounded	Kilgower William	Pte.	Wounded
Anderson James	Pte.	Wounded	McLuskie Edward	Pte.	Wounded
Browne John	Pte.	Wounded			

88th REGIMENT OF FOOT

NAME	RANK	CASUALTY	NAME	RANK	CASUALTY
Duffy Edward	Pte.	Killed	Gwynn Daniel	Pte.	Wounded
Kernon James	Pte.	Killed	Higgins John	Pte.	Wounded
Lyons Patrick	Pte.	Killed	Horrigan Thomas	Pte.	Wounded
Scanlon Maurice	Pte.	Killed	Killilea Thomas	Pte.	Wounded
Moore T.	Qrt/master	Wounded	McNab Peter	Pte.	Wounded
McNally George	Col/Sgt	Wounded	McClernan Alexander	Pte.	Wounded
Fallon James	Sergt.	Wounded	Scheal Patrick	Pte.	Wounded
Burke Peter	Pte.	Wounded	Shearman Thomas	Pte.	Wounded
Day Martin	Pte.	Wounded	Smith Constantine	Pte.	Wounded
Farrell Patrick	Pte.	Wounded	Tangney Maurice	Pte.	Wounded
Gallaher John	Pte.	Wounded	Cameron Hugh	Pte.	Missing
Grealy Michael	Pte.	Wounded			

93rd HIGHLANDERS

NAME	RANK	CASUALTY	NAME	RANK	CASUALTY
Abercrombie R.	Lieut.	Killed	Austin Alexander	Pte.	Wounded
Cameron John	Pte.	Killed	Aymers George	Pte.	Wounded
McLeod William	Pte.	Killed	Bain James	Pte.	Wounded
Paton Robert	Pte.	Killed	Burnie John	Pte.	Wounded
Wyllie William	Pte.	Killed	Burns John	Pte.	Wounded
McDonald Alexander	Sergt.	Wounded	Carson Thomas	Pte.	Wounded
Phillips David	Sergt.	Wounded	Chalmers James	Pte.	Wounded
Adams Robert	Pte.	Wounded	Feckney George	Pte.	Wounded

NOTES

The Battle of the Alma
93rd HIGHLANDERS

NAME	RANK	CASUALTY	NAME	RANK	CASUALTY
Ferguson William	Pte.	Wounded	Morrison William	Pte.	Wounded
Flanagan Neil	Pte.	Wounded	Munro D.	Pte.	Wounded
Garraty George	Pte.	Wounded	Nichol David	Pte.	Wounded
Gordon James	Pte.	Wounded	Paton William	Pte.	Wounded
Gordon John	Pte.	Wounded	Paul Alexander	Pte.	Wounded
Heggins John	Pte.	Wounded	Polson William	Pte.	Wounded
Leslie John	Pte.	Wounded	Polson Donald	Pte.	Wounded
McDonald William	Pte.	Wounded	Robertson Ramsay	Pte.	Wounded
McDonald Alexander	Pte.	Wounded	Ross George	Pte.	Wounded
McDonald John	Pte.	Wounded	Shaw James	Pte.	Wounded
McGunigall Hugh	Pte.	Wounded	Todd Alexander	Pte.	Wounded
McKay John	Pte.	Wounded	Torry John	Pte.	Wounded
McKinon John	Pte.	Wounded	Urquhart William	Pte.	Wounded
McPherson David	Pte.	Wounded	Stephen David	Sergt.	D.O.W.
Melville Donald	Pte.	Wounded			

95th REGIMENT OF FOOT

NAME	RANK	CASUALTY	NAME	RANK	CASUALTY
Dowdall G. J.	Capt.	Killed	Sims William	Pte.	Killed
Eddington J. G.	Capt.	Killed	Skinner Henry	Pte.	Killed
Eddington E. W.	Lieut.	Killed	Sullivan Daniel	Pte.	Killed
Polhill R. C.	Lieut.	Killed	Sullivan Patrick	Pte.	Killed
Kingsley J. C.	Lt/Adj.	Killed	Timson Thomas	Pte.	Killed
Braybrooke W. L.	Lieut.	Killed	Wells William	Pte.	Killed
(Ceylon Rifles attch 95th)			Woy Moses	Pte.	Killed
Blackshaw William	Sergt.	Killed	Smith W.	Lt/Col.	Wounded
Huggard Stephen	Sergt.	Killed	Hume H.	Major	Wounded
Woolnough Robert	Sergt.	Killed	Heyland A. T.	Brv/Mjr.	Wounded
Delaney John	Corpl.	Killed	Sargent J. W.	Capt.	Wounded
Matthews Andrew	Corpl.	Killed	Wing V.	Capt.	Wounded
Rogers Alfred	Corpl.	Killed	Gerard R.	Lieut.	Wounded
Avery Thomas	Pte.	Killed	Macdonald A.	Lieut.	Wounded
Bakewell William	Pte.	Killed	Braybrook B.	Ensign	Wounded
Branson Henry	Pte.	Killed	Brooke J. H.	Ensign	Wounded
Brooker Henry	Pte.	Killed	Boothby B. C.	Ensign	Wounded
Casey James	Pte.	Killed	Bazalgette E.	Ensign	Wounded
Chapman William	Pte.	Killed	Gordon A.	Surgeon	Wounded
Connor Michael	Pte.	Killed	Baghurst James	Sergt.	Wounded
Cross Abraham	Pte.	Killed	Davis George	Sergt.	Wounded
Donoghue Patrick	Pte.	Killed	Garrat George	Sergt.	Wounded
Frost Thomas	Pte.	Killed	Hodgson Thomas	Sergt.	Wounded
Fry Samuel	Pte.	Killed	Logan William	Sergt.	Wounded
Hagen Patrick	Pte.	Killed	McDowell Thomas	Sergt.	Wounded
Hall Thomas	Pte.	Killed	Murphy John	Sergt.	Wounded
Herr John	Pte.	Killed	Poulteney George	Sergt.	Wounded
Hodgskinson James	Pte.	Killed	Rontier William	Sergt.	Wounded
Johnstone John	Pte.	Killed	Walker R. G.	Sergt.	Wounded
Jeggett George	Pte.	Killed	Wetton Thomas	Sergt.	Wounded
Juff Peter	Pte.	Killed	Whaley Joseph	Sergt.	Wounded
McCann Hugh	Pte.	Killed	Aldworth Patrick	Corpl.	Wounded
McCarthy William	Pte.	Killed	Death Thomas	Corpl.	Wounded
Magenis Hugh	Pte.	Killed	Dulahan James	Corpl.	Wounded
Martin John	Pte.	Killed	Gunyon George J.	Corpl.	Wounded
Moon Henry	Pte.	Killed	Larkin Martin	Corpl.	Wounded
Murphy Thomas	Pte.	Killed	Seymour George	Corpl.	Wounded
Nelson James	Pte.	Killed	Walsh James	Corpl.	Wounded
Oldring Goldsmith	Pte.	Killed	Wilson Alfred	Corpl.	Wounded
Pegg Charles	Pte.	Killed	McElwer William	Drummer	Wounded
Reilly James	Pte.	Killed	Adams George	Pte.	Wounded
Ring John	Pte.	Killed	Anderson Thomas	Pte.	Wounded
Roddle Stephen	Pte.	Killed	Atkins Daniel	Pte.	Wounded
Shea John	Pte.	Killed	Barnett Joseph	Pte.	Wounded

NOTES

The Battle of the Alma

95th REGIMENT OF FOOT

NAME	RANK	CASUALTY	NAME	RANK	CASUALTY
Barry Richard	Pte.	Wounded	Karley Ephraim	Pte.	Wounded
Baxter Thomas	Pte.	Wounded	Keeling Francis	Pte.	Wounded
Beresford George	Pte.	Wounded	Lamb John	Pte.	Wounded
Bevis William	Pte.	Wounded	Leary Daniel	Pte.	Wounded
Bliss William	Pte.	Wounded	Levey Benjamin	Pte.	Wounded
Blythe Joseph	Pte.	Wounded	Lordon Jeremiah	Pte.	Wounded
Bonython Thomas	Pte.	Wounded	McArdie James	Pte.	Wounded
Boon Henry	Pte.	Wounded	McCastlin John	Pte.	Wounded
Booton Samuel	Pte.	Wounded	McCourt Robert	Pte.	Wounded
Bowers John	Pte.	Wounded	McGillicuddy James	Pte.	Wounded
Brennan Eugene	Pte.	Wounded	McKernar James	Pte.	Wounded
Brown Morris	Pte.	Wounded	McShean James	Pte.	Wounded
Burgess Joseph	Pte.	Wounded	Madden Thomas	Pte.	Wounded
Callaghan John	Pte.	Wounded	Mason Edward	Pte.	Wounded
Card Thomas	Pte.	Wounded	Monger John	Pte.	Wounded
Carter George	Pte.	Wounded	Montague Sydney C.	Pte.	Wounded
Clarke John	Pte.	Wounded	Murphy Joseph	Pte.	Wounded
Clarke Samuel	Pte.	Wounded	Norris Thomas	Pte.	Wounded
Collins Daniel	Pte.	Wounded	O'Keefe John	Pte.	Wounded
Cooknell John	Pte.	Wounded	Osborne James	Pte.	Wounded
Cooper George	Pte.	Wounded	Pearce Benjamin	Pte.	Wounded
Connor John	Pte.	Wounded	Philp Charles	Pte.	Wounded
Crouch John	Pte.	Wounded	Pollard George	Pte.	Wounded
Culbert William	Pte.	Wounded	Pratt Thomas	Pte.	Wounded
Daley Denis	Pte.	Wounded	Rangden Thomas	Pte.	Wounded
Daw Jesse	Pte.	Wounded	Rawlins Samuel	Pte.	Wounded
Day George	Pte.	Wounded	Reardon James	Pte.	Wounded
Delaney Thomas	Pte.	Wounded	Ripley James	Pte.	Wounded
Donnell William	Pte.	Wounded	Risby Samuel	Pte.	Wounded
Donoghue Jeremiah	Pte.	Wounded	Rose Charles	Pte.	Wounded
Downey James	Pte.	Wounded	Rose Joel	Pte.	Wounded
Farthing Robert	Pte.	Wounded	Russell John	Pte.	Wounded
Fielding James	Pte.	Wounded	Savin John	Pte.	Wounded
Flynn Matthew	Pte.	Wounded	Scott James	Pte.	Wounded
Golden James	Pte.	Wounded	Seaborn John	Pte.	Wounded
Goulden Thomas	Pte.	Wounded	Seckington Harry	Pte.	Wounded
Hale James	Pte.	Wounded	Shaw Frederick	Pte	Wounded
Harrison John	Pte.	Wounded	Shea Darby	Pte.	Wounded
Harrison Joseph	Pte.	Wounded	Shepperson William	Pte.	Wounded
Harrison Martin	Pte.	Wounded	Smith John	Pte.	Wounded
Hayes Patrick	Pte.	Wounded	Smith Nicholas	pte.	Wounded
Hazeldine John	Pte.	Wounded	Stewart James	Pte.	Wounded
Healy Thomas	Pte.	Wounded	Sullivan Eugene	Pte.	Wounded
Herlaha Denis	Pte.	Wounded	Trainor William	Pte.	Wounded
Hill John	Pte.	Wounded	Tunnicliffe John	Pte.	Wounded
Holmes Arthur	Pte.	Wounded	Turner John	Pte.	Wounded
Hollybrass Frederick	Pte.	Wounded	Ward Patrick	Pte.	Wounded
Irwin James	Pte.	Wounded	Ward Robert	Pte.	Wounded
Jacques John	Pte.	Wounded	Woodward Robert	Pte.	Wounded
Jones John	Pte.	Wounded	Groomsell William	Corpl.	Missing
Jones Thomas	Pte.	Wounded	Clements William	Pte.	Missing
Jones William	Pte.	Wounded	Wright Walter	Pte.	Missing

1st BATTALION RIFLE BRIGADE

NAME	RANK	CASUALTY
Rose Richard	Pte.	Wounded

NOTES

The Battle of the Alma
2nd BATTALION RIFLE BRIGADE

NAME	RANK	CASUALTY	NAME	RANK	CASUALTY
Simpson W.	Sergt.	Killed	Ford Thomas	Pte.	Wounded
Swallow James	Sergt.	Killed	Gray James	Pte.	Wounded
Robinson John	Corpl.	Killed	Griffiths —	Pte.	Wounded
Calton Henry	Pte.	Killed	Hawkins Richard	Pte.	Wounded
Finnucane Cornelius	Pte.	Killed	Hicks Joseph	Pte.	Wounded
Hexter Edward	Pte.	Killed	Howell Charles	Pte.	Wounded
Kennedy William	Pte.	Killed	Howley Patrick	Pte.	Wounded
McBride Michael	Pte.	Killed	Illman William	Pte.	Wounded
Pine Thomas	Pte.	Killed	Jones David	Pte.	Wounded
Rason Charles	Pte.	Killed	Kally Thomas	Pte.	Wounded
Robinson George	Pte.	Killed	Lloyd Richard	Pte.	Wounded
Earl of Errol	Capt.	Wounded	Long William	Pte.	Wounded
Lucas Lucas	Sergt.	Wounded	Marton Richard	Pte.	Wounded
Davis John	Bugler	Wounded	Mills William	Pte.	Wounded
Dyre Isaac	Bugler	Wounded	Mulligan William	Pte.	Wounded
Ebethurte George	Bugler	Wounded	Nailon Morris	Pte.	Wounded
Allen Thomas	Pte.	Wounded	Owen John	Pte.	Wounded
Beeton Augustus	Pte.	Wounded	Price Henry	Pte.	Wounded
Bennett James	Pte.	Wounded	Rhodes Charles	Pte.	Wounded
Burchill Jesse	Pte.	Wounded	Sand John	Pte.	Wounded
Cooley John	Pte.	Wounded	Stewart Alexander	Pte.	Wounded
Coombes George	Pte.	Wounded	Summers Richard	Pte.	Wounded
Cooper Henry	Pte.	Wounded	Taylor William	Pte.	Wounded
Coston Elijah	Pte.	Wounded	Warren George	Pte.	Wounded
Farrar William	Pte.	Wounded	Woolf Samuel	Pte.	Wounded

NOTES

THE HIGHLANDERS
ATTACKING THE RUSSIAN REDOUBT
AT THE
BATTLE OF ALMA.

Sir Colin Campbell, far ahead of his men, shouted to them with heroic emulation,
"We'll hae nane but Hieland bonnets here." *p.227*

BATTLE FIELD OF THE ALMA.
NIGHT AFTER THE BATTLE.

THE FIRST BOMBARDMENT OF SEBASTOPOL, FIRST BATTLE OF INKERMANN, AND MINOR ACTIONS

The following casualties occurred among the Officers, Non-Commissioned Officers and Men of the Army, published for October and early November 1854. In many cases the specific date of casualty was not given and the degree of wound not stated. The casualty dates listed indicate the following:-
1. Casualties subsequent to the opening of the Trenches before Sebastopol, 10th October 1854.
2. The First Bombardment of Sebastopol, 17th October 1854.
3. The First Battle of Inkermann, 26th October 1854 in which the 30th, 41st, 47th, 49th and 95th Regiments took part.
4. Minor skirmishes and desultory shelling by the enemy. (Refer to Chronological Events of the War. Appendix II).

Compiled from the London Gazette, dates as indicated against each entry.

ROYAL ARTILLERY

NAME	RANK	CASUALTY	DATE	LONDON GAZETTE
Spiers J.	Sergt.	Killed	24-10-54	16-11-54
Taylor F.	Sergt.	Killed	24-10-54	16-11-54
Fox William	A/Bombr.	Killed	22-10-54	16-11-54
Pocock A.	A/Bombr.	Killed	13/17-10-54	11-11-54
Devlin Joseph	Gunner	Killed	3-11-54	11-12-54
Element Alfred	Gunner	Killed	22-10-54	16-11-54
Hammond George	Gunner	Killed	2-11-54	11-12-54
Hodgeson J.	Gunner	Killed	23-10-54	16-11-54
Morrison R.	Gunner	Killed	23-10-54	16-11-54
Sweeney O.	Gnr.&Drvr.	Killed	18/21-10-54	7-11-54
Tinsley J.	Gnr.&Drvr.	Killed	18/21-10-54	7-11-54
Wyler R.	Gnr.&Drvr.	Killed	18/21-10-54	7-11-54
Maude G. A.	Capt.	W/D	25-10-54	16-11-54
Garland Robert	Sergt.	W/Sv	13/17-10-54	11-11-54
Mitchell J.	Sergt.	W/Sl	23-10-54	16-11-54
Moran J.	Sergt.	W/Sl	18/21-10-54	7-11-54
Mould John	Sergt.	W/D	25-10-54	16-11-54
Smith G.	Sergt	W/Sl	18/21-10-54	7-11-54
Organ H.	Corpl.	W/Sl	18/21-10-54	7-11-54
Walker J.	Corpl.	W/Sv	13/17-10-54	11-11-54
Blacker John	Bombr.	W/Sl	22-10-54	16-11-54

NOTES

The First Bombardment of Sebastopol, First Battle of Inkermann, and Minor Actions

ROYAL ARTILLERY

NAME	RANK	CASUALTY	DATE	LONDON GAZETTE
Dundas James	Bombr.	W/Sl	20-10-54	16-11-54
Kenan William	Bombr.	W/Sl	18/21-10-54	7-11-54
Lane W.	Bombr.	W/Sl	20-10-54	16-11-54
McFaddyen John	Bombr.	W/Sl	13/17-10-54	11-11-54
McPherson J.	Bombr.	W/Sl	18/21-10-54	7-11-54
Manns J. M.	Bombr.	W/Sv	24-10-54	16-11-54
Bake R.	A/Bombr.	W/Sv	13/17-10-54	11-11-54
Pinion W.	A/Bombr.	W/Sl	23-10-54	16-11-54
Solomon E.	A/Bombr.	W/Sv	13/17-10-54	11-11-54
Webber Henry	A/Bombr.	W/Sl	13/17-10-54	11-11-54
Bradley John	Gnr.&Drvr.	W/Sl	18/21-10-54	7-11-54
Carson J.	Gnr.&Drvr.	W/Sv	13/17-10-54	11-11-54
Crofts John	Gnr.&Drvr.	W/Sv	13/17-10-54	11-11-54
Cunningham C.	Gnr.&Drvr.	Wounded	18/21-10-54	7-11-54
Davis Hugh	Gnr.&Drvr.	Wounded	18/21-10-54	7-11-54
Dennison W.	Gnr.&Drvr.	Wounded	18/21-10-54	7-11-54
Devlin Patrick	Gnr.&Drvr	W/Sl	13/17-10-54	11-11-54
Galton William	Gnr.&Drvr.	Wounded	18/21-10-54	7-11-54
Gummie J.	Gnr.&Drvr.	W/Sl	13/17-10-54	11-11-54
Haggett T.	Gnr.&Drvr.	W/Sl	13/17-10-54	11-11-54
Hawkins C.	Gnr.&Drvr.	W/Sv	13/17-10-54	11-11-54
Hill John	Gnr.&Drvr.	Wounded	18/21-10-54	7-11-54
Honey John	Gnr.&Drvr	Wounded	18/21-10-54	7-11-54
Hughes J.	Gnr.&Drvr.	W/Sv	13/17-10-54	11-11-54
Light John	Gnr.&Drvr.	Wounded	18/21-10-54	7-11-54
McCawley D.	Gnr.&Drvr.	W/Sv	13/17-10-54	11-11-54
McKafferty J.	Gnr.&Drvr.	W/Sv	13/17-10-54	11-11-54
McKee Robert	Gnr.&Drvr.	W/Sl	29-10-54	26-11-54
Mallett R.	Gnr.&Drvr.	W/Sl	13/17-10-54	11-11-54
Mattison J.	Gnr.&Drvr.	Wounded	18/21-10-54	7-11-54
Murphy James	Gnr.&Drvr.	W/Sl	13/17-10-54	11-11-54
Nicholls Samuel	Gnr.&Drvr.	W/D	13/17-10-54	11-11-54
O'Neil W.	Gnr.&Drvr.	Wounded	18/21-10-54	7-11-54
Orr John	Gnr.&Drvr.	W/Sl	13/17-10-54	11-11-54
Orron J.	Gnr.&Drvr.	W/Sl	13/17-10-54	11-11-54
Sutherland A.	Gnr.&Drvr.	Wounded	18/21-10-54	7-11-54
Welsh J.	Gnr.&Drvr.	W/Sl	13/17-10-54	11-11-54
White J.	Gnr.&Drvr.	Wounded	18/21-10-54	7-11-54
Wilson J.	Gnr.&Drvr.	W/Sv	13/17-10-54	11-11-54
Withers J.	Gnr.&Drvr.	Wounded	18/21-10-54	7-11-54
Wyatt J.	Gnr.&Drvr.	Wounded	18/21-10-54	7-11-54
Bennett John	Gunner	W/Sv	22-10-54	16-11-54
Cator Samuel	Gunner	W/Sv	22-10-54	16-11-54
Cliburn John	Gunner	W/Sl	22-10-54	16-11-54
Coats R.	Gunner	W/Sv	23-10-54	16-11-54
Cunningham Charles	Gunner	W/Sl	2-11-54	11-12-54
Davidson William	Gunner	W/Sl	25-10-54	16-11-54
Death J.	Gunner	W/Sv	23-10-54	16-11-54
Dugan John	Gunner	W/Sl	22-10-54	16-11-54
Grey Thomas	Gunner	W/Sl	2-11-54	11-12-54
Gobsell Joseph	Gunner	W/Sl	25-10-54	16-11-54
Hannigan W.	Gunner	W/Sv	23-10-54	16-11-54
Jackson Arthur	Gunner	W/Sl	25-10-54	16-11-54
Kavanagh W.	Gunner	W/Sl	24-10-54	16-11-54
Kench E.	Gunner	W/Sl	24-10-54	16-11-54
Mitchell James	Gunner	W/Sl	22-10-54	16-11-54
Morley James	Gunner	W/Sl	29-10-54	26-11-54
Pemberton W.	Gunner	W/D	24-10-54	16-11-54
Preslee John	Gunner	W/Sl	22-10-54	16-11-54
Russell Robert	Gunner	W/Sl	20-10-54	16-11-54
Sims Henry	Gunner	W/Sl	22-10-54	16-11-54
Walsh D	Gunner	W/Sl	13/17-10-54	11-11-54
Williams John	Gsunner	W/Sl	22-10-54	16-11-54
Williams William	Gunner	W/Sl	29-10-54	26-11-54
Wilson William	Gunner	W/Sl	27-10-54	16-11-54

NOTES

The First Bombardment of Sebastopol, First Battle of Inkermann, and Minor Actions

ROYAL SAPPERS AND MINERS

NAME	RANK	CASUALTY	DATE	LONDON GAZETTE
Denholm William	Pte.	Killed	18/21-10-54	7-11-54
Bland J.	Pte.	W/D	24-10-54	16-11-54
Dilling James	Pte.	W/Sl	25-10-54	16-11-54
Hutton John	Pte.	W/Sl	30-10-54	16-11-54
Wheeler J.	Pte.	W/Sl	24-10-54	16-11-54

3rd BATTALION GRENADIER GUARDS

NAME	RANK	CASUALTY	DATE	LONDON GAZETTE
Bowell G.	Pte.	Killed	18/21-10-54	7-11-54
Bridle R.	Pte.	Killed	18/21-10-54	7-11-54
Malone J.	Pte.	Killed	18/21-10-54	7-11-54
Sergeant —	Sergt.	Wounded	18/21-10-54	7-11-54
Key W.	Corpl.	Wounded	18/21-10-54	7-11-54
Bacchus G.	Pte.	Wounded	18/21-10-54	7-11-54
Bridgman William	Pte.	Wounded	13/17-10-54	11-11-54
Cooper W.	Pte.	Wounded	18/21-10-54	7-11-54
Crickmay W.	Pte.	Wounded	18/21-10-54	7-11-54
East George	Pte.	Wounded	13/17-10-54	11-11-54
Fordham James	Pte.	Wounded	13/17-10-54	11-11-54
Gilbert Henry	Pte.	Wounded	13/17-10-54	11-11-54
Harman J.	Pte.	Wounded	18/21-10-54	7-11-54
Jackson W.	Pte.	Wounded	18/21-10-54	7-11-54
Laice Matthew	Pte.	Wounded	26-10-54	16-11-54
Luthers B.	Pte.	Wounded	18/21-10-54	7-11-54
Newton John	Pte.	Wounded	13/17-10-54	11-11-54
Steel John	Pte.	Wounded	13/17-10-54	11-11-54
Smith Elijah	Pte.	Wounded	13/17-10-54	11-11-54
Taylor William	Pte.	Wounded	13/17-10-54	11-11-54
Tibbitt Benjamin	Pte.	Wounded	13/17-10-54	11-11-54
Vine W.	Pte.	Wounded	18/21-10-54	7-11-54
Whetstone Thomas	Pte.	Wounded	13/17-10-54	11-11-54

1st BATTALION COLDSTREAM GUARDS

NAME	RANK	CASUALTY	DATE	LONDON GAZETTE
Bull S.	Pte.	Killed	18/21-10-54	7-11-54
Tipple S.	Pte.	Killed	18/21-10-54	7-11-54
Martin J.	Drummer	Wounded	18/21-10-54	7-11-54
Randle G.	Pte.	Wounded	18/21-10-54	7-11-54
Smith P.	Pte.	Wounded	18/21-10-54	7-11-54
Tooley William	Pte.	Wounded	1-11-54	16-11-54

1st BATTALION SCOTS FUSILIER GUARDS

NAME	RANK	CASUALTY	DATE	LONDON GAZETTE
Edy G.	Pte.	Wounded	18/21-10-54	7-11-54
Femister H.	Pte.	Wounded	18/21-10-54	7-11-54
Gartrie S.	Pte.	Wounded	18/21-10-54	7-11-54
Purvis J.	Pte.	Wounded	18/21-10-54	7-11-54
Watson J.	Pte.	Wounded	18/21-10-54	7-11-54

NOTES

The First Bombardment of Sebastopol, First Battle of Inkermann, and Minor Actions

1st BATTALION 1st REGIMENT OF FOOT

NAME	RANK	CASUALTY	DATE	LONDON GAZETTE
Webb William	Pte.	Killed	13/17-10-54	11-11-54
Bristow William	Pte.	Wounded	22-10-54	16-11-54
Goose William	Pte.	Wounded	13/17-10-54	11-11-54
Jones Thomas	Pte.	Wounded	13/17-10-54	11-11-54
Kenny Martin	Pte.	Wounded	13/17-10-54	11-11-54
Kernan Robert	Pte.	Wounded	26-10-54	16-11-54
Mulready James	Pte.	Wounded	13/17-10-54	11-11-54
Noonan William	Pte.	Wounded	23-10-54	16-11-54
Ray John	Pte.	Wounded	13/17-10-54	11-11-54

4th REGIMENT OF FOOT

NAME	RANK	CASUALTY	DATE	LONDON GAZETTE
Ewen H.	Pte.	Killed	18/21-10-54	7-11-54
Frawley J.	Pte.	Killed	18/21-10-54	7-11-54
Banks J.	Pte.	Killed	18/21-10-54	7-11-54
Calligan Patrick M.	Pte.	Killed	18/21-10-54	7-11-54
Cross J.	Pte.	Killed	18/21-10-54	7-11-54
Hagan J.	Pte.	Killed	18/21-10-54	7-11-54
Mulquearn M.	Pte.	Killed	18/21-10-54	7-11-54

7th REGIMENT OF FOOT

NAME	RANK	CASUALTY	DATE	LONDON GAZETTE
Linegar William	Corpl.	Killed	18/21-10-54	7-11-54
Blacker Charles	Corpl.	Wounded	18/21-10-54	7-11-54
Bretton Francis	Pte.	Wounded	27-10-54	16-11-54
Butler Edwin	Pte.	Wounded	25-10-54	16-11-54
Carney Edward	Pte.	Wounded	26-10-54	16-11-54
Ford John	Pte.	Wounded	22-10-54	16-11-54
Henry James	Pte.	Wounded	13/17-10-54	11-11-54
Hopes William	Pte.	Wounded	26-10-54	16-11-54
Kirk Thomas	Pte.	Wounded	22-10-54	16-11-54
Myland John	Pte.	Wounded	26-10-54	16-11-54
O'Connell William	Pte.	Wounded	26-10-54	16-11-54
Robinson James	Pte.	Wounded	22-10-54	16-11-54
Shepherd John	Pte.	Wounded	22-10-54	16-11-54
Tyne Patrick	Pte.	Wounded	22-10-54	16-11-54

19th REGIMENT OF FOOT

NAME	RANK	CASUALTY	DATE	LONDON GAZETTE
Dunn William	Sergt.	Killed	18/12-10-54	7-11-54
Campion Patrick	Col/Sgt.	Wounded	13/17-10-54	11-11-54
Austin John	Corpl.	Wounded	13/17-10-54	11-11-54
Cruikshank Thomas	Corpl.	Wounded	13/17-10-54	11-11-54
Hanlon Henry	Drummer	Wounded	13/17-10-54	11-11-54
Beer Jacob	Pte.	Wounded	18/21-10-54	7-11-54
Corbett John	Pte.	Wounded	13/17-10-54	11-11-54
Crowley William	Pte.	W/Sl	26-10-54	16-11-54
Dixson Thomas	Pte.	Wounded	13/17-10-54	11-11-54
Flinn James	Pte.	W/Sl	21-10-54	16-11-54
Gomm James	Pte.	W/Sl	26-10-54	16-11-54
Gun P. M. G.	Pte.	W/M	24-10-54	16-11-54

NOTES

The First Bombardment of Sebastopol, First Battle of Inkermann, and Minor Actions

19th REGIMENT OF FOOT

NAME	RANK	CASUALTY	DATE	LONDON GAZETTE
Haigh George	Pte.	Wounded	18/21-10-54	7-11-54
Keating Edward	Pte.	W/Sv	24-10-54	16-11-54
Loughlin Michael	Pte.	Wounded	13/17-10-54	11-11-54
Maher James	Pte.	Wounded	13/17-10-54	11-11-54
Reimy James	Pte.	Wounded	18/21-10-54	7-11-54

20th REGIMENT OF FOOT

NAME	RANK	CASUALTY	DATE	LONDON GAZETTE
Wosley James	Pte.	Killed	13/17-10-54	11-11-54
Wyatt Thomas	Pte.	Killed	13/17-10-54	11-11-54
Horsford James	Drummer	W/Sl	29-10-54	16-11-54
Akins George	Pte.	W/M	1-11-54	16-11-54
Dewell James	Pte.	Wounded	18/21-10-54	7-11-54
Humphries Charles	Pte.	W/Sl	1-11-54	16-11-54
Langley John	Pte.	Wounded	13/17-10-54	11-11-54
Lynch James	Pte.	W/Sl	25-10-54	16-11-54
Pemberton Samuel	Pte.	W/Sl	29-10-54	16-11-54
Riton James	Pte.	Wounded	13/17-10-54	11-11-54
Swan David	Pte.	W/Sl	22-10-54	16-11-54
Young G.	Pte.	Wounded	13/17-10-54	11-11-54

21st REGIMENT OF FOOT

NAME	RANK	CASUALTY	DATE	LONDON GAZETTE
Dumphey Fenton	Pte.	Killed	1-11-54	16-11-54
Wright John	Pte.	Killed	1-11-54	16-11-54
Bishop William	Pte.	Wounded	18/21-10-54	7-11-54
Brogan Robert	Pte.	Wounded	13/17-10-54	11-11-54
Kay John	Pte.	Wounded	13/17-10-54	11-11-54

23rd REGIMENT OF FOOT

NAME	RANK	CASUALTY	DATE	LONDON GAZETTE
Shine Owen	Pte.	Killed	18/21-10-54	7-11-54
Dawson James	Corpl.	Wounded	13/17-10-54	11-11-54
Atherson Edward	Pte.	Wounded	18/21-10-54	7-11-54
Calville John	Pte.	Wounded	26-10-54	16-11-54
Corfield William	Pte.	Wounded	13/17-10-54	11-11-54
Crowther Joseph	Pte.	Wounded	18/21-10-54	7-11-54
Davies David	Pte.	Wounded	13/17-10-54	11-11-54
Elvis William	Pte.	Wounded	18/21-10-54	7-11-54
Moulton George	Pte.	Wounded	13/17-10-54	11-11-54
Murphy James	Pte.	Wounded	13/17-10-54	11-11-54
Murren James	Pte.	Wounded	3-11-54	11-12-54
Ogilway James	Pte.	Wounded	13/17-10-54	11-11-54
Stack Thomas	Pte.	Wounded	18/21-10-54	7-11-54

NOTES

The First Bombardment of Sebastopol, First Battle of Inkermann, and Minor Actions

28th REGIMENT OF FOOT

NAME	RANK	CASUALTY	DATE	LONDON GAZETTE
Faulkner W.	Col/Sgt.	Killed	18/21-10-54	7-11-54
Door S.	Pte.	Killed	18/21-10-54	7-11-54
Bailey J.	Pte.	Wounded	18/21-10-54	7-11-54
Cavan F.	Pte.	Wounded	18/21-10-54	7-11-54
Daley P.	Pte.	Wounded	18/21-10-54	7-11-54
Flaherty Edmund	Pte.	W/Sl	25-10-54	16-11-54
Timpson J.	Pte.	Wounded	18/21-10-54	7-11-54

30th REGIMENT OF FOOT

NAME	RANK	CASUALTY	DATE	LONDON GAZETTE
Freeman Charles	Pte.	Killed	26-10-54	16-11-54
Hunter Robert	Pte.	Killed	26-10-54	16-11-54
Jenkinson Thomas	Pte.	Killed	26-10-54	16-11-54
Matthews Bryan	Pte.	Killed	26-10-54	16-11-54
Morris Patrick	Pte.	Killed	26-10-54	16-11-54
Rose George	Pte.	Killed	26-10-54	16-11-54
Smith George(4th)	Pte.	Killed	26-10-54	16-11-54
Sullivan Daniel	Sergt.	W/Sl	26-10-54	16-11-54
Delaney Thomas	Corpl.	W/Sl	26-10-54	16-11-54
Sharp John	Corpl.	W/Sv	26-10-54	16-11-54
Bennett David	Pte.	W/Sv	26-10-54	16-11-54
Brennan Edward	Pte.	W/Sv	26-10-54	16-11-54
Byng J.	Pte.	W/Sl	22-10-54	16-11-54
Doody Patrick	Pte.	W/Sl	26-10-54	16-11-54
Evans John	Pte.	W/Sl	26-10-54	16-11-54
Fisher Archibald	Pte.	W/Sl	26-10-54	16-11-54
Gibbins James	Pte.	W/D	26-10-54	16-11-54
Horgan Edward	Pte.	W/Sv	26-10-54	16-11-54
Kennedy Michael	Pte.	W/Sv	26-10-54	16-11-54
Kerr James	Pte.	W/Sv	26-10-54	16-11-54
Law John	Pte.	W/Sl	26-10-54	16-11-54
McCabe David	Pte.	W/D	26-10-54	16-11-54
McGinn Peter	Pte.	W/Sl	26-10-54	16-11-54
O'Brien William	Pte.	W/Sl	26-10-54	16-11-54
Regan Bartholomew	Pte.	W/Sv	26-10-54	16-11-54
Reynolds Charles	Pte.	W/Sv	26-10-54	16-11-54
Smith John(4th)	Pte.	W/Sl	26-10-54	16-11-54
Sturgeon Francis	Pte.	W/D	26-10-54	16-11-54
Tucker John	Pte.	W/Sv	26-10-54	16-11-54
Winimo William	Pte.	W/Sl	26-10-54	16-11-54

33rd REGIMENT OF FOOT

NAME	RANK	CASUALTY	DATE	LONDON GAZETTE
Woodcock John	Sergt.	Wounded	13/17-10-54	11-11-54
Bradley Patrick	Pte.	W/Sl	2-11-54	11-12-54
Brough Joseph	Pte.	Wounded	13/17-10-54	11-11-54
Campbell James	Pte.	Wounded	18/21-10-54	7-11-54
Dogherty Patrick	Pte.	Wounded	13/17-10-54	11-11-54
Greenwood William	Pte.	Wounded	13/17-10-54	11-11-54
Monaghan Daniel	Pte.	W/Sl	3-11-54	11-12-54
Swadkins James	Pte.	Wounded	18/21-10-54	7-11-54
Thrieston Patrick	Pte.	Wounded	13/17-10-54	11-11-54
Urquhart Joseph	Pte.	D.O.W.	3-11-54	11-12-54
Ward William	Pte.	Wounded	13/17-10-54	11-11-54
Weatherall J.	Pte.	Wounded	18/21-10-54	7-11-54

NOTES

The First Bombardment of Sebastopol, First Battle of Inkermann, and Minor Actions

38th REGIMENT OF FOOT

NAME	RANK	CASUALTY	DATE	LONDON GAZETTE
Sweeney Michael	Pte.	Killed	13/17-10-54	11-11-54
Smith John	Sergt.	Wounded	13/17-10-54	11-11-54
Bailie William	Pte.	W/Sl	3-11-54	11-12-54
Carroll Myles	Pte.	Wounded	18/21-10-54	7-11-54
Cogan Thomas	Pte.	W/Sl	3-11-54	11-12-54
Elliot Donald	Pte.	Wounded	13/17-10-54	11-11-54
Flinn Daniel	Pte.	Wounded	13/17-10-54	11-11-54
Humphreys Henry	Pte.	Wounded	13/17-10-54	11-11-54
Keeff John	Pte.	Wounded	13/17-10-54	11-11-54
Littin John	Pte.	Wounded	13/17-10-54	11-11-54
McCullogh William	Pte.	Wounded	13/17-10-54	11-11-54
McQuade William	Pte.	Wounded	13/17-10-54	11-11-54
Savery George	Pte.	Wounded	13/17-10-54	11-11-54
Wareham William	Pte.	Wounded	13/17-10-54	11-11-54

41st REGIMENT OF FOOT

NAME	RANK	CASUALTY	DATE	LONDON GAZETTE
Hoey P.	Pte.	Killed	18/21-10-54	7-11-54
Martin John	Pte.	Killed	26-10-54	16-11-54
Clough John	Pte.	W/Sv	26-10-54	16-11-54
Dudley Robert	Pte.	W/Sv	26-10-54	16-11-54
Donovan Daniel	Pte.	D.O.W.	26-10-54	16-11-54
Grace Michael	Pte.	W/Sl	26-10-54	16-11-54
Hanrahan Roger	Pte.	W/Sv	26-10-54	16-11-54
Keeffe Timothy	Pte.	W/Sv	26-10-54	16-11-54
Light Charles	Pte.	W/Sv	26-10-54	16-11-54
Lyons John	Pte.	Wounded	18/21-10-54	7-11-54
Madigan M.	Pte.	Wounded	18/21-10-54	7-11-54
Starkey M.	Pte.	W/Sv	24-10-54	16-11-54
Tilley William	Pte.	W/Sv	26-10-54	16-11-54

42nd REGIMENT OF FOOT

NAME	RANK	CASUALTY	DATE	LONDON GAZETTE
Rawkin William	Sergt.	Wounded	13/17-10-54	11-11-54
McKenzie D.	Corpl.	Wounded	18/21-10-54	7-11-54
Fox G.	Pte.	Wounded	18/21-10-54	7-11-54
Green Westrop	Pte.	W/Sl	3-11-54	11-12-54
McCready R.	Pte.	Wounded	18/21-10-54	7-11-54
Salmon Patrick	Pte.	Wounded	13/17-10-54	11-11-54

44th REGIMENT OF FOOT

NAME	RANK	CASUALTY	DATE	LONDON GAZETTE
Pither James	Corpl.	Killed	13/17-10-54	11-11-54
Neill F.	Drummer	Killed	18/21-10-54	7-11-54
Kennedy Thomas	Pte.	Killed	13/17-10-54	11-11-54
Warr William	Pte.	Killed	13/17-10-54	11-11-54
Holland James	Sergt.	Wounded	13/17-10-54	11-11-54
Simmons H.	Corpl.	Wounded	18/21-10-54	7-11-54
Young R.	Corpl.	Wounded	18/21-10-54	7-11-54
Black J.	Pte.	Wounded	18/21-10-54	7-11-54

NOTES

The First Bombardment of Sebastopol, First Battle of Inkermann, and Minor Actions

44th REGIMENT OF FOOT

NAME	RANK	CASUALTY	DATE	LONDON GAZETTE
Doole W.	Pte.	Wounded	18/21-10-54	7-11-54
Dunleary Nelson	Pte.	Wounded	13/17-10-54	11-11-54
Ford Benjamin	Pte.	W/Sl	31-10-54	16-11-54
Hooks Henry	Pte.	Wounded	13/17-10-54	11-11-54
Keane W.	Pte.	Wounded	13/17-10-54	11-11-54
McPeake T.	Pte.	Wounded	13/17-10-54	11-11-54
Shambrook Joseph	Pte.	Wounded	13/17-10-54	11-11-54
Thompson S.	Pte.	Wounded	13/17-10-54	11-11-54

47th REGIMENT OF FOOT

NAME	RANK	CASUALTY	DATE	LONDON GAZETTE
Flynn D.	Pte.	Killed	18/21-10-54	7-11-54
Hill T.	Pte.	Killed	18/21-10-54	7-11-54
Kerwan C.	Pte.	Killed	23-10-54	16-11-54
Pittman Frederick	Pte.	Killed	26-10-54	16-11-54
Bowler William	Corpl.	W/Sl	26-10-54	16-11-54
Cable T.	Corpl.	Wounded	18/21-10-54	7-11-54
Cantrill John	Pte.	W/Sl	26-10-54	16-11-54
Chittock Frederick	Pte.	Wounded	13/17-10-54	11-11-54
Donohoe John	Pte.	Wounded	13/17-10-54	11-11-54
Finlay Patrick	Pte.	W/Sv	26-10-54	16-11-54
Hanley Patrick	Pte.	Wounded	13/17-10-54	11-11-54
Houlihan William	Pte.	W/Sl	26-10-54	11-11-54
Mamard Patrick	Pte.	W/Sl	26-10-54	11-11-54
Mulligan Robert	Pte.	W/Sl	26-10-54	11-11-54
Neil John	Pte.	W/Sl	26-10-54	11-11-54

49th REGIMENT OF FOOT

NAME	RANK	CASUALTY	DATE	LONDON GAZETTE
Powell C. T.	Major	Killed	28-10-54	16-11-54
Hanley William	Pte.	Killed	13/17-10-54	11-11-54
Swayne George	Pte.	Killed	26-10-54	16-11-54
Armstrong William	Col/Sgt.	W/Sv	26-10-54	16-11-54
Campbell James	Corpl.	W/Sv	26-10-54	16-11-54
Dunn Daniel	Corpl.	W/Sv	26-10-54	16-11-54
Henry Charles	Corpl.	W/Sl	26-10-54	16-11-54
Sweeney Eugene	Drummer	W/Sv	26-10-54	16-11-54
Atherton James	Pte.	W/D	26-10-54	16-11-54
Brown William	Pte.	W/Sv	26-10-54	16-11-54
Cardiff James	Pte.	W/Sv	26-10-54	16-11-54
Cunningham P.	Pte.	Wounded	18/21-10-54	7-11-54
Donahy Thomas	Pte.	W/Sv	26-10-54	16-11-54
Fahy Thomas	Pte.	W/Sv	26-10-54	16-11-54
Fensome Thomas	Pte.	W/Sv	26-10-54	16-11-54
Jones John	Pte.	W/D	26-10-54	16-11-54
Jones Samuel	Pte.	W/Sv	26-10-54	16-11-54
Jordan Edward	Pte.	W/Sl	26-10-54	16-11-54
Lake John	Pte.	W/Sl	26-10-54	16-11-54
Lyons Michael	Pte.	W/D	26-10-54	16-11-54
Monaghan Thomas	Pte.	W/Sv	26-10-54	16-11-54
Murphy W.	Pte.	Wounded	18/21-10-54	7-11-54
Parker James	Pte.	W/Sv	26-10-54	16-11-54
Sable James	Pte.	W/Sv	26-10-54	16-11-74

NOTES

The First Bombardment of Sebastopol, First Battle of Inkermann, and Minor Actions

50th REGIMENT OF FOOT

NAME	RANK	CASUALTY	DATE	LONDON GAZETTE
Davis Samuel	Pte.	Wounded	13/17-10-54	11-11-54
Dignan John	Pte.	Wounded	13/17-10-54	11-11-54
Doherty Michael	Pte.	Wounded	13/17-10-54	11-11-54
Doyle Edward	Pte.	Wounded	13/17-10-54	11-11-54
Gray John	Pte.	Wounded	13/17-10-54	11-11-54
Wait J.	Pte.	W/Sv	23-10-54	16-11-54
Walsh Patrick	Pte.	Wounded	13/17-10-54	11-11-54
Wilson Thomas	Pte.	Wounded	18/21-10-54	7-11-54

57th REGIMENT OF FOOT

NAME	RANK	CASUALTY	DATE	LONDON GAZETTE
Carson James	Pte.	W/Sl	29-10-54	16-11-54
McFarlane Robert	Pte.	Wounded	13/17-10-54	11-11-54
McNamara A.	Pte.	W/Sl	26-10-54	16-11-54
Mullen Henry	Pte.	W/Sl	27-10-54	16-11-54
Murphy Michael	Pte.	Wounded	13/17-10-54	11-11-54
Phillips James	Pte.	Wounded	18/21-10-54	7-11-54

63rd REGIMENT OF FOOT

NAME	RANK	CASUALTY	DATE	LONDON GAZETTE
Brennan Joseph	Pte.	Killed	1-11-54	16-11-54
Preston Robert	Pte.	Killed	18/21-10-54	7-11-54
Field Thomas	Sergt.	Wounded	18/21-10-54	7-11-54
Clarke William	Corpl.	Wounded	18/21-10-54	7-11-54
Hannon John	Pte.	Wounded	18/21-10-54	7-11-54
Ives Robert	Pte.	Wounded	24-10-54	16-11-54
Leonard John	Pte.	Wounded	27-10-54	16-11-54

68th REGIMENT OF FOOT

NAME	RANK	CASUALTY	DATE	LONDON GAZETTE
Carroll Patrick	Pte.	Killed	13/17-10-54	11-11-54
Gallivan Michael	Pte.	Killed	25-10-54	16-11-54
Gwyer William	Pte.	Killed	13/17-10-54	11-11-54
Hore James	Pte.	Killed	13/17-10-54	11-11-54
Brown George	Pte.	Wounded	13/17-10-54	11-11-54
Crawley Patrick	Pte.	W/Sl	25-10-54	16-11-54
Hayes Stephen	Pte.	Wounded	18/21-10-54	7-11-54
Holden Patrick	Pte.	Wounded	13/17-10-54	11-11-54
Holder Patrick	Pte.	Wounded	18/21-10-54	7-11-54
Wilson James	Pte.	Wounded	13/17-10-54	11-11-54

77th REGIMENT OF FOOT

NAME	RANK	CASUALTY	DATE	LONDON GAZETTE
Dermett Charles	Corpl.	Killed	24-10-54	16-11-54
Mason John	Pte.	Killed	22-10-54	16-11-54
Fitzharris John	Col/Sgt.	Wounded	18/21-10-54	7-11-54
Gilliget Timothy M.	Pte.	W/Sl	3-11-54	11-12-54

NOTES

The First Bombardment of Sebastopol, First Battle of Inkermann, and Minor Actions

77th REGIMENT OF FOOT

NAME	RANK	CASUALTY	DATE	LONDON GAZETTE
Glynn Michael	Pte.	Wounded	18/21-10-54	7-11-54
Gulliford Edward	Pte.	Wounded	13-17-10-54	11-11-54
Long James	Pte.	W/Sl	31-10-54	16-11-54
Monaghan Gilbert	Pte.	Wounded	13/17-10-54	11-11-54
Parton Timothy	Pte.	Wounded	18/21-10-54	7-11-54
White Abraham	Pte.	Wounded	18/21-10-54	7-11-54

79th REGIMENT OF FOOT

NAME	RANK	CASUALTY	DATE	LONDON GAZETTE
Saunderson A.	Pte.	Wounded	18/21-10-54	7-11-54

88th REGIMENT OF FOOT

NAME	RANK	CASUALTY	DATE	LONDON GAZETTE
Matthewman John	Sergt.	Killed	13/17-10-54	11-11-54
Griffin Daniel	Pte.	Killed	13/17-10-54	11-11-54
Hugh John M.	Pte.	Killed	1-11-54	16-11-54
Hynes Michael	Pte.	Killed	13/17-10-54	11-11-54
Kilden James	Pte.	Killed	26-10-54	16-11-54
Leonard Peter	Pte.	Killed	13/17-10-54	11-11-54
McDonald Robert	Pte.	Killed	13/17-10-54	11-11-54
Perryman Michael	Pte.	Killed	13/17-10-54	11-11-54
McDonagh Michael	Sergt.	Wounded	13/17-10-54	11-11-54
Somers Edward	Sergt.	W/Sl	1-11-54	16-11-54
Anderson Alexander	Pte.	W/Sl	1-11-54	16-11-54
Burns Patrick	Pte.	Wounded	13/17-10-54	11-11-54
Bush John	Pte.	Wounded	13/17-10-54	11-11-54
Connolly Michael	Pte.	W/Sl	26-10-54	16-11-54
Cullen Patrick	Pte.	Wounded	13/17-10-54	11-11-54
Daly John	Pte.	Wounded	13/17-10-54	11-11-54
Doherty Timothy	Pte.	Wounded	13/17-10-54	11-11-54
Downs John	Pte.	W/Sv	1-11-54	16-11-54
English Edward	Pte.	Wounded	13/17-10-54	11-11-54
Ferris Morris	Pte.	Wounded	13/17-10-54	11-11-54
Foley Thomas	Pte.	Wounded	13/17-10-54	11-11-54
Garaghty Michael	Pte.	W/Sv	1-11-54	16-11-54
Kelly Thomas	Pte.	W/D	1-11-54	16-11-54
Kenny James	Pte.	Wounded	13/17-10-54	11-11-54
Knowles William	Pte.	W/Sl	1-11-54	16-11-54
Leonard Patrick	Pte.	Wounded	13/17-10-54	11-11-54
McMahon John	Pte.	W/Sl	1-11-54	16-11-54
Monarty Daniel	Pte.	Wounded	13/17-10-54	11-11-54
Morissey Patrick	Pte.	Wounded	13/17-10-54	11-11-54
O'Brien Thomas	Pte.	W/Sl	1-11-54	16-11-54
Purcell Bartholomew	Pte.	W/Sl	1-11-54	16-11-54
Savage Morris	Pte.	W/Sl	1-11-54	16-11-54

95th REGIMENT OF FOOT

NAME	RANK	CASUALTY	DATE	LONDON GAZETTE
Cardee Charles	Pte.	Killed	26-10-54	16-11-54
Conner Roger	Sgt/Mjr.	W/Sl	26-10-54	16-11-54
Baxter Thomas	Pte.	W/Sl	26-10-54	16-11-54

NOTES

The First Bombardment of Sebastopol, First Battle of Inkermann, and Minor Actions

95th REGIMENT OF FOOT

NAME	RANK	CASUALTY	DATE	LONDON GAZETTE
Clarke George	Pte.	W/Sl	26-10-54	16-11-54
Dalton James	Pte.	W/Sl	26-10-54	16-11-54
Doody John	Pte.	W/Sl	26-10-54	16-11-54
Elliott George	Pte.	W/Sl	26-10-54	16-11-54
Leggett Charles	Pte.	W/Sl	26-10-54	16-11-54
Leonard Michael	Pte.	Wounded	18/21-10-54	7-11-54
McElligott John	Pte.	W/Sl	26-10-54	16-11-54
Ombley Peter	Pte.	W/Sl	26-10-54	16-11-54

1st BATTALION RIFLE BRIGADE

NAME	RANK	CASUALTY	DATE	LONDON GAZETTE
Lewis Charles	Pte.	Killed	31-10-54	16-11-54
Mead John	Pte.	Killed	13/17-10-54	11-11-54
Powell James	Col/Sgt.	Wounded	13/17-10-54	11-11-54
Carter J.	Pte.	W/Sl	24-10-54	16-11-54
Goodfellow Robert	Pte.	Wounded	13/17-10-54	11-11-54
Lowe Joseph	Pte.	Wounded	13/17-10-54	11-11-54
Martin William	Pte.	W/Sl	31-10-54	16-11-54
Werton James	Pte.	W/Sl	13/17-10-54	11-11-54
Wright William	Pte.	W/Sl	25-10-54	16-11-54

2nd BATTALION RIFLE BRIGADE

NAME	RANK	CASUALTY	DATE	LONDON GAZETTE
Larrad J.	Sergt.	Killed	3-11-54	11-12-54
Campbell W.	Corpl.	Killed	13/17-10-54	11-11-54
Bishop John	Pte.	Killed	13/17-10-54	11-11-54
Carlow John	Pte.	Killed	13/17-10-54	11-11-54
Wilson John	Pte.	Killed	3-11-54	11-12-54
Bridgham R.	Sergt.	Wounded	18/21-10-54	7-11-54
Cupper J.	Corpl.	Wounded	18/21-10-54	7-11-54
Graham D.	Corpl.	W/Sl	26-10-54	16-11-54
McCarthy Daniel	Bugler	Wounded	13/17-10-54	11-11-54
Berry James	Pte.	Wounded	13/17-10-54	11-11-54
Cann George	Pte.	Wounded	13/17-10-54	11-11-54
Crevy Joseph	Pte.	Wounded	13/17-10-54	11-11-54
Crouch William	Pte.	W/Sl	26-10-54	16-11-54
Green Alfred	Pte.	W/Sl	13/17-10-54	11-11-54
Jackson W.	Pte.	W/M	24-10-54	16-11-54
Kent H.	Pte.	Wounded	18/21-10-54	7-11-54
Kerswell E.	Pte.	Wounded	18/21-10-54	7-11-54
Lynch W.	Pte.	Wounded	18/21-10-54	7-11-54
Muir R.	Pte.	Wounded	18/21-10-54	7-11-54
Parsons J.	Pte.	Wounded	18/21-10-54	7-11-54
Pinfold Thomas	Pte.	Wounded	13/17-10-54	11-11-54
Regan William	Pte.	Wounded	13/17-10-54	11-11-54
Rielly J.	Pte.	W/Sl	26-10-54	16-11-54
Rutson Joseph	Pte.	W/Sl	3-11-54	11-12-54
Smith Charles	Pte.	W/Sl	3-11-54	11-12-54
Taylor Charles	Pte.	Wounded	13/17-10-54	11-11-54
Waldron J.	Pte.	W/Sl	26-10-54	16-11-54
White James	Pte.	W/Sl	3-11-54	11-12-54

NOTES

THE GUARDS
WORKING IN THE TRENCHES
BEFORE SEBASTOPOL.

THE ACTION AT BALAKLAVA

The following casualties occurred among the Officers, Non-Commissioned Officers and Men of the Heavy and Light Regiments of Cavalry in the action at Balaklava, 25th October, 1854.
Compiled from the London Gazette (Officers 12th November, 1854. (Other Ranks) 16th December 1854.

STAFF

NAME	RANK	CASUALTY	NAME	RANK	CASUALTY
Earl of Lucan	Lieut/Gen.	W/Sl	Lockwood George	Captain	Killed (or missing)
Scarlett Hon J. Y.	Brig/Gen.	W/Sl	Maxse H. F.	Lieut.	W/Sl
Charteris Hon W.	Captain	Killed	Elliot A. I.	Lieut.	W/Sl

4th DRAGOON GUARDS

NAME	RANK	CASUALTY	NAME	RANK	CASUALTY
Ryan Thomas	Pte.	Killed	Anchinclass James	Pte.	W/Sl
Evans John	Troop Sgt/Mjr.	W/Sl	Preece Henry	Pte.	W/Sl
			Scanlon William	Pte.	W/D
Percy William	Sergt.	W/Sl			

5th DRAGOON GUARDS

NAME	RANK	CASUALTY	NAME	RANK	CASUALTY
Taylor James	Corpl.	Killed	Herbert Henry	Pte.	W/Sv
Callery Bernard	Pte.	Killed	Jenkins Joseph	Pte.	W/Sv
Swinfen F. H.	Lieut.	W/Sl	McCabe John	Pte.	W/Sv
Neville Hon G.	Cornet	W/Sv	Malone Edward	Pte.	W/Sv
McKeegan Charles	Corpl.	W/Sv	Morris William	Pte.	W/Sl
Babbington Charles	Pte.	W/Sv	Willson William	Pte.	W/Sv
Dickson G. H.	Pte.	W/Sl			

1st DRAGOONS

NAME	RANK	CASUALTY	NAME	RANK	CASUALTY
Middleton Charles	Pte.	Killed	Stacey George	Trumptr.	W/Sv
Shore Thomas	Pte.	Killed	Astlett J. R.	Pte.	W/Sv
Yorke John	Lt/Col.	W/Sv	Blake James	Pte.	W/Sv
Campbell George	Capt.	W/Sv	Kennedy B.	Pte.	W/Sl
Elmsall W. de	Capt.	W/Sv	Taylor George	Pte.	W/Sv
Hartopp W. W.	Cornet	W/Sv	Woodward Samuel	Pte.	W/Sl
Noake M.	Sergt.	W/Sv			

NOTES

The Action at Balaklava

2nd N B DRAGOONS

NAME	RANK	CASUALTY	NAME	RANK	CASUALTY
Clifford A. P.	Corpl.	Killed	Donaldson William	Pte.	W/Sv
Campbell Henry	Pte.	Killed	Fawke Walter	Pte.	W/Sl
Griffith H.D.	Lt/Col.	W/Sl	Foster Richard	Pte.	W/Sv
Clarke G. C.	Capt.	W/Sv	Galbraith McAdam	Pte.	W/Sv
Handley H. E.	Cornet	W/Sl	Gardiner A. D.	Pte.	W/Sv
Prendergast Lenox	Cornet	W/Sv	Glancy Charles	Pte.	W/Sl
Brown Matthew	Troop Sgt/Mjr.	W/Sl	Gofley Thomas	Pte.	W/Sl
			Hackett James	Pte.	W/Sl
Davidson James	Troop Sgt/Mjr.	W/Sl	Hammond William	Pte.	W/Sv
			Heywood William	Pte.	W/Sl
Dearden James	Troop Sgt/Mjr.	W/Sl	Hunter James	Pte.	W/Sl
			Jackson William	Pte.	W/Sv
Gibson David	Sergt.	W/Sv	Johnston William	Pte.	W/Sl
Kneath Thomas	Sergt.	W/Sv	Kerr Robert	Pte.	W/Sl
Wilson John	Sergt.	W/Sv	Knowles John	Pte.	W/Sl
Campbell Francis	Corpl.	W/Sv	Langdon Thomas	Pte.	W/Sl
Aitken James	Pte.	W/Sl	Livingstone Richard	Pte.	W/Sv
Alexander George	Pte.	W/Sl	Lochrie Henry	Pte.	W/Sl
Allen James	Pte.	W/Sl	Long A. S.	Pte.	W/Sv
Allis William J.	Pte.	W/Sv	McNee John	Pte.	W/Sl
Barnet Robert	Pte.	W/Sl	McPherson James	Pte.	W/Sl
Bothwicke James	Pte.	W/Sl	Marshall William	Pte.	W/Sl
Borland John	Pte.	W/Sl	Morrison William	Pte.	W/Sv
Burley Peter	Pte.	W/Sl	Seggie Williak	Pte.	W/Sv
Burns George	Pte.	W/Sl	Taylor James	Pte.	W/Sl
Caulfield William	Pte.	W/Sl	Thompson Robert	Pte.	W/Sv
Colter James	Pte.	W/Sl	Trail Thomas	Pte.	W/Sv
Connell William	Pte.	W/Sl	Ward Owen	Pte.	W/Sv
Currie Charles	Pte.	W/Sl	Watson James	Pte.	W/Sv
Davidson Donald	Pte.	W/Sl	Weir Alexander	Pte.	W/Sl
Davis William	Pte.	W/Sv			

6th DRAGOONS

NAME	RANK	CASUALTY	NAME	RANK	CASUALTY
Elliot Robert	Pte.	Killed	Clarke Charles	Pte.	W/Sv
Latimer Alexander	Pte.	Killed	Davis John	Pte.	W/Sl
Shields Alexander	T/S/M	W/Sl	Keane Robert	Pte.	W/Sl
Jeffries Richard	Sergt.	W/Sv	Lyons William	Pte.	W/Sl
Bolton Frederick	Sergt.	W/D	McCanna John	Pte.	W/Sl
Kidney John	Corpl.	W/Sl	Rourke Michael	Pte.	W/D
Backler James	Pte.	W/Sl	Turner Robert	Pte.	W/Sv
Breadins William	Pte.	W/Sl			

4th LIGHT DRAGOONS

NAME	RANK	CASUALTY	NAME	RANK	CASUALTY
Halkett J. T. D.	Major	Killed	Phelan Michael	Pte.	Killed
Sparke H. A.	Lieut	Killed	Robinson George	Pte.	Killed
Herbert Francis	T/S/M	Killed	Swan George	Pte.	Killed
Cambell Edward	Sergt.	Killed	Tomset Thomas	Pte.	Killed
Lynch Richard	Sergt.	Killed	Waight Charles	Pte.	Killed
Spence Henry	Corpl.	Killed	Brown G. J.	Capt.	W/Sv
Burns Thomas	Trmptr.	Killed	Hutton Thomas	Capt.	W/Sv
Lovelock Edward	Trmptr.	Killed	Jennings Henry	T/S/M	W/Sl
Donaldson James	Pte.	Killed	Heron Denis	Corpl.	W/Sl
Haxhall Daniel	Pte.	Killed	Armes Thomas	Pte.	W/Sl
Hutton Thomas	Pte.	Killed	Bradley Edward	Pte.	W/Sl
Marshall Charles	Pte.	Killed	Carrol Peter	Pte.	W/Sl
Moody Thomas	Pte.	Killed	Carter Joseph	Pte.	W/Sl

NOTES

The Action at Balaklava

4th LIGHT DRAGOONS

NAME	RANK	CASUALTY	NAME	RANK	CASUALTY
Croydon George	Pte.	W/Sl	Keenan William	Pte.	W/Sl
Devlin James	Pte.	W/Sv	Olley James	Pte.	W/Sl
Downing Frederick	Pte.	W/Sl	Phillips Joseph	Pte.	W/Sl
Gosbell Joseph	Pte.	W/Sv	Rogers Thomas	Pte.	W/Sl
Gray John	Pte.	W/Sl	Sutcliffe William	Pte.	W/Sl
Herbert Thomas	Pte.	W/Sl	Thorne William	Pte.	W/Sl
Hughes John	Pte.	W/Sl	Tyler James	Pte.	W/Sl
Jones William	Pte.	W/Sl	Whitby Joseph	Pte.	W/Sl

8th HUSSARS

NAME	RANK	CASUALTY	NAME	RANK	CASUALTY
Fitzgibbon J. C.	Lieut.	Killed	Clutterbuck D.	Lieut.	W/Sl
Clowes G.	Cornet	Killed	Seager Edward	Lt & Adj.	W/Sl
McCluer H.	T/S/M	Killed	Clarke —	T/S/M	W/Sl
Rielly Michael	Sergt.	Killed	Gray William	Trmp/Mjr.	W/Sl
Williams William	Sergt.	Killed	Sewell John	Corpl.	W/Sv
Donald William	Corpl.	Killed	Dunn John	Trmptr.	W/Sv
Adams Joshua	Pte.	Killed	Bray Francis	Pte.	W/D
Barry John	Pte.	Killed	Brown John	Pte.	W/Sv
Brennan Michael	Pte.	Killed	Cheshire Henry	Pte.	W/Sv
Dies James	Pte.	Killed	Clement James	Pte.	W/Sv
Finnegan Andrew	Pte.	Killed	Doolan Patrick	Pte.	W/D
Hanrahan Denis	Pte.	Killed	Fullon William	Pte.	W/Sl
Heffron Thomas	Pte.	Killed	Glendire R. O.	Pte.	W/Sv
Herbert Edmund	Pte.	Killed	Kennedy Richard	Pte.	W/Sv
Keating Matthew	Pte.	Killed	Kiterick Patrick	Pte.	W/Sl
McDonald Edward	Pte.	Killed	Ross Joseph	Pte.	W/Sv
Morris George	Pte.	Killed	Ryan William	Pte.	W/D
Waterer Charles	Pte.	Killed	Spain Christopher	Pte.	W/Sl
White John	Pte.	Killed	Tovamley Thomas	Pte.	W/Sv

11th HUSSARS

NAME	RANK	CASUALTY	NAME	RANK	CASUALTY
Jones J.	Sergt.	Killed	Wareham W.	Pte.	Killed
Jordan T.	Sergt.	Killed	Wooton G.	Pte.	Killed
France T.	Corpl.	Killed	Cook E. A.	Capt.	W/Sl
Allured C.	Pte.	Killed	Trevelyan	Lieut.	W/Sl
Brunton J.	Pte.	Killed	Houghton G. P.	Cornet	W/Sv
Bubb R.	Pte.	Killed	Bentley W.	Sergt.	W/Sl
Cooper C. B.	Pte.	Killed	Davies R.	Sergt.	W/Sl
Davis W.	Pte.	Killed	Lawson J.	Sergt.	W/Sv
Elder T.	Pte.	Killed	Cork C.	Corpl.	W/Sl
George J. M.	Pte.	Killed	Hudson E.	Corpl.	W/Sl
Gwinnell R.	Pte.	Killed	Kilvert J.	Corpl.	W/Sl
Horne G.	Pte.	Killed	Andrews D.	Pte.	W/Sl
Jackman J.	Pte.	Killed	Bingham J.	Pte.	W/Sl
Lazell R.	Pte.	Killed	Firth W.	Pte.	W/Sv
Larkin J.	Pte.	Killed	Glainster J.	Pte.	W/D
Levett R.	Pte.	Killed	Groome H.	Pte.	W/Sl
Purcell D.	Pte.	Killed	Jewell H.	Pte.	W/Sv
Shrive T.	Pte.	Killed	Jowett G.	Pte.	W/Sl
Shoppee L.	Pte.	Killed	Martin R.	Pte.	W/Sv
Spring W. H.	Pte.	Killed	Milburn S.	Pte.	W/Sv
Stephenson J.	Pte.	Killed	Pennington W. H.	Pte.	W/Sl
Wakelin H.	Pte.	Killed	Purvis J. C.	Pte.	W/Sv
Ward D.	Pte.	Killed	Roberts T.	Pte.	W/Sv

NOTES

The Action at Balaklava
11th HUSSARS

NAME	RANK	CASUALTY	NAME	RANK	CASUALTY
Shergold H.	Pte.	W/Sl	Turner G.	Pte.	W/D
Samer S.	Pte.	W/Sv	Walker W.	Pte.	W/Sl
Strutt T.	Pte.	W/Sl	Wilcox E.	Pte.	W/Sl
Taylor W.	Pte.	W/Sl	Young R.	Pte.	W/sv

13th LIGHT DRAGOONS

NAME	RANK	CASUALTY	NAME	RANK	CASUALTY
Oldham J. A.	Capt.	Killed	Watson James	Pte.	Killed
Goad T. H.	Capt.	Missing	Williams T. J.	Pte.	Killed
Montgomery H.	Cornet	Missing	Peake Frederick	Sergt.	W/Sv
Webster John	T/S/M	Killed	Brooks John	Pte.	W/Sv
Smith E. W. A.	Corpl.	Killed	Ethridge John	Pte.	W/Sv
Blackett Thomas	Pte.	Killed	Keen John	Pte.	W/Sv
Court Charles	Pte.	Killed	Moore Joseph	Pte.	W/D
Dorell William	Pte.	Killed	Pegler Henry	Pte.	W/Sv
Fraser Robert	Pte.	Killed	Rhodes Joseph	Pte.	W/Sv
Lawson William	Pte.	Killed	Sewell William	Pte.	W/Sv
McGorrine Thomas	Pte.	Killed	Wilde George	Pte.	W/Sl
Slattery James	Pte.	Killed	Williams George	Pte.	W/Sv

17th LANCERS

NAME	RANK	CASUALTY	NAME	RANK	CASUALTY
Winter J. P.	Capt.	K. or M.	Scarfe James	Sergt.	W/Sv
Thompson J. H.	Lieut.	K. or M.	Pyne John	Corpl.	W/Sl
Chadwick J.	Cornet & Adj	K. or M.	Taylor George	Corpl.	W/Sv
			Brown John	L/Cpl.	W/Sl
Talbot Edward	Sergt.	Killed	Brittain William	Trmptr.	W/D
Hall James	Corpl.	Killed	Landfred Martin	Trmptr.	W/Sl
Wrigley Cont.	Corpl.	Killed	Andrews John	Pte.	W/Sv
Aldows Charles	Pte.	Killed	Brown Peter	Pte.	W/Sv
Baker William	Pte.	Killed	Buck James	Pte.	W/Sl
Bow John	Pte.	Killed	Clifford Frederick	Pte.	W/D
Broom George	Pte.	Killed	Doyle William	Pte.	W/Sl
Brooks Walter	Pte.	Killed	Dudley Thomas	Pte.	W/Sv
Carter Henry	Pte.	Killed	Duggan John	Pte.	W/Sv
Corcoran Thomas	Pte.	Killed	Fegan Patrick	Pte.	W/Sl
Dollar Richard	Pte.	Killed	Foster Thomas	Pte.	W/D
Dowling Patrick	Pte.	Killed	Friend James	Pte.	W/Sl
Flowers George	Pte.	Killed	Gravenor John	Pte.	W/Sl
Gray Henry	Pte.	Killed	Hart John	Pte.	W/Sl
Harrison William	Pte.	Killed	Herriott George	Pte.	W/Sl
Jackson Robert	Pte.	Killed	Magee Thomas	Pte.	W/Sl
Lees John	Pte.	Killed	Mullen Thomas	Pte.	W/D
Ling Robert	Pte.	Killed	Mustard James	Pte.	W/Sl
McNeill Robert	Pte.	Killed	McNeill David	Pte.	W/Sv
Melrose Frederick	Pte.	Killed	O'Gorman James	Pte.	W/Sl
Mitton Charles	Pte.	Killed	Payne John	Pte.	W/Sl
Pearce Henry	Pte.	Killed	Pearson William	Pte.	W/Sv
Sewell Johnson	Pte.	Killed	Phelan William	Pte.	W/Sv
Stamage James	Pte.	Killed	Puvis William	Pte.	W/Sv
Wilson John	Pte.	Killed	Rafferty Patrick	Pte.	W/Sv
Morris William	Capt.	W/Sv	Soley Benjamin	Pte.	W/Sv
Webb A. F. C.	Capt.	W/Sv	Stanley David	Pte.	W/Sv
White Robert	Capt.	W/Sv	Stewart John	Pte.	W/Sv
Gordon Sir William	Lieut.	W/Sv	Watts James	Pte.	W/Sv

NOTES

The Action at Balaklava

The following Officers, Non-Commissioned Officers and Men were taken prisoner by the Russians during the action at Balaklava, 25th October 1854; those wounded are indicated.

Compiled from the London Gazette. 16th November 1854.

4th LIGHT DRAGOONS

NAME	RANK	CASUALTY	NAME	RANK	CASUALTY
Fowler William	Trp/Sgt/Mjr	Wounded	Fletcher Thomas	Pte.	Wounded
Thomas William	Corpl.	Wounded	Frederick Charles	Pte.	
Armstrong Joseph	Corpl.		King Thomas	Pte.	
Crawford Hugh	Trumpeter		Linser Thomas	Pte.	Wounded
Bagshaw James	Pte.		Lucas Thomas	Pte.	Wounded
Bolton James	Pte.		Normoyle James	Pte.	Wounded
Boxhall James	Pte.	Wounded	O'Brien Michael	Pte.	
Farquharson Robert	Pte.		Parks Samuel	Pte.	

8th HUSSARS

NAME	RANK	CASUALTY	NAME	RANK	CASUALTY
Clowes George	Cornet	Wounded	Horan Patrick	Pte.	
Taylor William	Corpl.	Wounded	Maccanon James	Pte.	Wounded
Berlin John	Pte.	Wounded	Palframan Richard	Pte.	
Bird William	Pte.		Perry William	Pte.	Wounded
Fitzgibbon John	Pte.	Wounded	Turner Edward	Pte.	Wounded

11th HUSSARS

NAME	RANK	CASUALTY	NAME	RANK	CASUALTY
Williams James	Corpl.	Wounded	Hyde Walter	Pte.	Wounded
Berry John	Pte.	Wounded	Parker Henry	Pte.	
Dryden John	Pte.	Wounded	Sheppard William	Pte.	Wounded
Henry N.	Pte.				

13th LIGHT DRAGOONS

NAME	RANK	CASUALTY	NAME	RANK	CASUALTY
Lincoln John	Trp/Sgt/Mjr		Duke William	Pte.	Wounded
Smith George	Trp/Sgt/Mjr	Wounded	Harris A.	Pte.	Wounded
Howard William	Trumpeter	Wounded	Hanlon Christopher	Pte.	Wounded
Benton William	Pte.	Wounded	Maccan John	Pte.	Wounded
Cook Thomas	Pte.	Wounded	Martin William	Pte.	Wounded
Cooper George	Pte.	Wounded	Warren Charles	Pte.	

17th LANCERS

NAME	RANK	CASUALTY	NAME	RANK	CASUALTY
Chadwick John	Lieut.	Wounded	McCallister James	Pte.	Wounded
Brown Thomas	Pte.	Wounded	Marshall Thomas	Pte.	Wounded
Edge Robert	Pte.	Wounded	Sharp Thomas	Pte.	Wounded
Ellis Henry	Pte.	Wounded	Tanner Alfred	Pte.	Wounded
Kirk William	Pte.	Wounded	Wightman James	Pte.	Wounded
Lyle John	Pte.	Wounded	Young Henry	Pte.	Wounded

OFFICERS OF THE COMMISSARIAT

NAME	RANK	NAME	RANK
Johnson Edmund	Issuer	Kerrs James	Issuer

NOTES

CHARGE OF HEAVY CAVALRY AT THE BATTLE OF BALAKLAVA
OCTOBER 25, 1854.

BRITISH LIGHT CAVALRY ATTACKING THE RUSSIAN GUNS AT THE BATTLE OF BALAKLAVA
Oct. 25th 1854.

EARL OF CARDIGAN.
COMMANDER IN THE CELEBRATED CAVALRY CHARGE AT BALAKLAVA, OCT. 25. 1854.

THE BATTLE OF INKERMANN

The following casualties occurred among the officers, Non-Commissioned Officers and Men of the Army during the Second Battle of Inkermann, 5th November 1854.

Compiled from the London Gazette, (Officers) 22nd November 1854.(Other Ranks) 11th December 1854.

STAFF

NAME	RANK	CASUALTY
1st Division		
Butler H. T.	Capt. D.A.A.G.	Killed
Bentinck H. J. W.	Major/General	W/Sl
Clifton T. H.	Capt.	W/Sl
2nd Division		
Allix W. K.	Capt.	Killed
Adams H. W.	Brigadier/Genrl.	W/Sv
Adams C.	Capt. A.D.C.	W/Sl
Gubbins J.	Capt. A.D.C.	W/Sv
Harding F. P.	Capt. A.D.C.	W/Sv
McDonald A.	Capt. A.D.C.	W/Sv
4th Division		
Cathcart Sir George	Lieut/General K.C.B.	Killed
Goldie T. L.	Brigadier/Genrl.	Killed
Seymour C.T.	Lieut/Colonel A.A.G.	Killed
Torrens W. H.	Brigadier/Genrl.	W/Sv
Maitland C. L. B.	Brevet/Major D.A.A.G.	W/Sv
Torrens H. D.	Lieut. A.D.C.	W/Sl
Light Division		
Brown Sir George	Lieut/General K.C.B.	W/Sv

4th LIGHT DRAGOONS

NO.	NAME	RANK	CASUALTY	NO.	NAME	RANK	CASUALTY
1065	Rickman James	Pte.	Killed	1130	Gillan David	Pte.	Wounded
1526	Wholman Charles	Pte.	Killed				

11th HUSSARS

NO.	NAME	RANK	CASUALTY	NO.	NAME	RANK	CASUALTY
1625	Wright George	Pte.	Killed	1102	Breese John	Sergt.	Wounded

NOTES

The Battle of Inkermann

17th LANCERS

NO.	NAME	RANK	CASUALTY	NO.	NAME	RANK	CASUALTY
	Clevland Archibald	Cornet	Killed	1567	Richardson John	Pte.	Wounded
985	Robinson R. F.	Pte.	Killed	1036	Swiney James	Pte.	Wounded

ROYAL ARTILLERY

NAME	RANK	CASUALTY	COMPANY	BATTALION
Fox Strangways T.	Brig/Gen.	Killed		
Townsend P.	Major	Killed		
Ousted Alfred	Sergt.	Killed	1	3
Tait James	Sergt.	Killed	5	11
West Alfred	Sergt.	Killed	6	11
Bell Charles	Corpl.	Killed	6	11
Brennan Edward	Gnr. & Drvr.	Killed	8	3
Brown W. (1st)	Gnr. & Drvr.	Killed	1	3
Cook James	Gnr. & Drvr.	Killed	4	11
Crowle Thomas	Gnr. & Drvr.	Killed	2	8
Ellis Benjamin Naylor	Gnr. & Drvr.	Killed	7	11
Gaston W. J.	Gnr. & Drvr.	Killed	4	12
Gushrie William	Gnr. & Drvr.	Killed	6	11
Jameson John	Gnr. & Drvr.	Killed	8	3
Marsh George	Gnr. & Drvr.	Killed	8	3
Mitchell William	Gnr. & Drvr.	Killed	8	3
Mundane R.	Gnr. & Drvr.	Killed	4	12
Taylor James	Gnr. & Drvr.	Killed	4	11
Gambier G.	Lt/Col.	W/Sl		
Baddeley J. F. L.	Capt. & Adj.	W/Sv		
Ingilby C. H.	Capt.	W/Sv		
Tupper G.	Capt.	W/Sl		
Crawford William	Col/Sgt.	W/Sl	4	12
Crowe William	Sergt.	W/Sl	4	12
Henry Alexander	Sergt.	W/Sl	4	11
Hillyard Thomas	Sergt.	W/Sl	4	11
McKown John	Sergt.	W/D	2	8
Walker David	Corpl.	W/Sv	8	3
Archdeacon James	Bomb.	W/Sl	6	11
Barnard F.	Bomb.	W/Sv	7	11
Bishop Abraham	Bomb.	W/Sl	4	11
Ewing S.	Bomb.	W/Sv	7	11
Haigh George	Bomb.	W/Sl	6	11
Newton Alfred	Bomb.	W/Sl	4	11
Keane R.	Trumptr.	W/Sl	4	12
Kerr William T.	Trumptr.	W/Sl	4	11
Craig James	Collar Maker	W/Sl	1	3
Elsdon J.	Collar Maker	W/Sl	4	12
Major Richard	Collar Maker	W/Sl	5	12
Finch Charles	Wheeler	W/Sl	4	11
Anson William	Gnr. & Drvr.	W/Sl	7	11
Barber John	Gnr. & Drvr.	W/Sl	4	11
Beattie J.	Gnr. & Drvr.	W/Sl	4	12
Bowring W.	Gnr. & Drvr.	W/Sl	4	12
Broadbent J.	Gnr. & Drvr.	W/Sl	4	12
Brown Samuel	Gnr. & Drvr.	W/Sl	4	11
Choat William	Gnr. & Drvr.	W/Sl	7	11
Close F.	Gnr. & Drvr.	W/Sl	4	12
Cook William	Gnr. & Drvr.	W/Sl	1	3
Cox J.	Gnr. & Drvr.	W/Sl	4	12
Curry Charles	Gnr. & Drvr.	W/Sv	4	12
Curtain Bernard	Gnr. & Drvr.	W/Sl	8	3
Cusick Richard	Gnr. & Drvr.	W/Sl	1	3
Davis Hugh	Gnr. & Drvr.	W/D	6	11
Denny Benjamin	Gnr. & Drvr.	W/Sl	5	11
Dodge John	Gnr. & Drvr.	W/Sl	1	3

NOTES

The Battle of Inkermann

ROYAL ARTILLERY

NAME	RANK	CASUALTY	COMPANY	BATTALION
Donoghoe Mathew	Gnr. & Drvr.	W/Sl	8	3
Dover George	Gnr. & Drvr.	W/Sl	8	3
Dunning W.	Gnr. & Drvr.	W/Sl	7	11
Fortune R.	Gnr. & Drvr.	W/Sl	4	12
Frost Edwin	Gnr. & Drvr.	W/Sl	8	3
Gleave Thomas	Gnr. & Drvr.	W/Sv	8	3
Green G.	Gnr. & Drvr.	W/Sl	4	12
Hambling T.	Gnr. & Drvr.	W/Sl	6	11
Hawkins Robert	Gnr. & Drvr.	W/Sv	8	3
Hookway J.	Gnr. & Drvr.	W/Sv	4	12
Hornsby James	Gnr. & Drvr.	W/Sl	6	11
Hunt John	Gnr. & Drvr.	W/Sl	2	8
Johnson W.	Gnr. & Drvr.	W/Sl	4	12
Jones Charles	Gnr. & Drvr.	W/Sl	4	11
Jones Thomas	Gnr. & Drvr.	W/Sl	4	11
Kirby Thomas	Gnr. & Drvr.	W/Sl	4	11
Logan A.	Gnr. & Drvr.	W/Sl	4	12
MacAteer T.	Gnr. & Drvr.	W/Sv	4	12
McAulay John	Gnr. & Drvr.	W/Sl	5	11
McConnell E.	Gnr. & Drvr.	W/Sl	4	12
McCord Thomas	Gnr. & Drvr.	W/Sv	8	3
McGrath J.	Gnr. & Drvr.	W/Sl	8	3
McIntyre James	Gnr. & Drvr.	W/Sl	8	3
McLemon J.	Gnr. & Drvr.	W/Sl	8	3
McNally James	Gnr. & Drvr.	W/Sl	8	3
Martin Robert	Gnr. & Drvr.	W/Sv	2	8
Mathews David	Gnr. & Drvr.	W/Sv	8	3
Murray Thomas	Gnr. & Drvr.	W/Sl	1	3
Niven William	Gnr. & Drvr.	W/Sv	7	11
Peters Henry	Gnr. & Drvr.	W/Sv	8	3
Pirie John	Gnr. & Drvr.	W/Sl	4	11
Prince B.	Gnr. & Drvr.	W/Sl	4	12
Roberts John	Gnr. & Drvr.	W/Sl	5	11
Robinson Richard	Gnr. & Drvr.	W/Sv	8	3
Robinson R.	Gnr. & Drvr.	W/Sv	8	3
Royals James	Gnr. & Drvr.	W/Sl	6	11
Russ Humphrey	Gnr. & Drvr.	W/Sv	6	11
Smithers William	Gnr. & Drvr.	W/Sl	4	11
Suttie John	Gnr. & Drvr.	W/Sl	1	3
Taylor John	Gnr. & Drvr.	W/Sv	6	11
Thomas T.	Gnr. & Drvr.	W/Sv	4	12
Toshack James	Gnr. & Drvr.	W/Sl	1	3
Villiers Arthur	Gnr. & Drvr.	W/Sl	4	11
Waterman W.	Gnr. & Drvr.	W/Sl	2	8
Wood Charles	Gnr. & Drvr.	W/Sl	8	3

AMBULANCE CORPS

NO.	NAME	RANK	CASUALTY
226	McDevitt James	Pte	W/Sv

3rd BATTALION GRENADIER GUARDS

NO.	NAME	RANK	CASUALTY	NO.	NAME	RANK	CASUALTY
	Pakenham E. W.	Lt/Col.	Killed	5540	Barton George	Corpl.	Killed
	Newman Sir R. L.	Capt.	Killed	4347	Davey John	Corpl.	Killed
	Neville Hon H. A.	Capt.	Killed	5090	Lomax Henry	Corpl.	Killed
2880	Algar John	Sergt.	Killed	5611	Medlicott Peter	Corpl.	Killed
4221	Cook Reuben	Sergt.	Killed	4998	Crotch Robert	Drummer	Killed
4822	Cowell John	Sergt.	Killed	5867	Andrews William	Pte.	Killed
3792	Parkinson Richard	Sergt.	Killed	5724	Bailey Thomas	Pte.	Killed

NOTES

The Battle of Inkermann
3rd BATTALION GRENADIER GUARDS

NO.	NAME	RANK	CASUALTY	NO.	NAME	RANK	CASUALTY
5530	Baldwin Squire	Pte.	Killed		Tipping A.	Capt.	W/Sv
5484	Bates George	Pte.	Killed		Ferguson Sir J.	Lieut.	W/Sl
3667	Bates William	Pte.	Killed		Sturt C. N.	Lieut.	W/Sv
4795	Beard William	Pte.	Killed	3503	Miner Richard	Col/Sgt.	W/Sl
5719	Beer Henry	Pte.	Killed	5829	Hughes James	Sergt.	W/Sl
5115	Bridgman William	Pte.	Killed	3933	Dawson Thomas	Sergt.	W/Sv
5339	Burrows German	Pte.	Killed	5318	Keeling James	Sergt.	W/Sl
3929	Charlot Richard	Pte.	Killed	4922	Rushent Thomas	Sergt.	W/Sv
5861	Columbine Peter	Pte.	Killed	3966	Walker William	Sergt.	W/Sl
5147	Compton Robert	Pte.	Killed	3863	Bowers William	Corpl.	W/Sv
4263	Cook Joseph	Pte.	Killed	4549	Clarke James	Corpl.	W/Sl
4994	Cooper James	Pte.	Killed	6140	Cowen Robert	Corpl.	W/Sl
4919	Cox George	Pte.	Killed	6304	Evans Alfred	Corpl.	W/Sl
4552	Crouchley John	Pte.	Killed	6272	Horsman Thomas	Corpl.	W/Sl
4874	Davis William	Pte.	Killed	4997	Horspool John	Corpl.	W/Sl
2938	Day Joseph	Pte.	Killed	1894	Lee James	Corpl.	W/Sl
6419	Dell James	Pte.	Killed	3376	Owen Benjamin	Corpl.	W/Sl
5281	Dible William	Pte.	Killed	3586	Swinburn John	Corpl.	W/Sl
6276	Dobinson Joseph	Pte.	Killed	5408	Wadsworth Joseph	Corpl.	W/Sv
4050	Eastaff George	Pte.	Killed	3044	Yates Frederick	Corpl.	W/Sv
5704	Filton Aaron	Pte.	Killed	5482	Robinson George	Drummer	W/Sv
6040	Flynn Peter	Pte.	Killed	3456	Adridge George	Pte.	W/Sv
4239	French Jacob	Pte.	Killed	3420	Allcock George	Pte.	W/Sv
6030	Fullerlove John	Pte.	Killed	4649	Ames James	Pte.	W/Sv
6393	Gathercole Walter	Pte.	Killed	5606	Archer Isaac	Pte.	W/Sl
4173	Guest John	Pte.	Killed	4666	Ashford Samuel	Pte.	W/Sv
5578	Hall William	Pte.	Killed	5069	Baker Henry	Pte.	W/Sv
3866	Hancock James	Pte.	Killed	4936	Baldwin James	Pte.	W/Sl
4080	Hansford Richard	Pte.	Killed	5330	Bancroft James	Pte.	W/Sl
6328	Heasman Jesse	Pte.	Killed	4589	Barrett Edward	Pte.	W/Sl
5916	Hebblethwaite James	Pte.	Killed	5400	Beck John	Pte.	W/Sv
5289	Henson William	Pte.	Killed	4716	Bedford James	Pte.	W/Sv
6253	Hill George	Pte.	Killed	6042	Benbow Charles	Pte.	W/Sl
5728	Hill James	Pte.	Killed	5937	Beying Edward	Pte.	W/Sl
6996	Holmes Joseph	Pte.	Killed	3889	Biles John	Pte.	W/Sl
4891	Howell Arthur	Pte.	Killed	4176	Blackwell William	Pte.	W/Sl
5995	Hughes Evan	Pte.	Killed	5885	Blow James	Pte.	W/Sv
6212	Lodge James	Pte.	Killed	4818	Boneham John	Pte.	W/Sv
6186	McGinnis William	Pte.	Killed	6422	Bowler George	Pte.	W/Sv
5392	Marginson James	Pte.	Killed	4962	Bradfield Thomas	Pte.	W/Sl
4948	Milnes Ellis	Pte.	Killed	4892	Challice Ezra	Pte.	D.O.W.
5409	Mustow Charles	Pte.	Killed	5953	Church Isaac	Pte.	W/Sv
6269	Neaton James	Pte.	Killed	5398	Clarke Joseph	Pte.	W/Sl
3439	Osmond Isaac	Pte.	Killed	4379	Clarke Thomas	Pte.	W/Sv
6229	Partridge William	Pte.	Killed	5817	Cook John	Pte.	W/Sv
5913	Piddlesden George	Pte.	Killed	5637	Cook Samuel	Pte.	W/Sv
6118	Rule Thomas	Pte.	Killed	5713	Cope William	Pte.	W/Sv
6057	Sellars Robert	Pte.	Killed	5640	Crickmay Edward	Pte.	W/Sl
4958	Sergeant Henry	Pte.	Killed	5703	Cripps Lewis	Pte.	W/Sv
6410	Shardlow Henry	Pte.	Killed	3584	Crook John	Pte.	W/Sl
4904	Sparrow James	Pte.	Killed	5141	Dennison Ephraim	Pte.	W/Sv
6289	Smith John	Pte.	Killed	6394	Dickinson Samuel	Pte.	W/Sl
3306	Smith Thomas	Pte.	Killed	3795	Dormer Daniel	Pte.	W/D
5511	Smith William	Pte.	Killed	5317	Dry William	Pte.	W/Sv
5307	Steel John	Pte.	Killed	5593	Dury Joseph	Pte.	W/Sl
6179	Thurlby Richard	Pte.	Killed	5965	Eady Moses	Pte.	W/Sl
4343	Turnhill Nathaniel	Pte.	Killed	6044	Edson John	Pte.	W/Sl
3522	Turner Robert	Pte.	Killed	6241	Elsley George	Pte.	W/Sl
5220	Trunby Richard	Pte.	Killed	3939	Frampton Edmund	Pte.	W/Sv
4274	Varney James	Pte.	Killed	4341	Gittins John	Pte.	W/Sv
5283	Woolven Henry	Pte.	Killed	5766	Greatorex William	Pte.	W/Sv
4780	Yeomans James	Pte.	Killed	6052	Green Edward	Pte.	W/Sl
	Hamilton F. W.	Colnl.	W/Sl	4653	Green George	Pte.	W/Sl
	Percy Hon H.	Lt/Col.	W/Sl	6090	Grime William	Pte.	W/Sl
	Bradford R.	Lt/Col.	W/Sl	5806	Grimshaw John	Pte.	W/Sv

NOTES

The Battle of Inkermann

3rd BATTALION GRENADIER GUARDS

NO.	NAME	RANK	CASUALTY	NO.	NAME	RANK	CASUALTY
5723	Guzett Charles	Pte.	W/Sv	4548	Palethorpe Thomas	Pte.	W/Sv
5316	Hall Benjamin	Pte.	W/Sl	4786	Palmer John	Pte.	W/Sv
4131	Hall George	Pte.	W/Sl	5935	Parsons James	Pte.	W/Sl
4220	Hall William	Pte.	W/Sv	4506	Patter Edward	Pte.	W/Sl
3224	Harper Richard	Pte.	W/Sl	4944	Pepper James	Pte.	W/Sl
3467	Hartley Abraham	Pte.	W/Sv	4528	Pepper Joseph	Pte.	W/Sl
5730	Hatter Charles	Pte.	W/Sl	5873	Piggot Charles	Pte.	W/Sv
6073	Hawkesley Charles	Pte.	W/Sl	4024	Price James	Pte.	W/Sl
6367	Hayes Samuel	Pte.	W/Sl	3193	Pryer Samuel	Pte.	W/Sl
3236	Hazleman John	Pte.	W/Sv	5013	Rixon James	Pte.	W/Sl
6364	Head John	Pte.	W/Sv	4491	Roberts John	Pte.	W/Sv
6202	Hills George	Pte.	W/Sv	3135	Rolfe Thomas	Pte.	W/Sl
5622	Hiscock James	Pte.	W/Sl	5423	Rudkin John	Pte.	W/Sl
5028	Hope John	Pte.	W/D	4596	Sawyer Timothy	Pte.	W/D
5276	Ivermee Charles	Pte.	W/Sl	5123	Shepherd Christopher	Pte.	W/Sl
5646	Jackett George	Pte.	W/Sl	5396	Skinner Thomas	Pte.	W/Sl
6851	Jennings William	Pte.	W/Sl	4132	Smith Charles	Pte.	W/Sl
5034	Jones Stephen	Pte.	W/Sl	4775	Smith George	Pte.	W/Sl
4567	Kennings William	Pte	W/Sv	4923	Sollis William	Pte.	W/Sl
5839	King William	Pte.	W/Sl	5183	Stafford James	Pte.	W/Sv
4450	Leason George	Pte.	D.O.W	4963	Symes Levi	Pte.	W/Sl
5073	Lewis Stephen	Pte.	W/Sl	5702	Talbot James	Pte.	W/Sl
3453	Lovely George	Pte.	W/Sl	3380	Taylor Frederick	Pte.	W/Sl
5485	Lovern William	Pte.	W/Sv	5417	Taylor William	Pte.	W/Sl
5666	Lucas William	Pte.	W/Sl	5651	Thake Alexander	Pte.	W/Sv
5301	Luker William	Pte.	W/Sv	4770	Thomas John	Pte.	W/Sl
5863	Luter George	Pte.	W/Sv	4740	Thornton Joseph	Pte.	W/Sl
6028	Major George	Pte.	W/Sv	4916	Tomlinson Joseph	Pte.	W/Sl
6027	Manfield Richard	Pte.	W/Sv	6026	Topp Henry	Pte.	W/Sv
5581	Manion Thomas	Pte.	W/Sl	6135	Turner William	Pte.	W/Sv
6354	Martin James	Pte.	W/Sv	4823	Upton Henry	Pte.	W/Sl
4965	Mattingley George	Pte.	W/Sl	3337	Vaill John	Pte.	W/Sl
5311	Meakin George	Pte.	W/Sv	5718	Wales Frederick	Pte.	W/Sl
5264	Middleton Robert	Pte.	W/Sv	6517	Warren Robert	Pte.	W/Sl
3737	Molton George	Pte.	W/Sl	5444	White Thomas	Pte.	W/Sv
4509	Morris John	Pte.	W/Sl	4514	Williams Charles	Pte,	W/Sl
4764	Murton William	Pte.	W/Sl	4072	Williams David	Pte.	W/Sv
4924	Naylor James	Pte.	W/Sl	5844	Williams John	Pte.	W/Sl
5711	Newbury John	Pte.	W/Sl	5981	Willingham Joseph	Pte.	W/Sl
5744	Nichols George	Pte.	W/Sv	5331	Woodery Thomas	Pte.	W/Sl
5634	North Thomas	Pte.	W/Sl	5132	Wright Charles	Pte.	W/Sl
6169	Nutting Robert	Pte.	W/Sl				

1st BATTALION COLDSTREAM GUARDS

NAME	RANK	CASUALTY	NAME	RANK	CASUALTY
Dawson Hon. T. V.	Lt/Col.	Killed	Brett William	Pte.	Killed
Cowell J. C.	Lt/Col.	Killed	Buckle George	Pte.	Killed
Bouverie H. M.	Capt.	Killed	Burton Robert	Pte.	Killed
Eliot Hon. G. C. C.	Capt.	Killed	Coleman George	Pte.	Killed
Mackinnon L. D.	Capt.	Killed	Coxon George	Pte.	Killed
Ramsden F. H.	Capt.	Killed	Dew Robert	Pte.	Killed
Disbrowe E. A.	Lieut.	Killed	Dowshard Samuel	Pte.	Killed
Greville C. H.	Lieut.	Killed	Elvin James	Pte.	Killed
Jacques Thomas	Col/Sgt.	Killed	Farrant James	Pte.	Killed
McLellan Alexander	Col/Sgt.	Killed	Ferguson Thomas	Pte.	Killed
Thomas Richard	Sergt.	Killed	Gay James	Pte.	Killed
Dobbe James	Corpl.	Killed	Gay William	Pte.	Killed
Conduct William	Corpl.	Killed	Green John	Pte.	Killed
Bates Thomas	Corpl.	Killed	Hanneford George	Pte.	Killed
Bassent Joseph	Pte.	Killed	Harpsley Joseph	Pte.	Killed
Baxter William	Pte.	Killed	Hewitt Thomas	Pte.	Killed
Boothby John	Pte.	Killed	Holt Robert	Pte.	Killed

NOTES

The Battle of Inkermann

1st BATTALION COLDSTREAM GUARDS

NAME	RANK	CASUALTY	NAME	RANK	CASUALTY
Hore John	Pte.	Killed	Booker Samuel	Pte.	W/Sl
Johnson William	Pte.	Killed	Breadbeer Henry	Pte.	W/Sl
Keitch Mark	Pte.	Killed	Brown James	Pte.	W/Sv
Killingley Thomas	Pte.	Killed	Burell William	Pte.	W/Sl
Kingsland George	Pte.	Killed	Burnett Samuel	Pte.	W/Sv
Last Joseph	Pte.	Killed	Burt John	Pte.	W/Sl
Lawes James	Pte.	Killed	Burtonwood Charles	Pte.	W/Sv
Lawrence George	Pte.	Killed	Calcott John	Pte.	W/Sl
Lawrence James	Pte.	Killed	Carter Josiah	Pte.	W/Sv
Lockwood Isaac	Pte.	Killed	Chamberlain Joseph	Pte.	W/Sv
Loving James	Pte.	Killed	Chandler James	Pte.	W/Sl
Manning George	Pte.	Killed	Clark Robert	Pte.	W/Sv
Manus Alfred	Pte.	Killed	Clarke George	Pte.	W/Sv
Melluish John	Pte.	Killed	Cooper George	Pte.	W/Sl
Murden George	Pte.	Killed	Cracknell George	Pte.	W/Sv
Murrell William	Pte.	Killed	Curds James	Pte.	W/Sl
Pailey William	Pte.	Killed	Davidson Thomas	Pte.	W/Sv
Payne George	Pte.	Killed	Divison William	Pte.	W/Sv
Pailing John	Pte.	Killed	Drew Simeon	Pte.	W/Sv
Pearson John	Pte.	Killed	Eade Henry	Pte.	W/Sv
Phillip James	Pte.	Killed	Farham William	Pte.	W/Sl
Poleman William	Pte.	Killed	Firman James	Pte.	W/Sv
Pratt James	Pte.	Killed	Foster Alfred	Pte.	W/Sv
Sharp James	Pte.	Killed	Foster Joseph	Pte.	W/Sv
Smith Robert	Pte.	Killed	Garrod William	Pte.	W/Sl
Smith William	Pte.	Killed	Gelding George	Pte.	W/Sv
Thornley William	Pte.	Killed	Gibbons Samuel	Pte.	W/Sv
Tibbles Robert	Pte.	Killed	Gibbs William	Pte.	W/Sv
Turner James	Pte.	Killed	Glasbrook Edward	Pte.	W/Sv
Utley Isaac	Pte.	Killed	Glasgow Alexander	Pte.	W/Sl
Webb Isaac	Pte.	Killed	Graves Thomas	Pte.	W/Sl
Westwick Leonard	Pte.	Killed	Green Edward	Pte.	D.O.W
Whitehead William	Pte.	Killed	Gould Wyndham	Pte.	W/Sl
Willey William	Pte.	Killed	Harriman Thomas	Pte.	W/Sv
Wilshire Job	Pte.	Killed	Hawkins Joseph	Pte.	W/Sv
Woodhams Able	Pte.	Killed	Hazlewood David	Pte.	W/Sl
Fitzroy Lord A. C. L.	Lt/Col.	W/Sv	Homeyard Edward	Pte.	W/Sl
Halkett J.	Lt/Col.	W/Sv	Holden Robert	Pte.	W/Sl
Upton Hon. G.	Col.	W/Sl	Hoy John	Pte.	W/Sl
Fielding Hon. P.	Capt.	W/Sv	Hughes Arthur	Pte.	W/Sv
Amherst Hon. W. A.	Lieut.	W/Sv	Hunter William	Pte.	W/Sl
Talbot A.	Sgt/Mjr.	W/Sl	Issot John	Pte.	W/Sl
Austin Thomas	Col/Sgt.	W/Sv	Johnson Alfred	Pte.	Missing
Geard Charles	Col/Sgt.	W/Sl	Jones David	Pte.	W/Sl
Walden George	Sergt.	W/Sv	Joy James	Pte.	W/Sv
Phillips Esau	Sergt.	W/Sl	Kain Elisha	Pte.	W/Sv
Russ James	Sergt.	W/Sl	Kellett Thomas	Pte.	W/Sl
Bridges Frederick	Corpl.	W/Sv	King John (Ist)	Pte.	W/Sv
Conduct William	Corpl.	W/D.O.W.	Landsbury Jonathan	Pte.	W/Sv
Empson Edward	Corpl.	W/Sv	Larke Edward	Pte.	W/Sv
Smith Frederick	Corpl.	W/Sl	Lewis Edward	Pte.	W/Sl
Thorn Thomas	Corpl.	W/Sv	Lucas John	Pte.	W/Sl
Youngman Edward	Corpl.	W/Sv	Machin William	Pte.	W/Sv
Howcroft George	Drummer	W/Sl	Mayhew George	Pte.	W/Sv
Price Alexander	Drummer	W/Sl	Meek George	Pte.	W/Sv
Adams John	Pte.	W/Sv	Mustern J.	Pte.	W/Sv
Aldous William	Pte.	W/Sv	Moxham John	Pte.	W/Sv
Allen John	Pte.	W/Sv	Moxham William	Pte.	W/Sv
Aneil John	Pte.	W/Sv	Newton Charles	Pte.	W/Sv
Arms John	Pte.	W/Sv	Neville Charles	Pte.	W/Sv
Barnard Emanuel	Pte.	W/Sl	Page Joseph	Pte.	W/Sv
Barrett Enoch	Pte.	W/Sv	Palmer James	Pte.	W/Sl
Berry Charles	Pte.	W/Sv	Parker Thomas	Pte.	W/Sv
Best George	Pte.	W/Sv	Parker Robert	Pte.	W/Sl
Birkhead Charles	Pte.	W/Sl	Parriment George	Pte.	W/Sv

NOTES

The Battle of Inkermann

1st BATTALION COLDSTREAM GUARDS

NAME	RANK	CASUALTY	NAME	RANK	CASUALTY
Parrington Thomas	Pte.	W/Sl	Seaman James	Pte.	W/Sv
Pettit Henry	Pte.	W/Sv	Sheldrake Frederick	Pte.	W/Sv
Potter Joel	Pte.	W/Sv	Styles James	Pte.	W/Sv
Powell Joseph	Pte.	W/Sv	Swift Jessey	Pte.	W/Sl
Prince Ezekiel	Pte.	W/Sl	Syms Thomas	Pte.	W/Sv
Pugsby Silas	Pte.	W/Sl	Tanswell William	Pte.	W/Sl
Quilter Robert	Pte.	W/Sv	Thetford John	Pte.	D.O.W.
Rawlings James	Pte.	W/Sl	Turner Henry	Pte.	W/Sl
Robinson Samuel	Pte.	W/Sl	Topley John	Pte.	W/Sl
Rogers George	Pte.	W/Sl	Washer George	Pte.	W/Sv
Rolfe James	Pte.	W/Sl	Ward Charles	Pte.	W/Sl
Rolph Jonathan	Pte.	W/Sl	Wildman Abner	Pte.	W/Sv
Rudd James	Pte.	W/Sl	Youle William	Pte.	W/Sv

1st BATTALION SCOTS FUSILIER GUARDS

NO.	NAME	RANK	CASUALTY	NO.	NAME	RANK	CASUALTY
	Blair J. H.	Lt/Col.	Killed	4218	Smart George	Pte.	Killed
2688	Jones Morgan	Sergt.	Killed	4216	Wallbridge W. W.	Pte.	Killed
3281	Taylor Alexander	Sergt.	Killed	3797	Wright George	Pte.	Killed
3806	Brown Daniel	Corpl.	Killed		Walker E. W. F.	Col.	W/Sv
2803	Ellis Thomas	Corpl.	Killed		Seymour Francis	Lt/Col.	W/Sl
4072	Molloy John	Corpl.	Killed		Baring F.	Capt.	W/Sv
4250	Thompson Peter	Corpl.	Killed		Gipps R.	Capt.	W/Sv
4121	Barbour Robert	Pte.	Killed		Shuckburgh G. T. F.	Capt.	W/Sl
2772	Beans Alexander	Pte.	Killed		Drummond H.	Capt/Adj.	W/Sv
2540	Brazill Peter	Pte.	Killed		Blane S. J.	Lieut.	W/Sl
3948	Campbell William	Pte.	Killed		Elkington A. G.	Ass/Surg.	W/Sl
3456	Case Henry	Pte.	Killed	3283	Cameron Kenneth	Sergt.	W/Sl
4053	Chalmers Thomas	Pte.	Killed	3370	Clew James	Sergt.	W/Sl
4313	Collison William	Pte.	Killed	3075	Craig James	Sergt.	W/Sl
2824	Davis Joseph	Pte.	Killed	3393	Dryden Robert	Sergt.	W/Sv
3019	Doull John	Pte.	Killed	2511	Gordon Cosmo C.	Sergt.	W/Sl
3849	Edy George	Pte.	Killed	3895	Guerin Joseph	Sergt.	W/Sl
2071	Elder Robert	Pte.	Killed	2858	Scott Ralph	Sergt.	W/Sl
3984	Fleming John	Pte.	Killed	2791	Sharp George	Sergt.	W/Sl
4510	Grant Peter	Pte.	Killed	3781	Bullock Emanuel	Corpl.	W/Sl
3056	Hailstone Edmund	Pte.	Killed	4357	Bullock George	Corpl.	W/Sl
1976	Harris Jesse	Pte.	Killed	4364	Day James	Corpl.	W/Sl
3795	Hill John	Pte.	Killed	2788	Dawes Edward	Corpl.	W/Sv
3336	Hunter Andrew	Pte.	Killed	3625	Manson David	Corpl.	W/Sl
3619	Irish Edmund	Pte.	Killed	4392	Moulton Charles J.	Corpl.	W/Sv
2038	Jamieson Walter	Pte.	Killed	4249	Poole Thomas J.	Corpl.	W/Sl
3953	Jennings William	Pte.	Killed	3856	Poyntz Joseph	Corpl.	W/Sl
4366	Johnson John	Pte.	Killed	4372	Stewart William	Corpl.	W/Sl
4453	Jones Robert	Pte.	Killed	2912	Juggins William	Drummer	W/Sv
2627	Keay John G.	Pte.	Killed	2702	Lilley John F.	Drummer	W/Sl
3089	Kennish George	Pte.	Killed	4465	Addison James	Pte.	W/Sl
4074	Lindores George	Pte.	Killed	4208	Alexander James	Pte.	W/Sl
4491	McClellan William	Pte.	Killed	4361	Alexander James	Pte.	W/Sv
4259	McDonald John	Pte.	Killed	2568	Austin John	Pte.	W/Sl
3670	McKay George	Pte.	Killed	3748	Baker William	Pte.	W/Sv
2998	McLean Archibald	Pte.	Killed	3311	Barnes William	Pte.	W/Sv
3652	Manson Peter	Pte.	Killed	4490	Barron Henry	Pte.	W/Sl
2782	Mealy John	Pte.	Killed	4296	Baverstock Daniel	Pte.	W/Sv
3090	Parker David	Pte.	Killed	4543	Beattie John	Pte.	W/Sl
4167	Parker Jesse	Pte.	Killed	4149	Brent Charles	Pte.	W/Sl
4160	Paterson Robert	Pte.	Killed	3679	Burns John	Pte.	W/Sl
2069	Perry William	Pte.	Killed	2799	Chase James	Pte.	W/Sl
3661	Rennie William	Pte.	Killed	2235	Clark Andrew	Pte.	W/Sl
4520	Rowe John	Pte.	Killed	4422	Clark James	Pte.	W/Sl
4016	Shiel Samuel	Pte.	Killed	3266	Collins David	Pte.	W/Sv
4169	Sibbold John	Pte.	Killed	3904	Condie George	Pte.	W/Sv

NOTES

The Battle of Inkermann

1st BATTALION SCOTS FUSILIER GUARDS

NO.	NAME	RANK	CASUALTY	NO.	NAME	RANK	CASUALTY
3638	Cooper John	Pte.	W/Sl	2924	Morant George	Pte.	W/Sv
4464	Cox William	Pte.	W/Sl	3838	Morgan James	Pte.	W/Sv
3159	Dickson Alexander	Pte.	W/Sv	4377	Motion John	Pte.	W/Sl
2603	Dinsmure William	Pte.	W/Sv	3050	Munro John	Pte.	W/Sv
3560	Dobson Robert	Pte.	W/Sl	4481	Neish John	Pte.	W/Sl
3718	Drummond Benjamin	Pte.	W/Sv	2999	Nobb Francis	Pte.	W/Sl
2594	Emery Jonathan	Pte.	W/Sv	4380	Packham Jesse	Pte.	W/Sv
3889	Finlayson William	Pte.	W/Sl	2030	Paine Thomas	Pte.	W/Sl
2952	Fletcher George	Pte.	W/Sl	1818	Parry William	Pte.	W/Sl
3774	Ford William	Pte.	W/Sl	3532	Partridge George	Pte.	W/Sv
2636	Forrest John	Pte.	W/Sv	3776	Peckham Alexander	Pte.	W/Sl
3425	Gabbot John	Pte.	W/Sl	4431	Pilley James	Pte.	W/Sl
4243	Gardyne James	Pte.	W/Sv	1335	Pye John	Pte.	W/Sl
2816	Gondon Alexander	Pte.	W/Sl	2161	Ranby Everett	Pte.	W/Sl
4007	Gowilay John	Pte.	W/Sl	3541	Randell James	Pte.	W/Sv
4428	Grier George	Pte.	W/Sl	3924	Reckie George	Pte.	W/Sl
3826	Guthrie John	Pte.	W/Sv	3624	Reed Charles	Pte.	W/Sl
3917	Hagardy John	Pte.	W/Sl	4429	Reed Richard	Pte.	W/Sl
3617	Hannah Alexander	Pte.	W/Sl	3959	Ridges John	Pte.	W/Sv
4069	Harris John	Pte.	W/Sv	4592	Roberts Henry	Pte.	W/Sl
3841	Hawkes William	Pte.	W/Sv	4206	Robertson William	Pte.	W/Sl
4483	Henderson John	Pte.	W/Sv	3304	Robinson Edward	Pte.	W/Sv
4252	Howden Alexander	Pte.	W/Sl	3964	Rugg George	Pte.	W/Sl
2727	Howes Charles	Pte.	W/Sl	4260	Sandford James	Pte.	W/Sv
4469	Howes Henry	Pte.	W/Sv	2796	Sharp John	Pte.	W/Sv
3726	Hope John	Pte.	W/Sl	3853	Smith George	Pte.	W/Sv
2823	Kidd James	Pte.	W/Sl	4398	Smith James	Pte.	W/Sv
3568	Knott William	Pte.	W/Sl	3983	Thomson William	Pte.	W/Sv
3937	Lockyer William	Pte.	W/Sl	3805	Trainer Francis	Pte.	W/Sv
3812	McAlfin Thomas	Pte.	W/Sl	4501	Whittaker Joseph	Pte.	W/Sv
2518	McCallum Archibald	Pte.	W/Sl	3672	Williams William	Pte.	W/Sl
3180	McDonald James	Pte.	W/Sl	4516	Wilson Joseph	Pte.	W/Sl
4153	McKay James(2nd)	Pte.	W/Sl	4418	Wilson Tullock	Pte.	W/Sl
3996	McKinnon William	Pte.	W/Sl	3049	Witcher Thomas	Pte.	W/Sl
3653	McNeul William	Pte.	W/Sv	3952	Woods John	Pte.	W/Sl
3395	Manson David	Pte.	W/Sv	4042	Wright Thomas	Pte.	W/Sl
4461	Marchant George	Pte.	W/Sv	4466	Wright William	Pte.	W/Sv
3039	Marsh Richard	Pte.	W/Sl	1847	Wyatt James	Pte.	W/Sv
3613	Marshall Charles	Pte.	W/Sl	6091	Barrett James	Pte.	Missing
2325	Meredith John	Pte.	W/Sl	4383	Bridge James	Pte.	Missing
2474	Minister Frederick	Pte.	W/Sl	5870	Brooks Abel	Pte.	Missing
3793	Moore Edwin	Pte.	W/Sv	5284	Hebberd George	Pte.	Missing

1st BATTALION 1st REGIMENT OF FOOT

NO.	NAME	RANK	CASUALTY
3177	Walsh J.	Pte.	Killed

7th REGIMENT OF FOOT

NO.	NAME	RANK	CASUALTY	NO.	NAME	RANK	CASUALTY
2015	Palmer Robert	Corpl.	Killed		Shipley R. Y.	Capt.	W/Sv
2289	Boardman James	Pte.	Killed		Butler H. W. P.	Lieut.	W/Sv
2799	Burnes John	Pte.	Killed		Jones L. J. F.	Ensign	W/Sl
1894	Dyer William	Pte.	Killed	1947	Sarjent Thomas	Sergt.	W/Sv
3424	Humphries George	Pte.	Killed	1775	Richards William	Sergt.	W/Sl
3252	King James	Pte.	Killed	1839	Joy William	Corpl.	W/Sl
2830	Roach Thomas	Pte.	Killed	2847	Thyme Thomas	Corpl.	W/Sv
2881	Woods Henry	Pte.	Killed	2612	Wood John Stanley	Corpl.	W/Sl
	Troubridge Sir T.	Major	W/Sv	2622	McQuire Edward	Drummer	W/Sv
	Rose E. H.	Capt.	W/Sl	2895	Atkinson John	Pte.	W/Sl

NOTES

The Battle of Inkermann

7th REGIMENT OF FOOT

NO.	NAME	RANK	CASUALTY	NO.	NAME	RANK	CASUALTY
1478	Barrack William	Pte.	W/Sv	3252	King James	Pte.	D.O.W
2461	Barry John	Pte.	W/Sl	2663	Lomas Herbert	Pte.	W/Sv
2592	Beck John	Pte.	W/Sv	2040	Martin John	Pte.	W/Sl
2042	Brabham Abraham K.	Pte.	W/Sl	3294	Mitchell Samuel	Pte.	W/Sl
2728	Brown Thomas(1st)	Pte.	W/Sl	1367	Mooney James	Pte.	W/Sv
3041	Brown Thomas(2nd)	Pte.	W/Sv	1686	Mothersdale James	Pte.	W/D
2237	Bullen Richard	Pte.	W/Sv	1308	Parke James	Pte.	W/Sv
2218	Butler John	Pte.	W/Sv	2941	Parsons James	Pte.	W/Sl
1235	Byrne Henry	Pte.	W/Sv	2736	Priestley Wilkinson	Pte.	W/Sv
2846	Chilton William	Pte.	W/Sl	2894	Reynolds Charles	Pte.	W/Sv
3102	Conran Peter	Pte.	W/D	1062	Senior Joseph	Pte.	W/Sl
3075	Cunningham William	Pte.	W/Sv	2442	Sergeant John	Pte.	W/D
2594	Diamond Joseph	Pte.	W/Sl	3287	Sexon Thomas	Pte.	W/Sv
2627	Donegan Patrick	Pte.	W/Sv	1694	Sharpe Samuel	Pte.	W/Sv
3344	Dowling Stephen	Pte.	W/Sv	3034	Smith William	Pte.	W/Sv
2262	Finley John	Pte.	W/Sl	3136	Sutton William	Pte.	W/D
3331	French William	Pte.	W/Sl	3193	Taylor William	Pte.	W/Sv
2398	Glover George	Pte.	W/Sl	2782	Tuckfield George	Pte.	W/Sv
2952	Grant William	Pte.	W/Sv	1507	Edwards Thomas	Corpl.	Missing
2731	Griffiths Richard	Pte.	W/Sl	3247	Argue Robert	Pte.	Missing
993	Hamson William	Pte.	W/Sv	3122	Britland Robert	Pte.	Missing
2680	Henry James	Pte.	W/Sv	1961	Kelson Thomas	Pte.	Missing
2950	Hurst John	Pte.	W/Sv	2030	Lynch Terence	Pte.	Missing
3079	Kelly Peter	Pte.	W/Sv	3006	Walsh James	Pte.	Missing

19th REGIMENT OF FOOT

NO.	NAME	RANK	CASUALTY	NO.	NAME	RANK	CASUALTY
	Ker James	Capt.	Killed	2953	Abbot Richard	Pte.	W/Sl
2426	Cooper Levi	Pte.	Killed	2660	Seal John	Pte.	W/Sl
1044	Madden Henry	Sgt/Maj.	W/Sl				

20th REGIMENT OF FOOT

NO.	NAME	RANK	CASUALTY	NO.	NAME	RANK	CASUALTY
	Dowling W. H.	Lieut.	Killed	3416	Rainbird Thomas	Pte.	Killed
2728	Botell George	Sergt.	Killed	2024	Slater William	Pte.	Killed
2875	Young Joseph	Sergt.	Killed	3550	Stebbins George	Pte.	Killed
2786	Wheeler Henry	Drummer	Killed	1768	Wallis William	Pte.	Killed
3586	Ashby Thomas	Pte.	Killed	2890	Whelan Martin	Pte.	Killed
2153	Berry James	Pte.	Killed	941	Wood Charles	Pte.	Killed
2582	Byford Samuel	Pte.	Killed	2071	McCarthy John	Pte.	D.O.W
2856	Carty Patrick	Pte.	Killed	3466	Poll Joseph	Pte.	D.O.W
3401	Clarke James	Pte.	Killed	2861	Sell William	Pte.	D.O.W
2550	Deffey Joseph	Pte.	Killed	3904	Vale John	Pte.	D.O.W
1931	Egan Patrick	Pte.	Killed	3202	Wagstaff John	Pte.	D.O.W
2334	Fallon Patrick	Pte.	Killed		Horn F.	Col.	W/Sl
1539	Humphries John	Pte.	Killed		Crofton H. D.	Br/Lt/Col	W/Sv
3143	Kelly Oliver	Pte.	Killed		Sharpe J. B.	Br/Maj.	W/Sv
3711	Hinton E. C.	Pte.	Killed		Butler C. R.	Capt.	W/Sv
2844	Masterton Thomas	Pte.	Killed		Wood W. T.	Capt.	W/Sl
3133	McDonough Bartholomew	Pte.	Killed		Bennett G.	Lieut.	W/Sv
					Padfield F.	Lt.&Adj.	W/Sl
3146	McGovern Terence	Pte.	Killed		Kekewich L.	Ensign	W/Sl
1569	Mereday Thomas	Pte.	Killed	1313	Mathieson John	Col/Sgt.	Wounded
3222	Moles Henry	Pte.	Killed	1603	Whybrow James	Col/Sgt.	Wounded
2355	Murray Patrick	Pte.	Killed	2601	Gibson Samuel	Sergt.	Wounded
1703	Patient William	Pte.	Killed	1797	Griffiths George W.	Sergt.	Wounded
3920	Payne Charles	Pte.	Killed	1314	Lawrie Andrea	Sergt.	Wounded
2780	Perry William	Pte.	Killed	1005	Parker Jesse	Sergt.	Wounded
2471	Poore Edward	Pte.	Killed	2031	Rolph Joseph	Sergt.	Wounded

NOTES

The Battle of Inkermann

20th REGIMENT OF FOOT

NO.	NAME	RANK	CASUALTY	NO.	NAME	RANK	CASUALTY
2760	Rule Arthur	Sergt.	Wounded	2706	Jackson Edward	Pte.	Wounded
1655	Smith James	Sergt.	Wounded	3842	Jakes George	Pte.	Wounded
2725	Best Frederick	Corpl.	Wounded	3749	Gennings Martin	Pte.	Wounded
3165	Campbell William	Corpl.	Wounded	2044	Jones Michael	Pte.	Wounded
3188	Gray James	Corpl.	Wounded	3860	Jones William	Pte.	Wounded
3448	Langmaid John S.	Corpl.	Wounded	3878	Kearns William	Pte.	Wounded
3302	Magrane Michael	Corpl.	Wounded	2115	Kennedy William	Pte.	Wounded
3402	O'Neill William	Corpl.	Wounded	2828	Kinsella John	Pte.	Wounded
3423	Osborne Isaac	Corpl.	Wounded	3161	Livermore William	Pte.	Wounded
1971	Thorn George	Corpl.	Wounded	3312	McDonough Edward	Pte.	Wounded
3189	Diggins William	Drummer	Wounded	1942	McGonegal James	Pte.	Wounded
2486	Adams William	Pte.	Wounded	1163	Mann William	Pte.	Wounded
861	Adams John M.	Pte.	Wounded	3819	Markham John	Pte.	Wounded
3884	Allen John	Pte.	Wounded	3243	May Walter	Pte.	Wounded
3289	Amos Alexander	Pte.	Wounded	2079	Meehan Patrick	Pte.	Wounded
3556	Ankor James	Pte.	D.O.W	3681	Merriot Edward	Pte.	Wounded
3910	Aifries John	Pte.	Wounded	1608	Morrell Christopher	Pte.	Wounded
2254	Baker Robert	Pte.	Wounded	3275	Mullen James	Pte.	Wounded
3136	Barnes George	Pte.	Wounded	3147	Murphy James	Pte.	Wounded
3821	Beard Benjamin	Pte.	Wounded	3492	Murphy John	Pte.	Wounded
2002	Bishop Benjamin	Pte.	Wounded	3395	Noble Joseph	Pte.	Wounded
3781	Bitton David	Pte.	Wounded	2543	Norman Robert	Pte.	Wounded
2508	Blake George	Pte.	Wounded	2813	Nowlan Patrick	Pte.	Wounded
3824	Bradford William	Pte.	D.O.W	3712	O'Brien Patrick	Pte.	Wounded
1784	Broadhurst Jonathan	Pte.	Wounded	3742	Osborne Henry	Pte.	Wounded
3411	Bunker Abraham	Pte.	Wounded	3243	Page Daniel	Pte.	Wounded
3635	Burgess Richard	Pte.	Wounded	3340	Pemberton Samuel	Pte.	Wounded
3755	Burman Thomas	Pte.	Wounded	3813	Penigar Edwin	Pte.	Wounded
3174	Cammerford George	Pte.	Wounded	3562	Petters John	Pte.	Wounded
996	Campbell James	Pte.	Wounded	3179	Pillson John	Pte.	Wounded
3265	Carroll Michael	Pte.	Wounded	2342	Reilly Denis	Pte.	Wounded
3449	Case Zachariah	Pte.	Wounded	3426	Rodgers James	Pte.	Wounded
3308	Casey John	Pte.	Wounded	2857	Roote Joseph	Pte.	Wounded
3386	Cawston William	Pte.	Wounded	2636	Rowland James	Pte.	Wounded
3627	Champion James	Pte.	Wounded	2720	Russell John	Pte.	Wounded
3482	Childs William	Pte.	Wounded	1897	Showler Henry	Pte.	Wounded
3149	Clancy Peter	Pte.	Wounded	1133	Simons Thomas	Pte.	Wounded
3176	Clarke James	Pte.	Wounded	1782	Smith John	Pte.	Wounded
3692	Connolly Daniel	Pte.	Wounded	2488	Stagg Henry	Pte.	Wounded
2426	Corte Simon	Pte.	Wounded	2413	Stokes James	Pte.	Wounded
3044	Couldry John	Pte.	Wounded	3766	Sullivan John	Pte.	Wounded
3578	Cowell James	Pte.	Wounded	3799	Suttell Edward	Pte.	Wounded
3726	Cox Henry	Pte.	Wounded	3452	Tadd William	Pte.	Wounded
3307	Delaney John	Pte.	Wounded	2568	Thomas Edward	Pte.	Wounded
3851	Dennis James	Pte.	Wounded	1064	Thorp John	Pte,	Wounded
3636	Dennis John	Pte.	Wounded	3180	Twissell John	Pte.	Wounded
2491	Devin Patrick	Pte.	Wounded	2669	Walls John	Pte.	Wounded
3858	Dewar Robert	Pte.	Wounded	3718	Weatherston John	Pte.	Wounded
2782	Eaton Richard	Pte.	Wounded	1724	Well William	Pte.	Wounded
3686	Falmer John	Pte.	Wounded	1132	Whiting William	Pte.	Wounded
3852	Flack Thomas	Pte.	Wounded	3769	Wiseman Edward	Pte.	Wounded
2549	French Sydney	Pte.	Wounded	2422	Wright Joseph	Pte.	Wounded
3565	Greenhill Jonathan	Pte.	Wounded	3506	Wright Frederick	Pte.	Wounded
1977	Halpin Thady	Pte.	Wounded	2626	Wyatt William	Pte.	Wounded
3509	Haly Patrick	Pte.	Wounded	1615	Hawkins John	Pte.	Missing
2773	Harnett Thomas	Pte.	Wounded	1507	Hobday William	Pte.	Missing
3600	Hoare Henry	Pte.	Wounded	2751	Houghton Henry	Pte.	Missing
3912	Holland George	Pte.	Wounded	3859	Love William	Pte.	Missing
1944	Huntley Harvey	Pte.	Wounded	3503	Mullins Michael	Pte.	Missing
2785	Ingram John	Pte.	Wounded	3691	Scott John	Pte.	Missing

NOTES

The Battle of Inkermann

21st REGIMENT OF FOOT

NO.	NAME	RANK	CASUALTY	NO.	NAME	RANK	CASUALTY
	Hart H. F. E.	Lieut.	Killed	2304	Dwyer Patrick	Pte.	Wounded
1088	Barker L. H.	Pte.	Killed	3446	Easey John B.	Pte.	Wounded
2388	Cooliss Michael	Pte.	Killed	3478	Elliot Charles	Pte.	Wounded
3561	Eager Tobias	Pte.	Killed	2903	Emery Thomas	Pte.	Wounded
3145	Grimes Robert	Pte.	Killed	3335	Freeth John	Pte.	Wounded
2532	Healey Denis	Pte.	Killed	2193	Gaynor John	Pte.	Wounded
2885	Lydiard John	Pte.	Killed	1999	Gulliver George	Pte.	Wounded
2524	Linahan Michael	Pte.	Killed	2329	Halloran Michael(1st)	Pte.	Wounded
1634	Mizen Thomas	Pte.	Killed	3398	Hargreaves Samuel	Pte.	Wounded
3353	Moran Patrick	Pte.	Killed	3306	Harborrow James	Pte.	Wounded
2618	Qualey William	Pte.	Killed	3345	Heley John	Pte.	Wounded
2637	Swift John	Pte.	Killed	3702	Henson Thomas	Pte.	Wounded
3197	Tift John	Pte.	Killed	2641	Hewitt Jonathan	Pte.	Wounded
3589	Warren John	Pte.	Killed	2875	Hewitt Alexander	Pte.	Wounded
2263	Whelan James	Pte.	Killed	3174	Hickey Michael	Pte.	Wounded
	Ainslie F. G.	Lt/Col.	W/Sv	2329	Hickey Michael(1st)	Pte.	Wounded
	Boldero G. W.	Capt.	W/Sv	1175	Hood George	Pte.	Wounded
	Killeen R.	Lieut.	W/Sl	3610	Hosey Thomas	Pte.	Wounded
	King H.	Lieut.	W/Sv	3479	Hughes Neal	Pte.	Wounded
	Stephens R.	Lieut.	W/Sv	3435	Jackson Alexander	Pte.	Wounded
	Templeman A.	Lieut.	W/Sl	3652	Johnson John	Pte.	Wounded
1865	Vousden Thomas	Sgt/Maj.	Wounded	3417	Jones Thomas	Pte.	Wounded
2145	Ellis Richatd	Col/Sgt.	Wounded	3135	Kite Isaac	Pte.	Wounded
1821	Walters William	Col/Sgt.	Wounded	1701	Leat William	Pte.	Wounded
1550	Yeates George	Col/Sgt.	Wounded	3454	Lewis Thomas	Pte.	Wounded
2290	Boulger Michael	Sergt.	Wounded	1412	Little Jacob	Pte.	Wounded
1019	Crichton John	Sergt.	Wounded	3614	McBride Joseph	Pte.	Wounded
2804	Flinn William	Sergt.	Wounded	2750	McCrae John	Pte.	Wounded
2192	Foster James	Sergt.	Wounded	3470	McDermott Robert	Pte.	Wounded
1572	Fox Phillip	Sergt.	Wounded	3613	McDonald Patrick	Pte.	Wounded
1530	Jordan John	Sergt.	Wounded	2587	McGlashan James	Pte.	Wounded
2492	Lannon Patrick	Sergt.	Wounded	3508	McTague Peter	Pte.	Wounded
2588	Powell Thomas	Sergt.	Wounded	2487	Mack Edmund	Pte.	D.O.W.
2845	Boag Thomas	Corpl.	Wounded	3373	Madden John	Pte.	Wounded
2414	Butler Patrick	Corpl.	Wounded	3527	Mageone John	Pte.	Wounded
2864	Anderson Thomas J.	Pte.	Wounded	2555	Mahony James	Pte.	Wounded
3326	Bentley Thomas	Pte.	Wounded	3588	Martin John	Pte.	Wounded
1643	Blackwell George	Pte.	Wounded	3124	Miller James	Pte.	Wounded
2593	Boland Mathew	Pte.	Wounded	2840	Newton James	Pte.	Wounded
3055	Booth James	Pte.	Wounded	3218	Patton John	Pte.	Wounded
2815	Bray Edward	Pte.	Wounded	3009	Preece William	Pte.	Wounded
1754	Bridges Charles	Pte.	Wounded	3584	Purdue Henry	Pte.	Wounded
1781	Bryce David	Pte.	Wounded	3726	Ryan John	Pte.	Wounded
3220	Burke Michael	Pte.	Wounded	3460	Sinnott Miles	Pte.	Wounded
3101	Byrne Michael	Pte.	Wounded	2311	Smith John(16)	Pte.	Wounded
2381	Campbell James(1st)	Pte.	Wounded	3126	Smith George(1st)	Pte.	Wounded
2826	Campbell James(2nd)	Pte.	Wounded	3233	Stubbings John	Pte.	Wounded
3419	Carr William	Pte.	Wounded	2900	Ward Joseph L.	Pte.	Wounded
3495	Cavanagh John	Pte.	Wounded	2590	Weedon John	Pte.	Wounded
3510	Cochlan Jeremiah	Pte.	Wounded	3168	Wilson Alexander	Pte.	Wounded
3172	Cock John.	Pte.	Wounded	3083	Wilson John	Pte.	Wounded
2484	Collins Michael	Pte.	Wounded	3359	Yockney Henry	Pte.	Wounded
3438	Crighton Thomas	Pte.	Wounded	3364	Thomas George	Pte.	Wounded
2686	Crisp Charles	Pte.	Wounded	3486	Boylan John	Pte.	Missing
2368	Crowley Patrick	Pte.	Wounded	3081	Chesterman George	Pte.	Missing
3573	Curley Daniel	Pte.	Wounded	3028	Gubb Charles	Pte.	Missing
3107	Dancey William G.	Pte.	Wounded	2431	Halloran James	Pte.	Missing
3258	Donohoe John	Pte.	Wounded	2949	Logan Robert	Pte.	Missing
3606	Drake Patrick	Pte.	Wounded	3099	McCourtie Michael	Pte.	Missing

NOTES

The Battle of Inkermann

23rd REGIMENT OF FOOT

NO.	NAME	RANK	CASUALTY	NO.	NAME	RANK	CASUALTY
3441	Batten J.	Pte.	Killed	3915	Kiley J.	Pte.	W/Sl
2660	Brown William	Pte.	Killed	2949	Lubey E.	Pte.	W/Sl
2894	Carr W.	Pte.	Killed	1426	McDarling T.	Pte.	W/D
1395	Gallagher V.	Pte.	Killed	3783	Mack J.	Pte.	W/Sv
3936	Hetherington J. H.	Pte.	Killed	3882	Reycroft T.	Pte.	W/Sv
2791	Saunders D.	Pte.	Killed	3802	Webb J.	Pte.	W/D
2763	Williams J.	Pte.	Killed	2834	Williams A.	Pte.	W/Sv
	Vane T. F.	Lieut.	W/Sl	2695	Wynn C.	Pte.	W/Sl
3346	Durkley R.	Sergt.	W/D		Duff J.	Lieut.	Missing
3637	Gamble J.	Sergt.	W/D	3253	Newman J.	Sergt.	Missing
3178	Bennett D.	Corpl.	W/Sv	3448	Birch J.	Pte.	Missing
3484	Aitken H.	Pte.	W/D	1311	Clarke R. W.	Pte.	Missing
3176	Butcher J.	Pte.	W/Sl	1903	Crook J.	Pte.	Missing
2055	Clarke M.	Pte.	W/Sl	1626	Gittens T.	Pte.	Missing
3552	Cose R.	Pte.	W/Sl	3482	Hill W.	Pte.	Missing
3603	Farnham F.	Pte.	W/Sv	3607	Lancaster W.	Pte.	Missing
1395	Gallagher —	Pte.	D.O.W	3547	Mandeville E.	Pte.	Missing
3993	Glasspool P.	Pte.	W/Sl	3477	Rhodes J.	Pte.	Missing
1676	Gosling G.	Pte.	W/Sv	2593	Sawford J.	Pte.	Missing
1925	Hawkins T.	Pte.	W/Sv	2076	Wilkington J.	Pte.	Missing
3984	Holland J.	Pte.	W/Sl	3980	Williams C.	Pte.	Missing

30th REGIMENT OF FOOT

NO.	NAME	RANK	CASUALTY	NO.	NAME	RANK	CASUALTY
	Connolly A.	Capt.	Killed	2441	Jameson William	Sergt.	W/Sl
	Gibson A.	Lieut.	Killed	2270	Loromore Patrick	Sergt.	W/Sl
2257	Dale Thomas	Pte.	Killed	2984	Johnson John(2nd)	Corpl.	W/Sv
2169	Davis William	Pte.	Killed	3533	McGlade Alexander	Corpl.	W/D
3296	Elliott John	Pte.	Killed	3314	McGrath Patrick	Corpl.	W/Sv
2667	Featherston John	Pte.	Killed	3255	Steohens Henry	Corpl.	W/Sl
3775	Fletcher David	Pte.	Killed	1866	Wedle Samuel	Corpl.	W/Sv
3732	Hands William	Pte.	Killed	3163	Young George	Corpl.	W/D
3819	Hutton John	Pte.	Killed	2626	Waters Michael	Drummer	W/Sv
3862	Ingles John	Pte.	Killed	3643	Adam James	Pte.	W/D
2024	McAllister George	Pte.	Killed	2847	Alexander James	Pte.	W/Sv
3836	McIntosh John	Pte.	Killed	3769	Allan John	Pte.	W/D
3995	Mcnurty Daniel	Pte.	Killed	3551	Behone Thomas	Pte.	W/Sl
2762	Manton William	Pte.	Killed	2975	Belcher Benjamin	Pte.	W/Sl
3789	Middlemas John	Pte.	Killed	3825	Bennett Thomas	Pte.	W/Sl
3098	Mohan John	Pte.	Killed	3881	Black John	Pte.	W/Sl
3625	Morgan William	Pte.	Killed	3378	Boughen Daniel	Pte.	W/Sl
3650	Rodway Joseph	Pte.	Killed	3384	Boughen Laurence	Pte.	W/Sl
3452	Scott Henry	Pte.	Killed	2542	Boyd Joseph	Pte.	W/Sl
3223	Sherry Daniel	Pte.	Killed	2633	Brady George	Pte.	W/Sl
3882	Simpson Donald	Pte.	Killed	3844	Browne James	Pte.	W/Sl
3771	Smith Thomas	Pte.	Killed	3774	Byers Thomas	Pte.	W/Sv
3584	Stills William	Pte.	Killed	3765	Campbell Malcolm	Pte.	W/Sl
3155	Swift John	Pte.	Killed	3217	Cannon James	Pte.	W/Sv
2814	Tearney Patrick	Pte.	Killed	2415	Carthrue John	Pte.	W/Sl
2168	Waldock Thomas	Pte.	Killed	3790	Carr Thomas	Pte.	W/Sv
3631	Willis John	Pte.	Killed	2263	Chambers Charles	Pte.	W/Sl
3247	English Patrick	Pte.	D.O.W	3140	Condon Michael	Pte.	W/D
	Mauleverer J. T.	Major	W/Sv	3072	Connor John(1)	Pte.	W/D
	Bayley P.	Capt.	W/Sv	2997	Corcoran Thomas	Pte.	W/Sv
	Dickson G.	Capt.	W/Sl	3987	Crane Thomas	Pte.	W/Sl
	Rose J.	Capt.	W/Sv	2105	Davidson Thomas	Pte.	W/Sl
	Ross Lewin J. D.	Lieut.	W/D	3795	Dove Robert	Pte.	W/Sl
2461	Gallagher William	Col/Sgt.	W/D	3416	Dunleary John	Pte.	W/Sl
2156	Thompson John	Col/Sgt.	W/D	3190	Egan Thomas	Pte.	W/Sl
1886	Dunn David	Sergt.	W/Sl	3792	Findlay Alexander	Pte.	W/Sv

NOTES

The Battle of Inkermann

30th REGIMENT OF FOOT

NO.	NAME	RANK	CASUALTY	NO.	NAME	RANK	CASUALTY
2938	Fitzpatrick Thomas	Pte.	W/D	3035	McMahon James	Pte.	W/Sl
3335	Fletcher Robert	Pte.	W/Sl	3241	Maher Thomas	Pte.	W/Sv
2341	Greaves William	Pte.	W/Sv	2713	Mahoney John	Pte.	W/Sv
3562	Green Joseph	Pte.	W/Sl	2652	Marshall Michael	Pte.	W/Sl
4023	Grimes Bernard	Pte.	W/Sv	3498	Mills Edward	Pte.	W/D
3136	Hallam Robert	Pte.	W/D	3312	Monaghan Edward	Pte.	W/Sv
3991	Halliday David	Pte.	W/Sv	3996	Mooney Patrick	Pte.	W/Sv
3573	Hammerton Joseph	Pte.	W/Sv	3358	Moore Thomas	Pte.	W/Sl
2805	Healey Paul	Pte.	W/Sl	3480	Morgan William	Pte.	W/Sv
3034	Hendry William	Pte.	W/Sv	2797	Okell William	Pte.	W/Sv
3446	Hennel Thomas	Pte.	W/Sv	3607	Palmer Charles	Pte.	W/Sl
3172	Hickey Patrick	Pte.	W/Sl	3418	Potter William	Pte.	W/Sv
2813	Hindley William	Pte.	W/Sl	2310	Powell Charles	Pte.	W/Sv
2750	Hughes Michael	Pte.	W/Sl	3353	Purcell Patrick	Pte.	W/Sl
3322	Hunt John	Pte.	W/Sv	2841	Rhodes Richard	Pte.	W/Sv
3552	Keilly John J.	Pte.	W/Sv	3672	Rodgers John	Pte.	W/Sv
3135	Lawless Michael	Pte.	W/Sv	3173	Ryan James	Pte.	W/D
3043	Leonard John	Pte.	W/Sl	2945	Ryan Thomas	Pte.	W/Sv
1521	Leverett Thomas	Pte.	W/Sl	3860	Sheddon Hugh	Pte.	W/Sv
2707	Long Michael	Pte.	W/Sl	3832	Shiels Alexander	Pte.	W/Sv
3428	Lunn James	Pte.	W/Sl	2563	Simpson Joseph	Pte.	W/Sl
4028	McCarthy Thomas	Pte.	W/D	3106	Smith Thomas(4)	Pte.	W/Sl
3794	McClean John	Pte.	W/Sl	3801	Turnbull George	Pte.	W/Sv
3816	McDonald Thomas	Pte.	W/D	3627	Ward William	Pte.	W/D
2638	McGarry Patrick	Pte.	W/Sl	3791	White John	Pte.	W/Sl
3120	McIntyre John	Pte.	W/Sv	3616	William John	Pte.	W/Sl
3820	McLean Donald	Pte.	W/Sl	3253	Wylie Andrew	Pte.	W/Sv

33rd REGIMENT OF FOOT

NO.	NAME	RANK	CASUALTY	NO.	NAME	RANK	CASUALTY
	Thorold Henry	Lieut.	Killed	2871	Gallagher James	Pte.	Wounded
	Nagle John	Sergt.	Killed	2296	Griffin John	Pte.	Wounded
2202	Burke William	Pte.	Killed	3087	Heywood Mathew	Pte.	Wounded
942	Chapman John	Pte.	Killed	1269	Hindle John	Pte.	Wounded
3183	Collings Maurice	Pte.	Killed	3270	Hoban Pierce	Pte.	Wounded
2613	Deery Thomas	Pte.	Killed	3191	Hogan Denis	Pte.	Wounded
1655	Finlay Edward	Pte.	Killed	3175	Hoolshan Michael	Pte.	Wounded
2090	Hilton John	Pte.	Killed	2983	Ireland John	Pte.	Wounded
2248	O'Hara Peter	Pte.	Killed	2986	Jugger Henry	Pte.	Wounded
2850	Riley William	Pte.	Killed	3350	Kelly Luke	Pte.	Wounded
2654	Tidd Thomas	Pte.	Killed	2093	Landers Michael	Pte.	Wounded
	Corbett F.	Lieut.	W/Sl	993	Latimer William	Pte.	Wounded
	Owens J.	Ensign	W/D	3216	Layton James	Pte.	Wounded
1063	Tomlinson George	Sgt/Maj.	Wounded	3413	Leary Patrick	Pte.	Wounded
1533	Brown George	Sergt.	Wounded	2923	Lewis James	Pte.	Wounded
2544	Clarke James	Corpl.	Wounded	3228	McCarthy Eugene	Pte.	Wounded
1515	Griffin James	Corpl.	Wounded	2756	McKinlay David	Pte.	Wounded
1672	Langstone Samuel	Corpl.	Wounded	1811	McLoughlan —	Pte.	Wounded
1134	Ainsworth John	Pte.	Wounded	2779	Marshall George	Pte.	Wounded
1842	Atkins Samuel	Pte.	Wounded	2774	Moore William	Pte.	Wounded
3254	Bryant James	Pte.	Wounded	3006	Mosley William	Pte.	Wounded
2574	Burnes Edward	Pte.	Wounded	3380	Rawley James	Pte.	Wounded
2708	Burnes James	Pte.	Wounded	2885	Robinson William	Pte.	Wounded
3266	Byatt Joseph	Pte.	Wounded	3112	Simpson James	Pte.	Wounded
2416	Charrell Samuel	Pte.	Wounded	3171	Smith John	Pte.	Wounded
3090	Dixon William	Pte.	Wounded	1934	Sullivan Humphrey	Pte.	Wounded
2184	Dobson John	Pte.	Wounded	973	Sutton Joseph	Pte.	Wounded
3452	Donoghue Joshua	Pte.	Wounded	3198	Thompson George	Pte.	Wounded
3338	Dwyer John	Pte.	Wounded	2660	Westwood Samuel	Pte.	Wounded
3128	Elliss William	Pte.	Wounded	2736	Wilson James	Pte.	Wounded
3184	Ellwood William	Pte.	Wounded	3337	Wynn James	Pte.	Wounded
2314	Fitzgerald James	Pte.	Wounded	3101	Pollard Thomas	Pte.	Missing

NOTES

The Battle of Inkermann

41st REGIMENT OF FOOT

NO.	NAME	RANK	CASUALTY	NO.	NAME	RANK	CASUALTY
	Carpenter G.	Lt/Col.	Killed	2133	Chegwin Noah	Pte.	W/D
	Richards E.	Capt.	Killed	2403	Connell Luke	Pte.	W/D
	Stirling J.	Lieut.	Killed	3088	Connors William	Pte.	W/Sv
	Swaby J. W.	Lieut.	Killed	2196	Corr William	Pte.	W/Sv
	Taylor A.	Lieut.	Killed	2732	Connihan Richard	Pte.	W/Sv
1510	Spence John	Sgt/Maj.	Killed	770	Creighton John	Pte.	W/Sv
2693	White James	Sergt.	Killed	2860	Crowley John	Pte.	W/Sv
1981	Jones Thomas	Corpl.	Killed	2844	Cullen Walter	Pte.	W/Sv
2377	Shaughnessy William	Corpl.	Killed	1837	Cumings James	Pte.	W/Sv
3495	Ball William	Pte.	Killed	1633	Dawson David	Pte.	W/Sv
1323	Benjamin James	Pte.	Killed	2122	Doherty Simon	Pte.	W/Sv
2728	Batford Thomas	Pte.	Killed	2361	Downes James	Pte.	W/Sv
1708	Bostock James	Pte.	Killed	2961	Duffy Thomas	Pte.	W/Sv
2635	Brodie Peter	Pte.	Killed	3146	Duggan Michael	Pte.	W/Sv
2433	Burnes James	Pte.	Killed	2121	Ellis John	Pte.	W/Sl
2804	Coghlan John	Pte.	Killed	3021	Feeney Thomas	Pte.	W/Sv
2139	Cooper James	Pte.	Killed	3384	Fletcher Henry	Pte.	W/D
2254	Daily John	Pte.	Killed	2093	Gollagher John	Pte.	W/Sv
3408	Daniels John	Pte.	Killed	2433	Gatey William	Pte.	W/Sv
1797	Davies Daniel	Pte.	Killed	3379	Glynn James	Pte.	W/Sv
1611	Evans Daniel	Pte.	Killed	3351	Gregg William	Pte.	W/Sv
2567	Evans Jonathan	Pte.	Killed	2821	Hall Benjamin	Pte.	W/Sv
3300	Falsey Patrick	Pte.	Killed	2687	Hayes Daniel	Pte.	W/Sv
2571	Finn William	Pte.	Killed	3400	Henderson Henry	Pte.	W/Sv
2849	Keefe Timothy	Pte.	Killed	1749	Hillson John	Pte.	W/Sv
1095	Kennedy William	Pte.	Killed	1425	Jenkins John	Pte.	W/D
2688	Lilles Thomas	Pte.	Killed	2422	Jones Thomas	Pte.	W/Sv
2294	Macdonald John	Pte.	Killed	3043	Kelly John	Pte.	W/Sv
2964	Meally Patrick	Pte.	Killed	3031	Lavelle John	Pte.	W/Sv
2974	Moran Martin	Pte.	Killed	3343	Lawler John	Pte.	W/Sv
1230	Murphy John	Pte.	Killed	1924	Lewis Mathew	Pte.	W/Sv
2798	Murphy Thomas	Pte.	Killed	3084	Lynch Denis	Pte.	W/Sv
3085	O'Brien Patrick	Pte.	Killed	2350	McCarthy Thomas	Pte.	W/Sl
3412	Olliver William	Pte.	Killed	3354	McGuire Patrick	Pte.	W/Sv
2458	Phillips Michael	Pte.	Killed	2946	McMahon James	Pte.	W/Sv
3038	Rielly Timothy	Pte.	Killed	3012	McPherson Thomas	Pte.	W/D
	Williams Thomas	Pte.	Killed	2749	Madigan John	Pte.	W/Sv
2120	Williams Griffiths	Pte.	Killed	2448	Maddigan Michael	Pte.	W/Sv
2272	Woods George	Pte.	Killed	2551	Mahoney Daniel	Pte.	W/Sv
	Bligh F. C.	Capt.	W/Sl	2963	Marsden William	Pte.	W/Sl
	Meredith H. W.	Capt.	W/Sl	2918	Martin Christopher	Pte.	W/Sv
	Rowlands Hugh	Capt.	W/Sl	2353	Martin William	Pte.	W/Sv
	Bush H. S.	Lieut.	W/Sv	1995	Messling Charles	Pte.	W/Sl
	Fitzroy G. R.	Lieut.	W/Sv	1235	Miles John	Pte.	W/Sv
	Johnston W.	Lieut.	W/Sl	2038	Mitchell John	Pte.	W/D
2626	Bolger David	Sergt.	W/Sv	1940	Moane James	Pte.	W/Sv
1829	Challen Thomas	Sergt.	W/Sl	2062	Morgan Richard	Pte.	W/Sv
2420	Hehir James	Sergt.	W/Sv	2381	Mulligan Lawrence	Pte.	W/Sv
1997	Jones James	Sergt.	W/Sv	2312	Murphy Michael	Pte.	W/Sv
2480	Bond John	Corpl.	W/Sv	2456	O'Brien John	Pte.	W/Sl
2424	Carroll Michael	Corpl.	W/D	2494	O'Connell Denis	Pte.	W/D
2316	Crawford William	Corpl.	W/Sl	3432	O'Leary Patick	Pte.	W/D
1744	Gee Daniel	Corpl.	W/D	1875	Perry Michael	Pte.	W/D
2549	Walshe Henry	Corpl.	W/Sv	3413	Power Martin	Pte.	W/Sv
2845	Walshe Patrick	Corpl.	W/Sv	2498	Quinn Michael	Pte.	W/Sv
2858	Carberry Michael	Drummer	W/Sv	2794	Reid William	Pte.	W/Sv
2919	Kean Patrick	Drummer	W/Sv	1332	Rickard John	Pte.	W/D
1313	Banton William	Pte.	W/Sv	1808	Rigbsy William	Pte.	W/Sv
3496	Barnett Francis	Pte.	W/Sv	3426	Riorden Daniel	Pte.	W/D
3499	Bragg William	Pte.	W/Sv	1192	Robinson Thomas	Pte.	W/Sv
3196	Buck John	Pte.	W/Sv	3393	Robinson Thomas	Pte.	W/D
2938	Butler Patrick	Pte.	W/Sv	2778	Ryder Edmund	Pte.	W/D
2573	Carroll William	Pte.	W/Sv	2890	Shaughnessy John	Pte.	W/Sv

NOTES

The Battle of Inkermann

41st REGIMENT OF FOOT

NO.	NAME	RANK	CASUALTY	NO.	NAME	RANK	CASUALTY
	Smith James	Pte.	W/Sv	1110	Vincent Thomas	Pte.	W/Sl
2090	Smith Thomas	Pte.	W/Sv	2882	Wade Patrick	Pte.	W/D
2497	Smullen Charles	Pte.	W/Sv	3374	Walsh James	Pte.	W/Sv
2113	Sully Henry	Pte.	W/Sv	1350	Welsman Robert	Pte.	W/D
3018	Sutcliffe James	Pte.	W/Sv	1399	White John	Pte.	W/Sv
2173	Sweeny Timothy	Pte.	W/Sl	2051	Wilson Joseph	Pte.	W/D
2259	Truston Martin	Pte.	W/Sv	3520	Wilson John	Pte.	W/Sv
2053	Thomas John	Pte.	W/Sv	1251	Yates William	Pte.	W/Sv

46th REGIMENT OF FOOT

NO.	NAME	RANK	CASUALTY	NO.	NAME	RANK	CASUALTY
2836	Byrnes Patrick	Pte.	Killed	2968	Byrnes Michael	Pte.	Wounded
2381	Clancy Thomas	Pte.	Killed	2170	Connelly Joseph	Pte.	Wounded
2369	Delany Edward	Pte.	Killed	3113	Cox William	Pte.	Wounded
2867	Dennison Joseph	Pte.	Killed	3077	Divine Michael	Pte.	Wounded
3112	Flynn Thomas	Pte.	Killed	922	Flaherty Patrick	Pte.	Wounded
3200	Johnson John	Pte.	Killed	3170	Fulcher John	Pte.	Wounded
1803	O'Brien Francis	Pte.	Killed	3367	Hall John	Pte.	Wounded
2974	Robinson George	Pte.	Killed	2641	Harbour Joseph	Pte.	Wounded
713	Sandelands John	Pte.	Killed	914	Harrowing Isaac	Pte.	Wounded
1179	Shipp Samuel	Pte.	Killed	1335	Kent George	Pte.	Wounded
2421	Tohey Thomas	Pte.	Killed	2338	Kepple Henry	Pte.	Wounded
	Hardy W.	Capt.	W/Sv	2860	McCullough James	Pte.	Wounded
	Hellier E. H.	Ensign	W/Sl	2486	Moylan Patrick	Pte.	Wounded
2622	Aldridge James	Corpl.	Wounded	1848	Painter John	Pte.	Wounded
2802	Harris John	Corpl.	Wounded	2218	Smith Frederick	Pte.	Wounded
2804	Armstrong Robert	Pte.	Wounded	1293	Stewart Robert	Pte.	Wounded
2811	Barry Patrick	Pte.	Wounded	1415	Thompson Samuel	Pte.	Wounded
2919	Brattion William	Pte.	Wounded	2824	Unaworth Daniel	Pte.	Wounded
2232	Brown William	Pte.	Wounded	1975	Walsh Michael	Pte.	Wounded
2890	Burns John	Pte.	Wounded	2950	Williams Edward	Pte.	Wounded

47th REGIMENT OF FOOT

NO.	NAME	RANK	CASUALTY	NO.	NAME	RANK	CASUALTY
2755	Bairstow Isaac	Corpl.	Killed	2219	Measures William	Corpl.	W/Sl
2309	Duke Benjamin	Corpl.	Killed	1866	Cross Charles	Corpl.	W/Sv
1657	Hooke Michael	Corpl.	Killed	2526	Graham James	Corpl.	W/Sl
2702	Byrne Michael	Pte.	Killed	2251	Harding Charles	Corpl.	W/D
2455	Connelley Miles	Pte.	Killed	2171	McBride William	Corpl.	W/Sv
2568	Connor Daniel	Pte.	Killed	2705	White Francis	Corpl.	W/Sl
2654	Daley John	Pte.	Killed	3157	Ball James	Pte.	W/Sv
2490	Fitzgibbon Joseph	Pte.	Killed	3097	Clarke David	Pte.	W/Sv
3072	Ford George	Pte.	Killed	2407	Clune Patrick	Pte.	W/Sl
2393	Gomm Worthy	Pte.	Killed	2120	Connors John	Pte.	W/Sv
3220	Hara Lawrence	Pte.	Killed	2888	Conolly John	Pte.	W/Sl
1978	Hawkins Joseph	Pte.	Killed	3142	Connolly Michael	Pte.	W/Sl
2876	Hennessy Patrick	Pte.	Killed	2264	Dillon John	Pte.	W/Sv
2694	Hollister Mark	Pte.	Killed	2000	Dobbin William	Pte.	W/D
3158	Kena Edmund	Pte.	Killed	3239	Dwyer Mathew	Pte.	W/Sl
2336	McNamara Patrick	Pte.	Killed	3643	Fisher William	Pte.	W/Sv
2261	Pound William	Pte.	Killed	2096	Gray John	Pte.	W/Sv
2495	Scott Peter	Pte.	Killed	2225	Hetherington William	Pte.	W/Sv
2639	Weaver Jesse	Pte.	Killed	2914	Hensworth William	Pte.	W/Sv
3030	Webb John	Pte.	Killed	2510	Hurkey John	Pte.	W/Sv
	Haly W. O'G	Lt/Col.	W/Sv	2475	Kilbride Thomas	Pte.	W/Sv
	Waddilove G.	Ensign	W/Sl	2827	Lean Thomas	Pte.	W/Sl
2226	Cunningham John	Sergt.	W/Sv	1919	Luff Joseph	Pte.	W/Sv
2015	Cochrane J. C.	Sergt.	W/Sv	2456	McCreesh Thomas	Pte.	W/Sv
2145	Keating John	Sergt.	W/Sv	2620	McLean Daniel	Pte.	W/Sv

NOTES

The Battle of Inkermann

47th REGIMENT OF FOOT

NO.	NAME	RANK	CASUALTY	NO.	NAME	RANK	CASUALTY
2793	McMahon John	Pte.	W/Sv	1261	Stockey Moses	Pte.	W/Sl
3175	Mitchell James	Pte.	W/Sl	2073	Taylor James	Pte.	W/Sv
2151	Moloney Henry	Pte.	W/Sv	1828	Taylor William	Pte.	W/Sv
3077	Moyniham Michael	Pte.	W/Sv	2234	Thompson Robert	Pte.	W/Sv
1626	O'Neil John	Pte.	W/Sl	2117	Trehy John	Pte.	W/Sv
1139	Rowley Henry	Pte.	W/Sv	2537	Uniacke Maurice	Pte.	W/Sl
1597	Saddler James	Pte.	W/Sv	1652	Walsh Thomas	Pte.	W/Sl
1510	Sedwick William	Pte.	W/Sl	2621	Ward Thomas	Pte.	W/D
2598	Sheehan Timothy	Pte.	W/Sv	2506	Hoyle Samuel	Corpl.	Missing
3096	Smith John	Pte.	W/Sv	3180	MacDonald Denis	Pte.	Missing

49th REGIMENT OF FOOT

NO.	NAME	RANK	CASUALTY	NO.	NAME	RANK	CASUALTY
	Dalton T. N.	Major	Killed	2190	Rogers Moses	Sergt.	W/Sv
	Armstrong A. S.	Lieut.	Killed	2997	Ryan William	Sergt.	W/Sv
1703	Brown Alexander	Col/Sgt.	Killed	1727	Burgoyne William	Corpl.	W/Sl
3025	Harding Robert	Sergt.	Killed	1442	Dwyer John	Corpl.	W/Sv
2496	Sunidge John	Sergt.	Killed	2197	Eade Thomas	Corpl.	W/Sv
3092	Hogan Michael	Corpl.	Killed	2450	Henry Charles	Corpl.	W/Sl
3111	Coleman Andrew	Drummer	Killed	3011	Ryan Anthont	Corpl.	W/Sl
2908	Anderson John	Pte.	Killed	838	Alexander James	Pte.	W/D
1961	Byrne William	Pte.	Killed	1997	Baker Edward	Pte.	W/D
3182	Connors John	Pte.	Killed	3555	Bennett John	Pte.	W/Sv
1994	Cooper Matthew	Pte.	Killed	2993	Brereton Richard	Pte.	W/Sv
2251	Corbet John	Pte.	Killed	1893	Bridgeman Henry	Pte.	W/Sv
2617	Cummings Michael	Pte.	Killed	1864	Brind Richard	Pte.	W/Sv
2651	Cushion John	Pte.	Killed	2571	Brogan Mathew	Pte.	W/Sv
3561	Day John	Pte.	Killed	2456	Burke John	Pte.	W/Sv
1452	East Henry	Pte.	Killed	2459	Burke Thomas	Pte.	W/Sv
2674	Farrel John	Pte.	Killed	2577	Burns Patrick	Pte.	W/Sv
2464	Folan Patrick	Pte.	Killed	2046	Campion Frederick	Pte.	W/Sl
2618	Graham Joshua	Pte.	Killed	1410	Carroll William	Pte.	W/Sv
2299	Gray James	Pte.	Killed	2198	Claves William	Pte.	W/Sv
1409	Harding John	Pte.	Killed	2339	Cockshin John	Pte.	W/Sv
1445	Higgins Francis	Pte.	Killed	2804	Coleman Ryan	Pte.	W/Sv
2404	Jeffrey John	Pte.	Killed	1140	Collins Joshua	Pte.	W/Sl
3466	Keny Thomas	Pte.	Killed	3063	Connors Michael	Pte.	W/Sv
2458	Kilkelly Thomas	Pte.	Killed	2842	Conolly James	Pte.	W/D
2941	Lawler John	Pte.	Killed	2899	Costin Edwin	Pte.	W/D
2174	Lewis Thomas	Pte.	Killed	3551	Croker Nehemiah	Pte.	W/D
2593	McDade Nathaniel	Pte.	Killed	3174	Crouch George	Pte.	W/Sl
3178	Micue Michael	Pte.	Killed	3041	Cunningham John	Pte.	W/Sl
928	Molloy William	Pte.	Killed	2605	Davidson William	Pte.	W/D
3079	Moloney William	Pte.	Killed	2447	Doran Bryan	Pte.	W/Sv
2273	Mumford Henry	Pte.	Killed	2553	Duncan Thomas	Pte.	W/Sv
3215	Murphy John	Pte.	Killed	2945	Dwyer Daniel	Pte.	W/Sv
2432	O'Brien Bartholomew	Pte.	Killed	2340	Eakins Robert	Pte.	W/Sv
3518	O'Brien Michael	Pte.	Killed	2921	Ennis James	Pte.	W/Sl
3005	O'Neil Owen	Pte.	Killed	3029	Fahy John	Pte.	W/Sv
1911	Palmer William	Pte.	Killed	1975	Flynn John	Pte.	W/Sv
3175	Robinson George	Pte.	Killed	2691	Gibbin Owen	Pte.	W/Sl
2254	Sage William	Pte.	Killed	2664	Grattan John	Pte.	W/Sl
2634	Smith John	Pte.	Killed	1505	Greves George	Pte.	W/Sv
3052	Somerville John	Pte.	Killed	2692	Hanlon James	Pte.	W/Sv
2662	Sweeny Martin	Pte.	Killed	2881	Hart Edward	Pte.	W/Sl
1905	Tanner John	Pte.	Killed	2275	Hemson David	Pte.	W/Sl
2122	Bullen William	Col/Sgt.	W/Sl	1823	Hitchcock Henry	Pte.	W/D
1333	O'Leary Michael	Col/Sgt.	W/Sl	1556	Hunter William	Pte.	W/Sl
2555	Cook Robert	Sergt.	W/Sv	1339	Jenkins Thomas	Pte.	W/Sv
2797	Devitt Michael	Sergt.	W/D	1919	Johnston George	Pte.	W/D
2913	Gunn John	Sergt.	W/Sl	2124	Keep Joseph	Pte.	W/Sv
2678	Robinson James	Sergt.	W/Sl	1914	Kinchin Richard	Pte.	W/D

NOTES

The Battle of Inkermann

49th REGIMENT OF FOOT

NO.	NAME	RANK	CASUALTY	NO.	NAME	RANK	CASUALTY
2854	Kirwan Patrick	Pte.	W/Sl	2668	O'Neill Daniell	Pte.	W/Sv
2841	Lambert John	Pte.	W/Sv	1005	Potton John	Pte.	W/Sv
3179	Ledden Richard	Pte.	W/Sv	2808	Quinn James	Pte.	W/Sv
3555	McAnliffe Cornelius	Pte.	W/Sv	3006	Rawlinson John	Pte.	W/Sl
1232	McDonald Michael	Pte.	W/Sv	2462	Rielly John	Pte.	W/Sl
2110	McEntee James	Pte.	W/Sv	2318	Rogers Henry	Pte.	W/Sv
2982	McGolding Michael	Pte.	W/Sv	2497	Ryan James	Pte.	W/Sv
3161	McGorman William	Pte.	W/Sv	2970	Ryan Patrick	Pte.	W/D
2539	McLoughlan James	Pte.	W/D	3235	Sayers John	Pte.	W/Sl
2686	McMahon James	Pte.	W/Sl	2043	Shean Robert	Pte.	W/Sv
1560	McMoreland William	Pte.	W/Sl	899	Shepperd John	Pte.	W/Sl
2779	McMullane Thomas	Pte.	W/Sv	2736	Smith George	Pte.	W/Sv
2627	McRory Gregory	Pte.	W/Sv	2891	Smith Thomas	Pte.	W/Sv
3482	Malone Loughlin	Pte.	W/Sl	3158	Stapleton Edward	Pte.	W/Sv
2629	Mangan John	Pte.	W/Sv	3438	Swatton George	Pte.	W/Sv
3080	Mason Edmund	Pte.	W/Sv	2405	Tahy John	Pte.	W/Sv
2730	Maynard William	Pte.	W/Sv	3511	Tipple Thomas	Pte.	W/Sv
1857	Minnell John	Pte.	W/Sv	1459	Thompson William	Pte.	W/Sv
2149	Moore Henry	Pte.	W/D	2871	Traynor Thomas	Pte.	W/Sv
2466	Morgans George	Pte.	W/Sv	2451	Tumey James	Pte.	W/Sv
2390	Mulvanny John	Pte.	W/Sl	3539	Vale Thomas	Pte.	W/Sl
2776	Murphy Thomas	Pte.	W/Sv	2022	West William	Pte.	W/Sv
2730	O'Brien Patrick	Pte.	W/Sl	2417	White Thomas	Pte.	W/Sv
2938	O'Connor John	Pte.	W/Sv	2509	Wright James	Pte.	W/Sl
2942	O'Loughlan Patrick	Pte.	W/Sv	3169	Young Henry	Pte.	W/Sv

50th REGIMENT OF FOOT

NO.	NAME	RANK	CASUALTY	NO.	NAME	RANK	CASUALTY
	Dashwood W. G.	Lieut.	Killed	3195	Bucks J.	Pte.	W/D
2645	Bricknell J.	Pte.	Killed	4037	Byrne T.	Pte.	W/Sv
3789	Cooper William	Pte.	Killed	3875	Furlong T.	Pte.	W/Sv
3819	Cronan B.	Pte.	Killed	3800	Gallagher Thomas	Pte.	W/Sv
4099	Daly J.	Pte.	Killed	3203	Leary Moses	Pte.	W/Sl
3706	Edge J.	Pte.	Killed	3608	Leitch A.	Pte.	W/Sl
4068	Lavery William	Pte.	Killed	1441	MacDonald T.	Pte.	W/Sl
3767	Mitchell R.	Pte.	Killed	3128	Macdonogh T.	Pte.	W/Sv
1643	Mooney J.	Pte.	Killed	3552	Mabson J.	Pte.	W/Sv
4106	Nagle J.	Pte.	Killed	2266	Manigan J.	Pte.	W/Sl
2858	Robertson D.	Pte.	Killed	2881	Mara T.	Pte.	W/Sl
2309	Slattery J.	Pte.	Killed	2539	Meaney P.	Pte.	W/Sv
3094	Smith W.	Pte.	Killed	4091	Nolan J.	Pte.	W/Sl
	Frampton H. J.	Capt.	W/Sl	2231	Parker R.	Pte.	W/Sv
1557	Frero J.	Drummer	W/Sl	3531	Rorke J.	Pte.	W/Sv
2128	Arnott A.	Pte.	W/Sv				

55th REGIMENT OF FOOT

NO.	NAME	RANK	CASUALTY	NO.	NAME	RANK	CASUALTY
2826	Baines Edmund	Corpl.	Killed	3587	Sim William	Pte.	Killed
3474	Smith Arthur	Corpl.	Killed	2848	Ward Moses	Pte.	Killed
3488	Anderson John	Pte.	Killed		Warren C. (C.B.)	Lt/Col.	W/Sv
3398	Bailey Samuel	Pte.	Killed		Daubeney H. C. B.	Brv/Col.	W/Sl
3505	Buist Andrew	Pte.	Killed		Barnston W.	Lieut.	W/Sv
2024	Caffrey Bernard	Pte.	Killed		Hume J. R.	Lieut.	W/Sv
2199	Carty Christopher	Pte.	Killed		Morgan G. A.	Lieut.	W/Sl
1604	Doherty Daniel	Pte.	Killed	2304	Boyle Michael	Sergt.	W/Sl
2255	Hatch William	Pte.	Killed	1609	Gaze Charles	Sergt.	W/Sl
2543	Keefe John	Pte.	Killed	1809	Higginson Thomas	Sergt.	W/Sl
3444	Keenan John	Pte.	Killed	1411	Madden Thomas	Sergt.	W/D
3108	Kitson James	Pte.	Killed	2417	Tunnicliffe James	Sergt.	W/Sv

NOTES

The Battle of Inkermann

55th REGIMENT OF FOOT

NO.	NAME	RANK	CASUALTY	NO.	NAME	RANK	CASUALTY
2624	Callaghan Patrick	Cpl.	W/Sl	2401	Harris John	Pte.	W/D
2709	Duff Arthur	Cpl.	W/Sl	3136	Howard John	Pte.	W/Sl
1499	Hardison Robert	Cpl.	W/Sv	2602	Hynes John	Pte.	W/Sv
3531	Hay Peter	Cpl.	W/D	3441	Jenkins William	Pte.	W/Sl
2474	Hickey Maurice	Cpl.	W/Sl	2758	Keefe John	Pte.	W/D
2068	Lakin John	Cpl.	W/Sl	3124	Kilbride Michael	Pte.	W/Sv
2535	Moriarty John	Cpl.	W/D	2781	Kirby Walter	Pte.	W/Sv
2978	Scott Thomas	Cpl.	W/Sv	2333	Knight James	Pte.	W/Sv
3484	Aitken James	Pte.	W/Sl	1782	Lilley Joseph	Pte.	W/Sl
3487	Anderson George	Pte.	W/Sv	3201	McCormack James	Pte.	W/Sl
3027	Andrews Thomas	Pte.	W/Sv	3546	McDougal John	Pte.	W/Sv
2599	Armstrong Benjamin	Pte.	W/Sv	3558	McKennan James	Pte.	W/Sv
2289	Armstrong George	Pte.	W/D	3562	McLeod Charles	Pte.	W/Sv
2491	Baddington James	Pte.	W/Sl	3067	Mahoney Daniel	Pte.	W/Sv
1201	Biddle John	Pte.	W/Sv	2437	Malone Edward	Pte.	W/Sl
2500	Brander Robert	Pte.	W/Sv	3458	May Thomas	Pte.	W/D
2813	Bridges George	Pte.	W/Sl	2979	O'Leary Edward	Pte.	W/D
3501	Browne Alexander	Pte.	W/D	2443	Paton Thomas	Pte.	W/Sl
2518	Byrne Patrick	Pte.	W/Sv	2374	Pearce John	Pte.	W/Sl
3451	Cauley Thomas	Pte.	W/Sv	2353	Prout Thomas	Pte.	W/D
3512	Christie Peter	Pte.	W/Sl	3199	Roberts George	Pte.	W/Sv
2110	Crowther William	Pte.	W/D	2964	Ryan David	Pte.	W/D
2889	Cutmore Levi	Pte.	W/Sv	3585	Shand Charles	Pte.	W/D
3419	Douglas John	Pte.	W/Sl	1269	Smith Felix	Pte.	W/Sl
2461	Dunn James	Pte.	W/Sv	2146	Sparkes John	Pte.	W/Sl
2508	Dunn James	Pte.	W/Sv	2476	Spillane Morris	Pte.	W/Sv
3423	Fitzgerald Michael	Pte.	W/Sv	1199	Starkey John	Pte.	W/Sv
2112	Fleming John	Pte.	W/Sl	3477	Stone Thomas	Pte.	W/Sl
1324	Fox Edward	Pte.	W/Sl	2346	Tye James	Pte.	W/Sl
2861	Gain William	Pte.	W/Sl	2171	Brown John	Pte.	Missing
970	Gordon Thomas	Pte.	W/Sl	3425	Francis James	Pte.	Missing
1309	Gresham Patrick	Pte.	W/Sl	2125	Johnston John	Pte.	Missing
3433	Haines George	Pte.	W/Sv	2337	Webb John	Pte.	Missing
1681	Harper Thomas	Pte.	W/D				

57th REGIMENT OF FOOT

NO.	NAME	RANK	CASUALTY	NO.	NAME	RANK	CASUALTY
	Stanley E.	Capt.	Killed	976	McNea William	Corpl.	Wounded
1239	Griffiths Hiram	Col/Sgt.	Killed	2262	Pickering Oswald	Corpl.	Wounded
2485	Gregory Aford	Sergt.	Killed	2208	Reynolds Thomas	Corpl.	Wounded
1494	McCann Felix	Sergt.	Killed	1450	Connors John	Drummer	Wounded
1372	Blood Thomas	Corpl.	Killed	2426	Bezar Zachariah	Pte.	Wounded
1813	Palmer Henry J.	Corpl.	Killed	3465	Billins William	Pte.	Wounded
2382	Morris Edward	Drummer	Killed	2820	Box Thomas	Pte.	Wounded
–	Clancy William	Pte.	Killed	1839	Brown John	Pte.	Wounded
2099	Foley Michael	Pte.	Killed	3222	Briggs William	Pte.	Wounded
–	Garner William	Pte.	Killed		Bland J. F.	Capt.	D.O.W.
2193	Geeghan Patrick	Pte.	Killed		Hague G. W.	Lieut.	W/D
2031	Hanna Hugh	Pte.	Killed		Venables C.	Lieut.	W/Sl
1150	Johnston William	Pte.	Killed	2439	Bright Robert	Pte.	Wounded
980	Murphy Michael	Pte.	Killed	1945	Bushell George	Pte.	Wounded
–	Ryan Thomas	Pte.	Killed	3093	Cannon John	Pte.	Wounded
2068	Temperley William	Pte.	Killed	2447	Carroll John	Pte.	Wounded
2351	Whelan John	Pte.	Killed	3564	Caskie Edward	Pte.	Wounded
1802	Jones John	Col/Sgt.	Wounded	2343	Charles William	Pte.	Wounded
1319	Hewitt Adam	Sergt.	D.O.W.	1623	Collins John	Pte.	Wounded
863	Betts William	Sergt.	Wounded	1899	Colquhoun Thomas	Pte.	Wounded
1570	Cross William	Sergt.	Wounded	2308	Conniff Patrick	Pte.	Wounded
1331	Dougall John	Sergt.	Wounded	2290	Conroy Michael	Pte.	Wounded
586	Place William	Sergt.	Wounded	2547	Cooke James	Pte.	Wounded
1633	Haggerty John	Corpl.	Wounded	2153	Costin Robert	Pte.	Wounded
2149	Laycock Joseph	Corpl.	Wounded	2308	Daly Martin	Pte.	Wounded

NOTES

The Battle of Inkermann

57th REGIMENT OF FOOT

NO.	NAME	RANK	CASUALTY	NO.	NAME	RANK	CASUALTY
1919	Doorley Patrick	Pte.	Wounded	1788	Kelter Hugh	Pte.	Wounded
2060	Doyle Patrick	Pte.	Wounded	2359	Lindsell John	Pte.	Wounded
2220	Drumm Hugh	Pte.	Wounded	1358	Leary Daniel	Pte.	Wounded
1754	Duff David	Pte.	Wounded	2140	Leonard James	Pte.	Wounded
2454	Duffield Robert	Pte.	Wounded	2239	Lynch John	Pte.	Wounded
2209	Ebbit Francis	Pte.	Wounded	1418	McClees James	Pte.	Wounded
3334	Edwards John	Pte.	Wounded	2282	McConnell William	Pte.	Wounded
1924	Epps John	Pte.	Wounded	1685	McEntee John	Pte.	Wounded
2318	Fannon Peter	Pte.	Wounded	2634	Molloy Martin	Pte.	Wounded
1824	Farrell Edward	Pte.	Wounded	1046	Murray Peter	Pte.	Wounded
2543	Foley James	Pte.	Wounded	2465	Navy William	Pte.	Wounded
2125	Foley John	Pte.	Wounded	2596	Neill Edward	Pte.	Wounded
2423	Gavaghan James	Pte.	Wounded	1829	Noble William	Pte.	Wounded
2107	Gill Patrick	Pte.	Wounded	1364	Poland Patrick	Pte.	Wounded
3522	Godin G. A.	Pte.	Wounded	1430	Reed John	Pte.	Wounded
905	Greenwood John	Pte.	Wounded	1179	Reed William	Pte.	Wounded
2005	Hanna Charles	Pte.	Wounded	2450	Ross Frederick	Pte.	Wounded
2331	Harn Michael	Pte.	Wounded	2345	Russell Thomas	Pte.	Wounded
1611	Harrison James	Pte.	Wounded	1912	Smart John	Pte.	Wounded
2105	Helforty James	Pte.	Wounded	2545	Wheatcroft Isaac	Pte.	Wounded
2389	Hobbins Samuel	Pte.	Wounded	2274	Wilson Mathew	Pte.	Wounded
3351	Jamieson John	Pte.	Wounded	2498	Wright William	Pte.	Wounded
2114	Keating James	Pte.	Wounded	2309	Gallagher John	Pte.	Missing

63rd REGIMENT OF FOOT

NO.	NAME	RANK	CASUALTY	NO.	NAME	RANK	CASUALTY
	Swyny E. S. T.	Lt/Col.	Killed	2693	McMahon James	Corpl.	Wounded
	Curtois G. C. W.	Lieut.	Killed	2828	Neil Patrick	Corpl.	Wounded
	Clutterbuck J. H.	Ensign	Killed	2527	Cunningham John	Drummer	Wounded
2238	McCann Edward	Corpl.	Killed	3712	McEvoy John	Drummer	Wounded
2505	Dougan George	Corpl.	Killed	1716	Ansell Thomas	Pte.	Wounded
3084	Coughlin Lawrence	Pte.	Killed	2594	Brady John	Pte.	Wounded
3142	Belwood Charles	Pte.	Killed	3392	Bennett William	Pte.	Wounded
2862	Green Michael	Pte.	Killed	2927	Burke John	Pte.	Wounded
2812	Jeffries Thomas	Pte.	Killed	2656	Cain Edward	Pte.	Wounded
2766	Jordan Edward	Pte.	Killed	2740	Carter Thomas	Pte.	Wounded
2977	King Thomas	Pte.	Killed	2903	Cody Patrick	Pte.	Wounded
2984	Murphy John	Pte.	Killed	3477	Coleman Patrick	Pte.	Wounded
3458	O'Brien Michael	Pte.	Killed	2716	Coughlin Michael	Pte.	Wounded
2245	Reilly Patrick	Pte.	Killed	2739	Cumlin Patrick	Pte.	Wounded
3039	Shea William	Pte.	Killed	2263	Daly John	Pte.	Wounded
2160	Stringer John	Pte.	Killed	3487	Daly Thomas	Pte.	Wounded
	Fairtlough C. E.	Capt.	W/Sl	3387	Davey John	Pte.	Wounded
	Harries Thomas	Capt.	W/Sl	2886	Donovan Humphrey	Pte.	Wounded
	Bennett R.	Lt & Adj.	W/Sv	2631	Doughen Martin	Pte.	Wounded
	Johns T.	Lieut.	W/Sl	3120	Doyle Thomas	Pte.	Wounded
	Newhenham W. H.	Lieut.	W/Sl	2120	Draper Charles	Pte.	Wounded
	Morgan T. K.	Ensign	W/Sv	2946	Evans William	Pte.	Wounded
	Tysden H. T.	Ensign	W/Sv	3343	Finn George	Pte.	Wounded
1901	Avery Francis	Col/Sgt.	Wounded	3298	Flaherty John	Pte.	Wounded
1423	Brophy John	Col/Sgt.	Wounded	1647	Flock William	Pte.	Wounded
1560	Hughes Robert	Col/Sgt.	Wounded	1680	Fone John	Pte.	Wounded
2348	Armstrong Edward	Sergt.	Wounded	3693	Fraser James	Pte.	Wounded
2375	Healy Jeremiah	Sergt.	Wounded	3424	Garrett George	Pte.	Wounded
2077	Prouse William	Sergt.	Wounded	1947	Grey Robert	Pte.	Wounded
2719	Roberts Arthur	Sergt.	Wounded	3000	Goodwin Abraham	Pte.	Wounded
1825	Shaw Joseph	Sergt.	Wounded	—	Hanchel Michael	Pte.	Wounded
2237	Wooton James	Sergt.	Wounded	3376	Hannan Timothy	Pte.	Wounded
2945	Dea John	Corpl.	Wounded	3523	Harris Richard	Pte.	Wounded
2427	Lovett David	Corpl.	Wounded	1120	Hill Edward	Pte.	Wounded
3295	Lyme Thomas	Corpl.	Wounded	3420	Humpage Joseph	Pte.	Wounded
2247	McElligott Patrick	Corpl.	Wounded	2839	Keefe Matthew	Pte.	Wounded

NOTES

The Battle of Inkermann
63rd REGIMENT OF FOOT

NO.	NAME	RANK	CASUALTY	NO.	NAME	RANK	CASUALTY
2639	Kelly William	Pte.	Wounded	3034	Pinson Thomas E.	Pte.	Wounded
1850	Knight Nathan	Pte.	Wounded	2008	Poundford Thomas	Pte.	Wounded
2938	Lennard John	Pte.	Wounded	2773	Puntell Thomas	Pte.	Wounded
2768	Lepper Patrick	Pte.	Wounded	3413	Reading George	Pte.	Wounded
2967	Lovett John	Pte.	Wounded	3066	Reilly Daniel	Pte.	Wounded
2717	McGrath Michael	Pte.	Wounded	3279	Ryan Edward	Pte.	Wounded
2990	McGrath Daniel	Pte.	Wounded	2124	Sheridan Charles	Pte.	Wounded
2787	McNamara John	Pte.	Wounded	3121	Smith Peter	Pte.	Wounded
2287	Mackillacuddy Wm.	Pte.	Wounded	2453	Smith John	Pte.	Wounded
2599	Mack Michael	Pte.	Wounded	2896	Stokes John	Pte.	Wounded
3236	Madden Patrick	Pte.	Wounded	3371	Sullivan Timothy	Pte.	Wounded
2696	Mann Richard	Pte.	Wounded	2980	Thorn William	Pte.	Wounded
3410	Marden John	Pte.	Wounded	3349	Toker John	Pte.	Wounded
3411	Mears William	Pte.	Wounded	2813	Varney James	Pte.	Wounded
2572	Moore Francis	Pte.	Wounded	3985	Whelan Patrick	Pte.	Wounded
2223	Murphy Michael	Pte.	Wounded	2009	Young Thomas	Pte.	Wounded
2845	Murray Thomas	Pte.	Wounded	2456	Bartlett George	Pte.	Missing
3478	Norton Patrick	Pte.	Wounded	2741	Kenny Michael	Pte.	Missing
2829	Nunane John	Pte.	Wounded	2278	Murphy Owen	Pte.	Missing
1517	O'Brien John	Pte.	Wounded	3018	O'Donnell Thomas	Pte.	Missing

68th REGIMENT OF FOOT

NO.	NAME	RANK	CASUALTY	NO.	NAME	RANK	CASUALTY
	Wynne H. G.	Major	Killed	3098	Coughlan John	Pte.	Wounded
	Barker F. G.	Lieut.	Killed	1411	Curran James	Pte.	Wounded
2838	Ashford William	Pte.	Killed	1035	Deacon James	Pte.	Wounded
2203	Blakeman Daniel	Pte.	Killed	2696	East Joseph	Pte.	Wounded
3252	Calderbank William	Pte.	Killed	2287	Ellis Charles	Pte.	Wounded
1575	Hitchcock Henry	Pte.	Killed	2691	Flinn Patrick	Pte.	Wounded
2913	Kinton John	Pte.	Killed	3435	Flynn John	Pte.	Wounded
3443	Longworthy George	Pte.	Killed	2862	Harman Anthony	Pte.	D.O.W.
3379	Malone James	Pte.	Killed	2871	Heald Richard	Pte.	Wounded
2805	Manly William	Pte.	Killed	2550	Hogan Lawrence	Pte.	Wounded
1388	Midgely Joseph	Pte.	Killed	1993	Jarvis Thomas	Pte.	Wounded
2723	Miller William	Pte.	Killed	3181	Lennan Patrick	Pte.	Wounded
3409	Owen Thomas	Pte.	Killed	3376	Lewis John	Pte.	Wounded
	Smith Harry	Lt/Col.	W/D	2970	Lyons James	Pte.	Wounded
	Cator J.	Lieut.	W/D	3172	McDonald William	Pte.	Wounded
1124	McKillop John	Bugle/Mjr.	Wounded	3199	Mande George	Pte.	D.O.W.
2414	Watkins John	Bugler	Wounded	2777	Moulton Alfred	Pte.	Wounded
3092	Clarke John	Corpl.	Wounded	3645	Rielly Andrew	Pte.	Wounded
2652	Delaney Peter	Corpl.	Wounded	1623	Ruscoe William	Pte.	Wounded
2372	Appleyard Edward	Pte.	Wounded	3048	Rushworth Richard	Pte.	Wounded
2892	Baskerville William	Pte.	Wounded	2466	Smith Joseph	Pte.	Wounded
1370	Buckley Terence	Pte.	Wounded	3109	Sullivan James	Pte.	Wounded
2102	Butcher William	Pte.	Wounded	3197	Taylor Ralph	Pte.	Wounded
3166	Cotton John	Pte.	Wounded	1673	Twoomey John	Pte.	Wounded

77th REGIMENT OF FOOT

NO.	NAME	RANK	CASUALTY	NO.	NAME	RANK	CASUALTY
	Nicholson J.	Capt.	Killed	3056	Field James	Pte.	Killed
1598	Castinux Mark	Sergt.	Killed	2426	Finlan John	Pte.	Killed
2187	Bernard Robert	Sergt.	Killed	2701	Johnson David	Pte.	Killed
2553	Barr Robert	Pte.	Killed	2247	Joyce James	Pte.	Killed
2925	Brown James	Pte.	Killed	2388	Kenna Thomas	Pte.	Killed
2918	Collins James	Pte.	Killed	2103	Lynch Patrick	Pte.	Killed
2116	Connor James	Pte.	Killed	2339	McGrath Patrick	Pte.	Killed
2697	Cook Richard	Pte.	Killed	1503	Richey Stewart	Pte.	Killed
2405	Costello John	Pte.	Killed	1960	Strange John	Pte.	Killed

NOTES

The Battle of Inkermann

77th REGIMENT OF FOOT

NO.	NAME	RANK	CASUALTY	NO.	NAME	RANK	CASUALTY
3076	Taylor Thomas	Pte.	Killed		Hutchinson William	Pte.	W/Sv
3081	Wise James	Pte.	Killed	1190	Joyce James	Pte.	W/Sl
2006	Beaumont Arthur	Sergt.	W/Sl	860	Kenneally Martin	Pte.	W/Sl
1846	Carty Patrick	Sergt.	W/Sv	2825	McAnliff Owen	Pte.	W/D
1702	Furnish James C.	Corpl.	W/Sl	2222	McGrath Thomas	Pte.	W/Sv
2181	Marshall Samuel	Corpl.	W/D	3087	McGrath William	Pte.	D.O.W.
—	Stringer Michael	Corpl.	W/D		Kneight Thomas	Pte.	W/Sv
1546	Walsh Samuel	Corpl.	W/Sl	3068	Newby James	Pte.	W/Sv
2598	Wilson James	Corpl.	W/Sl		Nicholson Robert	Pte.	W/Sv
2422	Fox Patrick	Drummer	W/Sv	1245	Nolan Joseph	Pte.	W/D
2073	Allum Joseph	Pte.	W/Sv	2645	Page George	Pte.	W/D
1660	Bancroft Joseph	Pte.	W/Sv	2965	Rafferty Owen	Pte.	W/Sv
2591	Burnell James	Pte.	W/Sl		Riddle William	Pte.	W/Sl
1675	Chance William	Pte.	W/Sl	2643	Smith James	Pte.	W/Sl
1440	Colclough Samuel	Pte.	W/Sv		Seckington George	Pte.	W/Sv
1781	Connell Thomas	Pte.	W/D	2793	Thompson Thomas	Pte.	W/Sv
2740	Dennison George	Pte.	W/Sv		Tiffin William	Pte.	W/D
3055	Fenson William	Pte.	D.O.W.		Vaughan William	Pte.	W/Sv
2687	Hall Wilson	Pte.	W/Sv	2431	Williams John	Pte.	W/Sv
2085	Horan Cornelius	Pte.	W/Sv	2945	Winterbottom Joseph	Pte.	W/Sv

88th REGIMENT OF FOOT

NO.	NAME	RANK	CASUALTY	NO.	NAME	RANK	CASUALTY
1302	O'Donnell R.	Sgt/Mjr.	Killed		Crosse J. G.	Capt.	W/Sl
993	Clements R.	Sergt.	Killed		Baynes H. J.	Lieut.	W/Sv
2557	Leary Timothy	Sergt.	Killed	2810	Glynn Patrick	Col/Sgt.	W/D
2575	Smith William	Sergt.	Killed	2811	Holmes J. J.	Col/Sgt.	W/Sv
2452	Kelly Thomas	Corpl.	Killed	1451	Carroll James	Sergt.	W/Sv
1303	Segrave William	Corpl.	Killed	1403	Connors John	Sergt.	W/Sl
3128	Breshnahan Daniel	Pte.	Killed	1066	Flynn A. O.	Sergt.	W/Sl
3297	Casey William	Pte.	Killed	2493	Foley Daniel	Sergt.	W/Sl
2669	Cassidy William	Pte.	Killed	1866	Madden Thomas	Sergt.	W/Sv
2242	Connaughton Michael	Pte.	Killed	920	Moore Patrick	Sergt.	W/Sl
2986	Connell George	Pte.	Killed	2707	Slattery M.	Sergt.	W/Sl
844	Connican Patrick	Pte.	Killed	1977	Clegg Michael	Corpl.	W/Sl
3120	Connolly Patrick	Pte.	Killed	2332	Conroy Thomas	Corpl.	W/Sv
2476	Faherty Martin	Pte.	Killed	2219	Gannon A.	Corpl.	W/Sl
3262	Ferguson Richard	Pte.	Killed	2701	Lyons Patrick	Corpl.	W/Sv
3076	Hartley Martin	Pte.	Killed	2650	O'Rourke James	Corpl.	W/Sl
3264	Hickey James	Pte.	Killed	2416	Keegan Michael	Corpl.	W/Sl
2835	Joyce Thomas	Pte.	Killed	1827	Cunningham S.	L/Cpl.	W/Sl
3195	Kavanagh John	Pte.	Killed	2426	Sullivan Thomas	L/Cpl.	W/Sl
2867	Kean Matthias	Pte.	Killed	2291	Grannon Richard	Drummer	W/Sl
1352	Lewis William	Pte.	Killed	836	Bernard James	Pte.	W/Sl
2961	Looney John	Pte.	Killed	1958	Bowles Francis	Pte.	W/Sl
1192	Lowry Thomas	Pte.	Killed	3007	Brennahan Patrick	Pte.	W/Sv
3173	Lyle Joseph	Pte.	Killed	2761	Brett William	Pte.	W/Sl
3177	McGregor Daniel	Pte.	Killed	3111	Brown John	Pte.	W/Sl
2088	McMahon John	Pte.	Killed	3112	Burke James	Pte.	W/Sl
1914	Mair John	Pte.	Killed	3387	Caggins Martin	Pte.	W/Sl
2009	Malone John	Pte.	Killed	3267	Cohig John	Pte.	W/Sv
1872	Murray Thomas	Pte.	Killed	3213	Condon David	Pte.	W/Sv
3556	Nan William	Pte.	Killed	2675	Connolly Gregory	Pte.	W/Sl
2908	Nash Patrick	Pte.	Killed	2467	Connors Michael	Pte.	W/Sl
3292	Nattall Walter	Pte.	Killed		Conry Thomas	Pte.	W/Sl
2687	Nee Coleman	Pte.	Killed	3323	Cox Michael	Pte.	W/Sl
3429	Nowlan James	Pte.	Killed	2134	Cummins Patrick	Pte.	W/Sv
1440	O'Brien Thomas	Pte.	Killed	3136	Daley John	Pte.	W/Sl
2956	O'Shaughnessy Patrick	Pte.	Killed	3454	Dawson John	Pte.	W/Sv
2889	Patty Martin	Pte.	Killed	2759	Dillon Thomas	Pte.	W/Sv
2452	Shea James	Pte.	Killed	2630	Dolan Anthony	Pte.	W/Sv
	Jeffreys E. R.	Lt/Col.	W/Sl	3108	Egan John	Pte.	W/Sl

NOTES

The Battle of Inkermann
88th REGIMENT OF FOOT

NO.	NAME	RANK	CASUALTY	NO.	NAME	RANK	CASUALTY
2975	Enright John	Pte.	W/Sl	2471	McGuire Patrick	Pte.	W/Sl
2139	Fallon John	Pte.	W/Sv	589	Mills William	Pte.	W/Sl
2654	Ferris Thomas	Pte.	W/Sv	2955	Moore John	Pte.	W/Sv
3043	Finnecan Thomas	Pte.	W/Sv	3102	Moore John	Pte.	W/Sv
2498	Fitzgerald Thomas	Pte.	W/Sv	2451	Mullens John	Pte.	W/Sl
2726	Flannagan Michael	Pte.	W/Sv	3279	Mulholland John	Pte.	W/Sv
2614	Gallaha Patrick	Pte.	W/Sl	2827	Neill Robert	Pte.	W/Sl
1282	German James	Pte.	W/Sl	2128	Noone Martin	Pte.	W/Sl
1947	Gilbride John	Pte.	W/Sv	2057	O'Brien Denis	Pte.	W/Sv
2852	Hackett William	Pte.	W/Sl	2772	O'Connor Michael	Pte.	W/Sv
3351	Hamilton William	Pte.	W/Sl	2123	O'Neil Michael	Pte.	W/Sv
1754	Hannon James	Pte.	W/Sv	2941	Price Edmund	Pte.	W/Sl
3226	Hogan Charles	Pte.	W/Sv	1640	Renny Denis	Pte.	W/D
2706	Hogan Connor	Pte.	W/Sl	2939	Spellman Michael	Pte.	W/Sv
2563	Hollands Michael	Pte.	W/D	2536	Spencer Philip	Pte.	W/Sv
2163	Joyce Patrick	Pte.	W/Sl	2945	Stock Patrick	Pte.	W/Sl
2909	Keating Thomas	Pte.	W/Sl	2884	Sullivan Roga	Pte.	W/Sl
2533	Lacey Edward	Pte.	W/Sv	2892	Sullivan Patrick	Pte.	W/Sl
2185	Lappin John	Pte.	W/Sv	2640	Tierney Thomas	Pte.	W/Sl
3167	Lodge James	Pte.	W/Sl	2764	Walsh John	Pte.	W/Sv
2964	Lynch Patrick	Pte.	W/Sl	3274	Weir James	Pte.	W/Sl
2830	McCay Patrick	Pte.	W/Sl				

95th REGIMENT OF FOOT

NO.	NAME	RANK	CASUALTY	NO.	NAME	RANK	CASUALTY
2265	Murphy James	Col/Sgt.	Killed	2032	Walsh James	Corpl.	W/Sl
977	Evans Edward	Sergt.	Killed	2374	Adam William	Pte.	W/Sl
2164	Aldworth Patrick	Corpl.	Killed	1991	Ahearn William	Pte.	W/Sv
2215	Clarke Robert	Corpl.	Killed	1597	Avis John	Pte.	W/Sv
2525	Purcell Michael	Corpl.	Killed	2579	Barber Frederick	Pte.	W/Sv
2963	Abraham Thomas	Pte.	Killed	2947	Booth John	Pte.	W/Sv
2400	Barnes James	Pte.	Killed	2240	Burnes Patrick	Pte.	W/Sv
2809	Carney Patrick	Pte.	Killed	2895	Byrne Michael	Pte.	W/Sv
2217	Carroll Michael	Pte.	Killed	1033	Campbell Florence	Pte.	W/Sv
2131	Christopher Joseph	Pte.	Killed	3007	Cantillon James	Pte.	W/Sv
3094	Daniels James	Pte.	Killed	1834	Carmody John	Pte.	W/Sv
3129	Denton Stephen	Pte.	Killed	2404	Carroll James	Pte.	W/Sl
3023	Dermody John	Pte.	Killed	2898	Carroll John	Pte.	W/Sv
2370	Duffy John	Pte.	Killed	2800	Chun Joseph	Pte.	W/Sv
2468	Dunn Thomas	Pte.	Killed	2837	Cocksedge Thomas	Pte.	W/Sl
2566	Griffiths Edward	Pte.	Killed	2003	Cody James	Pte.	W/Sv
3134	Harris William	Pte.	Killed	2148	Coffee Cornelius	Pte.	W/Sv
2697	Jones John	Pte.	Killed	2082	Conway Richard	Pte.	W/Sv
1769	Knights David	Pte.	Killed	2641	Conaughton Michael	Pte.	W/Sl
3110	Lacey David	Pte.	Killed	2942	Cottington George	Pte.	W/Sv
2988	Lovett Robert	Pte.	Killed	1688	Cuhill Thomas	Pte.	W/Sv
3094	Melvin William	Pte.	Killed	2478	Cuttle David	Pte.	D.O.W.
2997	Mullaney Michael	Pte.	Killed	2094	Donaghue Patrick	Pte.	W/Sv
2169	Newby William	Pte.	Killed	2112	Donovan Cornelius	Pte.	W/Sv
3034	Slark John	Pte.	Killed	2060	Downey James	Pte.	W/Sl
2523	Stewart James	Pte.	Killed	2143	Downey Michael	Pte.	W/Sv
1984	Wade George	Pte.	Killed	2290	Doyle Patrick	Pte.	W/D
	Champion J. G.	Major	W/Sv	1164	Duke Ezekiel	Pte.	W/Sv
	Hume H.	Major	W/Sl	3034	Fasedray John	Pte.	W/D
	Vialls G. C.	Capt.	W/Sl	2235	Fitzgerald James	Pte.	W/Sv
	McDonald A. J. J.	Lieut.	W/D	2913	Fosser George	Pte.	W/Sv
2077	Long John	Sergt.	W/Sv	3207	Giles William	Pte.	W/D
2817	Rowell William	Sergt.	W/Sv	3047	Glennon Francis	Pte.	W/Sv
1810	Connell John	Corpl.	W/Sv	2754	Golding James	Pte.	W/Sl
2708	Henderson George	Corpl.	W/Sv	3123	Golding Thomas	Pte.	W/D
2228	O'Sullivan John	Corpl.	W/Sv	2728	Gooding James	Pte.	W/Sv
1602	Paget John	Corpl.	W/Sv	2959	Green George	Pte.	W/Sv

NOTES

The Battle of Inkermann
95th REGIMENT OF FOOT

NO.	NAME	RANK	CASUALTY	NO.	NAME	RANK	CASUALTY
3131	Green Horatio	Pte.	W/Sl	1001	Percival Isaac	Pte.	W/D
2858	Gregg Samuel	Pte.	W/Sl	2349	Richardson Robert	Pte.	W/Sv
1967	Griffin Thomas	Pte.	W/Sl	1293	Richardson William	Pte.	W/D
3039	Grimminson James	Pte.	W/Sl	1766	Rose Charles	Pte.	W/Sv
3040	Grimminson Henry	Pte.	W/Sv	2841	Rosedale William	Pte.	W/D
1618	Hawkins Michael	Pte.	W/Sv	2140	Ryan Matthew	Pte.	W/Sv
2098	Hayes John	Pte.	W/Sv	1094	Ryan Cornelius	Pte.	W/Sv
1780	Hennesy Patrick	Pte.	W/Sv	3051	Shea Darby	Pte.	W/Sl
2721	Henry Edward	Pte.	W/Sv	3085	Shrives Isaac	Pte.	W/Sv
1608	Hoase George	Pte.	W/Sv	2514	Smith Charles	Pte.	W/Sv
2792	Holmes Arthur	Pte.	W/Sl	2221	Smith Charles	Pte.	W/Sv
1270	Hynes Edward	Pte.	W/D	2951	Smith John	Pte.	W/Sv
1606	Irvine John	Pte.	W/Sv	2857	Smith John	Pte.	W/Sv
2496	Jameson George	Pte.	W/Sv	2319	Spicer Thomas	Pte.	W/D
2518	Jeffries Robert	Pte.	W/Sl	2874	Sullivan John	Pte.	W/Sl
2666	Keeling George	Pte.	W/Sl	1947	Sullivan Patrick	Pte.	W/Sl
1850	Kenny Patrick	Pte.	W/D	2118	Sweeny James	Pte.	W/Sv
1515	Kerry John	Pte.	W/Sv	2781	Taylor George	Pte.	W/Sv
3036	Kilroy Thomas	Pte.	W/Sv	1389	Taylor Thomas	Pte.	W/D
1735	Lane Richard	Pte.	W/Sv	2640	Troubridge Richard	Pte.	W/Sl
3090	Leonard Michael	Pte.	W/Sv	1183	Urid Martin	Pte.	W/D
2977	Lepards William	Pte.	W/Sv	2926	Walker Philip	Pte.	W/Sv
2830	Lewis Thomas	Pte.	W/Sv	2559	Walker Thomas	Pte.	W/Sv
2732	Lock James	Pte.	W/Sv	3107	Walker William	Pte.	W/Sv
3170	Luke George	Pte.	W/Sv	2028	Walsh John	Pte.	W/Sv
1931	Lynch Thomas	Pte.	W/D	2882	Ward Patrick	Pte.	W/Sv
3193	McCullough Francis	Pte.	W/Sv	2241	Waring Hughber	Pte.	W/Sv
3086	Maher John	Pte.	W/D	1294	Waters Patrick	Pte.	W/Sv
1459	Medcalf Henry	Pte.	W/Sl	3055	Wheeler Eleazor	Pte.	W/Sl
3020	Morgan Michael	Pte.	W/Sv	2991	Wilson Henry	Pte.	W/Sl
3184	Morpe George	Pte.	W/Sv	2859	Winpenny C.	Pte.	W/Sv
2580	Nutbeen Henry	Pte.	W/Sl	2513	Woodward Robert	Pte.	W/D
2980	Payne Alfred	Pte.	W/Sv	3186	Wright William	Pte.	W/Sv
1392	Pegg John	Pte.	W/Sv	3244	Yarrow Francis	Pte.	W/Sv

1st BATTALION RIFLE BRIGADE

NO.	NAME	RANK	CASUALTY	NO.	NAME	RANK	CASUALTY
	Cartwright A. A.	Capt.	Killed		Flower C. S.	Lieut.	W/Sl
1450	Camer George	Col/Sgt.	Killed	2575	Green John	Col/Sgt.	Wounded
2643	Nosely George	Col/Sgt.	Killed	2058	McGrotty John	Col/Sgt.	Wounded
2664	Powell James	Col/Sgt.	Killed	3098	Forsyth John	Sergt.	Wounded
3389	Brett William	Sergt.	Killed	1346	Jerrom William	Sergt.	Wounded
1946	McCullen Thomas	Sergt.	Killed	2858	Vaughan John	Sergt.	Wounded
2009	Sills William	Sergt.	Killed	3362	Allen John	Corpl.	Wounded
1571	Goddard Charles	Corpl.	Killed	3587	Garfield Charles	Corpl.	Wounded
3159	Lee John	Corpl.	Killed	2466	Nightingale Henry	Corpl.	Wounded
3402	Birch John	Pte.	Killed	1870	Shaw Samuel	Corpl.	Wounded
3403	Bishop George	Pte.	Killed	1951	Taylor George	Corpl.	Wounded
3649	Bonham William	Pte.	Killed	2122	Huston Elijah	Bugler	Wounded
2465	Calderbank John	Pte.	Killed	3599	Adams David	Pte.	Wounded
2728	Davies William	Pte.	Killed	3455	Barker Henry	Pte.	Wounded
3670	Harris Emanuel	Pte.	Killed	3519	Barrow Charles	Pte.	Wounded
3280	Hickey Thomas	Pte.	Killed	2752	Beard Frederick	Pte.	Wounded
3603	McInerney Hugh	Pte.	Killed	2837	Beatty William	Pte.	Wounded
2900	McNamara Patrick	Pte.	Killed	1954	Benley Thomas	Pte.	Wounded
2804	Marley William	Pte.	Killed	2919	Bibby Henry	Pte.	Wounded
2624	Percival Alfred	Pte.	Killed	2162	Brown John	Pte.	Wounded
2870	Quinn Felix	Pte.	Killed	3282	Burgess John	Pte.	Wounded
2153	Scheoder John	Pte.	Killed	3644	Butler Patrick	Pte.	Wounded
2751	Trapp John	Pte.	Killed	3137	Button George	Pte.	Wounded
	Rooper E.	Major	W/Sv	3712	Caddy Joseph	Pte.	Wounded
	Coote Buller	Lieut.	W/Sl	3325	Carter George	Pte.	Wounded

NOTES

The Battle of Inkermann

1st BATTALION RIFLE BRIGADE

NO.	NAME	RANK	CASUALTY	NO.	NAME	RANK	CASUALTY
2191	Catchpole Charles	Pte.	Wounded	2973	Monyer Timothy	Pte.	Wounded
2813	Clews Cornelius	Pte.	Wounded	3632	Newbanks James	Pte.	Wounded
3613	Coakley John	Pte.	Wounded	3554	Palmer Cornelius	Pte.	Wounded
3250	Davies Daniel	Pte.	Wounded	3511	Petchley Thomas	Pte.	Wounded
3404	Denny Francis	Pte.	Wounded	3789	Porter Edward	Pte.	Wounded
2914	Doran William	Pte.	Wounded	3490	Powell Joseph	Pte.	Wounded
3625	Fuldeman Edward	Pte.	Wounded	3246	Pusday William	Pte.	Wounded
3680	Griloe Robert	Pte.	Wounded	3363	Rains Charles	Pte.	Wounded
2838	Hanify Michael	Pte.	Wounded	3004	Robesson George	Pte.	Wounded
3327	Hardy William	Pte.	Wounded	3231	Robinson James	Pte.	Wounded
2613	Harman Robert	Pte.	Wounded	3689	Saunders William	Pte.	Wounded
3206	Hayhoe Henry	Pte.	Wounded	3057	Simms William	Pte.	Wounded
2270	Head Robert	Pte.	Wounded	3011	Sheen John	Pte.	Wounded
3541	Healy David	Pte.	Wounded	2806	Sparks Peter	Pte.	Wounded
3219	Hodge William	Pte.	Wounded	2983	Stephens Alfred	Pte.	Wounded
2398	Hodges William	Pte.	Wounded	3067	Stokes Henry	Pte.	Wounded
3090	Home Thomas	Pte.	Wounded	3607	Stringer Patrick	Pte.	Wounded
1330	Horan Thomas	Pte.	Wounded	3237	Taylor Henry	Pte.	Wounded
2434	Hudson John	Pte.	Wounded	2574	Taylor John	Pte.	Wounded
3239	Jones Thomas	Pte.	Wounded	3495	Thompson Henry	Pte.	Wounded
3573	Kavanah Francis	Pte.	Wounded	3059	Tornlin Richard	Pte.	Wounded
2629	King John	Pte.	Wounded	3473	Walker William	Pte.	Wounded
3646	King Richard	Pte.	Wounded	3442	Watson Edward	Pte.	Wounded
1413	Knight Thomas	Pte.	Wounded	2325	Webb William	Pte.	Wounded
2886	McGee Joseph	Pte.	Wounded	2898	Whiting John	Pte.	Wounded
3506	Mack John	Pte.	Wounded	3589	Williams Robert	Pte.	Wounded
3390	Makepeace Samuel	Pte.	Wounded	3467	Willis Charles	Pte.	Wounded
3425	Martin Richard	Pte.	Wounded	2899	Wood William	Pte.	Wounded

2nd BATTALION RIFLE BRIGADE

NO.	NAME	RANK	CASUALTY	NO.	NAME	RANK	CASUALTY
	Malcolm L. W.	Lieut.	Killed	3992	Freeman Charles	Pte.	Wounded
2552	Batlett Henry	Pte.	Killed	3684	Grooves Charles	Pte.	Wounded
3793	Carey Joseph	Pte.	Killed	3504	Harvey George	Pte.	Wounded
3686	Hayward William	Pte.	Killed	3858	Herring John	Pte.	Wounded
3620	Jee Thomas	Pte.	Killed	2043	McCall B.	Pte.	Wounded
1806	Nilson John	Pte.	Killed	3816	McNabb R.	Pte.	Wounded
3872	Payne James	Pte.	Killed	3586	Marratt Edward	Pte.	Wounded
3870	Sheather Stephen	Pte.	Killed	1224	Midgeley George	Pte.	Wounded
2352	Westway John	Pte.	Killed	2773	Monk William	Pte.	Wounded
2747	McCarthy B.	Pte.	Killed	3499	Muggridge William	Pte.	Wounded
2891	Smith W. O.	Pte.	Killed	3031	Murray James	Pte.	Wounded
1272	Tierle William	Pte.	Killed	3716	Palmer Thomas	Pte.	Wounded
	Newdigate E.	Capt.	W/Sl	3327	Smith Charles	Pte.	Wounded
2309	Allen William	Pte.	Wounded	3886	Sutton Charles	Pte.	Wounded
2515	Bowring John	Pte.	Wounded	3677	Tracey Richard	Pte.	Wounded
3858	Burnes James	Pte.	Wounded	3802	Tucker Edward	Pte.	Wounded
2557	Careless William	Pte.	Wounded	3572	Wingfield Frederick	Pte.	Wounded
3528	Cook John	Pte.	Wounded	3711	Wright George	Pte.	Wounded

NOTES

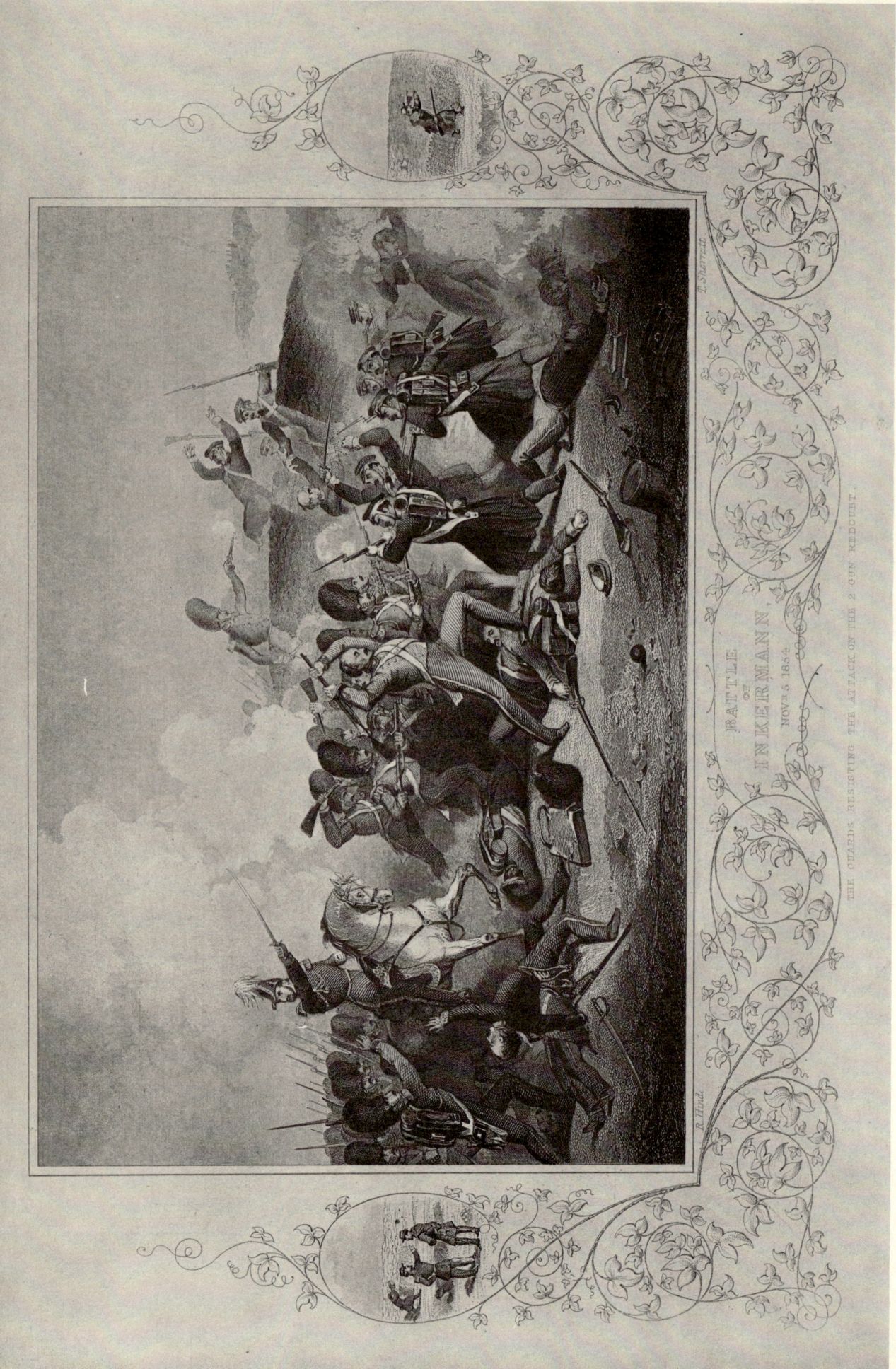

BATTLE OF INKERMANN
NOV. 5 1854
THE GUARDS RESISTING THE ATTACK ON THE 2 GUN REDOUBT

THE BATTLE OF INKERMANN.
Charge of the Guards.

THE ASSAULT ON THE QUARRIES

The following casualties occurred among the Officers, Non-Commissioned Officers and Men of the Army during the Assault on the Quarries in front of the Redan, 7th June 1855. Some casualties from enemy shelling in the three days prior to the Assault are included.
Compiled from the London Gazette 22nd June 1855.

ROYAL ARTILLERY

NO.	NAME	RANK	CASUALTY	DATE	LONDON GAZETTE
73	Broach William	Corpl.	Killed	7-6-55	22-6-55
1675	Baker George	Pte.	Killed	7-6-55	22-6-55
3345	Banham George	Pte.	Killed	7-6-55	22-6-55
526	Brown Thomas	Pte.	Killed	6-6-55	22-6-55
2242	Dalgleish Thomas	Pte.	Killed	6-6-55	22-6-55
1215	Harris James	Pte.	Killed	7-6-55	22-6-55
2277	Kelsey Samuel	Pte.	Killed	7-6-55	22-6-55
2371	McKenna Edward	Pte.	Killed	7-6-55	22-6-55
4015	Parr William	Pte.	Killed	7-6-55	22-6-55
3533	Rynes Lawrence	Pte.	Killed	6-6-55	22-6-55
—	Stevens Nathaniel	Pte.	Killed	6-6-55	22-6-55
	Adye Mortimer	Capt.	W/Sv	6-6-55	22-6-55
	Gordan A.	Capt.	W/Sl	6-6-55	22-6-55
	Keene J. E. K.	Lieut.	W/Sl	7-6-55	22-6-55
103	Mitchell Joseph	Col/Sgt.	W/Sl	7-6-55	22-6-55
1774	Ramsay John	Col/Sgt.	W/Sl	7-6-55	22-6-55
—	Dowling Daniel	Sergt.	W/Sl	7-6-55	22-6-55
8	Symons George	Sergt.	W/Sv	6-6-55	22-6-55
—	Taylor William	Sergt.	W/Sv	7-6-55	22-6-55
1099	Fails Thomas	Corpl.	W/Sv	6-6-55	22-6-55
954	Haigh Joseph	Corpl.	W/Sv	6-6-55	22-6-55
2134	Bligh Ephraim	Bomb.	W/Sl	6-6-55	22-6-55
1135	Bruce William	Bomb.	W/Sl	7-6-55	22-6-55
1779	Gibblet Richard	Bomb.	W/Sl	7-6-55	22-6-55
3223	Muirhead Graham	Bomb.	W/Sl	6-6-55	22-6-55
—	Robinson James	Bomb.	W/Sl	7-6-55	22-6-55
1657	Anderson David	Gnr. & Drvr.	W/Sl	7-6-55	22-6-55
2976	Baker William	Gnr. & Drvr.	W/Sl	6-6-55	22-6-55
2579	Bryan W.	Gnr. & Drvr.	W/Sl	7-6-55	22-6-55
1506	Buck George	Gnr. & Drvr.	W/Sl	6-6-55	22-6-55
3445	Eastley George	Gnr. & Drvr.	W/Sl	7-6-55	22-6-55
—	Elliott George	Gnr. & Drvr.	W/D	7-6-55	22-6-55

NOTES

The Assualt on the Quarries

ROYAL ARTILLERY

NO.	NAME	RANK	CASUALTY	DATE	LONDON GAZETTE
3685	Farr Henry	Gnr. & Drvr.	W/Sl	7-6-55	22-6-55
3011	Goodall Alexander	Gnr. & Drvr.	W/Sl	7-6-55	22-6-55
2985	Harper George	Gnr. & Drvr.	W/Sv	7-6-55	22-6-55
2277	Hughes Frederick	Gnr. & Drvr.	W/Sl	7-6-55	22-6-55
3266	Hughes Samuel	Gnr. & Drvr.	W/Sl	6-6-55	22-6-55
—	Jones John	Gnr. & Drvr.	W/Sl	7-6-55	22-6-55
2906	Kemp John	Gnr. & Drvr.	W/Sv	7-6-55	22-6-55
—	Kneler Edward	Gnr. & Drvr.	W/Sv	7-6-55	22-6-55
—	Love Hugh	Gnr. & Drvr.	W/Sl	7-6-55	22-6-55
2324	McCann Anthony	Gnr. & Drvr.	W/Sl	7-6-55	22-6-55
3068	McCourt William	Gnr. & Drvr.	W/Sl	7-6-55	22-6-55
382	McElveney Robert	Gnr. & Drvr.	W/Sv	6-6-55	22-6-55
—	McGrath James	Gnr. & Drvr.	W/Sv	7-6-55	22-6-55
—	McRae John	Gnr. & Drvr.	W/Sl	7-6-55	22-6-55
—	Medley Samuel	Gnr. & Drvr.	W/Sl	6-6-55	22-6-55
811	Muds James	Gnr. & Drvr.	W/Sv	7-6-55	22-6-55
—	Murphy Daniel	Gnr. & Drvr.	W/D	6-6-55	22-6-55
4099	Murray James	Gnr. & Drvr.	W/Sl	7-6-55	22-6-55
3219	Mustandley Isaac	Gnr. & Drvr.	W/Sl	7-6-55	22-6-55
—	Osgood Stephen	Gnr. & Drvr.	W/Sv	7-6-55	22-6-55
2389	Pratt Joseph	Gnr. & Drvr.	W/Sl	7-6-55	22-6-55
1764	Quinland John	Gnr. & Drvr.	W/Sv	7-6-55	22-6-55
4038	Quinn Edward	Gnr. & Drvr.	W/Sl	7-6-55	22-6-55
153	Regan John	Gnr. & Drvr.	W/Sl	7-6-55	22-6-55
3754	Reid Robert	Gnr. & Drvr.	W/Sl	6-6-55	22-6-55
2251	Robinson George	Gnr. & Drvr.	W/Sv	7-6-55	22-6-55
—	Scribbing Amos	Gnr. & Drvr.	W/Sv	7-6-55	22-6-55
—	Seagrave Samuel	Gnr. & Drvr.	W/Sl	7-6-55	22-6-55
2250	Smith George	Gnr. & Drvr.	W/Sl	6-6-55	22-6-55
2964	Smith William	Gnr. & Drvr.	W/Sl	7-6-55	22-6-55
1213	Williams Thomas	Gnr. & Drvr.	W/Sl	7-6-55	22-6-55
3628	Wilson John	Gnr. & Drvr.	W/Sl	6-6-55	22-6-55

ROYAL ENGINEERS

NO.	NAME	RANK	CASUALTY	DATE	LONDON GAZETTE
	Dawson G.	Capt.	Killed	6-6-55	22-6-55
	Lowry T. G.	Lieut.	Killed	7-6-55	22-6-55

ROYAL SAPPERS AND MINERS

NO.	NAME	RANK	CASUALTY	DATE	LONDON GAZETTE
2162	Fraser James	Corpl.	Killed	7-6-55	22-6-55
1680	McLeod A.	Col/Sgt.	W/Sl	6-6-55	22-6-55
505	Luxton Peter	2nd Corpl.	W/Sv	7-6-55	22-6-55
252	Cumming Walter	L/Cpl.	W/Sl	7-6-55	22-6-55
2084	Young Robert	L/Cpl.	W/Sv	7-6-55	22-6-55
336	Collings R.	Pte.	W/Sv	7-6-55	22-6-55
1444	Dines Samuel	Pte.	W/Sl	7-6-55	22-6-55
655	Hosie Alexander	Pte.	W/Sl	7-6-55	22-6-55
1312	McDonald William	Pte.	W/D	7-6-55	22-6-55
226	Patterson James	Pte.	W/Sl	6-6-55	22-6-55
1956	Patterson John	Pte.	W/Sl	6-6-55	22-6-55
746	Slade Peter	Pte.	W/Sv	6-6-55	22-6-55

NOTES

The Assault on the Quarries

2nd BATTALION 1st REGIMENT OF FOOT

NO.	NAME	RANK	CASUALTY	DATE	LONDON GAZETTE
	Muller B. H. E.	Capt.	Killed	7-6-55	22-6-55
2395	Richardson William	L/Sgt.	Killed	7-6-55	22-6-55
1847	Anthony John	Pte.	Killed	7-6-55	22-6-55
2215	Dans Alfred	Pte.	Killed	7-6-55	22-6-55
2289	Fagan John	Pte.	Killed	7-6-55	22-6-55
1934	Martin, John	Pte.	Killed	7-6-55	22-6-55
2080	Vial John	Pte.	Killed	7-6-55	22-6-55
1663	Wales Bernard	Pte.	Killed	7-6-55	22-6-55
	Bellew W.	Lieut.	W/D	7-6-55	22-6-55
	Legge M. A.	Lieut.	W/Sl	7-6-55	22-6-55
	Stewart J. E.	Lieut.	W/D	7-6-55	22-6-55
2547	Swiney John	Sergt.	W/Sl	7-6-55	22-6-55
1510	Moore, Harvey	L/Sgt.	W/Sl	7-6-55	22-6-55
2925	Anderton William	Pte.	W/Sl	7-6-55	22-6-55
2978	Barker James	Pte.	W/Sv	7-6-55	22-6-55
2938	Birley Thomas	Pte.	W/Sl	7-6-55	22-6-55
2999	Burnsides William	Pte.	W/D	7-6-55	22-6-55
1860	Chalmers John	Pte.	W/Sv	7-6-55	22-6-55
1728	Dack Robert	Pte.	W/Sl	7-6-55	22-6-55
2935	Donton James	Pte.	W/Sl	7-6-55	22-6-55
2667	Duggan Edmund	Pte.	W/Sl	7-6-55	22-6-55
2450	Ellis Thomas	Pte.	W/M	7-6-55	22-6-55
2682	Fincham Thomas	Pte.	W/Sl	7-6-55	22-6-55
2358	Fox James	Pte.	W/Sl	7-6-55	22-6-55
2954	Gosling Charles	Pte.	W/Sl	7-6-55	22-6-55
2624	Gough John	Pte.	W/Sl	7-6-55	22-6-55
2592	Hall Jacob	Pte.	W/D	7-6-55	22-6-55
2698	Hancock Joseph	Pte.	W/Sl	7-6-55	22-6-55
2616	Hansell George	Pte.	W/D	7-6-55	22-6-55
2900	Herbert Charles	Pte.	W/Sl	7-6-55	22-6-55
2322	Johnson James	Pte.	W/Sv	7-6-55	22-6-55
1943	Jones John	Pte.	W/D	7-6-55	22-6-55
3033	McCormack Michael	Pte.	W/Sl	7-6-55	22-6-55
2862	McCormack Thomas	Pte.	W/Sl	7-6-55	22-6-55
2600	McDermott John	Pte.	W/Sv	7-6-55	22-6-55
2871	McDonough Henry	Pte.	W/Sl	7-6-55	22-6-55
2376	McLaughlin Patrick	Pte.	W/Sv	7-6-55	22-6-55
2972	Maloney John	Pte.	W/D	7-6-55	22-6-55
2543	Mann Robert	Pte.	W/Sl	7-6-55	22-6-55
1801	Mitchell James	Pte.	W/Sl	7-6-55	22-6-55
1971	Moore John	Pte.	W/Sv	7-6-55	22-6-55
1978	Murray Hugh	Pte.	W/D	7-6-55	22-6-55
2700	Nunn George	Pte.	W/Sv	7-6-55	22-6-55
2984	Palmer John	Pte.	W/Sv	7-6-55	22-6-55
1653	Pattengill George	Pte.	W/Sv	7-6-55	22-6-55
1769	Pattie James	Pte.	W/Sl	7-6-55	22-6-55
2303	Porter Crozier	Pte.	W/Sl	7-6-55	22-6-55
2969	Quail Robert	Pte.	W/Sl	7-6-55	22-6-55
1630	Quantrill George	Pte.	W/Sl	7-6-55	22-6-55
931	Reid William	Pte.	W/Sl	7-6-55	22-6-55
2484	Seerie John	Pte.	W/Sl	7-6-55	22-6-55
2853	Shearman Martin	Pte.	W/Sv	7-6-55	22-6-55
2962	Sherdan John	Pte.	W/Sl	7-6-55	22-6-55
2310	Shore John	Pte.	W/Sl	7-6-55	22-6-55
1414	Sleep William	Pte.	W/Sl	7-6-55	22-6-55
2915	Steynor Charles	Pte.	W/D	7-6-55	22-6-55
3007	Sullivan Patrick	Pte.	W/Sl	7-6-55	22-6-55
2924	Thompson Thomas	Pte.	W/Sl	7-6-55	22-6-55
2887	Vincent Robert	Pte.	W/Sl	7-6-55	22-6-55
2556	Wall Jeremiah	Pte.	W/Sl	7-6-55	22-6-55
3020	Walsh Peter	Pte.	W/Sl	7-6-55	22-6-55
2858	Waters Patrick	Pte.	W/Sv	7-6-55	22-6-55

2nd BATTALION 1st REGIMENT OF FOOT

NOTES

The Assault on the Quarries

3rd REGIMENT OF FOOT

NO.	NAME	RANK	CASUALTY	DATE	LONDON GAZETTE
3140	Ryan Patrick	Pte.	Killed	7-6-55	22-6-55
	Ambrose G. J.	Capt.	W/D	7-6-55	22-6-55
	Breedon H. A.	Lieut.	W/Sl	6-6-55	22-6-55
2698	Dugan John	Sergt.	W/Sl	6-6-55	22-6-55
3103	Brarken Denis	Pte.	W/Sl	6-6-55	22-6-55
3516	Carty William	Pte.	W/Sl	7-6-55	22-6-55
3428	Dunbar James	Pte.	W/Sv	7-6-55	22-6-55
2179	Dwyer John	Pte.	W/Sl	6-6-55	22-6-55
2635	Fahey John	Pte.	W/Sv	7-6-55	22-6-55
2982	Gilbert Robert	Pte.	W/Sl	6-6-55	22-6-55
2991	Grimes Arthur	Pte.	W/Sl	7-6-55	22-6-55
3069	Holdroyd George	Pte.	W/Sl	6-6-55	22-6-55
3510	Homer William	Pte.	W/Sv	7-6-55	22-6-55
3538	Lee John	Pte.	W/Sv	7-6-55	22-6-55
3348	McDonald John	Pte.	W/D	7-6-55	22-6-55
—	McGovern Thomas	Pte.	W/Sl	6-6-55	22-6-55
2924	McGreal Edward	Pte.	W/Sv	6-6-55	22-6-55
2534	Martin William	Pte.	W/Sv	6-6-55	22-6-55
3187	Muldoon William	Pte.	W/Sl	6-6-55	22-6-55
3481	O'Brien John	Pte.	W/D	7-6-55	22-6-55
2675	Purcell Thomas	Pte.	W/Sl	6-6-55	22-6-55

4th REGIMENT OF FOOT

NO.	NAME	RANK	CASUALTY	DATE	LONDON GAZETTE
3241	Deneen Michael	Pte.	Killed	6-6-55	22-6-55
3420	Durant William	Pte.	W/D	6-6-55	22-6-55

7th REGIMENT OF FOOT

NO.	NAME	RANK	CASUALTY	DATE	LONDON GAZETTE
2920	Dobbie Wm. D.K.	Col/Sgt.	Killed	7-6-55	22-6-55
2809	Parker George	Corpl.	Killed	7-6-55	22-6-55
2255	Brown John	Pte.	Killed	7-6-55	22-6-55
2158	Cook William	Pte.	Killed	7-6-55	22-6-55
3080	Gilvey James	Pte.	Killed	7-6-55	22-6-55
3694	Hargreaves Thomas	Pte.	Killed	7-6-55	22-6-55
	Hornsell Joseph	Pte.	Killed	7-6-55	22-6-55
1506	Jagger Benjamin	Pte.	Killed	7-6-55	22-6-55
2242	Latimer Thomas	Pte.	Killed	7-6-55	22-6-55
3242	Thompson William	Pte.	Killed	7-6-55	22-6-55
3784	Ward James	Pte.	Killed	7-6-55	22-6-55
1499	Wilson Thomas	Pte.	Killed	7-6-55	22-6-55
	Mills Frederick	Major	W/Sl	7-6-55	22-6-55
	Turner W. W.	Capt.	W/Sl	7-6-55	22-6-55
	Jones H. M.	Lieut.	W/Sl	7-6-55	22-6-55
	Jones L. J. F.	Lieut.	W/Sl	7-6-55	22-6-55
	Waller G. H.	Lieut.	W/Sl	7-6-55	22-6-55
3225	Martin Henry	Sergt.	W/Sl	7-6-55	22-6-55
2381	Richmond Jonathan	Sergt.	W/Sl	7-6-55	22-6-55
1535	Stocks John	Sergt.	W/Sl	7-6-55	22-6-55
2432	Ross John	Corpl.	W/M	7-6-55	22-6-55
3227	Abbott Henry	Pte.	W/Sl	7-6-55	22-6-55

NOTES

The Assault on the Quarries

7th REGIMENT OF FOOT

NO.	NAME	RANK	CASUALTY	DATE	LONDON GAZETTE
3008	Adams George	Pte.	W/Sl	7-6-55	22-6-55
3416	Adams Robert	Pte.	W/Sv	7-6-55	22-6-55
3646	Anderson Peter	Pte.	W/Sl	7-6-55	22-6-55
2088	Arnott John	Pte.	W/D	7-6-55	22-6-55
3330	Bagshaw William	Pte.	W/Sl	7-6-55	22-6-55
3763	Barker George	Pte.	W/Sv	7-6-55	22-6-55
2925	Barrett William	Pte.	W/Sv	7-6-55	22-6-55
2903	Bath John	Pte.	W/Sv	7-6-55	22-6-55
3050	Bennett William	Pte.	W/Sl	7-6-55	22-6-55
3041	Brown Thomas	Pte.	W/Sl	7-6-55	22-6-55
3640	Clarke Thomas	Pte.	W/Sl	7-6-55	22-6-55
3055	Connell Thomas	Pte.	W/Sl	7-6-55	22-6-55
2357	Cronin John	Pte.	W/Sv	7-6-55	22-6-55
3696	Cross Robert	Pte.	W/Sl	7-6-55	22-6-55
3860	Denby John	Pte.	W/Sv	7-6-55	22-6-55
2928	Dickens Alfred	Pte.	W/Sl	7-6-55	22-6-55
2080	Donnolly Daniel	Pte.	W/Sl	7-6-55	22-6-55
1219	Doyle Arthur	Pte.	W/Sl	7-6-55	22-6-55
3379	Dunn Charles	Pte.	W/Sv	7-6-55	22-6-55
1131	Dunn James	Pte.	W/Sl	7-6-55	22-6-55
3470	Ford Patrick	Pte.	W/Sl	7-6-55	22-6-55
1249	Fox John	Pte.	W/Sv	7-6-55	22-6-55
3570	Frailey Timothy	Pte.	W/Sl	7-6-55	22-6-55
1780	Francis William	Pte.	W/Sv	7-6-55	22-6-55
3440	Franklin James	Pte.	W/Sv	7-6-55	22-6-55
3642	George James	Pte.	W/Sv	7-6-55	22-6-55
3310	Gleave Thomas	Pte.	W/Sl	7-6-55	22-6-55
2795	Goding William	Pte.	W/Sl	7-6-55	22-6-55
3142	Gormley James	Pte.	W/Sl	7-6-55	22-6-55
3531	Hampton John	Pte.	W/Sv	7-6-55	22-6-55
3689	Hanson Richard	Pte.	W/Sv	7-6-55	22-6-55
3375	Hargaddon Thomas	Pte.	W/Sl	7-6-55	22-6-55
3337	Hasson Robert	Pte.	W/Sl	7-6-55	22-6-55
3230	Jackson Thomas	Pte.	W/Sv	7-6-55	22-6-55
3597	Johnson William	Pte.	W/Sl	7-6-55	22-6-55
3146	Kavanagh Martin	Pte.	W/Sl	7-6-55	22-6-55
3558	Keenan John	Pte.	W/Sv	7-6-55	22-6-55
3477	Linegar Thomas	Pte.	W/Sl	7-6-55	22-6-55
3151	McDermott John	Pte.	W/Sl	7-6-55	22-6-55
2886	McGillicuday Thomas	Pte.	W/D	7-6-55	22-6-55
3214	McNamara Peter	Pte.	W/Sl	7-6-55	22-6-55
3243	Maiden John	Pte.	W/D	7-6-55	22-6-55
3298	Marsh Charles	Pte.	W/Sl	7-6-55	22-6-55
3715	Martin Peter	Pte.	W/Sv	7-6-55	22-6-55
3390	Mitchell William	Pte.	W/Sl	7-6-55	22-6-55
3149	Mulgrave Terence	Pte.	W/Sv	7-6-55	22-6-55
2519	Mulligan Michael	Pte.	W/D	7-6-55	22-6-55
2307	Murphy Hugh	Pte.	W/Sl	7-6-55	22-6-55
3005	Murphy James	Pte.	W/Sv	7-6-55	22-6-55
3443	Norman William	Pte.	W/Sv	7-6-55	22-6-55
2787	O'Sullivan Eugene	Pte.	W/Sl	7-6-55	22-6-55
3057	Owens Thomas	Pte.	W/Sv	7-6-55	22-6-55
3743	Palmons John	Pte.	W/Sv	7-6-55	22-6-55
3532	Pitsforth Joseph	Pte.	W/Sl	7-6-55	22-6-55
2282	Printy Patrick	Pte.	W/Sl	7-6-55	22-6-55
2874	Redman James	Pte.	W/Sv	7-6-55	22-6-55
3761	Reeder Frederick	Pte.	W/Sl	7-6-55	22-6-55
3012	Robinson George	Pte.	W/D	7-6-55	22-6-55
1376	Scanlon George	Pte.	W/Sv	7-6-55	22-6-55
3282	Sheridan John	Pte.	W/Sl	7-6-55	22-6-55
3745	Slater Thomas	Pte.	W/Sl	7-6-55	22-6-55
2049	Smith John	Pte.	W/Sl	7-6-55	22-6-55
2875	Smith Owen	Pte.	W/Sl	7-6-55	22-6-55
2908	Smith William	Pte.	W/Sl	7-6-55	22-6-55

NOTES

The Assault on the Quarries

7th REGIMENT OF FOOT

NO.	NAME	RANK	CASUALTY	DATE	LONDON GAZETTE
2709	Snowden Henry	Pte.	W/Sv	7-6-55	22-6-55
3164	Staines William	Pte.	W/D	7-6-55	22-6-55
3796	Sykes John	Pte.	W/Sv	7-6-55	22-6-55
3489	Whitham Charles	Pte.	W/Sv	7-6-55	22-6-55
3179	Williams Charles	Pte.	W/Sv	7-6-55	22-6-55
2803	Cardwell Thomas	Pte.	Missing	7-6-55	22-6-55
2683	Coverton Samuel	Pte.	Missing	7-6-55	22-6-55
1415	Hargreaves Jesse	Pte.	Missing	7-6-55	22-6-55
3672	Hargreaves Richard	Pte.	Missing	7-6-55	22-6-55
3254	Jones George	Pte.	Missing	7-6-55	22-6-55
3795	Parkin Matthew	Pte.	Missing	7-6-55	22-6-55
3397	Parsons James	Pte.	Missing	7-6-55	22-6-55
2834	Stephens Alfred	Pte.	Missing	7-6-55	22-6-55

14th REGIMENT OF FOOT

NO.	NAME	RANK	CASUALTY	DATE	LONDON GAZETTE
2806	Mulcahy Lawrence	Pte.	Killed	5-6-55	22-6-55

17th REGIMENT OF FOOT

NO.	NAME	RANK	CASUALTY	DATE	LONDON GAZETTE
	Boyd J. B. H.	Lieut.	W/Sl	4-6-55	22-6-55
2154	Connolly John	Sergt.	W/Sl	7-6-55	22-6-55
3227	Brown Peter	Pte.	W/Sl	7-6-55	22-6-55
3465	Burns James	Pte.	W/Sl	7-6-55	22-6-55
3232	Connolly Thomas	Pte.	W/Sl	7-6-55	22-6-55
2757	Menzies William	Pte.	W/Sl	7-6-55	22-6-55

18th REGIMENT OF FOOT

NO.	NAME	RANK	CASUALTY	DATE	LONDON GAZETTE
3147	Brody Patrick	Pte.	W/Sl	4-6-55	22-6-55
3177	Dolan John	Pte.	W/M	4-6-55	22-6-55
2727	Flannery Michael	Pte.	W/Sl	4-6-55	22-6-55
3555	Ford Johnson	Pte.	W/Sl	4-6-55	22-6-55
3701	Green Thomas	Pte.	W/Sl	4-6-55	22-6-55
2597	Hamilton James	Pte.	W/Sv	4-6-55	22-6-55
2417	Ryan Thomas	Pte.	W/Sl	4-6-55	22-6-55

19th REGIMENT OF FOOT

NO.	NAME	RANK	CASUALTY	DATE	LONDON GAZETTE
	Evans G. W.	Lieut.	W/Sv	7-6-55	22-6-55
3200	Rudd James	L/Cpl.	W/Sv	7-6-55	22-6-55
3313	Keans James	Pte.	W/Sl	7-6-55	22-6-55
2685	Lynch Richard	Pte.	W/Sl	6-6-55	22-6-55

NOTES

The Assault on the Quarries

20th REGIMENT OF FOOT

NO.	NAME	RANK	CASUALTY	DATE	LONDON GAZETTE
	Padfield F.	Lieut. & Adj.	W/Sv	7-6-55	22-6-55

23rd REGIMENT OF FOOT

NO.	NAME	RANK	CASUALTY	DATE	LONDON GAZETTE
2074	Clarke Henry	Pte.	Killed	7-6-55	22-6-55
4110	Campbell Hugh	Corpl.	W/Sl	7-6-55	22-6-55
4585	Barnes Thomas	Pte.	W/Sv	7-6-55	22-6-55
4384	Clarke William	Pte.	W/Sl	7-6-55	22-6-55
3440	Coyle Michael	Pte.	W/Sl	7-6-55	22-6-55
4094	Dewe Richard	Pte.	W/Sv	7-6-55	22-6-55
3250	Downey Joseph	Pte.	W/Sl	7-6-55	22-6-55
3776	Edden Richard	Pte.	W/Sl	7-6-55	22-6-55
4517	Hallaran William	Pte.	W/Sl	7-6-55	22-6-55
4487	Pugsley James	Pte.	W/D	6-6-55	22-6-55
3592	Roberts Thomas	Pte.	W/D	7-6-55	22-6-55

28th REGIMENT OF FOOT

NO.	NAME	RANK	CASUALTY	DATE	LONDON GAZETTE
4128	Dawson James	Pte.	Killed	7-6-55	22-6-55
2923	McNamara Thomas	Pte.	W/Sl	4-6-55	22-6-55
3558	O'Hara John	Pte.	W/Sl	4-6-55	22-6-55

30th REGIMENT OF FOOT

NO.	NAME	RANK	CASUALTY	DATE	LONDON GAZETTE
	Pennefather M.	Capt.	W/Sv	7-6-55	22-6-55

33rd REGIMENT OF FOOT

NO.	NAME	RANK	CASUALTY	DATE	LONDON GAZETTE
2680	Stewart William	Corpl.	Killed	7-6-55	22-6-55
1390	Iredale Henry	L/Cpl.	W/Sv	7-6-55	22-6-55
3217	Kilmister Edward	Pte.	W/Sl	7-6-55	22-6-55
3536	Murphy Timothy	Pte.	W/Sv	7-6-55	22-6-55
2650	Paul Alexander	Pte.	W/Sl	7-6-55	22-6-55

34th REGIMENT OF FOOT

NO.	NAME	RANK	CASUALTY	DATE	LONDON GAZETTE
	Lawrence H. M.	Lieut.	Killed	7-6-55	22-6-55
2160	Bradford Joseph	Pte.	Killed	7-6-55	22-6-55
3592	Carew Thomas	Pte.	Killed	7-6-55	22-6-55
2985	Hickton Henry S.	Pte.	Killed	7-6-55	22-6-55
2940	Kelly Peter	Pte.	Killed	7-6-55	22-6-55
3711	Lennox David	Pte.	Killed	7-6-55	22-6-55
3615	Metcalf Thomas	Pte.	Killed	7-6-55	22-6-55

NOTES

The Assault on the Quarries

34th REGIMENT OF FOOT

NO.	NAME	RANK	CASUALTY	DATE	LONDON GAZETTE
1684	Murphy John	Pte.	Killed	7-6-55	22-6-55
2518	Neal Atkinson	Pte.	Killed	7-6-55	22-6-55
2426	Sweeney Thomas	Pte.	Killed	7-6-55	22-6-55
	Peel J.	Capt.	W/Sv	7-6-55	22-6-55
	Westhead G. E. B.	Capt.	W/Sv	7-6-55	22-6-55
	Saunders T. H.	Lieut.	W/Sv	7-6-55	22-6-55
2425	Lambert Thomas	Sergt.	W/Sv	7-6-55	22-6-55
3036	Manmon John	Corpl.	W/Sl	7-6-55	22-6-55
3833	Wharton Joseph	Corpl.	W/M	7-6-55	22-6-55
3783	Beatty Alex	Pte.	W/Sv	7-6-55	22-6-55
3684	Begley Thomas	Pte.	W/Sl	6-6-55	22-6-55
3777	Bleakley John	Pte.	W/Sl	7-6-55	22-6-55
3173	Bunbery Thomas	Pte.	W/Sv	7-6-55	22-6-55
3566	Byrne Charles	Pte.	W/Sl	7-6-55	22-6-55
3134	Clarke Thomas	Pte.	W/Sv	7-6-55	22-6-55
2063	Collins Henry	Pte.	W/Sv	7-6-55	22-6-55
3819	Donovan Jeremiah	Pte.	W/Sv	6-6-55	22-6-55
3101	Dunn Michael	Pte.	W/Sl	7-6-55	22-6-55
2149	Farrar Henry	Pte.	W/Sv	7-6-55	22-6-55
3820	Fitzgerald Thomas	Pte.	W/Sv	7-6-55	22-6-55
3253	Fitzpatrick John	Pte.	W/Sl	7-6-55	22-6-55
4020	Gorman John	Pte.	W/Sv	7-6-55	22-6-55
3299	Hall John	Pte.	W/M	6-6-55	22-6-55
3726	Hankinson George	Pte.	W/Sv	7-6-55	22-6-55
3681	Higgins Patrick	Pte.	W/Sv	7-6-55	22-6-55
2912	Jones Lewis	Pte.	W/M	6-6-55	22-6-55
3283	Kelly Charles	Pte.	W/Sv	7-6-55	22-6-55
3996	Lawrence George	Pte.	W/Sv	7-6-55	22-6-55
3208	Lynch Patrick	Pte.	W/Sv	7-6-55	22-6-55
3713	McCarthy Daniel	Pte.	W/Sl	7-6-55	22-6-55
2424	McDonald Donald	Pte.	W/Sl	7-6-55	22-6-55
4038	McKenna James	Pte.	W/Sv	7-6-55	22-6-55
3398	Malone John	Pte.	W/Sv	7-6-55	22-6-55
3308	Norton Michael	Pte.	W/Sv	7-6-55	22-6-55
3626	Orrell George	Pte.	W/Sv	7-6-55	22-6-55
2169	Palmer John	Pte.	W/Sv	7-6-55	22-6-55
3428	Percival William	Pte.	W/D	6-6-55	22-6-55
3064	Reach Edward	Pte.	W/Sv	7-6-55	22-6-55
3716	Redman John	Pte.	W/Sv	7-6-55	22-6-55
3878	Regan Jeremiah	Pte.	W/Sv	7-6-55	22-6-55
3525	Rostron Joseph	Pte.	W/Sv	7-6-55	22-6-55
2284	Squires George	Pte.	W/D	6-6-55	22-6-55
3567	Thornton Richard	Pte.	W/Sv	7-6-55	22-6-55
3653	Wilkinson John	Pte.	W/Sl	7-6-55	22-6-55
3613	Wilson Charles	Pte.	W/Sv	7-6-55	22-6-55
3968	Butterfield Ben	Pte.	Missing	7-6-55	22-6-55
3963	Fannon Denis	Pte.	Missing	7-6-55	22-6-55
3657	Morris John	Pte.	Missing	7-6-55	22-6-55

38th REGIMENT OF FOOT

NO.	NAME	RANK	CASUALTY	DATE	LONDON GAZETTE
3114	Quinn John	Corpl.	W/Sl	7-6-55	22-6-55
3625	Baxter Adam	Pte.	W/Sl	7-6-55	22-6-55

NOTES

The Assault on the Quarries

39th REGIMENT OF FOOT

NO.	NAME	RANK	CASUALTY	DATE	LONDON GAZETTE
2796	Brandon Daniel	Pte.	W/Sv	4-6-55	22-6-55
2981	McCarthy Michael	Pte.	W/Sv	4-6-55	22-6-55

41st REGIMENT OF FOOT

NO.	NAME	RANK	CASUALTY	DATE	LONDON GAZETTE
	Dixon F. B.	Capt.	W/Sl	7-6-55	22-6-55
2068	Price George	Col/Sgt.	W/Sv	7-6-55	22-6-55
1104	Horner Charles	Corpl.	W/M	7-6-55	22-6-55
1814	Bowles Henry	Pte.	W/Sl	7-6-55	22-6-55
3278	Collins Bartholomew	Pte.	W/Sl	7-6-55	22-6-55
2602	Connors Andrew	Pte.	W/Sv	7-6-55	22-6-55
2523	Curran John	Pte.	W/Sl	7-6-55	22-6-55
3225	Doulan William	Pte.	W/Sl	7-6-55	22-6-55
3150	Ennis Michael	Pte.	W/Sl	7-6-55	22-6-55
3209	Keenale John	Pte.	W/Sl	7-6-55	22-6-55
2773	Lawler Michael	Pte.	W/Sl	7-6-55	22-6-55
3486	McDermott John	Pte.	W/Sv	7-6-55	22-6-55
2334	McKeough James	Pte.	W/Sl	7-6-55	22-6-55
2736	McMahon Thomas	Pte.	W/Sv	7-6-55	22-6-55
3782	Matthews Joseph	Pte.	W/Sl	7-6-55	22-6-55
2070	Meade James	Pte.	W/Sl	7-6-55	22-6-55
2083	Phillips John	Pte.	W/Sl	7-6-55	22-6-55
2209	Stubbe Samuel	Pte.	W/Sl	7-6-55	22-6-55
3422	Underwood Thomas	Pte.	W/Sl	7-6-55	22-6-55

44th REGIMENT OF FOOT

NO.	NAME	RANK	CASUALTY	DATE	LONDON GAZETTE
3266	Campbell James	Sergt.	W/M	6-6-55	22-6-55
3425	Carnt George	Pte.	W/Sl	6-6-55	22-6-55
3944	Murphy John	Pte.	W/Sl	6-6-55	22-6-55

46th REGIMENT OF FOOT

NO.	NAME	RANK	CASUALTY	DATE	LONDON GAZETTE
2634	Power Edward	Drummer	W/M	5-6-55	22-6-55

47th REGIMENT OF FOOT

NO.	NAME	RANK	CASUALTY	DATE	LONDON GAZETTE
2498	McGrath John	Sergt.	Killed	7-6-55	22-6-55
2362	Dean William	Corpl.	Killed	7-6-55	22-6-55
2234	Thomson Robert	L/Cpl.	Killed	7-6-55	22-6-55
1417	Brown William	Pte.	Killed	7-6-55	22-6-55
—	Buckley Daniel	Pte.	Killed	7-6-55	22-6-55
1909	Chittock Frederick	Pte.	Killed	7-6-55	22-6-55
1609	Cooke Thomas	Pte.	Killed	7-6-55	22-6-55
3099	Dowling William	Pte.	Killed	7-6-55	22-6-55
1816	Flanagan Patrick	Pte.	Killed	7-6-55	22-6-55
3070	Glennon Denis	Pte.	Killed	7-6-55	22-6-55
2118	Haly John	Pte.	Killed	7-6-55	22-6-55
1407	Henry William	Pte.	Killed	7-6-55	22-6-55

NOTES

The Assualt on the Quarries

47th REGIMENT OF FOOT

NO.	NAME	RANK	CASUALTY	DATE	LONDON GAZETTE
3266	Hodgins Michael	Pte.	Killed	7-6-55	22-6-55
2047	Hood George	Pte.	Killed	7-6-55	22-6-55
2785	Kelly John	Pte.	Killed	7-6-55	22-6-55
2758	Kelly Patrick	Pte.	Killed	7-6-55	22-6-55
3063	Kelly Stephen	Pte.	Killed	7-6-55	22-6-55
—	Long John	Pte.	Killed	7-6-55	22-6-55
2560	Murphy John	Pte.	Killed	7-6-55	22-6-55
3311	Murray Charles	Pte.	Killed	7-6-55	22-6-55
2728	Newton John	Pte.	Killed	7-6-55	22-6-55
3315	Noonan Michael	Pte.	Killed	7-6-55	22-6-55
3386	O'Neil Hugh	Pte.	Killed	7-6-55	22-6-55
2848	Shackey Patrick	Pte.	Killed	7-6-55	22-6-55
2997	Whealan Edward	Pte.	Killed	7-6-55	22-6-55
2868	White Michael	Pte.	Killed	7-6-55	22-6-55
	Villiers J.	Major	W/Sv	7-6-55	22-6-55
	Lowndes J. H.	Capt.	W/Sv	7-6-55	22-6-55
	Hunter F. W. F.	Capt.	W/Sv	7-6-55	22-6-55
	Irby J. J. C.	Lieut.	W/D	7-6-55	22-6-55
2064	Beatson Donald	Sergt.	W/Sv	7-6-55	22-6-55
1784	Stafford Reuben	Sergt.	W/Sl	7-6-55	22-6-55
2633	Grant William	Corpl.	W/Sl	7-6-55	22-6-55
1377	Lang George	Corpl.	W/Sl	7-6-55	22-6-55
3199	O'Loughlin John	Corpl.	W/Sl	7-6-55	22-6-55
3409	Beattie George	L/Cpl.	W/Sl	7-6-55	22-6-55
1674	Cleary John	L/Cpl.	W/Sl	7-6-55	22-6-55
3396	Bailey John	Pte.	W/Sl	7-6-55	22-6-55
3201	Barwell George	Pte.	W/Sv	7-6-55	22-6-55
3260	Brennan James	Pte.	W/Sv	7-6-55	22-6-55
3022	Campbell John	Pte.	W/Sl	7-6-55	22-6-55
3119	Carey Patrick	Pte.	W/Sv	7-6-55	22-6-55
2104	Carthy Daniel	Pte.	W/D	7-6-55	22-6-55
3056	Cawley Patrick	Pte.	W/Sl	7-6-55	22-6-55
3374	Chadwick Issachar	Pte.	W/Sl	7-6-55	22-6-55
3288	Chapman John	Pte.	W/Sl	7-6-55	22-6-55
3287	Clancy Lawrence	Pte.	W/Sv	7-6-55	22-6-55
2595	Clarke Philip	Pte.	W/Sl	7-6-55	22-6-55
2353	Coleman John	Pte.	W/Sv	7-6-55	22-6-55
2051	Coll Daniel	Pte.	W/Sv	7-6-55	22-6-55
2899	Connors Denis	Pte.	W/Sl	7-6-55	22-6-55
3308	Cunningham Thomas	Pte.	W/D	7-6-55	22-6-55
3098	Dunne Thomas	Pte.	W/Sv	7-6-55	22-6-55
2693	Filey James	Pte.	W/Sv	7-6-55	22-6-55
2855	Foley Daniel	Pte.	W/Sv	7-6-55	22-6-55
3152	Freeman Henry	Pte.	W/Sv	7-6-55	22-6-55
2957	Griffin Patrick	Pte.	W/Sl	7-6-55	22-6-55
1958	Griffiths John	Pte.	W/Sl	7-6-55	22-6-55
3045	Hanlon Denis	Pte.	W/Sl	7-6-55	22-6-55
3198	Harrington Jeremiah	Pte.	W/D	7-6-55	22-6-55
3410	Harrington William	Pte.	W/D	7-6-55	22-6-55
2584	Howard William	Pte.	W/Sl	7-6-55	22-6-55
2871	Keefe John	Pte.	W/Sv	7-6-55	22-6-55
2954	Keefe Thomas	Pte.	W/Sv	7-6-55	22-6-55
2433	Keenan Thomas	Pte.	W/Sv	7-6-55	22-6-55
2921	Kelly Thomas	Pte.	W/Sl	7-6-55	22-6-55
3282	Kennedy Daniel	Pte.	W/Sv	7-6-55	22-6-55
3340	Kennedy William	Pte.	W/Sl	7-6-55	22-6-55
3007	Kilham Thomas	Pte.	W/M	7-6-55	22-6-55
3309	Mahoney Patrick	Pte.	W/Sl	7-6-55	22-6-55
2181	Mitchell William	Pte.	W/Sv	7-6-55	22-6-55
3041	Morris Jonas	Pte.	W/Sl	7-6-55	22-6-55
3251	Murphy John	Pte.	W/Sv	7-6-55	22-6-55
3286	Nairn James	Pte.	W/Sl	7-6-55	22-6-55
1997	O'Flaherty Henry	Pte.	W/Sl	7-6-55	22-6-55
2160	Phelan Richard	Pte.	W/Sv	7-6-55	22-6-55
3508	Pitman John	Pte.	W/Sv	7-6-55	22-6-55

NOTES

The Assault on the Quarries

47th REGIMENT OF FOOT

NO.	NAME	RANK	CASUALTY	DATE	LONDON GAZETTE
3025	Reegan John	Pte.	W/M	7-6-55	22-6-55
2808	Ryan Thomas	Pte.	W/Sl	7-6-55	22-6-55
1704	Schofield William	Pte.	W/Sl	7-6-55	22-6-55
3207	Searson Thomas	Pte.	W/Sv	7-6-55	22-6-55
3179	Shea Patrick	Pte.	W/Sv	7-6-55	22-6-55
2236	Smith John	Pte.	W/Sv	7-6-55	22-6-55
2910	Tracey James	Pte.	W/Sl	7-6-55	22-6-55
2882	Treacy Carron	Pte.	W/D	7-6-55	22-6-55
2537	Uniacke Maurice	Pte.	W/Sl	7-6-55	22-6-55
2909	Walsh John	Pte.	W/D	7-6-55	22-6-55
3353	Walsh Robert	Pte.	W/Sv	7-6-55	22-6-55
2013	Wisdom Solomon	Pte.	W/Sl	7-6-55	22-6-55
3338	Connors Michael	Pte.	Missing	7-6-55	22-6-55
3356	Hogan Jeremiah	Pte.	Missing	7-6-55	22-6-55
3389	McDonald John	Pte.	Missing	7-6-55	22-6-55

49th REGIMENT OF FOOT

NO.	NAME	RANK	CASUALTY	DATE	LONDON GAZETTE
2886	McCoy Robert	Sergt.	Killed	7-6-55	22-6-55
3285	Roughan James	L/Cpl.	Killed	7-6-55	22-6-55
3275	Carney Michael	Pte.	Killed	7-6-55	22-6-55
3626	Healy Michael	Pte.	Killed	7-6-55	22-6-55
3181	Hoctor John	Pte.	Killed	7-6-55	22-6-55
2384	Kearnan John	Pte.	Killed	7-6-55	22-6-55
3472	Keeney Thomas	Pte.	Killed	7-6-55	22-6-55
2887	Kenney George	Pte.	Killed	7-6-55	22-6-55
2547	Leary Patrick	Pte.	Killed	7-6-55	22-6-55
3214	Long John	Pte.	Killed	7-6-55	22-6-55
1604	McArthur James	Pte.	Killed	7-6-55	22-6-55
3199	McCarthy Terence	Pte.	Killed	7-6-55	22-6-55
3572	Meldrum David	Pte.	Killed	7-6-55	22-6-55
3704	O'Halloran Patrick	Pte.	Killed	7-6-55	22-6-55
3332	Parker John	Pte.	Killed	7-6-55	22-6-55
3386	Raidy Michael	Pte.	Killed	7-6-55	22-6-55
2476	Spalane Moris	Pte.	Killed	7-6-55	22-6-55
	Armstrong J. W.	Major	W/Sv	7-6-55	22-6-55
	Marchant E. Le	Capt.	W/Sv	7-6-55	22-6-55
	Eustace T. F.	Lieut.	W/Sv	7-6-55	22-6-55
	Young W.	Lieut.	W/Sv	7-6-55	22-6-55
1843	Grundy William	Col/Sgt.	W/D	7-6-55	22-6-55
1783	Lonergan John	Col/Sgt.	W/D	7-6-55	22-6-55
2599	Barnes Charles	Sergt.	W/Sv	7-6-55	22-6-55
2376	Fennell George	Sergt.	W/Sv	7-6-55	22-6-55
2769	Hickey William	Sergt.	W/Sv	7-6-55	22-6-55
3060	Murphy Patrick	Sergt.	W/Sl	7-6-55	22-6-55
2643	Shea Richard	Sergt.	W/D	7-6-55	22-6-55
2699	Kinolty James	Corpl.	W/M	7-6-55	22-6-55
3122	New James	Corpl.	W/Sv	7-6-55	22-6-55
2812	Rooney Michael	Corpl.	W/Sv	7-6-55	22-6-55
2748	Burgess Joseph	Pte.	W/Sl	7-6-55	22-6-55
2031	Burke Joseph	Pte.	W/Sv	7-6-55	22-6-55
2983	Clarke Thomas	Pte.	W/Sv	7-6-55	22-6-55
3191	Connolly Michael	Pte.	W/Sl	7-6-55	22-6-55
3461	Corner Patrick	Pte	W/Sv	7-6-55	22-6-55
3174	Crouch George	Pte.	W/Sl	7-6-55	22-6-55
2262	Curry James	Pte.	W/Sl	7-6-55	22-6-55
3800	Curtain John	Pte.	W/Sv	7-6-55	22-6-55
2231	Dear George	Pte.	W/Sl	7-6-55	22-6-55
3348	Driscoll Timothy	Pte.	W/D	7-6-55	22-6-55
3537	Feagen Michael	Pte.	W/Sv	7-6-55	22-6-55
3625	Gaffney Thomas	Pte.	W/Sl	7-6-55	22-6-55
3598	Gallagher James	Pte.	W/Sv	7-6-55	22-6-55

NOTES

The Assault on the Quarries

49th REGIMENT OF FOOT

NO.	NAME	RANK	CASUALTY	DATE	LONDON GAZETTE
2311	Garvin Robert	Pte.	W/D	7-6-55	22-6-55
2784	Gibbons James	Pte.	W/Sl	7-6-55	22-6-55
2431	Green James	Pte.	W/Sv	7-6-55	22-6-55
3292	Greenan Patrick	Pte.	W/Sv	7-6-55	22-6-55
3324	Halvey Jeremiah	Pte.	W/Sv	7-6-55	22-6-55
2843	Heaslip Richard	Pte.	W/Sv	7-6-55	22-6-55
3202	Hill Edward	Pte.	W/Sv	7-6-55	22-6-55
3026	Jefries Edward	Pte.	W/Sv	7-6-55	22-6-55
2787	Keesham Michael	Pte.	W/Sv	7-6-55	22-6-55
2609	Kelly Timothy	Pte.	W/Sl	7-6-55	22-6-55
3127	Kenney Daniel	Pte.	W/Sv	7-6-55	22-6-55
2854	Kirwin Patrick	Pte.	W/D	7-6-55	22-6-55
3462	Lacey Patrick	Pte.	W/Sv	7-6-55	22-6-55
2764	Lee John	Pte.	W/Sv	7-6-55	22-6-55
2610	Lee Thomas	Pte.	W/Sv	7-6-55	22-6-55
2696	Little James	Pte.	W/M	7-6-55	22-6-55
3055	Long Thomas	Pte.	W/Sl	7-6-55	22-6-55
3369	McCormick Michael	Pte.	W/Sv	7-6-55	22-6-55
3622	McGee Patrick	Pte.	W/Sv	7-6-55	22-6-55
3481	McGrath James	Pte	W/Sv	7-6-55	22-6-55
2545	McKewer James	Pte.	W/Sv	7-6-55	22-6-55
3582	McMoran John	Pte.	W/D	7-6-55	22-6-55
3527	Martin Patrick	Pte.	W/Sv	7-6-55	22-6-55
3152	Moore Martin	Pte.	W/Sl	7-6-55	22-6-55
1338	Mulvaney Bernard	Pte.	W/Sv	7-6-55	22-6-55
2520	Murray Hugh	Pte.	W/M	7-6-55	22-6-55
2730	O'Brien Patrick	Pte.	W/Sv	7-6-55	22-6-55
3473	Patridge Richard	Pte.	W/Sv	7-6-55	22-6-55
2645	Ready James	Pte.	W/Sl	7-6-55	22-6-55
2964	Robinson James	Pte.	W/Sl	7-6-55	22-6-55
2357	Ryan Patrick	Pte.	W/Sv	7-6-55	22-6-55
3027	Shannon Patrick	Pte.	W/D	7-6-55	22-6-55
3220	Stack Thomas	Pte.	W/Sv	7-6-55	22-6-55
1577	Stevens James	Pte.	W/Sv	7-6-55	22-6-55
2898	Stratford James	Pte.	W/Sv	7-6-55	22-6-55
2549	Townsend William	Pte.	W/Sv	7-6-55	22-6-55
3318	Ward John	Pte.	W/Sl	7-6-55	22-6-55
3149	Whealan Martin	Pte.	W/Sv	7-6-55	22-6-55
3708	Wheat Charles	Pte.	W/Sv	7-6-55	22-6-55
2646	Keogh Mathew	Pte.	Missing	7-6-55	22-6-55

50th REGIMENT OF FOOT

NO.	NAME	RANK	CASUALTY	DATE	LONDON GAZETTE
3546	Gaffney John	Pte.	W/Sv	6-6-55	22-6-55
4272	Nicolls John	Pte.	W/Sl	6-6-55	22-6-55

55th REGIMENT OF FOOT

NO.	NAME	RANK	CASUALTY	DATE	LONDON GAZETTE
	Stone Richard J. T.	Lieut.	Killed	7-6-55	22-6-55
	Scott James	Lieut.	W/Sl	7-6-55	22-6-55
2882	Kendrick Henry	Sergt.	W/Sl	7-6-55	22-6-55
2324	Townsend William	L/Sgt.	W/Sv	7-6-55	22-6-55
2808	Britton William	Corpl.	W/Sv	7-6-55	22-6-55
3232	Delaney Martin	Corpl.	W/Sv	7-6-55	22-6-55
2851	Denman William	Corpl.	W/Sv	7-6-55	22-6-55
2691	Ely Henry	Corpl.	W/Sv	6-6-55	22-6-55

NOTES

The Assault on the Quarries

55th REGIMENT OF FOOT

NO.	NAME	RANK	CASUALTY	DATE	LONDON GAZETTE
2884	Rennie John	Corpl.	W/Sv	7-6-55	22-6-55
3495	Black Patrick	Pte.	W/Sv	7-6-55	22-6-55
3499	Bowie Allan	Pte.	W/D	7-6-55	22-6-55
3156	Boyd James	Pte.	W/D	7-6-55	22-6-55
3502	Brown Thomas	Pte.	W/D	7-6-55	22-6-55
1346	Casterton William	Pte.	W/D	7-6-55	22-6-55
3511	Chambles John	Pte.	W/Sl	7-6-55	22-6-55
1390	Downey James	Pte.	W/D	7-6-55	22-6-55
3216	Drawry John	Pte.	W/Sv	7-6-55	22-6-55
3382	Gannion Michael	Pte.	W/D	6-6-55	22-6-55
2994	Gaving John	Pte.	W/Sv	7-6-55	22-6-55
2012	Hopecroft Robert	Pte.	W/Sv	7-6-55	22-6-55
2820	Landers John	Pte.	W/Sl	7-6-55	22-6-55
3183	Lennon Peter	Pte.	W/Sv	7-6-55	22-6-55
3556	McKenzie Donald	Pte.	W/D	7-6-55	22-6-55
1494	Madden Patrick	Pte.	W/D	7-6-55	22-6-55
2336	Masson Saul	Pte.	W/Sv	7-6-55	22-6-55
3150	Minahan James	Pte.	W/D	7-6-55	22-6-55
3146	Neagle William	Pte.	W/D	7-6-55	22-6-55
3025	Reeve William	Pte.	W/Sl	7-6-55	22-6-55
3055	Ryan Patrick	Pte.	W/Sv	7-6-55	22-6-55
3588	Skinner Alexander	Pte.	W/Sv	7-6-55	22-6-55
3345	Smith James	Pte.	W/Sv	7-6-55	22-6-55
3012	Stone George	Pte.	W/Sv	7-6-55	22-6-55
3287	Walsh Patrick	Pte.	W/Sl	7-6-55	22-6-55
3604	Weir John	Pte.	W/Sl	7-6-55	22-6-55
3483	Wright Alexander	Pte.	W/Sl	7-6-55	22-6-55
2284	Meard Martin	Sergt.	Missing	7-6-55	22-6-55
1499	Hardison Robert	Corpl.	Missing	7-6-55	22-6-55
2909	Cotter John	Pte.	Missing	7-6-55	22-6-55
3303	Craig Robert	Pte.	Missing	7-6-55	22-6-55
3101	Flannery Hugh	Pte.	Missing	7-6-55	22-6-55
3318	Higgins Thomas	Pte.	Missing	7-6-55	22-6-55
2094	Mallart William	Pte.	Missing	7-6-55	22-6-55
3602	Watson George	Pte.	Missing	7-6-55	22-6-55

57th REGIMENT OF FOOT

NO.	NAME	RANK	CASUALTY	DATE	LONDON GAZETTE
3260	McPhee George	Pte.	W/Sv	7-6-55	22-6-55

62nd REGIMENT OF FOOT

NO.	NAME	RANK	CASUALTY	DATE	LONDON GAZETTE
	Dickson W. F.	Major	Killed	7-6-55	22-6-55
	Forster J. B.	Capt.	Killed	7-6-55	22-6-55
2240	Fennell Owen	Col/Sgt.	Killed	7-6-55	22-6-55
2932	Jones Thomas	Col/Sgt.	Killed	7-6-55	22-6-55
3691	Bailey John	Pte.	Killed	7-6-55	22-6-55
3333	Boylan John	Pte.	Killed	7-6-55	22-6-55
3313	Quigley John	Pte.	Killed	7-6-55	22-6-55
	Shearman R. A.	Lt./Col.	W/M	7-6-55	22-6-55
	Ingall W. L.	Capt.	W/Sl	7-6-55	22-6-55
3001	Ware George	Drummer	W/Sl	7-6-55	22-6-55
3369	Browne Edward	Pte.	W/Sl	7-6-55	22-6-55
3555	Crowley Patrick	Pte.	W/Sl	7-6-55	22-6-55
3559	Doyle John	Pte.	W/Sl	7-6-55	22-6-55
3260	Dunne Michael	Pte.	W/Sl	7-6-55	22-6-55

NOTES

The Assault on the Quarries

62nd REGIMENT OF FOOT

NO.	NAME	RANK	CASUALTY	DATE	LONDON GAZETTE
2753	Fanelly John	Pte.	W/Sv	7-6-55	22-6-55
3562	Halley John	Pte.	W/Sl	7-6-55	22-6-55
3695	Herbert John	Pte.	W/Sl	7-6-55	22-6-55
3330	McIntyre James	Pte.	W/Sl	7-6-55	22-6-55
2418	Newham William	Pte.	W/Sv	7-6-55	22-6-55
3266	O'Neill Owen	Pte.	W/Sl	7-6-55	22-6-55
3318	Richards John	Pte.	W/Sl	7-6-55	22-6-55
3707	Rowntree Thomas	Pte.	W/Sl	7-6-55	22-6-55
3406	Scott James	Pte.	W/Sl	7-6-55	22-6-55
2895	Sullivan Patrick	Pte.	W/Sv	7-6-55	22-6-55
3627	Thompson Andrew	Pte.	W/Sl	7-6-55	22-6-55
1701	Turner James	Pte.	W/Sl	7-6-55	22-6-55

68th REGIMENT OF FOOT

NO.	NAME	RANK	CASUALTY	DATE	LONDON GAZETTE
	Marshall James	Lieut.	Killed	7-6-55	22-6-55
3353	Caves Charles	Pte.	W/Sv	5-6-55	22-6-55
3398	Gannon Thomas	Pte.	W/Sv	7-6-55	22-6-55
1258	Mitchell Joseph	Pte.	W/Sv	4-6-55	22-6-55

77th REGIMENT OF FOOT

NO.	NAME	RANK	CASUALTY	DATE	LONDON GAZETTE
2877	Corcoran Michael	Pte.	Killed	7-6-55	22-6-55
2451	Durney Hugh	Pte.	Killed	7-6-55	22-6-55
3169	Watson Charles	Pte.	Killed	7-6-55	22-6-55
	Gilby B. D.	Capt.	W/Sl	7-6-55	22-6-55
	Dickson M. W.	Lieut.	W/Sv	7-6-55	22-6-55
3451	Coulan Thomas	Pte.	W/Sv	7-6-55	22-6-55
3428	Cousins Robert	Pte.	W/D	7-6-55	22-6-55
3253	Curry Peter	Pte.	W/Sv	7-6-55	22-6-55
2348	Hanlon John	Pte.	W/Sv	7-6-55	22-6-55
2964	Irvin David	Pte.	W/M	7-6-55	22-6-55
3415	Lyons John	Pte.	W/Sv	7-6-55	22-6-55
2819	Maher Patrick	Pte.	W/D	7-6-55	22-6-55
2970	Mollor James	Pte.	W/Sv	7-6-55	22-6-55
3537	Mooney John	Pte.	W/D	7-6-55	22-6-55
3251	Moore John	Pte.	W/Sl	7-6-55	22-6-55
1869	Mugrate Thomas	Pte.	W/Sv	7-6-55	22-6-55
1774	Woodward John	Pte.	W/Sl	7-6-55	22-6-55
2239	Wright Alexander	Pte.	W/Sv	7-6-55	22-6-55

88th REGIMENT OF FOOT

NO.	NAME	RANK	CASUALTY	DATE	LONDON GAZETTE
	Bayley Edward	Brevet/Mjr.	Killed	7-6-55	22-6-55
	Corbett Edmund	Capt.	Killed	7-6-55	22-6-55
	Wray Jackson	Capt.	Killed	7-6-55	22-6-55
	Webb E. H.	Lieut.	Killed	7-6-55	22-6-55
1921	Haverty John	Sergt.	Killed	7-6-55	22-6-55
2598	Sherlock Michael	Corpl.	Killed	7-6-55	22-6-55
2564	Brereton Thomas	Pte.	Killed	7-6-55	22-6-55
3212	Burke James	Pte.	Killed	7-6-55	22-6-55
1920	Cassidy Francis	Pte.	Killed	7-6-55	22-6-55

NOTES

The Assault on the Quarries

88th REGIMENT OF FOOT

NO.	NAME	RANK	CASUALTY	DATE	LONDON GAZETTE
2996	Fleming Dennis	Pte.	Killed	7-6-55	22-6-55
3345	Johnston Henry	Pte.	Killed	7-6-55	22-6-55
3232	Kelly Thomas	Pte.	Killed	7-6-55	22-6-55
3380	McSorley Owen	Pte.	Killed	7-6-55	22-6-55
2600	O'Donnell James	Pte.	Killed	7-6-55	22-6-55
3371	O'Neil Patrick	Pte.	Killed	7-6-55	22-6-55
2703	Ryan Michael	Pte.	Killed	7-6-55	22-6-55
3499	Size Richard	Pte.	Killed	7-6-55	22-6-55
	Maynard E. G.	Capt.	W/Sv	7-6-55	22-6-55
	Kenny C. A.	Lieut.	W/Sv	7-6-55	22-6-55
	Grier J. F.	Lieut.	W/Sl	7-6-55	22-6-55
2596	Dwyer Patrick	Col/Sgt.	W/Sv	7-6-55	22-6-55
1794	O'Shaugnassy Thomas	Col/Sgt.	W/Sv	7-6-55	22-6-55
3503	Kelly M.	Sergt.	W/Sv	7-6-55	22-6-55
946	Savage John	Sergt.	W/M	7-6-55	22-6-55
3189	Purcell Daniel	Corpl.	W/Sv	7-6-55	22-6-55
3064	Reilly John	Corpl.	W/Sv	7-6-55	22-6-55
2598	Rush James	Corpl.	W/Sl	7-6-55	22-6-55
3110	Sullivan Maurice	Corpl.	W/Sl	4-6-55	22-6-55
2737	McCann Michael	Drummer	W/Sl	7-6-55	22-6-55
3421	Barber George	Pte.	W/D	7-6-55	22-6-55
3549	Boyle Patrick	Pte.	W/D	7-6-55	22-6-55
3667	Bradley James	Pte.	W/Sv	7-6-55	22-6-55
3164	Burke John	Pte.	W/Sv	7-6-55	22-6-55
3070	Byrne James	Pte.	W/Sv	7-6-55	22-6-55
3658	Campbell John	Pte.	W/Sl	7-6-55	22-6-55
1669	Carson James	Pte.	W/Sl	7-6-55	22-6-55
3529	Cassidy Martin	Pte.	W/Sv	7-6-55	22-6-55
3467	Clinton Robert	Pte.	W/D	7-6-55	22-6-55
2466	Connolly Michael	Pte.	W/Sv	4-6-55	22-6-55
3127	Connors Henry	Pte.	W/Sv	7-6-55	22-6-55
2670	Connors John	Pte.	W/Sl	7-6-55	22-6-55
2864	Conway Denis	Pte.	W/Sv	7-6-55	22-6-55
3363	Cook Michael	Pte.	W/D	7-6-55	22-6-55
3445	Coyle William	Pte.	W/Sl	7-6-55	22-6-55
2613	Cunningham Martin	Pte.	W/Sl	7-6-55	22-6-55
2912	Donlan Thomas	Pte.	W/Sv	7-6-55	22-6-55
3541	Eckersley John	Pte.	W/Sv	7-6-55	22-6-55
3373	Fergusson William	Pte.	W/Sv	7-6-55	22-6-55
2775	Fogarty Patrick	Pte.	W/Sv	7-6-55	22-6-55
3522	Gillan Michael	Pte.	W/Sv	7-6-55	22-6-55
2645	Gleeson Michael	Pte.	W/Sl	7-6-55	22-6-55
3357	Grehan George	Pte.	W/D	7-6-55	22-6-55
3021	Higgins Patrick	Pte.	W/Sl	7-6-55	22-6-55
2909	Keating Thomas	Pte.	W/Sv	7-6-55	22-6-55
3069	Lilliman John	Pte.	W/Sv	7-6-55	22-6-55
3241	McDonald Owen	Pte.	W/Sv	7-6-55	22-6-55
2519	McDonogh Valentine	Pte.	W/Sv	7-6-55	22-6-55
3000	McMahon John	Pte.	W/Sv	7-6-55	22-6-55
2900	McMahon Patrick	Pte.	W/M	7-6-55	22-6-55
3108	Maddigan James	Pte.	W/Sv	7-6-55	22-6-55
3339	Monohan George	Pte.	W/Sv	7-6-55	22-6-55
2879	Nolan John	Pte.	W/Sl	7-6-55	22-6-55
3464	Nolan Timothy	Pte.	W/Sl	7-6-55	22-6-55
3677	O'Brien Thomas	Pte.	W/Sl	7-6-55	22-6-55
3354	Pattern James	Pte.	W/Sl	7-6-55	22-6-55
3780	Purcell Henry	Pte.	W/Sv	7-6-55	22-6-55
3474	Reid Richard	Pte.	W/Sv	7-6-55	22-6-55
3246	Rutter John	Pte.	W/Sv	7-6-55	22-6-55
3395	Sullivan Timothy	Pte.	W/Sv	7-6-55	22-6-55
3602	Sweeney Owen	Pte.	W/Sv	7-6-55	22-6-55
3098	Walker George	Pte.	W/Sl	7-6-55	22-6-55
3232	Walsh Richard	Pte.	W/Sv	7-6-55	22-6-55

NOTES

The Assault on the Quarries

88th REGIMENT OF FOOT

NO.	NAME	RANK	CASUALTY	DATE	LONDON GAZETTE
2725	Bourke Thady	Pte.	Missing	7-6-55	22-6-55
3654	Fitzgerald John	Pte.	Missing	7-6-55	22-6-55
3314	Hynes Bernard	Pte.	Missing	7-6-55	22-6-55
3595	Murtugh Anthony	Pte.	Missing	7-6-55	22-6-55
2137	Whitstone Michael	Pte.	Missing	7-6-55	22-6-55

89th REGIMENT OF FOOT

NO.	NAME	RANK	CASUALTY	DATE	LONDON GAZETTE
3514	Burke Patrick	Corpl.	W/Sl	4-6-55	22-6-55
3333	Burke Michael	Pte.	W/Sl	6-6-55	22-6-55
2949	Stalling Thomas	Pte.	W/Sl	4-6-55	22-6-55

90th REGIMENT OF FOOT

NO.	NAME	RANK	CASUALTY	DATE	LONDON GAZETTE
	Campbell R. P.	Lt./Col.	W/Sv	7-6-55	22-6-55
3720	Hannigan Daniel	L/Corpl.	W/Sv	7-6-55	22-6-55

95th REGIMENT OF FOOT

NO.	NAME	RANK	CASUALTY	DATE	LONDON GAZETTE
3321	Best Robert	Pte.	W/Sv	7-6-55	22-6-55
3314	Fisher Samuel	Pte.	W/Sv	7-6-55	22-6-55
2210	Hill Robert	Pte.	W/M	7-6-55	22-6-55
2794	Horn James	Pte.	W/M	7-6-55	22-6-55

96th REGIMENT OF FOOT

NO.	NAME	RANK	CASUALTY	DATE	LONDON GAZETTE
	Anderson C.	Lieut.	W/Sl	7-6-55	22-6-55

97th REGIMENT OF FOOT

NO.	NAME	RANK	CASUALTY	DATE	LONDON GAZETTE
3307	Breaney Matthew	Pte.	Killed	7-6-55	22-6-55
2922	Mason Moses	Pte.	Killed	7-6-55	22-6-55
	Mackesy E. R.	Lieut.	W/Sv	7-6-55	22-6-55
2209	Case John	Corpl.	W/Sl	7-6-55	22-6-55
3317	Downey Thomas	Pte.	W/Sv	7-6-55	22-6-55
3127	Drane Thomas	Pte.	W/Sl	7-6-55	22-6-55
3085	Fleming William	Pte.	W/Sl	7-6-55	22-6-55
2321	Gribbin John	Pte.	W/Sl	7-6-55	22-6-55
3469	Harbour Thomas	Pte.	W/Sl	7-6-55	22-6-55
3673	Kilcoin John	Pte.	W/Sl	7-6-55	22-6-55
3623	Perry James	Pte.	W/Sl	7-6-55	22-6-55
3585	Welch William	Pte.	W/Sl	7-6-55	22-6-55

NOTES

The Assault on the Quarries

1st BATTALION RIFLE BRIGADE

NO.	NAME	RANK	CASUALTY	DATE	LONDON GAZETTE
4002	Cartwright Thomas	Pte.	W/Sv	6-6-55	22-6-55
3596	Currie Peter	Pte.	W/D	6-6-55	22-6-55

2nd BATTALION RIFLE BRIGADE

NO.	NAME	RANK	CASUALTY	DATE	LONDON GAZETTE
3859	Wilkinson Joseph	Pte.	Killed	7-6-55	22-6-55
2077	Cook J.	Sergt.	W/Sl	4-6-55	22-6-55
2127	Booth John	Pte.	W/Sl	7-6-55	22-6-55
3648	Hillier F. J.	Pte.	W/Sl	7-6-55	22-6-55
3289	Jacobs Charles	Pte.	W/Sl	7-6-55	22-6-55
1617	Jones Thomas	Pte.	W/Sl	7-6-55	22-6-55
4199	King Robert	Pte.	W/Sl	7-6-55	22-6-55
3086	Longmire Henry	Pte.	W/Sv	7-6-55	22-6-55
4190	Moriarty John	Pte.	W/Sl	7-6-55	22-6-55
3105	Nutty Edward	Pte.	W/Sv	7-6-55	22-6-55
3776	Reilly John	Pte.	W/Sv	7-6-55	22-6-55
3727	Tench Edward	Pte.	W/Sl	7-6-55	22-6-55
3770	Wiseman Robert	Pte.	W/Sl	7-6-55	22-6-55

NOTES

THE FIRST ATTACK ON THE REDAN

The following casualties occurred among the Officers, Non-Commissioned Officers and men of the Army during the First Attack on the Redan, 18th June, 1855.
Compiled from the London Gazette, 3rd July, 1855 and 9th July, 1855.

STAFF

NAME	RANK	CASUALTY
3rd Division		
Eyre William C. B.	Major General	W/Sv
4th Division		
Campbell Sir J. Bart.	Major General	Killed
Snodgrass A.	Staff Captain (38th Foot)	W/Sv
Wortley Stuart	Br/Major D.A.Q.M.G. (1st Dgn Gds)	W/Sl

ROYAL ARTILLERY

NO.	NAME	RANK	CASUALTY	NO.	NAME	RANK	CASUALTY
—	Rose Alexander	Corpl.	Killed	2048	Allen Robert	Gnr.&Dvr.	W/Sv
3255	Arthur Thomas	Gnr.	Killed	104	Beattie William	Gnr.&Dvr.	W/D
54	Brennan Michael	Gnr.	Killed	—	Cormick William	Gnr.&Dvr.	W/Sv
3599	Harris Henry	Gnr.	Killed	2969	Doneghy John	Gnr.&Dvr.	W/D
—	Parker William	Gnr.	Killed	3355	Flood James	Gnr.&Dvr.	W/Sv
2316	Woode Joseph	Gnr.	Killed	2236	McIvor John	Gnr.&Dvr.	W/Sv
—	Williams W. J.	Capt.	W/Sl	2021	Ovenden William	Gnr.&Dvr.	W/Sl
2249	Heard William	Sergt.	W/Sl	3512	Perkins Thomas	Gnr.&Dvr.	W/Sv
—	Keown Thomas	Sergt.	W/Sv	2703	Robertson John	Gnr.&Dvr.	W/D
949	Ewing Samuel	Bombr.	W/Sv	—	Sparrow William	Gnr.&Dvr.	W/Sl
57	Symons Joseph	Bombr.	W/D				

ROYAL ENGINEERS

NO.	NAME	RANK	CASUALTY	NO.	NAME	RANK	CASUALTY
	Jesse William	Capt.	Killed		Jones Harry D.	Mjr/Gen.	W/Sl
	Graves T.	Lieut.	Killed		Tylden R.	Lt/Col.	W/Sv
	Murray James	Lieut.	Killed		Bourchier E. F.	Br/Mjr.	W/Sl

NOTES

The First Attack on the Redan

ROYAL SAPPERS AND MINERS

NO.	NAME	RANK	CASUALTY	NO.	NAME	RANK	CASUALTY
1027	Baker William	2nd/Cpl.	Killed	1257	Maycock Joseph	L/Cpl.	W/Sv
2124	Barnes Joseph	Pte.	Killed	2657	Pearson Edward	Pte.	W/Sl
1169	Eadie Robert	Pte.	Killed	854	Perie John	Pte.	W/Sl
2477	McNeil Thomas	Pte.	Killed	324	Preece William	Pte.	W/Sl
721	Rollings William	Pte.	Killed	2403	Spear Samuel	Pte.	W/Sv
1854	Dobbie William	Sergt.	W/Sl	767	Tickle Aaron	Pte.	W/Sv

AMBULANCE CORPS.

NO.	NAME	RANK	CASUALTY
469	McDonald William	Pte.	W/Sv

LAND TRANSPORT CORPS

NO.	NAME	RANK	CASUALTY	
1049	Anderson Andrew	2nd/Cl. Drv.	W/Sv	
1712	Begg James	Corpl.	W/Sl	Attd. from 9th Foot
2098	Egan James	Pte.	W/Sl	Attd. from 1st Foot

1st BATTALION COLDSTREAM GUARDS

NO.	NAME	RANK	CASUALTY	NO.	NAME	RANK	CASUALTY
4629	Slatter George	Pte.	W/Sl	4054	Stephenson Robert	Pte.	W/Sl

1st BATTALION SCOTS FUSILIER GUARDS

NO.	NAME	RANK	CASUALTY	NO.	NAME	RANK	CASUALTY
4931	Clark George	Pte.	Killed	4255	Cumming James	Pte.	W/D
5223	Clarke James	Pte.	Killed	4698	Drummond John	Pte.	W/Sv
5348	Davidson Archibald	Pte.	Killed	4903	Geddes James	Pte.	W/Sv
4800	Gibson Andrew	Pte.	Killed	4816	Kenworthy John	Pte.	W/Sl
4720	Brooker George	Pte.	W/Sl	4775	Laing Alexander	Pte.	W/Sl
4309	Carbine Joshua	Pte.	W/Sl	2930	Turnbull George	Pte.	W/Sl

1st BATTALION 1st FOOT

NO.	NAME	RANK	CASUALTY	NO.	NAME	RANK	CASUALTY
3041	Horan Patrick	Pte.	Killed	3179	Leonard Luke	Pte.	W/Sl
3331	Kennidy Luke	Pte.	Killed	2158	Treiney James	Pte.	W/Sv
2499	Burt Alexander	Pte.	W/Sl				

2nd BATTALION 1st FOOT

NO.	NAME	RANK	CASUALTY	NO.	NAME	RANK	CASUALTY
2383	Horne Lewis	Pte.	W/Sl	2988	Filden Thomas	Pte.	W/Sv
3038	Clarke Charles	Pte.	W/Sl	2365	Simpson William	Pte.	W/Sl

NOTES

The First Attack on the Redan

3rd REGIMENT OF FOOT

NO.	NAME	RANK	CASUALTY	NO.	NAME	RANK	CASUALTY
3293	Bailey Richard	Pte.	W/Sv	2499	Neal John	Pte.	W/Sv
2608	Butler Thomas	Pte.	W/Sv	3366	Newberry Andrew	Pte.	W/D

4th REGIMENT OF FOOT

NO.	NAME	RANK	CASUALTY	NO.	NAME	RANK	CASUALTY
3658	Cotton Bernard	Pte.	Killed	3533	Lindsay Alexander	Pte.	W/D
1363	Garrett George	Pte.	Killed	3478	McCarthy John	Pte.	W/D
3392	Hagan Patrick	Pte.	Killed	3397	McKenzie Gordon	Pte.	W/Sv
3163	Healey Michael	Pte.	Killed	2415	Maragh James	Pte.	W/D
3483	Lucas William	Pte.	Killed	3221	Murphy James	Pte.	W/Sv
1985	Swinter Thomas	Pte.	Killed	1754	Neaglee Edward	Pte.	W/D
	Cobbe H. C.	Colonel	W/Sv	2585	Ryan Patrick	Pte.	W/Sl
2049	Thatcher George	Corpl.	W/Sv	3798	Stephenson Thomas	Pte.	W/Sv
3508	Carroll Thomas	Pte.	W/Sl	3441	Tegg William	Pte.	W/Sv
3177	Collins Cornelius	Pte.	W/Sv	3281	Williams John	Pte.	W/Sl
3635	Hall Thomas	Pte.	W/Sv	3574	Wold Joseph	Pte.	W/Sv
3646	Hendey Robert	Pte.	W/Sv	3325	Watkins John	Pte.	Missing
3589	Lewis Thomas	Pte.	W/Sv	2998	Wood William	Pte.	Missing

7th REGIMENT OF FOOT

NO.	NAME	RANK	CASUALTY	NO.	NAME	RANK	CASUALTY
	Yea L. W.	Colonel	Killed	2735	Cawthorne William	Pte.	W/Sv
	Hobson J. S. C.	Lieut.&Adj.	D.O.W.	3750	Congreve William	Pte.	W/Sv
2215	Bergin Michael	Sergt.	Killed	3278	Connell John	Pte.	W/Sl
2097	Miller David	Sergt.	Killed	3241	Cook William	Pte.	W/Sv
2889	Williamson Frank	Sergt.	Killed	3712	Crawford William	Pte.	W/Sl
2042	Bramham A. K.	Corpl.	Killed	3377	Dorrington George	Pte.	W/Sv
3126	Bradshaw Charles	Pte.	Killed	2348	Doyle Thomas	Pte.	W/Sv
2901	Caine George	Pte.	Killed	3754	Ellams Richard	Pte.	W/Sv
3790	Lee John	Pte.	Killed	3719	Evans William	Pte.	W/Sl
3207	McCarroll Francis	Pte.	Killed	3080	Gaynor William	Pte.	W/Sl
3427	McIntire Robert	Pte.	Killed	2853	Gill Thomas	Pte.	W/Sv
2559	Nugent William	Pte.	Killed	1977	Goldsmith Thomas	Pte.	W/Sl
3407	Parker John	Pte.	Killed	3468	Hagan John	Pte.	W/Sv
2720	Steele Lawrence	Pte.	Killed	3786	Hague William	Pte.	W/Sv
3609	Thomas Alfred	Pte.	Killed	3220	Hill William	Pte.	W/Sl
3064	Whitehead Henry	Pte.	Killed	3183	Irwin Joseph	Pte.	W/Sl
3261	Williamson Thomas	Pte.	Killed	3661	Jones Charles	Pte.	W/Sl
	Pack A. J.	Major	W/Sv	3322	Jordan Patrick	Pte.	W/Sl
	Appleyard F.	Capt.	W/Sl	3210	Keogh Joseph	Pte.	W/Sl
	Browne Lord R.	Lieut.	W/Sl	3091	Leach Thomas	Pte.	D.O.W.
	Jones L. J. F.	Lieut	W/Sv	3790	Lee John	Pte.	W/Sl
	Fitzclarence Hon. E.	Lieut	W/D	3477	Linegar Thomas	Pte.	W/Sv
	Malan C.	Lieut	W/Sv	2207	McCartney Michael	Pte.	W/Sv
	Waller G. H.	Lieut	W/Sl	3801	McDonald John	Pte.	W/D
	Wright W. L. L. C.	Lieut	W/Sl	2999	McGuire John	Pte.	W/Sl
883	Bacon William	Sgt/Mjr.	W/Sl	2617	Manston William	Pte.	W/Sl
2623	Buck William	Corpl.	W/Sv	2436	Marshall William	Pte.	W/Sl
3262	Edwards Henry	Corpl.	W/Sl	3390	Mitchell William	Pte.	W/Sl
3426	Flack Samuel	Corpl.	W/Sl	3502	Nightingale Thomas	Pte.	W/Sl
1879	Hughes Matthew	Corpl.	W/Sv	3143	Palmer John	Pte.	W/D
2217	Nutley Andrew	Corpl.	W/Sl	3407	Parker John	Pte.	W/Sl
3070	Oakes Henry	Corpl.	W/Sv	3532	Pitsworth Joseph	Pte.	W/Sl
3759	Aspinal William	Pte.	W/Sl	3540	Platt John	Pte.	W/Sl
3251	Barnes Thomas	Pte.	W/Sl	1470	Robertson James	Pte.	W/Sv
3787	Bartell James	Pte.	W/Sv	1953	Rowle John	Pte.	W/Sv
3644	Blackhall John	Pte.	W/Sl	2930	Smith John (9)	Pte.	W/Sv

NOTES

The First Attack on the Redan

7th REGIMENT OF FOOT

NO.	NAME	RANK	CASUALTY	NO.	NAME	RANK	CASUALTY
2908	Smith William	Pte.	W/Sl	1967	Williamson Andrew	Pte.	W/Sl
2517	Stephens W. H.	Pte.	W/Sv	3805	Wynn John	Pte.	W/Sv
3779	Sykes Joseph	Pte.	W/Sl	3650	Young Joseph	Pte.	W/Sl
2933	Turner Robert	Pte.	W/Sl		Robinson N. D.	Lieut.	Missing
3596	Tyrrell Stephen	Pte.	W/Sv				

9th REGIMENT OF FOOT

NO.	NAME	RANK	CASUALTY	NO.	NAME	RANK	CASUALTY
	Smith Frederick	Capt.	D.O.W.	3679	Hagan Bernard	Pte.	W/Sl
2668	Flanigan Peter	Pte.	Killed	2855	Haughney John	Pte.	W/Sl
1458	Gaffy Luke	Pte.	Killed	3113	Hockenall Joseph	Pte.	W/Sl
	McQueen John	Lt.&Adj.	W/Sv	2962	Killeen James	Pte.	W/Sl
	Douglas A G.	Lieut.	W/Sl	3201	Kilroy Patrick	Pte.	W/Sl
2091	Gwinnett Richard	Sergt.	W/Sl	3296	Lindford Thomas	Pte.	W/Sl
1315	Nursey Robert	Sergt.	W/Sl	3689	Louch Henry	Pte.	W/Sl
2558	O'Neil John	Sergt.	W/Sl	1432	Loughlin James	Pte.	W/Sl
3358	Hall James	L/Cpl.	W/Sv	3329	Lyons John	Pte.	W/Sl
1715	Aldridge Zachariah	Pte.	W/Sv	3037	McDonald John	Pte.	W/Sl
3286	Andrews William	Pte.	W/Sv	2742	McMahon John	Pte.	W/Sl
3576	Arlott George	Pte.	W/Sl	3212	Minahen John	Pte.	W/Sl
3626	Barnard Thomas	Pte.	W/Sl	3590	Monaghan Michael	Pte.	W/Sl
3739	Beard John	Pte.	W/Sv	3312	Molloy Patrick	Pte.	W/Sv
3801	Burns Robert	Pte.	W/Sv	3476	Murphy Patrick	Pte.	W/Sl
3299	Byrne Michael	Pte.	W/Sl	1642	Muschamp Barker	Pte.	W/Sv
2111	Campbell James	Pte.	W/Sl	1525	Potter William	Pte.	W/Sl
3569	Connerly Timothy	Pte.	W/Sv	2060	Rackett William	Pte.	W/Sv
3648	Cook Henry	Pte.	W/Sv	3350	Reid William	Pte.	W/Sl
3046	Dolohery Simon	Pte.	W/Sl	2051	Schevenals Denis	Pte.	W/Sl
2576	Duffy Frank	Pte.	W/Sl	3630	Sullivan Patrick	Pte.	W/Sl
2057	Dunn Peter	Pte.	W/Sv	3659	Sullivan Patrick	Pte.	W/Sl
1734	Earnshaw John	Pte.	W/Sl	3387	Walsh Peter	Pte.	W/Sv
3272	Gray William	Pte.	W/Sl	1454	Wareing Joseph	Pte.	W/Sl
3593	Guthrie Thomas	Pte.	W/Sv	3281	White Thomas	Pte.	W/Sv

14th REGIMENT OF FOOT

NO.	NAME	RANK	CASUALTY	NO.	NAME	RANK	CASUALTY
1534	Lynch Michael	Pte.	Killed	1360	Rever Peter	Pte.	W/Sl
3412	Martin John	Pte.	Killed	3726	Smith Joseph	Pte.	W/Sv
3398	Thompson William	Pte.	Killed	3259	Sullivan John	Pte.	W/Sl
3241	Brown Thomas	Corpl.	W/D				

17th REGIMENT OF FOOT

NO.	NAME	RANK	CASUALTY	NO.	NAME	RANK	CASUALTY
	Croker J. L.	Capt.	Killed	1070	Borrett David	Sergt.	W/D
1707	Connell Michael	Sergt.	Killed	1633	Holt Edward	Sergt.	W/D
2893	King Patrick	Corpl.	Killed	1976	Patterson William	Sergt.	W/D
2974	Belton Morgan	Pte.	Killed	2784	Duffell James	Corpl.	W/Sv
2573	Dwyer John	Pte.	Killed	1357	Davis John	L/Cpl.	W/Sl
2952	Dwyer Martin	Pte.	Killed	2696	Faughnan Thomas	L/Cpl.	W/Sl
2988	Naughton Thomas	Pte.	Killed	3691	Anderson John	Pte.	W/Sl
3030	Robinson Charles	Pte.	Killed	3282	Arnold James	Pte.	W/Sl
2963	Sally William	Pte.	Killed	3156	Browning Robert	Pte.	W/Sl
2782	Stevens Henry	Pte.	Killed	3487	Burns Christopher	Pte.	W/Sl
2073	Colcliffe William	Col/Sgt.	W/Sl	2490	Carmody George	Pte.	W/Sv
1456	O'Leary William	Col/Sgt.	W/Sl	2542	Darcy Patrick	Pte.	W/Sv

NOTES

The First Attack on the Redan

17th REGIMENT OF FOOT

NO.	NAME	RANK	CASUALTY	NO.	NAME	RANK	CASUALTY
1355	Gilman Richard	Pte.	W/Sv	3555	McGuire James	Pte.	D.O.W.
3641	Gordon Bernard	Pte.	W/Sv	2439	McQuade James	Pte.	W/Sl
3127	Grimes Michael	Pte.	W/Sv	1582	Mellows James	Pte.	W/Sl
3190	Howard Richard	Pte.	W/Sl	3294	Moore John	Pte.	W/Sv
1118	Hynes Andrew	Pte.	W/Sl	2891	Parker Michael	Pte.	W/Sl
3249	Keough Thomas	Pte.	W/Sl	3027	Ruddell Francis	Pte.	W/Sv
2880	King Mathew	Pte.	W/D	2950	Scott Thomas	Pte.	W/Sl
3131	Kinna Nicholas	Pte.	W/D	2837	Stapleton Patrick	Pte.	W/Sl
3372	McAllister —	Pte.	W/Sl	2878	Walsh Patrick	Pte.	W/Sl
3387	McCarthy Patrick	Pte.	W/Sv				

18th REGIMENT OF FOOT

NO.	NAME	RANK	CASUALTY	NO.	NAME	RANK	CASUALTY
	Meurant J. W.	Lieut.	Killed	339	Owen Edward	Sgt.	W/Sv
1355	Mallow Thomas	Col/Sgt.	Killed	3310	Reside William	Sgt.	W/Sl
3105	Hortigan Michael	Corpl.	Killed	2975	Sheehan Richard	Sgt.	W/Sl
2939	Morgan George	Corpl.	Killed	2531	Stewart William	Sgt.	W/Sl
3739	Watson James	Corpl.	Killed	1680	Studdart Thomas	Sgt.	W/Sv
3011	Birmingham William	Pte.	Killed	2828	Dillon John	Corpl.	W/Sv
1669	Cautlin Michael	Pte.	Killed	3012	Kuniare Patrick	Corpl.	W/Sv
2664	Cotter Timothy	Pte.	Killed	2792	Leahy James	Corpl.	W/Sv
2207	Dowd Patrick	Pte.	Killed	3086	Newman Charles	Corpl.	W/Sv
1756	Gordon Robert	Pte.	Killed	3033	O'Connor Michael	Corpl.	W/Sv
5315	Gorman Michael	Pte.	Killed	1266	Sheedy Henry	Corpl.	W/Sl
2903	Hannigan Cornelius	Pte.	Killed	3569	Waters Robert	Corpl.	W/Sl
3191	Kearns Patrick	Pte.	Killed	3362	Cardwell William	Drummer	W/Sv
2128	Keelan Lawrence	Pte.	Killed	1050	McGrath Thomas	Drummer	W/Sl
2180	McCormick Thomas	Pte.	Killed	983	Molloy John	Drummer	W/Sl
3562	McEvoy Samuel	Pte.	Killed	2818	Abbott Patrick	Pte.	W/Sv
2340	Maloney Patrick	Pte.	Killed	3707	Baglin Richard	Pte.	W/Sl
3791	Moloney John	Pte.	Killed	2221	Bailey Thomas	Pte.	W/Sv
3618	Murphy Michael (2)	Pte.	Killed	1734	Brogan Michael	Pte.	W/Sv
3621	Murray James	Pte.	Killed	3508	Browne William	Pte.	W/Sv
3121	Pugh George	Pte.	Killed	2673	Bryan Peter	Pte.	W/D
3541	Quinn Bernard	Pte.	Killed	2085	Callaghan John	Pte.	W/Sl
2906	Reane Abraham	Pte.	Killed	1743	Carroll John	Pte.	W/Sv
3292	Rodgers James	Pte.	Killed	3398	Casey John	Pte.	W/Sl
	Clarke Kennedy J.	Major	W/Sl	1713	Cawley Michael	Pte.	W/Sv
	Armstrong A.	Capt.	W/Sl	3529	Church Alfred	Pte.	D.O.W.
	Cormick John	Capt.	W/D	3655	Clancy Charles	Pte.	W/Sv
	Hayman M. J.	Capt.	W/D	3194	Clancy John	Pte.	W/Sv
	Stephenson H. J.	Capt.	W/Sl	2962	Clayton Edward	Pte.	W/Sl
	Wilkinson J. G.	Capt.	W/Sl	3268	Coleman Jeremiah	Pte.	W/Sl
	Bryen Taylor W. O.	Lieut.	W/Sl	3638	Coleman John	Pte.	W/Sv
	Fearnley Fairfax	Lieut.	W/Sv	3047	Collins Michael	Pte.	W/Sl
	Hotham Charles	Lieut.	W/Sl	1971	Collins Patrick	Pte.	W/Sl
	Kemp W.	Lieut.	W/Sv	3349	Collins John	Pte.	W/Sv
1196	Orchard Isaac	Col/Sgt.	W/Sv	3794	Comisky Francis	Pte.	W/Sl
2155	Proctor James	Col/Sgt.	W/Sl	3197	Condon Michael	Pte.	W/Sl
2089	Widenham George	Col/Sgt.	W/D	3586	Connell Michael	Pte.	W/Sl
3331	Bartlett Frederick	Sgt.	W/Sl	3576	Connell Owen	Pte.	W/Sv
1774	Carroll Patrick	Sgt.	W/D	3378	Cotton John	Pte.	W/Sl
3332	Clarke George	Sgt.	W/Sv	3587	Coulter Thomas	Pte.	W/Sl
3871	Dunne Edward	Sgt.	W/Sl	2117	Cox John	Pte.	W/Sv
1960	Gleeson John	Sgt.	W/Sl	3226	Coyle Patrick	Pte.	W/Sl
1448	Grant John	Sgt.	W/Sv	2014	Cremin Michael	Pte.	W/Sv
2081	Hallissey John	Sgt.	W/Sv	3208	Cullinan Patrick	Pte.	W/Sv
2129	Keenan Charles	Sgt.	W/Sl	3794	Cumiskey Patrick	Pte.	W/Sl
3341	McCarthy Timothy	Sgt.	W/D	2877	Cummings Patrick	Pte.	W/Sl
2315	Morton Henry	Sgt.	W/Sv	2861	Curtin John	Pte.	W/Sl
1886	O'Donnell Thomas	Sgt.	W/Sl	2920	Dacy James	Pte.	W/Sl

NOTES

The First Attack on the Redan

18th REGIMENT OF FOOT

NO.	NAME	RANK	CASUALTY	NO.	NAME	RANK	CASUALTY
2090	Dennis James	Pte.	W/Sl	2652	Lynch James	Pte.	W/Sv
2934	Desmond Andrew	Pte.	W/Sl	1583	Mackay Michael	Pte.	W/Sv
2627	Desmond John	Pte.	W/Sl	2612	McCabe Hugh	Pte.	W/M
2999	Dimphy Thomas	Pte.	W/Sl	1824	McCarthy Dennis	Pte.	W/D
2160	Doherty Robert	Pte.	W/Sl	1390	McCarthy Charles	Pte.	W/Sv
2070	Donohoe Patrick	Pte.	W/Sl	2933	McCarthy John	Pte.	W/Sv
2213	Donovan Patrick	Pte.	W/Sv	2604	McCawley John	Pte.	W/Sv
3481	Dougherty John	Pte.	W/Sv	3112	McGaragle John	Pte.	W/Sv
3110	Dowd Patrick	Pte.	W/Sl	3489	McGavin Hugh	Pte.	W/Sl
2364	Downs John	Pte.	W/Sl	3401	McGawley Michael	Pte.	W/Sv
3028	Doyle John	Pte.	W/M	2045	McGowen John	Pte.	W/Sv
2398	Doyle Joseph	Pte.	W/Sl	3849	McGuire Michael	Pte.	W/Sv
2994	Driscoll Daniel	Pte.	W/Sl	3612	McGuinness John	Pte.	W/Sv
1913	Duggan John	Pte.	W/Sl	2080	McGuinness Henry	Pte.	W/Sv
3125	Dunn James	Pte.	W/Sl	3573	McHale Thomas	Pte.	W/Sv
2904	Edgill James	Pte.	W/Sv	3413	McKevill Owen	Pte.	W/Sl
3334	Edmonds Thomas	Pte.	W/Sv	1159	McLoughlin John	Pte.	W/Sl
3592	Edwards Moses	Pte.	W/Sv	3648	McNally James	Pte.	W/Sl
3780	Entwhistle Ralph	Pte.	W/M	2258	McNally Owen	Pte.	W/Sv
2069	Fallon William	Pte.	W/Sl	2705	Maher John	Pte.	W/Sv
3733	Farrell James	Pte.	W/Sl	3735	Maher William	Pte.	W/Sl
2643	Farrell Nicholas	Pte.	W/Sl	3225	Malley William	Pte.	W/Sv
2833	Fenton Roger	Pte.	W/M	1289	Mangan Thomas	Pte.	W/Sv
2910	Fielding Charles	Pte.	W/Sl	3554	Mansfield Henry	Pte.	W/Sl
2890	Finnegan Patrick	Pte.	W/Sv	3610	Marks James	Pte.	W/Sv
1922	Fitzgerald John	Pte.	W/Sv	3151	Masterton Peter	Pte.	W/Sv
2794	Flaherty Thomas	Pte.	W/D	3359	Medhurst Thomas	Pte.	W/Sl
3222	Flanagan Thomas	Pte.	W/Sl	2339	Milliard William	Pte.	W/Sv
2815	Fleming James	Pte.	W/Sv	3650	Moreland Charles	Pte.	W/Sv
4001	Foote George	Pte.	W/Sl	3461	Moriarty Maurice	Pte.	W/M
3594	Forster Joseph	Pte.	W/Sl	3316	Morrow John	Pte.	W/Sl
3494	Fry Charles	Pte.	W/Sl	1220	Mulready Thomas	Pte.	W/Sl
3207	Glamson Maurice	Pte.	W/Sl	2141	Murphy Patrick Charles	Pte.	W/Sl
3425	Good William	Pte.	W/Sl	1988	Murphy James	Pte.	W/Sl
3368	Goody Frederick	Pte.	W/Sl	3369	Murphy Patrick	Pte.	W/Sv
2946	Gorman Andrew	Pte.	W/Sv	2912	Murphy Timothy	Pte.	W/Sl
3076	Gultry James	Pte.	W/Sl	3416	Murphy Timothy	Pte.	W/Sl
1597	Haggarty Thomas	Pte.	W/Sv	3450	Nanton Henry	Pte.	W/Sv
3148	Hair Michael	Pte.	W/Sl	2510	Neill Hugh	Pte.	W/Sv
3183	Hallman Michael	Pte.	W/Sv	3402	Nunn James	Pte.	W/Sv
3009	Hardy Austin	Pte.	W/Sv	3353	O'Brien John	Pte.	W/Sv
2618	Harrington John (1)	Pte.	W/Sv	3626	O'Brien Peter	Pte.	W/D
3030	Harrington John (2)	Pte.	W/Sv	2943	O'Leary Thomas	Pte.	W/Sl
3784	Harris Richard	Pte.	W/Sl	3640	O'Sullivan John	Pte.	W/Sl
3743	Hasleton Thomas	Pte.	W/Sv	3056	Powell Henry	Pte.	W/Sl
3008	Hayes David	Pte.	W/Sv	3081	Prior Michael	Pte.	W/Sl
2893	Hayes John	Pte.	W/Sv	3494	Quillan Anthony	Pte.	W/Sl
2253	Hogan Dennis	Pte.	W/Sv	3142	Quinn Thomas	Pte.	W/Sl
3731	Howes William	Pte.	W/D	3734	Quinn William	Pte.	W/M
3602	Houston James	Pte.	W/Sl	3789	Rainey Wilford	Pte.	D.O.W.
3188	Hughes James	Pte.	W/Sv	2526	Reagan John	Pte.	W/Sv
3654	Hughes Peter	Pte.	W/Sv	3404	Reeves John	Pte.	W/Sv
3337	Jerman Lawrence	Pte.	W/Sv	1186	Roach John	Pte.	W/Sl
3795	Keane David	Pte.	W/Sv	3631	Roberts Thomas	Pte.	W/Sv
3576	Keilly Cornelius	Pte.	W/Sv	3492	Robinson David	Pte.	W/Sl
1702	Kennedy Michael	Pte.	W/Sl	3146	Rohan Thomas	Pte.	W/Sl
3037	Killeen George	Pte.	W/Sl	3389	Rourke Daniel	Pte.	W/Sl
3087	Kilty Patrick	Pte.	W/Sl	2127	Ryan John	Pte.	W/D
3525	Lancaster James	Pte.	W/Sl	3632	Ryan John	Pte.	W/Sl
2820	Langton Edward	Pte.	W/Sl	3561	Ryan Michael	Pte.	W/Sv
2917	Leary Patrick	Pte.	W/Sl	3950	Ryan Patrick	Pte.	W/D
2061	Leary Patrick	Pte.	W/Sl	3635	Scanlon Edward	Pte.	W/Sl
3459	Leary Timothy	Pte.	W/Sl	3346	Sessnan John	Pte.	W/D
3480	Lebart John	Pte.	W/Sl	3279	Shaw Martin	Pte.	W/D
3278	Lucas George	Pte.	W/Sl	2854	Sheehan Cornelius	Pte.	W/Sl

NOTES

The First Attack on the Redan

18th REGIMENT OF FOOT

NO.	NAME	RANK	CASUALTY	NO.	NAME	RANK	CASUALTY
2011	Sheehan Michael	Pte.	W/D	3406	Taffe Peter	Pte.	W/Sv
3391	Sherrock John	Pte.	W/Sv	3281	Thompson Henry	Pte.	W/Sl
3124	Shihy Jeremiah	Pte.	W/Sv	3813	Tighe John	Pte.	W/D
1612	Singleton Thadeus	Pte.	W/Sl	2953	Tobin Patrick	Pte.	W/Sv
2551	Slowey James	Pte.	W/Sv	2886	Walsh Edward	Pte.	W/Sv
3217	Smith Patrick	Pte.	W/Sl	3498	Walsh Robert	Pte.	W/Sl
3190	Smith Philip	Pte.	W/Sl	3407	Warwick William	Pte.	W/Sl
3134	Smyth Terence	Pte.	W/Sl	3726	Whelan Jeremiah	Pte.	W/Sl
3393	Spaulding Henry	Pte.	W/Sv	3326	Wiggins Joseph	Pte.	W/D
3453	Speight Joseph	Pte.	W/Sv	3075	Winne Patrick	Pte.	W/Sl
3322	Sullivan James	Pte.	W/Sv	3429	Wise Thomas	Pte.	W/Sv
3375	Sullivan Thomas	Pte.	W/Sl	2862	Woods John	Pte.	W/Sv
2399	Swift James	Pte.	W/Sv	2407	Ahern John	Pte.	Missing

19th REGIMENT OF FOOT

NO.	NAME	RANK	CASUALTY
2935	Watson George	Pte.	W/Sl

20th REGIMENT OF FOOT

NO.	NAME	RANK	CASUALTY	NO.	NAME	RANK	CASUALTY
3298	Palmer David	L/Sgt.	Killed	2821	Bryan John	Pte.	W/Sv
3962	McGorman James	Pte.	Killed	3185	Jones John	Pte.	W/Sl
3667	Paul Thomas	Pte.	Killed	3282	Mulcahy James	Pte.	W/Sl
	Evelegh F. C.	Lieut/Col.	W/Sl	3426	Rodgers James	Pte.	W/Sl
	O'Neil J. J. S.	Lieut	W/Sl	2421	Russell Charles	Pte.	W/Sl
	Holmes F. G.	Ensign	W/Sl	3522	Simmons Francis	Pte.	W/Sv
2881	Barnes David	Pte.	W/Sl	2591	Woods Henry	Pte.	W/Sv

21st REGIMENT OF FOOT

NO.	NAME	RANK	CASUALTY	NO.	NAME	RANK	CASUALTY
3487	Hartney John	Pte.	Killed	3546	Cassidey Owen	Pte.	W/Sl
—	Lawrence John	Pte.	Killed	3611	Donohoe Michael	Pte.	W/Sl
3298	Tracey Paul	Pte.	Killed	3118	Duff Henry	Pte.	W/Sl
	Image John G.	Lieut.	W/Sl	3133	Ford William	Pte.	W/Sl
1918	O'Farrell Michael	Sgt.	W/Sl	3823	Hancock Charles	Pte.	W/D
2588	Powell Thomas	Sgt.	W/Sl	3031	Leaming Moses	Pte.	W/Sl
2256	Robertson Thomas	Sgt.	W/Sl	2705	McFadon Edward	Pte.	W/D
2288	Griffin James	Corpl.	W/Sl	3456	Marsden Thomas	Pte.	W/Sl
3488	Harrington Michael	Corpl.	W/Sl	3482	Rutherford William	Pte.	W/Sl
3113	Sim James	Corpl.	W/Sv	2928	Smith Richard	Pte.	W/Sv
3008	Watkins Frederick	Corpl.	W/D	3181	Spencer Thomas	Pte.	W/Sl
3018	Cassidey John	Pte.	W/Sv	3563	Studders James	Pte.	W/D

23rd REGIMENT OF FOOT

NO.	NAME	RANK	CASUALTY
	Lysons D.	Lieut/Col.	W/Sv

NOTES

The First Attack on the Redan

28th REGIMENT OF FOOT

NO.	NAME	RANK	CASUALTY	NO.	NAME	RANK	CASUALTY
2302	Collins Michael	Corpl.	Killed	3525	Dumphy Richard	Pte.	W/Sl
3507	Collins Joshua	Pte.	Killed	3371	Dunn William	Pte.	W/Sv
2291	Davis Thomas	Pte.	Killed	4012	Earls Stephen	Pte.	W/Sl
3356	English Richard	Pte.	Killed	4144	Ellis Thomas	Pte.	W/Sv
3903	Lennard Owen	Pte.	Killed	3822	Farrell Timothy	Pte.	W/Sl
3259	Smith William	Pte.	Killed	3238	Fihely Dennis	Pte.	W/Sv
3534	Thompson Hugh	Pte.	Killed	4011	Fisher Edward	Pte.	W/Sl
3747	Tobin James	Pte.	Killed	3811	Heaton Joseph	Pte.	W/Sl
3467	Watson James	Pte.	Killed	3197	Hill Jonathan	Pte.	W/D
	Alpin J. G. R.	Capt.	W/Sl	3888	Johnston John	Pte.	W/Sv
	Godley H. R. C.	Capt.	W/Sv	3833	Kennedy Isaac	Pte.	W/Sl
	Malcolm J. D.	Capt.	W/Sv	3199	Lewis Robert	Pte.	W/D
	Brodigan Francis	Lieut.	W/Sv	3061	McCann John	Pte.	W/Sv
	Lennard C. E. B.	Lieut.	W/Sv	4074	McCann James	Pte.	W/Sv
2518	Lumsden Thomas	Sgt/Major	W/Sl	2474	McEvoy Patrick	Pte.	W/Sl
3083	Connell Michael	Corpl.	W/Sl	3691	Mahoney John	Pte.	Missing
1251	O'Brien Stephen	Drummer	W/Sl	3559	Malone Edward	Pte.	W/Sv
3727	Adams James	Pte.	W/Sv	4118	Miller Robert	Pte.	W/D
3406	Alders Matthew	Pte.	W/Sl	3138	Mooran John	Pte.	W/Sl
3872	Austin John	Pte.	W/Sl	4001	Murphy James	Pte.	W/Sl
3124	Baker Joseph	Pte.	W/Sl	3423	O'Neil Thomas	Pte.	W/D
3531	Belcher John	Pte.	W/Sv	3919	Pearson James	Pte.	W/D
3575	Blythe Edward	Pte.	W/Sv	1592	Rawlington Francis	Pte.	W/Sl
3972	Burke Thomas	Pte.	W/D	2834	Simmins Thomas	Pte.	W/Sl
2086	Clarke Peter	Pte.	W/Sv	2867	Sleeper Edward	Pte.	W/Sl
2341	Collins Denis	Pte.	W/Sl	1681	Smith Samuel	Pte.	W/D
3053	Cook John	Pte.	W/Sv	3798	Stigoll Henry	Pte.	W/D
2718	Coyle Lawrence	Pte.	W/D	3825	Sweeny William	Pte.	W/D
3728	Dean Thomas	Pte.	W/Sv	3801	Tattersall Henry	Pte.	Missing
3646	Doherty John	Pte.	W/Sv	4178	Webber Charles	Pte.	W/D
3022	Donnolly John	Pte.	Missing	3999	Williams Thomas	Pte.	W/Sl
3434	Doran James	Pte.	W/Sv				

30th REGIMENT OF FOOT

NO.	NAME	RANK	CASUALTY	NO.	NAME	RANK	CASUALTY
4032	Fitzgerald Edward	Pte.	W/Sl	3740	Savourd Michael	Pte.	W/Sv
4077	McGrath James	Pte.	W/Sl				

31st REGIMENT OF FOOT

NO.	NAME	RANK	CASUALTY	NO.	NAME	RANK	CASUALTY
2875	Gleeson Edward	Pte.	W/Sv	3779	Smith Charles	Pte.	W/Sv
2772	Miller John	Pte.	W/Sv	2599	Thomas George	Pte.	W/Sv
3027	Shaw George	Pte.	W/Sv				

33rd REGIMENT OF FOOT

NO.	NAME	RANK	CASUALTY	NO.	NAME	RANK	CASUALTY
	Bennett V	Lieut.	Killed	3562	Doherty Thomas	Pte.	Killed
1096	Chalmers John	Sergt.	Killed	3383	Dwyre John	Pte.	Killed
2910	Beebe Henry	Pte.	Killed	3419	Harrigan John	Pte.	Killed
2725	Boyd Andrew	Pte.	Killed	1989	McGrath Patrick	Pte.	Killed
2561	Daily William	Pte.	Killed	1811	McLoughlin Andrew	Pte.	Killed

NOTES

The First Attack on the Redan

33rd REGIMENT OF FOOT

NO.	NAME	RANK	CASUALTY	NO.	NAME	RANK	CASUALTY
3030	Whitehead Thomas	Pte.	Killed	2032	Gorman James	Pte.	W/Sl
	Johnstone J. D.	Lieut/Col.	W/Sv	3132	Hanley Joseph	Pte.	Missing
	Mundy G. V.	Lieut/Col.	W/Sl	3169	Henchan Martin	Pte.	W/D
	Quayle J. E. T.	Capt.	W/D	2334	Hickey Pierce	Pte.	W/Sl
	Wickham T.	Capt.	W/Sv	3054	Higginbottom Charles	Pte.	W/D
	Rogers J. T.	Lieut.	W/Sl	2287	Leslie William	Pte.	W/Sv
	Heyland —	Lieut.	Missing	3511	Lloyd Peter	Pte.	W/Sl
2282	Fitzgibbon Benjamin	Corpl.	W/Sl	2740	Lockhead Charles	Pte.	W/D
3344	Bird Timothy	Pte.	W/D	2771	McGrogan Thomas	Pte.	W/Sl
2595	Birtenshaw William	Pte.	W/Sv	3832	Maher Patrick	Pte.	W/Sl
3280	Coulter Hugh	Pte.	W/D	2074	Mathews William	Pte.	W/Sl
3428	Crotty Francis	Pte.	W/Sl	3456	Merriott Joshua	Pte.	W/Sl
3765	Daily Michael	Pte.	W/Sl	3591	Murphy Patrick	Pte.	W/D
3878	Davis Charles	Pte.	W/D	3242	Needham Peter	Pte.	W/Sl
2797	Deschamp William	Pte.	W/D	3120	Nolan John	Pte	W/Sv
3168	Dunn Joseph	Pte.	W/D	2801	Russell James	Pte.	W/Sl
3597	Feeley Michael	Pte.	W/D	1631	Walsh Patrick	Pte.	W/D
3160	Fenning James	Pte.	W/Sl	3620	Young William	Pte.	W/Sv
3671	Gleeson James	Pte.	W/Sv				

34th REGIMENT OF FOOT

NO.	NAME	RANK	CASUALTY	NO.	NAME	RANK	CASUALTY
	Hurt F.	Capt.	Killed	3416	Scanlon John	Pte.	Killed
	Robinson John	Capt.	Killed	3764	Shannon Bartholomew	Pte.	Killed
	Shiffner John	Capt.	Killed	3941	Smith John	Pte.	Killed
	Alt H. D.	Lieut.	Killed	2247	Smith William	Pte.	Killed
2421	Neal George	Corpl.	Killed	3138	Townsend George	Pte.	Killed
2573	Allen Christopher	Pte.	Killed	3191	Walsh William	Pte.	Killed
2346	Ball Thomas	Pte.	Killed	3822	Waugh William	Pte.	Killed
3359	Barrett James	Pte.	Killed		Gwilt J.	Capt.	W/Sl
3127	Booth Samuel	Pte.	Killed		Jordan J.	Capt.	W/Sv
2521	Camm Naylor	Pte.	Killed		Warry W.	Capt.	W/Sl
3585	Charlesworth Wm.	Pte.	Killed		Clayton R. J. B.	Lieut.	W/Sv
2706	Cocklan John	Pte.	Killed		Harman G. B.	Lieut.	W/Sv
3775	Coleman William	Pte.	Killed		Peel F.	Lieut.	W/Sl
2631	College William	Pte.	Killed	2102	Mortimer John	Sgt/Mjr.	W/Sl
4047	Connors James	Pte.	Killed	1823	Coote William	Col/Sgt.	W/Sl
3376	Cornwall Mark	Pte.	Killed	1863	Smith William	Col/Sgt.	W/Sv
3248	Dix John	Pte.	Killed	3285	Anderson George	Sgt.	W/Sv
3875	Feeley James	Pte.	Killed	1899	Brown Francis	Sgt.	W/Sv
1413	Featherstone John	Pte.	Killed	2335	Haydon John	Sgt.	W/Sl
3527	Fishwick John	Pte.	Killed	1518	Key John	Sgt.	W/Sv
4112	Gooding Robert	Pte.	Killed	2255	Lear Thomas	Sgt.	W/Sv
4036	Hailes Abraham	Pte.	Killed	2206	Mann Benjamin	Sgt.	W/Sv
3347	Hanley Michael	Pte.	Killed	2954	Pratt James	Sgt.	W/Sl
3451	Holden Thomas	Pte.	Killed	2984	Quirk William	Sgt.	W/Sl
3959	Howard George	Pte.	Killed	3274	Bartlett Charles	Corpl.	W/D
3923	Inkland William	Pte.	Killed	3867	McCoy John	Corpl.	W/Sv
3543	Lovejoy Thomas	Pte.	Killed	3673	Powell William	Corpl.	W/Sv
3896	McClean John	Pte.	Killed	3699	Tyrrell Patrick	Corpl.	W/Sl
3706	McDonald Edward	Pte.	Killed	3948	Whittington Thomas	Corpl.	W/Sv
3715	McGeady Patrick	Pte.	Killed	4004	Kettle Thomas	L/Cpl.	W/Sv
3732	Mahoney Patrick	Pte.	Killed	2236	Criddie William	Drummer	W/Sv
3722	Malone Thomas	Pte.	Killed	3020	Gleeson Edward John	Drummer	W/Sv
3605	Megson Joseph	Pte.	Killed	4088	Ackland Henry	Pte.	W/Sl
3776	Muldoon Joseph	Pte.	Killed	2423	Allen Mathew	Pte.	W/D
3315	Mulvie Patrick	Pte.	Killed	3320	Allison Alfred	Pte.	W/Sv
2551	Parker John	Pte.	Killed	1412	Andrews George	Pte.	W/Sv
1812	Parker George	Pte.	Killed	3582	Andrews George	Pte.	W/Sv
3559	Pendlebury William	Pte.	Killed	1876	Artlett Moses	Pte.	W/Sl
1813	Price Charles	Pte.	Killed	4013	Aughton John	Pte.	W/Sv
4011	Savory Samuel	Pte.	Killed	1625	Bailey Thomas	Pte.	W/D

NOTES

The First Attack on the Redan

34th REGIMENT OF FOOT

NO.	NAME	RANK	CASUALTY	NO.	NAME	RANK	CASUALTY
3161	Barber George	Pte.	W/Sl	4067	Hargreaves John	Pte.	W/Sl
2087	Barker Peter	Pte.	W/Sv	3867	Harney Patrick	Pte.	W/Sl
2667	Bath Charles	Pte.	W/Sl	2162	Harris George	Pte.	W/Sv
3807	Beatty James	Pte.	W/D	3460	Harrison William	Pte.	W/Sl
4023	Beck William	Pte.	W/Sv	3368	Hatfield Charles	Pte.	W/Sv
3684	Begley Thomas	Pte.	W/Sv	1448	Herrot John	Pte.	W/Sv
3266	Bellerton Richard	Pte.	W/D	3400	Heydon Thomas	Pte.	W/Sv
1887	Biggs Thomas	Pte.	W/Sl	3863	Higginson James	Pte.	W/Sv
3540	Blizzard Thomas	Pte.	W/Sl	1885	Hornsby Robert	Pte.	W/D
2472	Braines William	Pte.	W/Sl	3185	Horseman William	Pte.	W/D
4043	Brannan Eugene	Pte.	W/D	3331	Howells John	Pte.	W/D
3998	Brennon Patrick	Pte.	W/Sv	3770	Invar Edward	Pte.	W/Sv
3835	Brien Daniel	Pte.	W/Sv	3449	Jones William	Pte.	W/Sv
2495	Bryan William	Pte.	W/Sv	2559	King George	Pte.	W/Sl
3696	Bullock William	Pte.	W/Sv	1996	King William	Pte.	W/Sv
4025	Burke Thomas	Pte.	W/Sl	2649	Latham John	Pte.	W/Sv
3291	Cahill Thomas	Pte.	W/Sv	3189	Latham James	Pte.	W/Sv
3049	Cane John	Pte.	W/Sl	3730	Lindsay James	Pte.	W/Sl
3206	Carew Robert	Pte.	W/Sl	3747	McAleer James	Pte.	W/Sl
3381	Carter Edward	Pte.	W/Sv	2803	McBune Lewis	Pte.	W/Sv
2507	Ceary Michael	Pte.	W/Sv	4022	McCabe William	Pte.	W/Sv
3676	Codrington William	Pte.	W/D	3110	McDaid William	Pte.	W/D
3800	Coffee Michael	Pte.	W/Sl	8311	McDonald Patrick	Pte.	W/Sv
4028	Connolly James	Pte.	W/Sl	3858	McGibbons Francis	Pte.	W/D
3849	Connor Charles	Pte.	W/Sv	3871	McRone James	Pte.	W/Sv
3420	Consani Anthony	Pte.	W/Sl	2717	Maddigan Michael	Pte.	W/Sl
3610	Copley Edward	Pte.	W/Sl	3157	Millar Thomas	Pte.	W/Sv
3606	Cotterall Henry	Pte.	W/Sl	2382	Mitchell William	Pte.	W/Sl
3618	Courcey James	Pte.	W/Sv	3804	Muldoon John	Pte.	W/Sv
3307	Cox Michael	Pte.	W/Sl	3431	O'Connell John	Pte.	W/Sv
3508	Coyston George	Pte.	W/Sv	3344	Ogden William	Pte.	W/Sl
2480	Daley James	Pte.	W/D	2361	Osborne James	Pte.	W/Sv
1963	Daniels David	Pte.	W/Sv	3357	Overfield George	Pte.	W/Sv
3346	Davis Samuel	Pte.	W/Sl	4039	Palmer William	Pte.	W/Sv
2318	Devlin James	Pte.	W/Sl	1617	Pearson William	Pte.	W/Sl
3847	Donovan Michael	Pte.	W/Sv	3080	Perkins Joseph	Pte.	W/Sv
2944	Doyle James	Pte.	W/Sl	3414	Powell Michael	Pte.	W/D
1335	Duffy James	Pte.	W/D	2414	Roach John	Pte.	W/Sv
3761	Duffy Thomas	Pte.	W/Sv	3137	Robinson Joseph	Pte.	W/Sv
3824	Egan Patrick	Pte.	W/D	4054	Scholes Joseph	Pte.	W/Sv
3514	Elliott Thomas	Pte.	W/Sv	2403	Simpson John	Pte.	W/Sl
2981	Essey John	Pte.	W/Sv	3090	Simpson Patrick	Pte.	W/Sv
3423	Escott John	Pte.	W/Sv	3731	Slavin James	Pte.	W/D
2504	Evers James	Pte.	W/Sl	3960	Smyth Thomas	Pte.	W/Sl
4026	Flanagan Patrick	Pte.	W/Sv	3616	Snape William	Pte.	W/Sl
3865	Flavell James	Pte.	W/Sl	3668	Somerwood John	Pte.	W/D
3512	Flynn Patrick	Pte.	W/Sl	3175	Standrings Alexander	Pte.	W/Sv
3682	Foley John	Pte.	W/D	2501	Stonan Denis	Pte.	W/Sv
3073	Foster Henry	Pte.	W/Sv	3607	Stray William	Pte.	W/Sl
2091	Gates Charles	Pte.	W/D	3841	Sullivan David	Pte.	W/Sl
3306	Gill William	Pte.	W/Sl	3786	Toohill Hugh	Pte.	W/Sl
3220	Gladstone John	Pte.	W/D	4115	Tribet Francis	Pte.	W/Sv
3993	Goodliffe Charles	Pte.	W/Sv	2037	Trignor Terence	Pte.	W/Sl
4017	Gorman Thomas	Pte.	W/Sv	2458	Trotter Robert	Pte.	W/Sv
4097	Gouge J.	Pte.	W/D	2076	Upperton Anthony	Pte.	W/Sl
3497	Graham John	Pte.	W/Sl	3815	Ward James	Pte.	W/Sv
2769	Grant John	Pte.	W/D	3013	Wareham Alfred	Pte.	W/Sv
3528	Green Thomas	Pte.	W/D	1792	Walker John	Pte.	W/Sv
2530	Hacop William	Pte.	W/Sv	3554	Walmsley William	Pte.	W/Sl
3794	Haffy Robert	Pte.	W/D	2907	Wheeldon John	Pte.	W/Sl
3995	Hailey William	Pte.	W/D	2920	Whelan Thomas	Pte.	W/Sv
3408	Hall Richard	Pte.	W/D	4058	Whittaker Francis	Pte.	W/Sv
2479	Hall Thomas	Pte.	W/D	3604	Wildgoose William	Pte.	W/Sv
3612	Hanley George	Pte.	W/Sl	3490	Willcox James	Pte.	W/Sv
1145	Hanvey Patrick	Pte.	W/D	3937	Williamson David	Pte.	W/Sv

NOTES

The First Attack on the Redan

34th REGIMENT OF FOOT

NO.	NAME	RANK	CASUALTY	NO.	NAME	RANK	CASUALTY
3119	Williamson William	Pte.	W/D	3298	Wood John	Pte.	W/Sl
3324	Wilson Michael	Pte.	W/D				

38th REGIMENT OF FOOT

NO.	NAME	RANK	CASUALTY	NO.	NAME	RANK	CASUALTY
	Davies O. G. S.	Lieut.	Killed	1706	Cassidy Patrick	Pte.	W/Sv
2276	Baugh George	Sergt.	Killed	3381	Champion Alfred	Pte.	W/Sv
2007	Slater Edward	Sergt.	Killed	3420	Chandler Joseph	Pte.	W/Sv
3180	Goodman Henry	Corpl.	Killed	3136	Chettle William	Pte.	W/Sv
3050	Argue Samuel	L/Cpl.	Killed	3726	Clarke Henry	Pte.	Missing
2414	Bruce William	L/Cpl.	Killed	3541	Cleating Martin	Pte.	W/Sv
2471	Connor Charles	L/Cpl.	Killed	3844	Coady Martin	Pte.	W/Sv
3674	Grace John	L/Cpl.	Killed	4116	Coglin George	Pte.	W/Sv
3841	Bradley Charles	Pte.	Killed	3033	Collins James	Pte.	W/Sl
2399	Corrigan Thomas	Pte.	Killed	3607	Connolly Thomas	Pte.	Missing
1629	Farrett Patrick (Farrell)	Pte.	Killed	3561	Connors John	Pte.	W/Sv
				2145	Cox John	Pte.	W/Sl
1961	Gardner Samuel	Pte.	Killed	2596	Creagan William	Pte.	W/Sv
2067	Gratton John	Pte.	Killed	2858	Cullam Charles	Pte.	W/Sv
3544	Jones David	Pte.	Killed	3145	Cully Samuel	Pte.	W/Sl
3470	O'Brien Patrick	Pte.	Killed	3952	Cusick Thomas	Pte.	W/Sv
3356	Reed George	Pte.	Killed	3847	Dalton Peter	Pte.	Missing
1679	Rowley Samuel	Pte.	Killed	1444	Deevy James	Pte.	W/Sv
2641	Woods James	Pte.	Killed	3849	Denison Arthur	Pte.	W/Sv
	Lowth J. J.	Lieut/Col.	W/Sv	2989	Desmond Timothy	Pte.	W/Sv
	Addington Hon. C.	Capt.	W/Sv	3563	Dickson William	Pte.	W/Sv
	Daniel Ludford H.	Capt.	W/Sv	2850	Dignan John	Pte.	W/Sv
	Feilden H. B.	Lieut.	W/Sv	3074	Dix John	Pte.	W/Sv
	French J. B.	Lieut.	W/Sv	3733	Donington Charles	Pte.	W/Sv
981	Adams John	Col/Sgt.	W/Sl	2953	Dooley John	Pte.	W/D
2023	Jarrett James	Col/Sgt.	W/Sv	3408	Dorsey Charles	Pte.	W/Sv
985	Benett John	Pay/Sgt.	W/Sv	3017	Duff William	Pte.	W/Sv
2703	Clarke Andrew	Sergt.	W/Sl	3767	Dyer Thomas	Pte.	W/Sv
2599	Dunn William	Sergt.	W/D	1890	Emery John	Pte.	W/Sl
3260	McKenzie George	Sergt.	W/Sl	1737	Finn William	Pte.	Missing
4267	Stapleton William	Sergt.	W/Sl	3056	Flaherty Patrick	Pte.	W/Sl
1313	Window Samuel	Sergt.	W/Sv	4277	Fleckney William	Pte.	W/Sv
2133	Balderson William	Corpl.	W/Sl	3853	Geraghty John	Pte.	W/D
3218	Beryman John	Corpl.	W/Sv	2330	Gorman Patrick	Pte.	W/Sl
3640	Jeans William	Corpl.	W/D	4179	Halloran James	Pte.	W/Sv
3048	Prichard John	Corpl.	W/Sv	3676	Hine Richard	Pte.	W/Sv
3335	Rowe James	Corpl.	W/Sv	4235	Hodson Henry	Pte.	W/Sl
1868	Williams Thomas	Corpl.	W/Sv	2827	Hynes John	Pte.	W/Sl
3291	Bibby William	L/Cpl.	W/Sv	3711	Jenkins Daniel	Pte.	W/Sv
1080	Curran Edward	L/Cpl.	W/Sv	3921	Jones William	Pte.	W/Sv
3462	Allen James	Pte.	W/Sv	4299	Kedus Levi	Pte.	W/Sv
1092	Armstrong John	Pte.	W/Sv	3680	Keith Donald	Pte.	W/Sv
4211	Ball John	Pte.	W/Sl	3506	Kieffe John	Pte.	W/Sv
3838	Bandon William	Pte.	W/Sv	3904	King Henry	Pte.	W/Sv
4271	Barker Joseph	Pte.	W/Sv	2068	Kirwan Patrick	Pte.	W/Sl
4095	Batson William	Pte.	W/Sv	2524	Lane Nicholas	Pte.	W/Sv
1535	Bigham Alexander	Pte.	W/Sv	3103	Leonard Thomas	Pte.	W/Sv
2571	Bonnor Thomas	Pte.	W/D	3658	Long Edward	Pte.	W/Sv
4084	Bradley John	Pte.	W/Sv	2491	Lynch James	Pte.	W/Sl
3140	Brafford Joseph	Pte.	W/Sl	3238	McGartland Hugh	Pte.	W/Sv
3362	Brash John	Pte.	W/Sv	3817	McMahon James	Pte.	W/Sv
3497	Burke William	Pte.	W/Sv	3479	McNaulty Peter	Pte.	W/Sv
3498	Burns Jeremiah	Pte.	W/Sl	2882	McNeice William	Pte.	W/Sv
3706	Byrne Edward	Pte.	W/Sv	3866	McVeigh John	Pte.	W/Sv
3464	Campbell David	Pte.	W/Sv	3737	Magan Owen	Pte.	W/Sv
4092	Casey Thomas	Pte.	W/Sv	3510	Maguire Patrick	Pte.	W/Sv

NOTES

The First Attack on the Redan

38th REGIMENT OF FOOT

NO.	NAME	RANK	CASUALTY	NO.	NAME	RANK	CASUALTY
3755	Mead Michael	Pte.	W/Sv	3717	Shea James	Pte.	W/Sv
2920	Miller William	Pte.	W/Sv	2874	Sheeran Joseph	Pte.	W/Sv
3653	Milner David	Pte.	W/Sl	3657	Stapleton John	Pte.	W/Sv
3747	Mitchell Thomas	Pte.	W/Sv	2625	Stephenson James	Pte.	W/Sv
3869	Moore William	Pte.	W/D	3185	Stokely William	Pte.	W/Sv
3586	Newton George	Pte.	W/Sl	3983	Taggart Michael	Pte.	W/Sv
4303	Newton Isaac	Pte.	W/Sl	3437	Taylor George	Pte.	W/Sv
2144	Newell Benjamin	Pte.	W/Sv	1844	Torrington David	Pte.	W/Sl
3353	O'Callaghan Roderick	Pte.	W/Sv	4291	Travers David	Pte.	W/Sl
3158	O'Neil John	Pte.	W/Sv	2434	Tyrrell Arthur	Pte.	W/Sv
4011	Ostler Henry	Pte.	W/Sv	3879	Tyrrell Terence	Pte.	W/Sv
3685	Parchley William	Pte.	W/Sv	2687	Wall Patrick	Pte.	W/Sv
4100	Pearce George	Pte.	W/Sv	2803	Walsh Thomas	Pte.	W/Sv
3803	Peters Michael	Pte.	W/Sv	3444	Ward Alfred	Pte.	W/Sv
2944	Pinner John	Pte.	W/Sv	4208	Webster Thomas	Pte.	W/Sv
2333	Reilly Patrick	Pte.	W/Sv	3825	White Patrick	Pte.	W/Sv
2535	Rush William	Pte.	W/Sv	1929	Wright John	Pte.	W/Sv
1510	Scott John	Pte.	Missing	3692	Yates Samuel	Pte.	W/Sv
2541	Shannon Ephraim	Pte.	W/Sl				

39th REGIMENT OF FOOT

NO.	NAME	RANK	CASUALTY
3381	Pye Prince	Sergt.	W/Sl

41st REGIMENT OF FOOT

NO.	NAME	RANK	CASUALTY	NO.	NAME	RANK	CASUALTY
2992	Eddy Owen	Pte.	Killed	2515	Driscoll Timothy	Pte.	W/Sv
3450	Greig John	Pte.	Killed	2582	Hartnady Patrick	Pte.	W/Sl
	Goodwyn J. E.	Lieut/Col.	W/Sl	1772	Higgins William	Pte.	W/Sl
1605	Whitton Joseph	Sergt.	W/Sv	2097	Lewis William	Pte.	W/Sl
3029	Armsby George	Pte.	W/Sl	3292	Murphy Michael	Pte.	W/Sl
3454	Brennan James	Pte.	W/Sv	1808	Rigsby William	Pte.	W/Sl
3042	Byrne Edward	Pte.	W/Sv	3397	Ryan James	Pte.	W/Sv
3532	Collins Edward	Pte.	W/Sl	2750	Thomas John	Pte.	W/Sl

42nd REGIMENT OF FOOT

NO.	NAME	RANK	CASUALTY	NO.	NAME	RANK	CASUALTY
2737	Carr Hugh	Pte.	Killed	3057	Coull Andrew	Pte.	W/Sv
1303	Lowrie Alexander	Pte.	Killed	2610	Crone James	Pte.	W/Sl
3766	Dunsmore Robert	Corpl.	W/Sl	3360	Duncan John	Pte.	W/Sl
3014	Blanny George	Pte.	W/Sl	3098	Hadley Thomas	Pte.	W/Sl
3097	Brooks William	Pte.	W/Sl	3191	McEnnis Thomas	Pte.	W/Sl
3217	Cameron James	Pte.	W/Sv	2312	Williamson John	Pte.	W/Sl
3307	Campbell William	Pte.	W/D				

44th REGIMENT OF FOOT

NO.	NAME	RANK	CASUALTY	NO.	NAME	RANK	CASUALTY
	Agar Hon. C.	Capt.	Killed	2894	Bradley John	Pte.	Killed
	Caulfield F. W.	Capt.	Killed	2655	Browne John	Pte.	Killed
	Fenwick Bowes	Capt.	Killed	3491	Darby James	Pte.	Killed
3030	Bruce Robert	Corpl.	Killed	2754	Digby John	Pte.	Killed
3404	Smith Joseph	Drummer	Killed	3766	Gleeson George	Pte.	Killed
3391	Barns William	Pte.	Killed	3083	Knox John	Pte.	Killed

NOTES

The First Attack on the Redan

44th REGIMENT OF FOOT

NO.	NAME	RANK	CASUALTY	NO.	NAME	RANK	CASUALTY
3940	Leary Jeremiah	Pte.	Killed	3930	Foley Patrick	Pte.	W/Sl
4123	Sharpe Alexander	Pte.	Killed	2592	Ford Benjamin	Pte.	Missing
3815	Smith William	Pte.	Killed	3762	Gurrier George	Pte.	W/Sv
4048	Styles William	Pte.	Killed	3933	Hamilton John	Pte.	W/Sv
3228	Traynor John	Pte.	Killed	3687	Hawks Henry	Pte.	W/Sl
4017	Wilinshurst William	Pte.	Killed	3934	Haywood James	Pte.	W/Sv
3263	Wilson James	Pte.	Killed	4166	Hazell George	Pte.	W/Sl
	Spencer Hon. A. A.	Colonel	W/Sl	3255	Henry James	Pte.	W/Sl
	Mansfield W. H.	Capt.	W/D	3784	Hickey James	Pte.	W/Sv
	Howarth T. O.	Lieut.	W/Sv	4181	Hill John	Pte.	W/Sl
	Logan J.	Lieut.	W/Sv	3644	Hodge Thomas	Pte.	W/Sl
2550	Huntington Henry	Col/Sgt.	W/Sv	3874	Hogan Stephen	Pte.	W/Sl
3397	Cain James	Sergt.	W/Sl	3748	Hoorodd Joseph	Pte.	W/Sl
4048	Collins David	Sergt.	W/Sv	4025	Hughes Bernard	Pte.	W/Sv
2577	Dunne John	Sergt.	W/Sv	3829	Jaffrey James	Pte.	W/Sl
3062	Galloway Robert	Sergt.	W/D	3904	Johnstone John	Pte.	W/Sl
2264	Gomersall John	Sergt.	W/Sv	3738	Kebbe John	Pte.	Missing
2634	Kelly Oscar	Sergt.	W/Sv	3610	Keeley Daniel	Pte.	W/Sv
2310	McLean James	Sergt.	W/D	3519	Kelby James	Pte.	W/Sl
2973	Rolstone William	Sergt.	W/Sv	2650	Kiddell James	Pte.	W/D
2809	Walsh David	Sergt.	W/Sl	3558	Kirk Robert	Pte.	W/D
3059	Anderson Thomas	Corpl.	W/Sv	3280	McCaffrey Michael	Pte.	W/Sl
2088	Brophy Martin	Corpl.	W/Sl	2644	McCarthy Michael	Pte.	W/Sl
2903	Friend Abraham	Corpl.	W/Sv	3076	McCauley John	Pte.	W/Sv
2612	Friend James	Corpl.	W/Sv	4018	McElroy Reid	Pte.	W/Sl
3695	Murray Robert	Corpl.	W/Sl	4054	McGee Everard	Pte.	W/Sv
3426	Oxley James	Corpl.	W/Sl	3298	McInnis David	Pte.	W/Sl
3872	Simm Wright	Corpl.	W/Sv	2835	Martin James	Pte.	W/Sv
3707	Durr Thomas	Drummer	W/Sv	1821	Massey William	Pte.	W/Sl
2711	Jackson David	Drummer	W/Sv	3608	Meads James	Pte.	W/Sl
3892	Agar John	Pte.	W/Sl	3636	Moore John	Pte.	W/Sl
3216	Alexander James	Pte.	W/Sl	3470	Murphy Jeremiah	Pte.	W/D
3979	Ashton Thomas	Pte.	W/Sl	3588	Mullen Patrick	Pte.	W/D
4043	Ayres Jeremiah	Pte.	Missing	3378	Mylon John	Pte.	W/Sl
3430	Barrett William	Pte.	W/Sl	4036	Nelson John	Pte.	W/Sl
2524	Bath Patrick	Pte.	W/Sl	3407	Newton William	Pte.	W/Sl
4220	Beck Alexander	Pte.	W/Sv	3137	O'Briens James	Pte.	W/Sv
4102	Berriman Thomas	Pte.	W/Sv	3043	Patterson James	Pte.	W/Sl
4062	Berry John	Pte.	W/Sl	2762	Peak Charles	Pte.	W/Sv
3770	Bourke James	Pte.	W/Sv	3948	Perkins Joseph	Pte.	W/Sv
3894	Blaney John	Pte.	Missing	2453	Reilly Martin	Pte.	W/Sv
3785	Brady James	Pte.	W/Sv	2626	Richmond John	Pte.	W/Sl
3957	Brisnahan John	Pte.	W/Sv	2076	Robert Thomas	Pte.	W/D
3789	Bryan Peter	Pte.	W/Sv	3509	Rowley William	Pte.	W/Sl
2761	Burgess George F.	Pte.	W/Sl	1515	Samples James	Pte.	W/Sl
4213	Byford Edward	Pte.	Missing	3465	Scannell Michael	Pte.	W/Sv
3918	Callaghan John	Pte.	W/Sl	1818	Sculby Daniel	Pte.	W/Sv
3900	Campbell John	Pte.	W/Sv	3669	Seeley Walter	Pte.	W/Sv
4051	Carson James	Pte.	W/Sl	4132	Sergeant Joseph	Pte.	Missing
3920	Clancy Patrick	Pte.	W/Sl	3948	Shea John	Pte.	W/Sl
3637	Clarke Samuel	Pte.	W/D	3951	Shea Timothy	Pte.	W/Sv
2777	Coalman William	Pte.	W/Sl	3953	Sheean Michael	Pte.	W/Sv
3142	Conkey Hugh	Pte.	W/Sv	3617	Smith James	Pte.	W/Sv
2450	Crawford Alexander	Pte.	W/Sv	4066	Smith Patrick	Pte.	W/Sv
4106	Crawshaw Josiah	Pte.	Missing	3634	Stapleton William	Pte.	W/Sl
2696	Cullen William	Pte.	W/Sl	3134	Steele William	Pte.	W/Sl
2670	Curry John	Pte.	W/D	4230	Thomas James	Pte.	W/Sl
3265	Dougherty Andrew	Pte.	W/Sl	3228	Traynor John	Pte.	W/Sl
3847	Duggan John	Pte.	W/Sv	3898	Weaver Richard	Pte.	W/Sv
3837	Fadden Peter	Pte.	W/Sv	3835	Weston William	Pte.	W/Sl
3061	Finlay John	Pte.	W/Sv	2954	White James	Pte.	W/Sl
3808	Finn Michael	Pte.	W/Sv	3756	Williams George	Pte.	W/Sv
3157	Flattery Thomas	Pte.	W/Sv				

NOTES

The First Attack on the Redan

47th REGIMENT OF FOOT

NO.	NAME	RANK	CASUALTY	NO.	NAME	RANK	CASUALTY
2623	McGuire Michael	Corpl.	W/Sv	2011	McMillin Nathaniel	Pte.	W/Sv
3095	Gavan James	Pte.	W/Sv	1475	Shurrocks James	Pte.	W/D
2811	McMahon John	Pte.	W/Sl				

49th REGIMENT OF FOOT

NO.	NAME	RANK	CASUALTY	NO.	NAME	RANK	CASUALTY
3219	Donovan John	Pte.	Killed	2999	Kennen Patrick	Pte.	W/Sl
3230	Fortune William	Pte.	Killed	3297	Morrison Owen	Pte.	W/Sv

50th REGIMENT OF FOOT

NO.	NAME	RANK	CASUALTY	NO.	NAME	RANK	CASUALTY
4043	Perry William	Pte.	Killed	3929	Kearns Peter	Pte.	W/Sv
2809	Reghan James	Pte.	Killed	3682	Ryan James	Pte.	W/Sv
3329	Bennett Charles	Pte.	W/Sl	2610	Senior Patrick	Pte.	W/M

55th REGIMENT OF FOOT

NO.	NAME	RANK	CASUALTY	NO.	NAME	RANK	CASUALTY
2031	Trimmings James	Sergt.	W/Sv	3358	Sheedy Thomas	Pte.	W/Sl
3370	Love James	Pte.	W/Sl	2925	Tate Robert	Pte.	W/Sl
2947	Meelican Connor	Pte.	W/Sl	2198	Whelan Robert	Pte.	W/Sl
3472	Sandford Frederick	Pte.	W/Sl				

57th REGIMENT OF FOOT

NO.	NAME	RANK	CASUALTY	NO.	NAME	RANK	CASUALTY
	Shadforth Thomas	Lt/Col.	Killed		Slade A. F. A.	Lieut.	W/Sv
	Ashwin J. C.	Lieut.	Killed		Venables C.	Lieut.	W/Sv
1961	Fallon Patrick	Col/Sgt.	Killed	2121	Collins Richard	Col/Sgt	W/Sl
2985	Gardiner Stewart	Sergt.	Killed	1523	Mulloy John	Col/Sgt.	W/D
2569	Greening William	Sergt.	Killed	1745	Boyd John	Sergt.	W/Sv
1689	James John	Sergt.	Killed	1902	Capel Thomas	Sergt.	W/Sv
1573	Lewis Robert	Sergt.	Killed	2492	Connors Patrick	Sergt.	W/Sv
1410	Mullin John	Sergt.	Killed	2219	Flanagan John	Sergt.	W/Sv
1661	Macklin James	Corpl.	Killed	2101	Griffith William	Sergt.	W/Sv
3027	Broderick Andrew	Pte.	Killed	1592	Hamilton Robert	Sergt.	W/Sv
839	Carney James	Pte.	Killed	2170	Morgans John	Sergt.	W/Sv
2232	Corrigan Richard	Pte.	Killed	1222	Williams James	Sergt.	W/Sv
2414	Dolan James	Pte.	Killed	2124	Cahill Patrick	Corpl.	W/Sv
1824	Farrell Edward	Pte.	Killed	1342	Dawson Robert	Corpl.	W/Sv
3156	Ferguson Joseph	Pte.	Killed	3080	Gostling Richard	Corpl.	W/Sv
3251	Fraser Robert	Pte.	Killed	2106	Geogan John	Corpl.	W/Sv
2610	Hayes Jeremiah	Pte.	Killed	1677	Huggard Thomas	Corpl.	W/Sv
1833	Johnson William	Pte.	Killed	3077	Hughes William	Corpl.	W/Sv
2221	McAnnally Charles	Pte.	Killed	2659	Jess Thomas	Corpl.	W/Sv
2550	Manning Patrick	Pte.	Killed	1865	McEnter John	Corpl.	W/Sv
2297	Stevens Alfred	Pte.	Killed	2416	Shea John	Corpl.	W/Sv
2727	Twist Matthew	Pte.	Killed	2026	Austin Goddard	Pte.	W/Sv
	Earle A. M.	Capt.& Br/Mjr.	W/Sv	2728	Barrett John	Pte.	W/Sv
				3249	Beasley James	Pte.	W/Sv
	Lea F. P.	Capt.	W/Sv	3121	Blackwell George	Pte.	W/Sv
	Norman G. H.	Capt.	W/Sv	2903	Busfield Benjamin	Pte.	W/Sv
	StClair C. W.	Capt.	W/Sv	1951	Butler John	Pte.	W/Sl

NOTES

The First Attack on the Redan
57th REGIMENT OF FOOT

NO.	NAME	RANK	CASUALTY	NO.	NAME	RANK	CASUALTY
1892	Byrne John	Pte.	W/Sl	3233	McNevin William	Pte.	W/Sv
3236	Byron John	Pte.	W/Sv	2283	Magee John	Pte.	W/Sv
1819	Casey John	Pte.	W/D	2502	Maher Patrick	Pte.	W/Sv
2716	Connor Timothy	Pte.	W/Sv	3223	Mateer Joseph	Pte.	W/Sv
—	Delaney Patrick	Pte.	W/Sv	2648	Moriarty John	Pte.	W/Sv
2864	Dempsey John	Pte.	W/Sv	2505	Muraine John	Pte.	W/Sv
3142	Donnolly Patrick	Pte.	W/Sv	2512	Murphy John	Pte.	W/Sv
2597	Downey Dennis	Pte.	W/Sv	2683	Murphy Michael	Pte.	W/Sv
2408	Ellis Forth	Pte.	W/Sv	2471	Murphy Michael	Pte.	W/Sv
2793	Fain Timothy	Pte.	W/Sv	2501	Murray John	Pte.	W/Sv
2841	Fitzpatrick Michael	Pte.	W/Sv	2324	Nicholls Frederick	Pte.	W/Sv
2738	Gahan John	Pte.	W/Sv	2264	Nicholls John	Pte.	W/Sv
2109	Greaney Thomas	Pte.	W/Sl	2465	Noary William	Pte.	W/Sl
2463	Green Richard	Pte.	W/Sv	1683	O'Donnell Luke	Pte.	W/Sv
2376	Green Simeon	Pte.	W/Sv	2995	O'Neil Patrick	Pte.	W/Sv
2304	Griffith John	Pte.	W/D	2296	Pasfield John	Pte.	W/Sv
2789	Hayes John	Pte.	W/Sv	2974	Purcell John	Pte.	W/Sv
2527	Hegarty Cornelius	Pte.	W/Sv	2670	Rahilly Daniel	Pte.	W/Sl
2003	Holliday William	Pte.	W/Sv	2476	Rowe James	Pte.	W/Sv
2603	Huggill George	Pte.	W/Sv	2472	Rowe Richard	Pte.	W/Sv
3227	Inglis James	Pte.	W/Sv	2412	Ryan Patrick	Pte.	W/Sv
2353	Jones John	Pte.	W/Sv	—	Shannon Robert	Pte.	W/Sv
1940	Kinnerney William	Pte.	W/Sv	2779	Sheehan John	Pte.	W/Sv
2731	Long John	Pte.	W/Sv	2909	Spinks James	Pte.	W/Sv
2244	McCaffery Felix	Pte.	W/Sv	2697	Sullivan James	Pte.	W/Sv
2663	McCarley John	Pte.	W/Sv	2726	Sullivan Patrick	Pte.	W/Sv
1976	McCruise Charles	Pte.	W/Sv	2778	Thomas George	Pte.	W/Sl
3244	McDonald Andrew	Pte.	W/Sv	893	Ward Maurice	Pte.	W/Sv
3089	McFarlane Robert	Pte.	W/Sv	2736	Washington William	Pte.	W/Sl
2500	McGee John	Pte.	W/Sv	3161	Watson Matthew	Pte.	W/Sv
1738	McKenna Patrick	Pte.	W/Sv	2871	Woods John	Pte.	W/Sv

63rd REGIMENT OF FOOT

NO.	NAME	RANK	CASUALTY
2765	Madden John	Pte.	W/Sl

72nd REGIMENT OF FOOT

NO.	NAME	RANK	CASUALTY	NO.	NAME	RANK	CASUALTY
2963	Bell John	Pte.	W/D	960	McDonald John	Pte.	W/Sv
3136	Hall William	Pte.	W/Sl				

77th REGIMENT OF FOOT

NO.	NAME	RANK	CASUALTY	NO.	NAME	RANK	CASUALTY
3320	Harrington Thomas	Pte.	Killed	2679	Cooper John	Pte.	W/Sv
3507	Wolbridge Henry	Pte.	Killed	3230	McMullen Joseph	Pte.	W/Sl
2010	Housden Charles	Col/Sgt.	W/Sl	3299	Magee Henry	Pte.	W/Sl
3157	Cochrane Thomas	Pte.	W/D	1511	Rudling George	Pte.	W/Sv

88th REGIMENT OF FOOT

NO.	NAME	RANK	CASUALTY	NO.	NAME	RANK	CASUALTY
1367	Dempsey John	Pte.	Killed	1651	Farrell James	Pte.	W/Sl
	Browne G. R.	Capt.	W/D	2950	Kelliher Denis	Pte.	W/D
1283	Conroy Patrick	Pte.	W/D				

NOTES

The First Attack on the Redan

89th REGIMENT OF FOOT

NO.	NAME	RANK	CASUALTY
3152	Byron Patrick	Pte.	W/Sv

90th REGIMENT OF FOOT

NO.	NAME	RANK	CASUALTY	NO.	NAME	RANK	CASUALTY
3779	Dunham Thomas	Pte.	W/Sl	2894	Larner Robert	Pte.	W/Sv

93rd REGIMENT OF FOOT

NO.	NAME	RANK	CASUALTY	NO.	NAME	RANK	CASUALTY
2964	Dugind William	Pte.	W/Sl	2234	McKinnon John	Pte.	W/Sl
3290	Goff Andrew	Pte.	W/Sl	2596	Munro Duncan	Pte.	W/Sv
3373	McKenzie Findlay	Pte.	W/Sv	3292	Murdoch John	Pte.	W/Sl

97th REGIMENT OF FOOT

NO.	NAME	RANK	CASUALTY	NO.	NAME	RANK	CASUALTY
3119	Carthy Francis	Pte.	W/Sv	3441	Goolden Maurice	Pte.	W/Sl
2169	Dodd Thomas	Pte.	W/Sl	2540	Johns William	Pte.	W/Sl

1st BATTALION RIFLE BRIGADE

NO.	NAME	RANK	CASUALTY	NO.	NAME	RANK	CASUALTY
2086	Jerrow George	Sergt.	Killed	3989	Couch Thomas Deller	Pte.	Missing
3272	McEwan John	Corpl.	Killed	4537	Finch Wm. Dean	Pte.	W/Sv
3985	Cain Michael	Pte.	Killed	4120	Harrison Thomas	Pte.	W/Sv
4400	Flanery John	Pte.	Killed	2762	Jenkins Richard	Pte.	W/Sl
2859	Lines George	Pte.	Killed	3297	Lafferty Peter	Pte.	W/Sl
3971	Spreadborough Chas.	Pte.	Killed	4323	Oliver George	Pte.	W/Sv
	Boileau C. A. P.	Lieut.	W/Sv	4377	Parker George	Pte.	W/Sv
3933	Bright David	Pte.	W/Sl	1707	Robinson William	Pte.	W/Sv
3807	Browne William	Pte.	W/Sl	2952	Scott Henry	Pte.	W/Sl
3714	Collins Timothy	Pte.	W/Sl	3717	Russell Joseph	Pte.	W/Sl

2nd BATTALION RIFLE BRIGADE

NO.	NAME	RANK	CASUALTY	NO.	NAME	RANK	CASUALTY
	Forman E. F.	Capt.	Killed	3696	Lewis Patrick	Pte.	Killed
3524	Bridgland R.	Sergt.	Killed	4212	McPherson George	Pte.	Killed
3241	Murch H.	Sergt.	Killed	3973	Marriott William	Pte.	Killed
3088	Arnold F.	Pte.	Killed	3031	Murray James	Pte.	Killed
1578	Baker James	Pte.	Killed	3305	New Joseph	Pte.	Killed
3827	Barr William	Pte.	Killed	3587	Taylor Charles	Pte.	Killed
3354	Carr Edward	Pte.	Killed	4231	Thompson Joseph	Pte.	Killed
1193	Collins G.	Pte.	Killed	1639	Williams James	Pte.	Killed
4138	Corlis Thomas	Pte.	Killed		Blackett E.	Capt.	W/D
3876	Davis George	Pte.	Killed		Fremantle —	Lieut.	W/Sv
3844	Doherty A.	Pte.	Killed		Knox J. S.	Lieut.	W/D
2551	Duthie W.	Pte.	Killed	3181	Beech Richard	Sergt.	W/Sv
4184	Elliott John	Pte.	Killed	2628	Brambleby John	Sergt.	W/Sv
3293	Gray Charles	Pte.	Killed	3058	Lee James	Sergt.	W/Sl
3964	Howlett James	Pte.	Killed	1498	Newham John	Sergt.	W/Sl
4279	Jones Thomas	Pte.	Killed	2235	Barford F.	Corpl.	W/Sl

NOTES

The First Attack on the Redan

2nd BATTALION RIFLE BRIGADE

NO.	NAME	RANK	CASUALTY	NO.	NAME	RANK	CASUALTY
2830	Bennett Thomas	Corpl.	W/Sl	3537	King Henry	Pte.	W/Sv
1902	Dawson Thomas	Corpl.	W/Sv	3754	King Samuel	Pte.	W/Sv
2324	Morris John	Corpl.	W/Sl	3694	King Thomas	Pte.	W/Sv
3067	Redman John	Corpl.	W/Sl	3543	Lenton David	Pte.	W/Sv
4188	Algar Samuel	Pte.	W/Sv	3617	McCracken Samuel	Pte.	W/D
2356	Atkins John	Pte.	W/Sv	3752	McDonough Joseph	Pte.	W/Sl
3655	Blanchard William	Pte.	W/Sl	1628	Madley Isaac	Pte.	W/Sv
3635	Bowen F.	Pte.	W/Sv	3381	Maybry John	Pte.	W/Sv
1979	Brown Richard	Pte.	W/Sl	4186	Mitchell Alexandr	Pte.	W/Sv
3134	Brown William	Pte.	W/D	2859	Mould George	Pte.	W/Sv
3382	Bryant John	Pte.	W/Sv	4299	Murray Brien	Pte.	W/Sv
3840	Campbell James	Pte.	W/Sv	4016	Nicholls William	Pte.	W/Sv
3741	Clerke William Bird	Pte.	W/Sv	3713	Nix William	Pte.	W/Sv
3667	Cody Edward	Pte.	W/Sl	2665	Nugent Joseph	Pte.	W/Sl
3609	Cooper Matthew	Pte.	W/Sl	1433	Ovey Thomas	Pte.	W/Sv
3848	Davis Edward	Pte.	W/Sv	3351	Padgham Henry	Pte.	W/Sl
4128	Dolan John	Pte.	W/Sl	3953	Pinches Thomas	Pte.	W/Sl
3668	Donnelly Hugh	Pte.	W/Sl	3583	Preston Edward	Pte.	W/Sl
4277	Dove John	Pte.	W/Sl	3249	Price Emanuel	Pte.	W/Sv
3005	Dowling James	Pte.	W/Sl	3968	Ratican Luke	Pte.	W/Sl
3671	East Thomas	Pte.	W/Sv	3853	Salter William	Pte.	W/Sl
2459	Eaton Benjamin	Pte.	W/Sl	4026	Sewell Samuel	Pte.	W/Sl
3934	Elliott James	Pte.	W/Sv	3393	Shakespeare John	Pte.	W/Sl
4187	English William	Pte.	W/D	4314	Smith William	Pte.	W/Sl
2661	Franklin George	Pte.	W/Sv	2786	Stevens Samuel	Pte.	W/Sl
2364	Gibbins John	Pte.	W/Sv	2253	Sutherland —	Pte.	W/Sl
4095	Golsby Charles	Pte.	W/Sl	4094	Thompson William	Pte.	W/Sv
1579	Goodwin James	Pte.	W/Sl	4017	Till George	Pte.	W/Sv
3682	Green Robert	Pte.	W/Sv	4293	Toal Edward	Pte.	W/Sl
2776	Greenwood Frederick	Pte.	W/D	2222	Todd William	Pte.	W/Sl
4362	Hadley John	Pte.	W/Sl	3485	Vince Thomas	Pte.	W/Sl
4159	Hewitt Joseph	Pte.	W/Sv	3065	Warren James	Pte.	W/Sl
4098	Hobden William	Pte.	W/Sl	3735	White Henry	Pte.	W/Sv
3868	Ingham James	Pte.	W/D	4140	Whitley Joseph	Pte.	W/Sl
1670	Jones Thomas	Pte.	W/Sl	4062	Wild Thomas	Pte.	W/Sv
2876	Jordan Thomas	Pte.	W/Sv	3614	Winson Joseph	Pte.	W/Sv
2806	Kerr James	Pte.	W/Sl				

NOTES

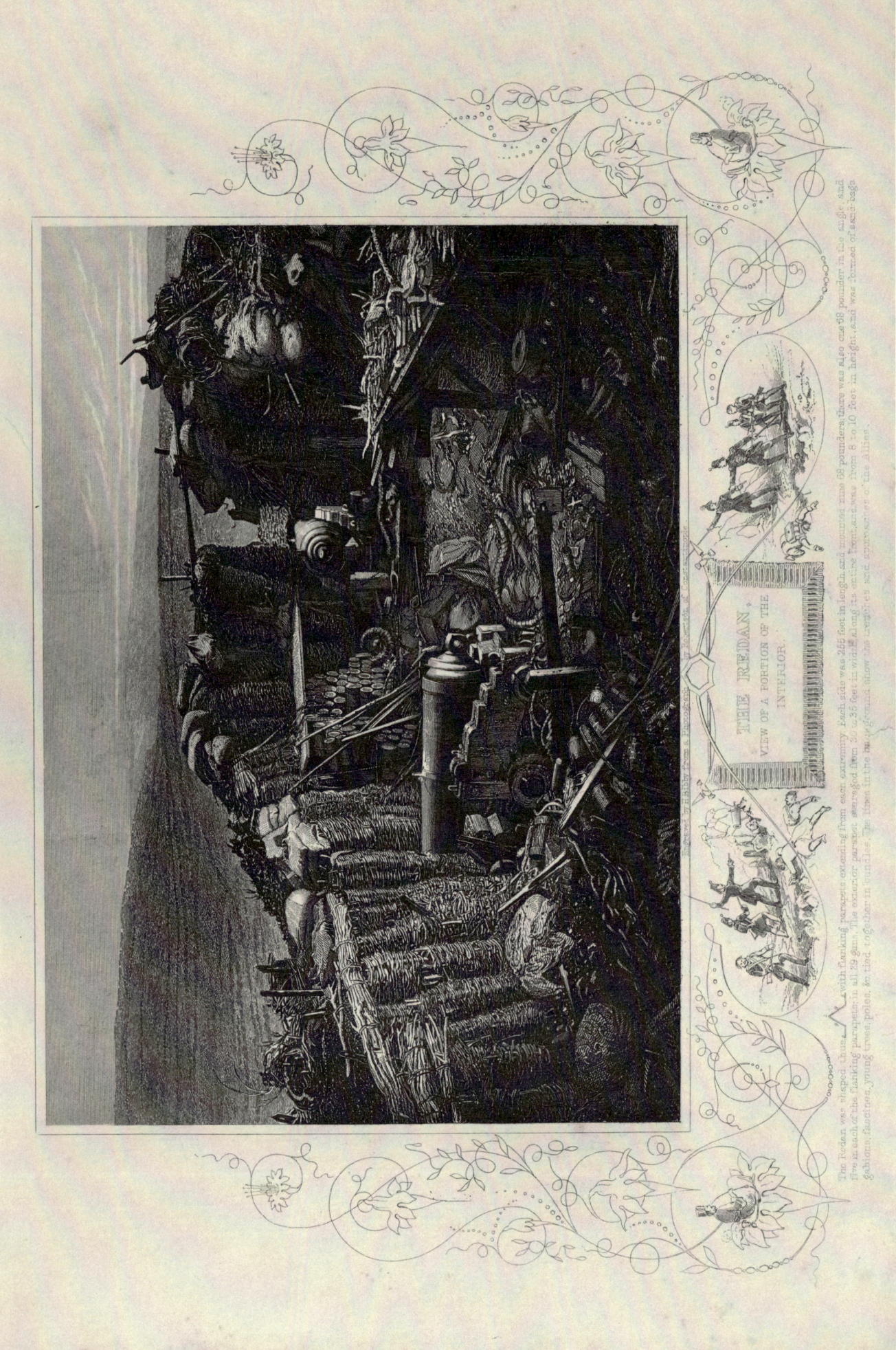

THE REDAN.
VIEW OF A PORTION OF THE INTERIOR.

The Redan was shaped thus ∧, with flanking parapets extending from each extremity. Each side was 255 feet in length, and mounted nine 68 pounders in the angle, and five in each of the flanking parapets; in all 29 guns. The exterior parados averaged from 30 to 35 feet in width along its entire front; its was from 8 to 10 feet in height, and was formed of sand bags, gabions, fascines, young trees, poles, &c., tied together in bundles. The lines in the rear formed above the parapets were commanders of the Allies.

THE FINAL ATTACK ON THE REDAN

The following casualties occurred among the Officers, Non-Commissioned Officers and Men of the Army during the Final Attack on the Redan, 8th September, 1855.
Compiled from the London Gazette 25th September 1855.

ROYAL ARTILLERY

NO.	NAME	RANK	CASUALTY	NO.	NAME	RANK	CASUALTY
	Shaw Robert	Corpl.	Killed		Birch William	Gunner	W/Sv
	Davis Isaac	Gnr.&Drvr.	Killed		Bower John	Gunner	W/Sl
	Eastley George	Gnr.&Drvr.	Killed		Brachen John	Gunner	W/Sl
	Hepperson Edward	Gnr.&Drvr.	Killed		Browne Samson	Gunner	W/Sv
	Tanner Patrick	Gnr.&Drvr.	Killed		Campkin Samuel	Gunner	W/Sl
	Fitzroy A. C. L.	Capt.	D.O.W.		Carlin John	Gunner	W/Sl
	Champion R. H.	Lieut.	W/Sv		Cockshort John	Gunner	W/Sv
	Tyler C. J.	Lieut.	W/Sl		Frass William	Gunner	W/Sv
	Armstrong William	Col/Sgt.	W/Sl		Harrison James	Gunner	W/Sl
	Agnew Samuel	Sergt.	W/Sl		Holmes Francis	Gunner	W/Sv
	Newall John	Sergt.	W/Sv		Lee Frederick	Gunner	W/Sl
	McDonald William	Corpl.	W/Sl		Lee James	Gunner	W/Sv
	Adams Alexander	Bombr.	W/Sv		McKanis Henry	Gunner	W/Sl
	Cambridge Daniel	Bombr.	W/Sv		McMullen William	Gunner	W/Sv
	Chambers George	Bombr.	W/Sl		Martin Joseph	Gunner	W/Sv
	Montague John	Bombr.	W/Sl		Massie James	Gunner	W/Sv
	Allen John (1st)	Gunner	W/Sv		O'Brien John	Gunner	W/Sv
	Allis John	Gunner	W/Sl		Randall Richard	Gunner	W/Sl
	Baillie Thomas	Gunner	W/Sl		Robinson John	Gunner	W/Sv
	Beggs James	Gunner	W/Sv		Smith William	Gunner	W/Sv

2nd BATTALION 1st REGIMENT OF FOOT

NO.	NAME	RANK	CASUALTY	NO.	NAME	RANK	CASUALTY
2340	Arbour Thomas	Pte.	Killed	1997	Brown Frederick	Pte.	W/Sl
	Gillum W. J.	Capt.	W/D	2892	Buchanan John	Pte.	W/D
	Caton R. B.	Lieut.	W/Sv	3011	Bunning William	Pte.	W/Sl
	Plunkett Hon. T. O. W.	Lieut.	W/Sl	2630	Comasky Patrick	Pte.	W/Sl
	Williams R. L.	Lieut.	W/Sv	2637	Dorling Robert	Pte.	W/Sl
1399	Heale Emanuel	Sgt/Mjr.	W/Sl	3429	Doyle Martin	Pte.	W/Sl
2493	Shelton William	Corpl.	W/Sv	2553	Hill William	Pte.	W/Sl
2315	Balmer William	Pte.	W/Sl	3175	Jones Robert	Pte.	W/Sv
3037	Batterbee George	Pte.	W/Sl	1292	Layton William	Pte.	W/Sl

NOTES

The Final Attack on the Redan

2nd BATTALION 1st REGIMENT OF FOOT

NO.	NAME	RANK	CASUALTY	NO.	NAME	RANK	CASUALTY
3143	Lover Walter	Pte.	W/Sv	2519	O'Brien Thomas	Pte.	W/D
2157	McDonald Thomas	Pte.	W/Sv	2292	Robinson George	Pte.	W/Sl
2502	McEvoy Michael	Pte.	W/Sv	2958	Smith John	Pte.	W/Sv
3030	McLoughlin James	Pte.	W/Sv	3195	Webb Richard	Pte.	W/Sl
2686	Matthews John	Pte.	W/Sl				

3rd REGIMENT OF FOOT

NO.	NAME	RANK	CASUALTY	NO.	NAME	RANK	CASUALTY
2298	Gardner Charles	Col/Sgt.	Killed	3096	Baron John	Pte.	W/Sv
2103	Barber Henry	Sergt.	Killed	3221	Bates Jacob	Pte.	W/Sv
2650	Curtain Daniel	Sergt.	Killed	3103	Brackin Denis	Pte.	W/Sl
2803	Jackson Johnson	Sergt.	Killed	2955	Brown Cornelius	Pte.	W/Sv
1232	Slaughter Charles	Sergt.	Killed	2728	Burke Michael	Pte.	W/Sv
2219	Hall Robert	Corpl.	Killed	1546	Campbell Frederick	Pte.	W/Sv
2194	O'Brien —	Corpl.	Killed	3165	Campbell Joseph	Pte.	W/Sv
2580	Stewart James	Corpl.	Killed	2518	Campbell William	Pte.	W/Sl
3527	Alman James	Pte.	Killed	3318	Carter Thomas	Pte.	W/Sl
3250	Bellone Edward	Pte.	Killed	2908	Cebeher Peter	Pte.	W/Sl
2961	Burke James	Pte.	Killed	1302	Clarke James	Pte.	W/Sv
3425	Coulter William	Pte.	Killed	1980	Collins John	Pte.	W/Sl
2262	Dandon James	Pte	Killed	1968	Collins Thomas	Pte.	W/Sv
2367	Day Edmund	Pte.	Killed	2736	Connor John	Pte.	W/Sl
2764	Dillon Michael	Pte.	Killed	3088	Cross Richard	Pte.	W/Sl
3511	Flynn Patrick	Pte.	Killed	3167	Cullin John	Pte.	W/Sl
2714	Gallagher Dennis	Pte.	Killed	3268	Cunningham Michael	Pte.	W/Sl
3140	Gallagher Dennis	Pte.	Killed	2156	Davis John	Pte.	W/Sl
3474 } 2104 }	Green Joseph	Pte.	Killed	3495	Dugan William	Pte.	W/Sl
2510	Homer William	Pte.	Killed	3139 } 3151 }	Dunn W. Mm.	Pte.	W/Sl
3347	Kanassan John	Pte.	Killed	3503	Egan Denis	Pte.	W/Sl
2666	Liston John	Pte.	Killed	3131	Ennis Thomas	Pte.	W/Sl
2618	McCaullig Patrick	Pte.	Killed	2683	Fitzgibbon Thomas	Pte.	W/Sl
3067	Mark John	Pte.	Killed	1454	Flanagan Thomas	Pte.	W/Sl
3206	Morrice James	Pte.	Killed	2722	Ford Michael	Pte.	W/Sl
3159	Murphy John	Pte.	Killed	2883	Fox John	Pte.	W/Sv
2342	O'Hanlan James	Pte.	Killed	2568 } 2124 }	Franklyn James	Pte.	W/D
1712 } 1645 }	Redwin George	Pte.	Killed	3203	Garrett Richard	Pte.	W/Sv
2851	Ryan Martin	Pte.	Killed	1283	Garvey James	Pte.	W/D
2023	Wilsden Henry	Pte.	Killed	2926	Gatley James	Pte.	W/Sl
2984	Wilson Frederick	Pte.	Killed	2217	Goodridge Ernest	Pte.	W/Sl
	Maude F. F.	Major	W/D	2006	Haig John	Pte.	W/Sl
	Dunbar P. J.	Capt.	W/Sl	2286	Hall John	Pte.	W/Sv
	Hood C.	Capt.	W/Sl	1830	Hammons Cornelius	Pte.	W/Sl
	Cox T. A.	Lieut.	W/Sl	2159	Hanley Elijah	Pte.	W/Sl
	Letts A. B.	Ensign	W/D	3263	Hanna Robert	Pte.	W/Sl
	Peachey H.	Ensign	W/Sv	3145 } 3192 }	Haroer Michael	Pte.	W/D
1670	Bowman Frederick	Sergt.	W/Sl				
1113	Hart William	Sergt.	W/Sv	2881	Hibbard John	Pte.	W/Sl
2408	Hayes William	Sergt.	W/Sl	2053	Hill George	Pte.	W/Sv
1976	O'Shea James	Sergt.	W/Sv	3273	Hoyd Thomas	Pte.	W/Sl
1187	Roach Richard	Sergt.	W/Sl	3464	Hughes John	Pte.	W/Sl
1990	Taylor Henry	Sergt.	W/Sl	3054	Hunt John	Pte.	W/Sv
2838 } 1437 }	Wilson William	Sergt.	W/Sl	2753	Hyland James	Pte.	W/Sl
				3007	Ireland William	Pte.	W/Sv
2401	Ford John	Corpl.	W/Sv	2359	Jephson Joseph	Pte.	W/Sl
3040	Gormby Michael	Corpl.	W/Sl	1687	Keel Isaac	Pte.	W/Sl
2687	Lynch Michael	Corpl.	W/Sl	3087	Key John	Pte.	W/Sl
3598	Fitzgerald Garrett	Drummer	W/Sl	2541	Kinley John	Pte.	W/D
2558	Healy Henry	Drummer	W/Sl	2769	Lawler Michael	Pte.	W/Sl
2412	Axom Thomas	Pte.	W/Sv	2386	Leahy Jeremiah	Pte.	W/Sv
3176	Balf James	Pte.	W/Sl	2835	McDermott Henry	Pte.	W/Sv
2516	Barnett Richard	Pte.	W/D	2781	McDonough Thomas	Pte.	W/Sl

NOTES

The Final Attack on the Redan

3rd REGIMENT OF FOOT

NO.	NAME	RANK	CASUALTY	NO.	NAME	RANK	CASUALTY
3080	McGann Peter	Pte.	W/Sl	2496	Slavin James	Pte.	W/Sl
3042	McKenny Owen	Pte.	W/Sl	3557	Speak Joseph	Pte.	W/Sl
3496 / 1506	McWilliams John	Pte.	W/Sl	1990	Taylor Henry	Pte.	W/Sl
				2142	Taylor William	Pte.	W/Sv
2335 / 2663	Merritt William	Pte.	W/Sv	3469 / 2415	Thompson William	Pte.	W/Sv
2975 / 2302	Miskell William	Pte.	W/Sv	2727	Tierney Joseph	Pte.	W/Sl
				3077	Tinnan Edward	Pte.	W/Sl
1973	Moore William	Pte.	W/Sl	2801	Toombs John	Pte.	W/D
2736	Morooney William	Pte.	W/Sl	3111	Tracey Denis	Pte.	W/Sl
2856	O'Brien John	Pte.	W/Sv	3486 / 2590	Wade John	Pte.	W/Sv
3486	Palmer Robert	Pte.	W/Sl				
3296	Pope John	Pte.	W/Sl	2921	Walsh John	Pte.	W/Sl
3056	Rea Edward	Pte.	W/Sv	2733	Walsh Thomas	Pte.	W/D
1979	Reardon Jeremiah	Pte.	W/Sl	3163	Wheatley William	Pte.	W/Sl
2314	Roberts Jason	Pte.	W/Sl	2055	Williams John	Pte.	W/Sv
3083	Savage John	Pte.	W/Sv	3068	Williams Thomas	Pte.	W/D
2022	Sexton Lawrence	Pte.	W/Sl	1963	Yates James	Pte.	W/Sv

Several men are shown with two or three regimental numbers, no explanation is given, but they had probably been transferred from another Regiment to the 3rd Foot.

7th REGIMENT OF FOOT

NO.	NAME	RANK	CASUALTY	NO.	NAME	RANK	CASUALTY
	Colt O.	Lieut.	Killed	3001	Adams S.	Pte.	W/Sl
	Wright L. L. G.	Lieut.	Killed	2993	Aniscow R.	Pte.	W/Sl
3111	Seddon A.	Sergt.	Killed	3885	Annell J.	Pte.	W/Sl
2511	Hargrave W.	Corpl.	Killed	3384	Arnold Robert	Pte.	Missing
1709	Harris W.	Drummer	Killed	3854	Bishop W.	Pte.	W/Sv
2867	Moore J. A.	Drummer	Killed	3948	Bond T.	Pte.	W/Sv
1219	Doyle A.	Pte.	Killed	3938	Bradley Thomas	Pte.	Missing
3977	Hudson W.	Pte.	Killed	3418	Bryson J.	Pte.	W/Sv
3389	Kirby F.	Pte.	Killed	3314	Clarke J.	Pte.	W/Sv
3713	McCabe J(2)	Pte.	Killed	2243	Collin M.	Pte.	W/D
3119	Madden P.	Pte.	Killed	4036	Cook G.	Pte.	W/Sv
3828	Maglin J.	Pte.	Killed	3323	Crute F.	Pte.	W/Sl
1827	Orton T.	Pte.	Killed	2214	Curry O.	Pte.	W/Sv
2068	Ryan J.	Pte.	Killed	3638	Davis Joseph	Pte.	Missing
3553	Scott J.	Pte.	Killed	3387	Fitzpatrick T.	Pte.	W/Sl
	Heyland J. R.	Br/Lt/Col.	W/Sv	3957	Foster Thomas	Pte.	Missing
	Turner W. W.	Br/Major	W/Sl	3737	Fuller S.	Pte.	W/D
	Hibbert H. P.	Capt.	W/Sv	3928	Garnett C.	Pte.	W/Sv
	Hickie J. F.	Capt.	W/Sv	4060	Gorman L.	Pte.	W/Sv
	Jones H. M.	Lieut.	W/D	4065	Gough J.	Pte.	W/D
883	Bacon W.	Sgt/Mjr.	W/Sv	3843	Griffin G.	Pte.	W/Sl
2842	Farrow W. H.	Sergt.	W/Sv	3316	Hackett B.	Pte.	W/D
3631	Fraser William	Sergt.	Missing	3746	Hollis W.	Pte.	W/Sv
3378	Going T.	Sergt.	W/Sl	3685	Hooten R.	Pte.	W/Sl
2191	Graham J.	Sergt.	W/Sv	4042	Jackson H.	Pte.	W/Sv
2423	Holmes F.	Sergt.	W/Sv	3202	Jenkins H.	Pte.	W/Sl
2424	Holmes R.	Sergt.	W/Sl	2336	Jones J.	Pte.	W/Sl
2269	Jowett W.	Sergt.	W/Sv	3948	Jones W.	Pte.	W/Sl
2010	McCann J.	Sergt.	W/D	3197	Kimberlin W.	Pte.	W/Sl
2826	Munro J.	Sergt.	W/Sl	3808	Kinch Isaac	Pte.	Missing
1535	Stocks John	Sergt.	Missing	3768	Leake J.	Pte.	W/Sl
2098	Whittle G.	Sergt.	W/Sv	3347	Lewis J.	Pte.	W/Sv
2612	Wood J. S.	Sergt.	W/Sv	2673	Lowe J.	Pte.	W/Sv
1799	Brooker T.	Corpl.	W/Sl	3669	McCarthy M.	Pte.	W/Sv
3142	Garmley J.	Corpl.	W/Sv	3945	McDonough P.	Pte.	W/Sv
2771	Henley G. W.	Corpl.	W/Sv	3114	McGinty E.	Pte.	W/D
2693	Settle T.	Corpl.	W/Sv	3214	McNamara Peter	Pte.	Missing

NOTES

The Final Attack on the Redan

7th REGIMENT OF FOOT

NO.	NAME	RANK	CASUALTY	NO.	NAME	RANK	CASUALTY
3791	Mahon P.	Pte.	W/Sv	2572	Shorland J.	Pte.	W/Sv
4032	Newsome N.	Pte.	W/Sv	3749	Smedley G.	Pte.	W/Sl
2941	Parsons J.	Pte.	W/Sv	3066	Smith G.	Pte.	W/Sl
3540	Platt S.	Pte.	W/Sv	2983	Smith J. (10)	Pte.	W/Sl
2411	Rider E.	Pte.	W/Sl	3855	Smith J.	Pte.	W/Sv
3071	Riding S.	Pte.	W/Sl	1576	Sweeney H.	Pte.	W/Sv
3400	Rose G.	Pte.	W/Sv	3927	Taylor William	Pte.	Missing
3958	Rutherford J.	Pte.	W/Sv	3522	Tierney J.	Pte.	W/Sv
1120	Saville R.	Pte.	W/Sv	3253	Warpole J.	Pte.	W/Sl
3817	Seivers H.	Pte.	W/D	3180	Webb J.	Pte.	W/Sv
1122	Sharp W.	Pte.	W/Sv	3947	Whittaker H.	Pte.	W/Sv
3979	Shaw H.	Pte.	W/Sv	3932	Whitten S.	Pte.	W/Sv
3941	Shaw T.	Pte.	W/D	3650	Young J.	Pte.	W/Sv

17th REGIMENT OF FOOT

NO.	NAME	RANK	CASUALTY	NO.	NAME	RANK	CASUALTY
3611	Brown John	Pte.	Killed	3461	Higginson John	Pte.	W/Sl
	Parker W. H.	Lieut.	W/Sl	2733	Hutchinson Henry	Pte.	W/D
	Thompson W. D.	Lieut.	W/D	3501	Johnson Richard	Pte.	W/Sl
2864	Brown John	Corpl.	W/Sl	3517	Larkin John	Pte.	W/Sl
2580	Bourke Joshua	Pte.	W/D	2607	McCabe John	Pte.	W/Sl
2608	Boyce William	Pte.	W/D	3681	McDermot Patrick	Pte.	W/D
3208	Clancey Michael	Pte.	W/Sv	2380	Nicholson Andrew	Pte.	W/Sv
2542	Darcy Patrick	Pte.	W/Sl	3828	O'Brien John	Pte.	W/Sv
2331	Denton George	Pte.	W/Sv	3708	Stephens Robert	Pte.	W/D
3211	Farrant Henry	Pte.	W/Sl	2630	Sullivan John	Pte.	W/Sv
3812	Fry John	Pte.	W/D				

19th REGIMENT OF FOOT

NO.	NAME	RANK	CASUALTY	NO.	NAME	RANK	CASUALTY
	Unett T.	Lt/Col.	D.O.W.	3556	Wilber George	Pte.	Killed
	Godfrey P.	Lieut.	Killed		Warden R.	Br/Mjr.	W/Sl
2382	Jannon Michael	Sergt.	Killed		Chippindall E.	Capt.	W/Sl
2092	Taffe Patrick	Sergt.	Killed		Bayley E. W. R.	Lieut.	W/Sl
1280	Weston Samuel	Sergt.	Killed		Goren A.	Lieut.	W/D
2674	Bromley William	Corpl.	Killed		Massy W. G. D.	Lieut.	W/D
2654	Morrish George	Corpl.	Killed		Molesworth R.	Lieut.	W/Sv
1960	Smith John	Corpl.	Killed		Martin R. C.	Ensign	W/Sv
2766	Aistin Charles	Pte.	Killed		Young W. W.	Ensign	W/Sv
3620	Baker Benjamin	Pte.	Killed	1381	Bell David	Act/Sgt/Mjr.	W/Sl
3103	Bowne Mathew	Pte.	Killed				
3004	Bromley George	Pte.	Killed	1513	Magner John	Col/Sgt.	W/D
2472	Brown John	Pte.	Killed	1417	Miller William	Col/Sgt.	W/Sl
3068	Cook Henry	Pte.	Killed	1360	Colgan James	Sergt.	W/Sl
3092	Curtis Thomas	Pte.	Killed	2584	Dodds James	Sergt.	W/Sl
3379	Dudley Patrick	Pte.	Killed	2805	Hogan George	Sergt.	W/Sv
2392	Farix Stephen	Pte.	Killed	2457	Horristall —	Sergt.	W/Sl
3381	Gaiter David	Pte.	Killed	1888	Murphy William	Sergt.	W/Sv
3256	Gaiter Thomas	Pte.	Killed	2242	Sherlock John	Sergt.	W/Sl
3400	Goulding James	Pte.	Killed	2901	McTaggart John	L/Sgt.	W/Sv
1052	Hennessy Philip	Pte.	Killed	1985	Maher Patrick	L/Sgt.	W/Sl
2480	Kennedy Patrick	Pte.	Killed	2769	Robins George	L/Sgt.	W/Sv
2601	Lahiff Stephen	Pte.	Killed	2644	Collins Edwin	Corpl.	W/Sl
1306	Norrish Patrick	Pte.	Killed	2075	Doyle Denis	Corpl.	W/Sv
2969	O'Connor Thomas	Pte.	Killed	2376	Doyle Edward	Corpl.	W/Sv
2850	Plant Thomas	Pte.	Killed	2584	Farrer Thomas	Corpl.	W/D
3167	Roberts George	Pte.	Killed	886	Gibson John	Corpl.	W/Sl
1478	Rourke Charles	Pte.	Killed	3388	Hardew Edwin	Corpl.	W/Sl
2779	Walsh John	Pte.	Killed.	2667	Keating Thomas	Corpl.	W/Sl

NOTES

The Final Attack on the Redan

19th REGIMENT OF FOOT

NO.	NAME	RANK	CASUALTY	NO.	NAME	RANK	CASUALTY
3063	Murphy Michael	Corpl.	W/Sv	2012	Harley John	Pte.	W/Sv
1464	Newall Andrew	Corpl.	W/Sv	3204	Hazle John	Pte.	W/Sv
1697	Robins Thomas	Corpl.	W/Sl	2548	Healy James	Pte.	W/Sv
2442	Smith William	Corpl.	W/Sl	2044	Herrity James	Pte.	W/Sl
2569	Strick Henry	Corpl.	W/Sv	2826	Hickey James	Pte.	W/Sl
3476	Ventham Charles	Corpl.	W/Sv	1856	Holland William	Pte.	W/Sl
2441	Hanton Henry	Drummer	W/Sl	2839	Hourighaid Jeremiah	Pte.	W/Sl
2953	Abbott Richard	Pte.	W/Sv	2740	Hutchings James	Pte.	W/Sv
3221	Ainge William	Pte.	W/Sl	1828	Ingram William	Pte.	W/Sv
3128	Anderson James	Pte.	W/Sv	2488	Jones Thomas	Pte.	W/Sv
3257	Anscombe Henry	Pte.	W/Sv	1354	Kennedy James	Pte.	W/Sv
2675	Ash Thomas	Pte.	W/Sv	3443	Lawrence Joseph	Pte.	W/Sv
3165	Barnard Francis	Pte.	W/D	2722	Levi Alexander	Pte.	W/Sv
2877	Beech Richard	Pte.	W/Sv	2685	Lynch Richard	Pte.	W/Sl
2697	Beer Jacob	Pte.	W/Sv	2142	Lynch William	Pte.	W/Sv
2976	Behan Thomas	Pte.	W/Sl	1884	Lyons Denis	Pte.	W/Sl
2768	Biercliff James	Pte.	W/Sv	3318	McCugh James	Pte.	W/Sl
3009	Bollen William	Pte.	W/Sl	3417	McDonald George	Pte.	W/Sv
3384	Box William	Pte.	W/Sl	2939	McDonald John	Pte.	W/Sl
3470	Brenan John	Pte.	W/Sv	3318	McHugh James	Pte.	W/Sv
1310	Broderick John	Pte.	W/Sv	3363	McNamara Michael	Pte.	W/Sl
1904	Brophy Patrick	Pte.	W/Sv	3397	McNamara Patrick	Pte.	W/Sv
2949	Brown John	Pte.	W/Sv	2719	McRoberts Abraham	Pte.	W/Sv
3511	Brown Thomas	Pte.	W/Sv	3378	Mack Michael	Pte.	W/Sv
2191	Bulger Patrick	Pte.	W/Sl	3340	Madden James	Pte.	W/Sv
4188	Burke John	Pte.	W/Sl	2830	Mexal John	Pte.	W/Sl
3464	Buro John	Pte.	W/Sl	3328	Mihill George	Pte.	W/Sv
2693	Caldwell John	Pte.	W/Sl	3210	Mitchell William	Pte.	W/Sl
3122	Campbell Robert	Pte.	W/Sl	3328	Mooney John	Pte.	W/Sv
3189	Carsen James	Pte.	W/Sv	3524	Moriarty Daniel	Pte.	W/D
1824	Chadwick William	Pte.	W/D	3316	Murphy James	Pte.	W/Sv
3236	Chivers Frederick	Pte.	W/Sl	3147	Murphy Patrick	Pte.	W/Sl
1477	Clare William	Pte.	W/Sv	3142	Murray Edward	Pte.	W/Sv
3292	Clarke John	Pte.	W/Sv	3179	Neil Henry	Pte.	W/Sv
2836	Clunke Patrick	Pte.	W/Sl	1995	Nelson Frederick	Pte.	W/Sv
1849	Collins Charles	Pte.	W/Sl	3271	Norwall Thomas	Pte.	W/Sl
2891	Connelly John	Pte.	W/Sl	1318	O'Connor James	Pte.	W/Sv
2343	Conway Martin	Pte.	W/Sl	3116	O'Hara Patrick	Pte.	W/Sl
1125	Cormick William	Pte.	W/Sv	3649	Ralph James	Pte.	W/Sv
3199	Cooper David	Pte.	W/Sv	3389	Reynolds John	Pte.	W/Sl
2366	Dacey John	Pte.	W/D	3440	Riggs Frederick	Pte.	W/Sv
3361	Daley Peter	Pte.	W/Sl	2784	Rixon George	Pte.	W/Sv
2832	Daly Michael	Pte.	W/Sl	3155	Robinson John	Pte.	W/Sv
3309	Darkin James	Pte.	W/Sl	2666	Rogers John	Pte.	W/Sv
3084	Dasson Henry	Pte.	W/Sv	2897	Saithings Anthony	Pte.	W/Sv
3426	Didman Frederick	Pte.	W/Sl	1961	Shaw William	Pte.	W/Sv
3062	Dobbin John	Pte.	W/Sl	1215	Shea Daniel	Pte.	W/Sv
2075	Dolan Francis	Pte.	W/Sv	2818	Shea Sinan	Pte.	W/Sv
2885	Donelly Patrick	Pte.	W/Sv	1333	Sherridan John	Pte.	W/Sv
1214	Doorley James	Pte.	W/Sl	3484	Simms Henry	Pte.	W/Sv
2505	Duffy James	Pte.	W/Sv	3639	Simpson Thomas	Pte.	W/Sv
2721	Evans Samuel	Pte.	W/Sv	1708	Stafford Michael	Pte.	W/Sv
2741	Faulkner Mathew	Pte.	W/Sl	3033	Stevens Henry	Pte.	W/Sv
3168	Fogarty William	Pte.	W/Sv	3047	Stillman Frederick	Pte.	W/Sv
3349	Frost Simon	Pte.	W/Sv	3367	Thaxted George	Pte.	W/Sl
3510	Geary Maurice	Pte.	W/Sv	3602	Tillman James	Pte.	W/Sv
2136	Gilgason John	Pte.	W/Sl	1836	Tinsley Joseph	Pte.	W/Sv
3015	Gilpin George	Pte.	W/Sv	2796	Toolair Thomas	Pte.	W/Sv
1891	Gorman James	Pte.	W/Sv	1466	Walsh James	Pte.	W/Sl
3555	Green John	Pte.	W/Sv	3504	Wardle Thomas	Pte.	W/Sv
3150	Grice James	Pte.	W/Sv	2657	Williams Thomas	Pte.	W/Sv
3075	Griffin John	Pte.	W/Sl	2043	Woodman Thomas	Pte.	W/Sl
3016	Griffin John	Pte.	W/Sv				
1106	Hallaran John	Pte.	W/Sl				
2204	Handley Anthony	Pte.	W/Sv				

NOTES

The Final Attack on the Redan

20th REGIMENT OF FOOT

NO.	NAME	RANK	CASUALTY	NO.	NAME	RANK	CASUALTY
	Chapman S. R.	Br/Major (Asst/Eng)	W/D	4125	Cates George	Pte.	W/Sl
				3697	Connolly Daniel	Pte.	W/Sl
1631	Fullmer Peter	Corpl.	W/Sl	4090	Joyce John	Pte.	W/Sl
3646	Barry Richard	Pte.	W/Sl	1879	Rea Edward	Pte.	W/Sl

21st REGIMENT OF FOOT

NO.	NAME	RANK	CASUALTY	NO.	NAME	RANK	CASUALTY
3229	Cavanagh Thomas	Pte.	Killed	3542	Donnolly Richard	Pte.	W/Sl
2777	Douglass William	Col/Sgt.	W/Sl	3254	Goodwin James	Pte.	W/Sl
2242	McAuliffe John	Corpl.	W/Sl	2618	Mahy Martin	Pte.	W/Sl
4052	Bell William	Pte.	W/Sl	2217	Weldon Thomas	Pte.	W/Sv

23rd REGIMENT OF FOOT

NO.	NAME	RANK	CASUALTY	NO.	NAME	RANK	CASUALTY
	Dyneley D.	Lt.&Adj.	Killed	3424	Welch John	Pte.	Killed
	Somerville R. H.	Lieut.	Killed	4630	Williams Luke	Pte.	Killed
1908	Gilloghy John	Col/Sgt.	Killed	4623	Williams Thomas	Pte.	Killed
3296	Ungless Thomas	Col/Sgt.	Killed	3812	Willington Thomas	Pte.	Killed
2776	Roberts Thomas	Sergt.	Killed	2467	Wright Thomas	Pte.	Killed
1075	Wilkinson John	Sergt.	Killed		Lysons D. CB.	Colonel	W/Sv
3341	Kelly John	Corpl.	Killed		Poole W. H.	Capt.	W/D
3271	Malone Edward	Corpl.	Killed		Vane F. F.	Capt.	W/Sv
4048	Barnes Thomas	Pte.	Killed		Beck C. H.	Lieut.	W/D
4578	Bath Noah	Pte.	Killed		Dare F. M. H.	Lieut.	W/Sv
4041	Biddle Robert	Pte.	Killed		Holden C. S.	Lieut.	W/D
—	Brading Joseph	Pte.	Killed		Millet L. E.	Lieut.	W/Sv
2410	Brown William	Pte.	Killed		O'Connor L.	Lieut.	W/D
3594	Churchill Henry	Pte.	Killed		Prevost S. G.	Lieut.	W/Sl
4583	Crutcher William	Pte.	Killed		Radcliffe H. D.	Lieut.	W/Sl
3166	Curren Mathew	Pte.	Killed		Tupper J. D. Vic.	Lieut.	W/Sv
4495	Davies Francis	Pte.	Killed		Williamson J.	Lieut.	W/Sv
4099	Doroman George	Pte.	Killed	1136	Smith W. H.	Sgt/Mjr.	W/Sv
3624	Fox Charles	Pte.	Killed	2307	Knight E.	Drum/Mjr.	W/Sl
3187	Frankham John	Pte.	Killed	2434	Coviton C.	Col/Sgt.	W/Sl
4763	Gardiner John	Pte.	Killed	1210	Handley W.	Col/Sgt.	W/Sl
4773	Giles Thomas	Pte.	Killed	1212	O'Neil J.	Col/Sgt.	W/Sv
4625	Harry Thomas	Pte.	Killed	1688	Danaline T.	Sergt.	W/Sl
3911	Hayes Patrick	Pte.	Killed	3660	Dawson J.	Sergt.	W/Sl
4777	Hobbs George	Pte.	Killed	1475	Juffrey T.	Sergt.	W/Sv
4632	Jervoise James	Pte.	Killed	2636	Parkinson W.	Sergt.	W/Sv
4467	John Davod	Pte.	Killed	4661	Seymour C.	Sergt.	W/Sv
3232	Jones Edward	Pte.	Killed	3321	Benbow C.	Corpl.	W/Sl
1888	Jones John Michael	Pte.	Killed	1669	Chadwick J.	Corpl.	W/Sv
4748	Jones William	Pte.	Killed	1330	Collins J.	Corpl.	W/Sl
4391	Lamb James	Pte.	Killed	4416	Patterson J.	Corpl.	W/Sl
4747	Lawless Thomas	Pte.	Killed	3822	Rickey W.	Corpl.	W/Sl
4135	Longman Robert	Pte.	Killed	1969	Stoate T.	Corpl.	W/Sl
2136	McCrum R. H.	Pte.	Killed	1252	Hicks C.	Drummer	W/Sv
3498	McEvery Thomas	Pte.	Killed	2692	James G.	Drummer	W/Sl
4734	Nasmyth John	Pte.	Killed	1028	Ross W.	Drummer	W/Sl
4133	O'Brien Timothy	Pte.	Killed	4366	Abbotson —	Pte.	W/Sv
3686	Payne Charles	Pte.	Killed	4426	Ashfield J.	Pte.	W/Sv
4344	Perkins Charles	Pte.	Killed	4947	Baker H.	Pte.	W/Sv
4743	Reid Samuel	Pte.	Killed	4834	Batchelor G.	Pte.	W/Sl
4486	Richards Richard	Pte.	Killed	4578	Bath N.	Pte.	W/Sv
2134	Robinson James	Pte.	Killed	4780	Beach J.	Pte.	W/Sv
4473	Stone Henry	Pte.	Killed	2892	Beamer T.	Pte.	W/Sl

NOTES

The Final Attack on the Redan

23rd REGIMENT OF FOOT

NO.	NAME	RANK	CASUALTY	NO.	NAME	RANK	CASUALTY
3702	Bentley W.	Pte.	W/Sl	4574	Musslewhite H.	Pte.	W/D
4267	Blessington P.	Pte.	W/Sv	3709	Nunan W.	Pte.	W/D
3899	Bowl J.	Pte.	W/Sl	4521	O'Leary P.	Pte.	W/Sv
4300	Box T.	Pte.	W/D	3568	O'Neil J.	Pte.	W/Sv
4706	Brown J.	Pte.	W/Sv	4404	Parker J.	Pte.	W/Sl
2879	Brown R.	Pte.	W/Sl	4171	Pearman C.	Pte.	W/D
4727	Cahill P.	Pte.	W/Sv	4595	Plant H.	Pte.	W/Sl
4028	Casey W.	Pte.	W/Sl	2101	Plummer A.	Pte.	W/Sl
4941	Clarke J.	Pte.	W/Sv	4140	Poulton G.	Pte.	W/Sl
2155	Clarke M.	Pte.	W/D	3481	Prebble W.	Pte.	W/D
4347	Clarke T.	Pte.	W/Sl	4143	Reed J.	Pte.	W/D
1315	Conway J.	Pte.	W/Sl	3595	Richardson J.	Pte.	W/Sl
4622	Corcoran P.	Pte.	W/Sv	1588	Ridden T.	Pte.	W/D
2820	Cullen T.	Pte.	W/Sl	4643	Roberts J.	Pte.	W/Sv
2762	Davies J.	Pte.	W/Sv	4707	Rody P.	Pte.	W/Sl
2789	Davies S. J.	Pte.	W/D	3806	Rowlands A.	Pte.	W/Sv
3204	Davies T.	Pte.	W/Sl	4786	Saunders A.	Pte.	W/Sl
4094	Dewe R.	Pte.	W/Sl	4762	Sheriff W.	Pte.	W/Sv
3558	Door A.	Pte.	W/Sl	4823	Silvester G.	Pte.	W/Sl
4753	Evans J.	Pte.	W/D	1459	Simpson E.	Pte.	W/Sl
4227	Faloon J.	Pte.	W/Sv	4582	Slade W.	Pte.	W/Sl
2683	Fielden W.	Pte.	W/Sl	4557	Smith J.	Pte.	W/Sl
4437	Fitzpatrick J.	Pte.	W/Sv	2127	Soseland N.	Pte.	W/Sv
3426	Ford R.	Pte.	W/Sl	4636	Sparks W.	Pte.	W/D
4663	Garrett J.	Pte.	W/Sl	2847	Spencer H.	Pte.	W/Sl
1401	Gerrighty T.	Pte.	W/Sv	4512	Stephens W.	Pte.	W/Sl
4773	Giles T.	Pte.	W/Sl	2406	Swan W.	Pte.	W/Sl
4737	Goddard W.	Pte.	W/Sv	4949	Thompson H.	Pte.	W/Sv
4742	Goodridge T.	Pte.	W/Sv	4820	Turner F.	Pte.	W/Sl
3814	Gordon E.	Pte.	W/D	—	Walker B.	Pte.	W/Sl
4518	Griffiths C.	Pte.	W/Sl	4450	Ward J.	Pte.	W/Sl
4448	Hanks J.	Pte.	W/D	4163	Webb R.	Pte.	W/D
1381	Hillen P.	Pte.	W/D	4711	Weldon W.	Pte.	W/Sl
4689	Hore E.	Pte.	W/Sl	3821	Weesh J.	Pte.	W/Sl
1899	Hughes D.	Pte.	W/Sl	1612	White W.	Pte.	W/D
3876	Hughes J.	Pte.	W/Sl	1845	Whiteside T.	Pte.	W/Sv
4829	Hughes T.	Pte.	W/Sv	4199	Williams C.	Pte.	W/D
1593	Hughes T.	Pte.	W/Sl	4624	Williams J.	Pte.	W/D
4525	Hunt W.	Pte.	W/D	4540	Williams T.	Pte.	W/D
4564	James J.	Pte.	W/Sl	4143	Wilmot F.	Pte.	W/D
4526	James W.	Pte.	W/Sv	2682	Wilton H.	Pte.	W/Sl
4612	Jay W.	Pte.	W/Sv	4599	Barrett Joseph	Pte.	Missing
4534	Johnston W.	Pte.	W/Sv	2119	Bedford Joseph	Pte.	Missing
4310	Jones E.	Pte.	W/Sv	4667	Brown George	Pte.	Missing
4092	Jones F.	Pte.	W/Sl	4877	Brown John	Pte.	Missing
4929	Jones J.	Pte.	W/D	4874	Clarke George	Pte.	Missing
4729	Jones W.	Pte.	W/Sl	4286	Constable Alfred	Pte.	Missing
2823	Kiernan J.	Pte.	W/Sl	4500	Davies William	Pte.	Missing
2704	Keough J.	Pte.	W/D	4348	Donovan Jeremiah	Pte.	Missing
2261	Keys W.	Pte.	W/Sv	4472	Dwyer Edwin	Pte.	Missing
3756	Kilroy J.	Pte.	W/D	1687	Fielding Burlace	Pte.	Missing
4910	Kirk J.	Pte.	W/Sv	4209	Folds William	Pte.	Missing
4290	Lamb R.	Pte.	W/Sl	4542	Hardson William	Pte.	Missing
4541	Lee T.	Pte.	W/D	4454	Jelly William	Pte.	Missing
4892	Leech G.	Pte.	W/Sl	4475	Jones John	Pte.	Missing
1671	Lourey P.	Pte.	W/D	4190	Martin William	Pte.	Missing
3295	McCarthy D.	Pte.	W/Sv	4895	Mason William	Pte.	Missing
4425	Manley H.	Pte.	W/D	4341	Perkins Henry	Pte.	Missing
3330	Mannion M.	Pte.	W/Sl	4654	Price William	Pte.	Missing
4021	Markham W.	Pte.	W/Sv	3476	Rush James	Pte.	Missing
3418	Martin A.	Pte.	W/Sv	4767	Singfield Samuel	Pte.	Missing
4721	Mooney J.	Pte.	W/D	4824	Smith William	Pte.	Missing
4022	Moran T.	Pte.	W/Sl	4299	Taylor David	Pte.	Missing
4595	Morris A.	Pte.	W/Sl	3525	Ware Henry	Pte.	Missing
4822	Mundy F.	Pte.	W/Sv	4834	Whilrican Maurice	Pte.	Missing
				4288	Whitehead Thomas	Pte.	Missing

NOTES

The Final Attack on the Redan

30th REGIMENT OF FOOT

NO.	NAME	RANK	CASUALTY	NO.	NAME	RANK	CASUALTY
	Patullo J. B.	Lt/Col.	Killed	2499	White J.	Drummer	W/Sl
	Stevenson J. C. N.	Capt.	Killed	2452	Ablett W.	Pte.	W/Sl
	Deane R. G.	Ensign	Killed	3680	Andrews J.	Pte.	W/Sv
2050	Collins James	Sgt/Mjr.	Killed	4066	Baker W.	Pte.	W/Sl
4088	Moore William	L/Sgt.	Killed	3803	Bird G.	Pte.	W/Sl
3070	Collins James	Corpl.	Killed	4240	Boyd W. J.	Pte.	W/D
4161	Ross John	Corpl.	Killed	3697	Breen L.	Pte.	W/Sv
3276	Corron H. C.	Drummer	Killed	3948	Broadrick —	Pte.	W/Sv
3994	Armstrong Edward	Pte.	Killed	3890	Brown T.	Pte.	W/Sv
3777	Besley William	Pte.	Killed	4434	Brown T.	Pte.	W/Sv
3881	Black John	Pte.	Killed	3363	Byrne J.	Pte.	W/Sl
3942	Brennan John	Pte.	Killed	3196	Byrne M.	Pte.	W/Sl
4068	Brien Simon	Pte.	Killed	3367	Byrne M.	Pte.	W/Sl
4080	Bryan Denis	Pte.	Killed	3963	Byrne M.	Pte.	W/Sl
3914	Burke John	Pte.	Killed	3968	Callaghan J.	Pte.	W/Sv
3965	Cantwell Edmund	Pte.	Killed	4030	Callaghan J.	Pte.	W/Sv
4283	Carr Samuel	Pte.	Killed	2874	Carey J.	Pte.	W/Sl
4310	Connell James	Pte.	Killed	4351	Coill J.	Pte.	W/Sv
4026	Connors Michael	Pte.	Killed	3228	Coffey D.	Pte.	W/Sl
3088	Dean William	Pte.	Killed	3930	Connell J.	Pte.	W/Sv
4118	Eastal Charles	Pte.	Killed	3929	Connell T.	Pte.	W/Sl
3883	Gillian James	Pte.	Killed	3920	Corbett D.	Pte.	W/Sv
2616	Granger Michael	Pte.	Killed	3670	Cronan J.	Pte.	W/Sl
3617	Hague William	Pte.	Killed	3549	Dalton M.	Pte.	W/Sl
2915	Hillary Henry	Pte.	Killed	3925	Dawson J.	Pte.	W/Sl
4065	Hurley John	Pte.	Killed	2025	Donaldson H.	Pte.	W/Sl
4348	Lade William	Pte.	Killed	3273	Donnell P.	Pte.	W/Sv
2707	Long Michael	Pte.	Killed	4216	Donnelly S.	Pte.	W/Sl
4352	Longbottom Wilberry	Pte.	Killed	4002	Doody P.	Pte.	W/Sv
3716	McCarthy Charles	Pte.	Killed	2240	Dyas D.	Pte.	W/Sv
4340	McGooking Edward	Pte.	Killed	3986	Evans J.	Pte.	W/Sl
4433	McKibben George	Pte.	Killed	4090	Fitzgerald P.	Pte.	W/Sl
4342	McQuirk Patrick	Pte.	Killed	4025	Gaffney M.	Pte.	W/Sl
4081	Martin James	Pte.	Killed	3853	Galbraith J.	Pte.	W/Sv
2974	Moore James	Pte.	Killed	2999	Gibbons J.	Pte.	W/Sv
2966	Munn John	Pte.	Killed	4337	Gribbins P.	Pte.	W/D
3380	Nowlan Michael	Pte.	Killed	2569	Hale J.	Pte.	W/Sv
3637	Palmer Charles	Pte.	Killed	3689	Hanrahan D.	Pte.	W/Sl
3437	Rawlins John	Pte.	Killed	2893	Harper F.	Pte.	W/Sv
4364	Riley John	Pte.	Killed	4268	Hawkins J.	Pte.	W/Sv
4325	Sergisson Erwin	Pte.	Killed	3153	Heade M.	Pte.	W/Sl
4335	Stewart John	Pte.	Killed	3034	Hendry W.	Pte.	W/Sl
3128	Watts George	Pte.	Killed	3236	Hill J.	Pte.	W/Sl
	Mauleverer J. T.	Lt/Col.	W/Sl	4124	Holborne C.	Pte.	W/Sl
	Campbell A.	Br/Mjr.	W/Sl	3661	Hunt G.	Pte.	W/Sl
	Pocock G. F. C.	Capt.	W/Sv	4273	Hunter H.	Pte.	W/Sl
	Austin A. J.	Lieut.	W/Sl	4118	Jameson J.	Pte.	W/Sl
	Field M. B.	Lieut.	W/Sv	4345	Johnson J.	Pte.	W/Sl
	Kerr W.	Lieut.	W/D	4198	Jute J.	Pte.	W/Sl
	Moorson C. J.	Lieut.	W/Sl	2956	Kelly M.	Pte.	W/Sv
	Sanders G. H.	Lieut.	W/Sv	3736	Keppel P.	Pte.	W/Sv
3376	McAllister H.	Col/Sgt.	W/Sv	4432	Lammond A.	Pte.	W/Sl
2769	McDonogh T.	Col/Sgt.	W/Sl	3840	Little J.	Pte.	W/Sl
2963	Tennant T.	Col/Sgt.	W/Sv	4050	Lloyd W.	Pte.	W/Sv
2747	Fitzgerald T.	Sergt.	W/Sv	4024	Lunn J.	Pte.	W/Sv
2103	McPhail J.	Sergt.	W/Sv	3092	Lynch D.	Pte.	W/Sv
2823	Symington J.	Sergt.	W/Sv	3734	McAnliff T.	Pte.	W/Sl
2542	Boyd J.	Corpl.	W/Sv	2047	McFarlane M.	Pte.	W/Sl
3709	Callaghan J.	Corpl.	W/Sv	4208	McGuire D.	Pte.	W/Sv
3820	McLean D.	Corpl.	W/Sl	3047	Maley E.	Pte.	W/Sv
2670	Mears J.	Corpl.	W/Sv	4204	Maloney M.	Pte.	W/Sv
3669	Mehaffy H.	Corpl.	W/Sl	2862	Martin C.	Pte.	W/Sl
2585	Rooke I.	Corpl.	W/Sl	4177	Mead P.	Pte.	W/Sl

NOTES

The Final Attack on the Redan

30th REGIMENT OF FOOT

NO.	NAME	RANK	CASUALTY	NO.	NAME	RANK	CASUALTY
2737	Michael N.	Pte.	W/D	4239	Russell M.	Pte.	W/Sl
3868	Miller F.	Pte.	W/Sv	3341	Ryder H.	Pte.	W/Sl
3484	Morgan W.	Pte.	W/Sv	3804	Smart A.	Pte.	W/Sv
2744	Mulligan W.	Pte.	W/Sl	3179	Smith T.	Pte.	W/Sv
3958	Murphy P.	Pte.	W/Sv	4217	Stenson T.	Pte.	W/D
2161	Neasmith T.	Pte.	W/Sl	2673	Stevens W.	Pte.	W/Sv
3786	O'Brien J.	Pte.	W/Sv	3592	Sullivan J. (1)	Pte.	W/Sl
3826	Parsons W.	Pte.	W/Sv	3761	Sullivan J. (3)	Pte.	W/Sl
4105	Peacock H.	Pte.	W/D	2864	Taylor J.	Pte.	W/Sv
4039	Power J.	Pte.	W/D	3344	Turner S.	Pte.	W/Sl
3237	Quigley P.	Pte.	W/Sv	3782	Veitch J.	Pte.	W/Sl
4285	Rainey J.	Pte.	W/Sv	3019	Vernon T.	Pte.	W/Sv
4269	Regan J.	Pte.	W/Sl	3169	Walsh P.	Pte.	W/Sv
4223	Rigsby W.	Pte.	W/D	1141	Webb D.	Pte.	W/Sl
3955	Roache T.	Pte.	W/Sl	4245	Whelan P.	Pte.	W/Sv
4277	Rourke P.	Pte.	W/Sv	3791	White J.	Pte.	W/Sv
4156	Russell J.	Pte.	W/Sl	4108	Young T.	Pte.	W/Sl

33rd REGIMENT OF FOOT

NO.	NAME	RANK	CASUALTY	NO.	NAME	RANK	CASUALTY
	Donovan H. G.	Lieut.	Killed	2679	Gardner J.	Pte.	W/Sl
3480	McLoughlin W.	Sergt.	Killed	2952	Gill M.	Pte.	W/Sv
3651	Connors J.	Pte.	Killed	3763	Gillespie D.	Pte.	W/Sv
3623	Hanley J.	Pte.	Killed	3131	Green J.	Pte.	W/Sl
3015	Harrison J.	Pte.	Killed	3476	Hackett T.	Pte.	W/Sv
3457	Hutty W.	Pte.	Killed	2222	Hartford K.	Pte.	W/Sv
2727	Kennedy J.	Pte.	Killed	3164	Healy T.	Pte.	W/Sv
3180	Monaghan M.	Pte.	Killed	1870	Higginson T.	Pte.	W/Sl
3879	Nash T.	Pte.	Killed	—	Hughes F.	Pte.	W/D
3525	Reagan M.	Pte.	Killed	3402	Keating J.	Pte.	W/Sl
2993	Smith R.	Pte.	Killed	3567	Keefe E.	Pte.	W/Sv
	Gough T. B.	Lt/Col.	W/D	3081	Laurence W.	Pte.	W/D
	Ellis H. D.	Capt.	W/Sl	3413	Leary P.	Pte.	W/Sl
	Trent J.	Lieut.	W/Sv	3752	Lee W.	Pte.	W/Sl
	Willis C. W.	Lieut.	W/Sl	2846	Lindy J.	Pte.	W/Sl
	Toseland G.	Lt.&Adj.	W/Sl	3065	Linnand T.	Pte.	W/Sv
2418	Reed P.	Col/Sgt.	W/Sv	2689	McCann H.	Pte.	W/D
1515	Griffin J.	Sergt.	W/Sl	3516	McCann P.	Pte.	W/Sl
1898	Hagan T.	Sergt.	W/Sv	3851	McCusker J.	Pte.	W/Sv
1806	Reidy J.	Sergt.	W/Sv	2854	McGregor C.	Pte.	W/Sv
2762	Tooley T.	Sergt.	W/Sv	3242	Needham P.	Pte.	W/Sl
1646	Londregan M.	Corpl.	W/Sv	2650	Paul A.	Pte.	W/Sl
3273	Bass E.	Pte.	W/Sv	3569	Quinn A.	Pte.	W/M
3918	Bavin W.	Pte.	W/Sl	3519	Quinn J.	Pte.	W/D
2158	Cahill P.	Pte.	W/Sl	3856	Ryan J.	Pte.	W/D
2028	Callaghan W.	Pte.	W/Sv	3595	Turner R.	Pte.	W/Sv
2406	Canavan J.	Pte.	W/D	3980	Walker J.	Pte.	W/Sv
3346	Clooney P.	Pte.	W/Sl	3290	Welch T.	Pte.	W/Sv
3280	Couxter H.	Pte.	W/Sv	2516	Wellington G.	Pte.	W/Sl
3089	Douglas W.	Pte.	W/Sl	2763	Wright J.	Pte.	W/D

34th REGIMENT OF FOOT

NO.	NAME	RANK	CASUALTY	NO.	NAME	RANK	CASUALTY
1625	Hull Thomas	Sergt.	Killed	2467	Harrison James	Col/Sgt.	W/Sv
2664	King George	Sergt.	Killed	2100	Woodcock Joseph	Col/Sgt.	W/Sl
2517	Bagbal John	Pte.	Killed	3058	Allis George	Sergt.	W/Sv
	Harris N. A.	Lieut.	W/Sv	3232	Cole Joseph	Sergt.	W/Sv
	Laurie J. D.	Lieut.	W/Sv	2828	Rawdon Joseph	Sergt.	W/Sl

NOTES

The Final Attack on the Redan

34th REGIMENT OF FOOT

NO.	NAME	RANK	CASUALTY	NO.	NAME	RANK	CASUALTY
2298	Ward George	Sergt.	W/Sl	3635	Lee Samuel	Pte.	W/Sv
3370	Benford Alfred	Corpl.	W/Sl	2750	Lindesay Andrew	Pte.	W/Sl
2280	Harper Frederick	Corpl.	W/Sl	4183	Logue Adam	Pte.	W/Sv
2159	Morton Joseph	Corpl.	W/Sv	3915	McAteer Robert	Pte.	W/Sv
1632	Swift John	Corpl.	W/Sv	3767	McCartney Robert	Pte.	W/Sv
2897	Egan Joseph	Drummer	W/Sl	3305	McMahon John	Pte.	W/Sv
1786	Artlett Moses	Pte.	W/Sl	3755	McTrienan Patrick	Pte.	W/Sl
3348	Barnes Enoch	Pte.	W/Sl	3694	Madden Thomas	Pte.	W/Sl
3549	Birch Francis	Pte.	W/Sl	3785	Moriarty Denis	Pte.	W/Sl
3707	Black James	Pte.	W/Sv	2415	Mulhorn Michael	Pte.	W/Sl
2383	Bowler Benjamin	Pte.	W/Sl	3932	Noble John	Pte.	W/Sv
3781	Brasloe Michael	Pte.	W/Sl	2200	Philips Edward	Pte.	W/Sl
4137	Brooks Henry	Pte.	W/Sv	2452	Potter Michael	Pte.	W/Sv
3526	Burns Thomas	Pte.	W/Sv	1814	Price George	Pte.	W/Sl
2722	Cook Charles	Pte.	W/Sl	4011	Savoy Samuel	Pte.	W/Sv
3484	Cottam John	Pte.	W/Sv	3783	Sherwin Patrick	Pte.	W/Sv
3561	Cross George	Pte.	W/Sv	3731	Slaven James	Pte.	W/Sv
3953	Emmett John	Pte.	W/Sv	3841	Sullivan David	Pte.	W/Sl
3701	Fagan Michael	Pte.	W/Sl	2196	Wallace Joseph	Pte.	W/Sl
3555	Hague John	Pte.	W/Sv	3490	Willott James	Pte.	W/Sl
3185	Horsman William	Pte.	W/Sv	4177	Hawthorne Benjamin	Pte.	Missing
3390	Hunter Charles	Pte.	W/Sl	2528	McGarrity James	Pte.	Missing
3475	Lacy Henry	Pte.	W/Sv	2647	Ryan Patrick	Pte.	Missing
3771	Lamb John	Pte.	W/Sv	4033	Sherwin Edward	Pte.	Missing
4180	Laxton Henry	Pte.	W/Sl	3388	Snow James	Pte.	Missing
3697	Lee John	Pte.	W/Sl	4135	Thorn Thomas	Pte.	Missing

41st REGIMENT OF FOOT

NO.	NAME	RANK	CASUALTY	NO.	NAME	RANK	CASUALTY
	Eman J. CB.	Lt/Col.	Killed	3393	Robinson Thomas	Pte.	Killed
	Every E.	Capt.	Killed	3438	Scott Robert	Pte.	Killed
	Lockhart J. A.	Capt.	Killed	2245	Walsh William	Pte.	Killed
1852	Fitzgerald L. E.	Col/Sgt.	Killed	3198	Woodward James	Pte.	Killed
2436	Emerson John	Sergt.	Killed		Pratt R.	Major	W/Sl
2900	Wall John	Sergt.	Killed		Rowlands H.	Capt.	W/Sl
2023	Walsh Thomas	Sergt.	Killed		Hamilton J. A.	Lt.&Adj.	W/Sl
3653	Bannister John	Pte.	Killed		Kingscote F.	Lieut.	W/Sv
2950	Brennan Patrick	Pte.	Killed		Maude R. E.	Lieut.	W/Sl
2441	Cassidy Matthew	Pte.	Killed	1450	Harris John	Sgt/Mjr.	W/Sv
1950	Cavanagh Patrick	Pte.	Killed	2742	Davis William	Col/Sgt.	W/Sv
3532	Collins Edward	Pte.	Killed	2748	Kelly James	Col/Sgt.	W/Sv
3200	Dawson Arthur	Pte.	Killed	1180	Bond Daniel	Sergt.	W/Sl
3371	Donohoe Thomas	Pte.	Killed	2336	Cadam John	Sergt.	W/Sv
3607	Dunne John	Pte.	Killed	3180	Casson William	Sergt.	W/Sl
1477	Farley Robert	Pte.	Killed	2015	Clarke William	Sergt.	W/Sl
3369	Flinn Denis	Pte.	Killed	2378	Dunnigan Patrick	Sergt.	W/Sl
1701	Hart Michael	Pte.	Killed	1993	Gruly Edwin	Sergt.	W/Sl
2182	Hodgskins Thomas	Pte.	Killed	2978	Hynes John	Sergt.	W/Sl
2619	Joyce Walter	Pte.	Killed	2981	Jennings Patrick	Sergt.	W/Sl
3705	Lawrence Henry	Pte.	Killed	1257	Jones Davis	Sergt.	W/Sl
3736	Long Charles	Pte.	Killed	2730	O'Neil James	Sergt.	W/Sv
3030	McDonald Joseph	Pte.	Killed	2781	Welland Joseph	Sergt.	W/Sv
2749	Madigan John	Pte.	Killed	3388	Allum Samuel	Corpl.	W/Sl
2551	Mahony Daniel	Pte.	Killed	3602	Conlan Patrick	Corpl.	W/Sl
2963	Marsden William	Pte.	Killed	2367	Dowling Francis	Corpl.	W/Sl
3659	Millott Thomas	Pte.	Killed	2630	Evans Charles	Corpl.	W/Sv
3524	Morrow William	Pte.	Killed	3148	Farrell John	Corpl.	W/Sv
2332	Murphy Samuel	Pte.	Killed	2907	Hare Samuel	Corpl.	W/Sv
2991	Perry Patrick	Pte.	Killed	2670	Lee Francis	Corpl.	W/Sl
3396	Philpott Richard	Pte.	Killed	2584	O'Dea Martin	Corpl.	W/Sv
3699	Purkins Alexander	Pte.	Killed	3028	Molloy Peter	Drummer	W/Sl
1890	Reeves Richard	Pte.	Killed	3572	Alford Edward	Pte.	W/Sv

NOTES

The Final Attack on the Redan

41st REGIMENT OF FOOT

NO.	NAME	RANK	CASUALTY	NO.	NAME	RANK	CASUALTY
3675	Allen Joseph	Pte.	W/Sl	3117	Langley Adam	Pte.	W/Sv
3285	Beads William	Pte.	W/Sv	2781	Leonard Martin	Pte.	W/Sv
1414	Bishop Joseph	Pte.	W/Sl	3346	Levinge Francis	Pte.	W/Sv
3243	Boland Dennis	Pte.	W/Sv	3642	Lewis Howell	Pte.	W/Sv
3285	Booth William	Pte.	W/Sv	3908	Lusk William	Pte.	W/Sv
1814	Bowles Henry	Pte.	W/Sl	3118	Lyons John	Pte.	W/Sv
3131	Brown Denis	Pte.	W/Sl	3156	McCormick Andrew	Pte.	W/Sl
3266	Calman Michael	Pte.	W/Sl	3197	McDale James	Pte.	W/Sv
3389	Carroll Thomas	Pte.	W/Sv	3094	McInnery James	Pte.	W/Sl
3700	Carter John	Pte.	W/Sv	2334	McKeough James	Pte.	W/D
2712	Clyde William	Pte.	W/Sv	2445	McMahon John	Pte.	W/Sv
2486	Connell Denis	Pte.	W/Sl	2429	McMahon Terence	Pte.	W/Sl
2711	Craine Charles	Pte.	W/Sl	3157	Mage George	Pte.	W/Sv
3070	Cranston Robert	Pte.	W/Sl	2918	Martin Christopher	Pte.	W/Sv
2487	Daley Patrick	Pte.	W/Sl	3782	Matthews Joseph	Pte.	W/Sl
2561	Darling Owen	Pte.	W/Sl	3445	Moloney John	Pte.	W/Sv
3166	Dealy Joseph	Pte.	W/Sv	3922	Monaghan Michael	Pte.	W/Sv
3145	Dempsey John	Pte.	W/Sl	3137	Moor Michael	Pte.	W/Sl
3165	Dingan William	Pte.	W/Sl	1919	Morgan Morgan	Pte.	W/Sl
3529	Doherty James	Pte.	W/Sl	2892	Murphy John	Pte.	W/Sv
2000	Draper John	Pte.	W/Sv	2726	Murray Charles	Pte.	W/Sl
2755	Edwards George	Pte.	W/Sl	3769	Nugent William	Pte.	W/Sv
3686	Elliot Thomas	Pte.	W/Sv	2456	O'Brien John	Pte.	W/Sl
3376	Eustace Michael	Pte.	W/Sv	3377	O'Meally James	Pte.	W/Sv
2902	Fitzgerald William	Pte.	W/Sv	3056	Perkins James	Pte.	W/Sl
2266	Flood John	Pte.	W/Sv	1792	Petley Thomas	Pte.	W/Sv
2011	Forbes Thomas	Pte.	W/D	3559	Phillips Daniel	Pte.	W/Sl
2699	Gaffney Michael	Pte.	W/D	3555	Reilly Thomas	Pte.	W/Sv
3473	Gaynor Patrick	Pte.	W/Sl	1903	Reynolds William	Pte.	W/Sv
2666	Giffaney Charles	Pte.	W/Sv	2302	Richards Michael	Pte.	W/Sv
2354	Grace Michael	Pte.	W/Sv	2829	Ritchie Matthew	Pte.	W/Sv
3140	Gready Peter	Pte.	W/Sl	2776	Robb William	Pte.	W/Sl
3351	Gregg William	Pte.	W/Sv	1650	Roe John	Pte.	W/Sl
3126	Hackett John	Pte.	W/Sl	2979	Rogan Martin	Pte.	W/Sv
2612	Hackett Patrick	Pte.	W/Sv	3468	Rooney John	Pte.	W/Sv
2661	Hagan Hugh	Pte.	W/Sl	2627	Sheehy James	Pte.	W/Sv
1749	Hallson John	Pte.	W/Sv	3704	Smith Ralph	Pte.	W/Sv
3365	Hammond William	Pte.	W/Sv	2482	Starkey Peter	Pte.	W/Sv
2507	Hanstan Richard	Pte.	W/Sl	3179	Stones John	Pte.	W/Sl
1726	Harris William	Pte.	W/Sv	3200	Tremble Patrick	Pte.	W/Sl
3831	Harrison John	Pte.	W/Sl	2726	Underwood Thomas	Pte.	W/Sl
2871	Hennessy Michael	Pte.	W/Sl	3557	Varo Edward	Pte.	W/Sl
2598	Henry John	Pte.	W/Sl	3106	Wall James	Pte.	W/Sv
2796	Herlihy Patrick	Pte.	W/Sl	3401	Sheean Benjamin	Corpl.	Missing
2555	Howard John	Pte.	W/Sl	3288	Cox David	Pte.	Missing
3077	Hughes John	Pte.	W/Sv	2214	Culbert John	Pte.	Missing
3291	Hunt James	Pte.	W/Sl	3586	Donnolly Thomas	Pte.	Missing
3510	Johnson James	Pte.	W/Sl	2535	Driscoll Michael	Pte.	Missing
3324	Johnston Thomas	Pte.	W/Sv	3335	Ennis Patrick	Pte.	Missing
2539	Jones John	Pte.	W/Sl	3502	Farrell Patrick	Pte.	Missing
3246	Kelly John	Pte.	W/Sv	1850	Higgin Myles	Pte.	Missing
3049	Kelly Thomas	Pte.	W/Sv	3768	Keen John	Pte.	Missing
3832	Kelly Timothy	Pte.	W/Sl	1210	Langham Samuel	Pte.	Missing
3132	Kennedy James	Pte.	W/Sl	3736	McMahon Thomas	Pte.	Missing
3420	Kennelly John	Pte.	W/Sl	3425	Neill Henry	Pte.	Missing
2305	Kiernan Michael	Pte.	W/Sl	2434	O'Hallaran Martin	Pte.	Missing
2335	Kilmurray James	Pte.	W/Sl	3725	Pratley Edward	Pte.	Missing
3439	Kingdom George	Pte.	W/Sl	3428	Roe James	Pte.	Missing
1545	Lane John	Pte.	W/Sv	3606	Smith John	Pte.	Missing

NOTES

The Final Attack on the Redan
42nd REGIMENT OF FOOT

NO.	NAME	RANK	CASUALTY	NO.	NAME	RANK	CASUALTY
2856	Crawford John	Corp.	Killed	3136	James Richard	Pte.	W/Sl
2230	White Peter	Sgt/Mjr.	W/Sl	2397	McKillop John	Pte.	W/D
2289	Dickson John	Corpl.	W/Sl	1151	McMillan Charles	Pte.	W/Sl
3567	Hadden William	L/Cpl.	W/Sl	3015	Mill Alexander	Pte.	W/Sl
2764	Morrison James	Drummer	W/Sl	2690	Mitchell James	Pte.	W/Sl
3096	Brien John	Pte.	W/Sl	3490	Neilson William	Pte.	W/Sl
2865	Colvin John	Pte.	W/Sl	3210	Roddis James	Pte.	W/Sl
1724	Cunningham Charles	Pte.	W/Sl	1197	Williamson John	Pte.	W/Sv
3202	Haynes William	Pte.	W/Sl	3727	Williamson John	Pte.	W/Sl
3618	Hope James	Pte.	W/Sl	2815	Wilson James	Pte.	W/Sl

46th REGIMENT OF FOOT

NO.	NAME	RANK	CASUALTY
3622	Williams John	Pte.	W/Sl

47th REGIMENT OF FOOT

NO.	NAME	RANK	CASUALTY	NO.	NAME	RANK	CASUALTY
1325	Davis Daniel	Pte.	Killed	1857	Jowles W.	Pte.	W/Sl
3514	Fletcher John	Pte.	Killed	3515	Kennedy J.	Pte.	W/Sl
2847	Cummins Michael	Pte.	Killed	1718	Lambert T.	Pte.	W/Sl
	Rooke W. F. G.	Br/Major	W/Sv	3068	McGrath J.	Pte.	W/Sl
2596	Cavanagh T.	Corpl.	W/Sv	3607	Martin P.	Pte.	W/Sl
2727	Melican E.	Corpl.	W/Sv	3164	Murphy F.	Pte.	W/Sl
2377	O'Loughlin C.	Corpl.	W/Sl	3167	Padget W.	Pte.	W/Sl
2694	Tiley J.	Corpl.	W/Sl	3463	Pearson J.	Pte.	W/Sl
3100	Ballia J.	Pte.	W/Sv	3122	Rielly T.	Pte.	W/Sv
3166	Barlow T.	Pte.	W/Sv	2102	Rourke P.	Pte.	W/Sl
2272	Bryan M.	Pte.	W/Sl	2169	Rush J.	Pte.	W/Sl
1899	Collins P.	Pte.	W/Sl	3233	Smith J.	Pte.	W/Sl
3437	Cotterall E.	Pte.	W/Sl	3436	Taylor S.	Pte.	W/Sl
2373	Douglass W.	Pte.	W/D	2963	Trussell E.	Pte.	W/Sl
3481	Fitzpatrick —	Pte.	W/Sl	3321	Wiggins J.	Pte.	W/Sl

48th REGIMENT OF FOOT

NO.	NAME	RANK	CASUALTY	NO.	NAME	RANK	CASUALTY
1351	Brown Thomas	Corpl.	W/Sl	3044	Cameron David	Pte.	W/Sl
2951	Thompson James	Corpl.	W/Sl	2731	Kelly Thomas	Pte.	W/Sl
2273	Byford Samuel	Pte.	W/Sl				

49th REGIMENT OF FOOT

NO.	NAME	RANK	CASUALTY	NO.	NAME	RANK	CASUALTY
	Rochfort G.	Capt.	Killed	3144	Connors J.	Pte.	W/Sl
3555	Bennett John	Pte.	Killed	2542	Deerne H.	Pte.	W/Sl
2883	Dougherty J.	Pte.	Killed	2553	Dixon F.	Pte.	W/Sl
	King J. H.	Br/Major	W/Sv	2895	Flood J.	Pte.	W/Sl
	Mitchell C.	Ensign	W/D	1958	Johnston J.	Pte.	W/Sl
2418	Fahy M.	Sergt.	W/Sv	3004	Laird D.	Pte.	W/Sl
2371	Gavagan J.	Sergt.	W/Sv	2792	Laverie O.	Pte.	W/Sl
2383	Messer J.	Corpl.	W/Sl	3156	Livock J.	Pte.	W/Sv
3671	Caldwell A.	Pte.	W/Sl	3105	McGarth E.	Pte.	W/D
3809	Cavanagh J.	Pte.	W/Sv	3716	McKenna M.	Pte.	W/Sl

NOTES

The Final Attack on the Redan

49th REGIMENT OF FOOT

NO.	NAME	RANK	CASUALTY	NO.	NAME	RANK	CASUALTY
2442	McQuade J.	Pte.	W/Sl	1622	Pendrigh A.	Pte.	W/Sv
2721	Mahoney T.	Pte.	W/Sv	3400	Reed C.	Pte.	W/Sv
2487	Martin J.	Pte.	W/Sv	3564	Toner P.	Pte.	W/Sl
2596	Meikle D.	Pte.	W/Sl	2121	Verrinder C.	Pte.	W/Sl
1973	Moroney T.	Pte.	W/Sv	1415	Walsh M.	Pte.	W/Sl
2390	Mulvaney J.	Pte.	W/Sl				

55th REGIMENT OF FOOT

NO.	NAME	RANK	CASUALTY	NO.	NAME	RANK	CASUALTY
	Cuddy W. H.	Br/Lt/Col.	Killed	1778	Ashton Joseph	Pte.	W/D
2696	Sayers Thomas	L/Sgt.	Killed	1205	Ashworthy Henry	Pte.	W/Sv
2825	Mekless George	Corpl.	Killed	3316	Barrett David	Pte.	W/Sv
2180	Barrett William	Pte.	Killed	2771	Bowen Stephen	Pte.	W/Sl
2399	Berryman William	Pte.	Killed	3788	Boyle James	Pte.	W/Sv
2919	Brown James	Pte.	Killed	3394	Boyle Michael	Pte.	W/Sv
3502	Brown Thomas	Pte.	Killed	3402	Brannan James	Pte.	W/Sl
3326	Burrell George	Pte.	Killed	2853	Bray Michael	Pte.	W/Sv
3336	Egan Joseph	Pte.	Killed	2813	Bridges George	Pte.	W/Sl
3078	Harman Henry	Pte.	Killed	2240	Brockhurst James	Pte.	W/Sl
1686	Haughton William	Pte.	Killed	3100	Brophy Patrick	Pte.	W/Sv
3728	Heavie George	Pte.	Killed	3769	Broughton William	Pte.	W/Sl
3442	McDowall William	Pte.	Killed	3687	Burns Michael	Pte.	W/Sv
3209	Minoge James	Pte.	Killed	3506	Byres Andrew	Pte.	W/D
3576	Morton Samuel	Pte.	Killed	3508	Campbell James	Pte.	W/Sv
3323	Paynes James	Pte.	Killed	3688	Carney James	Pte.	W/Sv
2837	Penny William	Pte.	Killed	3247	Carter William	Pte.	W/Sl
3465	Pine Patrick	Pte.	Killed	2576	Carty Thomas	Pte.	W/Sv
3471	Ryan Andrew	Pte.	Killed	3766	Channer Frederick	Pte.	W/Sv
3055	Ryan Patrick	Pte.	Killed	2373	Chapple William	Pte.	W/Sl
2991	Salter Thomas	Pte.	Killed	3512	Christie Peter	Pte.	W/Sv
3597	Summers John	Pte.	Killed	2923	Cleary John	Pte.	W/Sl
3036	Taylor Joseph	Pte.	Killed	3727	Clough William	Pte.	W/Sl
3609	Walsh Michael	Pte.	Killed	3281	Conolly John	Pte.	W/Sv
3603	Watson Morris	Pte.	Killed	3678	Cronan Patrick	Pte.	W/Sl
3271	White Michael	Pte.	Killed	3145	Cronigan Thomas	Pte.	W/Sv
3003	White William	Pte.	Killed	2495	Daser Michael (Alias Dea)	Pte.	W/Sv
	Cure A. C.	Major	W/Sv				
	Hume J. R.	Capt.	W/Sv	3515	Davidson James	Pte.	W/Sv
	Hume R.	Capt.	W/Sv	3742	Dillon Michael	Pte.	W/Sl
	Richards W. H.	Capt.	W/Sl	3420	Doyle John	Pte.	W/Sv
	Johnson W. B.	Lieut.	W/Sv	2508	Dunn James	Pte.	W/D
1591	Furphy James	Col/Sgt.	W/Sv	2780	Elliston John	Pte.	W/Sl
2446	Parsons William	Col/Sgt.	W/Sl	2870	Farrell John	Pte.	W/Sv
1528	Pope Peter	Col/Sgt.	W/Sl	3664	Flannagan James	Pte.	W/Sl
2229	Farren James	Sergt.	W/Sl	3523	Fleming Thomas	Pte.	W/Sv
2882	Hendrick —	Sergt.	W/Sv	2265	Flood James	Pte.	W/Sl
2177	McCloy Alexander	Sergt.	W/Sv	3122	Flynn Martin	Pte.	W/Sl
2648	Meara James	Sergt.	W/Sv	3645	Flynn Michael	Pte.	Missing
2539	White Charles	Sergt.	W/Sl	3109	Fogarty Martin	Pte.	W/Sv
2407	Armstrong William	Corpl.	W/Sl	3317	Foster Martin	Pte.	W/D
2629	Bussicott James	Corpl.	W/Sl	3371	Frawley John	Pte.	W/Sv
2689	Churchfield Joseph	Corpl.	W/Sv	3525	Gale Thomas	Pte.	W/Sv
3680	Cooke John	Corpl.	W/Sv	2523	Geary James	Pte.	W/Sl
3192	Fowler Joseph	Corpl.	W/Sv	3528	Grant George	Pte.	W/D
3764	Halgenfield Joseph	Corpl.	W/Sl	2788	Hennessey James	Pte.	W/Sl
3520	Hay Peter	Corpl.	W/Sv	2462	Henry Michael	Pte.	W/Sl
3160	Kennedy Ferdinand	Corpl.	W/Sv	1343	Herring William	Pte.	W/Sl
3625	Neyland Michael	Corpl.	W/Sl	3775	Hillier Frederick	Pte.	W/Sv
2905	O'Donnell John	Corpl.	W/Sv	3731	Hoare Jeremiah	Pte.	W/Sl
2868	Tierney David	Corpl.	W/Sl	3298	Hogan John	Pte.	W/Sl
2463	Toole Patrick	Corpl.	W/Sl	2738	Hogdin John	Pte.	W/Sv
2433	Walsh Maurice	Corpl.	W/Sv	3681	Hopkins John	Pte.	W/Sl

NOTES

The Final Attack on the Redan

55th REGIMENT OF FOOT

NO.	NAME	RANK	CASUALTY	NO.	NAME	RANK	CASUALTY
3439	Hughes Bryan	Pte.	W/Sv	2979	O'Leary Edward	Pte.	W/Sl
1841	Johnston Thomas	Pte.	W/Sl	2219	Osborne Thomas	Pte.	W/Sv
3239	Kennedy James	Pte.	W/Sl	3068	Parker James	Pte.	W/Sl
3124	Kilbride Michael	Pte.	W/Sl	2827	Parsons Charles	Pte.	W/Sv
1524	Legge John	Pte.	W/Sl	3307	Powell Isaac	Pte.	Missing
3183	Lennon Peter	Pte.	W/Sl	3268	Quilligan Michael	Pte.	W/Sv
3779	Lock Charles	Pte.	W/Sl	2807	Saunders Thomas	Pte.	W/Sl
3282	Lyons John	Pte.	W/Sv	3583	Scorgie William	Pte.	W/Sl
3542	McDiarmid Archibald	Pte.	W/Sv	3757	Seabright Benjamin	Pte.	Missing
2682	McIntyre Hugh	Pte.	W/Sv	2473	Sinnott Miles	Pte.	W/Sl
3558	McKinnon John	Pte.	W/Sv	3129	Spring James	Pte.	W/Sl
3705	McMahon John	Pte.	W/D	2739	Stephenson John	Pte.	W/Sl
2336	Magson Saul	Pte.	W/Sv	3593	Stevenson Thomas	Pte.	W/Sv
2503	Mahoney William	Pte.	W/Sl	3072	Stone Joseph	Pte.	W/Sv
1422	Matthews Frederick	Pte.	W/Sl	3820	Strong James	Pte.	W/Sl
3320	Meara William	Pte.	W/Sv	3390	Sullivan Timothy	Pte.	W/Sl
2947	Meclican Connor	Pte.	W/Sl	1614	Talbot William	Pte.	W/Sv
3369	Morrisey John	Pte.	W/Sv	2685	Walsh Timothy	Pte.	W/Sv
3617	Murtough John	Pte.	W/Sv	3604	Weir John	Pte.	W/Sv
3392	O'Grady Michael	Pte.	W/Sv	2132	Whealan James	Pte.	W/Sl
2553	O'Halloran John	Pte.	W/Sl	3506	Wilson Joseph	Pte.	W/Sv
2404	O'Leary Daniel	Pte.	W/D				

57th REGIMENT OF FOOT

NO.	NAME	RANK	CASUALTY	NO.	NAME	RANK	CASUALTY
2204	Morgan Henry	Pte.	Killed	2872	Powell Thomas	Corpl.	W/Sv
1965	Phelan Michael	Sergt.	W/Sv	3334	Sullivan Patrick	Pte.	W/Sv
1864	Kennedy Michael	Corpl.	W/Sv				

62nd REGIMENT OF FOOT

NO.	NAME	RANK	CASUALTY	NO.	NAME	RANK	CASUALTY
	Cox L. A.	Capt.	Killed	2560	Hayter John	Sergt.	W/Sv
	Blakiston L.	Lieut.	Killed	2418	Newham William	Sergt.	W/Sl
2113	Garrett Matthew	Sergt.	Killed	3069	Newman James	Sergt.	W/Sl
1508	Holmes William	Sergt.	Killed	2580	Biddiscombe Francis	Corpl.	W/Sl
2230	Norman George	Sergt.	Killed	3528	Corbett William	Corpl.	W/Sl
3375	Bunn John	Corpl.	Killed	3430	Elliott Francis	Corpl.	W/Sl
2598	Cleary John	Corpl.	Killed	2594	Hill William	Corpl.	W/Sl
3280	Lane John	Corpl.	Killed	3395	Smith William	Corpl.	W/Sv
3193	White John	Corpl.	Killed	3245	Trollope Thomas	Corpl.	W/Sv
3051	Treynor Henry	Drummer	Killed	3717	Stroud George	L/Cpl.	W/Sl
3477	Allen Thomas	Pte.	Killed	3369	Browne Edward	Pte.	W/Sl
3497	Bell James	Pte.	Killed	223-	Buchanan Robert	Pte.	W/Sv
1620	Bryant John	Pte.	Killed	3809	Campbell Patrick	Pte.	W/Sv
2250	Clarke James	Pte.	Killed	3816	Cassidy William	Pte.	W/Sv
3224	Costello Samuel	Pte.	Killed	3798	Coles Edwin	Pte.	W/Sl
2143	Flynn John	Pte.	Killed	3351	Conroy John	Pte.	W/Sl
2680	Jordan William	Pte.	Killed	2673	Crossly John	Pte.	W/Sl
3574	Magner Robert	Pte.	Killed	3677	Darknell James	Pte.	W/Sv
3284	Murphy Edward	Pte.	Killed	1672	Day John	Pte.	W/Sl
3760	Ritchins Joseph	Pte.	Killed	3678	Dickson Robert	Pte.	W/Sv
3766	Sandy John	Pte.	Killed	2925	Dixon Hezekiel	Pte.	W/Sl
2571	Strange Henry	Pte.	Killed	3815	Doherty James	Pte.	W/Sv
3506	Taggart James	Pte.	Killed	3334	Dunne John	Pte.	W/Sl
	Tyler L. B.	Lt/Col.	W/Sv	2551	Dunphy Stephen	Pte.	W/Sl
	Hunter E. H.	Capt.	W/Sl	1490	Dwyer John	Pte.	W/Sl
	Davenport W. B.	Lieut.	W/Sv	3692	Dyson John	Pte.	W/Sl
	Dring W.	Lieut.	W/Sl	1505	Everett Frederick	Pte.	W/Sv
2390	Young Joseph	Col/Sgt.	W/Sl	2769	Flynn Patrick	Pte.	W/Sv

NOTES

The Final Attack on the Redan

62nd REGIMENT OF FOOT

NO.	NAME	RANK	CASUALTY	NO.	NAME	RANK	CASUALTY
3587	Fox George	Pte.	W/Sv	3560	Perdue James	Pte.	W/Sl
2773	Frizzle James	Pte.	W/Sl	3724	Pike Henry	Pte.	W/Sl
3633	Gibberson William	Pte.	W/Sv	3394	Pole Alfred	Pte.	W/Sv
2960	Gorman Matthew	Pte.	W/Sl	3527	Power Edward	Pte.	W/Sv
3510	Healy John	Pte.	W/Sv	3495	Robinson John	Pte.	W/Sv
3561	Hedley Simeon	Pte.	W/Sl	2774	Robinson John	Pte.	W/Sl
3202	Hennessy Edmund	Pte.	W/Sv	3308	Russell John	Pte.	W/Sv
2685	Hewitt Robert	Pte.	W/Sl	3743	Short Henry	Pte.	W/Sv
3521	Higgins Michael	Pte.	W/Sv	3608	Skelly Thomas	Pte.	W/Sv
3049	Hume William	Pte.	W/Sv	3767	Slugg Solomon	Pte.	W/Sv
3758	Jones Joseph	Pte.	W/Sl	3562	Smith James	Pte.	W/Sl
3306	Kenny Joseph	Pte.	W/Sl	3520	Sullivan Jeremiah	Pte.	W/Sl
3288	King Patrick	Pte.	W/Sv	3580	Sullivan Maurice	Pte.	W/Sl
3530	Kirby Patrick	Pte.	W/Sl	2225	Tarrant James	Pte.	W/Sv
3523	Lawler John	Pte.	W/Sv	3820	Terriss Jacob	Pte.	W/Sl
3077	Lynch Patrick	Pte.	W/Sl	3537	Titball James	Pte.	W/Sv
3113	McCarthy John	Pte.	W/Sv	3569	Twigg John	Pte.	W/Sl
3742	McGrain Patrick	Pte.	W/Sl	3807	Webster James	Pte.	W/Sl
3754	McGrath James	Pte.	W/Sl	3417	Young Cornelius	Sergt.	Missing
3320	McIntyre James	Pte.	W/Sl	3277	Coleman Daniel	Corpl.	Missing
2849	McSharry John	Pte.	W/Sl	3736	Caffrey Hugh	Pte.	Missing
3165	Maguire Thomas	Pte.	W/Sl	3559	Doyle John	Pte.	Missing
3609	Middleton George	Pte.	W/Sl	3579	Driscoll Daniel	Pte.	Missing
2585	Mills Charles	Pte.	W/Sl	3314	Dwyer William	Pte.	Missing
3144	Mitchem John	Pte.	W/Sl	2819	Lough Michael	Pte.	Missing
2961	Mittendorf Charles F.	Pte.	W/Sl	3673	McLeod Michael	Pte.	Missing
3661	Morrissey James	Pte.	W/Sv	3814	Moore John	Pte.	Missing
3542	Neil James	Pte.	W/Sv	3396	Reddick George	Pte.	Missing

63rd REGIMENT OF FOOT

NO.	NAME	RANK	CASUALTY	NO.	NAME	RANK	CASUALTY
2617	Norton Martin	Pte.	Killed	1994	Crossley George	Pte.	W/Sl
	Lindesay P.	Lt/Col.	W/Sv	3704	Dowd Martin	Pte.	W/D
1992	Gillooly Michael	Sergt.	W/Sv	3796	Wood Charles	Pte.	W/Sl
3690	Coy William	Pte.	W/Sv				

68th REGIMENT OF FOOT

NO.	NAME	RANK	CASUALTY
3174	Long Michael	Pte.	W/Sl

72nd REGIMENT OF FOOT

NO.	NAME	RANK	CASUALTY	NO.	NAME	RANK	CASUALTY
2336	Robson John	Pte.	Killed				
	McDonald J.	Qrtr/Mstr.	W/Sv	3143	Johnston Peter	Pte.	W/Sl
2453	Jamieson Robert	Sergt.	W/Sl	3100	McCall James	Pte.	W/Sv
2351	McKenzie Donald	Corpl.	W/Sv	2330	McDonald Alexander	Pte.	W/Sl
3344	Chrystal Timothy	Pte.	W/Sl	3232	McGarry Patrick	Pte.	W/Sv
3119	Cuttrill Joseph	Pte.	W/Sl	3106	McIntyre John	Pte.	W/Sv
2782	Dodds John	Pte.	W/Sv	2736	McNeil Alexander	Pte.	W/Sl
3136	Hall William	Pte.	W/Sv	3208	Mathews Lawrence	Pte.	W/Sl
3254	Henderson John	Pte.	W/Sl	3436	Reilly James	Pte.	W/Sv
3086	Hogg Alexander	Pte.	W/Sl	1870	Sibbald William	Pte.	W/Sl
3146	Jack Daniel	Pte.	W/Sl	3161	Stewart Alexander	Pte.	W/Sv

NOTES

The Final Attack on the Redan

77th REGIMENT OF FOOT

NO.	NAME	RANK	CASUALTY	NO.	NAME	RANK	CASUALTY
	Parker W.	Capt.	Killed	1886	Delahunty Patrick	Pte.	W/Sv
1736	Maher Thomas	Col/Sgt.	Killed	3353	Donaldson James	Pte.	W/Sv
2391	Mann William	Sergt.	Killed	3218	Duffield John	Pte.	W/Sv
2392	Riches Thomas	Sergt.	Killed	2985	Fox James John	Pte.	W/Sv
3687	Wilton Thomas	Corpl.	Killed	2842	Gilchrist John	Pte.	W/Sv
3534	Buse George	Pte.	Killed	3261	Gold Charles	Pte.	W/Sl
2921	Cox James	Pte.	Killed	2775	Gorman Michael	Pte.	W/Sv
1162	Davin Stephen	Pte.	Killed	3547	Greer Archibald	Pte.	W/Sl
3540	Farney Henry	Pte.	Killed	3013	Gribben Henry	Pte.	W/Sv
3412	Fenton Denis	Pte.	Killed	3107	Hardinge Elliott	Pte.	W/Sv
3559	Hines Thomas	Pte.	Killed	3548	Keery Price	Pte.	W/Sv
1716	Hyde Thomas	Pte.	Killed	1865	Kenna Michael	Pte.	W/Sv
852	Lynch Bernard	Pte.	Killed	2954	Kilkenny Neil	Pte.	W/Sv
2806	Tivingstone Thomas	Pte.	Killed	2818	Lancastle George	Pte.	W/Sv
	Butts W. J.	Capt.	W/Sv	3555	McCulloch Isaiah	Pte.	W/Sv
	Knowles C. B.	Lieut.	W/Sv	1958	Maher John	Pte.	W/Sv
	Leggett W. G.	Lieut.	W/Sl	2545	Neil James	Pte.	W/Sv
	Waters M. A.	Lieut.	W/Sv	3035	Picton Thomas	Pte.	W/Sv
1708	Borritt Henry	Sgt/Mjr	W/Sv	3453	Riley Mathew	Pte.	W/Sv
1299	Fitzharris John	Col/Sgt.	W/Sv	3587	Roberts John	Pte.	W/Sv
2006	Beaumont Arthur	Sergt.	W/Sv	2684	Shaughnessy Mathew	Pte.	W/Sl
824	Bowden William	Sergt.	W/Sv	2857	Smiley James	Pte.	W/Sv
2380	Hope George	Sergt.	W/Sv	2988	Smith John	Pte.	W/Sv
2578	Mileman James	Sergt.	W/Sl	3185	Stone Francis	Pte.	W/Sv
2801	Rogers Terence	Corpl.	W/Sv	3242	Strain James	Pte.	W/Sl
2663	Steer George J.	Corpl.	W/Sv	3656	Tancred Robert	Pte.	W/Sv
2843	Thompson George	Corpl.	W/Sv	2756	Taylor Thomas	Pte.	W/Sv
3112	Armstrong John	Pte.	W/Sv	2989	Walker Joseph	Pte.	W/Sv
3405	Avoy James	Pte.	W/Sv	2128	Ward John	Pte.	W/Sv
3590	Baker Edward	Pte.	W/Sv	3148	Hanlan John	Sergt.	Missing
2870	Brophy Joseph	Pte.	W/Sv	2648	Fox William	Corpl.	Missing
2430	Carty John	Pte.	W/Sv	3392	Gallaway Hugh	Pte.	Missing
3155	Cassidy John	Pte.	W/Sv	1731	Greer John	Pte.	Missing
2840	Charleston Murdoch	Pte.	W/Sl	3500	Jones William	Pte.	Missing
3171	China James	Pte.	W/Sv	1973	Scullin Peter	Pte.	Missing
2014	Cotter John	Pte.	W/Sv	3604	Wilson William	Pte.	Missing
3510	Cotterell Henry	Pte.	W/Sv				

79th REGIMENT OF FOOT

NO.	NAME	RANK	CASUALTY	NO.	NAME	RANK	CASUALTY
3993	Auld John	Pte.	Killed	3682	Dunlop Thomas	Pte.	W/Sl
2368	McCormack John	Pte.	Killed	2346	McGregor James	Pte.	W/Sl
1258	Anderson John	Sergt.	W/D	3844	McLellan James	Pte.	W/Sl
2229	McKay Alexander	Sergt.	W/Sl	3169	Machray George	Pte.	W/D
2268	Borthwick James	Pte.	W/Sl	2215	Machray James	Pte.	W/D
3219	Bremer James	Pte.	W/Sl	2912	Machray James	Pte.	W/D
2977	Cruickshanks John	Pte.	W/Sl				

88th REGIMENT OF FOOT

NO.	NAME	RANK	CASUALTY	NO.	NAME	RANK	CASUALTY
	Grogan H. W.	Capt.	Killed	1963	Myers Michael	Pte.	Killed
2412	Flaherty John	Sergt.	Killed	2789	O'Brien Bartholomew	Pte.	Killed
1479	Price Samuel	Sergt.	Killed	2132	O'Donnel James	Pte.	Killed
2654	Conroy Thomas	Pte.	Killed	2632	O'Neill John	Pte.	Killed
3367	Dunleavy Thomas	Pte.	Killed	2941	Price James	Pte.	Killed
3630	Dunne Edward	Pte.	Killed	2892	Sullivan Patrick	Pte.	Killed
3729	Fahey Thomas	Pte.	Killed	2426	Sullivan Thomas	Pte.	Killed

NOTES

The Final Attack on the Redan

88th REGIMENT OF FOOT

NO.	NAME	RANK	CASUALTY	NO.	NAME	RANK	CASUALTY
	Maxwell G. V. CB.	Lt/Col.	W/Sv	3047	Horam Tully	Pte.	W/Sl
	Mauleverer B. B.	Capt.	W/Sv	3471	Keane Patrick	Pte.	W/Sv
	Beresford G. R.	Capt.	W/Sv	2951	Kelcher John	Pte.	W/D
	Hopton E.	Lieut.	W/Sv	3664	Kelly Joseph	Pte.	W/D
	Lambert W.	Lieut.	W/Sv	3362	Kelly Thomas	Pte.	W/Sv
	Scott L. C.	Lieut.	W/Sv	3425	Kenney John	Pte.	W/Sv
	Watson G. S.	Lieut.	W/Sv	3422	Lawson Michael	Pte.	W/Sv
	Walker G.	Ensign	W/Sv	2049	Lee John	Pte.	W/Sv
2199	Cooney Patrick	Sgt/Mjr.	W/Sv	3570	Lewis John	Pte.	W/D
1029	James John	Sergt.	W/Sv	3817	Lyons John	Pte.	W/Sv
1793	Mahon Patrick	Sergt.	W/Sl	3535	McAllister James	Pte.	W/D
2893	Millan Hugh	Sergt.	W/Sl	3870	McAvenna Edward	Pte.	W/Sl
2848	Prendible Thomas	Sergt.	W/Sl	2700	McCormick James	Pte.	W/Sl
3125	Prendible Thomas	Sergt.	W/Sv	3004	McDermott John	Pte.	W/Sl
2262	Warren Michael	Sergt.	W/Sv	3510	McKunn Michael	Pte.	W/Sv
2774	Condon James	Corpl.	W/Sv	3465	McLoughlan Charles	Pte.	W/Sv
1950	Connolly Patrick	Corpl.	W/Sv	2723	McNamara Patrick	Pte.	W/Sv
1995	Dolan Patrick	Corpl.	W/Sv	3922	McNamee James	Pte.	W/Sv
3536	Herlin James	Corpl.	W/Sv	3859	McNamee James	Pte.	W/Sv
2268	Quill John	Corpl.	W/Sv	3289	Mabe Charles	Pte.	W/Sv
1502	Carey Thomas	Drummer	W/Sv	3826	Maddigan James	Pte.	W/Sl
3329	Ashworth William	Pte.	W/Sv	2948	Marmion James	Pte.	W/Sl
3970	Beglan Michael	Pte.	W/Sv	3098	Mathew George	Pte.	W/Sv
3590	Bourke John	Pte.	W/Sl	3298	Mills William	Pte.	W/Sv
2761	Brett William	Pte.	W/Sl	3140	Moran Timothy	Pte.	W/Sv
3631	Briggey Patrick	Pte.	W/Sv	2997	Mulcahey Michael	Pte.	W/Sl
3256	Bryan George	Pte.	W/Sv	3936	Murnick Michael	Pte.	W/Sv
3890	Burnside John	Pte.	W/Sv	3933	Murphy Thomas	Pte.	W/Sl
2967	Canter James	Pte.	W/Sv	3204	Murray Dominic	Pte.	W/Sv
3389	Carney James	Pte.	W/Sv	2936	Nee Martin	Pte.	W/Sv
2925	Casry William	Pte.	W/Sv	3734	Neill Arthur	Pte.	W/D
2234	Clarke Charles	Pte.	W/Sl	2646	Nelly John	Pte.	W/Sv
3419	Coffee John	Pte.	W/Sl	4037	Noon Timothy	Pte.	W/Sl
3566	Connell James	Pte.	W/Sv	3880	O'Brien John	Pte.	W/Sv
2435	Connolly John	Pte.	W/Sv	2898	O'Rourke Patrick	Pte.	W/Sl
2844	Connors James	Pte.	W/Sv	3334	Patten James	Pte.	W/Sv
3547	Connors John	Pte.	W/Sv	3320	Platt Thomas	Pte.	W/Sv
2087	Connors John	Pte.	W/Sv	1208	Price John	Pte.	W/Sv
3018	Connors Patrick	Pte.	W/Sv	3780	Purcell Henry	Pte.	W/Sv
3661	Coogan John	Pte.	W/Sl	—	Quinlan William	Pte.	W/Sv
3684	Corbett Thomas	Pte.	W/Sl	3864	Quinn Daniel	Pte.	W/Sv
3546	Cox Thomas	Pte.	W/D	3848	Quinn James	Pte.	W/Sv
3742	Cummings Michael	Pte.	W/Sv	3588	Reilly Edward	Pte.	W/Sv
2971	Cunniff Michael	Pte.	W/Sv	3832	Reilly Thomas	Pte.	W/Sl
2978	Cunningham James	Pte.	W/Sv	3002	Rielly Thomas	Pte.	W/Sl
1852	Danaher Michael	Pte.	W/D	4016	Rooney Michael	Pte.	W/D
2017	Dowd Michael	Pte.	W/Sv	3417	Rutledge Richard	Pte.	W/Sv
3370	Doyle Christopher	Pte.	W/Sv	2913	Scanlon John	Pte.	W/Sl
4022	Dunn Patrick	Pte.	W/Sv	3250	Shannon Patrick	Pte.	W/Sv
911	Dunwoody William	Pte.	W/Sv	2633	Smith George	Pte.	W/Sv
3540	Falkner Francis	Pte.	W/Sv	3563	Smith George	Pte.	W/Sl
3629	Farley Lawrence	Pte.	W/Sv	2432	Stack Robert	Pte.	W/Sv
2713	Farrel James	Pte.	W/Sl	3395	Sullivan Timothy	Pte.	W/Sv
3835	Farrell John	Pte.	W/Sv	3098	Walker George	Pte.	W/Sl
—	Gannon Patrick	Pte.	W/Sv	3813	Walsh John	Pte.	W/Sv
3168	Gascoyne John	Pte.	W/Sl	4002	Whitehead William	Pte.	W/Sl
3459	Geage Samuel	Pte.	W/Sv	3562	Cullen Joseph	Corpl.	Missing
2463	Gennungs Edward	Pte.	W/Sv	3149	Bourke John	Pte.	Missing
3527	Graynaw Patrick	Pte.	W/Sl	3443	Colgan James	Pte.	Missing
1421	Gunning Andrew	Pte.	W/D	3330	Gaffrey Michael	Pte.	Missing
3962	Hallett Isaac	Pte.	W/Sl	2944	Griffen John	Pte.	Missing
3489	Handley Richard	Pte.	W/Sv	2971	Hayes William	Pte.	Missing
3538	Hawkins Henry	Pte.	W/Sv	—	Kelly Patrick	Pte.	Missing
2151	Higgins John	Pte.	W/Sl	3384	Kidd George	Pte.	Missing
3897	Holden John	Pte.	W/Sv	2518	King John	Pte.	Missing

NOTES

The Final Attack on the Redan

88th REGIMENT OF FOOT

NO.	NAME	RANK	CASUALTY	NO.	NAME	RANK	CASUALTY
1392	McGough James	Pte.	Missing	3894	Terrante William	Pte.	Missing
3072	McGuinness Bernard	Pte.	Missing	3571	Tibbing Patrick	Pte.	Missing
3517	Moore Thomas	Pte.	Missing	3909	Walsh James	Pte.	Missing
3400	O'Brien Edward	Pte.	Missing	1308	Ward Edward	Pte.	Missing
4019	Rooney Michael	Pte.	Missing	3912	Wright Henry	Pte.	Missing
2983	Sealy Andrew	Pte.	Missing				

90th REGIMENT OF FOOT

NO.	NAME	RANK	CASUALTY	NO.	NAME	RANK	CASUALTY
	Preston A.	Capt.	Killed	3929	Boyes J.	Pte.	W/Sv
	Vaughan H. M.	Capt.	Killed	3579	Brider W.	Pte.	W/Sv
	Swift A. D.	Lieut.	Killed	3388	Buckley D.	Pte.	W/Sv
	Wilmer H. F.	Lieut.	Killed	3976	Bumford J.	Pte.	W/Sl
2050	Ryan M.	Sergt.	Killed	3257	Carey M.	Pte.	W/Sv
2859	Handley H.	Corpl.	Killed	3275	Carey T.	Pte.	W/Sv
1921	Hickey T.	Pte.	Killed	2194	Carmagie D.	Pte.	W/Sv
3346	Murphy T.	Pte.	Killed	3814	Caves S.	Pte.	W/Sv
	Grove R.	Capt.	W/Sl	2419	Clancy W.	Pte.	W/Sv
	Perrin J.	Capt.	W/Sl	2970	Clements J.	Pte.	W/Sv
	Tinling W. B.	Capt.	W/Sv	3810	Coles T.	Pte.	W/Sv
	Wade J. H.	Capt.	W/Sv	3173	Collins M.	Pte.	W/Sl
	Deverill P. S.	Lieut.	W/Sv	3536	Comrie J.	Pte.	W/Sl
	Goodricke H. H.	Lieut.	W/Sv	3795	Cook A.	Pte.	W/Sv
	Grahame M.	Lieut.	W/Sl	3096	Cook J.	Pte.	W/Sv
	Haydock H. J.	Lieut.	W/Sl	3281	Cronan J.	Pte.	W/Sv
	Pigott Sir C. Bt.	Lieut.	W/Sv	3117	Crowrick T.	Pte.	W/Sv
	Rattray J. C.	Lieut.	W/Sv	2048	Cuddahy J.	Pte.	W/Sl
	Rous W. J.	Lieut.	W/Sl	2043	Cunningham P.	Pte.	W/Sl
1714	Bathurst A.	Col/Sgt.	W/Sv	3958	Dean W.	Pte.	W/Sv
2283	Fitzmaurice H.	Col/Sgt.	W/Sv	3229	Dogherty D.	Pte.	W/Sv
2268	King J.	Col/Sgt.	W/Sv	3922	Doyle J.	Pte.	W/Sv
3145	Burge R.	Sergt.	W/Sl	2994	Dunbar J.('79-90)	Pte.	W/Sl
2669	Canfor C.	Sergt.	W/Sv	2865	Eagles J.	Pte.	W/Sv
2005	Dobson W.	Sergt.	W/Sv	3961	England J.	Pte.	W/Sl
2978	Hutt H.	Sergt.	W/Sl	3149	English J.	Pte.	W/Sv
2853	Jefford H.	Sergt.	W/Sl	2100	English J.	Pte.	W/Sl
2609	Moyniham A.	Sergt.	W/Sl	2414	Etheridge G.	Pte.	W/Sv
2558	Riley T.	Sergt.	W/Sv	2529	Farday M.	Pte.	W/Sv
3162	Saunders R.	Sergt.	W/Sl	3440	Farrell P.	Pte.	W/Sl
2723	Williams J.	Sergt.	W/Sv	3390	Fay J.	Pte.	W/Sl
3189	Winstanley S.	Sergt.	W/Sv	3941	Fisher T.	Pte.	W/Sv
3236	Broadbridge R.	Corpl.	W/Sv	3321	Flewy T.	Pte.	W/Sv
2925	Donohue M.	Corpl.	W/Sl	3226	Fontaine H.	Pte.	W/Sv
2720	Hannafin D.	Corpl.	W/Sv	3500	Ford P.	Pte.	W/Sv
3536	Herling James	Corpl.	W/Sv	3753	Fuller H.	Pte.	W/Sl
3592	High H.	Corpl.	W/Sv	3647	Gentry J.	Pte.	W/Sv
2628	Hill H.	Corpl.	W/Sv	2628	Goldsmith J.	Pte.	W/Sv
2441	Miller W.	Corpl.	W/Sl	2148	Goodwin T.	Pte.	W/Sv
3481	Nicholls J.	Corpl.	W/Sv	3637	Graham A.	Pte.	W/Sv
2924	Salter W.	Corpl.	W/Sl	3683	Graham P.	Pte.	W/Sv
2922	Smith W.	Corpl.	W/Sv	3888	Grimwood J.	Pte.	W/Sv
2725	Allen R.	Pte.	W/Sl	3123	Harber T.	Pte.	W/Sv
2865	Allsop G.	Pte.	W/Sv	3488	Harding O.	Pte.	W/Sv
3337	Archer J.	Pte.	W/Sv	2987	Herlehey D.	Pte.	W/Sv
3872	Archer T.	Pte.	W/Sl	1600	Holness J.	Pte.	W/Sv
3532	Armott D.	Pte.	W/Sv	3940	Hughes J.	Pte.	W/Sv
3521	Bairnsfather W.	Pte.	W/Sv	3409	Inns T.	Pte.	W/D
3656	Battle M.	Pte.	W/Sl	3789	Jennings W.	Pte.	W/Sv
3689	Bellinger J.	Pte.	W/Sv	3484	Jones W.	Pte.	W/Sv
3266	Betts B.	Pte.	W/Sv	3391	Joyce P.	Pte.	W/Sv
3794	Beveridge W.	Pte.	W/Sv	3394	Kingston Edward	Pte.	W/Sl
3752	Binder J.	Pte.	W/Sv	2216	Kinross W.	Pte.	W/Sv

NOTES

The Final Attack on the Redan
90th REGIMENT OF FOOT

NO.	NAME	RANK	CASUALTY	NO.	NAME	RANK	CASUALTY
3345	Lawless J.	Pte.	W/Sl	3035	Whitmill J.	Pte.	W/Sv
3485	Lindo J.	Pte.	W/Sv	3600	William W.	Pte.	W/Sv
3617	Locke J.	Pte.	W/Sv	3802	Wright J.	Pte.	W/Sl
2515	Lomax C.	Pte.	W/Sv	2156	Bennett G.	Sergt.	Missing
3674	McKenzie D.	Pte.	W/Sl	2098	Dally J.	Sergt.	Missing
3668	McKeon T.	Pte.	W/Sv	2886	Kimpton J.	Sergt.	Missing
3359	McLelland J.	Pte.	W/Sv	2623	Walker F.	Sergt.	Missing
3974	McLeod W.	Pte.	W/Sl	3228	Dunning J.	Corpl.	Missing
1913	Marsh T.	Pte.	W/Sl	1441	Timmins T.	Corpl.	Missing
3718	Marshall J.	Pte.	W/Sv	3423	Anderson J.	Pte.	Missing
3020	Martin T.	Pte.	W/Sl	3517	Bell C.	Pte.	Missing
2541	Melbourne E.	Pte.	W/Sv	3580	Boreham E.	Pte.	Missing
3709	Mills J.	Pte.	W/Sv	3936	Breadmore J.	Pte.	Missing
3935	Mitchell J.	Pte.	W/Sv	3280	Bryan J.	Pte.	Missing
3718	Moore J.	Pte.	W/Sv	3846	Butler E.	Pte.	Missing
3751	Morris W.	Pte.	W/Sv	3916	Colledge H.	Pte.	Missing
3369	Nash J.	Pte.	W/Sv	3050	Currey J.	Pte.	Missing
3318	O'Brien E.	Pte.	W/Sv	3799	Denham T.	Pte.	Missing
3642	O'Neill J.	Pte.	W/Sl	1866	Donaldson D.	Pte.	Missing
3451	Petrie J.	Pte.	W/Sv	3990	Dyer M.	Pte.	Missing
3411	Pope J.	Pte.	W/Sv	3363	Edge P.	Pte.	Missing
1890	Purviss J.	Pte.	W/Sv	2698	Fuller W.	Pte.	Missing
3279	Redman J.	Pte.	W/Sv	3786	Hitch J.	Pte.	Missing
3259	Roe B.	Pte.	W/Sl	3776	Huckle J.	Pte.	Missing
3304	Rogers P.	Pte.	W/Sv	3307	Hurt E.	Pte.	Missing
2891	Rote H.	Pte.	W/Sv	2895	Ireland G.	Pte.	Missing
2308	Scott A.	Pte.	W/Sl	2943	Kippen A.	Pte.	Missing
3962	Seabright T.	Pte.	W/Sl	3418	McDiarmaid P.	Pte.	Missing
2804	Seymour J.	Pte.	W/Sv	3477	McDougall T.	Pte.	Missing
2918	Shepherd C.	Pte.	W/Sv	3824	Mathews H.	Pte.	Missing
3536	Simcrox P.	Pte.	W/Sv	2263	Meaden S.	Pte.	Missing
3719	Smith H.	Pte.	W/Sv	3667	Melaney W.	Pte.	Missing
3594	Squire J.	Pte.	W/Sv	2591	Moorman W.	Pte.	Missing
3764	Taverner W.	Pte.	W/Sv	3403	Murphy H.	Pte.	Missing
1966	Templeton A.	Pte.	W/Sv	3631	Payne A.	Pte.	Missing
3941	Thorndyke T.	Pte.	W/Sv	3480	Purcell J.	Pte.	Missing
3841	Tierney W.	Pte.	W/Sv	3762	Rourke J.	Pte.	Missing
3810	Turner I.	Pte.	W/Sv	1185	Shields A.	Pte.	Missing
3587	Vine J.	Pte.	W/Sv	3737	Slater W.	Pte.	Missing
3855	Walker B.	Pte.	W/Sv	3405	Stewart W.	Pte.	Missing
3340	Whelan M.	Pte.	W/Sv				

93rd REGIMENT OF FOOT

NO.	NAME	RANK	CASUALTY	NO.	NAME	RANK	CASUALTY
2243	Cowley Hugh	Pte.	Killed	2386	McGavie James	Pte.	W/Sv
3019	Wynn Oliver	Pte.	Killed	2640	McRae Donald	Pte.	W/Sl
1827	Massie John	Corpl.	W/Sv	1905	Walker Andrew	Pte.	W/Sl
1515	Cobb James	Pte.	W/Sv	2534	Walker Robert	Pte.	W/Sl
2333	Galloway John	Pte.	W/Sv				

95th REGIMENT OF FOOT

NO.	NAME	RANK	CASUALTY	NO.	NAME	RANK	CASUALTY
	Sargent J. N.	Capt.	W/Sl	3463	Burke Patrick	Pte.	W/Sv
	Parkinson C. F.	Lieut.	W/Sl	2926	Walker Philip	Pte.	W/Sv
1593	Woolnough Jonas	Col/Sgt.	W/Sv				

NOTES

The Final Attack on the Redan

97th REGIMENT OF FOOT

NO.	NAME	RANK	CASUALTY	NO.	NAME	RANK	CASUALTY
	Hancock Hon. H. R.	Lt/Col.	Killed	3458	Broadfoot Thomas	Pte.	W/Sv
	Welsford A. F.	Major	Killed	3159	Brown Edw. Pearson	Pte.	W/Sv
	Hutton J.	Capt.	Killed	3125	Brown John (1st)	Pte.	W/Sl
	McGregor A. D.	Lt.&Adj.	Killed	3662	Buxton William	Pte.	W/Sv
1218	Egan John	Col/Sgt.	Killed	1822	Cotterill John	Pte.	W/Sv
2172	Barnett Edward	Sergt.	Killed	3055	Chapman George	Pte.	W/Sl
2695	Dawson David	Drummer	Killed	3309	Clarke Patrick	Pte.	W/Sv
878	Hughes Patrick	Drummer	Killed	3467	Collins John	Pte.	W/Sv
3174	Anderson Charles	Pte.	Killed	2891	Connors John	Pte.	W/Sl
2751	Burns James	Pte.	Killed	1822	Correll John	Pte.	W/Sv
1986	Butler Patrick	Pte.	Killed	3748	Cox William	Pte.	W/Sl
2688	Frawley Daniel	Pte.	Killed	3144	Cunningham John	Pte.	W/Sl
2571	Frawley Michael	Pte.	Killed	3176	Dodd Robert	Pte.	W/Sv
1857	Hall Sampson	Pte.	Killed	2169	Dodd Thomas	Pte.	W/Sl
1847	Kennedy Daniel	Pte.	Killed	2358	Driver William	Pte.	W/Sv
1784	Kiernan James	Pte.	Killed	1357	Drury Daniel	Pte.	W/Sl
3258	McAlister Henry	Pte.	Killed	2951	Dunne Patrick	Pte.	W/Sv
3305	McManoman William	Pte.	Killed	1766	Dunne Peter	Pte.	W/Sv
3128	Panick William	Pte.	Killed	3738	Dutton John	Pte.	W/Sv
3502	Ramsden William	Pte.	Killed	1955	Farnham Stephen	Pte.	W/Sv
2826	Regan John	Pte.	Killed	3463	Farrell Lewis	Pte.	W/Sl
1098	Tancey Timothy	Pte.	Killed	3097	Fitzgerald Thomas	Pte.	W/Sv
3614	Tottle William	Pte.	Killed	1713	Fitzgerald William	Pte.	W/Sl
3903	Sherwood William	Pte.	Killed	1484	Flannery Patrick	Pte.	W/Sv
	Lumley C. H.	Capt.	W/D	3085	Fleming William	Pte.	W/Sv
	Sibthorp R. F. W.	Capt.	W/Sv	2750	Ford George	Pte.	W/Sv
	Woods H. G.	Capt.	W/Sl	1360	Fox James	Pte.	W/Sv
	Browne C. H.	Lieut.	W/Sl	3161	Gillandiers Francis	Pte.	W/Sl
	Fitzgerald M. G. B.	Lieut.	W/Sl	2461	Gilligan Patrick	Pte.	W/Sv
	Goodenough R. C.	Lieut.	W/Sv	3026	Gillon Michael	Pte.	W/Sv
	Hill J. E. D.	Ensign	W/Sl	2321	Gribbon John	Pte.	W/Sv
1342	Cusack John	Sgt/Mjr	W/Sl	3065	Gurley Patrick	Pte.	W/Sl
1115	Delaney Kiernan	Col/Sgt.	W/Sl	1773	Hallam Thomas	Pte.	W/Sl
1886	Lawless Peter	Col/Sgt.	W/Sv	3064	Hamilton John	Pte.	W/Sv
2428	Cavanagh Joseph	Sergt.	W/Sv	3838	Harris John	Pte.	W/Sl
1753	Edwards John	Sergt.	W/Sv	3859	Hayhurst William	Pte.	W/Sl
2006	Gilligan Terence	Sergt.	W/Sv	3074	Hennessy Timothy	Pte.	W/Sv
1330	Hanlan Peter	Sergt.	W/Sl	3498	Hepton John	Pte.	W/Sv
2216	Leckett Charles	Sergt.	W/Sv	3284	Hickey Timothy	Pte.	W/Sv
1297	Lee Isaac Henry	Sergt.	W/Sl	3398	Holland Henry	Pte.	W/Sv
3036	Madew Henry	Sergt.	W/D	1546	Hopkins John	Pte.	W/Sl
1430	Mooney John	Sergt.	W/Sv	3253	Huckle Robert	Pte.	W/Sl
2111	Newman William	Sergt.	W/Sv	3846	Hutchins William	Pte.	W/Sl
1317	Scott Walter	Sergt.	W/Sv	3696	Isaacs Frederick	Pte.	W/Sl
1849	Wedgworth Francis	Sergt.	W/Sl	3292	Jevery Michael	Pte.	W/Sv
2938	Fitzgerald James	Corpl.	W/Sl	2189	Johnston Peter	Pte.	W/Sv
2510	Garner Eli	Corpl.	W/Sl	3462	Jones George	Pte.	W/Sl
2993	Keely Daniel	Corpl.	W/Sv	3554	Jones John	Pte.	W/Sv
1502	Kemmy Michael	Corpl.	W/Sl	3605	Kain William	Pte.	W/Sv
2442	Martin James	Corpl.	W/Sl	2580	Keeley James	Pte.	W/Sv
2572	Murphy Michael	Corpl.	W/Sv	3407	Kelly John(2nd)	Pte.	W/Sl
3131	O'Connell Maurice	Corpl.	W/Sv	3112	Kennedy Alexander	Pte.	W/Sv
2589	O'Keefe David	Corpl.	W/Sl	3673	Kilcoin John	Pte.	W/Sl
2811	Pigeon John	Corpl.	W/Sv	3314	King Robert	Pte.	W/Sv
1950	Ragg William	Corpl.	W/Sl	3750	King Thomas	Pte.	W/Sv
2015	West Stephen	Corpl.	W/Sv	1049	Lancaster Joseph	Pte.	W/D
3966	Alborn William	Pte.	W/Sv	2889	Lane John	Pte.	W/Sl
3213	Barnes William	Pte.	W/Sv	2614	Loyd Edward	Pte.	W/Sl
3102	Beale William	Pte.	W/Sl	3123	McBriney James	Pte.	W/Sv
3435	Bennett William	Pte.	W/Sl	3674	McCarthy George	Pte.	W/Sl
1270	Bergin John	Pte.	W/Sv	2626	McCormick John	Pte.	W/Sv
2099	Biggins Thomas	Pte.	W/Sv	1839	McElligott Michael	Pte.	W/Sl
3845	Brewer Charles	Pte.	W/Sv	3181	McGrath William	Pte.	W/Sv

NOTES

The Final Attack on the Redan
97th REGIMENT OF FOOT

NO.	NAME	RANK	CASUALTY	NO.	NAME	RANK	CASUALTY
3304	McKeown Patrick	Pte.	W/Sl	3702	Williams Henry	Pte.	W/Sl
2586	McMahon Patrick	Pte.	W/Sv	3844	Wills John	Pte	W/Sv
1841	McNutty Patrick	Pte.	W/Sv	3080	Woods John	Pte.	W/Sv
1831	Manning Andrew	Pte.	W/Sv	2785	Danger James	Col/Sgt.	Missing
3306	Masterton Luke	Pte.	W/Sv	3525	Cullum Michael	Sergt.	Missing
2718	Moran James	Pte.	W/Sl	2072	Shea Daniel	Sergt.	Missing
3603	Morrison William	Pte.	W/Sl	2555	Walker Thomas	Sergt.	Missing
1139	Mulhall John	Pte.	W/Sl	2569	Duffy Thomas	Corpl.	Missing
2525	Murley Michael	Pte.	W/Sl	1369	Moore William	Corpl.	Missing
1091	Murphy Edward	Pte.	W/Sl	1129	Wilson William	Corpl.	Missing
3278	Newing Stephen	Pte.	W/Sv	3484	Blackmore Samuel	Pte.	Missing
1965	Nicholson John	Pte.	W/Sv	3889	Blunt Hiram	Pte.	Missing
3907	Nugent Patrick	Pte.	W/Sv	3495	Brown John (2)	Pte.	Missing
3973	Nugent Thomas	Pte.	W/Sv	—	Bungey William	Pte.	Missing
3289	O'Connor Patrick	Pte.	W/Sv	3543	Casey Daniel	Pte.	Missing
2970	O'Donnell George	Pte.	W/Sl	3663	Clay John	Pte.	Missing
3466	O'Neil John	Pte.	W/Sv	1607	Cook George	Pte.	Missing
2057	Parrin William	Pte.	W/Sl	1505	Donnelly James	Pte.	Missing
3500	Pearson James	Pte.	W/Sv	1765	Donohue John	Pte.	Missing
3871	Pearson Thomas	Pte.	W/Sv	3649	Donovan John	Pte.	Missing
3781	Powell William	Pte.	W/Sv	3353	Gammon William	Pte.	Missing
3539	Rielly James	Pte.	W/Sl	3441	Goolden Maurice	Pte.	Missing
3490	Rielly Philip	Pte.	W/Sv	3863	Hainton Robert	Pte.	Missing
3510	Robinson Thomas	Pte.	W/Sl	3225	Horton Edward	Pte.	Missing
3486	Ryan James	Pte.	W/Sv	1926	Hough William	Pte.	Missing
1527	Ryan Thomas	Pte.	W/Sv	2171	Johnston Thomas	Pte.	Missing
3684	Sanders John	Pte.	W/Sv	3084	Keefe Bartholomew	Pte.	Missing
3655	Shields John	Pte.	W/Sv	2781	Lee Thomas	Pte.	Missing
3661	Simpson Thomas	Pte.	W/Sv	3099	Little Robert	Pte.	Missing
3652	Sledden David	Pte.	W/Sl	2078	McCormick Jonathan	Pte.	Missing
2167	Smith Alexander W.	Pte.	W/D	2275	Marsden James	Pte.	Missing
3164	Smith George	Pte.	W/Sv	1925	Merle James	Pte.	Missing
1310	Smith Thomas	Pte.	W/Sl	2483	Murin John	Pte.	Missing
2537	Sullivan Denis	Pte.	W/Sv	1454	Murphy Thomas	Pte.	Missing
3801	Summers William	Pte.	W/Sv	3217	Ramsley Edward	Pte.	Missing
3708	Thomas William	Pte.	W/Sv	3431	Ratcliffe James	Pte.	Missing
1997	Thompson Charles	Pte.	W/Sv	3521	Robinshaw Stephen G.	Pte.	Missing
3297	Turley James	Pte.	W/Sv	3727	Russell John	Pte.	Missing
3283	Tyrrell John	Pte.	W/Sv	3464	Waterhouse Michael	Pte.	Missing
3743	Walker Samuel	Pte.	W/Sl	3641	Watkins Walter	Pte.	Missing
2146	Walker William	Pte.	W/D	3829	Wilmens Frederick	Pte.	Missing
3615	Whitehurst Eli	Pte.	W/Sv	3632	Wilton Josiah	Pte.	Missing

1st BATTALION RIFLE BRIGADE

NO.	NAME	RANK	CASUALTY	NO.	NAME	RANK	CASUALTY
2208	Holyland Thomas	Pte.	Killed	3400	Davis Edward	Pte.	W/Sl
4014	Weeks Frederick	Pte.	Killed	3555	Flannage Michael	Pte.	W/D
3504	Wilkinson Martin	Pte.	Killed	3827	Maloney John	Pte.	W/Sl
3269	Ackerman George	Pte.	W/Sl	4677	Webb T. W.	Pte.	W/Sl
4178	Davis Daniel	Pte.	W/Sl				

2nd BATTALION RIFLE BRIGADE

NO.	NAME	RANK	CASUALTY	NO.	NAME	RANK	CASUALTY
	Hammond M. M.	Capt.	Killed	2664	Everitt W.	Sergt.	Killed
	Ryder H. S.	Lieut.	Killed	2619	Farrell T.	Sergt.	Killed
	Dawson W.	Col/Sgt.	Killed	3343	Blishen H.	Corpl.	Killed
2356	Connor J.	Sergt.	Killed	1394	Bailey J.	Pte.	Killed

NOTES

The Final Attack on the Redan
2nd BATTALION RIFLE BRIGADE

NO.	NAME	RANK	CASUALTY	NO.	NAME	RANK	CASUALTY
4103	Birch G.	Pte.	Killed	3660	Carter T.	Pte.	W/Sl
4416	Bryant H.	Pte.	Killed	2248	Chapman H.	Pte.	W/Sl
4163	Cook E.	Pte.	Killed	3662	Chapman R.	Pte.	W/Sl
4195	Cook T.	Pte.	Killed	4549	Chapter H. T.	Pte.	W/D
4234	Donnelly S.	Pte.	Killed	3663	Clarey T.	Pte.	W/Sv
3820	Forsyth P.	Pte.	Killed	4172	Clarke R.	Pte.	W/Sv
4177	Howden R.	Pte.	Killed	5571	Clements J.	Pte.	W/Sv
2461	McDonald J.	Pte.	Killed	3335	Cokeley T.	Pte.	W/Sv
4338	Phipps R.	Pte.	Killed	4346	Cook M.	Pte.	W/Sv
3613	Sargent S.	Pte.	Killed	4395	Cook T.	Pte.	W/Sv
4505	Sumner C.	Pte.	Killed	3966	Cox E.	Pte.	W/Sl
3727	Tainsh E.	Pte.	Killed	2442	Cox G.	Pte.	W/Sv
2499	Thornhill A.	Pte.	Killed	4453	Crawley C.	Pte.	W/Sv
3641	Turner R.	Pte.	Killed	3790	Crosbie R.	Pte.	W/Sv
4256	Twiggs J.	Pte.	Killed	4380	Davis J.	Pte.	W/Sv
3485	Vince T.	Pte.	Killed	3920	Day R.	Pte.	W/Sv
4502	Ward W.	Pte.	Killed	4536	Dowden W.	Pte.	W/Sl
3888	Warner W.	Pte.	Killed	059	Evernden M.	Pte.	W/Sl
4042	Webster A.	Pte.	Killed	4646	Eyerr W.	Pte.	W/Sl
3519	Wilson R.	Pte.	Killed	2673	Fancourt H.	Pte.	W/Sv
	Woodford C.	Major	W/Sl	3820	Ferguson W.	Pte.	W/Sl
	Pellew Hon. B. R.	Capt.	W/Sl	3129	Finn H.	Pte.	W/Sv
	Borough R.	Lieut.	W/Sl	1676	Garner R.	Pte.	W/Sv
	Eccles W.	Lieut.	W/Sl	3726	Gatton P.	Pte.	W/Sv
	Eyre H.	Lieut.	W/Sl	3370	Goodall W.	Pte.	W/Sl
	Moore J. C.	Lieut.	W/Sl	3681	Graham W.	Pte.	W/Sv
	Playne F. C.	Lieut.	W/Sl	4088	Gunter T.	Pte.	W/Sv
	Riley F.	Lieut.	W/Sl	3687	Hannan H.	Pte.	W/Sl
1736	Waller J.	Sgt/Mjr.	W/Sv	4036	Harding R.	Pte.	W/Sl
2545	Skeates M.	Col/Sgt.	W/Sv	4643	Harris W.	Pte.	W/Sl
3177	Cook D.	Sergt.	W/Sv	3967	Haynes W.	Pte.	W/Sv
3890	James W.	Sergt.	W/Sv	4402	Herrity P.	Pte.	W/Sv
4244	Seaford J.	Sergt.	W/Sv	4197	Hicks W.	Pte.	W/D
2359	Thorogate W.	Sergt.	W/D	3289	Jacobs C.	Pte.	W/Sv
2959	Whiffen W.	Sergt.	W/Sv	2445	Johnson J.	Pte.	W/Sl
—	Blackstock H.	Corpl.	W/D	4635	Johnson S.	Pte.	W/Sv
2395	Carley H.	Corpl.	W/Sl	3923	Jones J.	Pte.	W/Sv
4416	Cowlishaw J.	Corpl.	W/Sl	2876	Jordan T.	Pte.	W/Sl
3106	Harris W.	Corpl.	W/Sl	4039	Key G.	Pte.	W/Sv
3042	Warren J.	Corpl.	W/Sl	4248	Lacey J.	Pte.	W/Sv
2599	West J.	Corpl.	W/Sl	4348	Lennard T.	Pte.	W/Sl
3071	Winchcombe J.	Corpl.	W/Sl	3540	Lenton D.	Pte.	W/Sl
2749	McCarthy D.	Bugler	W/Sl	3697	Lewis T.	Pte.	W/D
3986	Murray H.	Bugler	W/D	1022	Loughlin J.	Pte.	W/Sv
1456	Asher J.	Pte.	W/Sv	3153	Love S.	Pte.	W/Sl
4322	Banks H.	Pte.	W/Sv	3138	McDonald T.	Pte.	W/D
1556	Banks T.	Pte.	W/Sv	2074	McGee P.	Pte.	W/Sl
3653	Barrett R.	Pte.	W/Sl	3702	Mack J.	Pte.	W/Sv
4561	Beadle G.	Pte.	W/Sv	4560	Mack M.	Pte.	W/Sv
3051	Ben M.	Pte.	W/Sv	4157	Madgwick H.	Pte.	W/Sv
2570	Birkett W.	Pte.	W/D	4540	Martin M.	Pte.	W/Sv
4029	Blandford J.	Pte.	W/Sl	4339	Mason W.	Pte.	W/Sv
2127	Booth J.	Pte.	W/Sv	3304	Mason W.	Pte.	W/Sl
4028	Branning J.	Pte.	W/Sv	4003	Meredith W.	Pte.	W/Sl
4250	Brewster W.	Pte.	W/Sv	3050	Moore G.	Pte.	W/Sv
3107	Brown A.	Pte.	W/Sv	4620	Morris J.	Pte.	W/Sv
2589	Brown T.	Pte.	W/Sl	3842	Murray J.	Pte.	W/Sl
3589	Brown W.	Pte.	W/D	3892	Nash W.	Pte.	W/Sv
3823	Brown W.	Pte.	W/Sl	4198	Nasmyth R.	Pte.	W/Sl
4418	Bryant J.	Pte.	W/Sl	3300	Nichols S.	Pte.	W/Sv
3815	Buchanan H.	Pte.	W/D	3488	Nutt D.	Pte.	W/Sl
4281	Buckley H.	Pte.	W/Sv	3322	Palmer R.	Pte.	W/Sl
3808	Burke J.	Pte.	W/Sl	4673	Parkinson J.	Pte.	W/Sv
2416	Butt C.	Pte.	W/Sv	4173	Patterson J.	Pte.	W/Sv
4477	Cahill P.	Pte.	W/Sv	2454	Picken W.	Pte.	W/Sv

NOTES

The Final Attack on the Redan
2nd BATTALION RIFLE BRIGADE

NO.	NAME	RANK	CASUALTY	NO.	NAME	RANK	CASUALTY
3468	Pinfold T.	Pte.	W/Sv	3730	Waldron J.	Pte.	W/Sv
4364	Plant J.	Pte.	W/Sl	4547	Walton J.	Pte.	W/Sv
2869	Purcell J.	Pte.	W/Sl	2621	Ward T.	Pte.	W/Sv
3995	Radleigh J.	Pte.	W/Sl	3888	Warner W.	Pte.	W/Sl
4578	Riordan D.	Pte.	W/Sl	2969	Wesson J.	Pte.	W/Sv
4428	Saunders B.	Pte.	W/Sl	42-8	West J.	Pte.	W/Sl
4183	Saunders E.	Pte.	W/Sv	4391	White W.	Pte.	W/Sv
3775	Sawyer J.	Pte.	W/Sl	4201	Whitmore B.	Pte.	W/Sl
3911	Seaward S.	Pte.	W/Sl	4441	Wilkinson W.	Pte.	W/Sv
3309	Simpson A.	Pte.	W/Sv	3736	Williamson W.	Pte.	W/Sl
4273	Skinner R.	Pte.	W/Sl	1748	Wilson A.	Pte.	W/Sl
4210	Smith J.	Pte.	W/Sl	3738	Wilson W.	Pte.	W/Sl
4110	Spink J.	Pte.	W/Sl	3785	Wines J.	Pte.	W/Sv
4671	Trundell H.	Pte.	W/Sv	4463	Young T.	Pte.	W/Sv
4481	Turnstall D.	Pte.	W/D				

NOTES

GENERAL WINDHAM
IN THE REDAN.
SEPT 8TH 1855.

THE SECOND, THIRD, FOURTH, FIFTH AND FINAL BOMBARDMENT OF SEBASTOPOL, AND MINOR ACTIONS

The following casualties occurred among the Officers, Non-Commissioned Officers and Men of the Army in the period between The Battle of Inkermann, 5th November 1854, and the Final Attack on the Redan, 8th September 1855. The casualty dates listed, indicate the following:-
1. The Great Sortie of the Russians from Sebastopol, 22nd March 1855.
2. Second Bombardment of Sebastopol, April 9th 1855.
3. The Russian Rifle Pits Taken by a Detachment of the 77th Foot, April 19th 1855.
4. Third Bombardment of Sebastopol, 6th June 1855.
5. Fourth Bombardment of Sebastopol, 17th June 1855.
6. Fifth Bombardment of Sebastopol, 17th August 1855.
7. Final Bombardment of Sebastopol, September 5th 1855.
8. Various small engagements with the enemy and from desultory shelling. (Refer to Chronological Events of the War. Appendix II)

The Attack on the Quarries and the First and Final Attacks on the Redan are shown in their respective sections within this book

Compiled from the London Gazette dates as indicated against each entry.

ROYAL ARTILLERY

NO.	NAME	RANK	CASUALTY	DATE	LONDON GAZETTE
	Gordon A.	Capt.	Killed	5-7-55	17-5-55
	Oldfield Anthony	Capt.	Killed	17-8-55	31-8-55
	Snow E. G.	Capt.	Killed	6-9-55	18-9-55
	Luce E.	Lieut.	Killed	11-4-55	24-4-55
	Mitchell R. A.	Lieut.	Killed	14-4-55	1-5-55
—	Faust George	Col/Sgt.	Killed	10-4-55	24-4-55
1929	Morrison Alexander	Col/Sgt.	Killed	5-9-55	18-9-55
2145	Bratton James	Sergt.	Killed	20-4-55	4-5-55
—	Jamieson Alexander	Sergt.	Killed	13-4-55	1-5-55
31	Sutherland John	Sergt.	Killed	14-4-55	1-5-55
218	Boyd William	Corpl.	Killed	14-4-55	1-5-55
854	Brown Marshall	Bombr.	Killed	11-4-55	24-4-55
2932	Wilson Edward	Bombr.	Killed	11-8-55	24-8-55
—	Gunn James	A/Bombr.	Killed	26-4-55	15-5-55
2084	Callaghan Michael	Gnr.&Drvr.	Killed	11-4-55	24-4-55
2461	Denison James	Gnr.&Drvr.	Killed	5-4-55	20-4-55
—	Garrow Archibald	Gnr.&Drvr.	Killed	9-4-55	24-4-55
—	Hazzard William	Gnr.&Drvr.	Killed	9-4-55	24-4-55
—	Kendall Henry	Gnr.&Drvr.	Killed	10-4-55	24-4-55

NOTES

The Second, Third, Fourth, Fifth and Final Bombardment of Sebastopol, and Minor Actions

ROYAL ARTILLERY

NO.	NAME	RANK	CASUALTY	DATE	LONDON GAZETTE
2575	McIntyre James	Gnr.&Drvr.	Killed	10-4-55	24-4-55
–	Wren John	Gnr.&Drvr.	Killed	9-4-55	24-4-55
–	Armstrong Richard	Gunner	Killed	17-8-55	31-8-55
1760	Beckwith Henry	Gunner	Killed	11-6-55	26-6-55
–	Birch James	Gunner	Killed	14-4-55	1-5-55
–	Bird William	Gunner	Killed	23-8-55	4-9-55
3575	Bowie John	Gunner	Killed	11-6-55	26-6-55
2359	Cassidy William	Gunner	Killed	11-6-55	26-6-55
1650	Chambers John	Gunner	Killed	9-6-55	22-6-55
3366	Doherty Edward	Gunner	Killed	8-6-55	22-6-55
2686	Dougherty William	Gunner	Killed	5-9-55	18-9-55
–	Fanon Bernard	Gunner	Killed	11-6-55	26-6-55
–	Greer Alexander	Gunner	Killed	20-7-55	3-8-55
2984	Hamilton James	Gunner	Killed	16-4-55	1-5-55
–	Harvey James	Gunner	Killed	10-8-55	24-8-55
3233	Hatch Henry	Gunner	Killed	30-8-55	11-9-55
503	Henderson William	Gunner	Killed	26-4-55	15-5-55
–	Hodges George	Gunner	Killed	11-6-55	26-6-55
–	Jones George	Gunner	Killed	14-4-55	1-5-55
–	Keith James	Gunner	Killed	17-8-55	31-8-55
–	Kelly John	Gunner	Killed	11-6-55	26-6-55
60	King Thomas	Gunner	Killed	9-5-55	22-5-55
–	Lambert William	Gunner	Killed	23-8-55	4-9-55
1149	Lawley James	Gunner	Killed	14-4-55	1-5-55
–	McElwee Thomas	Gunner	Killed	11-6-55	26-6-55
2685	McManamy Patrick	Gunner	Killed	6-9-55	18-9-55
–	McQueen Michael	Gunner	Killed	16-4-55	1-5-55
4219	McQuillan Henry	Gunner	Killed	14-4-55	1-5-55
3595	Malley Peter	Gunner	Killed	25-7-55	7-8-55
–	Maull James	Gunner	Killed	12-6-55	26-6-55
1689	Metcliff Robert	Gunner	Killed	6-9-55	18-9-55
–	Minnies James	Gunner	Killed	17-8-55	31-8-55
–	Polson John	Gunner	Killed	12-4-55	24-4-55
4273	Quin John	Gunner	Killed	28-7-55	7-8-55
3202	Reid Roderick	Gunner	Killed	17-6-55	3-7-55
–	Simmonds William	Gunner	Killed	21-8-55	4-9-55
1960	Simpson Jonathan	Gunner	Killed	4-9-55	18-9-55
–	Walker J.	Gunner	Killed	7-9-55	25-9-55
–	Watson John	Gunner	Killed	17-8-55	31-8-55
–	Yates Jeremiah	Gunner	Killed	17-8-55	31-8-55
	Dickson C.	Lt/Col.	W/Sl	4-2-55	20-2-55
	Henry C. S.	Br/Mjr.	W/Sl	17-8-55	31-8-55
	Arbuthnot C. G.	Capt.	W/Sl	17-6-55	3-7-55
	Arbuthnot C. G.	Capt.	W/Sv	23-8-55	4-9-55
	Dickson P.	Capt.	W/Sl	20-8-55	4-9-55
	Conolly H. H.	Lieut.	W/Sl	9-6-55	22-6-55
	L'Estrange P. W.	Lieut.	W/Sv	12-4-55	24-4-55
	Price J. A.	Lieut.	W/Sl	1-9-55	18-9-55
	Roberts C. F.	Lieut.	W/Sl	2-9-55	18-9-55
	Scott C. E.	Lieut.	W/Sl	19-8-55	31-8-55
	Sinclair J.	Lieut.	W/Sv	10-4-55	24-4-55
	Tillard H. P.	Lieut.	W/Sl	17-6-55	3-7-55
	Winton F. W. de	Lieut.	W/Sl	23-8-55	4-9-55
	Cockerill R. W.	Asst/Surg.	W/Sl	14-4-55	1-5-55
–	Hamilton Joseph	Col/Sgt.	W/Sl	17-6-55	3-7-55
1603	Clark Angus	Sergt.	W/Sl	14-4-55	1-5-55
1987	Cornish Thomas	Sergt.	W/Sv	9-4-55	24-4-55
–	Fletcher Thomas	Sergt.	W/Sl	19-8-55	31-8-55
475	Hunter Alexander	Sergt.	W/Sl	17-3-55	30-3-55
–	Mansfield Joseph	Sergt.	W/Sl	17-8-55	31-8-55
2473	Pitchford Edward	Sergt.	W/Sl	17-6-55	3-7-55
3753	Ackland John	Corpl.	W/Sv	18-8-55	31-8-55
420	Byers John	Corpl.	W/Sl	10-4-55	24-4-55
–	Holyoak – (RMA Attch)	Corpl.	W/Sl	5-7-55	20-7-55
3019	Madden William	Corpl.	W/Sl	18-8-55	31-8-55

NOTES

The Second, Third, Fourth, Fifth and Final Bombardment of Sebastopol, and Minor Actions

ROYAL ARTILLERY

NO.	NAME	RANK	CASUALTY	DATE	LONDON GAZETTE
–	Sprowl Robert	Corpl.	W/Sl	17-8-55	31-8-55
2570	Steele Henry	Corpl.	W/Sl	17-6-55	3-7-55
2914	Taylor Robert	Corpl.	W/Sv	6-8-55	21-8-55
2711	West Francis	Corpl.	W/Sv	15-4-55	1-5-55
322	Aspindal Edward	Bombr.	W/Sl	17-6-55	3-7-55
–	Broomhead George	Bombr.	W/Sl	9-4-55	24-4-55
–	Cabb John	Bombr.	W/Sl	17-8-55	31-8-55
1846	Cameron Archibald	Bombr.	W/Sl	7-9-55	25-9-55
680	Cowdy Matthew	Bombr.	W/D	14-4-55	1-5-55
3214	Evans Thomas H.	Bombr.	W/Sl	11-6-55	26-6-55
–	Findlay A.	Bombr.	W/Sl	17-8-55	31-8-55
–	Ford Charles	Bombr.	W/Sl	17-8-55	31-8-55
389	Geaves Robert	Bombr.	W/Sl	15-4-55	1-5-55
–	Henry James	Bombr.	W/Sl	9-6-55	22-6-55
3201	Kelly Edward	Bombr.	W/Sv	7-9-55	25-9-55
3233	Kelly Adam	Bombr.	W/Sl	7-9-55	25-9-55
2648	Moffat Thomas	Bombr.	W/Sl	17-6-55	3-7-55
3767	Simpson William	Bombr.	W/Sl	18-8-55	31-8-55
–	Stanley Henry	Bombr.	W/Sl	17-8-55	31-8-55
–	StClair Edward	Bombr.	W/Sv	17-8-55	31-8-55
3323	Sweeney William	Bombr.	W/Sl	17-6-55	3-7-55
57	Symons Joseph	Bombr.	W/Sl	11-6-55	26-6-55
–	Thorburn Walter	Bombr.	W/Sv	17-8-55	31-8-55
–	Todd Andrew	Bombr.	W/Sv	17-8-55	31-8-55
2695	Watt John	Bombr.	W/Sv	5-9-55	18-9-55
–	Warrell Edward	Bombr.	W/Sl	5-9-55	18-9-55
2252	Wilson Robert	Bombr.	W/Sl	11-4-55	24-4-55
–	Zackey Daniel	Bombr.	W/Sl	5-9-55	18-9-55
–	Adam Alexander	A/Bombr.	W/Sl	13-4-55	1-5-55
–	Baines Thomas	A/Bombr.	W/Sl	17-6-55	3-7-55
–	Brown Alfred	A/Bombr.	W/Sl	13-4-55	1-5-55
792	Grant John	A/Bombr.	W/Sl	15-8-55	28-8-55
179	James Robert	A/Bombr.	W/Sl	24-4-55	15-5-55
–	Lloyd James	A/Bombr.	W/Sv	13-4-55	1-5-55
2702	McDonald Peter	A/Bombr.	W/Sv	16-4-55	1-5-55
3475	Balkwell Thomas	Gnr.&Drvr.	W/Sl	5-4-55	20-4-55
–	Bowers Samuel	Gnr.&Drvr.	W/Sl	24-3-55	10-4-55
–	Childs Thomas	Gnr.&Drvr.	W/Sl	9-4-55	24-4-55
2274	Clure Moses	Gnr.&Drvr.	W/Sv	9-4-55	24-4-55
–	Cullen Bernard	Gnr.&Drvr.	W/Sv	27-3-55	13-4-55
724	Dagin Joseph	Gnr.&Drvr.	W/Sv	9-4-55	24-4-55
1682	Davis Henry	Gnr.&Drvr.	W/Sv	6-4-55	20-4-55
–	Evans William	Gnr.&Drvr.	W/Sv	30-5-55	12-6-55
1692	Edgington James	Gnr.&Drvr.	W/Sl	9-4-55	24-4-55
3555	Flood James	Gnr.&Drvr.	W/Sv	6-4-55	20-4-55
5440	Hanson William	Gnr.&Drvr.	W/Sv	11-4-55	24-4-55
3205	Johnston Henry	Gnr.&Drvr.	W/Sl	9-4-55	24-4-55
3786	McBride Hugh	Gnr.&Drvr.	W/Sv	7-3-55	23-3-55
1350	Murray Ralph	Gnr.&Drvr.	W/Sl	24-3-55	10-4-55
–	Spence John	Gnr.&Drvr.	W/Sl	9-4-55	24-4-55
2252	Wilson Joseph	Gnr.&Drvr.	W/Sl	11-4-55	24-4-55
–	Armour James	Gunner	W/Sv	17-8-55	31-8-55
–	Astley Ralph	Gunner	W/Sl	25-8-55	7-9-55
2631	Baker James	Gunner	W/Sl	31-8-55	18-9-55
3976	Baker William	Gunner	W/Sl	16-4-55	1-5-55
4270	Banham William	Gunner	W/Sv	29-8-55	11-9-55
–	Batfield Robert	Gunner	W/Sl	17-8-55	31-8-55
–	Bennett William	Gunner	W/Sv	11-6-55	26-6-55
–	Boyd Robert	Gunner	W/Sl	9-6-55	22-6-55
–	Branton Charles	Gunner	W/Sl	30-8-55	11-9-55
2977	Brewer John	Gunner	W/Sv	25-7-55	7-8-55
3866	Brown James	Gunner	W/Sl	10-4-55	24-4-55
3723	Buckley Samuel	Gunner	W/Sl	20-4-55	4-5-55
1637	Burke Michael	Gunner	W/Sl	10-4-55	24-4-55
–	Burke Robert	Gunner	W/D	26-8-55	7-9-55

NOTES

The Second, Third, Fourth, Fifth and Final Bombardment of Sebastopol, and Minor Actions

ROYAL ARTILLERY

NO.	NAME	RANK	CASUALTY	DATE	LONDON GAZETTE
—	Burn John	Gunner	W/D	26-8-55	7-9-55
834	Burnside Robert	Gunner	W/Sl	12-6-55	22-6-55
1423	Burton Samuel	Gunner	W/D	31-5-55	12-6-55
—	Carroll Samuel	Gunner	W/Sl	11-8-55	24-8-55
—	Chapple John	Gunner	W/Sv	14-4-55	1-5-55
1920	Cleary Daniel	Gunner	W/Sv	16-6-55	3-7-55
—	Clench William	Gunner	W/Sl	20-8-55	4-9-55
4274	Close William	Gunner	W/Sl	1-9-55	18-9-55
—	Coles Robert	Gunner	W/Sl	20-8-55	4-9-55
3753	Collins W.	Gunner	W/Sl	6-8-55	21-8-55
4008	Connor James	Gunner	W/Sl	11-6-55	26-6-55
1535	Conolly Patrick	Gunner	W/Sl	17-4-55	1-5-55
2963	Cook William	Gunner	W/D	7-5-55	22-5-55
—	Cooper James	Gunner	W/Sv	23-8-55	4-9-55
—	Cowan James	Gunner	W/Sl	12-6-55	26-6-55
3194	Craig Thomas	Gunner	W/Sv	14-4-55	1-5-55
4644	Crease Joseph	Gunner	W/Sl	19-8-55	31-8-55
—	Croft Henry	Gunner	W/Sv	8-6-55	22-6-55
—	Davidson Joseph	Gunner	W/Sl	15-4-55	1-5-55
—	Deal William	Gunner	W/Sl	15-4-55	1-5-55
1222	Death James	Gunner	W/Sl	5-9-55	18-9-55
—	Dellison Jeremiah	Gunner	W/Sv	12-4-55	24-4-55
3780	Dick William	Gunner	W/Sl	14-4-55	1-5-55
—	Doggett Robert	Gunner	W/Sv	17-6-55	3-7-55
3302	Downey John	Gunner	W/Sl	3-9-55	18-9-55
—	Edmonton Alfred	Gunner	W/Sl	17-8-55	31-8-55
2106	Elvidge John	Gunner	W/Sl	22-8-55	4-9-55
—	Evans John	Gunner	W/Sv	16-4-55	1-5-55
2405	Evans Joseph	Gunner	W/Sl	17-6-55	3-7-55
—	Ferguson Daniel	Gunner	W/Sl	17-6-55	3-7-55
3532	Flood George	Gunner	W/Sv	7-9-55	25-9-55
—	Ford William	Gunner	W/Sl	16-4-55	1-5-55
—	Foy Patrick	Gunner	W/Sl	21-8-55	4-9-55
3923	Gadsby Philip	Gunner	W/Sv	7-8-55	21-8-55
—	Gardiner Alfred	Gunner	W/Sl	12-6-55	26-6-55
—	George John	Gunner	W/Sl	17-8-55	31-8-55
2607	Gray Alexander	Gunner	W/Sv	7-8-55	21-8-55
—	Grant William	Gunner	W/Sl	13-4-55	1-5-55
—	Green Benjamin	Gunner	W/Sl	8-6-55	22-6-55
—	Griffiths Richard	Gunner	W/Sl	16-4-55	1-5-55
61	Haddon Benjamin	Gunner	W/Sv	29-8-55	11-9-55
1436	Hale Robert	Gunner	W/Sl	10-4-55	24-4-55
3873	Hames Thomas	Gunner	W/Sv	15-8-55	28-8-55
533	Hardwick John	Gunner	W/Sl	11-8-55	24-8-55
—	Harper George	Gunner	W/Sl	14-4-55	1-5-55
2013	Harrison James	Gunner	W/Sl	9-6-55	22-6-55
—	Harrold John	Gunner	W/Sl	17-8-55	31-8-55
1599	Haslett James	Gunner	W/Sv	11-6-55	26-6-55
503	Henderson William	Gunner	W/Sl	10-4-55	24-4-55
1464	Hill Francis	Gunner	W/Sl	17-6-55	3-7-55
—	Holden Thomas	Gunner	W/Sl	14-4-55	1-5-55
—	Holdham Robert	Gunner	W/Sv	19-8-55	31-8-55
1595	Holland Thomas	Gunner	W/Sv	17-6-55	3-7-55
4181	Holmes Frederick	Gunner	W/Sl	28-7-55	7-8-55
—	Horigan Thomas	Gunner	W/Sl	17-8-55	31-8-55
—	Hornsby James	Gunner	W/Sl	10-4-55	24-4-55
—	Hovesdon William	Gunner	W/Sv	21-8-55	4-9-55
4073	Hubble William	Gunner	W/Sl	17-6-55	3-7-55
577	Hutton John	Gunner	W/Sl	14-4-55	1-5-55
222	Irwin William	Gunner	W/Sl	17-6-55	3-7-55
—	Iviss Edward	Gunner	W/Sv	14-4-55	1-5-55
3205	Johnson Henry	Gunner	W/Sl	16-4-55	1-5-55
—	Johnston David	Gunner	W/Sl	9-4-55	24-4-55
—	Jordan Thomas	Gunner	W/Sl	14-4-55	1-5-55

NOTES

The Second, Third, Fourth, Fifth and Final Bombardment of Sebastopol, and Minor Actions

ROYAL ARTILLERY

NO.	NAME	RANK	CASUALTY	DATE	LONDON GAZETTE
1967	Jordan James	Gunner	W/Sl	6-9-55	18-9-55
3559	Langley Henry	Gunner	W/Sv	14-4-55	1-5-55
2092	Langley Francis	Gunner	W/D	29-8-55	11-9-55
–	Laxton John	Gunner	W/Sl	23-8-55	4-9-55
–	Lewis John	Gunner	W/Sl	17-8-55	31-8-55
–	Lodge William	Gunner	W/Sl	18-8-55	31-8-55
1253	Loe Richard	Gunner	W/Sv	17-6-55	3-7-55
1944	Loggie Alexander	Gunner	W/D	11-6-55	26-6-55
3663	Longden George	Gunner	W/Sv	26-8-55	7-9-55
1752	Longwell John	Gunner	W/Sv	26-8-55	7-9-55
–	Loughrey John	Gunner	W/Sl	16-4-55	1-5-55
–	Lund Henry	Gunner	W/Sl	20-8-55	4-9-55
3610	Lynch Joseph	Gunner	W/D	9-6-55	22-6-55
3296	McAvis H.	Gunner	W/Sl	18-8-55	31-8-55
2963	McBeath James	Gunner	W/Sl	17-6-55	3-7-55
–	McCrea Robert	Gunner	W/Sl	11-6-55	26-6-55
–	McCullock John	Gunner	W/Sv	18-8-55	31-8-55
2685	McElhose Stewart	Gunner	W/Sv	17-4-55	1-5-55
3959	McFarline James	Gunner	W/Sl	6-9-55	18-9-55
4096	McGennis J.	Gunner	W/Sv	18-8-55	31-8-55
102	McGowan Terence	Gunner	W/Sv	5-9-55	18-9-55
2078	McGregor J.	Gunner	W/Sl	7-9-55	25-5-55
–	McIntyre Archibald	Gunner	W/Sv	8-6-55	22-6-55
–	McKay John	Gunner	W/Sv	11-6-55	26-6-55
–	McKee Daniel	Gunner	W/Sv	17-8-55	31-8-55
–	McKenna Patrick	Gunner	W/Sv	17-8-55	31-8-55
–	McLelland John	Gunner	W/Sl	6-9-55	18-9-55
–	McMann James	Gunner	W/Sl	22-8-55	4-9-55
–	Mabin William	Gunner	W/Sl	10-4-55	24-4-55
–	Martin Thomas	Gunner	W/Sl	13-4-55	1-5-55
960	Mays John	Gunner	W/Sv	24-4-55	15-5-55
–	Monsley William	Gunner	W/Sv	17-8-55	31-8-55
1618	Moore James	Gunner	W/Sl	17-4-55	1-5-55
2233	Moore John	Gunner	W/Sv	9-6-55	22-6-55
3736	Morely William	Gunner	W/Sl	17-6-55	3-7-55
–	Morsfold George	Gunner	W/Sv	8-6-55	22-6-55
–	Moss Alfred	Gunner	W/Sl	16-4-55	1-5-55
3406	Moss Francis	Gunner	W/Sl	11-8-55	24-8-55
–	Moulton William	Gunner	W/Sl	20-8-55	4-9-55
3651	Mountford Matthew	Gunner	W/Sl	6-9-55	18-9-55
–	Mulligan John	Gunner	W/Sv	17-8-55	31-8-55
–	Murray Thomas	Gunner	W/Sl	18-8-55	31-8-55
2707	Nicholson Donald	Gunner	W/Sl	2-9-55	18-9-55
3502	Oliver Richard	Gunner	W/Sv	12-4-55	24-4-55
–	O'Neil William	Gunner	W/Sl	12-4-55	24-4-55
2088	Obsorne William	Gunner	W/Sv	6-9-55	18-9-55
–	Pape George	Gunner	W/Sl	21-8-55	4-9-55
–	Parkinson George	Gunner	W/Sl	14-4-55	1-5-55
–	Parsons William	Gunner	W/Sl	8-6-55	22-6-55
–	Pawlyn William	Gunner	W/Sv	20-8-55	4-9-55
2292	Peters George	Gunner	W/Sl	6-9-55	18-9-55
–	Phelps William	Gunner	W/Sv	17-8-55	31-8-55
1414	Phillips Richard	Gunner	W/Sl	11-8-55	24-8-55
4271	Poke William	Gunner	W/Sl	26-8-55	7-9-55
–	Portch George	Gunner	W/Sl	16-4-55	1-5-55
–	Pristy Solomon	Gunner	W/Sl	4-7-55	20-7-55
1000	Rapwell Lancelot	Gunner	W/Sl	16-4-55	1-5-55
2684	Read Thomas	Gunner	W/Sl	23-8-55	4-9-55
3789	Redmond Patrick	Gunner	W/Sv	11-6-55	26-6-55
1168	Renshaw William	Gunner	W/Sv	9-6-55	22-6-55
552	Riley Wm. George	Gunner	W/Sl	16-4-55	1-5-55
–	Robert James	Gunner	W/Sl	14-4-55	1-5-55
2361	Rolle James	Gunner	W/Sl	28-8-55	11-9-55

NOTES

The Second, Third, Fourth, Fifth and Final Bombardment of Sebastopol, and Minor Actions

ROYAL ARTILLERY

NO.	NAME	RANK	CASUALTY	DATE	LONDON GAZETTE
4020	Russell William	Gunner	W/Sv	31-8-55	18-9-55
3995	Ruthwell Samuel	Gunner	W/Sl	13-8-55	28-8-55
–	Ruthwell Samuel	Gunner	W/Sl	22-8-55	4-9-55
–	Saunderson Jonathan	Gunner	W/Sl	17-8-55	31-8-55
3467	Sedgewick Thomas	Gunner	W/Sv	18-8-55	31-8-55
1810	Sharp James	Gunner	W/Sl	14-4-55	1-5-55
2078	Shepherd William	Gunner	W/Sl	17-6-55	3-7-55
–	Simpson James	Gunner	W/Sv	6-9-55	18-9-55
1807	Sims Samuel	Gunner	W/Sv	19-8-55	31-8-55
–	Sinclair William	Gunner	W/Sv	13-4-55	1-5-55
–	Smith Adam	Gunner	W/Sv	10-4-55	24-4-55
2488	Smith Andrew	Gunner	W/Sl	5-9-55	18-9-55
3071	Smith James	Gunner	W/D	23-8-55	4-9-55
3480	Smith John	Gunner	W/Sl	18-8-55	31-8-55
–	Spence John	Gunner	W/Sl	14-4-55	1-5-55
–	Spence William	Gunner	W/Sl	17-8-55	31-8-55
1503	Stewart George	Gunner	W/Sl	14-4-55	1-5-55
2983	Stewart James	Gunner	W/Sv	14-4-55	1-5-55
–	Taggett John	Gunner	W/Sl	14-4-55	1-5-55
–	Taylor Robert	Gunner	W/Sl	17-8-55	31-8-55
–	Tear Thomas	Gunner	W/Sv	13-4-55	1-5-55
2797	Thain Andrew	Gunner	W/Sv	3-9-55	18-9-55
–	Thompson Alexander	Gunner	W/Sl	9-6-55	22-6-55
–	Thompson William	Gunner	W/Sl	17-8-55	31-8-55
2040	Troddred Thomas	Gunner	W/Sl	16-4-55	1-5-55
–	Urquhart Hugh	Gunner	W/Sv	11-6-55	26-6-55
3787	Vigors George	Gunner	W/Sl	9-6-55	22-6-55
2267	Wallace John	Gunner	W/Sl	19-8-55	31-8-55
2061	Walsh James	Gunner	W/Sv	7-5-55	22-5-55
3421	Warner George	Gunner	W/Sv	13-4-55	1-5-55
–	Waterson T.	Gunner	W/Sv	7-9-55	25-9-55
–	Watkins Thomas	Gunner	W/Sl	17-8-55	31-8-55
–	Whitlow William	Gunner	W/Sl	17-8-55	31-8-55
–	Williams Richard	Gunner	W/Sl	17-8-55	31-8-55
3465	Williams Thomas	Gunner	W/Sl	22-8-55	4-9-55
–	Willicon John	Gunner	W/Sl	11-8-55	24-8-55
3628	Wilson John	Gunner	W/Sl	8-8-55	21-8-55
2316	Wood Joseph	Gunner	W/Sl	19-4-55	1-5-55
1674	Wordley Henry	Gunner	W/Sv	18-8-55	31-8-55
3596	Wright Richard	Gunner	W/Sv	14-4-55	1-5-55
3886	Yeo Thomas	Gunner	W/Sl	7-9-55	25-9-55
–	Young Henry	Gunner	W/Sv	18-8-55	31-8-55
–	Young John	Gunner	W/Sv	14-4-55	1-5-55

ROYAL ENGINEERS

NO.	NAME	RANK	CASUALTY	DATE	LONDON GAZETTE
	Craigie A. D.	Capt.	Killed	13-3-55	23-3-55
	Bambridge E.	Lieut.	Killed	4-4-55	20-4-55
	Carter J. H. S.	Lieut.	Killed	2-5-55	15-5-55
	Gordon J. W.	Br/Mjr.	W/Sv	22-3-55	3-5-55
	Armit L. J. A.	Capt.	W/Sv	4-4-55	20-4-55
	Browne J. F. M.	Capt.	W/Sv	26-8-55	7-9-55
	Grofton G.	Capt.	W/Sv	12-4-55	24-4-55
	King F. W.	Capt.	W/Sv	17-4-55	1-5-55
	Moleyns E. C. de	Capt.	W/Sl	5-7-55	20-7-55
	Owen H. C. C.	Capt.	W/D	19-4-55	1-5-55
	Baynes C. E. S.	Lieut.	W/D	19-4-55	1-5-55
	Graham A.	Lieut.	W/Sv	8-7-55	20-8-55
	Graham G.	Lieut.	W/Sl	13-4-55	1-5-55
	Graves T. M.	Lieut.	W/Sl	10-4-55	24-4-55
	Martin C. S.	Lieut.	W/D	24-11-54	11-12-54

NOTES

The Second, Third, Fourth, Fifth and Final Bombardment of Sebastopol, and Minor Actions

ROYAL ENGINEERS

NO.	NAME	RANK	CASUALTY	DATE	LONDON GAZETTE
	Montagu H.	Capt.	Missing	22-3-55	3-4-55
	James E. R.	Lieut.	Missing	2-7-55	20-7-55
	Green H (H.E.I.C.)	Capt.&Asst/Eng.	W/Sv	14-4-55	1-5-55

ROYAL SAPPERS AND MINERS

NO.	NAME	RANK	CASUALTY	DATE	LONDON GAZETTE
635	Wilson William	Sergt.	Killed	5-9-55	18-9-55
1147	Luke George	Corpl.	Killed	17-7-55	31-7-55
306	Ramsay A.	Corpl.	Killed	10-4-55	24-4-55
1157	Bell Charles	L/Cpl.	Killed	2-9-55	18-9-55
587	Miller John	L/Cpl.	Killed	25-7-55	7-8-55
3608	Pinch Richard	L/Cpl.	Killed	5-9-55	18-9-55
1030	Campbell Neil	Pte.	Killed	21-5-55	5-6-55
116	Coles Samuel	Pte.	Killed	9-12-54	29-12-54
1984	Collins William	Pte.	Killed	17-8-55	31-8-55
1907	Evans John	Pte.	Killed	19-4-55	1-5-55
1295	Gillard Nathaniel	Pte.	Killed	21-7-55	3-8-55
491	Lethbridge John	Pte.	Killed	15-4-55	1-5-55
151	McAsh Joseph	Pte.	Killed	13-4-55	1-5-55
1744	McNamara Michael	Pte.	Killed	18-8-55	31-8-55
2115	Masters Henry	Pte.	Killed	17-8-55	31-8-55
231	Miller John	Pte.	Killed	25-7-55	7-8-55
933	Morrison John	Pte.	Killed	2-9-55	18-9-55
2402	Rowlett Alfred	Pte.	Killed	26-7-55	7-8-55
1061	Russell Robert	Pte.	Killed	3-4-55	20-4-55
1150	Walsh Richard	Pte.	Killed	24-5-55	5-6-55
2434	Weir Alexander	Pte.	Killed	14-8-55	28-8-55
265	Wright John	Pte.	Killed	3-6-55	15-6-55
237	McDonald Henry	Col/Sgt.	W/Sl	19-4-55	1-5-55
1608	McLeod A.	Col/Sgt.	W/Sl	22-7-55	3-8-55
775	Castledine Benjamin	Sergt.	W/Sl	26-8-55	7-9-55
1745	Drew J. H.	Sergt.	W/Sl	10-11-54	11-12-54
725	Morant Philip	Sergt.	W/Sl	3-5-55	15-5-55
1995	Douglas James	Corpl.	W/Sl	25-6-55	10-7-55
1038	Lockwood Joseph	Corpl.	W/Sv	4-7-55	20-7-55
2198	Phillips Charles	2nd/Cpl.	W/Sv	4-9-55	18-9-55
1875	Smith Henry	2nd/Cpl.	W/Sv	17-8-55	31-8-55
2508	Swan William	2nd/Cpl.	W/Sv	20-5-55	5-6-55
503	Baker William	L/Cpl.	W/Sl	24-8-55	7-9-55
2729	Bridgman Richard	L/Cpl.	W/Sl	31-3-55	20-4-55
2282	Collins Joseph	L/Cpl.	W/Sv	2-7-55	17-7-55
596	Daft Stephen	L/Cpl.	W/Sv	15-6-55	3-7-55
1392	Finch Joseph	L/Cpl.	W/Sl	18-8-55	31-8-55
2601	Jenkins William	L/Cpl.	W/Sl	21-8-55	4-9-55
496	McGuire Edward	L/Cpl.	W/Sv	17-8-55	31-8-55
1164	Monds William	L/Cpl.	W/D	26-8-55	7-9-55
3608	Pinch Richard	L/Cpl.	W/Sl	26-7-55	7-8-55
140	Towell Peter	L/Cpl.	W/Sl	19-4-55	1-5-55
2611	Veal J.	L/Cpl.	W/Sl	6-4-55	20-4-55
624	Bastion J.	Pte.	W/Sv	10-4-55	24-4-55
2652	Bayne James	Pte.	W/Sl	12-4-55	24-4-55
1037	Boyce John	Pte.	W/Sl	4-9-55	18-9-55
391	Chesterman James	Pte.	W/Sl	6-9-55	18-9-55
627	Clubb George	Pte.	W/Sl	26-5-55	12-6-55
1004	Collins Francis	Pte.	W/Sl	27-7-55	7-8-55
1431	Colquhoune James	Pte.	W/Sl	26-8-55	7-9-55
104	Cuthbert D.	Pte.	W/Sv	27-2-55	16-3-55
1149	Delaney Peter	Pte.	W/Sl	17-8-55	31-8-55
262	Drummond James	Pte.	W/Sv	27-7-55	7-8-55
10	Eccles Thomas A.	Pte.	W/Sv	30-8-55	11-9-55

NOTES

The Second, Third, Fourth, Fifth and Final Bombardment of Sebastopol, and Minor Actions

ROYAL SAPPERS AND MINERS

NO.	NAME	RANK	CASUALTY	DATE	LONDON GAZETTE
1099	Fitzgerald Joshua	Pte.	W/D	2-9-55	18-9-55
2658	Gilchrist T.	Pte.	W/Sl	27-2-55	16-3-55
403	Giles John	Pte.	W/Sl	26-11-54	29-12-54
2591	Hobson George	Pte.	W/Sl	17-4-55	1-5-55
2291	Hodgkinson E.	Pte.	W/Sv	15-5-55	29-5-55
441	Jarrett Alfred	Pte.	D.O.W.	12-4-55	24-4-55
1514	Lang William	Pte.	W/Sv	10-6-55	22-6-55
1048	Lemming John	Pte.	W/Sl	17-4-55	1-5-55
1419	Lewis Edward	Pte.	W/Sl	10-7-55	24-7-55
212	Lincombe Thomas	Pte.	W/Sl	3-7-55	17-7-55
2255	Lloyd John	Pte.	W/Sl	17-8-55	31-8-55
113	McArthur Donald	Pte.	W/Sv	12-4-55	24-4-55
146	McCaughey Alexander	Pte.	W/Sl	17-4-55	1-5-55
2439	McFarlane Robert	Pte.	W/Sv	27-12-54	12-1-55
2477	McNeil Thomas	Pte.	W/Sv	3-4-55	20-4-55
2017	McRoberts John	Pte.	D.O.W.	14-6-55	26-6-55
946	Malcolm John	Pte.	W/Sl	8-6-55	22-6-55
2115	Masters H.	Pte.	W/Sl	16-3-55	30-3-55
1345	Mehan James	Pte.	W/Sl	10-7-55	24-7-55
725	Morant Philip	Pte.	W/Sl	3-5-55	15-5-55
580	Muir Thomas	Pte.	W/Sv	9-4-55	24-4-55
1506	Murphy John	Pte.	W/Sv	14-6-55	26-6-55
2009	Ralph William	Pte.	W/Sv	31-3-55	20-4-55
1211	Sharp Robert	Pte.	W/Sv	28-7-55	7-8-55
1890	Small William	Pte.	W/Sv	14-4-55	1-5-55
—	Small William	Pte.	W/D	16-6-55	3-7-55
1532	Sparks Alexander	Pte.	W/Sl	29-7-55	7-8-55
54	Stewart Roderick	Pte.	W/Sl	27-7-55	7-8-55
2278	Taylor William	Pte.	W/Sv	10-4-55	24-4-55
2526	Willis R.	Pte.	W/Sl	15-5-55	29-5-55
1205	Wood George	Pte.	W/Sl	24-5-55	5-6-55

AMBULANCE CORPS

NO.	NAME	RANK	CASUALTY	DATE	LONDON GAZETTE
226	McDevitt James	Pte.	W/Sv	2-12-54	29-12-54

LAND TRANSPORT CORPS

NO.	NAME	RANK	CASUALTY	DATE	LONDON GAZETTE
	Hudson Charles	Capt.	W/Sv	7-6-55	31-7-55

3rd BATTALION GRENADIER GUARDS

NO.	NAME	RANK	CASUALTY	DATE	LONDON GAZETTE
5699	Banks Richard	Pte.	Killed	27-6-55	10-7-55
7350	Birch Robert	Pte.	Killed	7-9-55	18-9-55
6758	Davis George	Pte.	Killed	11-7-55	24-7-55
7266	Dobson Thomas	Pte.	Killed	13-8-55	28-8-55
6250	Dunstar James	Pte.	Killed	7-9-55	18-9-55
7602	Fox Charles	Pte.	Killed	25-8-55	7-9-55
6752	Gilman Thomas	Pte.	Killed	29-7-55	10-8-55
8680	Gosling Elias	Pte.	Killed	5-9-55	18-9-55
6185	Hilch Edward	Pte.	Killed	7-9-55	18-9-55
6368	Miller Thomas	Pte.	Killed	4-8-55	17-8-55

NOTES

The Second, Third, Fourth, Fifth and Final Bombardment of Sebastopol, and Minor Actions

3rd BATTALION GRENADIER GUARDS

NO.	NAME	RANK	CASUALTY	DATE	LONDON GAZETTE
6922	Palmore James	Pte.	Killed	7-9-55	18-9-55
7323	Peat Henry	Pte.	Killed	25-8-55	7-9-55
7519	Richardson Richard	Pte.	Killed	16-8-55	28-8-55
6663	Stamford John	Pte.	Killed	13-8-55	28-8-55
6650	Wire John	Pte.	Killed	22-8-55	4-9-55
	Forbes Hon. W.	Capt.	W/Sl	28-8-55	11-9-55
	Verschoyle H. W.	Capt.	W/Sl	5-9-55	18-9-55
—	Bickrell William	Sergt.	W/Sl	30-8-55	11-9-55
4209	Davies James	Sergt.	W/Sl	3-9-55	18-9-55
4209	Davies James	Sergt.	W/Sl	5-7-55	17-7-55
4663	Drage Joseph	Sergt.	W/Sl	5-7-55	17-7-55
5558	Gamble William	Sergt.	W/Sv	16-8-55	28-8-55
4653	Marsh Thomas	Sergt.	W/Sv	29-7-55	10-8-55
6973	Brotherton Richard	Corpl.	W/D	11-7-55	24-7-55
3352	Bear Robert	Drummer	W/Sl	7-9-55	18-9-55
7314	Allinger John	Pte.	W/D	7-9-55	18-9-55
6744	Appleton Edward	Pte.	W/Sl	29-6-55	17-7-55
5337	Arbuthnot George	Pte.	W/Sv	30-8-55	11-9-55
4930	Baldwin James	Pte.	W/Sl	22-8-55	4-9-55
4418	Bandy Samuel	Pte.	W/Sl	7-8-55	21-8-55
6446	Barrett Robert	Pte.	W/Sl	4-7-55	17-7-55
6039	Beeteson William	Pte.	W/Sl	10-8-55	24-8-55
4310	Berry William	Pte.	W/Sv	7-9-55	18-9-55
6023	Bett Joseph	Pte.	W/Sl	4-9-55	18-9-55
7458	Bowland Frederick	Pte.	W/Sl	29-7-55	10-8-55
6422	Bowler George	Pte.	W/D	29-7-55	10-8-55
5189	Boxhall Charles	Pte.	W/Sl	4-9-55	18-9-55
6332	Butchers James	Pte.	W/D	13-8-55	28-8-55
6638	Calton John	Pte.	W/Sl	16-8-55	28-8-55
7035	Caulkin Thomas	Pte.	W/D	29-7-55	10-8-55
6703	Chapman Thomas	Pte.	W/Sv	4-7-55	17-7-55
3494	Clifford Alfred	Pte.	W/D	7-9-55	18-9-55
7197	Collings W. H.	Pte.	W/Sv	24-6-55	9-7-55
7245	Cox Caleb	Pte.	W/D	29-7-55	10-8-55
6861	Crew Joseph	Pte.	W/Sv	3-9-55	18-9-55
7748	Darington Thomas	Pte.	W/D	7-9-55	18-9-55
6459	Day John	Pte.	W/Sv	4-9-55	18-9-55
6606	Dean Charles	Pte.	W/Sv	4-7-55	17-7-55
5015	Eggleton Alfred	Pte.	W/Sl	4-9-55	18-9-55
6791	Ellingham Robert	Pte.	W/D	29-7-55	10-8-55
6672	Elsley William	Pte.	W/Sl	22-6-55	9-7-55
5229	Fielding Michael	Pte.	W/Sv	29-7-55	10-8-55
6858	Fletcher Moses	Pte.	W/Sl	16-8-55	28-8-55
—	Francis George	Pte.	W/Sv	5-9-55	18-9-55
2779	Graygoose Stephen	Pte.	W/Sl	25-8-55	7-9-55
5252	Harrison John	Pte.	W/Sl	22-8-55	4-9-55
6616	Hickling William	Pte.	W/Sl	16-8-55	28-8-55
5246	Higginson Charles	Pte.	W/Sl	16-8-55	28-8-55
6045	Higgs Amos	Pte.	W/Sv	22-8-55	4-9-55
6278	Holyrood William	Pte.	W/Sv	4-8-55	17-8-55
7515	Humphreys Thomas	Pte.	W/Sv	3-7-55	17-7-55
7220	Izzard Jesse	Pte.	W/Sl	22-8-55	4-9-55
4886	Jones Edward	Pte.	W/Sl	29-7-55	10-8-55
6510	Lawson Thomas	Pte.	W/Sl	3-9-55	18-9-55
1894	Lee James	Pte.	W/Sl	29-6-55	17-7-55
5391	Leger James	Pte.	W/Sv	7-9-55	18-9-55
4835	Lewis George	Pte.	W/Sl	22-8-55	4-9-55
5041	Lovegrove James	Pte.	W/Sv	7-9-55	18-9-55
6959	Lucas Henry	Pte.	W/Sv	19-8-55	31-8-55
6130	Marden Cuthbert	Pte.	W/D	3-9-55	18-9-55
7771	Marsden Thomas	Pte.	W/D	29-7-55	10-8-55
4947	Martin Henry	Pte.	W/Sv	19-8-55	31-8-55
6055	Mason Thomas	Pte.	W/Sl	29-6-55	17-7-55
4095	Masterman Cornelius	Pte.	W/Sv	7-9-55	18-9-55

NOTES

The Second, Third, Fourth, Fifth and Final Bombardment of Sebastopol, and Minor Actions

3rd BATTALION GRENADIER GUARDS

NO.	NAME	RANK	CASUALTY	DATE	LONDON GAZETTE
9580	Midden John	Pte	W/Sv	7-9-55	18-9-55
7578	Milliner Isaac	Pte.	W/Sv	5-7-55	17-7-55
6946	Naylor Seth	Pte.	W/D	11-7-55	24-7-55
6579	Newbury James	Pte.	W/Sl	10-8-55	24-8-55
6196	Notting Robert	Pte.	W/Sl	13-8-55	28-8-55
7066	Paine George	Pte.	W/Sv	28-8-55	11-9-55
3571	Palmer Anthony	Pte.	W/Sl	22-8-55	4-9-55
6948	Platt Thomas	Pte	W/Sl	16-8-55	28-8-55
3627	Pullen John	Pte.	W/Sv	4-8-55	17-8-55
6938	Robinson Edward	Pte.	W/Sl	30-8-55	11-9-55
7401	Sampson Thomas	Pte.	W/Sl	3-9-55	18-9-55
5123	Shepherd Charles	Pte.	W/Sl	4-8-55	17-8-55
7036	Sheppard Charles	Pte.	W/D	11-7-55	24-7-55
6965	Smith Charles	Pte.	W/Sv	1-8-55	14-8-55
6079	Smith Eliot	Pte.	W/Sl	17-7-55	31-7-55
3755	Smith Thomas	Pte.	W/Sv	30-8-55	11-9-55
6060	Spencer George	Pte.	W/Sv	26-7-55	7-8-55
6916	Stanley William	Pte.	W/Sl	1-9-55	18-9-55
3872	Suthers Benjamin	Pte.	W/D	14-7-55	27-7-55
6878	Symonds Charles	Pte.	W/Sv	28-8-55	11-9-55
5862	Tarrent James	Pte.	W/Sl	4-7-55	17-7-55
4004	Vemore Henry	Pte.	W/Sl	3-9-55	18-9-55
6336	Weedon Charles	Pte.	W/Sv	5-7-55	17-7-55
6871	Weir William	Pte.	W/D	29-7-55	10-8-55
6554	Wells Robert	Pte.	W/Sv	5-7-55	17-7-55
5031	Wesson George	Pte.	W/Sv	4-7-55	17-7-55
6751	Wickwar Samuel	Pte.	W/D	11-7-55	24-7-55
7442	Widdison Frederick	Pte.	W/Sl	29-7-55	10-8-55
6309	Williams Thomas	Pte.	W/Sv	13-8-55	28-8-55
6326	Withal George	Pte.	W/Sl	4-8-55	17-8-55

1st BATTALION, COLDSTREAM GUARDS

NO.	NAME	RANK	CASUALTY	DATE	LONDON GAZETTE
4161	Bolton George	Sergt.	Killed	22-8-55	4-9-55
4879	Copperwhite John	Pte.	Killed	19-8-55	31-8-55
4652	Harrison Thomas	Pte.	Killed	29-8-55	11-9-55
3941	Pass Joseph	Pte.	Killed	19-8-55	31-8-55
	Drummond R. Hon	Capt.	W/D	25-8-55	7-9-55
4457	Goodhand James	Corpl	W/Sl	17-7-55	31-7-55
2268	Trotter William	Corpl.	W/Sl	3-9-55	18-9-55
4000	Alexander James	Pte.	W/D	7-8-55	21-8-55
5293	Andrew William	Pte.	W/Sl	7-8-55	21-8-55
4505	Askew Parker	Pte.	W/Sl	3-9-55	18-9-55
4661	Baines Daniel	Pte.	W/Sv	25-8-55	7-9-55
4766	Baker William	Pte.	W/Sl	3-9-55	18-9-55
5676	Baldwin John	Pte.	W/Sv	23-7-55	7-8-55
4134	Ball Philip	Pte.	W/Sl	11-7-55	24-7-55
4561	Beasley Silvester	Pte.	W/Sl	28-8-55	11-9-55
4639	Beaton James	Pte.	W/Sv	9-7-55	24-7-55
7687	Brandon John	Pte.	W/Sv	23-7-55	7-8-55
—	Brewster Edward	Pte.	W/Sl	23-7-55	7-8-55
4806	Brown John	Pte.	W/Sl	19-8-55	31-8-55
5070	Bryant John	Pte.	W/Sl	3-9-55	11-9-55
4703	Buck Henry	Pte.	W/Sl	9-7-55	24-7-55
4583	Connell James	Pte.	W/Sl	9-7-55	24-7-55
3976	Cope John	Pte.	W/Sv	19-8-55	31-8-55
3078	Craven Hiram	Pte.	W/Sl	29-7-55	10-8-55
4634	Day Samuel	Pte.	W/Sl	29-7-55	10-8-55
4240	Dew Charles	Pte.	W/Sl	3-9-55	18-9-55
3974	Doherty John	Pte.	W/Sv	7-8-55	21-8-55

NOTES

The Second, Third, Fourth, Fifth and Final Bombardment of Sebastopol, and Minor Actions

1st BATTALION COLDSTREAM GUARDS

NO.	NAME	RANK	CASUALTY	DATE	LONDON GAZETTE
2626	Falkner James	Pte.	W/Sl	11-7-55	24-7-55
3542	Gibson Job	Pte.	W/D	7-7-55	20-7-55
4679	Gillespie Robert	Pte.	W/Sl	19-8-55	31-8-55
3984	Green George	Pte.	W/Sl	3-9-55	18-9-55
4575	Hansby Thomas	Pte.	W/Sv	19-8-55	31-8-55
4774	Hartlane John	Pte.	W/Sv	7-8-55	21-8-55
4711	Holden Robert	Pte.	W/Sv	22-8-55	4-9-55
4515	Hudson John	Pte.	W/Sv	10-8-55	24-8-55
4509	Kirkley Richard	Pte.	W/Sl	28-8-55	11-9-55
4665	Lamb George	Pte.	W/Sl	17-7-55	31-7-55
4707	Liffin Henry	Pte.	W/Sv	9-7-55	24-7-55
4259	Lissons John	Pte.	W/Sl	29-7-55	10-8-55
4580	Mason William	Pte.	W/Sl	29-7-55	10-8-55
2695	Moore George	Pte.	W/Sl	11-7-55	24-7-55
4517	Morley Henry	Pte.	W/Sv	9-7-55	24-7-55
5052	Moss James	Pte.	W/Sv	22-8-55	4-9-55
7542	Mountrey Charles	Pte.	W/D	23-7-55	7-8-55
4780	Old James	Pte.	W/Sv	22-8-55	4-9-55
4266	Oxpring David	Pte.	W/Sl	9-7-55	24-7-55
4491	Pacey Thomas	Pte.	W/Sl	17-7-55	31-7-55
3281	Patchett James	Pte.	W/Sl	9-7-55	24-7-55
3599	Phasey Alfred J.	Pte.	W/Sl	29-7-55	10-8-55
4973	Philpot George	Pte.	W/Sv	29-7-55	10-8-55
4265	Ploughman William	Pte.	W/Sv	11-7-55	24-7-55
3608	Podbury John	Pte.	W/Sv	29-7-55	10-8-55
1862	Rolph John	Pte.	W/Sl	9-7-55	24-7-55
3346	Russell John	Pte.	W/Sv	7-8-55	21-8-55
4632	Scott James	Pte.	W/Sl	20-7-55	3-8-55
4237	Smith Philip	Pte.	W/Sv	24-6-55	9-7-55
2509	Smith William	Pte.	W/Sv	7-8-55	21-8-55
3816	Sparrow Frederick	Pte.	W/Sl	11-7-55	24-7-55
4513	Spinks John	Pte.	W/Sl	19-8-55	31-8-55
4703	Taylor Abel	Pte.	W/Sl	22-8-55	4-9-55
5151	Thompson David	Pte.	W/D	7-8-55	21-8-55
4524	Turner Frederick	Pte.	W/Sl	22-8-55	4-9-55
3814	Turner Henry	Pte.	W/Sv	25-8-55	7-9-55
3447	Tyson William	Pte.	W/Sl	3-9-55	18-9-55
4642	Walsh James	Pte.	W/Sl	22-8-55	4-9-55
3601	White Joseph	Pte.	W/D	19-8-55	31-8-55
2108	Williamson W.	Pte.	W/Sl	11-7-55	24-7-55
—	Wilson William	Pte.	W/Sl	11-7-55	24-7-55

1st BATTALION, SCOTS FUSILIER GUARDS

NO.	NAME	RANK	CASUALTY	DATE	LONDON GAZETTE
	Drummond H.	Brv/Mjr.	Killed	13-8-55	28-8-55
	Buckley D. F. B.	Capt.	Killed	7-9-55	29-9-55
5276	Blinkhorn John	Pte.	Killed	10-8-55	24-8-55
4480	Carbine John	Pte.	Killed	4-7-55	17-7-55
4812	Davis Richard	Pte.	Killed	10-8-55	24-8-55
5039	Griffiths Evan	Pte.	Killed	10-8-55	24-8-55
4725	Hester William	Pte.	Killed	3-9-55	18-9-55
3020	James William	Pte.	Killed	9-6-55	22-6-55
2828	Kidd James	Pte.	Killed	14-7-55	27-7-55
5253	Knowles Thomas	Pte.	Killed	10-8-55	24-8-55
5051	McCabe John	Pte.	Killed	10-8-55	24-8-55
4116	McRoberts Thomas	Pte.	Killed	22-8-55	4-9-55
5226	Maxwell George	Pte.	Killed	26-7-55	7-8-55
4919	Ruice John	Pte.	Killed	19-8-55	31-8-55
4994	Sauceney William	Pte.	Killed	13-8-55	28-8-55
4658	Taylor Richard	Pte.	Killed	26-7-55	7-8-55

NOTES

The Second, Third, Fourth, Fifth and Final Bombardment of Sebastopol, and Minor Actions
1st BATTALION, SCOTS FUSILIER GUARDS

NO.	NAME	RANK	CASUALTY	DATE	LONDON GAZETTE
5095	Thomson Daniel	Pte.	Killed	4-8-55	17-8-55
	Seymour F.	Lt/Col.	W/Sv	25-8-55	7-9-55
	Baring F.	Capt.	W/Sl	19-8-55	31-8-55
	Coke Hon W. C. W.	Capt.	W/Sl	4-8-55	24-8-55
	Farquharson J. R.	Capt.	W/Sv	29-8-55	11-9-55
	Campbell A. C.	Lieut.	W/Sl	22-8-55	4-9-55
4062	Gilchrist Colin	Sergt.	W/Sl	2-9-55	18-9-55
4838	Gordan William	Corpl.	W/D	5-9-55	18-9-55
3553	McDougall James	Corpl.	W/D	19-8-55	31-8-55
5734	Murray John	Corpl.	W/Sv	10-8-55	24-8-55
4544	Parkinson William	Corpl.	W/Sv	5-9-55	18-9-55
3883	Skein Andrew	Corpl.	W/Sl	9-7-55	24-7-55
4635	Able James	Pte.	W/Sv	22-1-55	6-2-55
4680	Alder Enoch	Pte.	W/Sl	25-8-55	7-9-55
4208	Alexander James	Pte.	W/Sv	22-8-55	4-9-55
5371	Allen Peter	Pte.	W/Sv	7-9-55	25-9-55
4851	Baker Joseph	Pte.	W/Sl	25-8-55	7-9-55
5082	Bell William	Pte.	W/Sl	4-7-55	17-7-55
5202	Brown John	Pte.	W/Sv	19-8-55	31-8-55
4314	Brown William	Pte.	W/Sl	23-7-55	7-8-55
5017	Burns Thomas	Pte.	W/Sl	4-8-55	17-8-55
4849	Cairns Alexander	Pte.	W/D	22-8-55	4-9-55
2247	Cameron John	Pte.	W/Sv	22-8-55	4-9-55
3638	Cooper John	Pte.	W/Sl	22-8-55	4-9-55
4905	Coughlin Timothy	Pte.	W/Sl	11-7-55	24-7-55
4846	Dickein Henry	Pte.	W/Sl	19-8-55	31-8-55
2545	Dow James	Pte.	W/Sv	25-8-55	7-9-55
4843	Duff John	Pte.	W/Sl	11-7-55	24-7-55
3847	Forbes Duncan	Pte.	W/Sl	22-8-55	4-9-55
4664	Ford John	Pte.	W/Sl	25-8-55	7-9-55
4244	Frith Joseph	Pte.	W/Sv	11-7-55	24-7-55
5278	Garrett William	Pte.	W/Sl	9-7-55	24-7-55
4986	Harton Charles	Pte.	W/Sv	10-8-55	24-8-55
5303	Hatton George	Pte.	W/Sl	10-8-55	24-8-55
4848	Heron James	Pte.	W/Sl	4-7-55	17-7-55
4949	Hickey James	Pte.	W/Sl	4-9-55	18-9-55
5502	Hill Mark	Pte.	W/Sl	3-9-55	18-9-55
4532	Hopkins William	Pte.	W/Sl	27-6-55	10-7-55
4469	House Henry	Pte.	W/Sl	1-9-55	18-9-55
4721	Hurren Henry	Pte.	W/Sl	16-8-55	28-8-55
4923	Jones Peter	Pte.	W/D	26-7-55	7-8-55
5310	Jones Robert	Pte.	W/D	7-7-55	20-7-55
4686	Lewis Fred	Pte.	W/Sl	16-8-55	28-8-55
4183	Lynch Robert	Pte.	W/Sv	29-7-55	10-8-55
2518	McCallum Archibald	Pte.	W/Sl	22-8-55	4-9-55
4944	McCoureycan Daniel	Pte.	W/Sl	10-8-55	24-8-55
5050	McLean Angus	Pte.	W/Sv	22-8-55	4-9-55
4890	March Samuel	Pte.	W/Sl	9-7-55	24-7-55
3514	Millard Edwin	Pte.	W/Sv	24-6-55	9-7-55
5114	Offord John	Pte.	W/Sl	10-8-55	24-8-55
4003	Orchard W. H.	Pte.	W/Sl	29-7-55	10-8-55
3376	Payne William	Pte.	W/Sv	23-7-55	7-8-55
4343	Ramsay Peter	Pte.	W/Sl	29-7-55	10-8-55
4494	Robertson George	Pte.	W/Sl	29-6-55	17-7-55
5109	Russell William	Pte.	W/D	11-7-55	24-7-55
5196	Sains William	Pte.	W/Sl	22-8-55	4-9-55
5047	Sankey Thomas	Pte.	W/D	7-9-55	25-9-55
3716	Scott William	Pte.	W/Sl	14-7-55	27-7-55
4383	Scutt Clemence	Pte.	W/D	29-7-55	10-8-55
4394	Short Alexander	Pte.	W/Sl	26-7-55	7-8-55
5198	Simons Samuel	Pte.	W/Sl	23-7-55	7-8-55
4657	Smith George	Pte.	W/Sv	22-1-55	6-2-55
3853	Smith George	Pte.	W/Sv	5-9-55	18-9-55
4711	Smith Henry	Pte.	W/Sv	4-7-55	17-7-55

NOTES

The Second, Third, Fourth, Fifth and Final Bombardment of Sebastopol, and Minor Actions

1st BATTALION, SCOTS FUSILIER GUARDS

NO.	NAME	RANK	CASUALTY	DATE	LONDON GAZETTE
4397	Smith William	Pte.	W/Sl	9-7-55	24-7-55
5475	Spencer Thomas	Pte.	W/Sv	10-8-55	24-8-55
4628	Stanley Ephrain	Pte.	W/Sl	25-8-55	7-9-55
2685	Stevenson Andrew	Pte.	W/Sl	11-7-55	24-7-55
5059	Sturgeon John	Pte.	W/Sl	26-7-55	7-8-55
4279	Taylor James	Pte.	W/Sv	26-7-55	7-8-55
4713	Taylor William	Pte.	W/Sl	22-8-55	4-9-55
4615	Thomas Benjamin	Pte.	W/Sl	17-7-55	31-7-55
5234	Thompson Adam	Pte.	W/Sl	25-8-55	7-9-55
4710	Tipping Samuel	Pte.	W/Sl	26-7-55	7-8-55
5024	Wakeford Francis	Pte.	W/Sv	22-8-55	4-9-55
4531	Warmer George	Pte.	W/Sl	10-8-55	24-8-55
5297	Waters William	Pte.	W/D	11-7-55	24-7-55
4643	West William	Pte.	W/Sl	17-7-55	31-7-55
4019	Wood William	Pte.	W/Sv	1-9-55	18-9-55
5174	Worthington Henry	Pte.	W/Sl	25-8-55	7-9-55
3410	McGlachlan James	L/Sgt.	Missing	25-8-55	7-9-55
5044	Marin Patrick	Pte.	Missing	25-8-55	7-9-55

1st BATTALION, 1st REGIMENT OF FOOT

NO.	NAME	RANK	CASUALTY	DATE	LONDON GAZETTE
2980	Sullivan Daniel	Corpl.	Killed	17-5-55	29-5-55
2040	Horan Michael	L/Cpl.	Killed	3-8-55	17-8-55
2095	Daniel Edward	Pte.	Killed	14-12-54	9-1-55
3821	Garland Edward	Pte.	Killed	6-3-55	23-3-55
3063	Nelson Michael	Pte.	Killed	24-6-55	7-7-55
3923	Teender Joseph	Pte.	Killed	10-8-55	24-8-55
3387	Walker Thomas	Pte.	Killed	1-1-55	26-1-55
	Bell George	Colonel	W/Sl	14-2-55	2-3-55
1589	McDonell William	Col/Sgt.	W/Sl	28-8-55	11-9-55
2519	Smart John	Sergt.	W/Sl	12-12-54	9-1-55
2665	Wallace John	Sergt.	W/Sl	16-4-55	1-5-55
2812	Kanavan Michael	L/Sgt.	W/Sl	7-1-55	26-1-55
1280	Heher Michael	Corpl.	W/Sl	3-7-55	17-7-55
2768	Kelly James	Corpl.	W/Sl	29-3-55	13-4-55
1030	McMahon Michael	Corpl.	W/Sv	24-8-55	7-9-55
2980	Sullivan W.	Corpl.	W/Sv	19-8-55	31-8-55
3404	Carter John	L/Cpl.	W/Sv	28-8-55	11-9-55
2249	Norman Benjamin	L/Cpl.	W/Sl	30-12-54	26-1-55
3096	Adlam Joseph	Pte.	W/Sl	9-5-55	23-5-55
2692	Berry William	Pte.	W/Sv	16-5-55	29-5-55
3755	Booty Benjamin	Pte.	W/Sl	19-8-55	31-8-55
4172	Brackman Charles	Pte.	W/Sl	28-8-55	11-9-55
1434	Campbell John	Pte.	W/Sl	23-8-55	4-9-55
4087	Clinton Joseph	Pte.	W/Sl	28-8-55	11-9-55
4076	Connors John	Pte.	W/Sv	24-7-55	7-8-55
3780	Conway Thomas	Pte.	W/Sl	28-8-55	11-9-55
2608	Creagh John	Pte.	W/Sv	24-8-55	7-9-55
2916	Deanes Hugh	Pte.	W/Sl	7-9-55	25-9-55
3474	Dicky James	Pte.	W/Sv	24-7-55	7-8-55
3905	Donoghue Edward	Pte.	W/Sl	28-8-55	11-9-55
2971	Dow Henry	Pte.	W/Sl	1-1-55	26-1-55
3315	Driscoll Michael	Pte.	W/Sl	28-8-55	11-9-55
4028	Flat Joshua	Pte.	W/Sv	28-6-55	10-7-55
3966	Gregory William	Pte.	W/Sv	28-8-55	11-9-55
3279	Hamilton John	Pte.	W/Sl	3-7-55	17-7-55
3584	Harrison Thomas	Pte.	W/Sl	28-8-55	11-9-55
3327	Herbert James	Pte.	W/Sv	19-7-55	31-7-55
3862	Howard William	Pte.	W/Sl	13-7-55	27-7-55
3862	Howard William	Pte.	W/Sv	7-8-55	21-8-55

NOTES

The Second, Third, Fourth, Fifth and Final Bombardment of Sebastopol, and Minor Actions

1st BATTALION, 1st REGIMENT OF FOOT

NO.	NAME	RANK	CASUALTY	DATE	LONDON GAZETTE
3038	Howell Henry	Pte.	W/Sl	24-7-55	7-8-55
2256	Innes John	Pte.	W/Sv	12-12-54	9-1-55
1921	Jennings Michael	Pte.	W/Sl	28-8-55	11-9-55
3787	Johnson Thomas	Pte.	W/Sl	28-8-55	11-9-55
3295	Kane John	Pte.	W/Sl	28-8-55	11-9-55
2946	Kelly James	Pte.	W/Sl	7-9-55	25-9-55
2841	Kenny William	Pte.	W/Sv	8-11-54	4-12-54
3281	Lawler William	Pte.	W/Sv	23-1-55	9-2-55
3334	Leary Jeremiah	Pte.	W/Sl	24-7-55	7-8-55
2176	McGowan James	Pte.	W/Sl	15-5-55	29-5-55
2504	McSweeney Peter	Pte.	W/Sv	4-2-55	20-4-55
3906	Mathews James	Pte.	W/Sl	3-8-55	17-8-55
3375	Moran John	Pte.	W/Sl	7-1-55	26-1-55
2701	Morgan John	Pte.	W/Sl	10-12-54	26-1-55
2992	Mullins Thomas	Pte.	W/Sl	7-1-55	26-1-55
1789	Nichols Charles	Pte.	W/Sl	4-8-55	17-8-55
2215	Parker Isaac	Pte.	W/Sv	30-12-54	26-1-55
3826	Reeves George	Pte.	W/Sv	3-8-55	17-8-55
2070	Ryham Thomas	Pte.	W/Sl	2-5-55	15-5-55
2614	Salsbury William	Pte.	W/Sl	4-8-55	17-8-55
3640	Sewill Thomas	Pte.	W/D	3-8-55	17-8-55
3170	Silk Bryan	Pte.	W/Sv	4-2-55	20-2-55
3808	Smart John	Pte.	W/Sv	24-8-55	7-9-55
3289	Smith Frederick	Pte.	W/Sl	28-6-55	10-7-55
3711	Smith William	Pte.	W/Sv	7-8-55	21-8-55
2184	Walsh John	Pte.	W/Sl	30-11-54	26-12-54
3397	White John	Pte.	W/Sl	31-7-55	14-8-55

2nd BATTALION, 1st REGIMENT OF FOOT

NO.	NAME	RANK	CASUALTY	DATE	LONDON GAZETTE
1559	Armstrong John	Sergt.	Killed	17-8-55	28-8-55
3357	Connors J.	L/Cpl.	Killed	16-6-55	3-7-55
1907	Godbold James	L/Cpl.	Killed	9-7-55	24-7-55
2375	Rice John	L/Cpl.	Killed	17-7-55	31-7-55
3600	Brennan Martin	Pte.	Killed	16-6-55	3-7-55
2395	Cloonan Patrick	Pte.	Killed	10-5-55	23-5-55
3052	Daline Edward	Pte.	Killed	3-9-55	18-9-55
2130	Digley P.	Pte.	Killed	17-8-55	31-8-55
1950	Pipler Amos	Pte.	Killed	30-4-55	15-5-55
2575	Sculfer James	Pte.	Killed	3-6-55	15-6-55
2510	Shales William	Pte.	Killed	10-5-55	25-5-55
2027	Wakefield George	Pte.	Killed	10-5-55	25-5-55
3383	Wyves John	Pte.	Killed	28-5-55	12-6-55
	Byrne T. M.	Major	W/Sl	10-5-55	23-5-55
1909	Guran William	Sergt.	W/Sv	16-6-55	3-7-55
2129	Keane James	Sergt.	W/Sl	13-8-55	28-8-55
1418	Mulveny James	Sergt.	W/Sl	31-8-55	18-9-55
2506	Sweeney Michael	L/Sgt.	W/D	19-5-55	5-6-55
1683	Chilons George	Corpl.	W/Sl	9-7-55	24-7-55
2185	Wiseman B.	L/Cpl.	W/Sl	31-8-55	18-9-55
2118	McLeish James	Drummer	W/Sl	18-5-55	5-6-55
2165	Beattie William	Pte.	W/Sl	27-7-55	7-8-55
2537	Bone John	Pte.	W/Sv	26-7-55	7-8-55
2239	Bottomley Henry	Pte.	W/Sv	24-5-55	5-6-55
2964	Brennan Thomas	Pte.	W/Sl	25-8-55	7-9-55
2122	Buchanan David	Pte.	W/Sl	5-5-55	15-5-55
3270	Cannon Richard	Pte.	W/Sl	8-5-55	23-5-55
2535	Carey Patrick	Pte.	W/Sv	11-5-55	25-5-55
1094	Churchman Thomas	Pte.	W/D	17-7-55	31-7-55
2444	Clapwick John	Pte.	W/Sv	6-7-55	20-7-55

NOTES

The Second, Third, Fourth, Fifth and Final Bombardment of Sebastopol, and Minor Actions

2nd BATTALION, 1st REGIMENT OF FOOT

NO.	NAME	RANK	CASUALTY	DATE	LONDON GAZETTE
2630	Comasky Patrick	Pte.	W/Sl	12-5-55	25-5-55
2630	Comasky Patrick	Pte.	W/Sl	21-7-55	3-8-55
2582	Conton R.	Pte.	W/Sl	22-8-55	4-9-55
2687	Cook Daniel	Pte.	W/Sv	22-8-55	4-9-55
2852	Cowan Richard	Pte.	W/Sl	9-7-55	24-7-55
2688	Cross Thomas	Pte.	W/Sv	28-6-55	10-7-55
2344	Curley Thomas	Pte.	W/Sl	27-7-55	7-8-55
3071	Daly James	Pte.	W/Sl	22-8-55	4-9-55
1051	Davidson George	Pte.	W/Sl	22-5-55	5-6-55
2191	Dempsey John	Pte.	W/Sl	22-8-55	4-9-55
2151	Duffy Patrick	Pte.	W/Sv	10-5-55	23-5-55
3894	Faithfull Edward	Pte.	W/Sl	8-5-55	23-5-55
2824	Fitzgerald James	Pte.	W/Sv	22-6-55	9-7-55
2060	Fuller James	Pte.	W/Sl	28-6-55	10-7-55
3006	Gaffigan John	Pte.	W/Sl	26-7-55	7-8-55
2281	Harriatt John	Pte.	W/Sl	8-8-55	21-8-55
2562	Harrison John	Pte.	W/Sl	14-8-55	28-8-55
1888	Head John	Pte.	W/Sv	16-6-55	3-7-55
1780	Herbert Joseph	Pte.	W/Sl	8-8-55	21-8-55
1378	Hewitt Thomas	Pte.	W/Sl	26-7-55	7-8-55
2653	Howard Henry	Pte.	W/Sl	10-8-55	24-8-55
2398	Jordan Joseph	Pte.	W/Sl	21-7-55	3-8-55
3255	Lackey James	Pte.	W/Sv	7-8-55	21-8-55
2590	Lawler Daniel	Pte.	W/Sl	16-6-55	3-7-55
3869	McDonald John	Pte.	W/Sv	22-5-55	5-6-55
2157	McDonald Thomas	Pte.	W/Sl	18-5-55	5-6-55
2230	McKernard John	Pte.	W/Sl	3-9-55	18-9-55
2376	McLaughlin Pat	Pte.	W/Sl	10-8-55	24-8-55
3047	May William	Pte.	W/Sv	22-8-55	4-9-55
2815	Meally Michael	Pte.	W/Sv	22-6-55	9-7-55
2974	Melvin Owen	Pte.	W/Sv	16-6-55	3-7-55
2520	Mulretay James	Pte.	W/D	31-8-55	18-9-55
2520	Mulvahy James	Pte.	W/Sl	21-7-55	3-8-55
2029	Norman George	Pte.	W/D	17-7-55	31-7-55
4022	Norris Charles	Pte.	W/Sv	22-6-55	9-7-55
2775	Palmer Samuel	Pte.	W/Sl	22-8-55	4-9-55
2589	Patterson William	Pte.	W/Sl	14-8-55	28-8-55
2413	Pryde James	Pte.	W/Sl	17-7-55	31-7-55
2357	Ryan Patrick	Pte.	W/Sl	16-6-55	3-7-55
2601	Scully Peter	Pte.	W/Sl	27-4-55	15-5-55
2601	Scully Peter	Pte.	W/Sl	27-8-55	11-9-55
2601	Sealy Peter	Pte.	W/Sv	22-5-55	5-6-55
2823	Sheehan Michael	Pte.	W/Sl	22-6-55	9-7-55
1929	Sinnott Richard	Pte.	W/Sl	10-8-55	24-8-55
1260	Smith John	Pte.	W/Sl	15-5-55	29-5-55
2876	Stewart James	Pte.	W/Sl	23-5-55	5-6-55
2878	Sullivan John	Pte.	W/Sl	10-8-55	24-8-55
1436	Tozer Thomas	Pte.	W/Sl	21-7-55	3-8-55
2922	Walsh John	Pte.	W/Sl	28-6-55	10-7-55
2772	Whynd John	Pte.	W/Sl	10-8-55	24-8-55
2220	Young John	Pte.	W/Sl	15-5-55	29-5-55

3rd REGIMENT OF FOOT

NO.	NAME	RANK	CASUALTY	DATE	LONDON GAZETTE
1652	Brown Henry	Pte.	Killed	22-8-55	4-9-55
2854	Deakin Andrew	Pte.	Killed	8-7-55	20-7-55
3251	Dixon James	Pte.	Killed	9-6-55	22-6-55
3077	Dolan John	Pte.	Killed	31-5-55	12-6-55
3141	Farrell Peter	Pte	Killed	11-8-55	24-8-55
3065	Gill William	Pte.	Killed	26-6-55	10-7-55

NOTES

The Second, Third, Fourth, Fifth and Final Bombardment of Sebastopol, and Minor Actions

3rd REGIMENT OF FOOT

NO.	NAME	RANK	CASUALTY	DATE	LONDON GAZETTE
3560	Hagarty Patrick	Pte.	Killed	13-8-55	28-8-55
3126	Hodgins James	Pte.	Killed	26-6-55	10-7-55
3107	King John	Pte.	Killed	13-8-55	28-8-55
3147	McCarthy Charles	Pte.	Killed	15-5-55	29-5-55
3210	McGarvey Patrick	Pte.	Killed	13-8-55	28-8-55
2737	Neil John	Pte.	Killed	3-7-55	17-7-55
2751	Nicholson Dennis	Pte.	Killed	26-6-55	10-7-55
2920	Savell Anthony	Pte.	Killed	21-7-55	3-8-55
3172	Smith William	Pte.	Killed	8-6-55	22-6-55
3314	West James	Pte.	Killed	31-7-55	14-8-55
2627	Wilson George	Pte.	Killed	17-8-55	31-8-55
	Hood C.	Capt.	W/Sl	3-7-55	17-7-55
	Pownall W.	Capt.	W/Sv	28-5-55	12-6-55
	Walker M.	Capt.	W/D	9-6-55	22-6-55
	Burmingham H. G. C.	Lieut.	W/Sl	31-8-55	18-9-55
	Caldecott B. T.	Lieut.	W/Sl	17-8-55	31-8-55
	Dennis J. B.	Lieut.	W/M	17-8-55	31-8-55
2379	Cook Richard	Col/Sgt.	W/Sv	27-6-55	10-7-55
2800	Creaven Thomas	Sergt.	W/Sl	5-8-55	17-8-55
2752	Goggins John	Sergt.	W/Sl	22-8-55	4-9-55
2803	Jackson Johnson	Sergt.	W/Sv	6-7-55	20-7-55
1111	McCabe Peter	Sergt.	W/Sv	26-7-55	7-8-55
2051	Moyes John	Sergt.	W/Sl	8-6-55	22-6-55
880	Watson Charles	Sergt.	W/Sv	13-6-55	26-6-55
3528	Adams Henry	Corpl.	W/Sv	16-6-55	3-7-55
2548	Boreland Hugh	Corpl.	W/Sl	6-7-55	20-7-55
2811	Gallagher Peter	Corpl.	W/Sv	25-8-55	7-9-55
3469	Hewill John	Corpl.	W/Sv	9-7-55	24-7-55
2793	Kelly Thomas	Corpl.	W/Sl	11-8-55	24-8-55
3239	Neill William	Corpl.	W/Sl	10-7-55	24-7-55
2716	Simane Thomas	Corpl.	W/D	17-6-55	3-7-55
2893	Kennedy Patrick	Drummer	W/Sv	2-7-55	17-7-55
3542	Ainley Andrew	Pte.	W/Sv	9-8-55	21-8-55
2927	Allen James	Pte.	W/Sv	16-6-55	3-7-55
3178	Arkroyd John	Pte.	W/D	12-6-55	26-6-55
2492	Baily James	Pte.	W/Sl	13-6-55	26-6-55
3020	Barnett William	Pte.	W/Sv	28-5-55	12-6-55
3253	Baxter Hugh	Pte.	W/M	17-8-55	31-8-55
3537	Beardsell E.	Pte.	W/D	31-8-55	18-9-55
2765	Bennett Thomas	Pte.	W/Sv	30-6-55	17-7-55
3103	Bracken Denis	Pte	W/Sl	23-8-55	4-9-55
2955	Brown Cornelius	Pte.	W/Sv	20-5-55	5-6-55
3383	Campbell William	Pte.	W/Sl	8-7-55	20-7-55
2728	Carroll Patrick	Pte.	W/Sl	3-7-55	17-7-55
2020	Cates William	Pte.	W/M	20-5-55	5-6-55
2797	Clarke Patrick	Pte.	W/Sl	26-8-55	7-9-55
2914	Coleman Patrick	Pte.	W/D	8-7-55	20-7-55
3345	Connor Patrick	Pte.	W/Sl	16-6-55	3-7-55
2756	Connors John	Pte.	W/Sl	4-9-55	18-9-55
3571	Coombs James	Pte.	W/Sl	22-8-55	4-9-55
2787	Corbett James	Pte.	W/Sv	16-6-55	3-7-55
3137	Crany Denis	Pte.	W/Sv	25-8-55	7-9-55
2451	Cronin Michael	Pte.	W/Sl	9-6-55	22-6-55
2096	Crook Ephraim	Pte.	W/Sl	3-7-55	17-7-55
3268	Cunningham M.	Pte.	W/Sl	31-8-55	18-9-55
3509	Darragh James	Pte.	W/Sl	13-8-55	28-8-55
2367	Day Edmund	Pte.	W/Sl	29-5-55	12-6-55
3309	Dickens Richard	Pte.	W/Sl	26-7-55	7-8-55
2628	Donovan M.	Pte.	W/Sl	31-8-55	18-9-55
3428	Dunbar James	Pte.	W/M	26-8-55	7-9-55
2872	Dunne Denis	Pte	W/Sv	16-6-55	3-7-55
3555	Dutton William	Pte.	W/Sl	11-6-55	26-6-55
3078	Egan Bartholomew	Pte.	W/Sl	25-8-55	7-9-55
3074	Farrell John	Pte.	W/Sv	8-6-55	22-6-55

NOTES

The Second, Third, Fourth, Fifth and Final Bombardment of Sebastopol, and Minor Actions

3rd REGIMENT OF FOOT

NO.	NAME	RANK	CASUALTY	DATE	LONDON GAZETTE
3141	Farrell Peter	Pte.	W/Sl	26-6-55	7-8-55
2683	Fitzgibbon Thomas	Pte.	W/Sl	23-8-55	4-9-55
3550	Franklin James	Pte.	W/Sl	17-6-55	3-7-55
2811	Gallagher Matthew	Pte.	W/Sv	25-8-55	7-9-55
2999	Gallery Malachi	Pte.	W/D	25-8-55	7-9-55
2678	Gordan John	Pte.	W/Sl	28-8-55	11-9-55
3060	Green John	Pte.	W/Sv	28-8-55	11-9-55
3060	Green John	Pte.	W/Sl	15-8-55	28-8-55
3356	Gribbon George	Pte.	W/Sv	26-6-55	10-7-55
2802	Hallam Robert	Pte.	W/Sl	4-7-55	17-7-55
3494	Halloway E.	Pte.	W/Sl	31-8-55	18-9-55
2758	Hanlon Anthony	Pte.	W/D	17-6-55	3-7-55
2782	Hannery Patrick	Pte.	W/Sl	13-8-55	28-8-55
2131	Hanrahan James	Pte.	W/Sl	13-8-55	28-8-55
2996	Harper James	Pte.	W/Sl	22-8-55	4-9-55
2418	Harrigan John	Pte.	W/Sl	16-6-55	3-7-55
3471	Hayden Andrew	Pte.	W/Sv	8-6-55	22-6-55
3471	Hayden Andrew	Pte.	D.O.W.	9-6-55	22-6-55
3324	Homes George	Pte.	W/D.	13-8-55	28-8-55
3464	Hughes John	Pte.	W/Sl	17-8-55	31-8-55
3157	Jordan Peter	Pte.	W/Sl	20-5-55	5-6-55
3399	Katterns John	Pte.	W/Sl	26-7-55	7-8-55
2370	Kearns John	Pte.	W/Sl	8-6-55	22-6-55
2946	Keemury James	Pte.	W/D	22-8-55	7-9-55
3267	Kelly Robert	Pte.	W/Sl	9-6-55	22-6-55
2833	Kenny John	Pte.	W/Sl	8-6-55	22-6-55
2938	Kilcourse Thomas	Pte.	W/Sl	23-8-55	4-9-55
2704	Lawler Patrick	Pte.	W/Sl	26-8-55	7-9-55
3365	Lockhead Edward	Pte.	W/Sl	13-8-55	28-8-55
3520	Lovely Patrick	Pte.	W/Sl	13-8-55	28-8-55
2685	Lyons Patrick	Pte.	W/Sl	3-9-55	18-9-55
3512	McCrea Duncan	Pte.	W/Sl	5-8-55	17-8-55
3283	McCrowley John	Pte.	W/Sl	13-8-55	17-8-55
3086	McGann Thomas	Pte.	W/Sl	13-8-55	17-8-55
2889	McGough James	Pte.	W/D	26-6-55	10-7-55
2069	McGrath T.	Pte.	W/Sl	15-8-55	17-8-55
3042	McHenry Owen	Pte.	W/Sl	13-8-55	17-8-55
2875	McHugh Martin	Pte.	W/Sl	23-7-55	7-8-55
3512	McRae Duncan	Pte.	W/Sl	12-6-55	26-6-55
3429	Malcolm Hugh	Pte.	W/Sl	13-8-55	28-8-55
3523	Manvill Allen	Pte.	W/Sl	17-8-55	31-8-55
3067	Mark John	Pte.	W/Sl	9-8-55	21-8-55
3393	Miller Robert	Pte.	W/Sl	26-6-55	10-7-55
3302	Milton Thomas	Pte.	W/Sl	5-8-55	17-8-55
3262	Mitchell John	Pte.	W/Sl	31-5-55	12-6-55
2962	Monahan Peter	Pte.	W/Sl	2-9-55	18-9-55
1973	Moore William	Pte.	W/Sl	16-6-55	3-7-55
3423	Morrow Charles	Pte.	W/Sl	17-8-55	31-8-55
3557	Mullins M.	Pte.	W/Sl	31-8-55	18-9-55
3013	Murphy Thomas	Pte	W/Sl	3-9-55	18-9-55
2568	Murrell George	Pte	W/Sv	17-6-55	3-7-55
3106	Neill Luke	Pte.	W/Sv	25-8-55	7-9-55
3506	O'Keefe Dennis	Pte.	W/Sv	17-8-55	31-8-55
2365	Palmer D.	Pte.	W/Sl	31-8-55	18-9-55
3380	Potts Alexander	Pte.	W/Sl	13-8-55	28-8-55
2675	Purcell Thomas	Pte.	W/Sl	15-8-55	28-8-55
2894	Quirk John	Pte.	W/Sl	22-8-55	4-9-55
2931	Quirk John	Pte.	W/Sl	29-7-55	7-8-55
3545	Quornley William	Pte.	W/Sl	12-6-55	26-6-55
1712	Redwin George	Pte.	W/Sl	16-6-55	3-7-55
2705	Regan F.	Pte.	W/Sl	31-8-55	18-9-55
3355	Reid Hugh	Pte.	W/Sv	8-6-55	22-6-55
2360	Rourke Edward	Pte.	W/Sv	17-8-55	31-8-55
3083	Savage J.	Pte.	W/Sl	31-8-55	18-9-55

NOTES

The Second, Third, Fourth, Fifth and Final Bombardment of Sebastopol, and Minor Actions

3rd REGIMENT OF FOOT

NO.	NAME	RANK	CASUALTY	DATE	LONDON GAZETTE
3215	Schofield Tobias	Pte.	W/Sl	16-6-55	3-7-55
3494	Sherd James	Pte.	W/Sv	28-8-55	11-9-55
2003	Small John	Pte.	W/Sl	8-6-55	22-6-55
1985	Smith James	Pte.	W/Sl	3-7-55	17-7-55
3364	Stewart A.	Pte.	W/D	31-8-55	18-9-55
3364	Stewart Andrew	Pte.	W/Sl	15-8-55	28-8-55
2330	Tegg John	Pte.	W/Sv	26-8-55	7-9-55
3517	Thomas William	Pte.	W/Sl	16-8-55	28-8-55
3076	Tierney Patrick	Pte.	W/Sv	16-6-55	3-7-55
1910	Timms Edward	Pte.	W/Sv	26-6-55	10-7-55
2801	Toombs John	Pte.	W/Sl	20-5-55	5-6-55
2105	Tugwell Lewis	Pte.	W/D	17-8-55	31-8-55
3326	Walsh Thomas	Pte.	W/D	26-8-55	7-9-55
3092	Walsh Thomas	Pte.	W/Sl	3-9-55	18-9-55
	Ross C. C.	Capt.	Missing	31-8-55	18-9-55

4th REGIMENT OF FOOT

NO.	NAME	RANK	CASUALTY	DATE	LONDON GAZETTE
3343	Anglish John	Pte.	Killed	22-6-55	9-7-55
2155	Binson Thomas	Pte.	Killed	10-5-55	22-5-55
3605	Brett John	Pte.	Killed	10-5-55	22-5-55
3035	Finlay John	Pte.	Killed	6-8-55	21-8-55
3248	Green John	Pte.	Killed	8-1-55	26-1-55
3333	Hutchins Emanuel	Pte.	Killed	26-7-55	7-8-55
3408	Johnson John	Pte	Killed	28-8-55	11-9-55
1484	Jones John	Pte.	Killed	7-12-55	26-12-55
3217	Malline John	Pte.	Killed	26-6-55	10-7-55
3626	Ship Charles	Pte.	Killed	6-4-55	20-4-55
2084	Wallis James	Pte.	Killed	14-8-55	28-8-55
2478	William William	Pte.	Killed	6-9-55	18-9-55
	Paton James	Lieut.	W/Sl	26-7-55	7-8-55
3896	Hodgin John	Sergt.	W/Sv	7-8-55	21-8-55
1495	Hunt Joseph	Sergt.	W/Sl	12-5-55	25-5-55
3403	McLeod Michael	Sergt.	W/Sl	6-8-55	21-8-55
3411	Clarkson George	L/Sgt.	W/Sl	14-4-55	1-5-55
3197	Culligan John	L/Sgt.	W/Sl	14-4-55	1-5-55
2072	Clarkson John	Corpl.	W/Sl	22-6-55	9-7-55
3733	Warren William	Corpl.	W/Sv	26-7-55	7-8-55
3066	Brooks Leonard	Pte.	W/Sl	16-1-55	6-2-55
3641	Brown Charles F.	Pte.	W/Sv	26-7-55	7-8-55
3114	Campbell William	Pte.	W/Sl	14-4-55	1-5-55
3459	Candlen J.	Pte.	W/Sl	13-8-55	28-8-55
2114	Carron Patrick	Pte.	W/Sl	27-7-55	7-8-55
3235	Carry Thomas	Pte.	W/Sv	27-7-55	7-8-55
2734	Cookerton Daniel	Pte.	W/Sl	8-4-55	20-4-55
3060	Curley Michael	Pte.	W/Sv	24-7-55	7-8-55
3535	Dales John	Pte.	W/Sl	21-6-55	3-7-55
3487	Dawson William	Pte.	W/Sv	16-1-55	6-2-55
3494	Doolan William	Pte.	W/Sv	17-8-55	31-8-55
3561	Draper Edwin	Pte.	W/Sl	14-4-55	1-5-55
3619	Dunn Peter	Pte.	W/Sl	22-6-55	9-7-55
2361	Dunn Thomas	Pte.	W/Sl	22-6-55	9-7-55
2920	Edwards Robert	Pte.	W/Sl	17-8-55	31-8-55
3198	Fallan James	Pte.	W/Sl	21-6-55	3-7-55
2207	Fitzpatrick John	Pte.	W/Sv	21-6-55	3-7-55
3815	Galloway Robert	Pte.	W/Sv	26-7-55	7-8-55
1657	Gowan William	Pte.	W/Sl	7-12-55	26-12-55
3849	Hamilton Archibald	Pte.	W/Sl	6-7-55	20-7-55
3317	Heming Richard	Pte.	W/Sv	16-1-55	6-2-55
2461	Hewit Robert	Pte.	W/Sl	7-12-55	26-12-55

NOTES

The Second, Third, Fourth, Fifth and Final Bombardment of Sebastopol, and Minor Actions

4th REGIMENT OF FOOT

NO.	NAME	RANK	CASUALTY	DATE	LONDON GAZETTE
2430	Higgins Thomas	Pte.	W/Sl	22-6-55	9-7-55
2507	Homraghan M.	Pte.	W/Sl	13-8-55	28-8-55
1509	Hughes, Patrick	Pte.	W/Sl	3-9-55	18-9-55
2370	Hunt James	Pte.	W/Sl	17-8-55	31-8-55
3009	Hurdley William	Pte.	W/D	27-7-55	7-8-55
2558	Irving George	Pte.	W/D	14-8-55	28-8-55
3169	Jeffrey Michael	Pte.	W/Sv	28-2-55	16-3-55
3844	Johnson Samuel	Pte.	W/Sl	7-9-55	25-9-55
3213	Johnstone James	Pte.	W/Sv	14-4-55	1-5-55
2893	Jones Thomas	Pte.	W/Sl	22-6-55	9-7-55
3268	Kennedy John	Pte.	W/Sl	22-6-55	9-7-55
3564	Kincade George	Pte.	W/Sl	19-6-55	3-7-55
2488	Latchman C.	Pte.	W/Sv	17-8-55	31-8-55
3474	Laverlay James	Pte.	W/Sl	16-5-55	29-5-55
3672	McArragher Peter	Pte.	W/Sl	6-8-55	21-8-55
3468	McGravey James	Pte.	W/Sl	9-8-55	21-8-55
3011	McGuire John	Pte.	W/Sv	26-7-55	7-8-55
2956	McKenzie John	Pte.	W/Sv	7-7-55	20-7-55
3764	McKenzie William	Pte.	W/Sl	21-7-55	3-8-55
3187	McMahon James	Pte.	W/Sv	8-1-55	26-1-55
3478	McPherson Andrew	Pte.	W/Sl	16-5-55	29-5-55
3316	Martin Patrick	Pte.	W/Sl	16-8-55	28-8-55
3855	Mason Edwards	Pte.	W/Sv	26-7-55	7-8-55
3440	Mayhew Luke	Pte.	W/Sl	13-5-55	25-5-55
3040	Moir Alexander	Pte.	W/Sv	16-1-55	6-2-55
3167	Murphy Thomas	Pte.	W/D	21-6-55	3-7-55
3656	Norman William	Pte.	W/Sl	8-4-55	20-4-55
3665	Oaks George	Pte.	W/Sv	26-4-55	15-5-55
3847	O'Brien Francis	Pte.	W/Sv	24-7-55	7-8-55
3823	Pankin Alexander	Pte.	W/Sl	21-6-55	3-7-55
3575	Ran Patrick	Pte.	W/Sl	29-8-55	11-9-55
3823	Rankin Alexander	Pte.	W/Sv	24-7-55	7-8-55
3477	Reynolds G.	Pte.	W/Sv	12-8-55	24-8-55
1860	Richards William	Pte.	W/Sv	8-1-55	26-1-55
3146	Robertson William	Pte.	W/Sl	30-4-55	15-5-55
3312	Robinson H.	Pte.	W/Sl	13-8-55	28-8-55
3828	Rodway Samuel	Pte.	W/Sv	26-7-55	7-8-55
3515	Roe Patrick	Pte.	W/Sl	21-6-55	3-7-55
3165	Ross James	Pte.	W/D	3-9-55	18-9-55
3378	Ryan Dennis	Pte.	W/Sv	21-6-55	3-7-55
2995	Ryan John	Pte.	W/Sl	9-8-55	21-8-55
1358	Scammells Thomas	Pte.	W/Sl	21-6-55	3-7-55
3028	Shoueham James	Pte.	W/Sv	21-6-55	3-7-55
3500	Simpson William	Pte.	W/Sl	22-8-55	31-8-55
3421	Smith Daniel	Pte.	W/Sl	19-2-55	6-3-55
3287	Somers Bryan	Pte.	W/Sl	22-6-55	9-7-55
1425	Stanstie William	Pte.	W/Sv	7-9-55	20-7-55
2660	Stevens Samuel	Pte.	W/Sl	7-8-55	21-8-55
3109	Storey George	Pte.	W/Sl	8-4-55	20-4-55
3948	Thomas J.	Pte.	W/Sl	13-8-55	28-8-55
2495	Thompson Henry	Pte.	W/Sl	22-6-55	9-7-55
3438	Tongues John	Pte.	W/Sv	27-7-55	7-8-55
3372	Turner William	Pte.	W/Sv	14-4-55	1-5-55
3099	Urn William	Pte.	W/D	9-6-55	22-6-55
2687	Watkins William	Pte.	W/D	3-9-55	18-9-55
3284	Young Joseph	Pte.	W/Sl	4-3-55	16-3-55

7th REGIMENT OF FOOT

NO.	NAME	RANK	CASUALTY	DATE	LONDON GAZETTE
	Browne Hon C.	Capt.	Killed	22-3-55	3-4-55

NOTES

The Second, Third, Fourth, Fifth and Final Bombardment of Sebastopol, and Minor Actions

7th REGIMENT OF FOOT

NO.	NAME	RANK	CASUALTY	DATE	LONDON GAZETTE
3280	Bell William	Sergt.	Killed	19-3-55	3-4-55
3227	Abbot Henry	Pte.	Killed	7-9-55	25-9-55
3345	Brown John	Pte.	Killed	17-4-55	1-5-55
3372	Byrne Thomas	Pte.	Killed	27-4-55	15-5-55
3201	Cunningham Michael	Pte.	Killed	19-3-55	3-4-55
3458	Dancer Thomas	Pte.	Killed	12-7-55	24-7-55
3859	Hall John	Pte.	Killed	21-8-55	4-9-55
3915	King William	Pte.	Killed	29-8-55	11-9-55
3637	Langley Samuel	Pte.	Killed	7-9-55	25-9-55
3838	Lee George	Pte.	Killed	7-8-55	21-8-55
3571	Lyons Patrick	Pte.	Killed	30-7-55	14-8-55
3215	Murphy Michael	Pte.	Killed	1-5-55	15-5-55
3862	Newby John	Pte.	Killed	30-7-55	14-8-55
3756	Stokes James	Pte.	Killed	5-4-55	20-4-55
3919	Ward Charles	Pte.	Killed	3-9-55	18-9-55
	Cooper J. H.	Capt.	W/Sl	9-6-55	22-6-55
	Jones L. J. F.	Lieut.	W/Sl	27-3-55	13-4-55
	McHenry J.	Lieut.	W/Sv	22-3-55	3-4-55
3225	Martin Henry	Sergt.	W/Sv	31-8-55	18-9-55
2320	Finnegan Edward	Corpl.	W/Sv	5-4-55	20-4-55
2771	Henly George	Corpl.	W/Sl	10-6-55	22-6-55
2527	Hudson Matthew	Corpl.	W/Sv	22-3-55	3-4-55
3681	Marriott Cornelius	Corpl.	W/D	5-4-55	20-4-55
2698	Stannard Stephen	Corpl.	W/Sl	5-4-55	20-4-55
2598	Taylor Thomas	Corpl.	W/Sl	12-7-55	24-7-55
3330	Bagshaw William	Pte.	W/Sl	30-7-55	14-8-55
2461	Barry John	Pte.	W/Sv	9-5-55	18-5-55
3668	Bawdrey William	Pte.	W/Sv	13-3-55	16-3-55
2966	Begley Michael	Pte.	W/Sv	17-2-55	6-3-55
3050	Bennett William	Pte.	W/Sv	31-8-55	18-9-55
3997	Birch William	Pte.	W/Sl	5-8-55	17-8-55
2636	Boland James	Pte.	W/Sv	21-7-55	3-8-55
3009	Bowman Richard	Pte.	W/Sl	14-4-55	1-5-55
4049	Brown James	Pte.	W/Sl	14-8-55	28-8-55
3041	Brown Thomas	Pte.	W/Sv	24-8-55	7-9-55
4044	Byrne Edward	Pte.	W/Sv	6-8-55	21-8-55
3627	Carney John	Pte.	W/D	5-4-55	20-4-55
3943	Carpenter Joseph	Pte.	W/Sv	8-8-55	21-8-55
3131	Carty Thomas	Pte.	W/D	26-8-55	7-9-55
2160	Clements Robert	Pte.	W/Sv	10-5-55	18-5-55
3643	Clements William	Pte.	W/Sl	5-8-55	17-8-55
4079	Clinton Patrick	Pte.	W/D	30-7-55	14-8-55
3278	Connell John	Pte.	W/Sv	27-6-55	10-7-55
3867	Copley George	Pte.	W/Sl	9-5-55	18-5-55
3211	Daniels John	Pte.	W/Sv	22-3-55	3-4-55
3655	D'Arcy Patrick	Pte.	W/Sl	29-3-55	13-4-55
1940	Doyle Albert	Pte.	W/Sl	1-9-55	18-9-55
1669	Eales John	Pte.	W/Sv	15-5-55	29-5-55
1935	Elbon William	Pte.	W/Sl	6-9-55	18-9-55
3719	Evans William	Pte.	W/Sv	27-6-55	10-7-55
4111	Farmer Henry	Pte.	W/Sv	23-8-55	4-9-55
3771	Firth Charles	Pte.	W/Sv	24-4-55	15-5-55
3771	Frith Charles	Pte.	W/Sl	27-8-55	7-9-55
3869	Fisher Thomas	Pte.	W/Sv	6-9-55	18-9-55
3091	Fleming George	Pte.	W/Sv	12-5-55	25-5-55
3958	Forster William	Pte.	W/Sl	28-8-55	11-9-55
2803	Fowler John	Pte.	W/Sl	22-3-55	3-4-55
3889	Freeman George	Pte.	W/Sl	6-9-55	18-9-55
3572	Frenley Timothy	Pte.	W/Sv	29-8-55	11-9-55
3169	Gardiner William	Pte.	W/Sv	30-7-55	14-8-55
3408	Garling William	Pte.	W/Sv	19-3-55	3-4-55
3180	Gaynor William	Pte.	W/D	11-8-55	24-8-55
3768	Gillott William	Pte.	W/Sl	30-7-55	14-8-55
1977	Goldsmith Thomas	Pte.	W/D	11-8-55	24-8-55

NOTES

The Second, Third, Fourth, Fifth and Final Bombardment of Sebastopol, and Minor Actions

7th REGIMENT OF FOOT

NO.	NAME	RANK	CASUALTY	DATE	LONDON GAZETTE
3769	Graham William	Pte.	W/Sl	27-7-55	3-8-55
3785	Guest Philip	Pte.	W/Sv	6-5-55	18-5-55
2575	Hamlet Joseph	Pte.	W/D	9-8-55	21-8-55
2544	Harrison John	Pte.	W/Sv	30-8-55	11-9-55
3312	Haydon Thomas	Pte.	W/Sl	28-8-55	11-9-55
1819	Heaseltine Richard	Pte.	W/Sl	4-9-55	18-9-55
2680	Henry James	Pte.	W/Sv	31-8-55	18-9-55
3685	Hooton Richard	Pte.	W/Sl	17-8-55	31-8-55
2888	Humphrey George	Pte.	W/Sl	29-3-55	13-4-55
2006	Hunter John	Pte.	W/Sl	29-3-55	13-4-55
3851	Hutchison John	Pte.	W/Sv	22-3-55	3-4-55
3202	Jenkins Henry	Pte.	W/Sl	10-7-55	24-7-55
3810	Johnson James	Pte.	W/Sl	5-8-55	17-8-55
3146	Kavanagh Martin	Pte.	W/Sv	22-3-55	3-4-55
1192	Kelly Patrick	Pte.	W/Sv	30-7-55	14-8-55
1324	Kelly Thomas	Pte.	W/Sv	26-1-55	20-2-55
2951	Kerr John	Pte.	W/Sv	22-3-55	3-4-55
3206	Kerr John	Pte.	W/Sv	28-8-55	11-9-55
3371	Kinseld Martin	Pte.	W/Sl	14-8-55	28-8-55
3347	Lewis John	Pte.	W/Sv	9-6-55	22-6-55
3147	Lowe Samuel	Pte.	W/Sv	28-8-55	11-9-55
3647	McGarry Michael	Pte.	W/Sl	5-4-55	20-4-55
3647	McGarry Michael	Pte.	W/Sl	11-8-55	24-8-55
3232	Mason John	Pte.	W/Sl	27-6-55	10-7-55
3688	Mercer William	Pte.	W/Sl	27-7-55	3-8-55
298	Moore Cornelius	Pte.	W/Sv	13-6-55	26-6-55
3065	Moores Jonathan	Pte.	W/Sv	16-7-55	24-7-55
1035	Morgan Peter	Pte.	W/Sv	30-4-55	15-5-55
2859	Moroney John	Pte.	W/Sv	9-5-55	18-5-55
2763	Monsfield Anthony	Pte.	W/Sv	9-5-55	18-5-55
3944	Nathan John	Pte.	W/D	21-7-55	3-8-55
3502	Nightingale Thomas	Pte.	W/D	27-6-55	10-7-55
3602	Norman David	Pte.	W/Sv	6-5-55	18-5-55
3465	Pilkington William	Pte.	W/Sv	9-5-55	18-5-55
1968	Proctor Edward	Pte.	W/Sv	22-3-55	3-4-55
2864	Russell Vincent	Pte.	W/Sl	23-8-55	4-9-55
3762	Sawyer Anthony	Pte.	W/Sv	5-4-55	20-4-55
3619	Scott William	Pte.	W/Sv	21-7-55	3-8-55
3093	Shields Michael	Pte.	W/Sl	11-8-55	24-8-55
3817	Sievers Hazahel	Pte.	W/Sl	12-7-55	24-7-55
3745	Slater Thomas	Pte.	W/Sv	14-6-55	26-6-55
3166	Smith George	Pte.	W/Sv	13-6-55	26-6-55
2921	Spear George	Pte.	W/Sl	17-8-55	31-8-55
3587	Stevens William	Pte.	W/Sv	5-4-55	20-4-55
1788	Styles Andrew	Pte.	W/Sl	28-8-55	11-9-55
1576	Sweeney Hugh	Pte.	W/Sv	16-7-55	24-7-55
1734	Walker John	Pte.	W/Sl	30-7-55	14-8-55
3105	Wardell George	Pte.	W/Sv	30-4-55	15-5-55
3659	Williamson Peter	Pte.	W/Sv	5-4-55	20-4-55
	Howell William	Pte.	Missing	28-3-55	13-4-55

9th REGIMENT OF FOOT

NO.	NAME	RANK	CASUALTY	DATE	LONDON GAZETTE
3453	Campbell James	Pte.	Killed	4-9-55	18-9-55
2805	McCormick Brian	Pte.	Killed	18-8-55	31-8-55
2777	McGusheon Thomas	Pte.	Killed	18-8-55	31-8-55
3462	Sheady Michael	Pte.	Killed	14-4-55	1-5-55
3365	Toby William	Pte.	Killed	14-4-55	1-5-55
2374	Moss James	Sergt.	W/Sv	26-4-55	15-5-55
3419	Monaghan Michael	Corpl.	W/Sv	5-6-55	17-7-55

NOTES

The Second, Third, Fourth, Fifth and Final Bombardment of Sebastopol, and Minor Actions

9th REGIMENT OF FOOT

NO.	NAME	RANK	CASUALTY	DATE	LONDON GAZETTE
6446	Barrett Robert	Pte.	W/Sl	4-7-55	17-7-55
3181	Barry Patrick	Pte.	W/Sl	31-7-55	14-8-55
2219	Brownrigg Thomas	Pte.	W/Sl	7-9-55	25-9-55
3579	Case Richard	Pte.	W/Sl	22-4-55	4-5-55
6703	Chapman Thomas	Pte.	W/Sv	4-7-55	17-7-55
3537	Clifford Timothy	Pte.	W/Sv	22-7-55	3-8-55
1890	Crowther Joseph	Pte.	W/Sv	1-9-55	18-9-55
6606	Dean Charles	Pte.	W/Sv	4-7-55	17-7-55
2610	Dignam Michael	Pte.	W/Sv	13-7-55	27-7-55
3761	Elyne John	Pte.	W/Sl	2-9-55	18-9-55
3719	Finch William	Pte.	W/Sl	31-7-55	14-8-55
2886	Gallagher George	Pte.	W/Sv	24-6-55	9-7-55
3474	Grady John	Pte.	W/Sl	2-7-55	17-7-55
2244	Greenland J.	Pte.	W/D	11-8-55	24-8-55
3119	Hackenwell Joseph	Pte.	W/Sv	18-8-55	31-8-55
3220	Hagan Thomas	Pte.	W/Sv	15-8-55	28-8-55
1885	Hagarty Martin	Pte.	W/Sl	14-4-55	1-5-55
2374	Haighney John	Pte.	W/Sv	28-6-55	10-7-55
2577	McEvoy Keiron	Pte.	W/Sv	18-8-55	31-8-55
3538	Martin George	Pte.	W/Sv	16-8-55	28-8-55
—	Monaghan Stephen	Pte.	W/Sv	31-12-54	26-1-55
2941	Mulroney Peter	Pte.	W/Sl	6-3-55	23-3-55
2941	Mulvaney Peter	Pte.	W/Sl	21-7-55	3-8-55
2735	Murphy Maurice	Pte.	W/Sl	7-9-55	25-9-55
3571	O'Brien Michael	Pte.	W/Sl	9-8-55	21-8-55
3347	Pace Joseph	Pte.	W/Sv	14-4-55	1-5-55
3436	Power Patrick	Pte.	W/Sl	26-4-55	15-5-55
3566	Pratt Richard	Pte.	W/Sv	4-9-55	18-9-55
2706	Skilly John	Pte.	W/D	2-8-55	14-8-55
3483	Stenson Gilbert	Pte.	W/Sv	18-8-55	31-8-55
3541	Sullivan Daniel	Pte.	W/Sv	16-8-55	28-8-55
3259	Sullivan John	Pte.	W/D	6-9-55	18-9-55
5862	Tarrent James	Pte.	W/Sl	4-7-55	17-7-55
2669	Thomson Martin	Pte.	W/D	10-5-55	22-5-55
3475	Walsh Michael	Pte.	W/Sv	13-9-55	18-9-55
3650	Walsh William	Pte.	W/D	14-4-55	1-5-55
5031	Wesson George	Pte.	W/Sv	4-7-55	17-7-55
3352	Willshire William	Pte.	W/Sv	17-4-55	1-5-55

13th REGIMENT OF FOOT

NO.	NAME	RANK	CASUALTY	DATE	LONDON GAZETTE
1771	Tellman S.	Corpl.	W/Sl	7-9-55	25-9-55
3439	Barker John	Pte.	W/Sv	7-9-55	25-9-55
3596	Burton James	Pte.	W/Sl	7-9-55	25-9-55
3393	Coffey John	Pte.	W/Sv	7-9-55	25-9-55
3165	Hayes Thomas	Pte.	W/Sv	7-9-55	25-9-55
3503	Hobs James	Pte.	W/Sv	7-9-55	25-9-55
3429	McEnally T.	Pte.	W/Sl	7-9-55	25-9-55
3482	Murphy Patrick	Pte.	W/Sl	7-9-55	25-9-55
2919	Stokes Frederick	Pte.	W/Sl	7-9-55	25-9-55
2469	Sullivan Andrew	Pte.	W/Sl	7-9-55	25-9-55
2082	Whealan Thomas	Pte.	W/Sl	7-9-55	25-9-55

NOTES

The Second, Third, Fourth, Fifth and Final Bombardment of Sebastopol, and Minor Actions

14th REGIMENT OF FOOT

NO.	NAME	RANK	CASUALTY	DATE	LONDON GAZETTE
2996	Briordy Matthew	Pte.	Killed	26-4-55	15-5-55
3106	Callaghan Patrick	Pte.	Killed	4-5-55	15-5-55
3199	Flanagan Michael	Pte.	Killed	15-5-55	29-5-55
2961	Kennedy William	Pte.	Killed	11-8-55	24-8-55
3671	Lloyd John	Pte.	Killed	26-8-55	7-9-55
3738	Walker John	Pte.	Killed	4-5-55	15-5-55
3079	Casey John	Sergt.	W/D	11-8-55	24-8-55
2500	Prier H.	Sergt.	W/Sl	26-8-55	7-9-55
2842	Fegan C.	Corpl.	W/Sl	13-8-55	28-8-55
3133	Ryland William	Corpl.	W/Sl	14-4-55	1-5-55
3528	Barnwell James	Pte.	W/D	20-7-55	3-8-55
3638	Beathe James	Pte.	W/Sl	29-8-55	11-9-55
3552	Beattie James	Pte.	W/Sl	6-8-55	21-8-55
3666	Burke J.	Pte.	W/Sl	30-8-55	11-9-55
3371	Burke P.	Pte.	W/Sl	11-8-55	24-8-55
2648	Canty Patrick	Pte.	W/Sl	28-4-55	15-5-55
3678	Chambers J.	Pte.	W/Sl	13-8-55	28-8-55
2705	Clary Thomas	Pte.	W/Sv	24-5-55	5-6-55
3409	Connolly John	Pte.	W/Sv	14-8-55	28-8-55
3215	Conway T.	Pte.	W/Sv	12-8-55	24-8-55
3291	Crane Martin	Pte.	W/Sv	14-8-55	28-8-55
2979	Dennington Thomas	Pte.	W/Sv	14-8-55	28-8-55
3471	Dillon Robert	Pte.	W/Sv	27-5-55	12-6-55
3715	Fieldsen James	Pte.	W/D	14-8-55	28-8-55
3529	Flanagan Manin	Pte.	W/Sv	9-6-55	22-6-55
1334	Gordon Christopher	Pte.	W/D	6-9-55	18-9-55
2965	Green Michael	Pte.	W/D	6-9-55	18-9-55
3242	Harrison William	Pte.	W/M	27-4-55	15-5-55
3605	Hughes James	Pte.	W/Sl	14-8-55	28-8-55
2859	Hutton Peter	Pte.	W/Sl	6-9-55	18-9-55
3067	Lock William	Pte.	W/Sl	24-4-55	15-5-55
3835	McArdle John	Pte.	W/Sl	25-8-55	7-9-55
2869	McGovern Patrick	Pte.	W/Sv	26-4-55	15-5-55
3225	McGriffen R.	Pte.	W/Sl	11-8-55	24-8-55
2925	McKenzie Montgomery	Pte.	W/Sv	4-7-55	17-7-55
3240	McMahon P.	Pte.	W/Sl	11-8-55	24-8-55
3362	Malone John	Pte.	W/D	6-9-55	18-9-55
2902	Milin John	Pte.	W/Sv	9-6-55	22-6-55
3336	Murray Martin	Pte.	W/Sl	30-6-55	17-7-55
3700	Noonan Job	Pte.	W/Sl	13-8-55	28-8-55
2507	Price Thomas	Pte.	W/Sl	6-9-55	18-9-55
3175	Riley Patrick	Pte.	W/Sv	20-7-55	3-8-55
3324	Riley Thomas	Pte.	W/Sl	7-7-55	20-7-55
3536	Rourke H.	Pte.	W/Sl	26-8-55	7-9-55
3378	Taylor Michael	Pte.	W/Sl	23-7-55	7-8-55
3521	Woodhall Thomas	Pte.	W/Sl	24-4-55	15-5-55

17th REGIMENT OF FOOT

NO.	NAME	RANK	CASUALTY	DATE	LONDON GAZETTE
1686	Burton Henry	Corpl.	Killed	5-4-55	20-4-55
2283	Bastible Bartholomew	Pte.	Killed	12-7-55	24-7-55
2650	Byrnes Richard	Pte.	Killed	5-4-55	20-4-55
2311	Carolan Nicholas	Pte.	Killed	6-8-55	21-8-55
2644	Doyle John	Pte.	Killed	14-8-55	28-8-55
1988	Filan Anthony	Pte.	Killed	22-8-55	4-9-55
2442	Fisher George	Pte.	Killed	30-6-55	17-7-55
3689	Flaherty Michael	Pte.	Killed	16-5-55	29-5-55
1645	Higginson Charles	Pte.	Killed	21-4-55	4-5-55

NOTES

The Second, Third, Fourth, Fifth and Final Bombardment of Sebastopol, and Minor Actions

17th REGIMENT OF FOOT

NO.	NAME	RANK	CASUALTY	DATE	LONDON GAZETTE
3466	McCarthy John	Pte.	Killed	23-7-55	7-8-55
2290	McPartland Francis	Pte.	Killed	28-8-55	11-9-55
3206	Turner George	Pte.	Killed	17-6-55	3-7-55
	Williams R. E.	Lieut.	W/Sv	21-5-55	5-6-55
1420	Biddulph George	Sergt.	W/Sl	29-5-55	12-6-55
1411	Denahy Michael	Sergt.	W/Sl	12-7-55	24-7-55
2867	Hunt William	Sergt.	W/Sl	2-9-55	18-9-55
1357	Davis John	Corpl.	W/Sl	28-6-55	10-7-55
2498	Ford Edward	Corpl.	W/D	25-2-55	16-3-55
2257	Hemmings Eli	Corpl.	W/Sl	17-6-55	3-7-55
3064	McConnell William	Corpl.	W/Sv	23-5-55	5-6-55
2749	Riordan Patrick	Corpl.	W/Sl	8-6-55	22-6-55
3665	Swain Thomas	Corpl.	W/Sv	5-3-55	23-3-55
2776	Fowler John	L/Cpl.	W/Sv	8-8-55	21-8-55
2955	Black John	Pte.	W/Sv	23-7-55	7-8-55
3419	Bown Abraham	Pte.	W/D	8-6-55	22-6-55
2081	Brazill William	Pte.	W/Sl	1-8-55	14-8-55
2984	Brennan Michael	Pte.	W/Sv	8-6-55	22-6-55
3376	Bryan Patrick	Pte.	W/Sl	3-9-55	18-9-55
2638	Buckley Cornelius	Pte.	W/Sl	8-6-55	22-6-55
2986	Cain John	Pte.	W/Sl	5-7-55	17-7-55
2067	Cambridge Thomas	Pte.	W/Sl	29-7-55	7-8-55
2651	Carney Michael	Pte.	W/Sl	27-3-55	13-4-55
3279	Cassidy Henry	Pte.	W/Sl	24-8-55	7-9-55
3675	Clayton Henry	Pte.	W/Sl	19-8-55	31-8-55
2971	Connelly Patrick	Pte.	W/Sl	28-7-55	7-8-55
3386	Connor John	Pte.	W/Sv	13-8-55	28-8-55
3636	Cosgrove Thomas	Pte.	W/Sl	3-7-55	17-7-55
3768	Crawley Florence	Pte.	W/Sl	28-8-55	11-9-55
3179	Dowdall William	Pte.	W/Sl	3-8-55	17-8-55
3620	Estworthy Henry	Pte.	W/Sv	14-8-55	28-8-55
2643	Fitzgerald John	Pte.	W/Sl	1-7-55	17-7-55
3142	Galavin Patrick	Pte.	W/Sv	21-6-55	3-7-55
3253	Gallagher Patrick	Pte.	W/Sv	25-2-55	16-3-55
3621	Giddings James	Pte.	W/Sv	12-7-55	24-7-55
2316	Guest George	Pte.	W/Sl	5-4-55	20-4-55
2754	Hogan Matthew	Pte.	W/Sl	19-8-55	31-8-55
3184	Hogan Richard	Pte.	W/Sl	26-7-55	7-8-55
1691	Huddleston Peter	Pte.	W/Sv	17-2-55	6-3-55
2686	Kearns John	Pte.	W/Sv	6-8-55	21-8-55
3022	Keefe Daniel	Pte.	W/Sv	13-8-55	28-8-55
3506	Kelly Thomas	Pte.	W/Sl	29-7-55	7-8-55
3497	Kelly William	Pte.	W/Sv	12-7-55	24-7-55
2949	Kennedy John	Pte.	W/Sv	13-8-55	28-8-55
3380	Kennedy Patrick	Pte.	W/Sl	17-6-55	3-7-55
3164	Langford John	Pte.	W/Sv	30-7-55	14-8-55
2994	Loftos Thomas	Pte.	W/M	22-1-55	9-2-55
3669	Lynam Michael	Pte.	W/Sv	13-6-55	26-6-55
2585	McCabe John	Pte.	W/Sl	12-8-55	24-8-55
2977	McCowan Thomas	Pte.	W/Sl	19-8-55	31-8-55
3734	McLoughlin Michael	Pte.	W/Sl	23-7-55	7-8-55
3251	McMahon Patrick	Pte.	W/Sl	11-7-55	24-7-55
3361	Madden Peter	Pte.	W/Sv	27-7-55	7-8-55
2061	Maguire Edward	Pte.	W/Sl	21-5-55	5-6-55
3394	Manning George	Pte.	W/Sl	3-9-55	18-9-55
3673	Monaghan John	Pte.	W/Sl	12-7-55	24-7-55
3514	Murphy Patrick	Pte.	W/Sv	16-7-55	31-7-55
3526	Murphy Patrick	Pte.	W/Sv	27-7-55	7-8-55
2380	Nicholson Andrew	Pte.	W/Sl	29-5-55	12-6-55
3586	Nougher John	Pte.	W/D	23-7-55	7-8-55
2534	O'Brien Michael	Pte.	W/Sl	2-9-55	18-9-55
2920	Quin Patrick	Pte.	W/Sl	20-6-55	3-7-55
3443	Ryan William	Pte.	W/Sl	5-7-55	17-7-55
3078	Saunders James	Pte.	W/Sl	30-7-55	14-8-55

NOTES

The Second, Third, Fourth, Fifth and Final Bombardment of Sebastopol, and Minor Actions

17th REGIMENT OF FOOT

NO.	NAME	RANK	CASUALTY	DATE	LONDON GAZETTE
3374	Stewart Andrew	Pte.	W/Sl	14-6-55	26-6-55
3348	Thompson William	Pte.	W/Sl	3-9-55	18-9-55
3608	Townsend Francis	Pte.	W/Sl	2-9-55	18-9-55
2437	Walsh John	Pte.	W/Sl	30-7-55	14-8-55
3912	Walsh Michael	Pte.	W/Sl	5-8-55	17-8-55
3671	Walsh Thomas	Pte.	W/Sl	17-6-55	3-7-55
3577	Waters James	Pte.	W/Sl	22-6-55	9-7-55
3059	Winterbury Thomas	Pte.	W/Sl	8-6-55	22-6-55
3415	Young Henry	Pte.	W/Sl	22-6-55	9-7-55

18th REGIMENT OF FOOT

NO.	NAME	RANK	CASUALTY	DATE	LONDON GAZETTE
2982	Whelan Owen	Corpl.	Killed	14-3-55	23-3-55
2847	Cashman John	Pte.	Killed	20-6-55	3-7-55
3308	Clarke Joseph	Pte.	Killed	17-8-55	31-8-55
3109	Cormick William	Pte.	Killed	12-6-55	26-6-55
3252	Dignan Francis	Pte.	Killed	16-6-55	3-7-55
3424	Donovan Thomas	Pte.	Killed	26-8-55	7-9-55
3267	Flynn Alexander	Pte.	Killed	4-4-55	20-4-55
3354	Kavanagh Thomas	Pte.	Killed	26-8-55	7-9-55
2898	Kilcher Peter	Pte.	Killed	6-9-55	18-9-55
2715	Lynch John	Pte.	Killed	26-5-55	12-6-55
3186	Nolan John	Pte.	Killed	17-7-55	31-7-55
3043	Nugent Richard	Pte.	Killed	6-9-55	18-9-55
2965	O'Brien Dennis	Pte.	Killed	20-6-55	3-7-55
3404	Reeves John	Pte.	Killed	22-7-55	3-8-55
3699	Riley John	Pte.	Killed	26-8-55	7-9-55
3389	Rourke Daniel	Pte.	Killed	6-9-55	18-9-55
3190	Smyth Philip	Pte.	Killed	26-8-55	7-9-55
3324	Walpole Daniel	Pte.	Killed	6-5-55	18-5-55
2691	Collins Patrick	Sergt.	W/Sv	23-8-55	4-9-55
3330	Harvey John	Sergt.	W/Sl	6-9-55	18-9-55
2042	Hobbs John	Sergt.	W/D	12-6-55	26-6-55
2168	Hunter Nicholas	Sergt.	W/Sl	17-5-55	29-5-55
3468	Jackson Joseph	Sergt.	W/D	6-9-55	18-9-55
2129	Keenan Charles	Sergt.	W/Sl	6-9-55	18-9-55
2616	McKey Michael	Sergt.	W/D	15-6-55	3-7-55
2531	Stuart William	Sergt.	W/Sl	20-6-55	3-7-55
3045	Maddigan John	Corpl.	W/D	12-6-55	26-6-55
3610	Mark James	Corpl.	W/D	18-6-55	20-7-55
2997	Murphy Dennis	Corpl.	W/Sl	31-5-55	12-6-55
3086	Newman Charles	Corpl.	W/Sv	26-8-55	7-9-55
2790	Rouke Michael	Corpl.	W/Sv	17-8-55	31-8-55
2978	Ryan John	Corpl.	W/Sv	4-4-55	20-4-55
3641	Ashton Edward	Pte.	W/Sl	22-6-55	9-7-55
3577	Baker G.	Pte.	W/Sv	12-8-55	24-8-55
2637	Bannan Patrick	Pte.	W/Sv	18-6-55	20-7-55
3397	Brown William	Pte.	W/Sl	6-2-55	23-2-55
3063	Buckley Daniel	Pte.	W/D	12-6-55	26-6-55
3947	Buckley Jeremiah	Pte.	W/Sl	22-6-55	9-7-55
3564	Burley Patrick	Pte.	W/Sv	14-7-55	27-7-55
3085	Butler John	Pte.	W/D	2-9-55	18-9-55
3486	Byrnes Michael	Pte.	W/D	18-6-55	20-7-55
3059	Cautlin James	Pte.	W/Sv	4-8-55	17-8-55
3370	Collins Charles	Pte.	W/Sl	26-8-55	7-9-55
3047	Collins Michael	Pte.	W/Sl	9-8-55	21-8-55
2914	Conners John	Pte.	W/Sv	11-3-55	16-3-55
3221	Crowley Jeremiah	Pte.	W/Sv	18-6-55	20-7-55
3097	Curry John	Pte.	W/Sv	26-8-55	7-9-55
2991	Daly John	Pte.	W/Sv	21-6-55	3-7-55

NOTES

The Second, Third, Fourth, Fifth and Final Bombardment of Sebastopol, and Minor Actions

18th REGIMENT OF FOOT

NO.	NAME	RANK	CASUALTY	DATE	LONDON GAZETTE
2069	Fallan William	Pte.	W/Sv	22-7-55	3-8-55
3195	Farrelly Thomas	Pte.	W/Sl	12-6-55	26-6-55
3099	Flavohan Bartholomew	Pte.	W/Sv	17-7-55	31-7-55
1802	Fragon Thomas	Pte.	W/D	12-6-55	26-6-55
3494	Fry Charles	Pte.	W/Sl	26-7-55	7-8-55
3016	Fulham William	Pte.	W/Sl	12-6-55	26-6-55
3207	Glamson Maurice	Pte.	W/Sv	21-8-55	4-9-55
3240	Greenan Patrick	Pte.	W/Sl	13-6-55	26-6-55
3240	Greenan Patrick	Pte.	W/Sv	20-6-55	3-7-55
2822	Griffiths Henry	Pte.	W/Sl	4-4-55	20-4-55
2741	Halman John	Pte.	W/Sl	9-8-55	21-8-55
3204	Hamilton William	Pte.	W/Sv	17-8-55	31-8-55
3724	Haurahan Matthew	Pte.	W/D	18-6-55	20-7-55
3380	Henry John	Pte.	W/Sv	20-6-55	3-7-55
1171	Hopkins James	Pte.	W/Sv	10-5-55	22-5-55
3664	Hughes Peter	Pte.	W/Sl	31-5-55	12-6-55
3603	Jordan John	Pte.	W/Sv	18-6-55	20-7-55
3795	Kane Daniel	Pte.	W/Sl	26-8-55	7-9-55
3127	Keane Michael	Pte.	W/D	27-2-55	16-3-55
3314	Keefe Richard	Pte.	W/Sl	21-8-55	4-9-55
3357	Keeffe Boyle	Pte.	W/Sl	22-6-55	9-7-55
3555	Kerry John	Pte.	W/Sl	19-8-55	31-8-55
2146	Kinnelly Morris	Pte.	W/D	22-6-55	9-7-55
2535	Lawlor John	Pte.	W/Sl	17-8-55	31-8-55
2917	Leary Patrick	Pte.	W/Sl	13-6-55	26-6-55
3201	Linihan Thomas	Pte.	W/Sl	2-9-55	18-9-55
3448	Lyons John	Pte.	W/Sv	2-7-55	17-7-55
3696	McCann Hugh	Pte.	W/Sl	26-8-55	7-9-55
3864	McCrackin William	Pte.	W/Sl	19-8-55	31-8-55
3257	McDermott James	Pte.	W/Sl	12-6-55	26-6-55
3258	McGuire Patrick	Pte.	W/Sl	14-5-55	29-5-55
2576	McHale Thomas	Pte.	W/Sv	3-4-55	20-4-55
3013	McMahon Thomas	Pte.	W/Sl	14-7-55	27-7-55
3013	McMahon Thomas	Pte.	W/Sv	6-8-55	21-8-55
3095	Maher James	Pte.	W/Sl	11-6-55	26-6-55
3066	Maloney James	Pte.	W/Sl	14-5-55	29-5-55
3256	Marsh Robert	Pte.	W/Sv	20-6-55	3-7-55
3359	Medhurst Thomas	Pte.	W/Sl	4-8-55	17-8-55
3316	Morrow John	Pte.	W/Sl	14-7-55	27-7-55
2708	Mullhalley Peter	Pte.	W/D	12-6-55	26-6-55
3620	Murphy Jeremiah	Pte.	W/Sv	6-9-55	18-9-55
3386	Murray Dominic	Pte.	W/D	26-6-55	10-7-55
3353	O'Brien John	Pte.	W/Sv	17-7-55	31-7-55
2772	O'Brien Thomas	Pte.	W/Sv	18-6-55	20-7-55
3718	O'Connell Daniel	Pte.	W/Sl	4-8-55	17-8-55
3104	O'Donnell Patrick	Pte.	W/Sl	6-9-55	18-9-55
2948	O'Reegan James	Pte.	W/Sl	20-6-55	3-7-55
2948	O'Rogan James	Pte.	W/Sv	6-9-55	18-9-55
2424	Prendergrast Thomas	Pte.	W/Sv	11-6-55	26-6-55
3628	Quigley Martin	Pte.	W/Sv	26-8-55	7-9-55
2416	Quill Daniel	Pte.	W/Sv	18-6-55	20-7-55
2416	Quilley Daniel	Pte.	W/D	22-6-55	9-7-55
3157	Quilligan John	Pte.	W/Sl	26-8-55	7-9-55
2974	Quinn Thomas	Pte.	W/Sl	20-6-55	3-7-55
3509	Rowley Michael	Pte.	W/Sl	11-4-55	24-4-55
4157	Ryan Patrick	Pte.	W/D	2-9-55	18-9-55
1602	Singleton Thadeus	Pte.	W/Sl	17-8-55	31-8-55
2841	Small Aubred	Pte.	W/Sl	20-6-55	3-7-55
3134	Smyth Terence	Pte.	W/D	16-8-55	28-8-55
3393	Spaulding Henry	Pte.	W/D	18-6-55	20-7-55
2781	Stanley John	Pte.	W/Sl	4-8-55	17-8-55
3171	Storey George	Pte.	W/M	4-4-55	20-4-55
3020	Sullivan John	Pte.	W/Sl	2-9-55	18-9-55
3633	Sullivan Patrick	Pte.	W/D	12-6-55	26-6-55

NOTES

The Second, Third, Fourth, Fifth and Final Bombardment of Sebastopol, and Minor Actions

18th REGIMENT OF FOOT

NO.	NAME	RANK	CASUALTY	DATE	LONDON GAZETTE
2369	Sweeney Owen	Pte.	W/Sv	28-5-55	12-6-55
3428	Talbot Thomas	Pte.	W/Sv	20-6-55	3-7-55
3464	Toole Festus	Pte.	W/D	12-6-55	26-6-55
3232	Tracy John	Pte.	W/Sv	13-7-55	27-7-55
3394	Tue Henry	Pte.	W/Sv	18-6-55	20-7-55
3394	Tue Henry	Pte.	W/Sv	26-8-55	7-9-55
3465	Vyse Thomas	Pte.	W/Sv	16-6-55	3-7-55
3498	Walsh Robert	Pte.	W/D	21-8-55	4-9-55

19th REGIMENT OF FOOT

NO.	NAME	RANK	CASUALTY	DATE	LONDON GAZETTE
1756	Roe James	Corpl.	Killed	24-8-55	7-9-55
1963	Brown Patrick	Pte.	Killed	30-7-55	14-8-55
3355	Burke James	Pte.	Killed	25-8-55	7-9-55
1010	Donoghue Thomas	Pte.	Killed	10-4-55	24-4-55
3359	Doyle William	Pte.	Killed	13-8-55	28-8-55
2538	Kelly Jeremiah	Pte.	Killed	13-8-55	28-8-55
3559	McFadyen Bernard	Pte.	Killed	30-7-55	14-8-55
2849	Maddigan Thomas	Pte.	Killed	13-8-55	28-8-55
1844	Moore George	Pte.	Killed	5-8-55	17-8-55
2867	Reynolds John	Pte.	Killed	12-5-55	25-5-55
3412	Smith William	Pte.	Killed	13-8-55	28-8-55
	Warden R.	Brv/Mjr.	W/Sl	24-8-55	7-9-55
	Bayley E. R. W.	Lieut.	W/Sl	10-7-55	24-7-55
	Goren A.	Lieut.	W/Sl	28-7-55	7-8-55
2494	McClister Hugh	Sergt.	W/Sl	2-8-55	14-8-55
1912	Black Edward	Corpl.	W/Sv	29-12-54	26-1-55
2992	Costello William	Corpl.	W/Sl	27-6-55	10-7-55
2851	Crowe James	Corpl.	W/Sv	28-6-55	10-7-55
2667	Keating Thomas	Corpl.	W/Sl	10-6-55	22-6-55
2647	Keating Thomas	Corpl.	W/Sl	29-4-55	15-5-55
3090	Reed Samuel	Corpl.	W/Sl	2-9-55	18-9-55
1697	Robins Thomas	Corpl.	W/Sv	12-8-55	24-8-55
2188	Burke John	L/Cpl.	W/Sl	2-8-55	14-8-55
3286	Davis William	L/Cpl.	W/Sv	26-8-55	7-9-55
2796	Toolan Thomas	L/Cpl.	W/Sl	30-7-55	14-8-55
3087	Armstrong James	Pte.	W/Sl	14-8-55	28-8-55
2675	Ash Thomas	Pte.	W/Sv	11-5-55	25-5-55
2766	Austin Charles	Pte.	W/Sl	25-3-55	10-4-55
3232	Baldwise Patrick	Pte.	W/Sl	27-7-55	7-8-55
2464	Behan John	Pte.	W/Sl	27-8-55	11-9-55
3170	Behen James	Pte.	W/Sv	16-4-55	1-5-55
3428	Bennett Hugh	Pte.	W/Sv	15-2-55	2-3-55
3446	Bray Robert	Pte.	W/Sv	26-8-55	7-9-55
2835	Bridgeman John	Pte.	W/Sl	8-5-55	22-5-55
3232	Brown Thomas	Pte.	W/Sv	27-8-55	11-9-55
2335	Burke Patrick	Pte.	W/Sl	12-8-55	24-8-55
2552	Carroll Michael	Pte.	W/Sl	9-6-55	22-6-55
2789	Carter John	Pte.	W/Sl	31-8-55	18-9-55
2683	Clarke James	Pte.	W/Sl	29-8-55	11-9-55
3327	Collingwood Thomas	Pte.	W/Sl	13-7-55	24-7-55
3205	Collins Jeremiah	Pte.	W/D	14-8-55	28-8-55
2656	Connor Edward	Pte.	W/Sl	27-7-55	7-8-55
3199	Cooper David	Pte.	W/Sl	8-8-55	21-8-55
3123	Crompton William	Pte.	W/Sv	24-8-55	7-9-55
2851	Crowe James	Pte.	W/Sl	26-8-55	7-9-55
3461	Dickinson Thomas	Pte.	W/Sl	10-6-55	22-6-55
3140	Donnelly James	Pte.	W/Sv	22-4-55	4-5-55
1406	Dregan Andrew	Pte.	W/Sl	4-4-55	20-4-55
3519	Dugan William	Pte.	W/Sl	24-8-55	7-9-55

NOTES

The Second, Third, Fourth, Fifth and Final Bombardment of Sebastopol, and Minor Actions

19th REGIMENT OF FOOT

NO.	NAME	RANK	CASUALTY	DATE	LONDON GAZETTE
3406	Farrell Patrick	Pte.	W/D	29-8-55	11-9-55
2241	Feltus James	Pte.	W/Sv	29-6-55	17-7-55
3024	Frawley Michael	Pte.	W/Sv	15-12-54	9-1-55
3108	Garagan Francis	Pte.	W/Sv	13-8-55	28-8-55
2698	Gowing Charles	Pte.	W/Sl	7-7-55	20-7-55
2432	Hales Joseph	Pte.	W/Sl	6-4-55	20-4-55
1997	Hannigan Michael	Pte.	W/Sv	7-5-55	22-5-55
3251	Hawkins Daniel	Pte.	W/Sl	11-1-55	26-1-55
3297	Hayes William	Pte.	W/Sl	23-8-55	4-9-55
3279	Hayes William	Pte.	W/Sl	9-6-55	22-6-55
1612	Healy William	Pte.	W/Sv	29-6-55	17-7-55
2565	Hennessey Jeremiah	Pte.	W/Sl	29-8-55	11-9-55
2826	Hickey James	Pte.	W/Sv	30-7-55	14-8-55
2962	Higgins John	Pte.	W/Sv	3-5-55	15-5-55
3396	Holdsworth Henry	Pte.	W/M	27-7-55	7-8-55
3169	Holyoak Joseph	Pte.	W/Sv	6-8-55	21-8-55
1828	Ingram William	Pte.	W/Sl	27-7-55	7-8-55
3472	Kean Maurice	Pte.	W/Sl	11-6-55	26-6-55
2995	Kearney John	Pte.	W/Sl	6-2-55	23-2-55
2988	Kelly John	Pte.	W/Sl	13-8-55	28-8-55
2653	Lavery Hugh	Pte.	W/Sl	15-7-55	24-7-55
2804	Lee Peter	Pte.	W/Sv	27-7-55	7-8-55
2703	Liddle William	Pte.	W/Sl	18-8-55	31-8-55
1192	Lydon Michael	Pte.	W/Sv	8-8-55	21-8-55
2142	Lynch William	Pte.	W/Sl	13-8-55	28-8-55
2924	McHugh William	Pte.	W/Sv	30-7-55	14-8-55
2216	McHugh William	Pte.	W/Sv	30-7-55	14-8-55
3397	McNamara —	Pte.	W/Sv	9-6-55	22-6-55
2225	McNamara Patrick	Pte.	W/Sl	12-8-55	24-8-55
2853	Measures Thomas	Pte.	W/Sl	27-7-55	7-8-55
3276	Menzies William	Pte.	W/D	9-7-55	24-7-55
3336	Minahan Patrick	Pte.	W/Sv	24-8-55	7-9-55
2815	Morey William	Pte.	W/Sl	15-12-54	9-1-55
2632	Murgatroyd Joseph	Pte.	W/Sv	8-5-55	22-5-55
3316	Murphy Murphy	Pte.	W/Sl	24-8-55	7-9-55
2223	Murphy Thomas	Pte.	W/Sl	13-8-55	28-8-55
2464	Newcome Richard	Pte.	W/Sl	10-6-55	22-6-55
3175	O'Hara William	Pte.	W/Sl	23-8-55	4-9-55
2742	Osborne Frederick	Pte.	W/M	8-8-55	21-8-55
2553	Parker John	Pte.	W/Sl	13-8-55	28-8-55
2850	Plant Thomas	Pte.	W/Sl	10-7-55	24-7-55
1675	Pointing Edward	Pte.	W/Sv	11-5-55	25-5-55
3619	Reed George	Pte.	W/Sl	24-8-55	7-9-55
3183	Regan John	Pte.	W/Sl	15-7-55	24-7-55
2393	Riely James	Pte.	W/Sl	30-7-55	14-8-55
3148	Roach Michael	Pte.	W/Sv	14-6-55	26-6-55
3409	Rourke Thomas	Pte.	W/Sv	30-7-55	14-8-55
3409	Rourke Thomas	Pte.	W/Sl	29-8-55	11-9-55
3003	Royce George	Pte.	W/Sv	27-7-55	7-8-55
3225	Rush John	Pte.	W/M	9-6-55	22-6-55
3513	Russell George	Pte.	W/D	12-8-55	24-8-55
3000	Ryan Patrick	Pte.	W/Sl	27-7-55	7-8-55
2485	Sheehan John	Pte.	W/Sl	7-5-55	22-5-55
3264	Sullivan Owen	Pte.	W/Sv	14-8-55	28-8-55
2570	Thom Joseph	Pte.	W/Sl	22-7-55	3-8-55
2101	Tolan Michael	Pte.	W/Sv	29-4-55	15-5-55
2764	Tyler Edward	Pte.	W/Sv	29-4-55	15-5-55
3398	Walsh John	Pte.	W/Sl	14-6-55	26-6-55
3383	Wareing Thomas	Pte.	W/Sl	29-8-55	11-9-55
3383	Wareing Thomas	Pte.	W/Sl	30-7-55	14-8-55
2662	Weeden William	Pte.	W/Sl	27-7-55	7-8-55
3246	Wheatley Elijah	Pte.	W/Sl	29-8-55	11-9-55
3106	Wheelan John	Pte.	W/Sv	24-8-55	7-9-55
2926	Dawson James	Corpl.	Missing	13-8-55	28-8-55

NOTES

The Second, Third, Fourth, Fifth and Final Bombardment of Sebastopol, and Minor Actions

19th REGIMENT OF FOOT

NO.	NAME	RANK	CASUALTY	DATE	LONDON GAZETTE
	Voisey William	Pte.	Missing	19-12-54	9-1-55

20th REGIMENT OF FOOT

NO.	NAME	RANK	CASUALTY	DATE	LONDON GAZETTE
4072	Kavanagh John	L/Sergt.	Killed	12-7-55	24-7-55
3490	Drudge George	Pte.	Killed	25-12-54	12-1-55
3672	Ferney Thomas	Pte.	Killed	9-5-55	22-5-55
2769	Grannell John	Pte.	Killed	22-3-55	3-4-55
3842	Jokes George	Pte.	Killed	1-9-55	18-9-55
3114	Latham John	Pte.	Killed	24-8-55	7-9-55
3748	Mearns John	Pte.	Killed	22-3-55	3-4-55
4062	Sharpe Edwin	Pte.	Killed	1-9-55	18-9-55
3033	Fisher Harry	Corpl.	W/D	22-3-55	3-4-55
1977	Halpin Thady	Corpl.	W/Sl	22-3-55	3-4-55
2565	Smith Jacob	Corpl.	W/Sl	15-8-55	28-8-55
3157	Bray Patrick	Pte.	W/Sv	9-5-55	22-5-55
3456	Bryne Michael[1]	Pte.	W/D	22-3-55	3-4-55
3747	Doulan Martin	Pte.	W/Sl	25-12-54	12-1-55
2510	Duggan James	Pte.	W/Sl	25-12-54	12-1-55
3332	Eldridge John	Pte.	W/Sl	29-8-55	11-9-55
3628	Eoulston George	Pte.	W/Sv	2-12-54	26-12-54
3553	Flaherty Timothy	Pte.	W/Sv	30-7-55	14-8-55
3844	Fletcher Henry	Pte.	W/Sv	27-6-55	10-7-55
3539	Folen Peter	Pte.	W/Sl	25-7-55	7-8-55
3664	Golding Patrick	Pte.	W/Sl	22-3-55	3-4-55
3676	Hawkins James	Pte.	W/Sl	22-12-54	9-1-55
4060	Holmes William	Pte.	W/Sv	24-8-55	7-9-55
3548	Jennings Isaac	Pte.	W/Sv	22-12-54	9-1-55
2655	Johnson Lydney	Pte.	W/Sl	23-4-55	15-5-55
3833	Joyce William	Pte.	W/Sl	18-8-55	31-8-55
2834	Keating Patrick	Pte.	W/Sl	22-3-55	3-4-55
3807	Keefe Thomas	Pte.	W/Sv	22-12-54	9-1-55
3757	Lewis James	Pte.	W/Sl	22-3-55	3-4-55
1986	McCormack Thomas	Pte.	W/M	2-12-54	26-12-54
2497	McGrory John	Pte.	W/Sl	21-6-55	3-7-55
2178	Nolan Peter	Pte.	W/Sv	19-11-54	11-12-54
1296	O'Neil Michael	Pte.	W/Sl	18-8-55	31-8-55
3873	Perryer Henry	Pte.	W/Sv	25-7-55	7-8-55
3421	Prime Matthew	Pte.	W/Sv	26-11-54	26-12-54
3334	Rowe Peter	Pte.	W/Sl	22-3-55	3-4-55
3465	Russell James	Pte.	W/Sv	22-3-55	3-4-55
4073	Thompson William	Pte.	W/Sl	11-7-55	24-7-55
3186	Tickner William	Pte.	W/Sv	14-12-54	9-1-55
4065	Washington George	Pte.	W/Sl	12-8-55	24-8-55
3981	Watson George	Pte.	W/Sv	13-8-55	28-8-55
3424	Wheeler Charles	Pte.	W/Sl	26-11-54	26-12-54
2454	Whitmore John	Pte.	W/Sl	18-8-55	31-8-55
3940	Whitney William	Pte.	W/Sl	22-3-55	3-4-55
3323	Wilson Robert	Pte.	W/Sl	2-12-54	26-12-54
2591	Woods Henry	Pte.	W/Sv	24-8-55	7-9-55

21st REGIMENT OF FOOT

NO.	NAME	RANK	CASUALTY	DATE	LONDON GAZETTE
2353	McNamara Hugh	Sergt.	Killed	9-1-55	26-1-55
2291	Ryan William	Sergt.	Killed	9-1-55	26-1-55
3450	Byrne Michael	Pte.	Killed	22-6-55	9-7-55

NOTES

The Second, Third, Fourth, Fifth and Final Bombardment of Sebastopol, and Minor Actions

21st REGIMENT OF FOOT

NO.	NAME	RANK	CASUALTY	DATE	LONDON GAZETTE
2092	Fitzgerald Patrick	Pte.	Killed	19-6-55	3-7-55
3215	Kelly Patrick	Pte.	Killed	22-3-55	3-4-55
2705	McFaden Edward	Pte.	Killed	21-6-55	3-7-55
3004	Pearce William	Pte.	Killed	16-12-54	9-1-55
2196	Reily David	Pte.	Killed	31-12-54	26-1-55
—	Russell John	Pte.	Killed	19-4-55	1-5-55
3818	Tomlinson Hugh	Pte.	Killed	13-8-55	28-8-55
	Hawker S. W. H.	Capt.	W/Sl	22-6-55	9-7-55
	Lee V. H.	Lieut.	W/Sl	19-6-55	3-7-55
2290	Bougler Michael	Sergt.	W/Sl	16-12-54	9-1-55
2621	Lewis George	Sergt.	W/Sl	4-9-55	18-9-55
2996	Edwin George	L/Cpl.	W/Sv	4-8-55	17-8-55
3455	Bryan Thomas	Pte.	W/Sv	22-3-55	3-4-55
3220	Burke Michael	Pte.	W/Sl	22-6-55	9-7-55
3290	Carroll James	Pte.	W/Sl	13-1-55	2-2-55
3674	Carthy Charles	Pte.	W/Sl	20-8-55	4-9-55
3229	Cavanagh Thomas	Pte.	W/D	4-9-55	18-9-55
2403	Cavery Michael	Pte.	W/Sl	5-1-55	26-1-55
3856	Chalmers Alexander	Pte.	W/Sv	20-6-55	3-7-55
3205	Cleary James	Pte.	W/Sv	28-8-55	11-9-55
3725	Creed Charles	Pte.	W/Sl	9-1-55	26-1-55
1862	Curtis Uriah	Pte.	W/Sl	13-1-55	2-2-55
3461	Daley John	Pte.	W/Sl	4-9-55	18-9-55
3660	Doyle William	Pte.	W/D	4-9-55	18-9-55
2668	Faky Martin	Pte.	W/Sl	22-6-55	9-7-55
3200	Farrell Michael	Pte.	W/Sv	1-8-55	14-8-55
3631	Finn Michael	Pte.	W/Sv	22-3-55	3-4-55
3022	Flower William	Pte.	W/Sv	19-6-55	3-7-55
2676	Gough Francis	Pte.	W/Sl	13-1-55	2-2-55
3354	Hanrahan Patrick	Pte.	W/Sv	2-3-55	20-3-55
2632	Hickey Roger	Pte.	W/Sv	22-3-55	3-4-55
3129	Hogan Michael	Pte.	W/Sv	19-6-55	3-7-55
3105	Holdern Thomas	Pte.	W/Sv	16-12-54	9-1-55
3467	Horner John	Pte.	W/Sv	22-3-55	3-4-55
2773	Kain James	Pte.	W/Sl	13-1-55	2-2-55
2401	Kerny Anthony	Pte.	W/Sl	1-9-55	18-9-55
3302	McCallum James	Pte.	W/Sl	5-1-55	26-1-55
3668	McDonald John	Pte.	W/Sv	4-9-55	18-9-55
3736	McKenzie James	Pte.	W/Sv	18-8-55	31-8-55
3352	McManus Patrick	Pte.	W/Sv	21-6-55	3-7-55
3764	Millar William	Pte.	W/Sv	29-7-55	7-8-55
3274	Murphy Edwards	Pte.	W/Sv	4-9-55	18-9-55
2377	Powell Michael	Pte.	W/Sl	20-6-55	3-7-55
1933	Sartin George	Pte.	W/Sl	20-6-55	3-7-55
3323	Stone John	Pte.	W/Sv	22-6-55	9-7-55
2990	Wilkens Charles	Pte.	W/Sl	21-7-55	3-8-55
3886	Leahy Charles	Pte.	Missing	22-6-55	9-7-55
2143	McWiggin Hugh	Pte.	Missing	17-3-55	30-3-55
3231	Ryan Patrick	Pte.	Missing	22-6-55	9-7-55

23rd REGIMENT OF FOOT

NO.	NAME	RANK	CASUALTY	DATE	LONDON GAZETTE
	Owen W.	Lieut.	Killed	29-6-55	17-7-55
3907	Shave John	Corpl.	Killed	17-8-55	31-8-55
2709	Arnott John	Pte.	Killed	24-8-55	7-9-55
4697	Aubrey Alfred	Pte.	Killed	29-8-55	11-9-55
3442	Bennett James	Pte.	Killed	22-7-55	3-8-55
2314	Brumwell William	Pte.	Killed	31-7-55	14-8-55
3904	Bryan Thomas	Pte.	Killed	5-9-55	18-9-55
2930	Clayton William	Pte.	Killed	2-9-55	18-9-55

NOTES

The Second, Third, Fourth, Fifth and Final Bombardment of Sebastopol, and Minor Actions

23rd REGIMENT OF FOOT

NO.	NAME	RANK	CASUALTY	DATE	LONDON GAZETTE
4911	Edger Henry	Pte.	Killed	24-8-55	7-9-55
4927	Edwards George	Pte.	Killed	24-8-55	7-9-55
4856	Elms Henry	Pte.	Killed	24-8-55	7-9-55
4749	Foley William	Pte.	Killed	2-9-55	18-9-55
3112	Gough James	Pte.	Killed	15-8-55	28-8-55
4425	Harvey James	Pte.	Killed	25-4-55	1-5-55
2500	Hollister Robert	Pte.	Killed	16-4-55	1-5-55
4580	Holmes William	Pte.	Killed	29-6-55	17-7-55
3838	Jones Thomas	Pte.	Killed	9-6-55	22-6-55
2871	McGrorey James	Pte.	Killed	1-6-55	15-6-55
1333	McMahon James	Pte.	Killed	20-12-54	9-1-55
4162	Maskell Peter	Pte.	Killed	19-4-55	1-5-55
4588	Neville Thomas	Pte.	Killed	19-4-55	1-5-55
3837	Panting Josiah	Pte.	Killed	10-1-55	26-1-55
4543	Reese Thomas	Pte.	Killed	18-8-55	31-8-55
1591	Russell Samuel	Pte.	Killed	2-9-55	18-9-55
4532	Ryan John	Pte.	Killed	17-4-55	1-5-55
4480	Willis James	Pte.	Killed	9-6-55	22-6-55
	Bigge T. S.	Lieut.	W/Sl	24-8-55	7-9-55
3337	Casey Timothy	Sergt.	W/Sv	1-9-55	18-9-55
3354	Chamberlain Daniel	Sergt.	W/Sv	28-8-55	11-9-55
4232	Nixon Frederick	Sergt.	W/Sl	1-3-55	16-3-55
1669	Chadwick James	Corpl.	W/Sl	25-8-55	7-9-55
1708	Gibbs David	Corpl.	W/Sv	25-6-55	10-7-55
1706	Gibbs David	Corpl.	W/D	18-8-55	31-8-55
2214	Horner Sampson	Corpl.	W/Sv	10-6-55	22-6-55
2822	Rickey William	Corpl.	W/Sl	10-5-55	22-5-55
3307	Watts William	Corpl.	W/Sv	21-7-55	3-8-55
3804	Windsor Samuel	Corpl.	W/Sv	6-9-55	18-9-55
2695	Wyns Charles	Corpl.	W/Sv	24-8-55	7-9-55
3538	Morris Frederick	L/Cpl.	W/D	23-8-55	4-9-55
3886	Arden William	Pte.	W/Sv	17-8-55	31-8-55
4947	Bailey John	Pte.	W/Sv	28-8-55	11-9-55
4754	Bailey Thomas	Pte.	W/Sv	28-8-55	11-9-55
4609	Ball Henry	Pte.	W/Sv	3-5-55	15-5-55
4578	Ball Levi	Pte.	W/Sl	5-8-55	17-8-55
1106	Ball Thomas	Pte.	W/Sv	20-12-54	9-1-55
3924	Begley George	Pte.	W/Sl	28-8-55	11-9-55
4115	Bewistock William	Pte.	W/Sv	6-9-55	18-9-55
4269	Blessington Peter	Pte.	W/Sl	25-6-55	10-7-55
2745	Bohan Michael	Pte.	W/Sv	25-6-55	10-7-55
4393	Bond John	Pte.	W/Sv	8-7-55	20-7-55
4761	Bowcott Edward	Pte.	W/Sv	23-8-55	4-9-55
2410	Brown William	Pte.	W/D	5-5-55	18-5-55
3849	Buckingham Edward	Pte.	W/Sv	20-12-54	9-1-55
2196	Butcher George	Pte.	W/Sl	23-8-55	4-9-55
4287	Carroll Patrick	Pte.	W/Sv	30-8-55	11-9-55
4349	Chalkley Robert	Pte.	W/Sv	14-6-55	26-6-55
4866	Chant Daniel	Pte.	W/Sv	30-8-55	11-9-55
3423	Collins Timothy	Pte.	W/Sl	29-8-55	11-9-55
4522	Conway Jeremiah	Pte.	W/Sv	15-8-55	28-8-55
4489	Davies David	Pte.	W/Sl	10-6-55	22-6-55
3768	Davies John	Pte.	W/Sv	15-6-55	3-7-55
4432	Davies Richard	Pte.	W/Sv	28-8-55	11-9-55
2929	Dix Matthias	Pte.	W/D	29-8-55	11-9-55
4416	Donovan Patrick	Pte.	W/Sv	30-8-55	11-9-55
2862	Driscoll Dennis	Pte.	W/Sv	28-8-55	11-9-55
4472	Dwyer Edmund	Pte.	W/Sl	18-8-55	31-8-55
4621	Evans Thomas	Pte.	W/D	23-8-55	4-9-55
2817	Farmer John	Pte.	W/Sl	20-12-54	9-1-55
2817	Farmer John	Pte.	W/Sl	17-8-55	31-8-55
4149	Fowler John	Pte.	W/Sv	3-8-55	17-8-55
4107	Gambridge Joseph	Pte.	W/Sv	30-8-55	11-9-55
4466	Goodwin James	Pte.	W/Sv	21-5-55	5-6-55

NOTES

The Second, Third, Fourth, Fifth and Final Bombardment of Sebastopol, and Minor Actions

23rd REGIMENT OF FOOT

NO.	NAME	RANK	CASUALTY	DATE	LONDON GAZETTE
4503	Griffith John	Pte.	W/Sl	24-8-55	7-9-55
1905	Hainstock Robert	Pte.	W/Sv	15-8-55	28-8-55
1232	Hanwood John	Pte.	W/Sv	30-8-55	11-9-55
4043	Harrington George	Pte.	W/Sl	11-8-55	24-8-55
4421	Haynes Lock	Pte.	W/Sv	29-4-55	15-5-55
4234	Heggerty Patrick	Pte.	W/Sl	19-4-55	1-5-55
1381	Hillen Patrick	Pte.	W/Sv	25-6-55	10-7-55
1912	Hollerook James	Pte.	W/Sl	25-7-55	7-8-55
4192	Holt Thomas	Pte.	W/Sv	6-9-55	18-9-55
4502	Hudson William	Pte.	W/Sl	10-6-55	22-6-55
3876	Hughes Joseph	Pte.	W/Sv	20-12-54	9-1-55
4758	Hughes Richard	Pte.	W/Sv	29-6-55	17-7-55
4632	Jarvoise James	Pte.	W/Sl	29-6-55	17-7-55
4491	Jenkins William	Pte.	W/Sv	12-5-55	25-5-55
4491	Jenkins William	Pte.	W/D	10-6-55	22-6-55
4032	Jones David	Pte.	W/Sv	5-5-55	18-5-55
4556	Jones John	Pte.	W/Sl	21-5-55	5-6-55
4661	Jutner Henry	Pte.	W/Sl	6-9-55	18-9-55
3184	Kemish George	Pte.	W/Sv	28-8-55	11-9-55
4054	Kempster Arthur	Pte.	W/Sv	28-8-55	11-9-55
2903	Labon Joseph	Pte.	W/Sv	21-7-55	3-8-55
4598	Long James	Pte.	W/Sl	29-8-55	11-9-55
2278	Lowery Richard	Pte.	W/Sv	10-5-55	22-5-55
4336	Lunt Thomas	Pte.	W/Sl	5-5-55	18-5-55
4370	McCoughall —	Pte.	W/Sv	15-8-55	28-8-55
4403	McElwain John	Pte.	W/Sl	5-9-55	18-9-55
2676	McGosling John	Pte.	W/Sl	10-6-55	22-6-55
2354	Meton George	Pte.	W/Sl	11-8-55	24-8-55
4586	Millar William	Pte.	W/Sv	15-8-55	28-8-55
4721	Mooney John	Pte.	W/Sl	18-8-55	31-8-55
2504	Murphy James	Pte.	W/Sv	17-8-55	31-8-55
4212	Narley George	Pte.	W/Sv	21-7-55	3-8-55
4040	Newell James	Pte.	W/Sv	20-12-54	9-1-55
4400	Oliver George	Pte.	W/Sv	6-9-55	18-9-55
3568	O'Neil John	Pte.	W/Sl	14-4-55	1-5-55
3866	Owens Fred	Pte.	W/D	5-9-55	18-9-55
4129	Randall Joseph	Pte.	W/Sv	23-8-55	4-9-55
4543	Rees Thomas	Pte.	W/Sl	10-6-55	22-6-55
4880	Richardson David	Pte.	W/D	3-8-55	17-8-55
4662	Roberts George	Pte.	W/Sv	20-6-55	3-7-55
4516	Robinson Edwin	Pte.	W/Sv	30-7-55	14-8-55
4707	Rody Patrick	Pte.	W/Sv	24-8-55	7-9-55
3435	Rooke Shaderick	Pte.	W/Sl	10-6-55	22-6-55
1213	Ryan Matthew	Pte.	W/Sl	27-6-55	10-7-55
4524	Saunders George	Pte.	W/D	5-9-55	18-9-55
4557	Smith John	Pte.	W/Sl	10-6-55	22-6-55
3332	Stafford Stephen	Pte.	W/Sv	19-4-55	1-5-55
1534	Stokes Thomas	Pte.	W/D	10-6-55	22-6-55
4129	Such John	Pte.	W/Sl	19-4-55	1-5-55
4007	Swadling Robert	Pte.	W/Sv	6-9-55	18-9-55
3310	Symonds Thomas	Pte.	W/Sl	20-8-55	4-9-55
4092	Taylor William	Pte.	W/Sv	25-4-55	15-5-55
3902	Vaughan Michael	Pte.	W/Sl	17-8-55	31-8-55
4724	Wallis John	Pte.	W/Sv	28-8-55	11-9-55
3840	Warren John	Pte.	W/Sv	26-8-55	7-9-55
3781	Watkins Thomas	Pte.	W/Sv	20-12-54	9-1-55
3307	Watts William	Pte.	W/Sl	20-12-54	9-1-55
4649	West Thomas	Pte.	W/Sl	18-8-55	31-8-55
4593	Weston Richard	Pte.	W/Sv	12-5-55	25-5-55
4242	Whayling Patrick	Pte.	W/Sl	17-4-55	1-5-55
4242	Whelan Patrick	Pte.	W/Sl	17-8-55	31-8-55
4518	White Richard	Pte.	W/Sv	10-6-55	22-6-55
4749	Williams Frelin	Pte.	W/Sl	2-9-55	18-9-55
4422	Williams Henry	Pte.	W/Sv	2-7-55	17-7-55

NOTES

The Second, Third, Fourth, Fifth and Final Bombardment of Sebastopol, and Minor Actions

23rd REGIMENT OF FOOT

NO.	NAME	RANK	CASUALTY	DATE	LONDON GAZETTE
3314	Wood George R.	Pte.	W/Sv	30-8-55	11-9-55
4268	Woodall John	Pte.	W/Sl	17-8-55	31-8-55
2719	Buckingham Edward	Pte.	Missing	20-12-54	9-1-55
3552	Cose Robert	Pte.	Missing	20-12-54	9-1-55
2122	Fell Matthew	Pte.	Missing	20-12-54	9-1-55
3818	Fogarty Patrick	Pte.	Missing	20-12-54	9-1-55
2521	Gilmore John	Pte.	Missing	20-12-54	9-1-55
3565	Golling Thomas	Pte.	Missing	20-12-54	9-1-55
3692	Hudson Ambrose	Pte.	Missing	20-12-54	9-1-55
3595	Munt Thomas	Pte.	Missing	20-12-54	9-1-55
2489	Sparks George	Pte.	Missing	20-12-54	9-1-55
2889	Thompson John	Pte.	Missing	20-12-54	9-1-55

28th REGIMENT OF FOOT

NO.	NAME	RANK	CASUALTY	DATE	LONDON GAZETTE
3573	Bates Henry	Pte.	Killed	3-9-55	18-9-55
3763	Chiverton Francis	Pte.	Killed	1-5-55	15-5-55
3505	Connor Thomas	Pte.	Killed	24-6-55	9-7-55
3580	Cryon Michael	Pte.	Killed	11-4-55	24-4-55
4005	Dogwell James	Pte.	Killed	22-7-55	3-8-55
1973	Edward John	Pte.	Killed	1-5-55	15-5-55
3584	Fitzgerald Michael	Pte.	Killed	29-11-54	26-12-54
4283	Marshall Richard	Pte.	Killed	3-9-55	18-9-55
3660	Mulhorn Joseph	Pte.	Killed	17-8-55	31-8-55
	Baumgartner R. J.	Lt/Col.	W/Sl	17-8-55	31-8-55
	Morgan Hill F.	Lieut.	W/Sv	3-6-55	15-6-55
	Smyth E. S. R.	Lt. & Adj.	W/Sl	21-8-55	4-9-55
3970	Faller C. H.	Sergt.	W/Sl	15-6-55	3-7-55
3042	Flynn Patrick	Sergt.	W/Sl	17-8-55	31-8-55
2927	Carr Bernard	Corpl.	W/Sl	1-5-55	15-5-55
3726	Bellington John	Pte.	W/Sv	25-2-55	16-3-55
3968	Boyd James	Pte.	W/Sl	4-4-55	20-4-55
4127	Cantwell Patrick	Pte.	W/Sv	18-8-55	31-8-55
3676	Coleman James	Pte.	W/Sl	11-12-54	9-1-55
3505	Connor Thomas	Pte.	W/Sv	6-9-55	18-9-55
3655	Conroy Joseph	Pte.	W/Sv	15-6-55	3-7-55
3385	Duffy M.	Pte.	W/Sl	12-8-55	24-8-55
3991	Firth G.	Pte.	W/Sv	11-8-55	24-8-55
3490	Foster John	Pte.	W/Sl	3-9-55	18-9-55
3766	Gayritty Thomas	Pte.	W/Sv	16-6-55	3-7-55
2964	Hogan Patrick	Pte.	W/Sv	25-1-55	9-2-55
3859	Jackson Thomas	Pte.	W/Sv	19-8-55	31-8-55
3973	Locke George	Pte.	W/D	24-6-55	9-7-55
3670	McGainey Richard	Pte.	W/Sv	24-1-55	9-2-55
3928	Mackamara Thomas	Pte.	W/Sl	16-6-55	3-7-55
3841	Moon Thomas	Pte.	W/Sv	17-11-54	11-12-54
3483	Mountain Samuel	Pte.	W/Sl	29-5-55	12-6-55
3291	O'Neile James	Pte.	W/Sv	17-11-54	11-12-54
3674	Quinn John	Pte.	W/Sl	13-6-55	26-6-55
3500	Rogers John	Pte.	W/Sl	22-1-55	9-2-55
2632	Smith Charles	Pte.	W/Sl	22-12-54	9-1-55
1946	Smith Thomas	Pte.	W/Sv	1-5-55	15-5-55
1992	Steale James	Pte.	W/Sl	29-11-54	26-12-54
4009	Thomas Matthew	Pte.	W/Sl	1-5-55	15-5-55
3611	Toomey Michael	Pte.	W/Sl	11-12-54	9-1-55

NOTES

The Second, Third, Fourth, Fifth and Final Bombardment of Sebastopol, and Minor Actions

30th REGIMENT OF FOOT

NO.	NAME	RANK	CASUALTY	DATE	LONDON GAZETTE
3805	Douglas Charles	L/Cpl.	Killed	3-2-55	20-2-55
2630	Cleary Walter	Drummer	Killed	5-9-55	18-9-55
3664	Bowles John	Pte.	Killed	9-1-55	26-1-55
3202	Cann George	Pte.	Killed	28-8-55	11-9-55
3856	Carey Daniel	Pte.	Killed	11-4-55	24-4-55
3414	Clarke Edmund	Pte.	Killed	10-7-55	24-7-55
3864	Cree James	Pte.	Killed	2-9-55	18-9-55
3339	Dawson Richard	Pte.	Killed	2-9-55	18-9-55
4109	Dowell Robert	Pte.	Killed	10-7-55	24-7-55
3903	Dunn James	Pte.	Killed	20-8-55	4-9-55
2650	Enright Patrick	Pte.	Killed	9-1-55	26-1-55
2955	Ganly Patrick	Pte.	Killed	4-4-55	20-4-55
3773	Hunter Thomas	Pte.	Killed	2-9-55	18-9-55
4247	Ingram Arthur	Pte.	Killed	22-8-55	4-9-55
3485	Kemp Moses	Pte.	Killed	22-8-55	4-9-55
2823	Lennon Thomas	Pte.	Killed	5-9-55	18-9-55
3658	Richardson Henry	Pte.	Killed	22-8-55	4-9-55
2158	Still Alexander	Pte.	Killed	10-8-55	24-8-55
3967	Walsh Thomas	Pte.	Killed	24-4-55	15-5-55
	Forbes J.	Lt. & Adj.	W/M	31-8-55	18-9-55
3081	Delaney Thomas	Sergt.	W/D	16-4-55	18-5-55
2645	Hashim Frederick	Sergt.	W/Sl	9-6-55	22-6-55
3709	Callaghan James	Corpl.	W/Sl	4-9-55	18-9-55
2071	Cole Alexander	Corpl.	W/Sl	26-4-55	15-5-55
3517	Hardy John	Corpl.	W/D	5-9-55	18-9-55
4092	Laird William	Corpl.	W/Sl	1-4-55	20-4-55
2820	McLean Donald	Corpl.	W/Sl	21-7-55	3-8-55
3909	Thompson John	Corpl.	W/Sv	6-7-55	20-7-55
3671	Boreland Alexander	L/Cpl.	W/Sv	5-5-55	18-5-55
3292	Pollard James	L/Cpl.	W/Sv	5-5-55	18-5-55
3837	Tyrie Robert	L/Cpl.	W/Sv	20-8-55	4-9-55
2115	Smith James	Drummer	W/Sv	28-6-55	10-7-55
2499	White James	Drummer	W/Sl	10-8-55	24-8-55
3680	Andrews James	Pte.	W/Sv	22-8-55	4-9-55
3994	Armstrong Edward	Pte.	W/Sl	20-8-55	4-9-55
4013	Barry James	Pte.	W/Sv	11-8-55	24-8-55
2606	Bott Isaac	Pte.	W/D	9-7-55	24-7-55
3748	Bowler William	Pte.	W/Sv	9-6-55	22-6-55
3844	Brown James	Pte.	W/Sv	2-9-55	18-9-55
4414	Brown Michael	Pte.	W/Sl	2-9-55	18-9-55
3588	Burnford Joseph	Pte.	W/Sl	9-4-55	24-4-55
4030	Callaghan John	Pte.	W/Sl	13-3-55	23-3-55
3977	Castle Joseph	Pte.	W/Sl	12-7-55	24-7-55
3937	Cavanagh Patrick	Pte.	W/Sl	14-3-55	23-3-55
3613	Chamberlain Michael	Pte.	W/Sv	19-4-55	1-5-55
4212	Close Thomas	Pte.	W/Sl	16-8-55	28-8-55
4200	Collins Patrick	Pte.	W/Sv	22-8-55	4-9-55
3756	Connell Patrick	Pte.	W/Sl	13-4-55	1-5-55
3733	Connolly Michael	Pte.	W/D	2-9-55	18-9-55
2909	Cowley James	Pte.	W/Sv	25-7-55	7-8-55
3954	Cunningham Daniel	Pte.	W/Sl	2-9-55	18-9-55
3554	Desmond John	Pte.	W/M	16-4-55	1-5-55
3443	Donnell Patrick	Pte.	W/Sl	15-6-55	3-7-55
3755	Ducey Patrick	Pte.	W/Sv	20-5-55	5-6-55
4031	Dwyer Jeremiah	Pte.	W/Sv	11-8-55	24-8-55
3204	Dyball James	Pte.	W/Sv	28-8-55	11-9-55
3830	Edwards John	Pte.	W/Sl	25-8-55	7-9-55
3571	Filstead John	Pte.	W/Sv	13-3-55	23-3-55
4032	Fitzgerald Edward	Pte.	W/Sl	17-8-55	31-8-55
3655	Glackin William	Pte.	W/Sl	2-7-55	17-7-55
3855	Graham Peter	Pte.	W/Sv	10-4-55	24-4-55
2419	Green Robert	Pte.	W/Sv	22-8-55	4-9-55

NOTES

The Second, Third, Fourth, Fifth and Final Bombardment of Sebastopol, and Minor Actions

30th REGIMENT OF FOOT

NO.	NAME	RANK	CASUALTY	DATE	LONDON GAZETTE
4023	Grimes Bernard	Pte.	W/Sl	31-3-55	20-4-55
4071	Harrington Michael	Pte.	W/Sv	19-4-55	1-5-55
3723	Hayes David	Pte.	W/D	23-8-55	4-9-55
4124	Holborn Charles	Pte.	W/Sl	30-4-55	15-5-55
3171	Holmes William	Pte.	W/Sv	27-6-55	10-7-55
2718	Horgan Edward	Pte.	W/Sl	25-8-55	7-9-55
3157	Johnson Terence	Pte.	W/Sl	23-8-55	4-9-55
4274	Kavanagh Thomas	Pte.	W/Sv	27-6-55	10-7-55
2956	Kelly Michael	Pte.	W/Sl	23-8-55	4-9-55
3017	Kiely Thomas T.	Pte.	W/Sl	25-8-55	7-9-55
3932	Leah William	Pte.	W/Sv	27-6-55	10-7-55
3205	Long Mathew	Pte.	W/Sl	5-8-55	17-8-55
3947	Loughran Patrick	Pte.	W/Sl	10-8-55	24-8-55
3989	McGuire Michael	Pte.	W/Sl	26-4-55	15-5-55
4081	Martin James	Pte.	W/Sl	5-5-55	18-5-55
3654	Midhurst William	Pte.	W/Sl	16-8-55	28-8-55
2663	Mullins Edward	Pte.	W/Sv	8-6-55	22-6-55
3159	Ogden William	Pte.	W/Sl	4-3-55	16-3-55
3851	Parker James	Pte.	W/Sv	18-7-55	31-7-55
2627	Perkins Alfred	Pte.	W/Sl	4-9-55	18-9-55
2558	Pither Edmund	Pte.	W/Sl	1-7-55	17-7-55
4269	Regan John	Pte.	W/Sl	25-8-55	7-9-55
3658	Richardson Henry	Pte.	W/Sl	9-5-55	22-5-55
3915	Roodier John	Pte.	W/Sl	16-8-55	28-8-55
3901	Shannon Jeremiah	Pte.	W/Sl	2-9-55	18-9-55
3731	Sheehan Patrick	Pte.	W/Sl	2-9-55	18-9-55
3099	Sheppard George	Pte.	W/Sl	8-4-55	20-4-55
2039	Smith James	Pte.	W/Sl	15-6-55	3-7-55
2644	Startup Robert	Pte.	W/Sl	2-9-55	18-9-55
1614	Strip William	Pte.	W/Sv	25-1-55	9-2-55
3876	Sutherland Samuel	Pte.	W/Sl	5-9-55	18-9-55
3109	Vernon John	Pte.	W/Sl	6-3-55	23-3-55
3675	Walker Matthew	Pte.	W/D	17-8-55	31-8-55
3624	Ward James	Pte.	W/Sl	28-6-55	10-7-55
	Driscoll Patrick	Pte.	Missing	5-5-55	18-5-55

31st REGIMENT OF FOOT

NO.	NAME	RANK	CASUALTY	DATE	LONDON GAZETTE
	Anderson Charles	Capt.	Killed	4-9-55	18-9-55
2997	Behan Thomas	Col/Sgt.	Killed	4-8-55	17-8-55
2990	Thompson John	Sergt.	Killed	13-8-55	28-8-55
—	Atrell F. S.	Corpl.	Killed	7-9-55	25-9-55
2815	Gilman Thomas	Pte.	Killed	29-7-55	7-8-55
3811	Glennon Michael	Pte.	Killed	7-7-55	20-7-55
3378	Goon James	Pte.	Killed	17-8-55	31-8-55
1937	Hickey John	Pte.	Killed	4-9-55	18-9-55
3601	James John	Pte.	Killed	6-9-55	18-9-55
—	Jones Thomas	Pte.	Killed	15-7-55	27-7-55
3554	Lang Benjamin	Pte.	Killed	7-7-55	20-7-55
2984	Larkin Philip	Pte.	Killed	27-7-55	7-8-55
3435	McIlroy Michael	Pte.	Killed	7-7-55	20-7-55
3404	Neil Edward	Pte.	Killed	13-8-55	28-8-55
3967	Neile Edward	Pte.	Killed	17-8-55	31-8-55
2843	Oaten Henry	Pte.	Killed	5-8-55	17-8-55
2444	Potter William	Pte.	Killed	17-8-55	31-8-55
3703	Richards Henry	Pte.	Killed	17-8-55	31-8-55
2997	Behan Thomas	Col/Sgt.	W/Sl	30-7-55	14-8-55
2074	Foley James	Col/Sgt.	W/Sl	13-8-55	28-8-55
2719	Forrest James	Sergt.	W/Sl	4-8-55	17-8-55
1741	Lee Samuel	Sergt.	W/Sl	20-7-55	3-8-55

NOTES

The Second, Third, Fourth, Fifth and Final Bombardment of Sebastopol, and Minor Actions

31st REGIMENT OF FOOT

NO.	NAME	RANK	CASUALTY	DATE	LONDON GAZETTE
3889	McCarthy Dennis	Sergt.	W/Sl	17-8-55	31-8-55
3647	Malony William	Sergt.	W/Sl	17-8-55	31-8-55
2705	Gibson Thomas	Corpl.	W/Sv	28-6-55	10-7-55
3468	McMarry James	Corpl.	W/Sl	8-7-55	20-7-55
—	Prevost E.	Corpl.	W/Sl	7-9-55	25-9-55
3099	Roberts William	Corpl.	W/Sl	4-8-55	17-8-55
3201	White Patrick	Corpl.	W/Sl	17-8-55	31-8-55
3184	Cunningham M	Drummer	W/Sv	7-9-55	25-9-55
3310	Fox Patrick	Drummer	W/Sl	4-7-55	17-7-55
—	Holder James	Drummer	W/Sl	7-9-55	25-9-55
—	Martin S.	Drummer	W/Sv	7-9-55	25-9-55
3895	Anderson Joshua	Pte.	W/Sv	29-8-55	11-9-55
4538	Barnes George	Pte.	W/Sl	4-7-55	17-7-55
3756	Bliss James	Pte.	W/Sl	14-7-55	27-7-55
3262	Boyle Terence	Pte.	W/Sl	26-7-55	7-8-55
2728	Brennan Edward	Pte.	W/Sv	29-8-55	11-9-55
3656	Brickston John	Pte.	W/Sv	26-7-55	7-8-55
3705	Brien J.	Pte.	W/Sv	7-9-55	25-9-55
3530	Cardell Thomas	Pte.	W/Sl	4-8-55	17-8-55
2455	Cardle John	Pte.	W/Sl	17-8-55	31-8-55
3643	Clay John	Pte.	W/D	26-7-55	7-8-55
3599	Coleman George	Pte.	W/Sl	13-8-55	28-8-55
3700	Cooke Richard	Pte.	W/Sl	7-8-55	21-8-55
3354	Cremour Owen	Pte.	W/Sl	26-7-55	7-8-55
3041	Critchley William	Pte.	W/Sl	4-8-55	17-8-55
3808	Cuthbert Thomas	Pte.	W/D	2-9-55	18-9-55
3728	Daily John	Pte.	W/Sl	7-7-55	20-7-55
3876	Dalury Cornelius	Pte.	W/Sl	17-8-55	31-8-55
1867	Devoy John	Pte.	W/Sv	15-7-55	27-7-55
2518	Dockett Solomon	Pte.	W/Sl	20-8-55	4-9-55
3763	Dunn Patrick	Pte.	W/Sl	13-8-55	28-8-55
3413	Fee James	Pte.	W/Sv	2-9-55	18-9-55
3747	Flannagan John	Pte.	W/Sl	17-8-55	31-8-55
1932	Hammond Thomas	Pte.	W/Sl	26-7-55	7-8-55
3344	Haughton H.	Pte.	W/Sl	7-9-55	25-9-55
3345	Haynes Wilson	Pte.	W/D	17-6-55	3-7-55
2578	Heaginey Martin	Pte.	W/Sl	8-7-55	20-7-55
2943	Hogan Martin	Pte.	W/Sl	21-8-55	4-9-55
2810	Holmes Patrick	Pte.	W/Sv	14-8-55	28-8-55
3232	Horan William	Pte.	W/Sv	30-6-55	17-7-55
—	Howard Edward	Pte.	W/Sv	4-7-55	17-7-55
3855	Hutton Charles	Pte.	W/Sl	4-9-55	18-9-55
2585	Jenner John	Pte.	W/Sl	8-7-55	20-7-55
3440	Jones Thomas	Pte.	W/Sl	28-6-55	10-7-55
3975	Keane Edward	Pte.	W/Sl	29-8-55	11-9-55
3717	Kelly William	Pte.	W/Sv	29-8-55	11-9-55
3793	Keogh Malichi	Pte.	W/Sl	4-9-55	18-9-55
3400	Kernan Terence	Pte.	W/Sl	4-9-55	18-9-55
3596	Laxton Charles	Pte.	W/D	17-6-55	3-7-55
2875	Leeson Edward	Pte.	W/Sl	4-8-55	17-8-55
2956	Lockhurst Jesse	Pte.	W/Sv	16-8-55	28-8-55
3266	McBarron Michael	Pte.	W/Sl	26-7-55	7-8-55
3796	McCabe J.	Pte.	W/Sl	7-9-55	25-9-55
3957	McGrath Peter	Pte.	W/Sl	16-8-55	28-8-55
3957	McGrath Peter	Pte.	W/Sl	25-8-55	7-9-55
3412	McGuire John	Pte.	W/Sv	8-7-55	20-7-55
3439	McNab Patrick	Pte.	W/Sl	4-9-55	18-9-55
2851	McQuade John	Pte.	W/Sl	30-7-55	14-8-55
2207	Madden John	Pte.	W/Sl	4-9-55	18-9-55
1107	Maloney Edward	Pte.	W/Sv	29-8-55	11-9-55
3819	Matthews John	Pte.	W/D	29-8-55	11-9-55
—	Miller John	Pte.	W/Sv	9-7-55	24-7-55
3025	Mooney John	Pte.	W/Sl	20-7-55	3-8-55
3264	Mulhern James	Pte.	W/Sl	26-7-55	7-8-55

NOTES

The Second, Third, Fourth, Fifth and Final Bombardment of Sebastopol, and Minor Actions

31st REGIMENT OF FOOT

NO.	NAME	RANK	CASUALTY	DATE	LONDON GAZETTE
3715	Murphy Patrick	Pte.	W/Sv	16-8-55	28-8-55
1506	Neagle Patrick	Pte.	W/Sv	13-8-55	28-8-55
3425	Paris Henry	Pte.	W/Sl	7-8-55	21-8-55
3832	Perrin Matthew	Pte.	W/Sl	16-8-55	28-8-55
1298	Prince Lewis	Pte.	W/Sl	17-8-55	31-8-55
3972	Proctor James	Pte.	W/Sl	4-9-55	18-9-55
2716	Purcell Thomas	Pte.	W/Sl	2-9-55	18-9-55
2157	Rennox Joseph	Pte.	W/Sl	5-8-55	17-8-55
2682	Roberts J.	Pte.	W/Sl	7-9-55	25-9-55
3101	Rosney Denis	Pte.	W/Sv	20-8-55	4-9-55
3789	Rowlands Thomas	Pte.	W/Sv	29-8-55	11-9-55
2276	Ryan Michael	Pte.	W/Sl	16-8-55	28-8-55
3706	Shaw James	Pte.	W/Sl	16-8-55	28-8-55
3720	Sheridan Michael	Pte.	W/Sl	4-8-55	17-8-55
3174	Spellman James	Pte.	W/Sv	4-9-55	18-9-55
2346	Strain Hugh	Pte.	W/Sl	26-7-55	7-8-55
3333	Talbot John	Pte.	W/Sl	27-7-55	7-8-55
3364	Timlin Francis	Pte.	W/Sl	25-8-55	7-9-55
3305	Tracey John	Pte.	W/Sl	4-9-55	18-9-55
3148	Wade Thomas	Pte.	W/Sl	23-8-55	4-9-55
3603	Walton Henry	Pte.	W/Sl	4-8-55	17-8-55
3455	Wardle John	Pte.	W/Sv	26-7-55	7-8-55
3431	Weekly John	Pte.	W/Sl	4-8-55	17-8-55
3110	Weir James	Pte.	W/Sv	4-8-55	17-8-55
3423	Woods William	Pte.	W/D	18-7-55	31-7-55

33rd REGIMENT OF FOOT

NO.	NAME	RANK	CASUALTY	DATE	LONDON GAZETTE
	Marsh Ham St V.	Lt. & Adj.	Killed	24-6-55	9-7-55
2212	Mara John	Corpl.	Killed	18-8-55	31-8-55
3316	Blair James	Pte.	Killed	22-3-55	3-4-55
3684	Burrows William	Pte.	Killed	1-8-55	14-8-55
3610	Craig William	Pte.	Killed	12-6-55	26-6-55
3837	Harris Richard	Pte.	Killed	20-6-55	3-7-55
3206	Herson John	Pte.	Killed	25-6-55	10-7-55
2522	Holroyd Timothy	Pte.	Killed	20-12-54	9-1-55
3861	Joyce James	Pte.	Killed	22-8-55	4-9-55
2554	Keefe John	Pte.	Killed	22-3-55	3-4-55
2715	Key Joseph	Pte.	Killed	12-6-55	26-6-55
3645	King William	Pte.	Killed	3-6-55	15-6-55
3685	Kirby Edmund	Pte.	Killed	22-3-55	3-4-55
3659	Lownes George	Pte.	Killed	28-8-55	11-9-55
2513	McGarry Stephen	Pte.	Killed	20-12-54	9-1-55
3538	Ryan Edward	Pte.	Killed	5-8-55	17-8-55
3663	Ryan William	Pte.	Killed	23-4-55	15-5-55
3728	Sullivan Thomas	Pte.	Killed	5-7-55	17-7-55
3537	Wilson Thomas	Pte.	Killed	12-6-55	26-6-55
3469	Worrell Richard	Pte.	Killed	20-6-55	3-7-55
	Mundy G. V.	Brevet Lt/Col.	W/Sl	3-6-55	15-6-55
	Ellis H. D.	Capt.	W/Sl	15-8-55	28-8-55
	Donovan E. W.	Capt.	W/Sv	15-4-55	1-5-55
	Prescott E. B.	Lieut.	W/Sv	15-8-55	28-8-55
	Thompson J.	Lieut.	W/Sl	3-6-55	15-6-55
3474	Long Denis	L/Cpl.	W/Sl	15-4-55	1-5-55
3479	Noonan William	L/Cpl.	W/Sl	11-8-55	24-8-55
4040	Anderson J.	Pte.	W/D	28-8-55	11-9-55
2176	Brazel Patrick	Pte.	W/D	5-8-55	17-8-55
3260	Byett Joseph	Pte.	W/Sv	26-6-55	10-7-55
3505	Callaghan Owen	Pte.	W/Sv	23-4-55	15-5-55
3810	Clarke James	Pte.	W/D	9-8-55	21-8-55

NOTES

The Second, Third, Fourth, Fifth and Final Bombardment of Sebastopol, and Minor Actions

33rd REGIMENT OF FOOT

NO.	NAME	RANK	CASUALTY	DATE	LONDON GAZETTE
3031	Clifford Daniel	Pte.	W/Sl	27-7-55	7-8-55
2883	Cole William	Pte.	W/Sv	10-6-55	22-6-55
3536	Coleman John	Pte.	W/Sv	11-4-55	24-4-55
2027	Condrick John	Pte.	W/Sv	11-8-55	24-8-55
2019	Connelly James	Pte.	W/Sv	28-8-55	11-9-55
3787	Davis Charles	Pte.	W/Sl	11-8-55	24-8-55
3364	Dickinson Edward	Pte.	W/Sl	20-12-54	9-1-55
3087	Dineen John	Pte.	W/Sv	20-12-54	9-1-55
3743	Donnelly P.	Pte.	W/Sv	28-8-55	11-9-55
3261	Downey Timothy	Pte.	W/Sv	17-4-55	1-5-55
3575	Doyle Thomas	Pte.	W/Sv	16-4-55	1-5-55
3072	Duffy Michael	Pte.	W/Sl	28-8-55	11-9-55
3170	Fitzgerald John	Pte.	W/Sv	20-12-54	9-1-55
3129	Flattery Thomas	Pte.	W/Sv	25-7-55	7-8-55
3411	Fowler William	Pte.	W/Sl	15-4-55	1-5-55
3302	Gallagher James	Pte.	W/M	10-6-55	22-6-55
2032	Gorman James	Pte.	W/Sl	28-8-55	11-9-55
2686	Herbert George	Pte.	W/Sv	25-8-55	7-9-55
2644	Jackson Charles	Pte.	W/Sl	26-6-55	10-7-55
3435	Jessop Thomas	Pte.	W/Sl	26-6-55	10-7-55
3485	Keenon John	Pte.	W/Sl	15-6-55	3-7-55
3444	Kelly Patrick	Pte.	W/Sl	12-5-55	25-5-55
3784	Kerr James	Pte.	W/Sl	28-8-55	11-9-55
3090	Larkins Daniel	Pte.	W/Sl	15-4-55	1-5-55
3574	Leary John	Pte.	W/Sv	28-8-55	11-9-55
3104	Lynch D.	Pte.	W/Sl	28-8-55	11-9-55
3730	Lyndsay J.	Pte.	W/Sl	28-8-55	11-9-55
3382	McDermott John	Pte.	W/Sl	21-7-55	3-8-55
3212	McGuffey William	Pte.	W/Sl	12-5-55	25-5-55
2710	McLean John	Pte.	W/Sl	28-8-55	11-9-55
2982	Mayse John	Pte.	W/D	30-8-55	11-9-55
3217	Mills J.	Pte.	W/Sv	28-8-55	11-9-55
2833	Monaghan Thomas	Pte.	W/D	9-8-55	21-8-55
3835	Murphy Martin	Pte.	W/Sv	28-8-55	11-9-55
3156	O'Connell Daniel	Pte.	W/Sl	24-6-55	9-7-55
3196	Pukett Peter	Pte.	W/Sl	27-7-55	7-8-55
2023	Ray Charles	Pte.	W/Sl	15-8-55	28-8-55
3263	Richards Aaron	Pte.	W/Sl	15-6-55	3-7-55
3529	Ring Timothy	Pte.	W/Sl	27-7-55	7-8-55
3838	Ryan Denis	Pte.	W/M	5-8-55	17-8-55
3373	Ryan James	Pte.	W/Sv	17-4-55	1-5-55
3375	Smith James	Pte.	W/Sl	8-8-55	21-8-55
3849	Smith Matthew	Pte.	W/Sl	4-9-55	18-9-55
3369	Sullivan Bartholomew	Pte.	W/D	1-9-55	18-9-55
2346	Swain Robert	Pte.	W/Sv	1-9-55	18-9-55
3248	Taylor Ewan	Pte.	W/Sv	11-8-55	24-8-55
3516	Tobin Michael	Pte.	W/D	22-6-55	9-7-55
3577	Veins Thomas	Pte.	W/Sv	20-12-54	9-1-55
3828	Walker Thomas	Pte.	W/D	5-8-55	17-8-55
4146	Wilkins J.	Pte.	W/Sv	28-8-55	11-9-55
3707	Williams George	Pte.	W/Sv	12-5-55	25-5-55
3549	Woodthorpe William	Pte.	W/Sv	10-6-55	22-6-55
–	Baldwin Thomas	Pte.	Missing	20-12-54	9-1-55
–	Smith Henry	Pte.	Missing	20-12-54	9-1-55
3101	Pollard Thomas	Pte.	P.O.W.	5-11-54	29-5-55

34th REGIMENT OF FOOT

NO.	NAME	RANK	CASUALTY	DATE	LONDON GAZETTE
	Jordan W. W.	Lieut.	Killed	22-3-55	3-4-55
3281	Bentley Henry	Pte.	Killed	27-7-55	7-8-55

NOTES

The Second, Third, Fourth, Fifth and Final Bombardment of Sebastopol, and Minor Actions

34th REGIMENT OF FOOT

NO.	NAME	RANK	CASUALTY	DATE	LONDON GAZETTE
3535	Blackburn John	Pte.	Killed	6-4-55	20-4-55
1315	Bloxham George	Pte.	Killed	20-12-54	9-1-55
3231	Briggs Samuel	Pte.	Killed	13-6-55	26-6-55
3688	Buckey Simon	Pte.	Killed	17-5-55	29-5-55
3280	Byrne Michael	Pte.	Killed	15-4-55	1-5-55
2880	Callaghan William	Pte.	Killed	11-3-55	23-3-55
2981	Essey John	Pte.	Killed	6-7-55	20-7-55
2444	Gately Thomas	Pte.	Killed	15-3-55	23-3-55
3163	Heap Frederick	Pte.	Killed	17-4-55	1-5-55
3891	Heritage William	Pte.	Killed	15-3-55	23-3-55
3535	Huntingdon John	Pte.	Killed	25-7-55	7-8-55
2416	Kennedy Thomas	Pte.	Killed	8-5-55	22-5-55
3679	McCarthy Charles	Pte.	Killed	6-9-55	18-9-55
2199	Maycock John	Pte.	Killed	17-8-55	31-8-55
3677	Murray Francis	Pte.	Killed	7-5-55	22-5-55
2276	Nicholson James	Pte.	Killed	3-9-55	18-9-55
2534	Pinkard Richard	Pte.	Killed	23-4-55	15-5-55
*3527	Ward William	Pte.	Killed	13-7-55	27-7-55
3733	Watts Henry	Pte.	Killed	20-12-54	9-1-55
*3518	Thorton Thomas	Pte.	Killed	26-8-55	7-9-55
	Bale H. E.	Capt.	W/Sv	5-4-55	20-4-55
	Maxwell James	Capt.	W/Sv	25-5-55	12-6-55
	Boyce A. W.	Lieut.	W/Sl	11-6-55	26-6-55
	Laurie J. D.	Lieut.	W/Sl	25-8-55	7-9-55
	Lawrence H. M.	Lieut.	W/Sl	8-5-55	22-5-55
3138	Allen David	Sergt.	W/Sv	1-9-55	18-9-55
2743	Gridley John	Sergt.	W/D	3-4-55	20-4-55
3380	Strachan George	Sergt.	W/Sv	20-12-54	9-1-55
1062	Watson Alexander	Sergt.	W/Sl	4-7-55	17-7-55
2247	Willett B.	Sergt.	W/Sl	7-3-55	23-3-55
1004	Hope David	Corpl.	W/Sl	4-7-55	17-7-55
3869	McCoy John	Corpl.	W/Sv	31-8-55	18-9-55
3445	McCrickly James	Corpl.	W/Sv	22-3-55	3-4-55
3363	Stroud Samuel	Corpl.	W/Sv	9-6-55	22-6-55
3835	Wharton Joseph	Corpl.	W/Sl	5-4-55	20-4-55
2880	Wilcox Edwin	Corpl.	W/Sl	17-4-55	1-5-55
3812	Carr Richard	L/Cpl.	W/D	2-5-55	15-5-55
3114	Dunn William	Drummer	W/D	21-7-55	3-8-55
3533	Ashton George	Pte.	W/D	11-5-55	25-5-55
3113	Atchison George	Pte.	W/Sv	29-4-55	15-5-55
3144	Bates Jeremiah	Pte.	W/D	28-2-55	16-3-55
3375	Bowcott Edward	Pte.	W/Sv	20-12-54	9-1-55
3725	Boyce William	Pte.	W/D	9-7-55	24-7-55
2422	Breedon Joseph	Pte.	W/Sv	16-7-55	31-7-55
2948	Broply Clemence	Pte.	W/D	31-8-55	18-9-55
2395	Buckingham Philip	Pte.	W/Sv	29-8-55	11-9-55
3536	Burns Thomas	Pte.	W/Sl	3-4-55	20-4-55
3805	Campbell Hugh	Pte.	W/Sv	5-4-55	20-4-55
4139	Cardin Samuel	Pte.	W/Sl	29-8-55	11-9-55
3054	Caremore Joseph	Pte.	W/Sl	18-8-55	31-8-55
2507	Carey Michael	Pte.	W/Sv	15-7-55	27-7-55
1778	Chandler Isaac	Pte.	W/Sv	9-5-55	22-5-55
3415	Chapman Thomas	Pte.	W/Sv	3-7-55	17-7-55
3876	Coffey Timothy	Pte.	W/Sv	3-7-55	17-7-55
3376	Connall Monk	Pte.	W/Sv	22-3-55	3-4-55
3848	Connell Bartholomew	Pte.	W/Sv	20-12-54	9-1-55
4059	Cook James	Pte.	W/Sv	15-7-55	27-7-55
2477	Cook William	Pte.	W/Sl	6-4-55	20-4-55
3613	Copley William	Pte.	W/Sv	21-8-55	4-9-55
2837	Cormac James	Pte.	W/Sv	13-6-55	26-6-55
1991	Curry Daniel	Pte.	W/Sl	17-8-55	31-8-55
4115	Dally William	Pte.	W/Sv	15-7-55	27-7-55
2983	Day John	Pte.	W/Sv	5-5-55	18-5-55
3223	Donnelly Peter	Pte.	W/Sv	18-8-55	31-8-55

NOTES

The Second, Third, Fourth, Fifth and Final Bombardment of Sebastopol, and Minor Actions

34th REGIMENT OF FOOT

NO.	NAME	RANK	CASUALTY	DATE	LONDON GAZETTE
3914	Doyle Owen	Pte.	W/Sl	29-8-55	11-9-55
2477	Dwyer John	Pte.	W/Sv	9-5-55	22-5-55
3601	Dyer John	Pte.	W/Sv	13-5-55	25-5-55
2876	Earley Bernard	Pte.	W/Sl	16-7-55	31-7-55
3824	Egan Patrick	Pte.	W/D	29-8-55	11-9-55
3936	Farnan D.	Pte.	W/Sv	2-8-55	14-8-55
3253	Fitzpatrick John	Pte.	W/D	5-9-55	18-9-55
4823	Flannagan Patrick	Pte.	W/Sl	30-3-55	20-4-55
2832	Freeman George	Pte.	W/Sl	29-6-55	17-7-55
2327	Fulwell George	Pte.	W/D	12-5-55	25-5-55
3354	Gannon James	Pte.	W/Sl	24-8-55	7-9-55
3857	Gornan William	Pte.	W/D	29-4-55	15-5-55
2601	Harligan Robert	Pte.	W/Sl	21-8-55	4-9-55
4187	Harris Joseph	Pte.	W/Sl	29-8-55	11-9-55
3889	Hazlewood James	Pte.	W/Sv	13-6-55	26-6-55
3400	Heydon Thomas	Pte.	W/Sv	22-3-55	3-4-55
1615	Hinscoe Ralph	Pte.	W/Sl	27-4-55	15-5-55
3650	Hitchins Thomas	Pte.	W/Sv	20-12-54	9-1-55
1647	Hughes Robert	Pte.	W/Sv	18-3-55	30-3-55
3773	Humphries Andrew	Pte.	W/Sv	18-3-55	30-3-55
3505	Hutton William	Pte.	W/Sv	22-3-55	3-4-55
3084	Igo John	Pte.	W/Sl	27-6-55	10-7-55
3244	Keenahan William	Pte.	W/D	15-7-55	27-7-55
3651	King Joseph	Pte.	W/Sl	16-7-55	31-7-55
2871	Latimer David	Pte.	W/Sv	17-8-55	31-8-55
2734	Loft Thomas	Pte.	W/Sl	4-7-55	17-7-55
3129	Logne John	Pte.	W/Sl	16-7-55	31-7-55
3129	Logne John	Pte.	W/Sv	13-6-55	26-6-55
3543	Lovejoy Thomas	Pte.	W/Sl	27-4-55	15-5-55
1966	Lynch James	Pte.	W/Sv	22-3-55	3-4-55
3208	Lynch Patrick	Pte.	W/Sl	7-5-55	22-5-55
3983	McAteer Robert	Pte.	W/Sl	18-5-55	5-6-55
4022	McCabe William	Pte.	W/Sl	17-4-55	1-5-55
3679	McCarthy Charles	Pte.	W/Sl	13-6-55	26-6-55
3778	McCreagh Peter	Pte.	W/Sv	20-12-54	9-1-55
2119	McGowan James	Pte.	W/Sv	29-4-55	15-5-55
3307	McMahon John	Pte.	W/Sl	11-8-55	24-8-55
3237	McNamara Patrick	Pte.	W/Sv	8-4-55	20-4-55
3734	Mahoney Peter	Pte.	W/Sv	18-4-55	1-5-55
3003	Mansfield Joseph	Pte.	W/D	29-4-55	15-5-55
3506	Morris Henry	Pte.	W/Sl	31-8-55	18-9-55
3693	Morris John	Pte.	W/Sv	3-4-55	20-4-55
2607	Morton J.	Pte.	W/Sl	8-8-55	21-8-55
1335	Munro Jonathan	Pte.	W/Sl	4-7-55	17-7-55
3648	Murphy Charles	Pte.	W/D	24-8-55	7-9-55
3737	Murphy James	Pte.	W/Sv	9-5-55	22-5-55
3235	Noland Christopher	Pte.	W/Sv	5-4-55	20-4-55
2414	Roach John	Pte.	W/Sl	29-4-55	15-5-55
3137	Robinson Joseph	Pte.	W/Sl	3-5-55	15-5-55
3489	Rostron Christopher	Pte.	W/Sl	23-4-55	15-5-55
3548	Rostron H.	Pte.	W/Sl	16-7-55	31-7-55
4015	Short Patrick	Pte.	W/Sl	3-5-55	15-5-55
2786	Silk W.	Pte.	W/Sl	26-8-55	7-9-55
3290	Smith William	Pte.	W/Sv	19-4-55	1-5-55
3147	Spruce Robert	Pte.	W/Sv	25-6-55	10-7-55
2316	Taylor Charles	Pte.	W/D	26-6-55	10-7-55
3044	Thompson James	Pte.	W/Sl	5-8-55	17-8-55
3518	Thornton Thomas	Pte.	W/Sl	18-8-55	31-8-55
2669	Todd Michael	Pte.	W/D	3-5-55	15-5-55
2477	Tremble Richard	Pte.	W/D	3-5-55	15-5-55
3271	Turbady Michael	Pte.	W/Sv	11-5-55	25-5-55
3665	Vinning Sidney	Pte.	W/Sl	18-3-55	30-3-55
3554	Walmsley W.	Pte.	W/Sl	8-8-55	21-8-55
3687	Walsh Richard	Pte.	W/Sl	13-6-55	26-6-55

NOTES

The Second, Third, Fourth, Fifth and Final Bombardment of Sebastopol, and Minor Actions

34th REGIMENT OF FOOT

NO.	NAME	RANK	CASUALTY	DATE	LONDON GAZETTE
3200	Ward Joseph	Pte.	W/Sv	22-3-55	3-4-55
4046	Wetherall James	Pte.	W/Sl	21-7-55	3-8-55
3977	White Thomas	Pte.	W/Sv	6-8-55	21-8-55
3900	Whittaker Alfred	Pte.	W/D	12-5-55	25-5-55
3988	Whittle Matthew	Pte.	W/Sl	5-9-55	18-9-55
3818	Willox James	Pte.	W/Sl	29-5-55	12-6-55
3608	Wilson William	Pte.	W/Sl	29-6-55	17-7-55
3298	Wood John	Pte.	W/Sl	19-5-55	5-6-55
3298	Wood John	Pte.	W/Sl	31-8-55	18-9-55
2025	Worstall Josiah	Pte.	W/D	3-5-55	15-5-55
3701	Young Peter	Pte.	W/Sv	15-4-55	1-5-55
	Kelly R. D.	Brevet Lt/Col.	P.O.W.	22-3-55	3-4-55
	Byron J.	Lieut.	Missing	20-12-54	9-1-55
2419	Bonham John	Pte.	Missing	22-3-55	3-4-55
4020	Healy Martin	Pte.	Missing	22-3-55	3-4-55
3168	Robinson Wm. Henry	Pte.	Missing	22-3-55	3-4-55
3275	Willis William	Pte.	Missing	22-3-55	3-4-55

38th REGIMENT OF FOOT

NO.	NAME	RANK	CASUALTY	DATE	LONDON GAZETTE
3299	Flaherty James	Sergt.	Killed	21-5-55	5-6-55
2031	McGhee R.	Sergt.	Killed	4-8-55	17-8-55
3871	Murdoch John	L/Cpl.	Killed	15-5-55	29-5-55
3624	Blair Alexander	Pte.	Killed	20-12-54	9-1-55
3945	Donnelly Patrick	Pte.	Killed	6-12-55	29-12-55
3481	Kerr Duncan	Pte.	Killed	6-12-55	29-12-55
3928	Wooding J.	Pte.	Killed	11-8-55	24-8-55
	Vaughan J. C.	Capt.	W/Sv	15-6-55	3-7-55
	Dickins C. A. S.	Lieut.	W/Sv	2-7-55	17-7-55
	Gaynor Constantine S.	Lieut.	W/Sv	21-2-55	16-3-55
3227	Egan Owen	Sergt.	W/Sl	4-9-55	18-9-55
2754	Neill James	Sergt.	W/Sv	4-12-54	29-12-54
1313	Winden Samuel	Sergt.	W/Sl	28-1-55	29-12-55
2313	Simins John	L/Sgt.	W/Sv	27-5-55	12-6-55
2123	Baldwin William	Corpl.	W/Sl	15-11-55	11-12-55
2969	Bell Joseph	L/Cpl.	W/Sv	30-12-54	26-1-55
2634	Meehan Owen	L/Cpl.	W/Sl	21-5-55	5-6-55
2558	Mullins James	L/Cpl.	W/Sl	20-4-55	4-5-55
2632	Quicke Michael	L/Cpl.	W/Sl	16-4-55	1-5-55
3939	Swan Alfred	L/Cpl.	W/Sv	11-6-55	26-6-55
2857	Williams John	L/Cpl.	W/Sv	2-5-55	15-5-55
4139	Antill Robert	Pte.	W/Sv	21-6-55	3-7-55
3790	Archer William	Pte.	W/Sl	20-4-55	4-5-55
3206	Atkins James	Pte.	W/Sl	22-12-54	9-1-55
3695	Baigent George	Pte.	W/Sl	15-6-55	3-7-55
2828	Bird Michael	Pte.	W/Sv	15-1-55	6-2-55
3792	Boot Joseph	Pte.	W/Sv	18-8-55	31-8-55
4273	Bright James	Pte.	W/Sl	5-9-55	18-9-55
4101	Burke Thomas	Pte.	W/Sl	21-5-55	5-6-55
3091	Carroll John	Pte.	W/Sv	30-3-55	20-4-55
4092	Casey Thomas	Pte.	W/Sl	17-4-55	1-5-55
3814	Collins Thomas	Pte.	W/Sv	14-2-55	27-2-55
3635	Cooke John	Pte.	W/Sv	19-8-55	31-8-55
3139	Crozier William	Pte.	W/Sl	10-12-55	29-12-55
4037	Cumer William	Pte.	W/Sl	24-5-55	5-6-55
3979	Deverett Joseph	Pte.	W/Sl	15-3-55	23-3-55
3850	Dignan John	Pte.	W/Sl	20-4-55	4-5-55
3493	Donovan Dennis	Pte.	W/Sv	11-1-55	26-1-55
3331	Dudman Charles	Pte.	W/Sv	28-8-55	11-9-55
3622	Elsip Edwin	Pte.	W/Sv	23-1-55	9-2-55

NOTES

The Second, Third, Fourth, Fifth and Final Bombardment of Sebastopol, and Minor Actions

38th REGIMENT OF FOOT

NO.	NAME	RANK	CASUALTY	DATE	LONDON GAZETTE
1737	Finn William	Pte.	W/Sl	22-11-54	11-12-54
2557	Fitzgibbon Austin	Pte.	W/Sl	23-1-55	9-2-55
3542	Frawley William	Pte.	W/Sv	7-1-55	26-1-55
3993	Grey Thomas	Pte.	W/Sl	3-9-55	18-9-55
3811	Groghagan James	Pte.	W/Sl	24-8-55	7-9-55
2699	Hague Thomas	Pte.	W/D	4-9-55	18-9-55
2727	Haines John	Pte.	W/D	28-6-55	10-7-55
3856	Hamilton David	Pte.	W/Sv	16-4-55	1-5-55
1623	Hannaforth John	Pte.	W/Sl	28-11-54	29-12-54
3523	Haynes Francis	Pte.	W/Sv	12-3-55	23-3-55
3857	Healy Matthew	Pte.	W/Sv	19-8-55	31-8-55
3171	Hendley George	Pte.	W/Sl	23-8-55	4-9-55
3347	Hoban Daniel	Pte.	W/Sv	15-6-55	3-7-55
3677	Holmes James	Pte.	W/Sv	17-7-55	31-7-55
3678	Hughes John	Pte.	W/Sv	21-6-55	3-7-55
3085	Hunt Cornelius	Pte.	W/Sv	16-1-55	6-2-55
3377	Ibbs William	Pte.	W/Sl	28-11-55	29-12-55
3338	Kidler George	Pte.	W/Sv	18-12-55	29-12-55
3690	Linnahan Joseph	Pte.	W/Sl	5-8-55	17-8-55
3529	Lowe Thomas	Pte.	W/Sv	19-8-55	31-8-55
3835	McCabe William	Pte.	W/Sv	11-6-55	26-6-55
3892	McCarthy Denis	Pte.	W/Sl	21-7-55	3-8-55
4048	McCasker John	Pte.	W/Sl	21-6-55	3-7-55
4048	McCasker John	Pte.	W/Sl	15-5-55	29-5-55
3150	McConnell Alexander	Pte.	W/Sv	5-7-55	17-7-55
3863	McGrickian John	Pte.	W/Sl	29-7-55	7-8-55
3282	Malpas William	Pte.	W/Sl	20-12-55	26-12-55
3382	Manson Edward	Pte.	W/Sv	28-4-55	15-5-55
2976	Mayle Patrick	Pte.	W/Sl	5-8-55	17-8-55
3868	Miller John	Pte.	W/Sv	28-4-55	15-5-55
1166	Nicholson N.	Pte.	W/Sl	11-8-55	24-8-55
3558	Nugent John	Pte.	W/Sl	28-11-55	29-12-55
3353	O'Callaghan Roderick	Pte.	W/Sl	3-9-55	18-9-55
3482	O'Neil Hugh	Pte.	W/Sl	17-8-55	31-8-55
3327	Paisingham James	Pte.	W/Sv	22-12-54	9-1-55
3979	Peverett Joseph	Pte.	W/Sl	15-3-55	27-3-55
3791	Rice William	Pte.	W/Sv	9-7-55	24-7-55
3942	Ricker John	Pte.	W/Sv	26-4-55	15-5-55
3335	Rowe James	Pte.	W/Sl	19-8-55	31-8-55
2156	Sell John	Pte.	W/Sv	20-12-55	26-12-55
3489	Shearman James	Pte.	W/Sv	23-1-55	9-2-55
1232	Smith Owen	Pte.	W/Sl	24-8-55	7-9-55
3606	Stiesson W.	Pte.	W/Sv	29-7-55	7-8-55
3989	Sullivan Daniel	Pte.	W/Sl	24-8-55	7-9-55
3718	Sutton Frederick B.	Pte.	W/Sl	24-8-55	7-9-55
3112	Thompson Robert	Pte.	W/Sv	4-9-55	18-9-55
3931	Tullison Timothy	Pte.	W/Sl	11-5-55	25-5-55
3422	Tyler Charles	Pte.	W/Sl	19-3-55	3-4-55
4165	Walker John	Pte.	W/Sl	21-6-55	3-7-55
2561	Wilson John	Pte.	W/Sl	18-12-55	26-12-55
3077	Woodley James	Pte.	W/Sv	15-1-55	11-12-55
4214	Wright William	Pte.	W/Sl	26-7-55	7-8-55

39th REGIMENT OF FOOT

NO.	NAME	RANK	CASUALTY	DATE	LONDON GAZETTE
	Mannsell E. B.	Capt.	Killed	10-7-55	24-7-55
2810	Roan William	Corpl.	Killed	25-7-55	7-8-55
3322	Phillips William	L/Cpl.	Killed	26-7-55	7-8-55
2920	Kennedy W.	Pte.	Killed	11-8-55	24-8-55
3109	O'Callaghan James	Pte.	Killed	25-2-55	16-3-55

NOTES

The Second, Third, Fourth, Fifth and Final Bombardment of Sebastopol, and Minor Actions

39th REGIMENT OF FOOT

NO.	NAME	RANK	CASUALTY	DATE	LONDON GAZETTE
1709	Rudd James	Col/Sgt.	W/Sv	29-3-55	10-4-55
2773	Terniey Patrick	L/Sgt.	W/Sl	20-7-55	3-8-55
1602	Breen James	Corpl.	W/Sv	10-7-55	24-7-55
3384	Field Joseph	Corpl.	W/M	19-6-55	3-7-55
1787	Green George	Corpl.	W/Sl	30-6-55	17-7-55
2366	Kenelly Daniel	Corpl.	W/Sv	15-4-55	1-5-55
1487	O'Maley Thomas	Corpl.	W/Sl	15-7-55	27-7-55
2937	Togg George	Corpl.	W/M	12-4-55	24-4-55
3703	Allen P.	Pte.	W/Sl	11-8-55	24-8-55
3657	Asern Charles	Pte.	W/Sl	10-7-55	24-7-55
2464	Behan John	Pte.	W/Sl	10-5-55	22-5-55
2258	Brennan P.	Pte.	W/Sl	11-8-55	24-8-55
2428	Brown Joseph	Pte.	W/Sl	26-8-55	7-9-55
3325	Cane James	Pte.	W/Sl	26-7-55	7-8-55
3704	Connors Michael	Pte.	W/Sl	10-7-55	24-7-55
3136	Emery John	Pte.	W/Sl	10-5-55	22-5-55
3021	Fell Peter	Pte.	W/Sv	12-4-55	24-4-55
3338	Finneran Patrick	Pte.	W/Sl	10-7-55	24-7-55
3332	Flynn Patrick	Pte.	W/Sl	2-7-55	17-7-55
3458	Gologhy Thomas	Pte.	W/Sl	25-5-55	12-6-55
3491	Hunter Samuel	Pte.	W/Sl	16-8-55	7-9-55
3844	Hullett Charles	Pte.	W/Sl	10-7-55	24-7-55
3484	Jones George	Pte.	W/Sl	16-8-55	28-8-55
2195	Kileahy Patrick	Pte.	W/Sl	26-7-55	7-8-55
2437	Lynam J.	Pte.	W/Sl	11-8-55	24-8-55
2980	McCarthy Cornelius	Pte.	W/Sl	20-7-55	3-8-55
3382	McEwen John	Pte.	W/Sl	26-7-55	7-8-55
3572	Mitchell Robert	Pte.	W/Sl	2-8-55	14-8-55
3658	Morgan William	Pte.	W/Sl	7-4-55	20-4-55
2544	Neil James	Pte.	W/Sl	30-6-55	17-7-55
3511	Neville Patrick	Pte.	W/Sl	22-5-55	5-6-55
3511	Neville Patrick	Pte.	W/Sl	10-7-55	24-7-55
2774	Quill Daniel	Pte.	W/Sl	1-5-55	15-5-55
2360	Ridewood Alfred	Pte.	W/Sl	15-4-55	1-5-55
3927	Ryan M.	Pte.	W/D	11-8-55	24-8-55
3256	Ryan Michael	Pte.	W/Sl	23-5-55	5-6-55
1996	Stober Robert	Pte.	W/Sl	15-7-55	27-7-55
3697	Swales Joseph	Pte.	W/Sv	20-7-55	3-8-55
3493	Sullivan Daniel	Pte.	W/Sl	14-6-55	26-6-55
3804	Wright William	Pte.	W/Sl	14-8-55	28-8-55

41st REGIMENT OF FOOT

NO.	NAME	RANK	CASUALTY	DATE	LONDON GAZETTE
1908	Dungan Peter	Col/Sgt.	Killed	23-8-55	4-9-55
2161	Lee John	Corpl.	Killed	26-5-55	12-6-55
3499	Bragg William	Pte.	Killed	4-9-55	18-9-55
3073	Carroll Francis	Pte.	Killed	5-9-55	18-9-55
3634	Conlon Michael	Pte.	Killed	27-7-55	7-8-55
3502	Connolly John	Pte.	Killed	23-4-55	15-5-55
2247	Cunningham Patrick	Pte.	Killed	12-3-55	23-3-55
3701	Dodge Thomas	Pte.	Killed	1-9-55	18-9-55
2815	Fitzgibbons James	Pte.	Killed	9-5-55	22-5-55
3366	Harman Thomas	Pte.	Killed	8-8-55	21-8-55
1815	Jones George	Pte.	Killed	4-9-55	18-9-55
2984	Kary Patrick	Pte.	Killed	31-8-55	18-9-55
2864	Kean John	Pte.	Killed	23-4-55	15-5-55
2492	Keefe Dennis	Pte.	Killed	15-6-55	3-7-55
3009	McGoldrick William	Pte.	Killed	18-5-55	5-6-55
3515	McReady John	Pte.	Killed	23-8-55	4-9-55
2646	Maitland William	Pte.	Killed	21-4-55	1-5-55

NOTES

The Second, Third, Fourth, Fifth and Final Bombardment of Sebastopol, and Minor Actions

41st REGIMENT OF FOOT

NO.	NAME	RANK	CASUALTY	DATE	LONDON GAZETTE
1239	Phelps George	Pte.	Killed	7-12-54	26-12-54
3194	Regan James	Pte.	Killed	30-7-55	14-8-55
3235	Reynolds Bernard	Pte.	Killed	20-3-55	9-4-55
3625	Reynolds Patrick	Pte.	Killed	23-8-55	4-9-55
1808	Rigsby William	Pte.	Killed	26-8-55	7-9-55
3695	Weeble William	Pte.	Killed	22-6-55	9-7-55
3520	Wilson John	Pte.	Killed	30-7-55	14-8-55
	Graham L.	Bvt./Mjr.	W/Sv	29-8-55	11-9-55
	Baird James	Lieut.	W/Sl	9-6-55	22-6-55
1263	Fitzpatrick John	Col/Sgt.	W/D	16-4-55	1-5-55
1666	Anderson James	Sergt.	W/Sl	17-8-55	31-8-55
1778	Clunn William	Sergt.	W/Sv	27-6-55	10-7-55
1383	Corfield George	Sergt.	W/Sv	30-4-55	15-5-55
2316	Crawford William	Sergt.	W/Sl	13-8-55	28-8-55
2404	Ford Daniel	Sergt.	W/Sv	5-5-55	18-5-55
2698	Hurley Patrick	Sergt.	W/Sv	2-3-55	16-3-55
3388	Allum Samuel	Corpl.	W/Sv	20-4-55	4-5-55
2746	Creedon John	Corpl.	W/Sl	4-8-55	17-8-55
1255	Davies James	Corpl.	W/Sl	20-4-55	4-5-55
2367	Dowling Francis	Corpl.	W/Sl	17-8-55	31-8-55
2267	Ivers Richard	Corpl.	W/Sl	13-3-55	23-3-55
2584	O'Dea Martin	Corpl.	W/Sl	4-8-55	17-8-55
2959	Putland Henry	Corpl.	W/Sl	10-8-55	24-8-55
2138	Valentine John	Corpl.	D.O.W.	2-4-55	20-4-55
2197	Wilson John	L/Cpl.	W/Sl	13-6-55	26-6-55
2858	Carberry Michael	Drummer	W/Sl	23-7-55	7-8-55
3029	Armsby George	Pte.	W/Sl	29-6-55	17-7-55
3044	Banbury William	Pte.	W/Sl	16-8-55	28-8-55
3653	Bannister John	Pte.	W/Sl	8-8-55	21-8-55
1414	Bishop Joseph	Pte.	W/Sv	3-7-55	17-7-55
3243	Boland Denis	Pte.	W/Sl	4-7-55	17-7-55
1199	Bolter Thomas	Pte.	W/D	8-8-55	21-8-55
3024	Bourke John	Pte.	W/Sl	30-7-55	14-8-55
3747	Bowles Jacob	Pte.	W/Sv	13-7-55	27-7-55
3663	Brennan Maurice	Pte.	W/Sl	16-8-55	28-8-55
2997	Bunly Robert	Pte.	W/Sl	16-8-55	28-8-55
2430	Burke John	Pte.	W/M	20-4-55	4-5-55
3367	Burke Patrick	Pte.	W/Sv	4-9-55	18-9-55
2367	Burke Patrick	Pte.	W/Sv	18-2-55	6-3-55
2186	Butler Thomas	Pte.	W/Sv	27-8-55	11-9-55
3603	Byrne John	Pte.	W/Sl	16-8-55	28-8-55
3266	Callinan Michael	Pte.	W/Sl	30-7-55	14-8-55
2321	Carney Michael	Pte.	W/Sl	30-7-55	14-8-55
2220	Carter Benjamin	Pte.	W/Sl	10-8-55	24-8-55
3571	Cashman Timothy	Pte.	W/Sl	15-8-55	28-8-55
3681	Chapman William	Pte.	W/D	25-8-55	7-9-55
3207	Colgan Richard	Pte.	W/Sl	8-5-55	22-5-55
3207	Colgan Richard	Pte.	W/Sl	10-8-55	24-8-55
2486	Connell Denis	Pte.	W/Sv	29-4-55	15-5-55
3702	Conolly Thomas	Pte.	W/Sv	22-8-55	4-9-55
3460	Conway Michael	Pte.	W/Sv	26-4-55	15-5-55
3460	Conway Michael	Pte.	W/Sl	30-7-55	14-8-55
2653	Coughlan William	Pte.	W/Sv	20-4-55	4-5-55
3450	Creig John	Pte.	W/Sv	15-4-55	1-5-55
3205	Crougham James	Pte.	W/Sv	9-4-55	24-4-55
3234	Cunningham Patrick	Pte.	W/Sl	25-8-55	7-9-55
3356	Curry Thomas	Pte.	W/Sl	25-8-55	7-9-55
2280	Davis John	Pte.	W/Sv	9-5-55	22-5-55
1831	Davis Thomas	Pte.	W/Sv	29-4-55	15-5-55
3200	Dawson Arthur	Pte.	W/Sl	10-8-55	24-8-55
2122	Doherty Simon	Pte.	W/Sv	22-8-55	4-9-55
2361	Downes James	Pte.	W/Sl	14-3-55	23-3-55
2518	Driscoll Timothy	Pte.	W/Sl	10-5-55	22-5-55
3815	Dunnigan Richard	Pte.	W/Sl	8-8-55	21-8-55

NOTES

The Second, Third, Fourth, Fifth and Final Bombardment of Sebastopol, and Minor Actions

41st REGIMENT OF FOOT

NO.	NAME	RANK	CASUALTY	DATE	LONDON GAZETTE
3150	Ennie Michael	Pte.	W/Sl	23-7-55	7-8-55
3150	Ennie Michael	Pte.	W/Sl	4-9-55	18-9-55
3335	Ennis Patrick	Pte.	W/Sl	21-4-55	4-5-55
3386	Erwin Andrew	Pte.	W/Sl	17-8-55	31-8-55
2364	Evans John	Pte.	W/Sl	14-3-55	23-3-55
2609	Farmer John	Pte.	W/Sv	3-1-55	26-1-55
3330	Fenwick George	Pte.	W/D	20-4-55	4-5-55
3476	Ferguson Christopher	Pte.	W/Sl	15-4-55	1-5-55
3476	Ferguson Christopher	Pte.	W/D	25-5-55	12-6-55
3273	Gaffney John	Pte.	W/Sl	20-4-55	4-5-55
1817	Garrard Edward	Pte.	W/Sl	20-4-55	4-5-55
2279	Gee G. P.	Pte.	W/Sv	4-8-55	17-8-55
3140	Gready Peter	Pte.	W/Sl	10-5-55	22-5-55
3351	Greg William	Pte.	W/Sl	17-8-55	31-8-55
3446	Henry John	Pte.	W/Sl	21-4-55	4-5-55
3446	Henry John	Pte.	W/Sl	25-8-55	7-9-55
2796	Herlihy Patrick	Pte.	W/Sl	24-6-55	9-7-55
3260	Hickey John	Pte.	W/Sv	4-7-55	17-7-55
2680	Hughes James	Pte.	W/Sl	10-8-55	24-8-55
3766	Hughes John	Pte.	W/Sv	20-7-55	3-8-55
3178	Jackson Henry	Pte.	W/Sv	25-5-55	12-6-55
3284	Jeffers Patrick	Pte.	W/Sv	22-8-55	4-9-55
3652	Jones John	Pte.	W/Sl	12-8-55	24-8-55
2619	Joyce Walter	Pte.	W/Sl	17-7-55	31-7-55
2709	Kearney Pat	Pte.	W/Sl	29-4-55	15-5-55
2984	Keary Pat	Pte.	W/Sv	30-4-55	15-5-55
3122	Kennedy James	Pte.	W/Sl	27-4-55	15-5-55
2838	Kennedy Jason	Pte.	D.O.W	26-4-55	15-5-55
33097	Lewis William	Pte.	W/Sl	11-6-55	26-6-55
3545	Lowry Pat	Pte.	W/Sv	10-5-55	22-5-55
3621	Lowther John	Pte.	W/Sl	22-8-55	4-9-55
3513	McAlpine Allen	Pte.	W/Sl	25-5-55	12-6-55
2811	McBride Patrick	Pte.	W/Sl	25-8-55	7-9-55
3139	McGee Patrick	Pte.	W/Sv	29-7-55	7-8-55
3643	McGrath James	Pte.	W/Sl	5-7-55	17-7-55
3643	McGrath James	Pte.	W/Sv	29-7-55	7-8-55
3443	McGrath James	Pte.	W/Sv	10-8-55	24-8-55
3628	McNamara Henry	Pte.	W/Sv	28-6-55	10-7-55
3012	McPherson Thomas	Pte.	W/Sl	27-6-55	10-7-55
3515	McReady John	Pte.	W/Sl	29-4-55	15-5-55
3153	Maguire George	Pte.	W/Sv	9-6-55	22-6-55
3455	Malony John	Pte.	W/Sl	21-4-55	4-5-55
3593	Mannix William	Pte.	W/Sv	4-8-55	17-8-55
3120	Mara Patrick	Pte.	W/Sv	5-5-55	18-5-55
2425	Markey Francis	Pte.	W/Sv	28-12-54	12-1-55
3650	Moore John	Pte.	W/Sl	21-6-55	3-7-55
3471	Morgan Christopher	Pte.	W/Sl	20-4-55	4-5-55
2689	Morresy Edward	Pte.	W/Sv	31-8-55	18-9-55
2786	Mulachy William	Pte.	W/Sl	25-5-55	12-6-55
3635	Murphy Michael	Pte.	W/Sl	5-9-55	18-9-55
1887	Murray Anthony	Pte.	W/Sl	9-6-55	22-6-55
1887	Murray Anthony	Pte.	W/Sv	23-7-55	7-8-55
2738	Navin John	Pte.	W/Sl	14-3-55	23-3-55
1801	Nelson Charles	Pte.	W/Sl	31-8-55	18-9-55
1164	Nowland Pat	Pte.	W/Sl	21-4-55	4-5-55
2434	O'Halloran Pat	Pte.	W/Sl	29-4-55	15-5-55
3223	O'Reilly Patrick	Pte.	W/Sl	8-7-55	20-7-55
3696	Pace James	Pte.	W/Sv	8-8-55	21-8-55
3413	Power Martin	Pte.	W/Sv	10-5-55	22-5-55
3329	Rainbird William	Pte.	W/Sv	5-9-55	18-9-55
3175	Really Patrick	Pte.	W/Sv	1-9-55	18-9-55
3414	Reed Alfred	Pte.	W/Sv	8-8-55	21-8-55
2940	Regan Denis	Pte.	W/Sv	27-4-55	15-5-55
2302	Richardson Michael	Pte.	W/Sl	8-8-55	21-8-55

NOTES

The Second, Third, Fourth, Fifth and Final Bombardment of Sebastopol, and Minor Actions

41st REGIMENT OF FOOT

NO.	NAME	RANK	CASUALTY	DATE	LONDON GAZETTE
2979	Rogan Martin	Pte.	W/Sl	20-4-55	4-5-55
3541	Skinner Robert	Pte.	W/Sl	21-4-55	4-5-55
2405	Smullen Patrick	Pte.	W/Sl	25-8-55	7-9-55
3128	Sullivan John	Pte.	W/Sl	22-8-55	4-9-55
3488	Sullivan John	Pte.	W/Sv	24-4-55	15-5-55
2320	Sutherland John	Pte.	W/Sv	7-5-55	22-5-55
3552	Takey Martin	Pte.	W/Sl	18-4-55	1-5-55
2740	Thomas John	Pte.	W/Sv	23-4-55	15-5-55
2387	Tipler William	Pte.	W/Sl	27-8-55	11-9-55
3200	Tremble Pat	Pte.	W/Sl	29-4-55	15-5-55
1355	Turner Henry	Pte.	W/Sl	21-4-55	4-5-55
1355	Turner Henry	Pte.	W/Sv	17-8-55	31-8-55
3560	Walker George	Pte.	W/Sl	9-6-55	22-6-55
1725	Williams John	Pte.	W/Sl	4-5-55	18-5-55
1866	Wilson Joseph	Pte.	W/D	8-8-55	21-8-55
3381	Woodrough Thomas	Pte.	W/Sl	5-5-55	18-5-55
1729	Wormington Thomas	Pte.	W/Sl	5-5-55	18-5-55

42nd REGIMENT OF FOOT

NO.	NAME	RANK	CASUALTY	DATE	LONDON GAZETTE
	Fraser R. A.	Capt.	Killed	17-7-55	31-7-55
3235	Mahoney Michael	L/Cpl.	Killed	1-8-55	14-8-55
2774	Baxter Alexander	Pte.	Killed	17-7-55	31-7-55
3137	Clarke John	Pte.	Killed	16-8-55	28-8-55
3389	Gray William	Pte.	Killed	23-6-55	9-7-55
3100	Hanrahan Patrick	Pte.	Killed	19-8-55	31-8-55
3776	McDonald Robert	Pte.	Killed	13-8-55	28-8-55
3400	McLeod Alexander	Pte.	Killed	4-7-55	17-7-55
3194	Milne John	Pte.	Killed	11-7-55	24-7-55
3162	Muir John	Pte.	Killed	26-7-55	7-8-55
3462	Sutherland Daniel	Pte.	Killed	17-7-55	31-7-55
	Ward W. C.	Capt.	W/Sl	13-8-55	28-8-55
	Hesketh W. D.	Ensign	W/Sl	16-8-55	28-8-55
1866	Forsyth Samuel	Sergt.	W/Sl	17-7-55	31-7-55
2089	Smith John	Corpl.	W/D	17-7-55	31-7-55
1728	Blillock John	L/Cpl.	W/Sv	26-7-55	7-8-55
1986	Hartley Joseph	L/Cpl.	W/Sl	8-7-55	20-7-55
2851	Hossack Alexander	L/Cpl.	W/Sl	1-7-55	17-7-55
1520	Ingram Robert	L/Cpl.	W/Sv	4-8-55	17-8-55
2117	Barclay William	Pte.	W/D	29-6-55	17-7-55
3377	Bolger James	Pte.	W/Sl	24-6-55	9-7-55
2897	Brown Robert	Pte.	W/Sl	16-8-55	28-8-55
3352	Chalmers William	Pte.	W/Sv	13-8-55	28-8-55
3388	Connell Hugh	Pte.	W/Sv	16-8-55	28-8-55
3513	Cook Henry	Pte.	W/Sv	3-7-55	17-7-55
3229	Cooper Samuel	Pte.	W/Sl	8-7-55	20-7-55
2817	Crombie Andrew	Pte.	W/Sv	24-6-55	9-7-55
3462	Cruickshanks William	Pte.	W/Sv	17-7-55	31-7-55
2347	Douglas David	Pte.	W/Sv	27-6-55	10-7-55
3172	Dunlop David	Pte.	W/Sl	11-7-55	24-7-55
3241	Fegan John	Pte.	W/D	1-8-55	14-8-55
3112	Fitzgerald Richard	Pte.	W/Sv	17-7-55	31-7-55
3517	Formby John	Pte.	W/Sl	7-8-55	21-8-55
3024	Fraser Donald	Pte.	W/Sl	23-7-55	7-8-55
2566	Gilchrist James	Pte.	W/D	16-8-55	28-8-55
1751	Graham John	Pte.	W/Sl	19-8-55	31-8-55
2959	Hamilton William	Pte.	W/Sl	11-7-55	24-7-55
3094	Hannua Festus	Pte.	W/Sv	7-8-55	21-8-55
2103	Herron Alexander	Pte.	W/Sl	1-8-55	14-8-55
3101	Holder Thomas	Pte.	W/Sl	29-6-55	17-7-55

NOTES

The Second, Third, Fourth, Fifth and Final Bombardment of Sebastopol, and Minor Actions

42nd REGIMENT OF FOOT

NO.	NAME	RANK	CASUALTY	DATE	LONDON GAZETTE
1732	Ingram Peter	Pte.	W/Sv	19-8-55	31-8-55
2225	Jack James	Pte.	W/Sl	16-8-55	28-8-55
2585	Jack Robert	Pte.	W/Sl	13-8-55	28-8-55
3593	Logan James	Pte.	W/Sl	7-8-55	21-8-55
3325	Luckins William	Pte.	W/Sl	26-6-55	10-7-55
1913	McCulloch Daniel	Pte.	W/Sl	13-8-55	28-8-55
2247	McDonald David	Pte.	W/D	27-6-55	10-7-55
3356	McDonald Donald	Pte.	W/Sl	7-8-55	21-8-55
2369	McDougall Duncan	Pte.	W/Sv	7-8-55	21-8-55
2908	McDougall D.	Pte.	W/D	20-7-55	3-8-55
1915	McFarlane A.	Pte.	W/Sv	20-7-55	3-8-55
3523	McLaren Thomas	Pte.	W/D	22-8-55	4-9-55
2976	McLeod Angus	Pte.	W/Sl	26-7-55	7-8-55
2094	McNair Robert	Pte.	W/Sl	10-8-55	24-8-55
3700	McNeil Neil	Pte.	W/Sv	7-8-55	21-8-55
2536	Martin Thomas	Pte.	W/Sv	2-7-55	17-7-55
1768	Miller Robert	Pte.	W/Sl	20-7-55	31-7-55
3569	Milne Alexander	Pte.	W/Sl	23-7-55	7-8-55
3094	Noonan John	Pte.	W/Sl	22-8-55	4-9-55
3384	O'Neil James	Pte.	W/Sl	29-7-55	7-8-55
2997	Rennie William	Pte.	W/Sl	20-7-55	3-8-55
2336	Thompson Thomas	Pte.	W/Sl	29-7-55	7-8-55
3092	Warner John	Pte.	W/Sl	1-8-55	14-8-55
1127	Willack Matthew	Pte.	W/Sv	2-7-55	17-7-55
1197	Williamson John	Pte.	W/Sl	11-7-55	24-7-55
1197	Williamson John	Pte.	W/Sl	19-8-55	31-8-55
3620	Dick William	L/Cpl.	Missing	7-8-55	21-8-55

44th REGIMENT OF FOOT

NO.	NAME	RANK	CASUALTY	DATE	LONDON GAZETTE
2535	Claire Matthew	Pte.	Killed	20-1-55	6-2-55
4016	Feagan James	Pte.	Killed	13-8-55	28-8-55
1978	Greenfield Thomas	Pte.	Killed	1-2-55	20-2-55
2262	McNamara M.	Pte.	Killed	25-2-55	16-3-55
3164	Patterson James	Pte.	Killed	13-8-55	28-8-55
	Thoroton L.	Capt.	W/Sl	28-7-55	7-8-55
2634	Kelly Oscar	Sergt.	W/Sl	19-8-55	31-8-55
2932	McIlroy Isaac	Sergt.	W/Sl	13-2-55	2-3-55
2590	White Smythson	L/Sgt.	W/Sl	15-8-55	28-8-55
3820	Courtenay William	Corpl	W/Sv	4-12-54	29-12-54
3366	Torpy Patrick	Corpl	W/Sl	23-11-54	29-12-54
3338	Trodan Patrick	Corpl.	W/D	1-5-55	15-5-55
3796	Evans John	L/Cpl.	W/Sl	28-7-55	7-8-55
4089	Arnold Humphrey	Pte.	W/Sv	20-6-55	3-7-55
3674	Baker John	Pte.	W/Sl	9-11-55	11-12-55
4205	Baker Joseph	Pte.	W/Sl	20-3-55	3-4-55
3805	Bergin Robert	Pte.	W/Sv	20-11-55	11-12-55
3239	Burns John	Pte.	W/Sl	8-1-55	2-2-55
1650	Canthers Robert	Pte.	W/Sl	28-6-55	10-7-55
—	Chambers Alexander	Pte.	W/Sv	16-6-55	3-7-55
3677	Conolly Patrick	Pte.	W/Sv	8-6-55	22-6-55
3184	Dixon James	Pte.	W/Sl	14-8-55	28-8-55
3617	Dudgeon John	Pte.	W/Sl	23-11-54	29-12-54
3147	Dugan James	Pte.	W/Sl	4-8-55	17-8-55
3923	Dunohy Thomas	Pte.	W/Sl	14-8-55	28-8-55
3769	Elliot John	Pte	W/Sv	8-6-55	22-6-55
2779	Evans Charles	Pte.	W/Sv	9-11-55	11-12-55
3195	Firkins John	Pte.	W/Sv	8-6-55	22-6-55
3845	Griffiths Richard	Pte.	W/Sv	24-3-55	10-4-55
2513	Hullohan Patrick	Pte.	W/Sv	4-1-55	26-1-55

NOTES

The Second, Third, Fourth, Fifth and Final Bombardment of Sebastopol, and Minor Actions

44th REGIMENT OF FOOT

NO.	NAME	RANK	CASUALTY	DATE	LONDON GAZETTE
3649	Keefe W.	Pte.	W/Sv	13-8-55	28-8-55
2506	Kelly Festus	Pte.	W/Sv	12-1-55	2-2-55
3757	Kelly John	Pte.	W/D	1-5-55	15-5-55
3939	Leahy John	Pte.	W/Sv	5-8-55	17-8-55
1867	Lewis William	Pte.	W/Sl	20-11-55	11-12-55
4266	McCarthy John	Pte.	W/Sl	5-7-55	17-7-55
3076	McCaughley John	Pte.	W/Sl	10-8-55	24-8-55
2133	McManus John	Pte.	W/Sv	25-5-55	12-6-55
3039	McPeake Thomas	Pte.	W/Sl	10-8-55	24-8-55
4192	Mansfield William	Pte.	W/Sl	2-5-55	15-5-55
3537	Matson A.	Pte.	W/Sl	25-1-55	9-2-55
1819	Mitchell William	Pte.	W/M	21-6-55	3-7-55
2651	Onions James	Pte.	W/Sv	10-8-55	24-8-55
2001	Pegg William	Pte.	W/Sl	21-6-55	3-7-55
2360	Porter John	Pte.	W/Sv	27-12-54	12-1-55
3834	Saddler Thomas	Pte.	W/Sv	9-3-55	23-3-55
1410	Stephenson William	Pte.	W/Sv	4-12-54	29-12-54
4026	Sturgeon A.	Pte.	W/Sl	7-9-55	25-9-55
3955	Tailer Edward	Pte.	W/Sl	1-5-55	15-5-55
3100	Tawks Alfred	Pte.	W/Sv	18-12-54	9-1-55
2843	Toole John	Pte.	W/Sv	8-6-55	22-6-55
3156	Travers Richard	Pte.	W/Sv	12-1-55	2-2-55
4193	Walker J.	Pte.	W/Sv	13-8-55	28-8-55
2954	White J.	Pte.	W/D	13-8-55	28-8-55
3552	Wilkinson John	Pte.	W/Sl	28-7-55	7-8-55

46th REGIMENT OF FOOT

NO.	NAME	RANK	CASUALTY	DATE	LONDON GAZETTE
	Curtis F. J.	Lieut.	Killed	2-5-55	15-5-55
2150	Dignam George	Sergt.	Killed	4-12-54	29-12-54
2456	O'Brien Thomas	L/Cpl.	Killed	5-9-55	18-9-55
2960	Bowell John	Pte.	Killed	5-9-55	18-9-55
2798	Carter Joshua	Pte.	Killed	23-7-55	7-8-55
2918	Curran William	Pte.	Killed	18-4-55	1-5-55
2975	Kelly Thomas	Pte.	Killed	10-1-55	26-1-55
3512	Small Sampson	Pte.	Killed	16-5-55	29-5-55
3059	Spencer Michael	Pte.	Killed	18-4-55	1-5-55
3383	Thomas John	Pte.	Killed	17-12-54	9-1-55
	Campbell C. F.	Major & Ass. Eng.	W/Sl	28-7-55	7-8-55
1742	Brommell William	Sergt.	W/Sv	21-12-54	9-1-55
2152	Gloed Henry	Sergt.	W/Sv	21-4-55	4-5-55
1991	Grogan William	Sergt.	W/Sv	17-8-55	31-8-55
1682	Huid Rodolphus	Sergt.	W/Sv	24-8-55	7-9-55
2456	O'Brien Thomas	L/Cpl.	W/Sv	17-8-55	31-8-55
1632	Aldridge Peter	Pte.	W/Sl	4-12-54	29-12-54
3479	Beard Joshua	Pte.	W/Sv	27-8-55	11-9-55
3143	Connor Nicholas	Pte.	W/Sl	4-12-54	29-12-54
2143	Cook William	Pte.	W/Sl	4-12-54	29-12-54
3138	Coppinge William	Pte.	W/Sv	31-7-55	14-8-55
2604	Crowley Oliver	Pte.	W/Sl	30-11-54	29-12-54
2871	Cunningham Patrick	Pte.	W/Sl	11-7-55	24-7-55
3107	Donald John	Pte.	W/Sl	1-9-55	18-9-55
2976	Galvin Patrick	Pte.	W/Sl	11-7-55	24-7-55
2649	Glynn William	Pte.	W/Sl	19-11-54	11-12-54
3122	Grady Mark	Pte.	W/Sl	30-7-55	14-8-55
2450	Griffiths John	Pte.	W/Sv	4-12-54	29-12-54
3516	Hanlon James	Pte.	W/Sl	8-6-55	22-6-55
2772	Hawthorn Arthur	Pte.	W/Sl	4-12-54	29-12-54
3190	Holmes John	Pte.	W/Sv	4-12-54	29-12-54

NOTES

The Second, Third, Fourth, Fifth and Final Bombardment of Sebastopol, and Minor Actions

46th REGIMENT OF FOOT

NO.	NAME	RANK	CASUALTY	DATE	LONDON GAZETTE
3347	Howe William	Pte.	W/Sv	15-8-55	28-8-55
3495	Lightfoot Henry	Pte.	W/Sl	4-9-55	18-9-55
3406	McMahon Francis	Pte.	W/Sl	4-9-55	18-9-55
3257	Maher Michael	Pte.	W/Sl	11-7-55	24-7-55
2148	Martin William	Pte.	W/Sv	11-5-55	25-5-55
3344	Ossington Thomas	Pte.	W/Sv	23-6-55	9-7-55
2862	Papworth Joseph	Pte.	W/Sl	6-8-55	21-8-55
3215	Paul Matthew	Pte.	W/Sl	9-6-55	22-6-55
3281	Phillips Alfred	Pte.	W/Sl	10-1-55	26-1-55
3650	Pullen George	Pte.	W/Sv	8-8-55	21-8-55
3156	Reardon Michael	Pte.	W/Sv	23-7-55	7-8-55
3109	Ryan Thomas	Pte.	W/D	24-8-55	7-9-55
3497	Sanders Richard	Pte.	W/Sl	4-9-55	18-9-55
3462	Smith Thomas	Pte.	W/D	11-5-55	25-5-55
3344	Steptoe John	Pte.	W/Sl	1-9-55	18-9-55
2792	Tyson John	Pte.	W/Sv	24-8-55	7-9-55
3420	Wilson Jabey	Pte.	W/Sl	8-6-55	22-6-55

47th REGIMENT OF FOOT

NO.	NAME	RANK	CASUALTY	DATE	LONDON GAZETTE
1946	Godfrey Joseph	Sergt.	Killed	10-2-55	27-2-55
2184	Keefe John	Sergt.	Killed	12-7-55	24-7-55
2538	Mullins Michael	Sergt.	Killed	11-6-55	26-6-55
1979	Sweeney Hugh	Corpl.	Killed	28-3-55	13-4-55
2681	Bransfield William	Pte.	Killed	3-7-55	17-7-55
3348	Brennan Michael	Pte.	Killed	7-12-54	29-12-54
2765	Collins John	Pte.	Killed	26-7-55	7-8-55
3314	Dooley John	Pte.	Killed	20-8-55	4-9-55
3262	Drennan Michael	Pte.	Killed	22-3-55	3-4-55
3091	Forsyth John	Pte.	Killed	5-5-55	18-5-55
2932	Griffin Eugene	Pte.	Killed	5-1-55	26-1-55
1887	James Peter	Pte.	Killed	20-7-55	3-8-55
3154	Kelly Michael	Pte.	Killed	20-8-55	4-9-55
2891	Lowan Andrew	Pte.	Killed	10-8-55	24-8-55
3257	Mahar Michael	Pte.	Killed	27-8-55	11-9-55
3048	Multy Hugh	Pte.	Killed	17-8-55	31-8-55
3185	Murphy Thomas	Pte.	Killed	18-5-55	5-6-55
2026	Newman John	Pte.	Killed	10-8-55	24-8-55
2557	O'Donnell John	Pte.	Killed	21-7-55	3-8-55
2633	Parker Francis	Pte.	Killed	28-6-55	10-7-55
2229	Preston James	Pte.	Killed	7-7-55	20-7-55
3182	Ryan Thomas	Pte.	Killed	25-8-55	7-9-55
2285	Spiller Thomas H.	Pte.	Killed	5-1-55	26-1-55
3361	Thompson John K.	Pte.	Killed	30-5-55	12-6-55
1269	Weir Robert	Pte.	Killed	12-7-55	24-7-55
	Roper Thomas	Capt.	W/Sl	15-7-55	27-7-55
	Cattley A. G.	Ensign	W/Sl	12-7-55	24-7-55
2533	Gill William	Sergt.	W/Sl	9-6-55	22-6-55
3154	Hunter Thomas	Sergt.	W/Sl	20-8-55	4-9-55
2304	Tomlinson William	Sergt.	W/Sv	12-6-55	26-6-55
1861	Collopy William	Corpl.	W/Sl	10-8-55	24-8-55
2541	Densey John	Corpl.	W/Sv	31-8-55	18-9-55
2832	Doulon Thomas	Corpl.	W/Sl	10-7-55	24-7-55
2954	Keefe Thomas	Corpl.	W/Sl	19-8-55	31-8-55
2402	Glynn Michael	L/Cpl.	W/Sv	14-8-55	28-8-55
3494	Agnew Samuel	Pte.	W/Sv	27-8-55	11-9-55
2466	Anderson James	Pte.	W/Sl	8-7-55	20-7-55
2466	Anderson James	Pte.	W/Sl	4-8-55	17-8-55
2086	Archibald Andrew	Pte.	W/Sl	11-6-55	26-6-55
3166	Barber Thomas	Pte.	W/Sl	14-7-55	27-7-55

NOTES

The Second, Third, Fourth, Fifth and Final Bombardment of Sebastopol, and Minor Actions

47th REGIMENT OF FOOT

NO.	NAME	RANK	CASUALTY	DATE	LONDON GAZETTE
3377	Barry James	Pte.	W/Sv	20-4-55	4-5-55
1759	Bath Edward	Pte.	W/Sl	25-6-55	10-7-55
2551	Blake Richard	Pte.	W/Sv	12-6-55	26-6-55
3272	Brien Michael	Pte.	W/Sl	31-8-55	18-9-55
2256	Broadbent George	Pte.	W/Sv	3-7-55	17-7-55
3495	Brumley Thomas	Pte.	W/D	13-8-55	28-8-55
3168	Byrne Patrick	Pte.	W/Sv	12-6-55	26-6-55
2980	Carroll Michael	Pte.	W/Sl	12-6-55	26-6-55
3408	Caulfield Michael	Pte.	W/D	17-8-55	31-8-55
3056	Cawley Patrick	Pte.	W/Sv	20-8-55	4-9-55
3342	Christopher William	Pte.	W/Sl	10-8-55	24-8-55
2390	Clancy James	Pte.	W/D	24-4-55	15-5-55
2595	Clarke Philip	Pte.	W/Sv	18-2-55	6-3-55
3032	Connors Bernard	Pte.	W/Sv	10-5-55	22-5-55
2760	Cooney John	Pte.	W/Sv	17-8-55	31-8-55
3074	Cormick Michael	Pte.	W/Sl	7-1-55	26-1-55
3074	Cormick Michael	Pte.	W/Sl	20-4-55	4-5-55
3062	Cotton Michael	Pte.	W/Sl	10-8-55	24-8-55
3195	Creehan Thomas	Pte.	W/Sl	2-12-54	29-12-54
2528	Cronin Benjamin	Pte.	W/Sv	27-8-55	11-9-55
2029	Delaney Daniel	Pte.	W/Sl	8-6-55	22-6-55
2264	Dillon John	Pte.	W/Sv	19-5-55	12-6-55
2865	Dolan Patrick	Pte.	W/Sl	29-8-55	11-9-55
2925	Dunne Michael	Pte.	W/Sv	26-3-55	13-4-55
2996	Dwyer John	Pte.	W/Sv	20-4-55	4-5-55
2313	Eyre William	Pte.	W/Sl	21-7-55	3-8-55
3681	Fitzpatrick Charles	Pte.	W/Sl	30-8-55	11-9-55
3438	Fitzpatrick William	Pte.	W/Sv	17-8-55	31-8-55
3147	Flanery Patrick	Pte.	W/Sv	2-1-55	26-1-55
2370	Forde Thomas	Pte.	W/Sl	2-9-55	18-9-55
2402	Glynn Michael	Pte.	W/Sl	30-7-55	14-8-55
3250	Gorman James	Pte.	W/Sl	16-8-55	28-8-55
3095	Govan Thomas	Pte.	W/Sv	30-12-54	26-1-55
3334	Griffin John	Pte.	W/Sl	11-7-55	24-7-55
3256	Griffin Patrick	Pte.	W/Sv	24-4-55	15-5-55
2957	Griffin Patrick	Pte.	W/Sl	11-6-55	26-6-55
2165	Grimshaw John	Pte.	W/Sv	2-9-55	18-9-55
2080	Hales Thomas	Pte.	W/D	2-9-55	18-9-55
3293	Helden Archibald	Pte.	W/Sl	19-8-55	31-8-55
3117	Holyoak Joseph	Pte.	W/Sl	15-7-55	27-7-55
1967	Hopkins George	Pte.	W/Sv	14-6-55	26-6-55
3222	Hunbury Thomas	Pte.	W/Sv	29-8-55	11-9-55
2954	Keefe Thomas	Pte.	W/Sl	19-8-55	31-8-55
3481	Kelly John	Pte.	W/Sl	17-8-55	31-8-55
2523	Kelly Michael	Pte.	W/Sv	1-8-55	14-8-55
3282	Kennedy Daniel	Pte.	W/Sv	27-8-55	11-9-55
2967	Kennedy Mathew	Pte.	W/Sv	2-3-55	16-3-55
2870	Lawler William	Pte.	W/Sl	2-9-55	18-9-55
2891	Lohan Andrew	Pte.	W/Sl	28-6-55	10-7-55
3074	McCormick Michael	Pte.	W/Sl	7-1-55	26-1-55
2823	McDonald Dennis	Pte.	W/Sl	29-5-55	12-6-55
2585	McDonald Michael	Pte.	W/Sl	26-7-55	7-8-55
3339	McGrath Patrick	Pte.	W/Sv	29-8-55	11-9-55
2016	McGuire James	Pte.	W/D	2-9-55	18-9-55
2217	McMahon Joseph	Pte.	W/Sv	2-1-55	26-1-55
3433	McNamara John	Pte.	W/Sl	14-6-55	26-6-55
3264	Malon Martin	Pte.	W/Sv	27-8-55	11-9-55
2211	Marshall Joseph	Pte.	W/Sv	30-12-54	26-1-55
3238	Marshall William	Pte.	W/Sl	28-8-55	11-9-55
3393	Mayo Charles	Pte.	W/Sl	13-8-55	28-8-55
3001	Mophett James	Pte.	W/Sv	18-4-55	1-5-55
3458	Muirhead John	Pte.	W/Sl	3-7-55	17-7-55
3446	Mulcahy Thomas	Pte.	W/Sl	20-7-55	3-8-55
2896	Murphy William	Pte.	W/D	20-8-55	4-9-55

NOTES

The Second, Third, Fourth, Fifth and Final Bombardment of Sebastopol, and Minor Actions

47th REGIMENT OF FOOT

NO.	NAME	RANK	CASUALTY	DATE	LONDON GAZETTE
3130	Neil Michael	Pte.	W/Sl	25-8-55	7-9-55
3274	Newman William	Pte.	W/Sl	23-8-55	4-9-55
2505	O'Donnell Patrick	Pte.	W/Sl	12-6-55	26-6-55
3472	O'Hara James	Pte.	W/Sl	20-7-55	3-8-55
2499	Powell John	Pte.	W/Sv	25-5-55	12-6-55
1650	Rideford Joseph	Pte.	W/Sv	10-7-55	24-7-55
3311	Riley James	Pte.	W/Sv	20-8-55	4-9-55
3347	Roach John	Pte.	W/Sl	1-8-55	14-8-55
3189	Ross John	Pte.	W/Sv	1-8-55	14-8-55
3186	Ryan Charles	Pte.	W/Sv	2-5-55	15-5-55
3351	Shaughnessy James	Pte.	W/Sv	8-5-55	22-5-55
3315	Slater John	Pte.	W/Sl	31-8-55	18-9-55
1705	Spilsbury John	Pte.	W/Sv	14-7-55	27-7-55
2244	Stokes William	Pte.	W/Sv	26-7-55	7-8-55
2839	Sullivan Patrick	Pte.	W/Sv	27-8-55	11-9-55
3482	Sweeney Thomas	Pte.	W/Sv	16-8-55	28-8-55
3075	Tully John	Pte.	W/Sv	24-4-55	15-5-55
3127	Turney Thomas	Pte.	W/D	20-8-55	4-9-55
3280	Wall Edward	Pte.	W/Sl	10-8-55	24-8-55
3306	Ward James	Pte.	W/Sv	30-5-55	12-6-55
2705	White Francis	Pte.	W/Sv	1-8-55	14-8-55
3295	White James	Pte.	W/Sl	15-4-55	1-5-55
2868	White John	Pte.	W/Sl	14-2-55	2-3-55
3406	Whittaker Thomas	Pte.	W/Sv	30-6-55	10-7-55
2193	Windsor William	Pte.	W/Sl	6-7-55	20-7-55
3217	Woodhouse Philip	Pte.	W/Sv	9-5-55	22-5-55
2436	Wright Joseph	Pte.	W/Sv	11-7-55	24-7-55

48th REGIMENT OF FOOT

NO.	NAME	RANK	CASUALTY	DATE	LONDON GAZETTE
3203	Hyndman James	Pte.	Killed	17-7-55	31-7-55
3276	McManus William	Pte.	Killed	28-5-55	12-6-55
2632	Meakin Thomas	Pte.	Killed	14-7-55	31-7-55
2968	Richardson Thomas	Pte.	Killed	28-4-55	15-5-55
2721	Ridgeway Thomas	Pte.	Killed	17-7-55	31-7-55
	Horne E. G.	Lieut. & Adj.	W/Sl	20-8-55	4-9-55
1366	Corrigan Denis	Sergt.	W/Sv	9-7-55	24-7-55
1759	Kennedy Michael	Sergt.	W/Sv	7-8-55	21-8-55
2535	Moran Michael	Sergt.	W/Sl	18-8-55	31-8-55
2022	Patterson Henry	Sergt.	W/Sl	20-8-55	4-9-55
2118	Robinson John	Sergt.	W/Sv	15-8-55	28-8-55
2358	Cary James	L/Sgt.	W/Sv	10-7-55	24-7-55
2725	Berrill Jonathan	Pte.	W/Sl	2-8-55	14-8-55
2740	Berwick Robert	Pte.	W/Sv	27-4-55	15-5-55
3057	Bishery George	Pte.	W/Sl	25-7-55	7-8-55
2448	Delaney Edward	Pte.	W/Sv	21-6-55	3-7-55
2640	Donovan Jeremiah	Pte.	W/Sl	21-8-55	4-9-55
1868	Faulkner William	Pte.	W/Sl	19-8-55	31-8-55
3221	Forsyth Irwine	Pte.	W/Sv	16-8-55	28-8-55
3130	Graham George	Pte.	W/Sl	27-8-55	11-9-55
3171	Hadson James	Pte.	W/Sl	25-7-55	7-8-55
1935	Haggis Nathaniel	Pte.	W/Sl	16-5-55	29-5-55
2896	Halliwell William	Pte.	W/Sv	14-8-55	28-8-55
2612	Harris James	Pte.	W/Sl	28-5-55	12-6-55
2281	Healy Martin	Pte.	W/Sl	26-8-55	7-9-55
3211	Ismay Joseph	Pte.	W/Sl	30-5-55	12-6-55
1738	Kelly Daniel	Pte.	W/Sv	13-7-55	27-7-55
2284	Kidley Samuel	Pte.	W/Sv	21-8-55	4-9-55
2903	Knight William	Pte.	W/Sl	15-8-55	28-8-55
2991	Laney William	Pte.	W/Sl	27-8-55	11-9-55

NOTES

The Second, Third, Fourth, Fifth and Final Bombardment of Sebastopol, and Minor Actions

48th REGIMENT OF FOOT

NO.	NAME	RANK	CASUALTY	DATE	LONDON GAZETTE
2468	Lawlor Walter	Pte.	W/Sl	27-5-55	12-6-55
1058	Lewis Thomas	Pte.	W/Sv	1-9-55	18-9-55
3021	Little Francis	Pte.	W/Sv	1-8-55	14-8-55
3236	McKenzie James	Pte.	W/Sl	18-7-55	31-7-55
1376	McManus H.	Pte.	W/Sl	7-8-55	21-8-55
3045	Mathews Lawrence	Pte.	W/Sv	29-6-55	17-7-55
2575	Montgomery Samuel	Pte.	W/Sl	28-7-55	7-8-55
1970	Moore John	Pte.	W/Sl	4-9-55	18-9-55
3034	Mullin James	Pte.	W/Sv	16-5-55	29-5-55
2576	Murdock Thomas	Pte.	W/Sv	31-7-55	14-8-55
3114	O'Neil John	Pte.	W/Sv	2-9-55	18-9-55
3019	Ostell Thomas	Pte.	W/Sl	21-6-55	3-7-55
2924	Parker George	Pte.	W/Sv	15-8-55	28-8-55
3091	Redpath David	Pte.	W/Sv	9-5-55	22-5-55
2671	Rider Edward	Pte.	W/Sl	19-8-55	31-8-55
2474	Roarke John	Pte.	W/Sl	7-7-55	20-7-55
3120	Sheefield William	Pte.	W/Sl	9-7-55	24-7-55
1678	Slattery John	Pte.	W/Sl	18-7-55	31-7-55
3146	Smith William	Pte.	W/Sl	24-7-55	7-8-55
2161	Smith William	Pte.	W/Sv	14-6-55	26-6-55
3105	Somerville John	Pte.	W/Sv	14-7-55	27-7-55
3155	Taylor Robert	Pte.	W/Sl	2-8-55	14-8-55
2269	Treacy John	Pte.	W/Sl	19-8-55	31-8-55
2445	Walsh Thomas	Pte.	W/Sl	28-5-55	12-6-55
2980	Wells William	Pte.	W/Sl	14-5-55	29-5-55
2708	West James	Pte.	W/Sv	29-6-55	17-7-55
2634	Woodward Thomas	Pte.	W/Sl	13-5-55	25-5-55
3180	Wright John	Pte.	W/Sv	18-7-55	31-7-55
2952	Young John	Pte.	W/Sv	21-6-55	3-7-55

49th REGIMENT OF FOOT

NO.	NAME	RANK	CASUALTY	DATE	LONDON GAZETTE
1154	Headen Henry	Sergt.	Killed	21-4-55	4-5-55
2318	Sharman David	Sergt.	Killed	10-1-55	26-1-55
3456	Moore Bernard	L/Sgt.	Killed	21-6-55	3-7-55
2304	Campbell James	Corpl.	Killed	13-5-55	25-5-55
2201	Kent William	Corpl.	Killed	5-5-55	18-5-55
3515	Pickards Francis	Corpl.	Killed	30-8-55	11-9-55
2688	Smith William	L/Cpl.	Killed	19-4-55	1-5-55
3368	Ash Andrew	Pte.	Killed	5-5-55	18-5-55
2014	Atherton James	Pte.	Killed	28-6-55	10-7-55
3267	Barrett William	Pte.	Killed	4-9-55	18-9-55
2894	Bradley William	Pte.	Killed	19-4-55	1-5-55
2437	Burke John	Pte.	Killed	28-4-55	15-5-55
2519	Burns Joseph	Pte.	Killed	17-6-55	3-7-55
3723	Cannan Dennis	Pte.	Killed	29-8-55	11-9-55
2511	Carey Patrick	Pte.	Killed	9-6-55	22-6-55
3138	Collins James	Pte.	Killed	27-7-55	7-8-55
3370	Connolly John	Pte.	Killed	29-8-55	11-9-55
914	Creighan Patrick	Pte.	Killed	5-5-55	18-5-55
2629	Donaghy Thomas	Pte.	Killed	17-6-55	3-7-55
3103	Dowde Michael	Pte.	Killed	28-5-55	12-6-55
2815	Edwards James	Pte.	Killed	23-12-54	9-1-55
3560	Fogarty Patrick	Pte.	Killed	12-7-55	24-7-55
3547	Godfrey Thomas	Pte.	Killed	21-6-55	3-7-55
3458	Guest Henry	Pte.	Killed	7-12-54	29-12-54
3744	Halfpenny Patrick	Pte.	Killed	6-7-55	20-7-55
3353	Kelly John	Pte.	Killed	11-6-55	26-6-55
3948	Kelly Michael	Pte.	Killed	24-4-55	4-5-55
3571	McGrury Michael	Pte.	Killed	11-4-55	24-4-55

NOTES

The Second, Third, Fourth, Fifth and Final Bombardment of Sebastopol, and Minor Actions

49th REGIMENT OF FOOT

NO.	NAME	RANK	CASUALTY	DATE	LONDON GAZETTE
1274	Morrow John	Pte.	Killed	17-8-55	31-8-55
2430	Radford George	Pte.	Killed	25-8-55	7-9-55
3521	Reilly Lawrence	Pte.	Killed	9-6-55	22-6-55
1741	Tinnicliff Thed	Pte.	Killed	10-6-55	22-6-55
3251	White Owen	Pte.	Killed	3-6-55	15-6-55
2364	White William	Pte.	Killed	26-4-55	15-5-55
	Chatfield G. K.	Lieut.	W/Sl	3-9-55	18-9-55
	Rochfort G.	Lieut.	W/Sv	5-5-55	18-5-55
	Mitchell C.	Ensign	W/Sl	10-7-55	24-7-55
2947	Cable Thomas	Sergt.	W/Sl	9-6-55	22-6-55
3102	Costello John	Sergt.	W/Sv	28-8-55	11-9-55
1442	Dwyer John	Sergt.	W/Sv	12-7-55	24-7-55
2412	Pollard Edmund	Sergt.	W/Sv	19-8-55	31-8-55
1566	Hunter William	L/Sgt.	W/Sl	19-8-55	31-8-55
3099	Connolly Martin	Corpl.	W/Sv	5-5-55	18-5-55
2624	Rielly William	Corpl.	W/Sl	10-6-55	22-6-55
2243	Willis Thomas	Corpl.	W/Sl	26-4-55	15-5-55
3280	McAnliffe Morris	L/Cpl.	W/Sl	9-6-55	22-6-55
3230	Varley William	L/Cpl.	W/Sl	12-6-55	26-6-55
3229	Allan James	Pte.	W/D	13-4-55	1-5-55
3426	Allen David	Pte.	W/Sl	11-6-55	26-6-55
2014	Atherton James	Pte.	W/Sl	31-5-55	12-6-55
3768	Ball George	Pte.	W/Sv	17-8-55	31-8-55
1598	Bird William	Pte.	W/Sv	30-3-55	20-4-55
3230	Boyland Thomas	Pte.	W/Sl	17-6-55	3-7-55
2839	Braughall John	Pte.	W/Sv	31-5-55	12-6-55
3197	Brereton Edward	Pte.	W/D	19-4-55	1-5-55
3791	Brogan Michael	Pte.	W/Sl	24-7-55	7-8-55
3497	Burchall William	Pte.	W/Sv	15-4-55	1-5-55
3456	Cardiff James	Pte.	W/D	28-6-55	10-7-55
3253	Cavanagh John	Pte.	W/Sv	5-5-55	18-5-55
1181	Chance Charles	Pte.	W/D	26-7-55	7-8-55
2983	Clerk Michael	Pte.	W/Sl	4-4-55	20-4-55
3377	Connors Darby	Pte.	W/D	19-4-55	1-5-55
3228	Courtney Frederick	Pte.	W/Sv	5-5-55	18-5-55
3432	Crowe Patrick	Pte.	W/Sl	9-6-55	22-6-55
2611	Cummins Michael	Pte.	W/Sl	1-7-55	17-7-55
3325	Cussen John	Pte.	W/Sl	25-8-55	7-9-55
2807	Delaney John	Pte.	W/Sl	27-4-55	15-5-55
2177	Doughty Samuel	Pte.	W/Sv	11-4-55	24-4-55
3264	Doyle Patrick	Pte.	W/Sv	5-5-55	18-5-55
3783	Driscoll Edward	Pte.	W/Sv	28-8-55	11-9-55
3009	Duffy Patrick	Pte.	W/Sl	11-6-55	26-6-55
2029	Duffy Thomas	Pte.	W/Sl	14-8-55	28-8-55
3780	Edwards Isaac	Pte.	W/Sl	17-6-55	3-7-55
2755	Edwards John	Pte.	W/Sv	6-5-55	18-5-55
3580	Egan John	Pte.	W/Sv	7-4-55	20-4-55
3382	Fallen Thomas	Pte.	W/Sv	10-7-55	24-7-55
2493	Farrell James	Pte.	W/Sl	15-4-55	1-5-55
3323	Farrell Michael	Pte.	W/Sv	3-12-54	29-12-54
3416	Farquhar Peter	Pte.	W/Sv	5-5-55	18-5-55
1987	Fensome Thomas	Pte.	W/Sv	17-6-55	3-7-55
3311	Ford William	Pte.	W/Sv	26-7-55	7-8-55
3598	Gallagher Thomas	Pte.	W/Sv	14-8-55	28-8-55
3332	Gay David	Pte.	W/Sl	29-8-55	11-9-55
3574	Gormanly James	Pte.	W/Sv	5-5-55	18-5-55
2664	Gratton John	Pte.	W/Sv	27-7-55	7-8-55
3719	Greenan John	Pte.	W/D	26-7-55	7-8-55
1300	Greer Samuel	Pte.	W/Sl	17-6-55	3-7-55
3379	Haley James	Pte.	W/D	24-7-55	7-8-55
3445	Haley John	Pte.	W/D	21-6-55	3-7-55
3294	Hall William	Pte.	W/Sl	26-5-55	12-6-55
3715	Hamil Saunders	Pte.	W/Sl	14-8-55	28-8-55
2692	Handlin James	Pte.	W/Sl	8-8-55	21-8-55

NOTES

The Second, Third, Fourth, Fifth and Final Bombardment of Sebastopol, and Minor Actions

49th REGIMENT OF FOOT

NO.	NAME	RANK	CASUALTY	DATE	LONDON GAZETTE
2235	Hare John	Pte.	W/D	21-5-55	5-6-55
3834	Harrington Florence	Pte.	W/Sl	9-6-55	22-6-55
3385	Healy Peter	Pte.	W/D	19-4-55	1-5-55
2824	Hourigan Nicholas	Pte.	W/D	12-5-55	25-5-55
3483	Hutchinson James	Pte.	W/Sl	25-8-55	7-9-55
3209	James William	Pte.	W/Sv	5-5-55	18-5-55
3209	James William	Pte.	W/Sl	6-7-55	20-7-55
3353	Kelly John	Pte.	W/Sl	5-5-55	18-5-55
3655	Kemp Thomas	Pte.	W/Sl	21-4-55	4-5-55
3408	Kennedy James	Pte.	W/D	21-5-55	5-6-55
3556	Kenney Michael	Pte.	W/Sv	2-1-55	26-1-55
3475	Kenny Patrick	Pte.	W/D	20-7-55	3-8-55
3137	Kilfoyle John	Pte.	W/Sl	6-7-55	20-7-55
3838	Lane James	Pte.	W/Sl	29-8-55	11-9-55
3463	Lennon James	Pte.	W/Sv	8-8-55	21-8-55
3433	Linahan Denis	Pte.	W/Sl	5-5-55	18-5-55
3585	Linahan Jual	Pte.	W/Sv	5-5-55	18-5-55
2544	McDonald James	Pte.	W/Sl	9-6-55	22-6-55
1408	McDonnell John	Pte.	W/D	12-7-55	24-7-55
3597	McGann Patrick	Pte.	W/D	17-8-55	31-8-55
3597	McGann Patrick	Pte.	W/Sl	29-8-55	11-9-55
3340	McMahon Martin	Pte.	W/Sl	4-9-55	18-9-55
2741	McMahon Patrick	Pte.	W/D	29-8-55	11-9-55
2741	McMahon Patrick	Pte.	W/Sv	24-5-55	5-6-55
3103	McNeil James	Pte.	W/Sl	5-5-55	18-5-55
2465	Madden Patrick	Pte.	W/Sl	31-5-55	12-6-55
3320	Mahoney Daniel	Pte.	W/Sl	25-8-55	7-9-55
3522	Mapley Emanuel	Pte.	W/Sl	26-7-55	7-8-55
3871	Mickey John	Pte.	W/Sv	2-8-55	14-8-55
3297	Morrison Owen	Pte.	W/Sl	29-1-55	20-2-55
3379	Morrow James	Pte.	W/Sl	5-9-55	18-9-55
3509	Mullins Michael	Pte.	W/Sl	12-5-55	25-5-55
3509	Mullins Michael	Pte.	W/Sv	17-8-55	31-8-55
2390	Mulvaney John	Pte.	W/Sl	5-5-55	18-5-55
2730	O'Brien Patrick	Pte.	W/Sv	10-4-55	24-4-55
2668	O'Neill Daniel	Pte.	W/Sv	17-8-55	31-8-55
3591	Osborne Richard	Pte.	W/Sv	6-7-55	20-7-55
2309	Prendergast Patrick	Pte.	W/Sv	15-4-55	1-5-55
2857	Radmell Henry	Pte.	W/Sl	26-6-55	10-7-55
2832	Ready Michael	Pte.	W/Sv	12-7-55	24-7-55
3412	Rielly Peter	Pte.	W/Sl	8-8-55	21-8-55
2964	Robertson James	Pte.	W/Sv	29-8-55	11-9-55
1271	Rogers Michael	Pte.	W/Sl	5-5-55	18-5-55
3828	Russell Henry	Pte.	W/D	10-7-55	24-7-55
3477	Rutledge Thomas	Pte.	W/D	17-3-55	30-3-55
3717	Stinson William	Pte.	W/Sv	19-8-55	31-8-55
3021	Sullivan Dennis	Pte.	W/Sv	28-6-55	10-7-55
3636	Swail William	Pte.	W/Sv	29-8-55	11-9-55
1640	Thomson Robert	Pte.	D.O.W	25-4-55	15-5-55
3313	Toole John	Pte.	W/D	19-4-55	1-5-55
1081	Toomey James	Pte.	W/Sl	10-7-55	24-7-55
2992	Treasey John	Pte.	W/Sv	22-4-55	4-5-55
3636	Treasey Thomas	Pte.	W/Sl	5-5-55	18-5-55
2349	Trench Thomas	Pte.	W/Sv	28-6-55	10-7-55
2537	Uniacke Maurice	Pte.	W/Sl	25-8-55	7-9-55
3246	Walsh Thomas	Pte.	W/Sv	25-8-55	7-9-55
3668	Watts James	Pte.	W/D	19-8-55	31-8-55
3330	White Henry	Pte.	W/Sl	9-6-55	22-6-55
3760	White John	Pte.	W/Sl	20-7-55	3-8-55
3348	Wickham Edward	Pte.	W/Sl	24-7-55	7-8-55
2678	Robinson James	Sergt.	Missing	6-5-55	18-5-55
2857	Bannon Patrick	Pte.	Missing	6-5-55	18-5-55

NOTES

The Second, Third, Fourth, Fifth and Final Bombardment of Sebastopol, and Minor Actions

50th REGIMENT OF FOOT

NO.	NAME	RANK	CASUALTY	DATE	LONDON GAZETTE
1289	Clifford Thomas	Q.M.S.	Killed	13-4-55	1-5-55
3079	Howarth James	Sergt.	Killed	20-12-54	9-1-55
3105	Andrews Thomas	L/Sgt.	Killed	18-12-54	9-1-55
3396	Inglefield Benjamin	Corpl.	Killed	20-12-54	9-1-55
3468	Barry James	Pte.	Killed	31-8-55	18-9-55
4028	Bradley George	Pte.	Killed	5-12-54	29-12-54
4191	Carmichael James	Pte.	Killed	20-12-54	9-1-55
3175	Collis James	Pte.	Killed	20-12-54	9-1-55
4048	Connolly Stephen	Pte.	Killed	20-12-54	9-1-55
3902	Cooney Patrick	Pte.	Killed	20-12-54	9-1-55
4189	Cotter John	Pte.	Killed	2-12-54	29-12-54
4082	Dalton Thomas	Pte.	Killed	24-4-55	15-5-55
2488	Derming Samuel	Pte.	Killed	20-12-54	9-1-55
3069	Doherty Owen	Pte.	Killed	2-12-54	29-12-54
4072	Flynn John	Pte.	Killed	24-4-55	15-5-55
3858	Heard Daniel	Pte.	Killed	15-11-54	11-12-54
2999	Keefe Timothy	Pte.	Killed	20-12-54	9-1-55
3734	McDonald Lewis	Pte.	Killed	2-12-54	29-12-54
4123	McNamara Thomas	Pte.	Killed	13-4-55	1-5-55
4007	Mailey James	Pte.	Killed	20-12-54	9-1-55
3392	Moran James	Pte.	Killed	20-12-54	9-1-55
3726	Nagle Richard	Pte.	Killed	2-12-54	29-12-54
3373	Rohan Timothy	Pte.	Killed	15-11-54	11-12-54
1573	Shelley Patrick	Pte.	Killed	15-11-54	11-12-54
3994	Thompson Patrick	Pte.	Killed	20-12-54	9-1-55
3985	Thompson Samuel	Pte.	Killed	20-12-54	9-1-55
3757	Wood Edward	Pte.	Killed	20-12-54	9-1-55
	Moller J. O.	Major	D.O.W.	18-12-54	9-1-55
3431	O'Brien Thomas	Sergt.	W/Sl	13-4-55	1-5-55
3385	Stevenson James	Sergt.	W/Sv	3-8-55	17-8-55
3444	Upton Herbert	Sergt.	W/Sl	18-11-54	11-12-54
2951	Brett James	Corpl.	W/Sl	6-12-54	29-12-54
3396	Inglefield Benjamin	Corpl.	W/Sl	2-12-54	29-12-54
3315	McNamara Martin	Corpl.	W/Sl	31-7-55	14-8-55
3983	Wright Christopher	Corpl.	W/Sl	31-8-55	18-9-55
3633	Flading John	L/Cpl.	W/Sv	24-8-55	7-9-55
3393	O'Brien Michael	L/Cpl.	W/Sl	25-8-55	7-9-55
3584	Archer John	Pte.	W/Sl	27-7-55	7-8-55
4182	Barrett Robert	Pte.	W/Sv	20-12-54	9-1-55
3641	Blackley Mark	Pte.	W/Sl	31-7-55	14-8-55
3006	Brace John	Pte.	W/Sl	20-12-54	9-1-55
2940	Buckley Jeremiah	Pte.	W/Sv	20-12-54	9-1-55
3092	Cliff Thomas	Pte.	W/Sl	26-7-55	7-8-55
2832	Connors Patrick	Pte.	W/Sl	20-12-54	9-1-55
2832	Connors Patrick	Pte.	W/Sv	26-7-55	7-8-55
3393	Coombs George	Pte.	W/Sv	2-12-54	29-12-54
3103	Cooney William	Pte.	W/D	2-12-54	29-12-54
3718	Crawshaw Henry	Pte.	W/Sv	20-12-54	9-1-55
3441	Cummins Michael	Pte.	W/Sl	20-12-54	9-1-55
4238	Darragh John	Pte.	D.O.W.	18-12-54	9-1-55
1979	Doran William	Pte.	W/Sv	18-12-54	9-1-55
4063	Dougherty James	Pte.	W/Sv	14-12-54	9-1-55
2675	Duncan Peter	Pte.	W/D	2-12-54	29-12-54
3125	Garden Joseph	Pte.	W/Sv	18-11-54	11-12-54
3142	Gormley James	Pte.	W/Sv	20-12-54	9-1-55
4139	Grogan James	Pte.	W/Sl	7-5-55	22-5-55
3567	Groom Miles	Pte.	W/D	2-12-54	29-12-54
3889	Harryman Thomas	Pte.	W/D	2-12-54	29-12-54
3579	Hatton Joseph	Pte.	W/Sv	14-12-54	9-1-55
3747	Hunter John	Pte.	W/Sl	2-12-54	29-12-54
4019	Judge Michael	Pte.	W/Sl	13-4-55	1-5-55
2626	Kenny Thomas	Pte.	W/Sv	18-11-54	11-12-54

NOTES

The Second, Third, Fourth, Fifth and Final Bombardment of Sebastopol, and Minor Actions

50th REGIMENT OF FOOT

NO.	NAME	RANK	CASUALTY	DATE	LONDON GAZETTE
3136	Lawler John	Pte.	W/Sv	26-7-55	7-8-55
2818	McCarthy Charles	Pte.	W/Sl	20-12-54	9-1-55
3947	Macdonald John	Pte.	W/Sl	30-11-54	29-12-54
3689	Maloney Thomas	Pte.	W/Sv	20-12-54	9-1-55
3922	Mangin Thomas	Pte.	W/Sl	14-7-55	27-7-55
3453	Nicholson Michael	Pte.	W/Sv	20-12-54	9-1-55
3042	O'Brien Patrick	Pte.	W/Sl	20-12-54	9-1-55
1851	Price William	Pte.	W/Sl	20-12-54	9-1-55
4074	Robinson John	Pte.	W/Sl	18-11-54	11-12-54
1959	Taylor John	Pte.	W/Sl	20-12-54	9-1-55
3988	Taylor Oswald	Pte.	W/Sv	20-12-54	9-1-55
3647	Taylor Thomas	Pte.	W/Sl	6-12-54	29-12-54
3941	Toker Joseph	Pte.	W/Sv	20-12-54	9-1-55
3949	Toole Patrick	Pte.	W/Sl	24-8-55	7-9-55
3132	Wade James	Pte.	W/Sl	14-7-55	27-7-55
4115	Walcroft William	Pte.	W/Sv	18-12-54	9-1-55
4204	Wallis Michael	Pte.	W/Sl	20-12-54	9-1-55
3507	Walsh Christopher	Pte.	W/Sv	20-12-54	9-1-55
2271	Ward John	Pte.	W/Sv	20-12-54	9-1-55
	Frampton H. J.	Capt.	Missing	20-12-54	9-1-55
	Clarke M. A.	Lieut.	Missing	20-12-54	9-1-55
2864	Callaghan Timothy	Corpl.	Missing	20-12-54	9-1-55
1111	Bryan George	Pte.	Missing	2-12-54	29-12-54
3277	Callaghan John	Pte.	Missing	20-12-54	9-1-55
3429	Coreoran Thomas	Pte.	Missing	20-12-54	9-1-55
1583	Curnery Patrick	Pte.	Missing	2-12-54	29-12-54
4097	Dagan Mathew	Pte.	Missing	20-12-54	9-1-55
4000	Doyle George	Pte.	Missing	20-12-54	9-1-55
3155	Hattigan Edward	Pte.	Missing	20-12-54	9-1-55
3665	Howarth James	Pte.	Missing	2-12-54	29-12-54
2956	McAnliffe Lawrence	Pte.	Missing	20-12-54	9-1-55
3932	Sinett Thomas	Pte.	Missing	20-12-54	9-1-55

55th REGIMENT OF FOOT

NO.	NAME	RANK	CASUALTY	DATE	LONDON GAZETTE
	Elton F. C.	Capt.	Killed	10-8-55	24-8-55
2577	Kemp George	Corpl.	Killed	12-7-55	24-7-55
1462	Powell Thomas	Corpl.	Killed	2-9-55	18-9-55
3272	Bourke Patrick	Pte.	Killed	6-1-55	26-1-55
3298	Delivett Thomas	Pte.	Killed	17-4-55	1-5-55
3137	Hennesy Jeremiah	Pte.	Killed	18-4-55	1-5-55
3224	Howe Charles	Pte.	Killed	24-5-55	5-6-55
2003	Jukes John	Pte.	Killed	24-5-55	5-6-55
2646	McGrath Thomas	Pte.	Killed	23-12-54	9-1-55
2724	McGuire John	Pte.	Killed	10-3-55	23-3-55
3266	McMahon John	Pte.	Killed	23-12-54	9-1-55
3619	Martin Peter	Pte.	Killed	11-6-55	26-6-55
3224	Moran John	Pte.	Killed	20-5-55	5-6-55
3260	O'Connors Daniel	Pte.	Killed	25-12-54	12-1-55
3654	Wiley Edward	Pte.	Killed	12-7-55	24-7-55
	Evans C. H.	Lieut.	W/D	4-8-55	17-8-55
	Trevor J. W.	Lieut.	W/D	19-4-55	1-5-55
2624	Callaghan Patrick	Sergt.	W/Sl	4-8-55	17-8-55
2762	Champion S.	Sergt.	W/Sl	9-6-55	22-6-55
2882	Kendrick Henry	Sergt.	W/Sl	19-4-55	1-5-55
2177	McCloy Alexander	Sergt.	W/Sv	22-4-55	1-5-55
3547	McGarry Robert	Sergt.	W/Sl	4-8-55	17-8-55
2284	Meaner Martin	Sergt.	D.O.W.	9-6-55	22-6-55
3429	Gorman William	L/Sgt.	W/Sv	17-7-55	31-7-55
2798	Holdick Benjamin	L/Sgt.	W/Sl	4-8-55	17-8-55

NOTES

The Second, Third, Fourth, Fifth and Final Bombardment of Sebastopol, and Minor Actions

55th REGIMENT OF FOOT

NO.	NAME	RANK	CASUALTY	DATE	LONDON GAZETTE
2276	Fetton William	Corpl.	W/Sl	11-6-55	26-6-55
3573	Miller George	Corpl.	W/Sv	2-8-55	14-8-55
2103	Smith Joseph	Corpl.	W/Sv	27-7-55	7-8-55
2868	Tierney Daniel	Corpl.	W/Sv	4-8-55	17-8-55
2030	Blee Joseph	L/Cpl.	W/Sl	10-2-55	23-2-55
2834	Burke Edmund	L/Cpl.	W/Sl	27-4-55	4-5-55
2839	Evers Richard	Drummer	W/Sv	30-6-55	17-7-55
3611	Adams Henry	Pte.	W/Sl	4-8-55	17-8-55
3484	Aitken James	Pte.	W/D	17-8-55	31-8-55
3489	Anderson Robert	Pte.	W/Sv	21-7-55	3-8-55
3489	Anderson Robert	Pte.	W/Sl	2-9-55	18-9-55
2491	Baddington James	Pte.	W/Sl	4-4-55	20-4-55
2286	Bell Robert	Pte.	W/Sl	2-9-55	18-9-55
2315	Bloomfield Edward	Pte.	W/Sl	4-8-55	17-8-55
3500	Brander Robert	Pte.	W/Sl	30-6-55	17-7-55
2139	Broderick Denis	Pte.	W/Sl	26-7-55	7-8-55
3168	Burke James	Pte.	W/Sv	23-8-55	4-9-55
3243	Burke Thomas	Pte.	W/Sv	13-4-55	1-5-55
2877	Burke William	Pte.	W/Sv	20-5-55	5-6-55
3696	Cain John	Pte.	W/Sl	4-8-55	17-8-55
3508	Calder Robert	Pte.	W/Sv	8-6-55	22-6-55
3508	Calder Robert	Pte.	W/Sl	9-6-55	22-6-55
2985	Clarke Thomas	Pte.	W/Sl	24-7-55	7-8-55
3359	Connolly Patrick	Pte.	W/Sl	11-4-55	24-4-55
3259	Conway William	Pte.	W/Sl	4-8-55	17-8-55
3217	Cronan John	Pte.	W/Sl	4-8-55	17-8-55
2082	Crowther Charles	Pte.	W/Sl	26-7-55	7-8-55
2082	Crowther Charles	Pte.	W/Sl	29-7-55	7-8-55
2889	Culmore Levi	Pte.	W/Sl	9-6-55	22-6-55
3269	Curry Thomas	Pte.	W/Sv	19-4-55	1-5-55
3297	Dagan William	Pte.	W/Sl	4-8-55	17-8-55
2802	Dally James	Pte.	W/D	19-4-55	1-5-55
2721	Davis Richard	Pte.	W/D	23-7-55	7-8-55
3653	Dawson George	Pte.	W/D	1-4-55	20-4-55
1787	Dean Alfred	Pte.	W/Sl	23-7-55	7-8-55
3216	Drawry John	Pte.	W/Sl	1-4-55	20-4-55
3210	Drury John	Pte.	W/Sl	13-5-55	25-5-55
3098	Edge Matthew	Pte.	W/D	14-5-55	29-5-55
2385	Ellis John	Pte.	W/Sl	11-6-55	26-6-55
3103	Fahey William	Pte.	W/Sl	29-7-55	7-8-55
3520	Fairlie William	Pte.	W/D	20-4-55	1-5-55
3421	Farrell Michael	Pte.	D.O.W.	15-3-55	23-3-55
3664	Flannagan James	Pte.	W/Sl	7-7-55	20-7-55
3670	Flannagan Michael	Pte.	W/Sl	17-8-55	31-8-55
2994	Gareing Thomas	Pte.	W/D	2-8-55	14-8-55
2900	Gloster Thomas	Pte.	W/D	11-6-55	26-6-55
3079	Gordan John	Pte.	W/Sl	3-5-55	15-5-55
3527	Graham Thomas	Pte.	W/Sl	4-8-55	17-8-55
3195	Groves Samuel	Pte.	W/D	7-7-55	20-7-55
2967	Guering Patrick	Pte.	W/Sl	14-3-55	23-3-55
3187	Hagger Stephen	Pte.	W/D	1-4-55	20-4-55
3720	Hale John	Pte.	W/Sv	10-6-55	22-6-55
3116	Hanley William	Pte.	W/Sl	4-8-55	17-8-55
2462	Healy Michael	Pte.	W/Sv	1-7-55	17-7-55
3614	Hickey David	Pte.	W/D	11-6-55	26-6-55
3228	Hogan John	Pte.	W/Sl	29-7-55	7-8-55
2537	Hollshan Thomas	Pte.	W/Sl	27-7-55	7-8-55
3239	Kennedy James	Pte.	W/Sl	23-7-55	7-8-55
2955	Kenny John	Pte.	W/Sv	16-8-55	28-8-55
3112	Lane Charles	Pte.	W/Sl	29-7-55	7-8-55
1776	Larrett William	Pte.	W/Sl	10-1-55	26-1-55
1665	Lawrence James	Pte.	W/Sl	14-3-55	23-3-55
3447	Learey Jeremiah	Pte.	W/Sl	4-8-55	17-8-55
3331	Lewis Thomas	Pte.	W/Sl	27-6-55	10-7-55

NOTES

The Second, Third, Fourth, Fifth and Final Bombardment of Sebastopol, and Minor Actions

55th REGIMENT OF FOOT

NO.	NAME	RANK	CASUALTY	DATE	LONDON GAZETTE
3541	McBeath William	Pte.	W/D	26-6-55	10-7-55
3666	McCann James	Pte.	W/Sl	4-8-55	17-8-55
2165	McDonald Michael	Pte.	W/Sl	1-7-55	17-7-55
3166	McDonald Patrick	Pte.	W/Sl	29-7-55	7-8-55
3563	McIntosh John	Pte.	W/Sl	11-6-55	26-6-55
3335	McKenna James	Pte.	W/Sl	19-4-55	1-5-55
3564	McLeod Joshua	Pte.	W/D	9-6-55	22-6-55
3565	McLury John	Pte.	W/D	11-6-55	26-6-55
3747	McNatty William	Pte.	W/Sl	23-7-55	7-8-55
3566	McNaughton John	Pte.	W/D	14-8-55	28-8-55
3568	McPhail Thomas	Pte.	W/Sv	2-9-55	18-9-55
3320	Mara William	Pte.	W/Sl	4-8-55	17-8-55
2995	Martin Thomas	Pte.	W/Sv	29-7-55	7-8-55
3212	Meehan Michael	Pte.	W/Sl	14-4-55	1-5-55
3573	Miller George	Pte.	W/Sl	14-3-55	23-3-55
2472	Mortel William	Pte.	W/Sv	3-9-55	18-9-55
2472	Mortile William	Pte.	W/Sl	4-8-55	17-8-55
3244	Nugent Edward	Pte.	W/Sv	17-12-54	9-1-55
2309	Oriel John	Pte.	W/D	23-7-55	7-8-55
3048	O'Reilly Thomas	Pte.	W/Sl	4-8-55	17-8-55
2701	Parker Philip	Pte.	W/Sl	25-12-54	12-1-55
3323	Payne James	Pte.	W/Sl	2-9-55	18-9-55
2073	Philips Giles	Pte.	W/Sl	19-4-55	1-5-55
3294	Raulinson Charles	Pte.	W/Sl	11-5-55	25-5-55
3025	Reeve William	Pte.	W/Sl	26-7-55	7-8-55
2664	Rutridge Patrick	Pte.	W/Sl	23-8-55	4-9-55
3799	Shortt Charles	Pte.	W/Sl	4-9-55	18-9-55
1377	Singleton John	Pte.	W/Sv	12-3-55	23-3-55
3638	Slattery Thomas	Pte.	W/Sl	7-7-55	20-7-55
3193	Smith Thomas	Pte.	W/Sl	28-6-55	10-7-55
2820	Steadman Thomas	Pte.	W/Sl	4-8-55	17-8-55
3596	Stirling James	Pte.	W/D	11-6-55	26-6-55
1185	Taylor John	Pte.	W/D	26-4-55	4-5-55
3673	Thompson John	Pte.	W/D	11-6-55	26-6-55
3225	Vincent John	Pte.	W/Sl	21-7-55	3-8-55
3604	Weir John	Pte.	W/Sl	9-6-55	22-6-55
3003	White William	Pte.	W/Sl	7-7-55	20-7-55
3483	Wright Alexander	Pte.	W/Sv	2-9-55	18-9-55
3203	Mahoney Michael	L/Cpl.	Missing	7-12-54	29-12-54
3180	Greahan Martin	Pte.	Missing	7-12-54	29-12-54
1827	Osborn Thomas	Pte.	Missing	7-12-54	29-12-54
1394	O'Sullivan William	Pte.	Missing	7-12-54	29-12-54
3194	Preston James	Pte.	Missing	7-12-54	29-12-54
2927	Rendy Jeremiah	Pte.	Missing	7-12-54	29-12-54

56th REGIMENT OF FOOT

NO.	NAME	RANK	CASUALTY	DATE	LONDON GAZETTE
2458	Bright William	Pte.	Killed	5-9-55	18-9-55
3505	Buckingham John	Pte.	Killed	1-9-55	18-9-55
1972	Green J.	Pte.	Killed	7-9-55	25-9-55
3748	Lukey Jacob	Pte.	Killed	5-9-55	18-9-55
2993	Soley W.	Pte.	Killed	7-9-55	25-9-55
2813	Woods A.	Pte.	Killed	7-9-55	25-9-55
	Philips E. W.	Lieut.	W/Sl	5-9-55	18-9-55
2064	Emmett Arthur	Sergt.	W/D	4-9-55	18-9-55
4068	Bethell Joseph	Pte.	W/Sv	1-9-55	18-9-55
4132	Bright David	Pte.	W/Sl	5-9-55	18-9-55
3649	Butler James	Pte.	W/Sv	4-9-55	18-9-55
4084	Cummins Edward	Pte.	W/Sl	4-9-55	18-9-55
1440	Deliway Daniel	Pte.	W/Sl	29-8-55	11-9-55

NOTES

The Second, Third, Fourth, Fifth and Final Bombardment of Sebastopol, and Minor Actions

56th REGIMENT OF FOOT

NO.	NAME	RANK	CASUALTY	DATE	LONDON GAZETTE
3435	Flake Henry	Pte.	W/D	4-9-55	18-9-55
3846	Jones William	Pte.	W/D	4-9-55	18-9-55
3744	Lincham J.	Pte.	W/Sl	7-9-55	25-9-55
2351	Spicer W.	Pte.	W/Sl	7-9-55	25-9-55
1628	Virller Richard	Pte.	W/Sl	6-9-55	18-9-55

57th REGIMENT OF FOOT

NO.	NAME	RANK	CASUALTY	DATE	LONDON GAZETTE
1947	Kyle John	Sergt.	Killed	1-1-55	26-1-55
1349	Magee John	Sergt.	Killed	8-4-55	22-4-55
2553	Bennett Thomas	Pte.	Killed	24-12-54	9-1-55
3139	Conroy John	Pte.	Killed	26-8-55	7-9-55
3095	Dunn Daniel	Pte.	Killed	31-5-55	12-6-55
3176	Dwaddle James	Pte.	Killed	10-6-55	22-6-55
3197	Fennell Paul	Pte.	Killed	17-7-55	31-7-55
2226	Graham Alexander	Pte.	Killed	20-4-55	4-5-55
1419	Graham James	Pte.	Killed	24-12-54	9-1-55
2557	Jones John	Pte.	Killed	22-3-55	3-4-55
—	McCasspin Hugh	Pte.	Killed	24-12-54	9-1-55
3085	Mackleravey Hugh	Pte.	Killed	2-9-55	18-9-55
2811	Mullen John	Pte.	Killed	24-12-54	9-1-55
1954	Murphy Charles	Pte.	Killed	14-12-54	9-1-55
3253	Murray Foster	Pte.	Killed	20-4-55	4-5-55
2795	Nowlan John	Pte.	Killed	14-12-54	9-1-55
2594	Ryan Martin	Pte.	Killed	1-1-55	26-1-55
3125	Smith Felix	Pte.	Killed	22-3-55	3-4-55
2313	Walsh Robert	Pte.	Killed	1-1-55	26-1-55
2278	Webb Thomas	Pte.	Killed	24-12-54	9-1-55
	Mitchell George	Lieut.	W/D	18-3-55	30-3-55
2562	Bosworth William	Sergt.	W/Sv	10-8-55	24-8-55
2101	Griffiths William	Sergt.	W/Sl	8-12-54	29-12-54
1627	McDougall Alexander	Sergt.	W/Sl	8-12-54	29-12-54
1768	Waldie William	Sergt.	W/D	17-8-55	31-8-55
2275	Burns James	Corpl.	W/Sl	23-5-55	5-6-55
1296	Fieldins E.	Corpl.	W/Sl	20-11-54	11-12-54
3106	McGrury Henry	L/Cpl.	W/Sv	21-7-55	3-8-55
2151	Adley James	Pte.	W/Sv	16-6-55	3-7-55
2470	Anderson Thomas	Pte.	W/Sl	16-6-55	3-7-55
2279	Baisey William	Pte.	W/Sl	21-5-55	5-6-55
1946	Bardon John	Pte.	W/Sl	25-4-55	4-5-55
2765	Barry Patrick	Pte.	W/Sl	5-5-55	18-5-55
2479	Bates Stephen	Pte.	W/Sl	12-12-54	9-1-55
1917	Campbell John	Pte.	W/Sv	20-6-55	3-7-55
2840	Carroll Christopher	Pte.	W/Sl	22-12-54	9-1-55
1948	Carson Hance	Pte.	W/Sv	24-7-55	7-8-55
2318	Clarke George	Pte.	W/Sv	30-6-55	17-7-55
—	Cleary J.	Pte.	W/Sv	20-11-54	11-12-54
2804	Curtain Edmond	Pte.	W/D	21-4-55	4-5-55
1822	Derham John	Pte.	W/Sv	26-8-55	7-9-55
1647	Doyle Simon	Pte.	W/Sv	12-12-54	9-1-55
2461	Dullart Nicholas	Pte.	W/Sv	31-7-55	14-8-55
2796	Fagan William	Pte.	W/Sl	24-12-54	9-1-55
3748	Foley John	Pte.	W/Sv	22-3-55	3-4-55
3178	Frost Anthony	Pte.	W/Sv	20-6-55	3-7-55
2602	Goddin John	Pte.	W/Sv	11-4-55	24-4-55
1034	Golding Peter	Pte.	W/Sl	14-12-54	9-1-55
3207	Gray William	Pte.	W/Sv	2-9-55	18-9-55
1646	Hanley Michael	Pte.	W/Sl	14-12-54	9-1-55
2538	Hardgrave John	Pte.	W/Sl	14-8-55	28-8-55
1404	Herbert John	Pte.	W/Sv	1-1-55	26-1-55

NOTES

The Second, Third, Fourth, Fifth and Final Bombardment of Sebastopol, and Minor Actions

57th REGIMENT OF FOOT

NO.	NAME	RANK	CASUALTY	DATE	LONDON GAZETTE
2254	Hill Samuel	Pte.	W/Sl	25-4-55	4-5-55
2755	Hoolahan Martin	Pte.	W/Sv	9-6-55	22-6-55
2603	Huggill George	Pte.	W/D	27-8-55	11-9-55
3305	Hynes Patrick	Pte.	W/Sv	9-1-55	26-1-55
2763	Keefe Richard	Pte.	W/Sv	8-8-55	21-8-55
2015	Kelly John	Pte.	W/Sl	24-7-55	7-8-55
2178	Kelly Thomas	Pte.	W/Sl	8-12-54	29-12-54
—	Lewis James	Pte.	W/Sv	22-5-55	5-6-55
3224	Liddle Alexander	Pte.	W/Sv	24-8-55	7-9-55
1069	McBurney Harry	Pte.	W/Sl	27-8-55	7-9-55
2282	McConnell William	Pte.	W/Sl	14-12-54	9-1-55
3252	McIntosh George	Pte.	W/Sv	17-7-55	31-7-55
3013	McNamara John	Pte.	W/Sv	10-8-55	24-8-55
2805	McNamara Patrick	Pte.	W/Sv	28-6-55	10-7-55
2863	Manley John	Pte.	W/Sv	24-7-55	7-8-55
2420	Mulrooney Patrick	Pte.	W/Sv	9-1-55	26-1-55
2511	Murphy John	Pte.	W/Sl	8-12-54	29-12-54
2471	Murphy Michael	Pte.	W/Sl	8-12-54	29-12-54
2501	Murray John	Pte.	W/Sv	2-4-55	20-4-55
2296	Pasfield John	Pte.	W/Sl	20-4-55	4-5-55
3241	Peacock James	Pte.	W/Sv	22-3-55	3-4-55
2170	Redmond Patrick	Pte.	W/Sl	14-12-54	9-1-55
3177	Reid William	Pte.	W/Sv	22-5-55	5-6-55
2598	Rowe Nicholas	Pte.	W/Sv	17-8-55	31-8-55
3071	Sewell Richard	Pte.	W/Sl	4-12-54	29-12-54
2119	Shanks Gilbert	Pte.	W/Sv	27-7-55	7-8-55
3400	Sheehan John	Pte.	W/D	10-8-55	24-8-55
2751	Sheehan Timothy	Pte.	W/Sv	23-5-55	5-6-55
—	Smith Hugh	Pte.	W/Sv	18-11-54	11-12-54
3011	Smith William	Pte.	W/Sv	10-8-55	24-8-55
2448	Stagpool Martin	Pte.	W/Sv	28-4-55	4-5-55
1480	Thompson Henry	Pte.	W/Sv	12-12-54	9-1-55
3184	Thompson John	Pte.	W/Sv	24-7-55	7-8-55
1618	Traynor Thomas	Pte.	W/Sl	1-1-55	26-1-55
—	Williams Edward	Pte.	W/Sv	20-11-54	11-12-54
3194	Wright William	Pte.	W/Sl	18-8-55	31-8-55
1411	Holden Thomas	Sergt.	Missing	26-12-54	12-1-55
2307	Locke William	Sergt.	Missing	22-3-55	3-4-55
2478	Bales Edward	Pte.	Missing	22-3-55	3-4-55
2912	Clarke Charles	Pte.	Missing	1-1-55	26-1-55
2250	King Hugh	Pte.	Missing	26-12-54	12-1-55
	Carruthers John	Volunteer Reg No. not known	W/Sl	14-12-54	9-1-55

62nd REGIMENT OF FOOT

NO.	NAME	RANK	CASUALTY	DATE	LONDON GAZETTE
	White G. J.	Lieut.	Killed	3-5-55	15-5-55
3577	Donovan Patrick	Pte.	Killed	24-4-55	15-5-55
2592	Fitzgerald Patrick	Pte.	Killed	28-5-55	12-6-55
3518	Furlong John	Pte.	Killed	21-4-55	4-5-55
3117	Gunter Leighton	Pte.	Killed	18-12-54	9-1-55
2741	Lynch Patrick	Pte.	Killed	30-4-55	15-5-55
3530	Noonan John	Pte.	Killed	4-4-55	20-4-55
	Shearman R. A.	Lt/Col.	W/Sl	21-4-55	4-5-55
	Cubitt C. C.	Lieut.	W/Sl	28-6-55	10-7-55
	Forster J. B.	Capt.	W/Sl	15-3-55	23-3-55
—	Sirten Samuel	Corpl.	W/Sl	4-9-55	18-9-55
3295	Smith William	Corpl.	W/Sl	17-8-55	31-8-55

NOTES

The Second, Third, Fourth, Fifth and Final Bombardment of Sebastopol, and Minor Actions

62nd REGIMENT OF FOOT

NO.	NAME	RANK	CASUALTY	DATE	LONDON GAZETTE
3502	Amos David	Pte.	W/Sv	24-4-55	15-5-55
3743	Bellymore James	Pte.	W/D	4-9-55	18-9-55
—	Bermingham Michael	Pte.	W/Sl	20-7-55	3-8-55
3706	Berry James	Pte.	W/Sl	29-7-55	7-8-55
3570	Bunting Joseph	Pte.	W/Sl	15-4-55	1-5-55
2662	Collier John	Pte.	W/Sl	13-4-55	1-5-55
3649	Collins William	Pte.	W/Sv	4-1-55	26-1-55
—	Conroy Michael	Pte.	W/Sl	9-7-55	24-7-55
3557	Crown M.	Pte.	W/Sl	15-4-55	1-5-55
3205	Early Patrick	Pte.	W/Sv	22-5-55	5-6-55
2998	Fitzgerald Thomas	Pte.	W/Sl	4-1-55	26-1-55
3693	Freeman William	Pte.	W/Sl	29-7-55	7-8-55
3168	Grey William	Pte.	W/Sl	28-6-55	10-7-55
3132	Harrison William	Pte.	W/Sl	15-4-55	1-5-55
3720	Heywood William	Pte.	W/Sl	27-8-55	11-9-55
2311	Keating Daniel	Pte.	W/Sl	15-8-55	28-8-55
3290	Kelly John	Pte.	W/Sv	10-5-55	22-5-55
3563	Kerby Patrick	Pte.	W/Sl	11-4-55	24-4-55
3800	King James	Pte.	W/Sl	2-9-55	18-9-55
3426	Kufe Thomas	Pte.	W/Sv	4-3-55	16-3-55
3267	Lee William	Pte.	W/Sl	24-7-55	7-8-55
3675	McGibbon Donald	Pte.	W/Sl	21-7-55	3-8-55
3335	McKenna Thomas	Pte.	W/Sl	15-4-55	1-5-55
1673	McLaughlin John	Pte.	W/Sv	28-4-55	15-5-55
3639	McLoughlin Joseph	Pte.	W/Sl	15-8-55	28-8-55
3775	Madden James	Pte.	W/D	29-8-55	11-9-55
3528	Maher John	Pte.	W/Sl	2-9-55	18-9-55
3405	Mark Patrick	Pte.	W/Sl	24-4-55	15-5-55
2752	Nixon Adam	Pte.	W/Sv	28-5-55	12-6-55
3583	Perdue Henry	Pte.	W/Sl	24-7-55	7-8-55
3491	Ratty James	Pte.	W/Sl	14-4-55	1-5-55
3596	Reilly Hugh	Pte.	W/Sl	15-3-55	23-3-55
3668	Ross Henry	Pte.	W/Sl	27-7-55	7-8-55
3707	Rountree Thomas	Pte.	W/Sl	10-6-55	22-6-55
3442	Ruddle John	Pte.	W/Sv	21-7-55	3-8-55
3638	Simpson George	Pte.	W/Sv	23-4-55	15-5-55
2519	Stranford James	Pte.	W/D	4-8-55	17-8-55
3797	Surten Samuel	Pte.	W/Sl	4-9-55	18-9-55
3279	Swift William	Pte.	W/Sl	6-2-55	23-2-55

63rd REGIMENT OF FOOT

NO.	NAME	RANK	CASUALTY	DATE	LONDON GAZETTE
	Harrison G. N.	Brevet Major	Killed	7-7-55	20-7-55
3645	Browne Thomas	Pte.	Killed	22-8-55	4-9-55
3071	Mahon Edward	Pte.	Killed	23-8-55	4-9-55
	Higginbotham C.	Major	W/Sv	24-8-55	7-9-55
2002	Bourke Patrick	Sergt.	W/Sl	4-9-55	18-9-55
3549	Ball James	Pte.	W/Sv	16-7-55	31-7-55
3436	Caffrey Richard	Pte.	W/Sl	4-8-55	17-8-55
3384	Carey Edward	Pte.	W/Sv	16-7-55	31-7-55
3342	Carr William	Pte.	W/Sv	23-8-55	4-9-55
3785	Fitzpatrick John	Pte.	W/Sv	27-8-55	11-9-55
2487	Goodwin Hugh	Pte.	W/Sl	8-8-55	21-8-55
2821	Griffin Michael	Pte.	W/Sl	20-8-55	4-9-55
3591	Hampkin Stephen	Pte.	W/D	23-8-55	4-9-55
2311	Keating David	Pte.	W/Sl	15-8-55	28-8-55
3508	Lakey Francis	Pte.	W/Sl	4-8-55	17-8-55
3259	Leonard William	Pte.	W/Sl	23-11-54	11-12-54
3596	Lodge Benjamin	Pte.	W/Sv	23-8-55	4-9-55
3649	McFarlane Walter	Pte.	W/Sv	27-6-55	10-7-55

NOTES

The Second, Third, Fourth, Fifth and Final Bombardment of Sebastopol, and Minor Actions

63rd REGIMENT OF FOOT

NO.	NAME	RANK	CASUALTY	DATE	LONDON GAZETTE
3639	McLoughlin Joseph	Pte.	W/Sl	15-8-55	28-8-55
3227	Mulcahey Richard	Pte.	W/Sl	4-8-55	17-8-55
3153	Reilly John	Pte.	W/Sl	20-8-55	4-9-55
2675	Rorr William	Pte.	W/Sl	10-8-55	24-8-55
2675	Rorr William	Pte.	W/Sl	23-8-55	4-9-55
2695	Tuthill Francis	Pte.	W/Sl	20-8-55	4-9-55
2456	Bartlett George	Pte.	Missing		refer to the Battle of Inkermann, p. 61.
2741	Kenny Michael	Pte.	Missing		
2278	Murphy Owen	Pte.	Missing		
3018	O'Donald Thomas	Pte.	Missing		

68th REGIMENT OF FOOT

NO.	NAME	RANK	CASUALTY	DATE	LONDON GAZETTE
	Edwards R. L.	Capt.	Killed	11-5-55	25-5-55
2165	Ashby Robert	Pte.	Killed	11-5-55	25-5-55
2220	Bowers John	Pte.	Killed	15-8-55	28-8-55
3300	Forbes James	Pte.	Killed	9-6-55	22-6-55
3058	Gaffney William	Pte.	Killed	23-11-54	11-12-54
3668	Graham John	Pte.	Killed	10-8-55	24-8-55
3439	Hardyman William	Pte.	Killed	21-5-55	5-6-55
2952	McGeever Owen	Pte.	Killed	11-5-55	25-5-55
2882	Moyses Frederick	Pte.	Killed	8-6-55	22-6-55
2710	Murphy Stephen	Pte.	Killed	30-7-55	14-8-55
1391	Rustrick Thomas	Pte.	Killed	11-5-55	25-5-55
3049	Sales John	Pte.	Killed	10-8-55	24-8-55
3548	Simmons John	Pte.	Killed	11-5-55	25-5-55
3005	Tailey William	Pte.	Killed	11-5-55	25-5-55
3626	Toole Thomas	Pte.	Killed	28-7-55	7-8-55
3527	Turner James	Pte.	Killed	10-8-55	24-8-55
3580	Wheeler John	Pte.	Killed	26-7-55	7-8-55
2851	Wright John	Pte.	Killed	2-1-55	26-1-55
	Battiscombe H.	Lieut.	W/Sl	12-1-55	2-2-55
1522	Whelan James	Col/Sgt.	W/Sv	29-5-55	12-6-55
2328	Hasford James	Sergt.	W/Sv	20-8-55	4-9-55
2754	Glinane Thomas	Corpl.	W/Sv	11-5-55	25-5-55
3383	Ralph Edward	Corpl.	W/Sv	11-5-55	25-5-55
2910	Donoghue Roderick	L/Cpl.	W/Sv	19-8-55	31-8-55
2970	Lyons James	L/Cpl.	W/Sv	13-12-54	9-1-55
3018	Alsop Thomas	Pte.	W/Sl	9-6-55	22-6-55
3672	Asken James	Pte.	W/Sl	21-8-55	4-9-55
3571	Bailie Richard	Pte.	W/Sv	11-5-55	25-5-55
3188	Baxter John	Pte.	W/Sl	20-8-55	4-9-55
3133	Beard Stry	Pte.	W/Sl	4-9-55	18-9-55
2220	Bearnes John	Pte.	W/Sv	29-7-55	7-8-55
3425	Bonus Peter	Pte.	W/Sl	3-7-55	17-7-55
3424	Brennan John	Pte.	W/Sv	11-5-55	25-5-55
3701	Brown Joseph	Pte.	W/Sv	26-7-55	7-8-55
3501	Bush William	Pte.	W/Sv	11-5-55	25-5-55
2832	Byrne John	Pte.	W/Sl	12-1-55	2-2-55
2080	Campbell Benjamin	Pte.	W/Sl	11-5-55	25-5-55
3409	Carmody John	Pte.	W/Sv	29-7-55	7-8-55
3788	Carwood William	Pte.	W/Sl	20-8-55	4-9-55
2945	Connors John	Pte.	W/Sl	29-7-55	7-8-55
2858	Crimmins Thomas	Pte.	W/Sl	11-5-55	25-5-55
3203	Davidson James	Pte.	W/Sv	11-5-55	25-5-55
3676	Delaney James	Pte.	W/Sl	6-8-55	21-8-55
3438	Doyle Patrick	Pte.	W/Sv	11-5-55	25-5-55
2346	Duff Thomas	Pte.	D.O.W.	11-5-55	25-5-55
3529	Duggan John	Pte.	W/D	11-5-55	25-5-55
3394	Ellis William	Pte.	W/Sl	11-5-55	25-5-55

NOTES

The Second, Third, Fourth, Fifth and Final Bombardment of Sebastopol, and Minor Actions

68th REGIMENT OF FOOT

NO.	NAME	RANK	CASUALTY	DATE	LONDON GAZETTE
1868	Faulkner William	Pte.	W/Sl	19-8-55	31-8-55
3256	Ferris William	Pte.	W/Sv	11-5-55	25-5-55
3398	Gannon Thomas	Pte.	W/Sv	8-6-55	22-6-55
3398	Gannon Thomas	Pte.	W/Sl	26-8-55	4-9-55
2784	Gorry William	Pte.	W/Sv	6-8-55	21-8-55
3668	Graham John	Pte.	W/Sl	10-8-55	24-8-55
3091	Graham Robert	Pte.	W/Sl	12-1-55	2-2-55
3068	Hampshire Joseph	Pte.	W/Sl	12-1-55	2-2-55
2888	Hick Paul	Pte.	W/Sl	12-1-55	2-2-55
3328	Hilton James	Pte.	W/Sv	11-5-55	25-5-55
3241	Johnstone Thomas	Pte.	W/Sl	2-12-54	29-12-54
2717	Joyce Bartholomew	Pte.	W/D	11-5-55	25-5-55
2321	Kelly Joseph	Pte.	W/Sl	19-8-55	31-8-55
3338	Keogh Hugh	Pte.	W/Sl	21-8-55	4-9-55
3217	Lalley Patrick	Pte.	W/Sl	4-4-55	20-4-55
3263	Lawrison John	Pte.	W/Sl	13-12-54	9-1-55
3299	McDonald William	Pte.	W/Sv	11-5-55	25-5-55
3274	McElwain Samuel	Pte.	W/Sv	27-7-55	7-8-55
3591	McGowan James	Pte.	W/Sv	19-7-55	31-7-55
2987	McGowan M.	Pte.	W/Sl	4-9-55	18-9-55
3619	McKeevenny Thomas	Pte.	W/Sv	19-8-55	31-8-55
3336	Mack James	Pte.	W/Sv	12-1-55	2-2-55
2934	Molloy James	Pte.	W/D	11-5-55	25-5-55
2343	Murrell Thomas	Pte.	W/Sl	3-7-55	17-7-55
1539	Reardon Cornelius	Pte.	W/Sl	17-8-55	31-8-55
2799	Richardson Robert	Pte.	W/D	1-7-55	17-7-55
2671	Rider Edward	Pte.	W/Sl	19-8-55	31-8-55
1724	Riley John	Pte.	W/D	16-8-55	28-8-55
3252	Rogerson John	Pte.	W/Sv	28-4-55	15-5-55
2758	Ross Charles	Pte.	W/Sl	11-5-55	25-5-55
3049	Sales John	Pte.	W/Sl	10-8-55	24-8-55
3415	Sandys Robert	Pte.	D.O.W.	11-5-55	25-5-55
3617	Slowcroft Adam	Pte.	W/Sl	18-8-55	31-8-55
2999	Stead Frederick	Pte.	W/Sl	4-9-55	18-9-55
2269	Treacy John	Pte.	W/Sl	19-8-55	31-8-55
3210	Wallace Thomas	Pte.	W/Sv	25-6-55	10-7-55
2251	Walsh Joseph	Pte.	W/Sl	9-6-55	22-6-55
2231	Walsh Mark	Pte.	W/D	11-5-55	25-5-55
2235	Watkinson William	Pte.	D.O.W.	11-5-55	25-5-55
2533	Whenman Levi	Pte.	W/Sv	11-5-55	25-5-55
3566	Wilson Thomas	Pte.	W/Sv	3-7-55	17-7-55
2322	Woollfe Richard	Pte.	W/Sv	12-1-55	2-2-55
3212	Wright Thomas	Pte.	W/Sl	28-3-55	13-4-55
3007	Wyatt Thomas	Pte.	W/Sl	6-8-55	21-8-55
2722	Cooper William	Sergt.	Missing	12-1-55	2-2-55
3351	Binder Benjamin	L/Cpl.	Missing	12-1-55	2-2-55
2202	Harwood John	L/Cpl.	Missing	12-1-55	2-2-55
3146	Adams William	Pte.	Missing	12-1-55	2-2-55
3451	Baker John	Pte.	Missing	12-1-55	2-2-55
3253	Byron James	Pte.	Missing	12-1-55	2-2-55
2941	Clarke John	Pte.	Missing	12-1-55	2-2-55
2388	Eve John	Pte.	Missing	12-1-55	2-2-55
3368	Farrell Thomas	Pte.	Missing	12-1-55	2-2-55
3481	Field George	Pte.	Missing	12-1-55	2-2-55
3488	Mason Edward	Pte.	Missing	12-1-55	2-2-55
3187	Menagh James	Pte.	Missing	12-1-55	2-2-55
3404	Moher James	Pte.	Missing	12-1-55	2-2-55
2513	Tolley William	Pte.	Missing	12-1-55	2-2-55
2314	Wooley Robert	Pte.	Missing	11-5-55	25-5-55

NOTES

The Second, Third, Fourth, Fifth and Final Bombardment of Sebastopol, and Minor Actions

72nd REGIMENT OF FOOT

NO.	NAME	RANK	CASUALTY	DATE	LONDON GAZETTE
3015	Gilbert Charles	Pte.	Killed	8-7-55	20-7-55
1127	Law Alexander	Pte.	Killed	19-8-55	31-8-55
3044	McIntosh Donald	Pte.	Killed	13-8-55	28-8-55
1133	Merrilees Alexander	Pte.	Killed	5-7-55	17-7-55
2574	Patten John	Pte.	Killed	11-7-55	24-7-55
	Campbell J. T.	Lieut.	W/Sl	20-8-55	4-9-55
2744	McGilvray John	L/Sgt.	W/Sl	4-8-55	17-8-55
3411	McAleer A.	Corpl.	W/D	13-8-55	28-8-55
3133	Atkinson James	Pte.	W/Sl	26-6-55	10-7-55
3174	Barr John	Pte.	W/Sv	7-8-55	21-8-55
3064	Birkmyre William	Pte.	W/Sl	7-8-55	21-8-55
3117	Brown William	Pte.	W/Sv	10-8-55	24-8-55
1870	Campbell John	Pte.	W/Sv	4-8-55	17-8-55
2973	Chalmers William	Pte.	W/Sl	7-8-55	21-8-55
1848	Chisholm William	Pte.	W/Sl	13-8-55	28-8-55
3025	Clarke Andrew	Pte.	W/Sl	26-7-55	7-8-55
2956	Davidson James	Pte.	W/Sl	16-6-55	3-7-55
2448	Duff John	Pte.	W/Sl	3-7-55	17-7-55
2972	Dunchie Maitland	Pte.	W/Sl	26-7-55	7-8-55
1490	McCue Thomas	Pte.	W/Sl	22-8-55	4-9-55
3228	McDonald John	Pte.	W/D	13-8-55	28-8-55
2674	McDonald Neil	Pte.	W/Sl	13-8-55	28-8-55
3121	McKee Hugh	Pte.	W/D	4-8-55	17-8-55
3191	McMillan George	Pte.	W/Sl	16-8-55	28-8-55
2988	Marshall David	Pte.	W/Sv	29-7-55	7-8-55
3052	Murray James	Pte.	W/Sv	20-7-55	3-8-55
2943	Orr John	Pte.	W/Sl	5-7-55	17-7-55
3051	Patterson Robert	Pte.	W/Sl	23-7-55	7-8-55
3362	Reid James	Pte.	W/Sv	10-8-55	24-8-55
3424	Taylor John	Pte.	W/Sl	2-7-55	17-7-55
3304	White William	Pte.	W/Sl	20-7-55	3-8-55
3107	Youle John	Pte.	W/Sl	5-7-55	17-7-55

77th REGIMENT OF FOOT

NO.	NAME	RANK	CASUALTY	DATE	LONDON GAZETTE
	Egerton T. G.	Colonel	Killed	19-4-55	1-5-55
	Lempriere A.	Capt.	Killed	19-4-55	1-5-55
	Pechell W. H. C. G.	Capt.	Killed	3-9-55	18-9-55
2083	Casey Daniel	Sergt.	Killed	27-7-55	7-8-55
911	Loughlin John	Sergt.	Killed	3-9-55	18-9-55
1025	Despard John	L/Cpl.	Killed	21-8-55	4-9-55
3478	Heartley John	L/Cpl.	Killed	1-7-55	17-7-55
1437	Bennett Owen	Drummer	Killed	2-5-55	15-5-55
3380	Braziel Thomas	Pte.	Killed	22-3-55	3-4-55
2629	Brown William James	Pte.	Killed	17-2-55	6-3-55
1969	Bryan Patrick	Pte.	Killed	25-7-55	7-8-55
2617	Burfoot Francis	Pte.	Killed	15-3-55	23-3-55
3118	Cair William	Pte.	Killed	5-8-55	17-8-55
3083	Charleton Charles	Pte.	Killed	22-3-55	3-4-55
3482	Conelly William	Pte.	Killed	3-8-55	17-8-55
2769	Dinan Patrick	Pte.	Killed	15-8-55	24-8-55
3286	Dodd Alfred	Pte.	Killed	25-5-55	12-6-55
2829	Doyle Patrick	Pte.	Killed	25-7-55	7-8-55
3661	Hanlon John	Pte.	Killed	19-7-55	31-7-55
3657	Hutchinson John	Pte.	Killed	31-8-55	18-9-55
3350	Jackson George	Pte.	Killed	19-4-55	1-5-55
3437	Kimble Thomas	Pte.	Killed	19-4-55	1-5-55
2025	Leahy James	Pte.	Killed	19-4-55	1-5-55

NOTES

The Second, Third, Fourth, Fifth and Final Bombardment of Sebastopol, and Minor Actions

77th REGIMENT OF FOOT

NO.	NAME	RANK	CASUALTY	DATE	LONDON GAZETTE
3460	McCart John	Pte.	Killed	6-9-55	18-9-55
3344	Murphy Thomas	Pte.	Killed	30-5-55	12-6-55
3358	Murray John	Pte.	Killed	27-2-55	16-3-55
3339	Parker George	Pte.	Killed	19-4-55	1-5-55
3110	Prior Richard	Pte.	Killed	22-3-55	3-4-55
3074	Sharpe William	Pte.	Killed	3-9-55	18-9-55
3318	Stewart Alexander	Pte.	Killed	19-4-55	1-5-55
2064	Sullivan Michael	Pte.	Killed	19-4-55	1-5-55
2556	Wiggins Thomas	Pte.	Killed	10-6-55	22-6-55
3096	Williams George	Pte.	Killed	3-9-55	18-9-55
2711	Woodward George	Pte.	Killed	29-5-55	12-6-55
	Gilby B. D.	Capt.	W/Sl	19-4-55	1-5-55
	Morgan C. B.	Lieut.&Adj.	W/Sl	19-4-55	1-5-55
	Armstrong R. P.	Lieut.	W/Sl	17-8-55	31-8-55
	Fosberry W. T. E.	Lieut.	W/D	2-8-55	14-8-55
1702	Furnish James C.	Col/Sgt.	W/D	9-6-55	22-6-55
1952	Dunn Thomas	Sergt.	W/D	9-6-55	22-6-55
1750	Kirk William	Sergt.	W/Sl	14-8-55	28-8-55
1871	Larkman Isaac	Sergt.	W/Sl	27-7-55	7-8-55
3164	McNally James	Sergt.	W/Sv	19-4-55	1-5-55
2600	Park John	Sergt.	W/D	19-4-55	1-5-55
1601	Seerett William	Sergt.	W/Sv	3-5-55	15-5-55
3375	Stone George	Sergt.	W/Sv	14-8-55	28-8-55
2127	Tookey James	Sergt.	W/D	19-4-55	1-5-55
2142	Colgan Thomas	Corpl.	W/Sv	4-9-55	18-9-55
2846	Leonard J.	Corpl.	W/Sl	30-8-55	11-9-55
2542	Spence Thomas	Corpl.	W/Sv	2-8-55	14-8-55
2780	Witherspool Henry	Corpl.	W/Sv	17-4-55	1-5-55
3371	Hands Benjamin	L/Cpl.	W/Sv	8-8-55	21-8-55
1877	Kain Frederick	L/Cpl.	W/D	19-4-55	1-5-55
3414	Adcock Thomas	Pte.	W/Sl	10-6-55	22-6-55
2035	Ahern Patrick	Pte.	W/Sl	20-8-55	4-9-55
3400	Allen William	Pte.	W/Sl	24-7-55	7-8-55
2841	Baker David	Pte.	W/Sl	27-7-55	7-8-55
1277	Barber George	Pte.	W/Sl	8-8-55	21-8-55
2489	Barlow William	Pte.	W/Sl	15-6-55	3-7-55
3337	Bennett Francis	Pte.	W/Sv	19-4-55	1-5-55
2472	Bennett John	Pte.	W/Sl	27-7-55	7-8-55
3665	Betson Joseph	Pte.	W/D	20-8-55	4-9-55
3115	Bougham Patrick	Pte.	W/Sv	22-3-55	3-4-55
2500	Bowler Michael	Pte.	W/D	24-7-55	7-8-55
2862	Brannagan Patrick	Pte.	W/Sv	3-9-55	18-9-55
3685	Brooks George	Pte.	W/Sl	11-8-55	24-8-55
3044	Brooks Henry	Pte.	W/Sl	18-8-55	31-8-55
2520	Brown John M.	Pte.	W/Sv	19-4-55	1-5-55
3116	Bryan John	Pte.	W/Sl	27-7-55	7-8-55
3116	Bryan John	Pte.	W/Sl	3-9-55	18-9-55
3279	Bush Samuel	Pte.	W/Sv	5-9-55	18-9-55
2827	Campbell John	Pte.	W/Sv	18-4-55	1-5-55
3118	Carr William	Pte.	W/Sl	5-8-55	17-8-55
2940	Carson Samuel	Pte.	W/Sv	18-4-55	1-5-55
1217	Churchill William	Pte.	W/Sv	2-8-55	14-8-55
2871	Clarke James	Pte.	W/D	11-3-55	23-3-55
2875	Close Alexander	Pte.	W/Sv	19-4-55	1-5-55
3050	Connell Timothy	Pte.	W/Sv	11-3-55	23-3-55
2828	Coonahan John	Pte.	W/Sl	5-7-55	17-7-55
3276	Croney William	Pte.	W/Sv	19-4-55	1-5-55
3499	Cropp William	Pte.	W/Sl	11-8-55	24-8-55
1886	Delahunty Patrick	Pte.	W/Sl	20-8-55	4-9-55
2661	Dickey William	Pte.	W/Sl	18-8-55	31-8-55
2141	Dimond John	Pte.	W/Sl	19-4-55	1-5-55
3122	Donohue Thomas	Pte.	W/Sv	22-3-55	3-4-55
2903	Dougherty Hugh	Pte.	W/Sv	19-4-55	1-5-55
3435	Dunn William	Pte.	W/Sv	22-3-55	3-4-55

NOTES

The Second, Third, Fourth, Fifth and Final Bombardment of Sebastopol, and Minor Actions

77th REGIMENT OF FOOT

NO.	NAME	RANK	CASUALTY	DATE	LONDON GAZETTE
3435	Dunn William	Pte.	W/D	5-7-55	17-7-55
3227	Elderkin William	Pte.	W/Sv	19-4-55	1-5-55
2784	Erlam James	Pte.	W/Sl	28-3-55	13-4-55
2836	Farrell Michael	Pte.	W/Sl	25-7-55	7-8-55
2836	Farrell Michael	Pte.	W/Sv	28-8-55	11-9-55
1270	Fathen James	Pte.	W/Sl	27-7-55	7-8-55
2830	Faulkner John	Pte.	W/Sv	30-7-55	14-8-55
3689	Ferris John	Pte.	W/Sl	30-7-55	14-8-55
3392	Galloway Hugh	Pte.	W/Sv	19-4-55	1-5-55
2996	Grady Patrick	Pte.	W/Sl	28-3-55	13-4-55
3258	Grange William	Pte.	W/D	15-3-55	23-3-55
3125	Green Robert	Pte.	W/Sl	24-8-55	7-9-55
2625	Greneway George	Pte.	W/Sl	30-5-55	12-6-55
3433	Hackett William	Pte.	W/Sv	22-3-55	3-4-55
3468	Hamilton Robert	Pte.	W/Sl	31-8-55	18-9-55
2662	Hanajin John	Pte.	W/D	24-7-55	7-8-55
3187	Hawks W.	Pte.	W/Sv	30-8-55	11-9-55
3478	Heartly George	Pte.	W/Sv	19-4-55	1-5-55
2032	Hennessy Lawrence	Pte.	W/Sv	19-4-55	1-5-55
3322	Hoolahan Michael	Pte.	W/D	5-4-55	20-4-55
3478	Huntly George	Pte.	W/Sl	30-3-55	20-4-55
1973	Johnson Charles	Pte.	W/Sv	27-7-55	7-8-55
3496	Johnson Thomas	Pte.	W/Sl	20-8-55	4-9-55
3341	Jones Thomas	Pte.	W/Sv	5-4-55	20-4-55
3341	Jones Thomas	Pte.	W/Sv	19-4-55	1-5-55
3423	Joseph Michael	Pte.	W/D	20-8-55	4-9-55
2084	Joy Robert	Pte.	W/Sl	20-8-55	4-9-55
3669	Joyce Michael	Pte.	W/Sv	25-7-55	7-8-55
2547	Kelly Michael	Pte.	W/Sv	6-9-55	18-9-55
3454	Kelly Peter	Pte.	W/Sv	12-7-55	24-7-55
3443	Kennally John	Pte.	W/Sl	20-8-55	4-9-55
2817	Kilkenny Patrick	Pte.	W/Sv	19-4-55	1-5-55
3127	King Patrick	Pte.	W/Sv	19-4-55	1-5-55
3128	Kirkman Thomas	Pte.	W/Sv	6-9-55	18-9-55
2476	Knox Thomas H.	Pte.	W/Sv	19-4-55	1-5-55
1871	Larkman Isaac	Pte.	W/Sl	27-7-55	7-8-55
2098	Lennox William	Pte.	W/Sv	15-8-55	28-8-55
2861	McCabe Peter	Pte.	W/Sl	8-8-55	21-8-55
3320	McCallum Alexander	Pte.	W/Sv	19-4-55	1-5-55
3477	McCarthy Charles	Pte.	W/Sv	19-4-55	1-5-55
3374	McCarthy Patrick	Pte.	W/Sv	23-8-55	4-9-55
2963	McClusky Robert	Pte.	W/Sl	3-9-55	18-9-55
3399	McCormack Daniel	Pte.	W/Sv	12-7-55	24-7-55
2892	McDonald Philip	Pte.	W/D	20-8-55	4-9-55
3460	McGarth John	Pte.	W/Sv	10-6-55	22-6-55
3653	McGillam John	Pte.	W/D	23-8-55	4-9-55
3129	McGuire Brian	Pte.	W/Sl	23-8-55	4-9-55
3535	McIlvena Adam	Pte.	W/Sl	12-7-55	24-7-55
2552	McKneight Thomas	Pte.	W/D	13-2-55	3-3-55
2963	McLusky Robert	Pte.	W/Sv	22-3-55	3-4-55
2041	McMahon Francis	Pte.	W/D	28-8-55	11-9-55
3593	McMullen William	Pte.	W/Sv	20-8-55	4-9-55
1578	McVicker Neil	Pte.	W/Sv	17-8-55	31-8-55
2135	Magrath John	Pte.	W/Sv	27-2-55	16-3-55
1328	Mahon J.	Pte.	W/Sl	30-8-55	11-9-55
2898	Malcolm Henry	Pte.	W/Sl	30-3-55	20-4-55
2898	Malcolm Henry	Pte.	W/Sv	30-8-55	11-9-55
3361	Maurice James	Pte.	W/Sv	6-9-55	18-9-55
3361	Meince James	Pte.	W/D	5-4-55	20-4-55
1202	Mitchell Patrick	Pte.	W/Sl	17-8-55	31-8-55
3649	Mitchell Samuel	Pte.	W/Sl	17-8-55	31-8-55
3449	Montgomery Richard	Pte.	W/Sl	15-6-55	3-7-55
2452	Moore John	Pte.	W/Sv	27-2-55	16-3-55
724	Morcan Michael	Pte.	W/Sv	24-7-55	7-8-55

NOTES

The Second, Third, Fourth, Fifth and Final Bombardment of Sebastopol, and Minor Actions

77th REGIMENT OF FOOT

NO.	NAME	RANK	CASUALTY	DATE	LONDON GAZETTE
3425	Mulholland Daniel	Pte.	W/Sv	3-9-55	18-9-55
3474	Mullin Roger	Pte.	W/D	3-7-55	17-7-55
3109	Mulrooney James	Pte.	W/Sv	20-8-55	4-9-55
2805	Murgason Henry	Pte.	W/Sv	19-4-55	1-5-55
3019	Murray John	Pte.	W/Sv	5-4-55	20-4-55
3682	Naughton John	Pte.	W/D	23-8-55	4-9-55
3132	Nicholls Jessey	Pte.	W/D	22-4-55	4-5-55
2794	Oliver Thomas	Pte.	W/D	22-4-55	4-5-55
3699	Owens Daniel	Pte.	W/D	14-8-55	28-8-55
3339	Parker John	Pte.	W/Sl	30-7-55	14-8-55
3311	Patten John	Pte.	W/D	7-5-55	22-5-55
2980	Pierry John	Pte.	W/D	7-5-55	22-5-55
1589	Powell James	Pte.	W/D	23-4-55	15-5-55
3069	Pratt William	Pte.	W/Sv	20-8-55	4-9-55
2681	Pullen Richard	Pte.	W/Sl	5-7-55	17-7-55
3461	Quinn John	Pte.	W/Sv	12-7-55	24-7-55
3453	Reilly Michael	Pte.	W/Sv	7-7-55	20-7-55
2795	Reynolds Michael	Pte.	W/Sl	16-4-55	1-5-55
3360	Robinson J.	Pte.	W/D	30-8-55	11-9-55
2656	Roland William	Pte.	W/D	2-8-55	14-8-55
2778	Rurden Daniel	Pte.	W/D	13-2-55	3-3-55
3308	Saul John	Pte.	W/Sv	19-4-55	1-5-55
2752	Sayer James	Pte.	W/Sv	19-4-55	1-5-55
3239	Scott J.	Pte.	W/Sv	30-8-55	11-9-55
3664	Slater George	Pte.	W/Sv	15-8-55	28-8-55
3004	Smith Edward	Pte.	W/D	17-8-55	31-8-55
2988	Smith John	Pte.	W/Sl	2-8-55	14-8-55
3384	Stanton William	Pte.	W/Sv	3-7-55	17-7-55
3375	Stone George	Pte.	W/Sv	14-8-55	28-8-55
3694	Story Robert	Pte.	W/D	17-8-55	31-8-55
3265	Sullivan Owen	Pte.	W/Sl	17-8-55	31-8-55
3138	Talbot Matthew	Pte.	W/Sl	28-3-55	13-4-55
3357	Taylor Stewart	Pte.	W/Sv	19-4-55	1-5-55
3581	Thompson J.	Pte.	W/Sv	30-8-55	11-9-55
3100	Tobin Dennis	Pte.	W/Sl	17-8-55	31-8-55
2544	Toohey Patrick	Pte.	W/Sv	19-4-55	1-5-55
2851	Tracey Edmund	Pte.	W/Sl	2-7-55	17-7-55
3099	Tracey William	Pte.	W/Sv	19-4-55	1-5-55
3161	Trawley John	Pte.	W/D	7-7-55	20-7-55
2466	Tuney James	Pte.	W/Sv	6-9-55	18-9-55
1335	Tyrrol James	Pte.	W/Sv	19-4-55	1-5-55
2735	Underwood Richard	Pte.	W/Sl	20-8-55	4-9-55
3387	Walker Richard	Pte.	W/Sv	19-4-55	1-5-55
3168	Walker Stephen	Pte.	W/Sv	19-4-55	1-5-55
2912	Walsh Michael	Pte.	W/Sl	17-8-55	31-8-55
2128	Ward John	Pte.	W/Sl	28-8-55	11-9-55
3389	Warner Thomas	Pte.	W/Sv	14-8-55	28-8-55
2958	Webb Francis	Pte.	W/Sv	19-4-55	1-5-55
3321	Whelan Patrick	Pte.	W/Sv	19-4-55	1-5-55
2913	White William	Pte.	W/Sl	3-9-55	18-9-55
3473	Wiley Robert	Pte.	W/Sl	16-3-55	30-3-55
3043	Williams George	Pte.	W/D	20-8-55	4-9-55
1505	Wilson William	Pte.	W/Sl	3-9-55	18-9-55
2239	Wright A.	Pte.	W/Sl	30-8-55	11-9-55
3409	Wright John W.	Pte.	W/Sl	15-8-55	28-8-55
3094	Wright Joseph	Pte.	W/Sv	3-9-55	18-9-55
3297	Collins John	Pte.	Missing	22-3-55	3-4-55
3235	Lynn John	Pte.	Missing	22-3-55	3-4-55
3277	McCrinim David	Pte.	Missing	31-8-55	18-9-55
2166	O'Sullivan Richard	Pte.	Missing	22-3-55	3-4-55

NOTES

The Second, Third, Fourth, Fifth and Final Bombardment of Sebastopol, and Minor Actions

79th REGIMENT OF FOOT

NO.	NAME	RANK	CASUALTY	DATE	LONDON GAZETTE
3893	Beaton John	Pte.	Killed	23-6-55	9-7-55
3932	Conn George	Pte.	Killed	13-8-55	28-8-55
3860	McBean Leslie	Pte.	Killed	27-6-55	10-7-55
3109	Marshall David	Pte.	Killed	19-8-55	31-8-55
	McBarnet D. H.	Lieut.	W/Sl	20-8-55	31-8-55
	Lundy E. L.	Asst. Surgeon	W/Sl	29-7-55	7-8-55
1260	McLaren J.	Sergt.	W/Sl	13-8-55	28-8-55
3307	Brown John	Corpl.	W/Sl	22-8-55	4-9-55
4023	Bewley Edward	Pte.	W/Sl	10-8-55	24-8-55
3864	Brodie Peter	Pte.	W/Sl	16-8-55	28-8-55
2510	Campbell Hugh	Pte.	W/Sv	5-7-55	17-7-55
3437	Douglas William	Pte.	W/Sv	10-8-55	24-8-55
4040	Gemmell William	Pte.	W/Sl	10-8-55	24-8-55
2455	Gortley James	Pte.	W/Sl	19-8-55	31-8-55
4018	Gray Peter	Pte.	W/D	13-8-55	28-8-55
3497	Hamilton James	Pte.	W/Sl	6-7-55	20-7-55
3221	Hastie William	Pte.	W/Sv	19-8-55	31-8-55
3205	Howden Charles	Pte.	W/D	13-8-55	28-8-55
3447	Kelly William	Pte.	W/Sl	19-8-55	31-8-55
2479	Leath Thomas	Pte.	W/Sl	6-7-55	20-7-55
3522	Lindsey James	Pte.	W/Sl	19-8-55	31-8-55
3932	Logan James	Pte.	W/Sl	10-8-55	24-8-55
3623	McCulloch Charles	Pte.	W/Sl	19-8-55	31-8-55
3200	McDonald James	Pte.	W/Sl	10-8-55	24-8-55
2707	McDonald Robert	Pte.	W/Sl	29-7-55	7-8-55
3631	McGinty William	Pte.	W/Sl	29-7-55	7-8-55
3150	McGregor David	Pte.	W/Sl	26-7-55	7-8-55
3864	McKenzie John	Pte.	W/Sl	1-8-55	14-8-55
3762	McMillan James	Pte.	W/Sl	19-8-55	31-8-55
3495	McVey Hugh	Pte.	W/Sl	17-7-55	31-7-55
3562	Maxwell Alexander	Pte.	W/Sl	19-8-55	31-8-55
2250	Mitchell William	Pte.	W/Sl	26-7-55	7-8-55
3185	Rea Robert	Pte.	W/Sl	4-8-55	17-8-55
2479	Seath Thomas	Pte.	W/Sl	19-8-55	31-8-55
3556	Stewart Robert	Pte.	W/Sv	10-8-55	24-8-55
3640	Sweeney James	Pte.	W/Sl	29-7-55	7-8-55
4080	Urquhart John	Pte.	W/D	4-8-55	17-8-55
3601	Vershaw George	Pte.	W/Sl	5-7-55	17-7-55
3902	Wallace Robert	Pte.	W/Sv	10-8-55	24-8-55
3312	Watson John	Pte.	W/Sv	5-7-55	17-7-55

88th REGIMENT OF FOOT

NO.	NAME	RANK	CASUALTY	DATE	LONDON GAZETTE
	Preston H. B.	Lieut.	Killed	14-4-55	1-5-55
3165	Downie John	Corpl.	Killed	10-5-55	22-5-55
2720	Houlihom John	Corpl.	Killed	11-1-55	26-1-55
3015	Connors Martin	Pte.	Killed	14-6-55	26-6-55
3703	Dowd Thomas	Pte.	Killed	10-5-55	22-5-55
3805	Feegan Patrick	Pte.	Killed	18-8-55	31-8-55
3875	Gilgan Philip	Pte.	Killed	25-7-55	7-8-55
3167	Gordan Alexander	Pte.	Killed	25-7-55	7-8-55
2982	Hanley John	Pte.	Killed	8-7-55	20-7-55
1921	Hough John	Pte.	Killed	18-8-55	31-8-55
3554	Jones John	Pte.	Killed	19-7-55	31-7-55
3406	Kennedy John Wm.	Pte.	Killed	8-5-55	22-5-55
2762	Knowles William	Pte.	Killed	25-6-55	10-7-55
3796	McMullan John	Pte.	Killed	25-8-55	7-9-55
3352	Mahoney Edward	Pte.	Killed	4-9-55	18-9-55

NOTES

The Second, Third, Fourth, Fifth and Final Bombardment of Sebastopol, and Minor Actions

88th REGIMENT OF FOOT

NO.	NAME	RANK	CASUALTY	DATE	LONDON GAZETTE
3238	Montague Edward	Pte.	Killed	8-7-55	20-7-55
3774	Motton Frederick	Pte.	Killed	25-2-55	16-3-55
2727	O'Connors Michael	Pte.	Killed	28-8-55	11-9-55
3318	Riley John	Pte.	Killed	25-8-55	7-9-55
3111	Roberts John	Pte.	Killed	27-8-55	11-9-55
2396	Sherlock Michael	Pte.	Killed	2-6-55	15-6-55
3740	White Thomas	Pte.	Killed	21-7-55	3-8-55
	Steevens N.	Capt.	W/Sl	28-7-55	7-8-55
1096	Cunniff Charles	Sergt.	W/Sv	19-4-55	1-5-55
2412	Flaherty John	Sergt.	W/Sv	21-7-55	3-8-55
2812	Hopkins William	Sergt.	W/Sl	14-4-55	1-5-55
3341	Liddell Andrew	Sergt.	W/Sv	19-4-55	1-5-55
3514	Melville James	Sergt.	W/Sl	22-3-55	3-4-55
2620	Connolly Patrick	Corpl.	W/Sl	29-6-55	17-7-55
3165	Downie John	Corpl.	W/Sl	5-4-55	20-4-55
1056	Fahey Timothy	Corpl	W/D	14-8-55	28-8-55
2857	Fitzgerald John	Corpl.	W/Sv	29-6-55	17-7-55
3064	Riely John	Corpl.	W/Sv	26-8-55	7-9-55
2878	Ward B.	Corpl.	W/Sv	3-9-55	18-9-55
3172	Hueston Henry	L/Cpl.	W/Sv	23-4-55	15-5-55
3737	McCarra Michael	Drummer	W/Sv	18-8-55	31-8-55
3146	Allman John	Pte.	W/Sl	27-7-55	7-8-55
2438	Baker Thomas	Pte.	W/Sv	4-7-55	17-7-55
3619	Blacklock Charles	Pte.	W/Sl	9-7-55	24-7-55
3160	Brown William	Pte.	W/Sl	21-7-55	3-8-55
878	Bryan T.	Pte.	W/Sv	3-9-55	18-9-55
3149	Burke John	Pte.	W/Sl	8-7-55	20-7-55
2047	Cannon James	Pte.	W/D	10-5-55	22-5-55
3389	Carney James	Pte.	W/Sl	5-7-55	17-7-55
3679	Carter Thomas	Pte.	W/D	14-4-55	1-5-55
3110	Clacherty Patrick	Pte.	W/Sl	9-5-55	22-5-55
3779	Clarke Andrew	Pte.	W/D	9-7-55	24-7-55
2903	Cockerry Daniel	Pte.	W/Sv	27-2-55	16-3-55
3814	Collins John	Pte.	W/Sl	12-7-55	24-7-55
2047	Connors James	Pte.	W/Sl	17-4-55	1-5-55
2890	Connors William	Pte.	D.O.W.	10-5-55	22-5-55
2677	Cottingham Patrick	Pte.	W/Sv	3-9-55	18-9-55
1428	Cox James	Pte.	W/Sv	3-9-55	18-9-55
3143	Cullmane John	Pte.	W/Sv	14-4-55	1-5-55
3143	Cullmane John	Pte.	W/Sl	18-7-55	31-7-55
3742	Cummins Michael	Pte.	W/Sl	10-5-55	22-5-55
3931	Dacey John	Pte.	W/Sl	18-8-55	31-8-55
3912	Donlan Thomas	Pte.	W/Sl	3-5-55	15-5-55
2943	Donoghue John	Pte.	W/Sl	10-5-55	22-5-55
3836	Duhig Patrick	Pte.	W/Sv	24-6-55	9-7-55
3797	Farrell Edward	Pte.	W/Sv	26-8-55	7-9-55
3835	Farrell John	Pte.	W/D	3-9-55	18-9-55
2887	Foley Patrick	Pte.	W/Sv	23-4-55	15-5-55
3019	Fuly Michael	Pte.	W/D	18-8-55	31-8-55
3783	Fury John	Pte.	W/Sl	24-8-55	7-9-55
3224	Garry Michael	Pte.	W/Sv	18-8-55	31-8-55
3682	Gavin Peter	Pte.	W/D	3-9-55	18-9-55
3299	Gavin William	Pte.	W/Sv	18-11-54	11-12-54
2944	Griffin John	Pte.	W/Sv	9-5-55	22-5-55
3755	Griffin John	Pte.	W/D	4-7-55	17-7-55
3263	Hagarty John	Pte.	W/Sl	19-5-55	5-6-55
3560	Hartney Patrick	Pte.	W/Sl	8-8-55	21-8-55
2806	Holland Harry	Pte.	W/Sl	29-6-55	17-7-55
1961	Hough John	Pte.	W/Sl	14-3-55	23-3-55
3690	Huntley William	Pte.	W/Sl	14-3-55	23-3-55
2891	Hyth Richard	Pte.	W/Sv	25-8-55	7-9-55
3595	Keenan Michael	Pte.	W/Sv	8-7-55	20-7-55
1138	Kennedy Patrick	Pte.	W/Sv	5-7-55	17-7-55
3089	Keoghan Patrick	Pte.	W/Sl	5-9-55	18-9-55

NOTES

The Second, Third, Fourth, Fifth and Final Bombardment of Sebastopol, and Minor Actions

88th REGIMENT OF FOOT

NO.	NAME	RANK	CASUALTY	DATE	LONDON GAZETTE
3131	Low John	Pte.	W/D	26-8-55	7-9-55
3448	Lynch Robert	Pte.	W/D	4-7-55	17-7-55
2959	Lyrught James	Pte.	W/Sv	2-4-55	20-4-55
3935	McCormack Edward	Pte.	W/Sv	3-9-55	18-9-55
3674	McGindley John	Pte.	W/Sv	23-2-55	16-3-55
3646	McGuire John	Pte.	W/Sv	16-4-55	1-5-55
3140	McKeon Robert	Pte.	W/Sl	26-8-55	7-9-55
3765	McLoughlan Thomas	Pte.	W/Sl	26-8-55	7-9-55
3465	McLoughlin George	Pte.	W/Sl	18-7-55	31-7-55
3149	McMahon Daniel	Pte.	W/Sv	9-2-55	27-2-55
1792	McManus Thomas	Pte.	W/Sv	26-8-55	7-9-55
3379	McNamara Charles	Pte.	W/Sl	9-7-55	24-7-55
1657	McTag John	Pte.	W/D	3-9-55	18-9-55
1831	Malone Edward	Pte.	W/Sl	12-7-55	24-7-55
3208	Meough Thomas	Pte.	W/Sv	18-7-55	31-7-55
2997	Mulcahy Michael	Pte.	W/Sl	11-8-55	24-8-55
3685	Mullins James	Pte.	W/Sl	11-8-55	24-8-55
3699	Munro Donal	Pte.	W/Sl	2-4-55	20-4-55
3358	Murphy Patrick	Pte.	W/D	14-8-55	28-8-55
3933	Murphy Thomas	Pte.	W/Sl	18-7-55	31-7-55
3238	Murphy Edward	Pte.	W/Sv	11-8-55	24-8-55
3732	Murray James	Pte.	W/D	21-7-55	3-8-55
3726	Murray James	Pte.	W/D	13-6-55	26-6-55
3586	Nayle Joseph	Pte.	W/Sl	8-7-55	20-7-55
3643	Nelson Richard	Pte.	W/D	15-4-55	1-5-55
2991	Nevill James	Pte.	W/Sv	21-7-55	3-8-55
3461	Noffin Martin	Pte.	W/Sl	3-3-55	16-3-55
4037	Noone John	Pte.	W/Sl	19-7-55	31-7-55
2874	O'Brien John	Pte.	W/Sl	17-8-55	31-8-55
3573	O'Callaghan Charles	Pte.	W/Sl	12-7-55	24-7-55
2772	O'Connor Michael	Pte.	W/Sl	18-11-54	11-12-54
3205	O'Hara John	Pte.	W/Sv	26-5-55	12-6-55
3966	Platten Thomas	Pte.	W/Sv	14-8-55	28-8-55
3368	Pollard Edwin	Pte.	W/Sv	21-7-55	3-8-55
3508	Provens Samuel	Pte.	W/Sv	8-8-55	21-8-55
3780	Purcell Henry	Pte.	W/Sv	18-8-55	31-8-55
3832	Quinlan Edward	Pte.	W/Sl	26-8-55	7-9-55
3617	Quinn Daniel	Pte.	W/Sl	12-3-55	23-3-55
3848	Quinn James	Pte.	W/Sl	12-7-55	24-7-55
3848	Quinn James	Pte.	W/Sv	14-8-55	28-8-55
3676	Quinn James	Pte.	W/Sl	11-8-55	24-8-55
2105	Rielly Edward	Pte.	W/Sl	9-7-55	24-7-55
1895	Russell Michael	Pte.	W/Sl	14-8-55	28-8-55
3113	Sheehan Patrick	Pte.	W/Sl	26-8-55	7-9-55
3633	Smith George	Pte.	W/Sl	11-8-55	24-8-55
3563	Smith George	Pte.	W/Sl	29-5-55	12-6-55
3759	Smith James	Pte.	W/D	9-5-55	22-5-55
3840	Smith Matthew	Pte.	W/Sv	13-6-55	26-6-55
3009	Sullivan Eugene	Pte.	W/D	17-4-55	1-5-55
1026	Walsh John	Pte.	W/Sl	8-1-55	26-1-55
1491	Walsh M.	Pte.	W/Sv	3-9-55	18-9-55
4002	Whitehead William	Pte.	W/Sl	14-8-55	28-8-55
3792	Wilson Thomas	Pte.	W/Sv	4-7-55	17-7-55

89th REGIMENT OF FOOT

NO.	NAME	RANK	CASUALTY	DATE	LONDON GAZETTE
2819	Kennedy Michael	Pte.	Killed	8-5-55	22-5-55
2605	Nicholson Henry	Pte.	Killed	4-5-55	18-5-55
2926	Williamson Henry	Pte.	Killed	19-1-55	6-2-55
2483	Hampton Michael	Col/Sgt.	W/Sl	11-5-55	25-5-55

NOTES

The Second, Third, Fourth, Fifth and Final Bombardment of Sebastopol, and Minor Actions

89th REGIMENT OF FOOT

NO.	NAME	RANK	CASUALTY	DATE	LONDON GAZETTE
2395	Carruthers James	Sergt.	W/Sv	30-4-55	15-5-55
1708	McDougill Thomas	Sergt.	W/Sv	25-8-55	7-9-55
1378	Nagle Joseph	Sergt.	W/Sv	8-6-55	22-6-55
3508	Burke Mathew	Corpl.	W/D	4-8-55	17-8-55
3133	Farrell John	Corpl.	W/Sl	20-6-55	3-7-55
1266	Hinchey William	Corpl.	W/Sl	16-8-55	28-8-55
3039	Lambert Michael	Corpl.	W/Sv	11-5-55	25-5-55
3149	Love William	Corpl.	W/D	28-4-55	15-5-55
2837	Mooney Michael	Corpl.	W/Sl	21-8-55	4-9-55
1728	Palmer William	Corpl.	W/Sv	8-4-55	20-4-55
1605	Perry William	Corpl.	W/Sl	29-3-55	13-4-55
2981	Power Michael	Corpl.	W/Sl	2-8-55	14-8-55
3508	Burke Mathew	L/Cpl.	W/Sv	7-4-55	20-4-55
2937	Patterson Henry	L/Cpl.	W/Sl	9-6-55	22-6-55
2685	Atkinson Samuel	Pte.	W/Sv	9-4-55	24-4-55
2491	Atkinson William	Pte.	W/Sv	30-4-55	15-5-55
2631	Bell Alexander	Pte.	W/Sl	14-4-55	1-5-55
3267	Brine James	Pte.	W/Sl	8-5-55	22-5-55
3515	Broadbent Thomas	Pte.	W/Sv	30-4-55	15-5-55
3070	Burke David	Pte.	W/Sl	19-7-55	31-7-55
3286	Burke William	Pte.	W/Sl	7-5-55	22-5-55
2521	Carpenter James	Pte.	W/Sl	2-8-55	14-8-55
3097	Cary Daniel	Pte.	W/Sv	15-7-55	27-7-55
2306	Clarke George	Pte.	W/Sl	3-8-55	17-8-55
3119	Cormack Patrick	Pte.	W/Sl	28-8-55	11-9-55
1509	Cox John	Pte.	W/Sv	4-7-55	17-7-55
3538	Cummings Charles	Pte.	W/Sv	8-5-55	22-5-55
3230	Dixon John	Pte.	W/Sv	31-7-55	14-8-55
2321	Dixon Thomas	Pte.	W/Sv	28-4-55	15-5-55
3603	Dowd Philip	Pte.	W/D	4-7-55	17-7-55
3298	Faunce James	Pte.	W/Sv	9-6-55	22-6-55
3346	Fisher John	Pte.	W/Sl	2-8-55	14-8-55
3015	Flynn James	Pte.	W/Sv	31-7-55	14-8-55
3382	Gaffney Bernard	Pte.	W/Sv	8-5-55	22-5-55
3012	Gason James	Pte.	W/Sl	2-8-55	14-8-55
2571	Green Joseph	Pte.	W/Sv	11-5-55	25-5-55
3510	Hanagan Dennis	Pte.	W/Sl	2-8-55	14-8-55
3511	Hayes Thomas	Pte.	W/Sl	28-8-55	11-9-55
2747	Houston William	Pte.	W/Sl	19-1-55	6-2-55
2670	Jones Moses	Pte.	W/Sl	20-4-55	4-5-55
1249	Jordan Alexander	Pte.	W/D	20-6-55	3-7-55
3122	Kelly John	Pte.	W/Sl	3-7-55	17-7-55
3489	Kelly John	Pte.	W/Sl	17-2-55	16-3-55
2660	Knowles John	Pte.	W/Sv	17-2-55	16-3-55
2881	Londrigan James	Pte.	W/Sl	10-7-55	24-7-55
2972	Loughlin John	Pte.	W/Sl	22-12-54	9-1-55
3305	McKewn Michael	Pte.	W/Sl	4-7-55	17-7-55
2520	McQuilty Robert	Pte.	W/Sl	19-7-55	31-7-55
2609	Molony John	Pte.	W/Sv	28-8-55	11-9-55
3449	Moran John	Pte.	W/Sv	9-6-55	22-6-55
3186	Muley Thomas	Pte.	W/Sl	5-1-55	26-1-55
2465	Murray William	Pte.	W/Sv	13-2-55	2-3-55
1188	Nugent James	Pte.	W/Sl	22-12-54	9-1-55
3101	Quinlan Michael	Pte.	W/Sv	4-9-55	18-9-55
3270	Quinn James	Pte.	W/D	14-5-55	29-5-55
3234	Roek A. W.	Pte.	W/Sv	24-7-55	7-8-55
2429	Smith Samuel	Pte.	W/Sl	24-7-55	7-8-55
3519	Spiers George	Pte.	W/D	19-7-55	31-7-55
3098	Steele Robert	Pte.	W/D	4-5-55	18-5-55
1061	Wall John	Pte.	W/Sl	17-3-55	3-4-55
3501	Ward Jeremiah	Pte.	D.O.W.	14-3-55	21-3-55
3250	White George	Pte.	W/Sv	24-7-55	7-8-55
	Hill Arundel E.	Capt.	Missing	28-3-55	13-4-55

NOTES

The Second, Third, Fourth, Fifth and Final Bombardment of Sebastopol, and Minor Actions

90th REGIMENT OF FOOT

NO.	NAME	RANK	CASUALTY	DATE	LONDON GAZETTE
2649	Cook William	Pte.	Killed	3-4-55	20-4-55
3028	Cusack John	Pte.	Killed	6-9-55	18-9-55
3043	Fowler Thomas	Pte.	Killed	28-8-55	11-9-55
3624	Garretty Patrick	Pte.	Killed	3-9-55	18-9-55
3420	Goldie William	Pte.	Killed	10-4-55	24-4-55
3847	McAuliffe Timothy	Pte.	Killed	27-8-55	11-9-55
3873	McCrea Joseph	Pte.	Killed	6-9-55	18-9-55
2127	Martin James	Pte.	Killed	14-8-55	28-8-55
3553	Plummer Peter	Pte.	Killed	27-8-55	11-9-55
3502	Runham Frederick	Pte.	Killed	9-5-55	22-5-55
3867	Wells Henry	Pte.	Killed	28-8-55	11-9-55
	Grahame N.	Lieut.	W/Sl	8-8-55	21-8-55
	Nunn J. J.	Lieut.	W/Sl	10-6-55	22-6-55
	Rous W. J.	Lieut.	W/Sl	26-8-55	7-9-55
	Barr J.	Ensign	W/Sl	27-3-55	13-4-55
	Smith C.	Capt.	W/Sl	2-9-55	18-9-55
	Wolseley C. J.	Capt. & Ass. Eng.	W/Sv	30-8-55	11-9-55
2978	Hutt Henry	Sergt.	W/Sv	10-6-55	22-6-55
2723	Williams J.	Sergt.	W/Sl	18-7-55	31-7-55
2313	Carruthers William	Corpl.	W/Sv	22-3-55	3-4-55
2817	Clarke E.	Corpl.	W/Sv	26-8-55	7-9-55
2545	Dridge John	Corpl.	W/Sl	10-6-55	22-6-55
2816	Heritage James	Corpl.	W/Sl	14-8-55	28-8-55
2845	Hott Henry	Corpl.	W/Sl	23-8-55	4-9-55
3143	Humphreys George	Corpl.	W/Sv	6-9-55	18-9-55
2352	Lenane John	Corpl.	W/D	26-8-55	7-9-55
3478	Wickens Charles	L/Cpl.	W/Sl	16-6-55	3-7-55
3339	Adams Phillip	Pte.	W/Sv	16-4-55	1-5-55
3147	Andrews John	Pte.	W/Sv	11-6-55	26-6-55
2514	Bailey Thomas	Pte.	W/Sl	7-7-55	20-7-55
2102	Bartlett Joseph	Pte.	W/Sl	1-9-55	18-9-55
3582	Boyle Christopher	Pte.	W/Sv	26-8-55	7-9-55
3354	Brennan Thomas	Pte.	W/D	4-5-55	18-5-55
3943	Buchenough George	Pte.	W/Sv	24-8-55	7-9-55
3318	Buckley Daniel	Pte.	W/Sl	22-3-55	3-4-55
3025	Burke Patrick	Pte.	W/Sv	8-8-55	21-8-55
3410	Butler James	Pte.	W/Sv	10-4-55	24-4-55
3868	Carr James	Pte.	W/Sl	28-8-55	11-9-55
2932	Carrol Michael	Pte.	W/Sl	3-9-55	18-9-55
2719	Carruthers John	Pte.	W/Sv	10-5-55	22-5-55
3608	Carter William	Pte.	W/Sv	16-6-55	3-7-55
2097	Carty Michael	Pte.	W/Sv	16-7-55	31-7-55
2898	Clements James	Pte.	W/Sv	26-8-55	7-9-55
3424	Cochrane Alexander	Pte.	W/Sv	7-7-55	20-7-55
3616	Connell Edward	Pte.	W/Sv	26-8-55	7-9-55
3296	Coonan James	Pte.	W/D	8-8-55	21-8-55
3317	Crowrick Joseph	Pte.	W/Sl	5-8-55	17-8-55
3973	Cummings Francis	Pte.	W/Sv	26-8-55	7-9-55
3829	Davis William	Pte.	W/Sv	26-6-55	10-7-55
2796	Davis William	Pte.	W/Sv	9-7-55	24-7-55
3565	Duffy James	Pte.	W/Sl	16-7-55	31-7-55
2067	Dwyer Patrick	Pte.	W/Sv	19-7-55	31-7-55
3208	Elvin Mathew	Pte.	W/Sv	8-8-55	21-8-55
2392	Fahey Thomas	Pte.	W/Sv	2-5-55	15-5-55
2584	Fair John	Pte.	W/Sv	26-8-55	7-9-55
2454	Finn Patrick	Pte.	W/Sl	10-7-55	24-7-55
3490	Fletcher James	Pte.	W/Sv	18-5-55	5-6-55
3753	Fuller Henry	Pte.	W/Sl	10-7-55	24-7-55
1853	Gall John	Pte.	W/Sl	26-8-55	7-9-55
3271	Geoghan Thomas	Pte.	D.O.W.	3-4-55	20-4-55
2864	Green George	Pte.	W/Sv	16-7-55	31-7-55
3949	Halls John	Pte.	W/Sl	26-8-55	7-9-55

NOTES

The Second, Third, Fourth, Fifth and Final Bombardment of Sebastopol, and Minor Actions

90th REGIMENT OF FOOT

NO.	NAME	RANK	CASUALTY	DATE	LONDON GAZETTE
2665	Hampton William	Pte.	W/D	22-8-55	4-9-55
1917	Harper Joseph	Pte.	W/Sv	27-4-55	15-5-55
2223	Hartill John	Pte.	D.O.W.	19-2-55	6-3-55
2119	Henton James	Pte.	W/Sl	19-8-55	31-8-55
3324	Hepburn Peter	Pte.	W/Sv	25-4-55	15-5-55
2852	Hines John	Pte.	W/Sl	8-8-55	21-8-55
2827	Hobbs James	Pte.	W/Sv	15-2-55	2-3-55
3382	Hodge William	Pte.	W/Sv	9-4-55	24-4-55
3492	Hunter William	Pte.	W/Sl	10-6-55	22-6-55
1914	Johnson William	Pte.	W/Sl	5-5-55	18-5-55
3655	Jordan James	Pte.	W/Sv	9-5-55	22-5-55
2379	Kelly T.	Pte.	W/Sv	19-4-55	1-5-55
3146	Kimming Richard	Pte.	W/Sv	9-7-55	24-7-55
3531	Lynch Dennis	Pte.	W/Sl	23-8-55	4-9-55
3730	McCartney Alfred	Pte.	W/Sl	1-9-55	18-9-55
3359	McCleland James	Pte.	W/Sv	12-4-55	24-4-55
3430	McDogle Andrew	Pte.	W/Sv	15-8-55	28-8-55
3711	McDonald Patrick	Pte.	W/Sv	26-8-55	7-9-55
3251	McGinty William	Pte.	W/Sv	26-8-55	7-9-55
3668	McKeon John	Pte.	W/Sv	11-6-55	26-6-55
3678	McKeon John	Pte.	W/Sl	28-8-55	11-9-55
3566	McNamara Patrick	Pte.	W/Sv	26-8-55	7-9-55
3547	McNeil Daniel	Pte.	W/Sv	26-8-55	7-9-55
3432	Marshall Hugh	Pte.	W/Sv	25-7-55	7-8-55
3577	Martin Patrick	Pte.	W/Sl	23-8-55	4-9-55
2675	Miley John	Pte.	W/Sl	30-6-55	17-7-55
2909	Miller William	Pte.	W/Sv	25-4-55	15-5-55
3457	Murdoch David	Pte.	W/D	3-5-55	15-5-55
3256	Nevin Michael	Pte.	W/Sl	8-1-55	26-1-55
2602	Nicholson John	Pte.	W/Sl	22-3-55	2-4-55
2602	Nicholson John	Pte.	W/D	19-4-55	1-5-55
2046	Norris William	Pte.	W/Sv	5-7-55	17-7-55
2411	Nowlan John	Pte.	W/Sv	15-4-55	1-5-55
1419	Nunn James	Pte.	W/Sl	3-7-55	17-7-55
3288	O'Malley Michael	Pte.	W/Sv	26-8-55	7-9-55
3198	Osborne John	Pte.	W/Sl	28-8-55	11-9-55
2752	Oxley Samuel	Pte.	W/Sv	26-8-55	7-9-55
3950	Palmer Robert	Pte.	W/Sl	26-8-55	7-9-55
3679	Pawin David	Pte.	W/Sv	16-4-55	1-5-55
3491	Pearce William	Pte.	W/Sv	8-8-55	21-8-55
3284	Phelan Dennis	Pte.	W/Sl	27-3-55	13-4-55
3513	Rice John	Pte.	W/D	12-6-55	26-6-55
3678	Riley George	Pte.	W/Sv	26-8-55	7-9-55
3678	Riley Patrick	Pte.	W/Sv	26-8-55	7-9-55
2678	Robbins James	Pte.	W/Sl	10-6-55	22-6-55
2439	Ryan Michael	Pte.	W/Sv	3-7-55	17-7-55
2992	Sizer William	Pte.	W/D	31-5-55	12-6-55
2193	Smith Peter	Pte.	W/Sv	27-3-55	13-4-55
3286	Thornton Michael	Pte.	W/Sv	5-4-55	20-4-55
3757	Tibb Joseph	Pte.	W/Sv	14-8-55	28-8-55
3165	Toomey Andrew	Pte.	W/Sv	4-5-55	18-5-55
3154	Turner Joseph	Pte.	W/Sv	15-4-55	1-5-55
3472	West Abraham	Pte.	W/Sl	27-3-55	13-4-55
2938	Young Thomas	Pte.	W/Sl	7-2-55	23-2-55

93rd REGIMENT OF FOOT

NO.	NAME	RANK	CASUALTY	DATE	LONDON GAZETTE
2795	Ferguson James	Pte.	Killed	22-8-55	4-9-55
2689	Finlayson Peter	Pte.	Killed	22-8-55	4-9-55
2734	Fraser Donald	Pte.	Killed	6-8-55	21-8-55

NOTES

The Second, Third, Fourth, Fifth and Final Bombardment of Sebastopol, and Minor Actions

93rd REGIMENT OF FOOT

NO.	NAME	RANK	CASUALTY	DATE	LONDON GAZETTE
3221	Gibson Charles	Pte.	Killed	4-7-55	17-7-55
3066	Green George	Pte.	Killed	23-6-55	9-7-55
1809	Kennedy John	Pte.	Killed	29-7-55	7-8-55
3072	Wedderspoon James	Pte.	Killed	6-8-55	21-8-55
2326	McDonald John	Sergt.	W/Sl	7-8-55	21-8-55
2036	Forbes John	Corpl.	W/Sv	13-7-55	27-7-55
2515	Kiddie James	Corpl.	W/Sv	17-7-55	31-7-55
2423	McKay Angus	Piper	W/Sv	2-7-55	17-7-55
3155	Agnew Alexander	Pte.	W/Sv	3-7-55	17-7-55
2906	Bain John	Pte.	W/Sv	22-8-55	4-9-55
2788	Barclay Alexander	Pte.	W/Sv	7-8-55	21-8-55
1852	Baxter Robert	Pte.	W/Sl	29-7-55	7-8-55
3255	Blackhall Alexander	Pte.	W/Sl	29-6-55	17-7-55
3159	Campbell William	Pte.	W/Sl	17-7-55	31-7-55
3299	Cathro Peter	Pte.	W/Sl	19-8-55	31-8-55
1340	Chalmers John	Pte.	W/Sv	2-7-55	17-7-55
2695	Dingwall Alexander	Pte.	W/Sv	8-7-55	20-7-55
3539	Dowgall John	Pte.	W/D	8-7-55	20-7-55
3175	Fairlee James	Pte.	W/Sl	20-7-55	3-8-55
3470	Foal Edward	Pte.	W/Sl	26-6-55	10-7-55
3265	Griffin Thomas	Pte.	W/Sl	19-8-55	31-8-55
2994	Hansil James	Pte.	W/Sv	22-8-55	4-9-55
2731	Hardy William	Pte.	W/Sv	3-7-55	17-7-55
3146	Jarrett Henry	Pte.	W/Sv	22-8-55	4-9-55
3584	Leitch John	Pte.	W/Sl	19-8-55	31-8-55
3196	McCulloch John	Pte.	W/Sl	22-8-55	4-9-55
2697	McFadden Donald	Pte.	W/Sv	28-6-55	10-7-55
2100	McKay John	Pte.	W/Sv	3-7-55	17-7-55
3216	McLarty Hugh	Pte.	W/D	13-8-55	28-8-55
3082	McLusky Thomas	Pte.	W/Sv	22-6-55	9-7-55
2439	McNab John	Pte.	W/Sl	29-6-55	17-7-55
2685	Matheson Roderick	Pte.	W/Sl	22-8-55	4-9-55
3287	Middleton Thomas	Pte.	W/Sv	19-8-55	31-8-55
3097	Moodie John	Pte.	W/Sv	16-8-55	28-8-55
3531	Mortimer Samuel	Pte.	W/Sv	22-6-55	9-7-55
2407	Neil Edward	Pte.	W/Sl	19-8-55	31-8-55
1776	Patterson James	Pte.	W/Sv	20-7-55	3-8-55
1778	Pulton John	Pte.	W/Sl	13-7-55	27-7-55
2923	Ross Alexander	Pte.	W/Sv	29-7-55	7-8-55
2178	Ross David	Pte.	W/Sv	13-8-55	28-8-55
3231	Ross George	Pte.	W/Sv	29-6-55	17-7-55
3455	Salmond James	Pte.	W/Sl	13-8-55	28-8-55
2062	Thompson William	Pte.	W/Sv	13-8-55	28-8-55
3160	Urquhart William	Pte.	W/D	16-8-55	28-8-55
3271	Winters Hugh	Pte.	W/D	8-7-55	20-7-55
	MacGowan J. A.	Brevet/Mjr.	Missing	7-8-55	21-8-55

95th REGIMENT OF FOOT

NO.	NAME	RANK	CASUALTY	DATE	LONDON GAZETTE
	Fraser L.	Capt.	Killed	31-8-55	18-9-55
2197	McGrath Maurice	Sergt.	Killed	5-8-55	17-8-55
2548	Brown John	Col/Sgt.	Killed	28-8-55	11-9-55
1718	Collins Dennis	Pte.	Killed	11-8-55	24-8-55
	Weild R.	Lieut.	W/Sv	22-8-55	4-9-55
1073	McElliott John	Sergt.	W/Sl	31-7-55	14-8-55
2185	Murphy John	Sergt.	W/Sl	30-11-54	29-12-54
1873	Sparks William	Sergt.	W/Sl	24-7-55	7-8-55
2892	Cluney F. F.	Col/Sgt.	W/Sl	23-7-55	7-8-55
3461	Claypole Henry	Corpl.	W/Sl	15-7-55	27-7-55
3340	Johnston Henry	Corpl.	W/Sl	14-7-55	27-7-55

NOTES

The Second, Third, Fourth, Fifth and Final Bombardment of Sebastopol, and Minor Actions

95th REGIMENT OF FOOT

NO.	NAME	RANK	CASUALTY	DATE	LONDON GAZETTE
2620	Reaney Patrick	Corpl.	W/Sl	19-8-55	31-8-55
3421	Byrne John	L/Cpl.	W/Sv	19-8-55	31-8-55
3514	Long Thomas	L/Cpl.	W/Sl	26-8-55	4-9-55
3394	Baxter Alexander	Pte.	W/Sv	24-7-55	7-8-55
3271	Braden John	Pte.	W/Sv	24-7-55	7-8-55
3097	Callaghan James	Pte.	W/Sl	29-7-55	7-8-55
3579	Cartwright William	Pte.	W/Sl	4-9-55	18-9-55
3352	Cooper Thomas	Pte.	W/Sv	16-8-55	28-8-55
2176	Dwyes Michael	Pte.	W/Sv	30-7-55	14-8-55
1358	Fletcher Andrew	Pte.	W/Sl	23-7-55	7-8-55
2999	Harris John	Pte.	W/Sl	16-8-55	28-8-55
3477	Harris Nathaniel	Pte.	W/Sl	2-9-55	18-9-55
3504	Hickling William	Pte.	W/D	11-8-55	24-8-55
3403	Jennings Edward	Pte.	W/Sl	5-7-55	17-7-55
3470	Langhan Isaac	Pte.	W/Sl	23-7-55	7-8-55
3436	McArteny Joseph	Pte.	W/Sv	8-7-55	20-7-55
2099	McCarthy Patrick	Pte.	W/Sl	24-7-55	7-8-55
3584	Martin Edwin	Pte.	W/Sl	27-8-55	11-9-55
3248	Monaghan Peter	Pte.	W/Sv	2-8-55	14-8-55
3494	Moorhead John	Pte.	W/Sv	8-7-55	20-7-55
3093	Mulvill M.	Pte.	W/Sl	31-8-55	18-9-55
3428	Osborne Henry	Pte.	W/Sl	14-7-55	27-7-55
3062	Pickles James	Pte.	W/Sv	22-8-55	4-9-55
3487	Robb James	Pte.	W/Sl	31-8-55	18-9-55
3400	Shannett John	Pte.	W/Sv	27-7-55	7-8-55
3276	Shearman George	Pte.	W/D	5-8-55	17-8-55
3289	Smith James	Pte.	W/Sl	4-9-55	18-9-55
3368	Smith John	Pte.	W/Sl	5-8-55	17-8-55
3500	Sodon Francis	Pte.	W/Sv	18-7-55	31-7-55
2407	Stairatt James	Pte.	W/Sl	31-8-55	18-9-55
3338	Stewart H.	Pte.	W/Sv	31-8-55	18-9-55
1853	Sullivan Eugene	Pte.	W/Sv	23-7-55	7-8-55
2815	Swan James	Pte.	W/Sl	4-8-55	17-8-55
3471	Thomson Isaac	Pte.	W/Sl	22-8-55	4-9-55
2300	Thorley James	Pte.	W/Sl	31-12-54	26-1-55

97th REGIMENT OF FOOT

NO.	NAME	RANK	CASUALTY	DATE	LONDON GAZETTE
	Vicars H. S. J.	Capt.	Killed	22-3-55	3-4-55
	Preston G. B.	Lieut.	Killed	30-8-55	11-9-55
3438	O'Grady Patrick	Sergt.	Killed	31-8-55	18-9-55
3249	Evans G.	Corpl.	Killed	26-8-55	7-9-55
2464	Hart John	Corpl.	Killed	31-8-55	18-9-55
2439	Libenrood Henry	Corpl.	Killed	10-6-55	22-6-55
2064	Steevens James	L/Cpl.	Killed	22-3-55	3-4-55
1307	Alexander George	Pte.	Killed	22-3-55	3-4-55
3536	Bennett John	Pte.	Killed	27-8-55	11-9-55
3361	Calton George	Pte.	Killed	14-6-55	26-6-55
1967	Connors Michael	Pte.	Killed	2-6-55	12-6-55
1486	Corbet Edward	Pte.	Killed	30-4-55	15-5-55
2951	Crough Michael	Pte.	Killed	25-4-55	15-5-55
1028	Fry Stephen	Pte.	Killed	25-8-55	7-9-55
1957	Gillon George	Pte.	Killed	22-3-55	3-4-55
3615	Jay Henry	Pte.	Killed	28-7-55	7-8-55
1327	Keogh George	Pte.	Killed	6-4-55	20-4-55
2181	Kiely Thomas	Pte.	Killed	24-8-55	7-9-55
3443	Knight James	Pte.	Killed	15-4-55	1-5-55
1366	McAllister John	Pte.	Killed	9-8-55	21-8-55
3923	Massey James	Pte.	Killed	31-8-55	18-9-55
3456	Moore Michael	Pte.	Killed	30-3-55	20-4-55

NOTES

The Second, Third, Fourth, Fifth and Final Bombardment of Sebastopol, and Minor Actions

97th REGIMENT OF FOOT

NO.	NAME	RANK	CASUALTY	DATE	LONDON GAZETTE
1266	Murphy Patrick	Pte.	Killed	31-8-55	18-9-55
3294	Pepper Patrick	Pte.	Killed	12-4-55	24-4-55
3487	Pond James	Pte.	Killed	31-5-55	12-6-55
3462	Richardson John	Pte.	Killed	31-8-55	18-9-55
3331	Simonton William	Pte.	Killed	30-8-55	11-9-55
1959	Turton Robert	Pte.	Killed	19-12-54	9-1-55
1811	Widows John	Pte.	Killed	9-3-55	23-3-55
	Brinkley M.	Lieut.	W/Sv	30-8-55	11-9-55
	Derman W.	Lieut. & Adj.	W/M	18-8-55	31-8-55
	Ware G. H. H.	Lieut.	W/Sv	30-8-55	11-9-55
3023	Morrin Peter	Sergt.	W/Sv	5-4-55	20-4-55
2694	Traise Robert	Sergt.	W/Sl	31-3-55	20-4-55
3049	Bruce Silvanus	Corpl.	W/Sv	14-6-55	26-6-55
3762	Bull George	Corpl.	W/Sl	30-8-55	11-9-55
3127	Drane Thomas	Corpl.	W/Sl	30-8-55	11-9-55
2938	Fitzgerald James	Corpl.	W/Sl	27-7-55	7-8-55
2277	Hagan Denis	Corpl.	W/Sl	12-6-55	26-6-55
3478	McHugh John	Corpl.	W/Sl	22-3-55	3-4-55
1426	Marks Thomas	Corpl.	W/Sl	9-8-55	21-8-55
2188	Norton Michael	Corpl.	W/Sl	31-8-55	18-9-55
3674	Flowers William	L/Cpl.	W/Sv	2-9-55	18-9-55
3765	Grundey William	L/Cpl.	W/Sl	12-6-55	26-6-55
3088	Hickey John	L/Cpl.	W/Sl	14-6-55	26-6-55
1869	Arkwright J.	Pte.	W/Sv	26-8-55	7-9-55
3534	Ball Ralph	Pte.	W/Sv	12-6-55	26-6-55
3102	Ball William	Pte.	W/Sl	27-6-55	10-7-55
3414	Barker Edward	Pte.	W/Sl	21-8-55	4-9-55
1385	Bartley Robert	Pte.	W/Sv	12-8-55	24-8-55
3501	Broderick Thomas	Pte.	W/Sv	30-8-55	11-9-55
1986	Butler Patrick	Pte.	W/Sv	22-3-55	3-4-55
3119	Carty Francis	Pte.	W/Sl	14-3-55	23-3-55
3427	Collins James	Pte.	W/Sl	31-7-55	14-8-55
2518	Collins Matthew	Pte.	W/Sl	27-7-55	7-8-55
2583	Cookesay Thomas	Pte.	W/Sl	11-8-55	24-8-55
3063	Cooney Hugh	Pte.	W/Sv	19-7-55	3-8-55
3000	Coyle Patrick	Pte.	W/Sv	12-6-55	26-6-55
1758	Dempsey John	Pte.	W/Sl	23-5-55	5-6-55
1348	Doad William	Pte.	W/D	12-6-55	26-6-55
3127	Drane Thomas	Pte.	W/Sl	30-8-55	11-9-55
2443	Duffy James	Pte.	W/Sv	3-1-55	26-1-55
3249	Evans George	Pte.	W/Sv	8-4-55	20-4-55
1955	Farnham Stephen	Pte.	W/Sl	19-4-55	1-5-55
1955	Farnham Stephen	Pte.	W/Sl	9-8-55	21-8-55
3523	Farrell Thomas	Pte.	W/Sl	22-3-55	3-4-55
3525	Fitchett George	Pte.	W/Sl	21-8-55	4-9-55
3699	Forward James	Pte.	W/Sv	11-8-55	24-8-55
2623	Franklin John	Pte.	W/D	15-4-55	1-5-55
2087	Galvin Edward	Pte.	W/Sv	30-8-55	11-9-55
2461	Gilligan Patrick	Pte.	W/Sl	10-6-55	22-6-55
3433	Glynn John	Pte.	W/Sl	22-3-55	3-4-55
3221	Goodwin Thomas	Pte.	W/Sv	17-4-55	1-5-55
3627	Graham George	Pte.	W/Sl	25-7-55	7-8-55
3064	Hamilton John	Pte.	W/Sl	22-3-55	3-4-55
2779	Hanley Thomas	Pte.	W/Sv	12-6-55	26-6-55
3254	Hargreaves James	Pte.	W/Sl	14-3-55	23-3-55
3350	Heron John	Pte.	W/Sv	22-3-55	3-4-55
2715	Holden Hugh	Pte.	W/Sl	31-8-55	18-9-55
3220	Howland John	Pte.	W/Sv	11-5-55	25-5-55
3553	Irewing Nicholas	Pte.	W/Sl	27-3-55	13-4-55
2451	Jago John	Pte.	W/Sl	11-8-55	24-8-55
2171	Johnston Thomas	Pte.	W/Sl	9-8-55	21-8-55
2946	Joyce James	Pte.	W/Sl	17-8-55	31-8-55
3084	Keefe Bartholomew	Pte.	W/Sl	31-8-55	18-9-55
4065	Knowles William	Pte.	W/Sv	6-9-55	18-9-55

NOTES

The Second, Third, Fourth, Fifth and Final Bombardment of Sebastopol, and Minor Actions

97th REGIMENT OF FOOT

NO.	NAME	RANK	CASUALTY	DATE	LONDON GAZETTE
1776	Kyberd Benjamin	Pte.	W/Sv	22-3-55	3-4-55
2792	Langley Thomas	Pte.	W/Sv	27-7-55	7-8-55
3007	Lawell John	Pte.	W/Sl	11-8-55	24-8-55
3417	Lightbown Thomas	Pte.	W/Sl	31-8-55	18-9-55
3258	McAllister Henry	Pte.	W/Sl	8-8-55	21-8-55
2166	McDonald John	Pte.	W/Sv	25-8-55	7-9-55
3472	McGee James	Pte.	W/Sv	23-8-55	4-9-55
2199	McGenniss Edward	Pte.	W/D	12-6-55	26-6-55
1323	McKinlan —	Pte.	W/Sv	26-8-55	7-9-55
3470	McLoughlin William	Pte.	W/Sl	13-4-55	1-5-55
2165	Maloney Mitchell	Pte.	W/Sv	27-4-55	15-5-55
2165	Maloney Mitchell	Pte.	W/Sv	26-8-55	7-9-55
2720	Manning Thomas	Pte.	W/Sv	30-8-55	11-9-55
3089	Manokes Francis	Pte.	W/Sl	30-6-55	17-7-55
3089	Manokes Francis	Pte.	W/Sl	31-8-55	18-9-55
3055	Manville William	Pte.	W/Sv	9-8-55	21-8-55
1426	Marks Thomas	Pte.	W/Sv	30-8-55	11-9-55
3597	Merritt Charles	Pte.	W/Sv	30-6-55	17-7-55
3491	Milton James	Pte.	W/Sl	31-3-55	20-4-55
2853	Mullally John	Pte.	W/Sl	30-1-55	21-2-55
2520	Murley Mitchell	Pte.	W/Sl	17-4-55	1-5-55
2714	Newan Jabey	Pte.	W/Sl	27-3-55	13-4-55
3500	Pearson James	Pte.	W/Sv	16-4-55	1-5-55
3269	Philips William	Pte.	W/Sl	8-8-55	21-8-55
3665	Quant William	Pte.	W/Sv	25-4-55	15-5-55
3070	Quinn William	Pte.	W/Sv	10-6-55	22-6-55
3431	Ratcliffe James	Pte.	W/Sl	8-8-55	21-8-55
3445	Rothwell Thomas	Pte.	W/Sl	11-8-55	24-8-55
2536	Sally Patrick	Pte.	W/Sl	9-7-55	24-7-55
3104	Sheastone Charles	Pte.	W/Sv	11-5-55	25-5-55
3120	Smith Robert	Pte.	W/Sl	2-8-55	14-8-55
3060	Taylor John	Pte.	W/Sl	2-9-55	18-9-55
3664	Trotter James	Pte.	W/Sv	11-8-55	24-8-55
3757	Tuff George	Pte.	W/Sv	9-8-55	21-8-55
3355	Wells Daniel	Pte.	W/Sv	11-8-55	24-8-55
3632	Wilton Joseph	Pte.	W/Sv	9-8-55	21-8-55
3301	Weaver H.	Pte.	Missing	22-3-55	3-4-55

1st BATTALION, RIFLE BRIGADE

NO.	NAME	RANK	CASUALTY	DATE	LONDON GAZETTE
	Tryon H.	Lieut.	Killed	20-11-54	11-12-54
2937	Devitt Michael	Sergt.	Killed	12-4-55	24-4-55
3083	Allen Robert	Pte.	Killed	22-11-54	11-12-54
2102	Barge Thomas	Pte.	Killed	20-11-54	11-12-54
2995	Beale Robert	Pte.	Killed	20-11-54	11-12-54
3310	Blanchard James	Pte.	Killed	22-8-55	4-9-55
3450	Borrowdale William	Pte.	Killed	5-1-55	26-1-55
3319	Boxhall George	Pte.	Killed	20-11-54	11-12-54
3220	Brayley John	Pte.	Killed	20-11-54	11-12-54
3160	Brown George	Pte.	Killed	12-4-55	24-4-55
4368	Bryans James	Pte.	Killed	12-4-55	24-4-55
4394	Burrier John	Pte.	Killed	10-8-55	24-8-55
2905	Cairney Peter	Pte.	Killed	9-8-55	21-8-55
3734	Calvey Patrick	Pte.	Killed	16-4-55	1-5-55
3427	Carr Thomas	Pte.	Killed	22-11-54	11-12-54
3283	Carter James	Pte.	Killed	20-11-54	11-12-54
3430	Delaney John	Pte.	Killed	3-8-55	17-8-55
3325	Dod John	Pte.	Killed	20-11-54	11-12-54
2296	Eagle John	Pte.	Killed	12-4-55	24-4-55
3040	Evans William	Pte.	Killed	12-4-55	24-4-55

NOTES

The Second, Third, Fourth, Fifth and Final Bombardment of Sebastopol, and Minor Actions

1st BATTALION, RIFLE BRIGADE

NO.	NAME	RANK	CASUALTY	DATE	LONDON GAZETTE
3937	Fall Thomas	Pte.	Killed	16-5-55	29-5-55
2961	Fox James	Pte.	Killed	20-11-54	11-12-54
1940	Graham James	Pte.	Killed	5-1-55	26-1-55
2978	Henry James	Pte.	Killed	20-11-54	11-12-55
3990	Jeffereys John	Pte.	Killed	11-8-55	24-8-55
3727	Lane James	Pte.	Killed	15-11-54	11-12-54
3487	Leggett James	Pte.	Killed	15-1-55	6-2-55
3412	Mulford Thomas	Pte.	Killed	17-12-54	9-1-55
3152	Mulock Charles	Pte.	Killed	17-12-54	9-1-55
3191	Ninds William	Pte.	Killed	29-7-55	7-8-55
2705	O'Sullivan George	Pte.	Killed	23-11-54	11-12-54
3370	Randall John	Pte.	Killed	2-12-54	29-12-54
1590	Smith Henry B.	Pte.	Killed	14-6-55	26-6-55
3071	Wright George	Pte.	Killed	14-6-55	26-6-55
	Churchill C. H. S.	Capt.	W/Sl	22-11-54	11-12-54
	Morgan F. C.	2nd Lieut.	W/Sl	22-11-54	11-12-54
2414	Gibson William	Sergt.	W/Sl	9-8-55	21-8-55
2723	Barwell Samuel	Corpl.	W/Sv	11-12-54	9-1-55
3248	Brooks Richard	Corpl.	W/Sv	21-12-54	9-1-55
3080	Feakins William	Corpl.	W/Sl	28-12-54	12-1-55
3002	Goad Charles	Corpl.	W/Sv	22-11-54	11-12-54
2233	Hall William	Corpl.	W/Sl	23-11-54	11-12-54
3267	Reid Ishmael	Corpl.	W/Sv	2-1-55	26-1-55
3736	Ward Thomas	Corpl.	W/Sl	10-7-55	24-7-55
3089	Bailey Charles	Pte.	W/Sv	21-12-54	9-1-55
3477	Bailey W. D.	Pte.	W/Sv	22-11-54	11-12-54
3688	Baker Charles	Pte.	W/Sv	2-1-55	26-1-55
3466	Barker John	Pte.	W/Sv	4-12-54	29-12-54
3574	Barron Charles	Pte.	W/Sv	10-12-54	29-12-54
2971	Bartley Thomas	Pte.	W/Sv	2-1-55	26-1-55
3386	Barwell William	Pte.	W/Sl	27-11-54	29-12-54
2712	Baxter Joseph	Pte.	W/Sv	20-11-54	11-12-54
3547	Bowes William	Pte.	W/Sl	27-6-55	10-7-55
3128	Brady Edward	Pte.	W/Sv	3-9-55	18-9-55
2750	Bray Thomas	Pte.	W/Sl	26-12-54	12-1-55
3349	Brown Ellis	Pte.	W/Sl	2-12-54	29-12-54
4563	Bunting John	Pte.	W/Sv	26-3-55	13-4-55
3326	Burrow Henry	Pte.	W/Sl	26-7-55	7-8-55
3920	Cain Thomas	Pte.	W/D	24-6-55	9-7-55
4606	Caleb Thomas	Pte.	W/Sl	9-8-55	21-8-55
3439	Campbell Frederick	Pte.	W/Sl	20-11-54	11-12-54
3075	Cartwright Charles	Pte.	W/D	11-8-55	24-8-55
5946	Cherry John	Pte.	W/Sv	21-8-55	4-9-55
4593	Clark George	Pte.	W/D	5-7-55	17-7-55
3311	Clarke Daniel	Pte.	W/Sl	10-7-55	24-7-55
3815	Cleus Cornelius	Pte.	W/D	6-8-55	21-8-55
3613	Coakley John	Pte.	W/D	4-12-54	29-12-54
3586	Collins Peter	Pte.	W/Sl	22-11-54	11-12-54
2935	Conolly John	Pte.	W/Sl	31-3-55	20-4-55
4233	Cooper Charles	Pte.	W/Sl	22-8-55	4-9-55
4468	Cunningham Edward	Pte.	W/D	2-8-55	14-8-55
3779	Davies William	Pte.	W/Sl	28-6-55	10-7-55
3779	Davies William	Pte.	W/Sl	3-8-55	17-8-55
3530	Dogherty Patrick	Pte.	W/D	31-7-55	14-8-55
3882	Dyer Edmund	Pte.	W/Sl	23-1-55	9-2-55
2682	Eagle Walter	Pte.	W/Sv	2-1-55	26-1-55
4901	Ellis James	Pte.	W/Sv	15-8-55	28-8-55
4478	Evamy Julian	Pte.	W/Sl	21-8-55	4-9-55
4478	Evamy Julian	Pte.	W/Sl	4-9-55	18-9-55
4284	Farquharson	Pte.	W/Sl	9-8-55	21-8-55
3281	Field James	Pte.	W/Sl	7-7-55	20-7-55
2893	Flynn John	Pte.	W/Sv	20-11-54	11-12-54
2599	Gibbons Charles	Pte.	W/Sv	22-11-54	11-12-54
4569	Green John	Pte.	W/Sl	11-8-55	24-8-55

NOTES

The Second, Third, Fourth, Fifth and Final Bombardment of Sebastopol, and Minor Actions

1st BATTALION, RIFLE BRIGADE

NO.	NAME	RANK	CASUALTY	DATE	LONDON GAZETTE
3086	Griffiths James	Pte.	W/Sl	20-11-54	11-12-54
4630	Halden Hugh	Pte.	W/Sl	10-8-55	24-8-55
2966	Hammond George	Pte.	W/Sl	4-12-54	29-12-54
2838	Hanfry Michael	Pte.	W/Sv	20-11-54	11-12-54
4411	Hardmy William	Pte.	W/Sv	4-9-55	18-9-55
3701	Hart Frederick	Pte.	W/Sl	18-12-54	9-1-55
3662	Hawkins Edward	Pte.	W/Sv	20-11-54	11-12-54
4272	Hitchang Richard	Pte.	W/Sv	4-9-55	18-9-55
4060	Holden Samuel	Pte.	W/Sv	27-7-55	7-8-55
4567	Holland Thomas	Pte.	W/Sv	12-4-55	24-4-55
4637	Honeyball Isaac	Pte.	W/Sv	10-7-55	24-7-55
3273	Hopkins James	Pte.	W/Sl	22-11-54	11-12-54
3001	Howard Arthur	Pte.	W/Sl	20-11-54	11-12-54
—	Hudson Edwin	Pte.	W/Sv	2-12-54	29-12-54
3208	Hughes Patrick	Pte.	W/Sl	22-11-54	11-12-54
3482	Hutchinson Thomas	Pte.	W/Sv	22-11-54	11-12-54
3170	Hutton William	Pte.	W/Sv	20-11-54	11-12-54
2865	Jesson Christopher	Pte.	W/Sl	20-11-54	11-12-54
3313	Johnson Richard	Pte.	W/Sv	20-11-54	11-12-54
3674	Jones George	Pte.	W/Sv	9-8-55	21-8-55
3672	Jones John	Pte.	W/Sv	2-1-55	26-1-55
3569	Keough Patrick	Pte.	W/Sl	27-11-54	29-12-54
3441	King John	Pte.	W/Sl	20-11-54	11-12-54
3262	Knapp Charles	Pte.	W/Sl	22-11-54	11-12-54
4439	Lawrence William	Pte.	W/D	12-8-55	24-8-55
4102	Lord James	Pte.	W/Sv	16-5-55	29-5-55
3564	McAuliffe Timothy	Pte.	W/Sl	15-11-54	11-12-54
2838	McConnell Peter	Pte.	W/Sl	9-6-55	22-6-55
2878	McDonnell Peter	Pte.	W/Sl	6-8-55	21-8-55
2124	McNalty Patrick	Pte.	W/Sl	20-11-54	11-12-54
3831	Madauld James	Pte.	W/Sv	10-7-55	24-7-55
4630	Malden Hugh	Pte.	W/Sl	10-8-55	24-8-55
3776	Martin George	Pte.	W/Sl	10-8-55	24-8-55
5236	Mathews Robert	Pte.	W/Sl	6-8-55	21-8-55
2131	Mathyr John	Pte.	W/Sv	15-11-54	11-12-54
3258	Matson John	Pte.	W/Sl	22-11-54	11-12-54
3758	Mickle Richard	Pte.	W/Sv	15-8-55	28-8-55
3850	Moore John	Pte.	W/Sl	12-4-55	24-4-55
2972	Musgrove John	Pte.	W/Sl	26-7-55	7-8-55
2972	Musgrove John	Pte.	W/Sv	30-7-55	14-8-55
3214	New Charles	Pte	W/Sv	23-11-54	11-12-54
2298	Page William	Pte.	W/Sl	23-11-54	11-12-54
3139	Parlar Henry	Pte.	W/Sv	31-8-55	18-9-55
3565	Ralph Henry	Pte.	W/Sl	23-1-55	9-2-55
3161	Roberts William	Pte.	W/Sl	11-4-55	24-4-55
3628	Robins John	Pte.	W/Sl	22-11-54	11-12-54
2798	Robinson James	Pte.	W/Sl	25-6-55	10-7-55
3018	Russell Robert	Pte.	W/Sv	20-11-54	11-12-54
3329	Russell William	Pte.	W/Sv	3-8-55	17-8-55
3555	Simmons Cornelius	Pte.	W/Sv	22-11-54	11-12-54
3677	Simons James	Pte.	W/Sl	22-11-54	11-12-54
3385	Staffin Isaac	Pte.	W/Sl	18-8-55	31-8-55
3099	Sutton George	Pte.	W/Sl	22-11-54	11-12-54
2723	Swindell Thomas	Pte.	W/Sl	11-12-54	9-1-55
3338	Thorns George	Pte.	W/Sv	22-11-54	11-12-54
4396	Turner George	Pte.	W/Sv	28-6-55	10-7-55
3316	Turner John	Pte.	W/Sv	20-11-54	11-12-54
3987	Wells William	Pte.	W/Sl	8-8-55	21-8-55
3318	Weston John	Pte.	W/Sl	22-11-54	11-12-54
4649	Wheeler James	Pte.	W/Sv	20-6-55	3-7-55
3545	White Francis	Pte.	W/Sl	20-11-54	11-12-54
2898	Whiting John	Pte.	W/Sl	20-7-55	3-8-55
3295	Whitlock Robert	Pte.	W/Sl	20-11-54	11-12-54
3820	Wilden John	Pte.	W/Sl	19-8-55	31-8-55

NOTES

The Second, Third, Fourth, Fifth and Final Bombardment of Sebastopol, and Minor Actions

1st BATTALION, RIFLE BRIGADE

NO.	NAME	RANK	CASUALTY	DATE	LONDON GAZETTE
3422	Willoughby William	Pte.	W/D	8-8-55	21-8-55
3630	Wilmot John	Pte.	W/Sv	22-11-54	11-12-54
2679	Wood Josiah	Pte.	W/Sv	2-1-55	26-1-55
2989	Wren John	Pte.	W/Sv	21-7-55	3-8-55

Corpl. Samuel Barwell & Pte. Thomas Swindell have same Reg. No.

2nd BATTALION, RIFLE BRIGADE

NO.	NAME	RANK	CASUALTY	DATE	LONDON GAZETTE
	Woodford E. S. G.	Lieut.	Killed	30-6-55	17-7-55
	Hart George	Sergt.	Killed	3-6-55	15-6-55
3379	Shea Dennis	Corpl.	Killed	18-8-55	31-8-55
3287	Smith Thomas	Corpl.	Killed	15-4-55	1-5-55
2891	Smith W. O.	Corpl.	Killed	25-5-55	5-6-55
3493	Baker Frederick	Pte.	Killed	25-7-55	7-8-55
3525	Bates John	Pte.	Killed	3-7-55	17-7-55
3260	Cooper William	Pte.	Killed	16-6-55	3-7-55
2742	Dench George	Pte.	Killed	14-6-55	26-6-55
4146	Heard William	Pte.	Killed	10-6-55	22-6-55
2516	Heritage John	Pte.	Killed	16-6-55	3-7-55
4061	Jones Alfred	Pte.	Killed	10-6-55	22-6-55
3533	Jones John	Pte.	Killed	14-6-55	26-6-55
3767	King Patrick	Pte.	Killed	6-9-55	18-9-55
4409	McCann James	Pte.	Killed	2-9-55	18-9-55
4300	McCarthy J	Pte.	Killed	5-4-55	20-4-55
1563	McQuinn W.	Pte.	Killed	16-6-55	3-7-55
3946	Martin James	Pte.	Killed	3-7-55	17-7-55
4070	Mitchell William	Pte.	Killed	3-7-55	17-7-55
3976	Packer James	Pte.	Killed	6-9-55	18-9-55
4073	Rogers John	Pte.	Killed	22-7-55	3-8-55
4481	Tunstall David	Pte.	Killed	18-8-55	31-8-55
3729	Turner Thomas	Pte.	Killed	4-5-55	18-5-55
	Cary L. S. T. M.	Lieut.	W/Sv	1-9-55	18-9-55
	Norris W.	Lieut.	W/Sv	16-4-55	1-5-55
	Playne F. C.	Lieut.	W/Sv	31-5-55	12-6-55
1571	Marsh Charles	Col/Sgt.	W/Sl	26-8-55	7-9-55
1709	Brodd William	Sergt.	W/D	1-5-55	15-5-55
2077	Cook Joseph	Sergt.	W/Sl	26-8-55	7-9-55
2426	Cherry Joseph	Sergt.	W/Sv	5-9-55	18-9-55
2619	Farrell Thomas	Sergt.	W/Sl	25-7-55	7-8-55
2619	Farrell Thomas	Sergt.	W/Sl	23-8-55	4-9-55
1029	Harrywood John	Sergt.	W/Sv	1-9-55	18-9-55
1253	Voke George	Sergt.	W/Sv	27-1-55	20-2-55
2716	Ellis Robert	Corpl.	W/D	4-4-55	20-4-55
2629	Johnson Thomas	Corpl.	W/Sv	12-7-55	24-7-55
3089	Parnell George	Corpl.	W/Sl	6-9-55	18-9-55
2783	Rowe Joseph	Corpl.	W/Sl	17-8-55	31-8-55
3728	Turney James	A/Cpl.	W/Sl	20-8-55	4-9-55
2783	Rowe Joseph	A/Cpl.	W/Sl	22-4-55	4-5-55
3547	Eite J.	Bugler	W/Sl	17-8-55	31-8-55
4160	Arnitt Henry	Pte.	W/Sl	22-4-55	4-5-55
4021	Balantine James	Pte.	W/Sl	21-8-55	4-9-55
4137	Barker William	Pte.	W/D	6-9-55	18-9-55
4090	Bate John	Pte.	W/Sl	12-6-55	26-6-55
2940	Bateman Charles	Pte.	W/Sv	23-8-55	4-9-55
2191	Battle Thomas	Pte.	W/Sv	12-4-55	24-4-55
4054	Beard James	Pte.	W/Sv	5-9-55	18-9-55
4463	Beck William	Pte.	W/Sv	28-8-55	11-9-55
2014	Bendall Henry	Pte.	W/Sv	22-6-55	9-7-55
3912	Bennett Elijah	Pte.	W/Sl	29-6-55	17-7-55
2558	Bennett William	Pte.	W/Sl	24-7-55	7-8-55

NOTES

The Second, Third, Fourth, Fifth and Final Bombardment of Sebastopol, and Minor Actions

2nd BATTALION, RIFLE BRIGADE

NO.	NAME	RANK	CASUALTY	DATE	LONDON GAZETTE
4070	Bland Septimus	Pte.	W/Sl	16-6-55	3-7-55
4070	Bland Septimus	Pte.	W/Sl	30-6-55	17-7-55
4070	Bland Septimus	Pte.	W/D	17-8-55	31-8-55
3656	Bolter Joseph	Pte.	W/Sl	30-4-55	15-5-55
3642	Bone Thomas	Pte.	W/Sl	17-8-55	31-8-55
2660	Boor James	Pte.	W/Sl	6-9-55	18-9-55
4267	Boyle Thomas	Pte.	W/Sl	23-8-55	4-9-55
3795	Bradshaw J.	Pte.	W/Sl	21-7-55	3-8-55
3093	Breen Thomas	Pte.	W/Sl	1-9-55	18-9-55
4453	Brent James	Pte.	W/Sv	23-8-55	4-9-55
3320	Brent John	Pte.	W/D	23-8-55	4-9-55
4179	Brockbridge Adam	Pte.	W/Sl	12-7-55	24-7-55
4179	Brockbridge Adam	Pte.	W/Sl	17-8-55	31-8-55
4423	Brockville Henry	Pte.	W/D	5-9-55	18-9-55
3593	Buckley Michael	Pte.	W/Sl	28-8-55	11-9-55
4332	Buirns James	Pte.	W/Sl	3-7-55	17-7-55
3383	Cable George	Pte.	W/Sv	16-6-55	3-7-55
4306	Campbell James	Pte.	W/Sl	24-7-55	7-8-55
2990	Carden Frederick	Pte.	W/Sv	17-8-55	31-8-55
3817	Carroll John	Pte.	W/Sl	6-9-55	18-9-55
3660	Carter Thomas	Pte.	W/Sv	10-6-55	22-6-55
2748	Cates James	Pte.	W/Sl	1-9-55	18-9-55
4007	Cattrell Joseph	Pte.	W/Sv	26-8-55	7-9-55
4688	Cavanagh Patrick	Pte.	W/Sv	6-9-55	18-9-55
3662	Chapman Richard	Pte.	W/Sv	25-7-55	7-8-55
4164	Childs J.	Pte.	W/Sl	3-7-55	17-7-55
4164	Childs J.	Pte.	W/Sv	23-8-55	4-9-55
3396	Church William	Pte.	W/Sv	5-9-55	18-9-55
4033	Clarke Joseph	Pte.	W/Sv	3-7-55	17-7-55
4023	Codes Enoch	Pte.	W/Sv	23-8-55	4-9-55
3950	Coles Henry	Pte.	W/Sv	10-6-55	22-6-55
3254	Collins Samuel	Pte.	W/Sl	17-8-55	31-8-55
3609	Cooper Mathew	Pte.	W/Sv	14-8-55	28-8-55
3665	Corran John	Pte.	W/Sv	20-7-55	3-8-55
3338	Cox Daniel	Pte.	W/Sv	3-7-55	17-7-55
3510	Crittle James	Pte.	W/Sv	5-9-55	18-9-55
3790	Crosby James	Pte.	W/Sl	19-7-55	31-7-55
4586	Cumbert Thomas	Pte.	W/Sv	3-7-55	17-7-55
4666	Daly Thomas	Pte.	W/Sv	28-8-55	11-9-55
4343	Day George	Pte.	W/Sl	29-6-55	17-7-55
2650	Deasley William	Pte.	W/Sv	16-6-55	3-7-55
4432	Denton John	Pte.	W/Sv	23-8-55	4-9-55
4392	Duckett Charles	Pte.	W/Sl	31-8-55	18-9-55
4272	Dwyer Edward	Pte.	W/Sv	20-7-55	3-8-55
2257	Edmunds William	Pte.	W/Sv	10-6-55	22-6-55
3822	Ferguson William	Pte.	W/Sl	10-8-55	24-8-55
4121	Finch George	Pte.	W/Sv	13-8-55	28-8-55
4301	Fisher James	Pte.	W/Sl	29-6-55	17-7-55
3675	Flynn Thomas	Pte.	W/D	21-4-55	4-5-55
4178	Franklin Thomas	Pte.	W/Sv	18-3-55	30-3-55
4025	French Arthur	Pte.	W/Sl	6-5-55	18-5-55
4025	French Arthur	Pte.	W/Sv	14-8-55	28-8-55
3679	Garvey James	Pte.	W/Sv	6-9-55	18-9-55
4020	Gillard Emanuel	Pte.	W/Sl	17-3-55	30-3-55
4475	Goddard Samuel	Pte.	W/Sv	23-8-55	4-9-55
4455	Golby Charles	Pte.	W/Sl	26-8-55	7-9-55
4472	Gough Richard	Pte.	W/Sl	1-9-55	18-9-55
3681	Graham William	Pte.	W/Sl	17-8-55	31-8-55
3753	Gray James	Pte.	W/Sl	6-9-55	18-9-55
3539	Green John	Pte.	W/Sl	6-8-55	21-8-55
4269	Green Samuel	Pte.	W/Sl	3-7-55	17-7-55
4269	Green Samuel	Pte.	W/Sl	23-8-55	4-9-55
4269	Green Samuel	Pte.	W/Sv	28-8-55	11-9-55
2526	Grey John	Pte.	W/Sl	24-7-55	7-8-55

NOTES

The Second, Third, Fourth, Fifth and Final Bombardment of Sebastopol, and Minor Actions

2nd BATTALION, RIFLE BRIGADE

NO.	NAME	RANK	CASUALTY	DATE	LONDON GAZETTE
3104	Grier Joseph	Pte.	W/Sl	29-6-55	17-7-55
4080	Gunter Joseph	Pte.	W/Sl	21-7-55	3-8-55
4685	Hannan Henry	Pte.	W/Sl	23-8-55	4-9-55
4257	Harlock Charles	Pte.	W/Sv	14-6-55	26-6-55
3607	Harrison Thomas	Pte.	W/Sl	1-9-55	18-9-55
4195	Hathaway Thomas	Pte.	W/Sl	5-8-55	17-8-55
4218	Hawkins Richard	Pte.	W/D	5-9-55	18-9-55
3957	Hayward Henry	Pte.	W/Sv	15-6-55	3-7-55
2446	Herbert Henry	Pte.	W/Sl	11-6-55	26-6-55
2446	Herbert Henry	Pte.	W/Sv	14-8-55	28-8-55
3903	Hill Samuel	Pte.	W/D	5-4-55	20-4-55
3648	Hillier Thomas	Pte.	W/Sv	23-8-55	4-9-55
3869	Hine Alfred	Pte.	W/Sl	21-5-55	5-6-55
3869	Hine William	Pte.	W/Sl	23-8-55	4-9-55
3633	Howe Charles	Pte.	W/Sv	3-7-55	17-7-55
4417	Hudson William	Pte.	W/Sl	23-8-55	4-9-55
3688	Humpston Robert	Pte.	W/Sl	22-4-55	4-5-55
3289	Jacobs Charles	Pte.	W/Sl	17-8-55	31-8-55
4204	Jennings William	Pte.	W/Sl	24-7-55	7-8-55
4635	Johnstone Samuel	Pte.	W/Sl	17-8-55	31-8-55
3631	Kelly John	Pte.	W/Sl	3-7-55	17-7-55
3691	Kelly John	Pte.	W/Sl	21-6-55	3-7-55
3987	Kent Edward	Pte.	W/Sl	17-8-55	31-8-55
2937	Kent Richard	Pte.	W/Sl	14-6-55	26-6-55
4124	King Florence	Pte.	W/Sv	14-6-55	26-6-55
4245	Lacey Job	Pte.	W/Sl	16-5-55	29-5-55
4649	Langridge Henry	Pte.	W/Sl	1-9-55	18-9-55
3366	Lawn John	Pte.	W/Sv	3-7-55	17-7-55
4340	Lennard Thomas	Pte.	W/Sl	17-8-55	31-8-55
4521	Lewis Charles	Pte.	W/D	12-8-55	24-8-55
3307	Little John	Pte.	W/Sl	17-8-55	31-8-55
4044	Lodge Alfred	Pte.	W/Sv	23-8-55	4-9-55
3572	Long James	Pte.	W/Sl	3-7-55	17-7-55
3975	Long John	Pte.	W/Sl	24-7-55	7-8-55
3117	McCarthy Daniel	Pte.	W/Sl	17-8-55	31-8-55
4633	McEvoy Frederick	Pte.	W/Sv	17-8-55	31-8-55
2046	McGuire Patrick	Pte.	W/Sv	22-3-55	3-4-55
3752	Macdonnell James	Pte.	W/Sv	28-7-55	7-8-55
3752	Macdonnell James	Pte.	W/D	14-8-55	28-8-55
4022	Maggs William	Pte.	W/D	30-6-55	17-7-55
3584	Marrett Edward	Pte.	W/Sl	28-7-55	7-8-55
3304	Mason William	Pte.	W/Sl	3-9-55	18-9-55
3832	Milline Henry	Pte.	W/Sl	20-1-55	6-2-55
4520	Monk George	Pte.	W/Sv	26-8-55	7-9-55
3892	Morgan George	Pte.	W/Sl	17-8-55	31-8-55
3815	Mortimer G.	Pte.	W/Sv	22-6-55	9-7-55
2850	Mortimore George	Pte.	W/Sv	29-7-55	7-8-55
3830	Muir Robert	Pte.	D.O.W.	10-6-55	22-6-55
4129	Newman Walter	Pte.	W/Sl	20-1-55	6-2-55
2665	Nugent Joseph	Pte.	W/Sl	23-8-55	4-9-55
2726	Palled Peter	Pte.	W/Sl	9-8-55	21-8-55
1649	Parkinson John	Pte.	W/D	23-8-55	4-9-55
3996	Parkinson Thomas	Pte.	W/D	28-4-55	15-5-55
3071	Payne Moses	Pte.	W/Sv	25-7-55	7-8-55
3328	Perkins William	Pte.	W/Sl	22-4-55	4-5-55
3977	Perry Samuel	Pte.	W/Sv	24-7-55	7-8-55
3908	Philips William	Pte.	W/Sl	30-6-55	17-7-55
3511	Philips Joseph	Pte.	W/Sl	5-9-55	18-9-55
3988	Phillips William	Pte.	W/Sl	17-8-55	31-8-55
3953	Pinches Thomas	Pte.	W/Sl	31-8-55	18-9-55
4084	Pitt George	Pte.	W/D	28-5-55	12-6-55
4322	Ranks Henry	Pte.	W/Sl	21-8-55	4-9-55
4114	Ranson John	Pte.	W/Sv	28-8-55	11-9-55
3626	Reeves Henry	Pte.	W/Sv	3-7-55	17-7-55

NOTES

The Second, Third, Fourth, Fifth and Final Bombardment of Sebastopol, and Minor Actions

2nd BATTALION, RIFLE BRIGADE

NO.	NAME	RANK	CASUALTY	DATE	LONDON GAZETTE
3626	Reeves Henry	Pte.	W/Sl	3-9-55	18-9-55
1815	Richards William H.	Pte.	W/Sl	25-7-55	7-8-55
3919	Rigby Charles	Pte.	W/D	10-6-55	22-6-55
4072	Robertson Thomas	Pte.	W/Sl	3-9-55	18-9-55
3514	Robinson Thomas	Pte.	W/Sv	17-8-55	31-8-55
4002	Roge William	Pte.	W/Sl	12-7-55	24-7-55
3853	Salter William	Pte.	W/Sl	28-7-55	7-8-55
3853	Salter William	Pte.	W/Sv	5-9-55	18-8-55
2719	Scott Frederick	Pte.	W/Sv	1-8-55	14-8-55
3084	Scott William	Pte.	W/Sl	1-9-55	18-9-55
3724	Semple Robert	Pte.	W/Sv	24-6-55	9-7-55
3309	Simpson James	Pte.	W/Sl	23-8-55	4-9-55
4362	Smith John	Pte.	W/Sv	12-7-55	24-7-55
3632	Soper Lewis	Pte.	W/Sl	1-9-55	18-9-55
3939	Stephens Thomas	Pte.	W/Sl	13-3-55	23-3-55
4246	Strachan John	Pte.	W/Sl	1-9-55	18-9-55
4579	Sullivan James	Pte.	W/Sv	6-9-55	18-9-55
3726	Sutton Peter	Pte.	W/Sv	17-8-55	31-8-55
3323	Thomas John	Pte.	W/Sv	11-4-55	24-4-55
4099	Thompson Frederick	Pte.	W/Sv	10-6-55	22-6-55
4171	Thornly James	Pte.	W/Sl	13-3-55	23-3-55
4171	Thornly James	Pte.	W/Sl	20-7-55	3-8-55
4481	Tunstall Daniel	Pte	W/Sl	12-7-55	24-7-55
4256	Twiggs John	Pte.	W/Sl	21-4-55	4-5-55
2017	Underwood James	Pte.	W/Sl	15-7-55	27-7-55
4283	Venables Thomas	Pte.	W/Sl	1-9-55	18-9-55
4467	Walkinshaw A.	Pte.	W/Sv	30-7-55	14-8-55
3985	Wall Robert	Pte.	W/Sv	24-5-55	5-6-55
3895	Wallace James	Pte.	W/Sl	5-9-55	18-9-55
4547	Walton John	Pte.	W/Sl	23-8-55	4-9-55
4548	Walton William	Pte.	W/Sl	24-7-55	7-8-55
3732	Warren Henry	Pte.	W/Sl	27-6-55	10-7-55
4598	Watkinson John	Pte.	W/Sl	3-7-55	17-7-55
4147	Weeles John	Pte.	W/Sl	21-5-55	5-6-55
3947	Weller George	Pte.	W/Sl	1-9-55	18-9-55
3801	Welsh William	Pte.	W/D	21-5-55	5-6-55
3627	Westley Thomas	Pte.	W/Sv	6-9-55	18-9-55
3627	Westly John	Pte.	W/Sl	17-8-55	31-8-55
4355	White Henry	Pte.	W/Sl	3-7-55	17-7-55
2241	White John	Pte.	W/Sl	17-8-55	31-8-55
2428	Wild James	Pte.	W/Sv	24-6-55	9-7-55
4503	Wilmingham James	Pte.	W/Sl	5-9-55	18-9-55
4063	Wilson George	Pte.	W/Sl	19-7-55	31-7-55
3759	Wilson Henry	Pte.	W/Sl	17-8-55	31-8-55
4507	Wilson Robert	Pte.	W/Sl	1-9-55	18-9-55
3884	Woods Thomas	Pte.	W/Sl	16-7-55	31-7-55
3884	Wood Thomas	Pte.	W/Sl	28-8-55	11-9-55
3065	Warren John	Pte.	W/Sl	30-6-55	17-7-55
4052	Wright Henry	Pte.	W/Sl	15-4-55	1-5-55
3820	Young Joseph	Pte.	W/Sl	21-6-55	3-7-55

NOTES

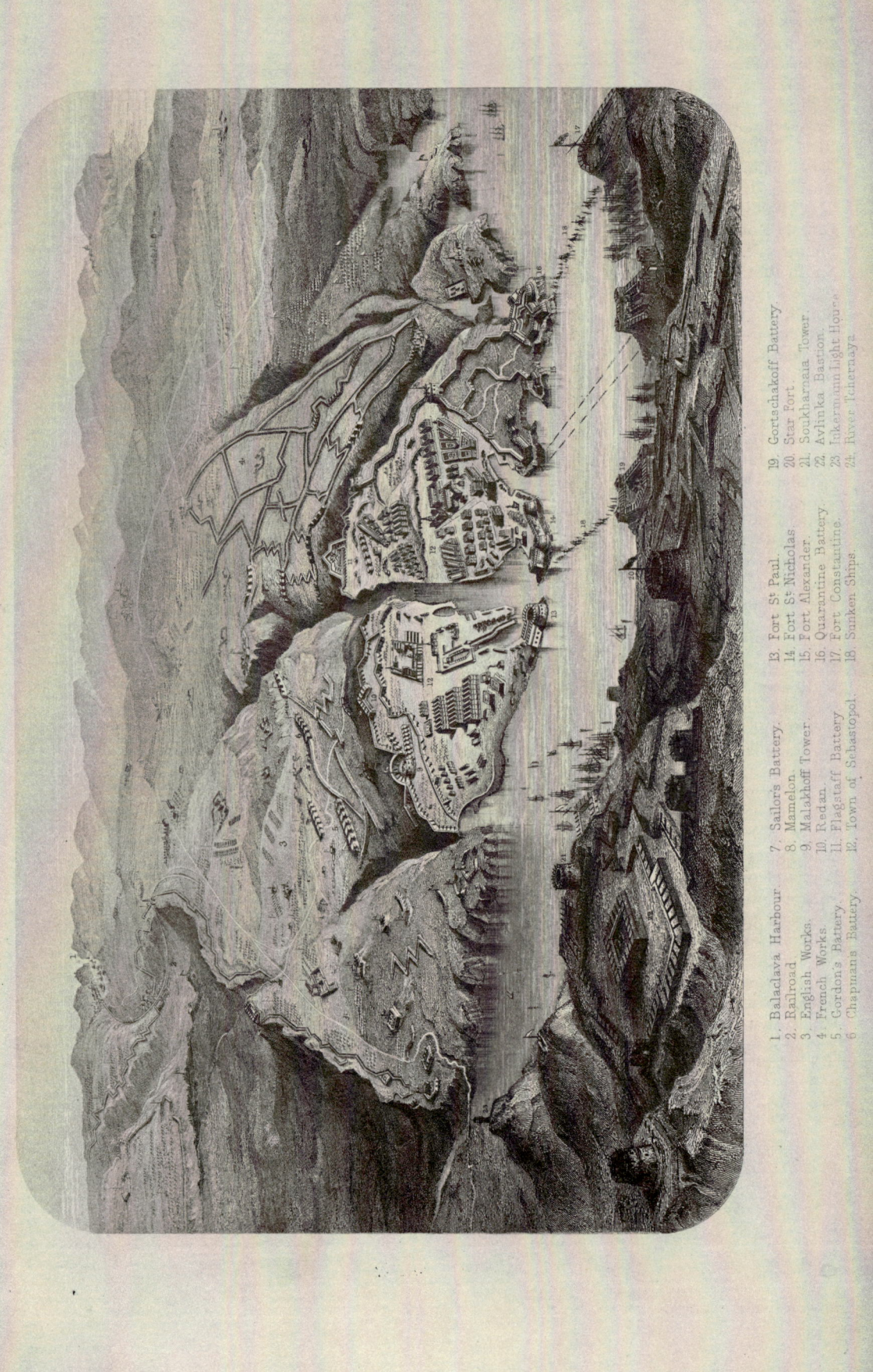

PLAN OF ATTACK & DEFENCES OF THE SOUTH & NORTH SIDES OF HARBOUR & TOWN OF SEBASTOPOL.

1. Balaclava Harbour
2. Railroad
3. English Works
4. French Works
5. Gordon's Battery
6. Chapmans Battery
7. Sailor's Battery
8. Mamelon
9. Malakhoff Tower
10. Redan
11. Flagstaff Battery
12. Town of Sebastopol
13. Fort St Paul
14. Fort St Nicholas
15. Fort Alexander
16. Quarantine Battery
17. Fort Constantine
18. Sunken Ships
19. Gortschakoff Battery
20. Star Fort
21. Soukharnaia Tower
22. Avlinka Bastion
23. Inkerman Light House
24. River Tchernaya

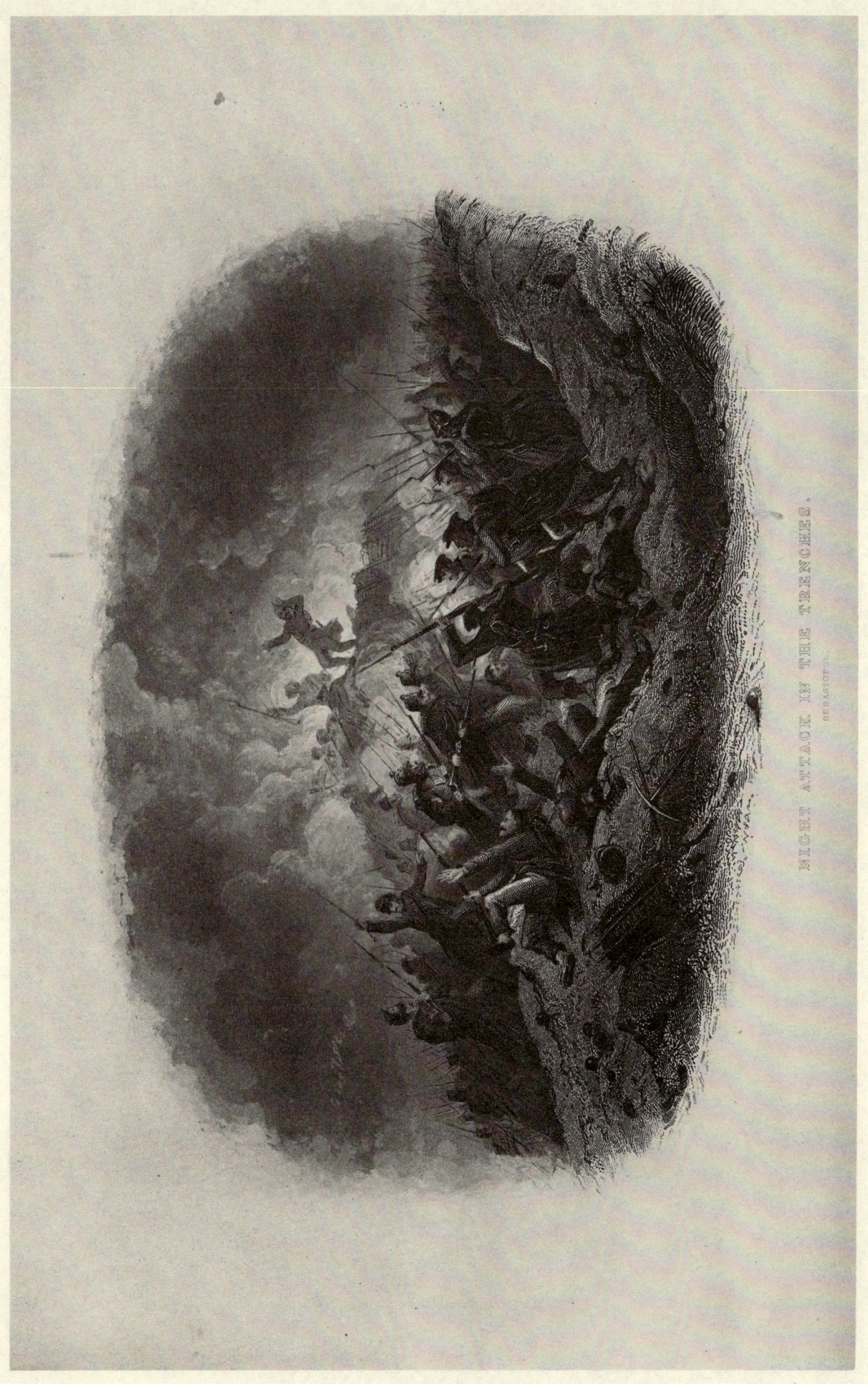

NIGHT ATTACK IN THE TRENCHES.
SEBASTOPOL.

RETREAT OF THE RUSSIANS
FROM THE SOUTH SIDE OF SEBASTOPOL.
Sept. 8, 1855.

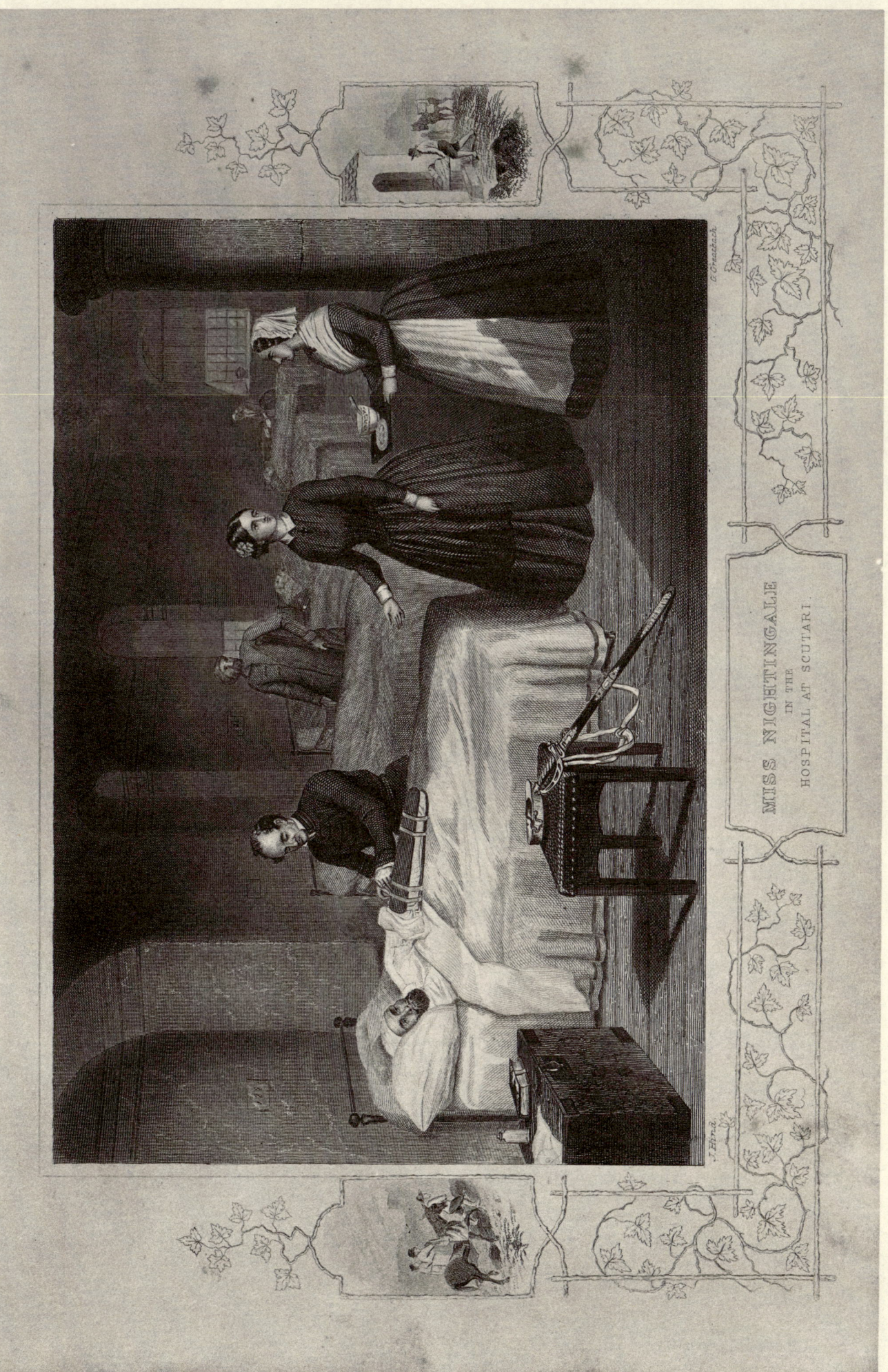

MISS NIGHTINGALE IN THE HOSPITAL AT SCUTARI.

THE QUEEN RECEIVING THE GUARDS AT BUCKINGHAM PALACE ON THEIR RETURN FROM THE CRIMEA.

THE MAGAZINE EXPLOSION AT THE FRENCH SIEGE TRAIN

The following casualties occurred among the Officers, Non-Commissioned Officers and Men of the Army who were encamped near the French Artillery Park during the accidental ignition of the magazine, 15th November, 1855.

Compiled from the London Gazette 27th November, 1855.

ROYAL ARTILLERY

NAME	RANK	CASUALTY	NAME	RANK	CASUALTY
Langley William	Corpl.	Killed	Cox John	Gunner	W/Sv
Lackie Daniel	Bombr.	Killed	Downy John	Gunner	W/Sl
Hemsley James	Gunner	Killed	Foy Patrick	Gunner	W/Sl
McCrae John	Gunner	Killed	McDonald Patrick	Gunner	W/Sl
Spence William	Gunner	Killed	Mallin James	Gunner	W/Sl
Targoose Samuel	Gunner	Killed	Marshall Robert	Gunner	W/Sv
Dawson W. J.	Lieut.	W/D	Pardmore James	Gunner	W/Sl
Roberts F. C.	Lieut.	W/D	Pickup Henry	Gunner	W/Sv
Cooper John	Col/Sgt.	W/Sv	Ross William	Gunner	W/Sl
Fitzsimmons C. G.	Col/Sgt.	W/Sl	Ryan Edward	Gunner	W/Sl
Russell William	Corpl.	W/Sl	Wodsworth Edward	Gunner	W/Sv
Hemp James	Bombr.	W/Sv	Wright John	Gunner	W/D
King James	A/Bombr.	W/Sl			

FIELD TRAIN DEPARTMENT

NAME	RANK	CASUALTY	NAME	RANK	CASUALTY
Yellon G.	Dept/Asst/Commissary	Killed	Brooks George	Civil Artificer	W/Sv
Dickson John	Sgt/Conductor	Killed	Wells Henry	Civil Artificer	W/Sv
Hodds H.	Dept/Asst/Commissary	W/Sv	Devine Walter	Gunner	W/Sl
Collins Henry	Quarter Master Sergeant	W/Sl	Hughes John	Gunner	W/Sv
Churcher Thomas	Sergt.	W/Sv	McCann Anthony	Gunner	W/Sv
Sands William	Sergt.	W/Sl	McKrevey William	Gunner	W/Sv
Boggie James	Store Conductor	W/Sv	McYork John	Gunner	W/Sv
Buchanan Joseph	Store Conductor	W/Sl	Perry James	Gunner	W/Sv
Findlay James	Store Conductor	W/Sl	Peters James	Gunner	W/Sv
McFaddyen James	Store Conductor	W/D	Young George	Gunner	W/Sv

NOTES

The Magazine Explosion at the French Siege Train

7th REGIMENT OF FOOT

NO.	NAME	RANK	CASUALTY	NO.	NAME	RANK	CASUALTY
3249	Boyle Charles	Pte.	Killed	2863	Hobson Samuel	Pte.	W/Sl
3281	Johnson Joseph	Corpl.	W/Sl	4231	Jackson Alfred	Pte.	W/Sl
2728	Browne Thomas	Pte.	W/Sl	4025	Kerry George	Pte.	W/Sl
3469	Buckley James	Pte.	W/Sl	4074	Lansley Charles	Pte.	W/Sl
3131	Carty Thomas	Pte.	W/Sl	3120	Michan Edward	Pte.	W/Sv
2012	Cassidy Andrew	Pte.	W/Sl	3032	Sweeney Patrick	Pte.	W/Sl
3580	Evans George	Pte.	W/Sl	3483	Wright Charles	Pte.	W/Sl

19th REGIMENT OF FOOT

NO.	NAME	RANK	CASUALTY	NO.	NAME	RANK	CASUALTY
1214	Doorly James	Corpl.	W/Sv	2763	Herwood Edwin	Pte.	W/Sv
887	Beech William	Pte.	W/Sl	2987	O'Brien Jeremiah	Pte.	W/Sv
2693	Caldwell John	Pte.	W/Sl	2485	Sheehan John	Pte.	W/Sl
3596	Gearedd John	Pte.	W/Sl	3319	Somerville Robert	Pte.	W/Sl

21st REGIMENT OF FOOT

NO.	NAME	RANK	CASUALTY
3854	Keely Timothy	Pte.	W/Sv

23rd REGIMENT OF FOOT

NO.	NAME	RANK	CASUALTY	NO.	NAME	RANK	CASUALTY
4660	Morris George	Pte.	Killed	1885	Owens William	Pte.	W/Sv
4839	Sheppard Mark	Pte.	Killed	4474	Parker Thomas	Pte.	W/Sl
2956	Duskin James	Pte.	W/Sv	4419	Wheeler John	Pte.	W/Sv
4045	Hutchings Charles	Pte.	W/D	4574	White Richard	Pte.	W/Sl

33rd REGIMENT OF FOOT

NO.	NAME	RANK	CASUALTY	NO.	NAME	RANK	CASUALTY
3692	McKay Alexander	L/Cpl.	Killed	3656	Howley Edward	Pte.	W/Sv
3873	Bell John	Pte.	Killed	3931	Hutchins James	Pte.	W/Sv
3181	Battison John	Pte.	W/Sl	3505	Leary Patrick	Pte.	W/Sv
3513	Bell Francis	Pte.	W/Sv	3906	Lyons Joseph	Pte.	W/Sl
3599	Callaghan Michael	Pte.	W/Sl	3103	McGuire Patrick	Pte.	W/Sl
3020	Fatham Samuel	Pte.	W/Sl	3624	McLoughlin John	Pte.	W/Sl
2785	Hodgins James	Pte.	W/D	3194	O'Connor John	Pte.	W/Sl
3153	Hotham Thomas	Pte.	W/Sv	2220	Welsh Patrick	Pte.	W/D

34th REGIMENT OF FOOT

NO.	NAME	RANK	CASUALTY	NO.	NAME	RANK	CASUALTY
3904	McLean William	Pte.	Killed	2931	Kelly Charles	Pte.	W/Sl
4110	Bradford Richard	Pte.	W/Sv	1546	Kelly John	Pte.	W/Sl
4130	Carey Absolom	Pte.	W/Sv	1966	Lynch James	Pte.	W/Sl
2334	Corner William	Pte.	W/Sl	2165	Pinkard William	Pte.	W/Sl
3625	Crumpton Arthur	Pte.	W/Sv	1813	Price George	Pte.	W/Sl
3162	Eyre Alexander	Pte.	W/Sl	4016	Ward Thady	Pte.	W/Sl
3882	Fowhey James	Pte.	W/Sl	2139	Weldon George	Pte.	W/Sl
1448	Henob John	Pte.	W/Sv				

NOTES

The Magazine Explosion at the French Siege Train

41st REGIMENT OF FOOT

NO.	NAME	RANK	CASUALTY
2397	Latty Joseph	Pte.	Killed

47th REGIMENT OF FOOT

NO.	NAME	RANK	CASUALTY	NO.	NAME	RANK	CASUALTY
1654	Wallace Charles	Col/Sgt.	W/Sl	2871	Keefe John	Pte.	W/D
2513	Wilson John	Col/Sgt.	W/Sl	2193	Windsor William	Pte.	W/Sl
2852	Rice William	L/Cpl.	W/Sl				

49th REGIMENT OF FOOT

NO.	NAME	RANK	CASUALTY	NO.	NAME	RANK	CASUALTY
674	Irwin John	Pte.	Killed	2841	Lambert John	Pte.	W/Sv
3159	Cunningham Patrick	Pte.	W/Sv				

77th REGIMENT OF FOOT

NO.	NAME	RANK	CASUALTY	NO.	NAME	RANK	CASUALTY
3609	Davison John	Pte.	Killed	3326	Bloomer James	Pte.	W/Sl
3229	Freeman John	Pte.	Killed	3721	Danton Thomas	Pte.	W/Sl
3524	White Joseph	Pte.	Killed	1189	Lynch Peter	Pte.	W/Sl
3520	Ashford George	Pte.	W/Sl	3546	McNamara Michael	Pte.	W/Sl
2472	Bennett John	Pte.	W/Sl				

88th REGIMENT OF FOOT

NO.	NAME	RANK	CASUALTY	NO.	NAME	RANK	CASUALTY
3896	McHugh John	Sergt.	W/Sl	3594	McDermott Christopher	Pte.	W/D

90th REGIMENT OF FOOT

NO.	NAME	RANK	CASUALTY	NO.	NAME	RANK	CASUALTY
3162	Sanders Robert	Sergt.	W/Sl	3826	Lambert W.	Pte.	W/Sv
2651	Cross Frank	Corpl.	W/Sl				

1st BATTALION RIFLE BRIGADE

NO.	NAME	RANK	CASUALTY	NO.	NAME	RANK	CASUALTY
3204	Pesket Charles	Sergt.	W/Sv	2919	Smith William	Sergt.	W/Sl

2nd BATTALION RIFLE BRIGADE

NO.	NAME	RANK	CASUALTY	NO.	NAME	RANK	CASUALTY
4466	Powell William	Pte.	Killed	2257	Edmonds William	Pte.	W/Sv
	Eccles W. H.	Lieut.	W/Sl	4169	Payne John	Pte.	W/Sl
	Reade J. B. C.	Ass/Surg.	W/Sl	3615	Smith William	Pte.	W/Sl
3941	Edwards John	Corpl.	W/Sv				

NOTES

THE ROYAL NAVY
AND
ROYAL MARINES

THE BOMBARDMENT OF SEBASTOPOL BY THE NAVAL SQUADRON

The following casualties occurred among the Officers, Non-Commissioned Officers and Men while serving in H.M. Ships of the Naval Squadron during the bombardment of the Forts on the North Side of Sebastopol Harbour, 17th October, 1854.

Compiled from the London Gazette 5th November, 1854.

H.M.S. AGAMEMNON

NAME	RANK	CASUALTY	NAME	RANK	CASUALTY
Grey Robert	Bosun's Mate	Killed	Mason Philip	Boy 2nd Cl.	W/Sl
			McCarthy John	OS	W/Sl
Pogson William	AB	Killed	Mundy John	R.M.	W/Sl
Smith John	AB	Killed	Parker John	OS	W/Sv
Spicer Jesse	OS	Killed	Plafair William	OS	W/Sv
Gaussen Thomas S.	Lieut.	W/Sl	Reeves William	Boy 1st Cl.	W/Sl
Boyle Perry	OS	W/Sl	Ringe Augustus	AB	W/Sl
Bremner Robert	OS	W/Sl	Ruan Thomas	R.M.	W/Sl
Burton John	OS	W/D	Smith Patrick	OS	W/Sv
Chaplin William	AB	W/D	Spiers John	Yeo. of Sig.	W/Sv
Ellis John	AB	W/Sl	Tope James	Adm. Dom.	W/Sv
Epps Daniel	Boy 1st Cl.	W/Sl	Warnford William	Bomb. R.M.A.	W/Sl
Hammond Edward	OS	W/Sl	Whitby George	OS	W/D
Hayes Thomas	Yeo. of Sig.	W/Sl	Woolacott George	OS	W/Sv
Martin John	Stoker	W/Sl	Yonge Duke de	Naval Cadet	W/Sl

H.M.S. ALBION

NAME	RANK	CASUALTY	NAME	RANK	CASUALTY
Chase P.	Lieut.	Killed	Barlow Robert	OS	W/Sl
Bickford Thomas	Coxswn.	Killed	Bennett John	LS	W/Sl
Keepe James	OS	Killed	Bowden Thomas	Capt. Mizentop	W/Sv
Lees James	OS	Killed	Bragg Charles	Boy 1st Cl.	W/Sl
Parker John	OS	Killed	Bufton James	AB	W/Sl
Pound John	OS	Killed	Carne William H.	Capt. Mizentop	W/Sl
Shropshell John	Cook's Mate	Killed	Carroll John	LS	W/Sl
Turnbull James	OS	Killed	Chandler William	OS	W/Sl
Valding Lewis	Capt. Maintop	Killed	Chapman William	Qrtr/Mstr.	W/Sl
Abrams John	AB	W/Sl	Coster Mil.	Capt's Cook	W/Sl
Arthur George	AB	W/Sl	Dolby Samuel	AB	W/Sl
Anderson Edward	Carp. Crew	W/Sl	Donald William	OS	W/Sl

NOTES

The Bombardment of Sebastopol by the Naval Squadron

H.M.S. ALBION

NAME	RANK	CASUALTY	NAME	RANK	CASUALTY
Donovan Cosr.	AB	W/Sv	Mixey John	AB	W/Sl
Dutton John	LS	W/Sl	Moorhead William	AB	W/Sl
Fourtaldi Fon.	AB	W/Sv	Murray John	AB	W/Sl
Fuller Matthew	Boy 2nd Cl.	W/Sl	Neal William	OS	W/Sv
Griffiths James	AB	W/Sl	Newman Henry	OS	W/Sl
Grohegan Thomas	AB	W/Sv	Nuther Charles	AB	W/Sl
Gumbeell William	OS	D.O.W.	Paul Mr	Master	W/Sl
Hanson James	Cooprs Crew	W/Sl	Penny Robert	Fifer (RM)	W/Sl
Hanson Peter	AB	W/Sl	Pine John	AB	W/Sl
Harris George	Caukrs Mate	W/Sv	Purrington Samuel	OS	W/Sl
Hazel John	OS	W/Sl	Ridell John	Mrn (RM)	W/Sl
Heddon Thomas	OS	W/Sl	Rosnia Henry	AB	W/Sl
Isaacs James	Cox. 1st Barge	W/Sv	Rundell William	OS	W/Sv
Janhemson Luke	Blacksmith	W/Sl	Sampson William	AB	W/Sl
Jenkins Samuel	AB	W/Sv	Solomon Charles	Mrn (RM)	W/Sl
Johnson Henry	AB	W/Sl	Sullivan Stephen	AB	W/Sl
Jordan Joel	AB	W/Sv	Symcock Richard	AB	W/Sl
Keegun John	AB	W/Sl	Treagy William	Boy 2nd Cl.	W/Sl
Lanaghan Alexander	Boy 1st Cl.	W/Sl	Thomas Joseph	OS	W/Sl
Lillicrap James	OS	W/Sl	Thornborough John	S.B. Attndt.	W/Sv
McClure Stuart	Capt. Aftr/Gd	W/D	Thorne Mr	Paymaster	W/Sl
McConnell Alexander	AB	W/Sl	Tull Daniel	Mrn (RM)	W/Sl
McDonald John	AB	W/Sv	Wall James	OS	W/Sv
McFarlane Robert	AB	W/Sv	West John	OS	W/Sv
McLean John	AB	W/Sl	Westoby John	Boy 1st Cl.	W/Sl
Marshall William	Boy 1st Cl.	W/Sl	Wicks John	Blacksmith's Mate	W/Sl
Mason R. D.	Surgeon	W/Sl			
Melville Peter	AB	W/Sl	Williamson William	AB	W/Sl
Mitchell James	AB	W/Sl			

H.M.S. ARETHUSA

NAME	RANK	CASUALTY	NAME	RANK	CASUALTY
Craig Charles	OS	Killed	Johnson John	AB	W/Sv
Edwards A.	Boy	Killed	Old John	AB	W/Sl
Hunt Thomas	Qtr/Mstr.	Killed	Orchard George	AB	W/Sl
Turnbull Henry	AB	Killed	Roach George	Mrn (RM)	W/Sl
Cansey John	Mrn (RM)	W/Sl	Rose John	AB	W/Sl
Critchell Osborne	Boy	W/Sl	Thorn Thomas	Bosun's Mate	W/Sl
Finesser Daniel	OS	W/Sl	Tong Frederick	AB	W/Sl
Harrison Thomas	Mrn (RM)	W/Sl	Webber Richard	Mrn (RM)	W/Sl
Jenkins William	OS	W/Sl	Yarnold Charles	Mrn (RM)	W/Sl

H.M.S. BELLEROPHON

NAME	RANK	CASUALTY	NAME	RANK	CASUALTY
Cantrell William	AB	Killed	Hill Afred	OS	W/Sl
Claringbold John	OS	Killed	Hill William	AB	W/Sl
Johns Robert	Cox	Killed	Joy Thomas	—	W/Sv
Porter Edward	OS	Killed	Lisk Simon	OS	W/Sl
Foster M.	Midshipman	W/Sv	Payne William	Boy 2nd Cl.	W/Sl
Austin James	OS	W/Sl	Saner Adam J.	Bandsman	W/Sl
Byng Daniel	OS	W/Sv	Smith James	Cox	W/Sl
Chandlers Richard	Mrn (RM)	W/Sl	Stone William	Boy 1st Cl.	W/Sl
Daniels Edward	OS	W/Sl	Wintlebryth George	OS	W/Sv
Fisher Alfred	Boy 1st Cl.	W/Sv			

NOTES

The Bombardment of Sebastopol by the Naval Squadron

H.M.S. BRITANNIA

NAME	RANK	CASUALTY	NAME	RANK	CASUALTY
Vaughan James W.	Lieut.	W/Sv	Parkyn William	AB	W/Sv
Andrews John	AB	W/Sl	Rickord Joseph	Boy 1st Cl.	W/Sl
Carey William	Bandsman	W/Sl	Synnett James	OS	W/Sl
Gradidge Martin	OS	W/Sl	Varo William	Boy 2nd Cl.	W/Sv
McNeill William	AB	W/Sv			

H.M.S. CYCLOPS

NAME	RANK	CASUALTY
Baldock Joseph	—	W/Sv

H.M.S. FIREBRAND

NAME	RANK	CASUALTY	NAME	RANK	CASUALTY
Besfer William	Stoker	W/Sl	Stewart W. H.	Capt.	W/Sv
Featherstone Charles	Yeo. of Sig.	W/Sv	Wyatt Joseph	Capt. Aftr./GD.	W/Sl
Magee James	Armourer	W/Sl			

H.M.S. LONDON

NAME	RANK	CASUALTY	NAME	RANK	CASUALTY
Cantin Michael	OS	Killed	Hooper John	AB	W/Sl
Conner Patrick	OS	Killed	Johnstone Alexander	AB	W/Sl
Penfold Henry	AB	Killed	Knight Richard	Mrn (RM)	W/Sl
Sans George	AB	Killed	Lewis Stephen	AB	W/Sv
Stephens Charles E.	Lieut.	W/Sl	Lowe Thomas	Mrn (RM)	W/Sv
Bailey James	OS	W/Sl	Marshall James	Capt. Foretop	W/Sl
Bates James	AB	W/Sv	Newman John	AB	W/Sl
Burr Charles	Bosun's Mate	W/Sl	Sharp Stephen	Mrn (RM)	W/Sl
Collins Richard	OS	W/Sl	Sutters Joshua	Mrn (RM)	W/Sv
Cottle Robert C.	AB	W/Sv	Wilson James	AB	W/Sv
Grubb James	OS	W/Sl	Wilson William	AB	W/Sv

H.M.S. NIGER

NAME	RANK	CASUALTY	NAME	RANK	CASUALTY
Palmer Edward	Boy	Killed	Hills Edward	Mrn (RM)	W/Sl
Arnold John	AB	W/Sv	Reid Renhew	Mrn (RM)	W/Sv
Avery Benjamin	Boy	W/Sl			

H.M.S. QUEEN

NAME	RANK	CASUALTY	NAME	RANK	CASUALTY
Curtis John	Boy 1st Cl.	Killed	Newman Henry	OS	W/Sv
Bayley Daniel	OS	W/Sl	Pinhorn James	OS	W/Sl
Johns William	Bosun's Mate	W/Sl	Rogers Jonathan	OS	W/Sl
Lambard Charles	AB	W/Sl	Sheppard John	Mrn (RM)	W/Sv

NOTES

The Bombardment of Sebastopol by the Naval Squadron

H.M.S. RETRIBUTION

NAME	RANK	CASUALTY	NAME	RANK	CASUALTY
Barber George	OS	W/Sl	Coleman F.	OS	W/Sl

H.M.S. RODNEY

NAME	RANK	CASUALTY	NAME	RANK	CASUALTY
Coombes Simon	OS	W/Sv	Lisle Robert	AB	W/Sv

H.M.S. SAMPSON

NAME	RANK	CASUALTY	NAME	RANK	CASUALTY
Cook Stephen	Capt. Maintop	W/Sl	Mahony John	AB	Killed
Feast James	Stoker	W/Sl			

H.M.S. SANSPAREIL

NAME	RANK	CASUALTY	NAME	RANK	CASUALTY
Madden Charles	Midshipman	Killed	Harris James	Boy 1st. Col.	W/Sl
Bell William	AB	Killed	Healey John	AB	W/Sl
Carr James	AB	Killed	Henwright Timothy	AB	W/Sv
Cullen Thomas	AB	Killed	Higgins David	AB	W/Sv
Dicker George	AB	Killed	Hobling John	AB	W/Sv
Downs Thomas	Boy 1st Cl.	Killed	Howard Thomas	AB	W/Sv
Durham John	AB	Killed	Jackson Thomas	OS	W/Sl
Hamlyn Henry	Sailmkrs Crew	Killed	Johns John	Boy 1st Cl.	W/Sv
Heard John	AB	Killed	Jones Robert	AB	W/Sv
Hicks Swafren	AB	Killed	Joyce James	AB	W/Sv
Shirvell James	AB	Killed	Keaffe John	AB	W/Sv
Anderson W. H.	Lieut.	W/Sl	Kenn William	AB	W/Sl
Bull James	Lieut.	W/Sv	Kennelly Michael	AB	W/Sl
Anderson James	AB	W/Sl	King John	LS	W/Sv
Avery Henry	Boson's Mate	W/Sv	Langley William	Boy 2nd Cl.	W/Sv
Babbage Frederick	AB	W/Sv	Lord Thomas	Ldg. Stkr.	W/Sl
Blake Alfred	AB	W/Sl	McColley William	Ldg. Stkr.	W/Sl
Bouncehall Joseph	AB	W/Sl	McDonald Oliver	AB	W/Sl
Boundy John	Mrn (RM)	W/Sl	Miller George	AB	W/Sv
Bryant Thomas	AB	W/Sv	Moon George	Boy 1st Cl.	W/Sv
Burt William	AB	W/Sv	Osborne Charles	AB	W/Sv
Bytheway William	Bomb (RM)	W/Sl	Page Henry	AB	W/Sl
Cairns John	AB	W/Sv	Parkinson C.	2nd Master	W/Sl
Carlyon Henry	Stoker	W/Sv	Parr William	Capt. Mizentop	W/Sl
Cartmell Joseph	Capt. of the Yd.	W/Sl	Pearson Frederick	AB	W/Sv
Childs Thomas	AB	W/Sv	Pearson William	OS	W/Sl
Clinch Thomas	AB	W/Sl	Pound James	AB	W/Sv
Cudlip Nicholas	AB	W/Sv	Richards Thomas	Boy 1st Cl.	W/Sl
Donovan Jeremiah	AB	W/Sl	Rickard William	AB	W/Sv
Fitzgerald Patrick	Bandsman	W/Sv	Sark John	AB	W/Sl
Forward William	AB	W/Sl	Shirwell Thomas	Bosun's Mate	W/Sv
Gallien William	AB	W/Sl	Skillicorn Edward	OS	W/Sl
Gibson John	AB	W/Sv	Todd George	Gunner (RM)	W/Sl
Gordon Abraham	Bosun's Mate	W/Sv	Williams John	AB	W/Sl
Harrington Denis	AB	W/Sv	Williams Thomas	AB	W/Sl

NOTES

The Bombardment of Sebastopol by the Naval Squadron

H.M.S. SPHINX

NAME	RANK	CASUALTY
Tracey James	OS	Drowned during action

H.M.S. SPITEFUL

NAME	RANK	CASUALTY	NAME	RANK	CASUALTY
Thornton Edward	OS	Killed	Cason James	Boy 1st Cl.	W/Sl
Winterburn William	Bomb. (RM)	Killed	George Frederick	Mrn (RM)	W/Sl
Kyanston A. F.	Cdmr.	W/Sl	Glover Robert	Gunner (RM)	W/Sl
Purvis F. R.	Lieut.	W/Sl	Ingram Mr	Gunner	W/Sl
Baillie Mr	Midshipman	W/Sl	Sate Charles	OS	W/Sv
Bailie Charles	AB	W/Sl			

H.M.S. TERRIBLE

NAME	RANK	CASUALTY	NAME	RANK	CASUALTY
Harrison Thomas	OS	Killed	Henright James	OS	W/Sl
Darch Henry	RM	W/Sl	Heritage Michael	RM	W/Sl
Fergusson William	RM	W/Sl	Riley Thomas	RM	W/Sv
Finn John	AB	W/Sl	Warner Henry	RM	W/Sl
Gasson Alfred	OS	W/Sv			

H.M.S. TRAFALGAR

NAME	RANK	CASUALTY	NAME	RANK	CASUALTY
Goff Charles	Pte. RM	W/Sl	Larkins Thomas	OS	W/Sl

H.M.S. TRITON

NAME	RANK	CASUALTY	NAME	RANK	CASUALTY
Lloyd Henry	Lieut.	W/D	Murray Thomas	Boy 1st Cl.	W/Sl
Hiscut Charles	Pte. RM	W/Sv	Winch Joel	Carp. Mate	W/D
Jumney W.	AB	W/Sl			

H.M.S. VENGEANCE

NAME	RANK	CASUALTY	NAME	RANK	CASUALTY
Hick Richard	LS	W/Sl	James William	AB	W/Sl

NOTES

ADMIRAL
SIR EDMUND LYONS,
COMMANDER OF THE BRITISH FLEET
IN THE BLACK SEA.

ADMIRAL SIR E. LYONS
IN
THE AGAMEMNON,
ATTACKING FORT CONSTANTINE.
Oct. 17, 1854.

THE
NAVAL BRIGADE

The following casualties occurred among the Officers, Non-Commissioned Officers and Men serving in the Naval Brigade ashore during the war in the Crimea. The casualties are listed under their parent ships and the dates given indicate the following: The Bombardment of Sebastopol from the Trenches; The Battle of Inkermann; The Storming of the Quarries; The Assaults on the Redan; and desultory shelling and minor assaults by the enemy, 1854 – 1855. (Refer to Chronological Events of the War. Appendix II).

Compiled from the London Gazette; dates as indicated against each entry.

H.M.S. ALBION

NAME	RANK	CASUALTY	DATE	LONDON GAZETTE
Hammet Lacon U.	Cmdr.	Killed	17-8-55	29-8-55
Kidd S. C.	Lieut.	Killed	18-6-55	29-6-55
Barry William	AB	Killed	17-8-55	29-8-55
Carnes James	Capt. Maintop	Killed	3-9-55	22-9-55
Millar William	AB	Killed	9-4-55	24-4-55
Smith Sidney	AB	Killed	20-10-54	7-11-54
Wood John	AB	Killed	5-11-54	22-11-54
Maitland H. L. A. H.	Lieut.	W/Sv	8-9-55	22-9-55
Dowell William M.	Lieut.	W/Sv	22-10-54	7-11-54
Atkinson James	AB	W/Sl	19-8-55	29-8-55
Bunting William	LS	W/Sv	6-9-55	18-9-55
Collings Michael	AB	D.O.W.	8.9.55	22.9.55
Crays William H.	Bosun's Mate	W/Sv	18-6-55	29-6-55
Daly John	AB	W/Sv	17-8-55	29-8-55
Dominey James	AB	W/Sl	27-8-55	18-9-55
Fomey Henry	AB	W/Sl	17-8-55	29-8-55
Foster John	AB	W/Sl	20-10-54	7-11-54
Glass William	Capt. Focsle.	W/Sl	3-11-54	22-11-54
Glass William	AB	W/Sl	24-7-55	10-8-55
Glenn William	AB	W/Sl	17-8-55	29-8-55
Hall William	AB	W/Sl	20-10-54	7-11-54
Hamilton William	OS	W/Sv	13-11-54	11-12-54
Huxstable Charles	AB	W/Sv	11-4-55	24-4-55
Lowe George	OS	W/Sl	20-10-54	7-11-54
Murphy Charles	OS	W/Sl	17-10-54	7-11-54
Oatling Charles	OS	W/Sl	27-8-55	18-9-55
Pidoux Henry	AB	W/Sv	20-10-54	7-11-54
Reeves Thomas	Gnr's. Mate	W/Sl	8-9-55	22-9-55
Rollings William	OS	W/Sl	13-4-55	24-4-55

NOTES

The Naval Brigade
H.M.S. ALBION

NAME	RANK	CASUALTY	DATE	LONDON GAZETTE
Rouse Mathew	AB	W/Sl	8-9-55	22-9-55
Ryder Nathaniel	AB	W/Sv	17-8-55	29-8-55
Saunders Richard	AB	W/Sl	7-6-55	19-6-55
Simmons James	AB	W/Sv	18-6-55	29-6-55
Wallace Richard	AB	W/D	18-10-54	7-11-54
Walsh Charles	LS	W/Sv	19-8-55	29-8-55
Warden John	AB	W/Sl	8-9-55	22-9-55
Wheeler William	AB	W/Sl	20-10-54	7-11-54

H.M.S. ARETHUSA

NAME	RANK	CASUALTY	DATE	LONDON GAZETTE
Blakeney Michael	AB	Killed	17-10-54	7-11-54
Brown Joseph	Sailmkr's Crew	Killed	18-10-54	7-11-54
Lander Thomas	AB	W/Sv	18-10-54	7-11-54
Walker William	AB	W/Sl	1-11-54	16-11-54
William Thomas	AB	W/Sl	22-10-54	7-11-54

H.M.S. BEAGLE

NAME	RANK	CASUALTY	DATE	LONDON GAZETTE
Rae (or Rice) Austin	AB	W/Sv	18-10-54	7-11-54

H.M.S. BELLEROPHON

NAME	RANK	CASUALTY	DATE	LONDON GAZETTE
Vincent Francis	AB	Killed	17-10-54	7-11-54
Alexander William	AB	W/Sv	19-10-54	7-11-54
Cosey John	AB	W/Sv	19-10-54	7-11-54
Curtis John	AB	W/Sl	17-10-54	7-11-54
Heddon Thomas	AB	W/Sv	17-10-54	7-11-54
Matthews Cornelius	AB	W/Sl	19-10-54	7-11-54
Paterson Henry	AB	W/Sv	20-10-54	7-11-54
Proudfoot James	AB	W/Sv	19-10-54	7-11-54
Supple William	AB	W/Sl	20-10-54	7-11-54

H.M.S. BRITANNIA

NAME	RANK	CASUALTY	DATE	LONDON GAZETTE
Greathed George	Lieut.	Killed	20-10-54	7-11-54
Harris James	AB	Killed	9-11-54	11-12-54
Naylor William	AB	Killed	18-10-54	7-11-54
Steel —	Lieut.	W/Sl	24-10-54	12-11-54
Brock Philip	Mate	W/Sl	3-11-54	22-11-54
Brown James	Bosun's Mate	W/Sv	22-10-54	7-11-54
Henry William	AB	W/Sl	9-11-54	11-12-54
Herris Joseph	2nd Mate	W/Sl	5-11-54	22-11-54
Hinin Ricard	AB	W/Sv	20-10-54	7-11-54
Killarney Bernard	AB	W/Sl	18-10-54	7-11-54
Latto Edward	AB	W/Sv	18-10-54	7-11-54
Lewis Francis	AB	W/Sl	18-10-54	7-11-54
McCredie Thomas	AB	W/Sl	17-10-54	7-11-54

NOTES

The Naval Brigade

H.M.S. BRITANNIA

NAME	RANK	CASUALTY	DATE	LONDON GAZETTE
Williams John	AB	W/Sl	30-10-54	16-11-54
Worrell Thomas	Carp. Crew	W/Sv	18-10-54	7-11-54
Wrann Thomas	AB	W/Sv	3-11-54	22-11-54

H.M.S. DAUNTLESS

NAME	RANK	CASUALTY	DATE	LONDON GAZETTE
Parsons Mr	Mate	W/Sv	18-6-55	29-6-55

H.M.S. DIAMOND

NAME	RANK	CASUALTY	DATE	LONDON GAZETTE
Churchill Edward	Capt. Maintop	Killed	17-10-54	7-11-54
Kakeman William	Capt. Maintop	Killed	17-10-54	7-11-54
Radmore James	AB	Killed	18-6-55	29-6-55
Cave Mr	Lieut.	W/Sv	18-6-55	29-6-55
Mitchell Alfred	Lieut.	W/Sv	20-10-54	7-11-54
Mitchell Alfred	Lieut.	W/Sv	9-6-55	22-6-55
Daniels Mr	Midshipman	W/Sl	6-6-55	19-6-55
Anthony Nathaniel	AB	W/D	18-10-54	7-11-54
Buchan John	AB	W/Sl	18-10-54	7-11-54
Dowling William	AB	W/Sv	19-10-54	7-11-54
Dunning Trevor	AB	W/Sl	24-10-54	12-11-54
Dunning Trevor	AB	W/Sl	7-4-55	20-4-55
Hoggins William	AB	W/Sv	18-10-54	7-11-54
Hoskins William	Caulker	W/Sl	8-8-55	24-8-55
Hughes John	AB	W/Sv	7-6-55	19-6-55
Ingarthen James	Bosun's Mate	W/Sv	17-10-54	7-11-54
Knott Arthur	CM	W/D	19-10-54	7-11-54
McCann William	AB	W/Sl	18-10-54	7-11-54
Matson William	AB	W/Sv	18-10-54	7-11-54
Nixon John	AB	W/Sv	18-6-55	29-6-55
Purton Daniel	Capt. Maintop	W/Sv	18-6-55	29-6-55
Quin Barney	OS	W/Sl	8-9-55	22-9-55
Selby Mr	Mate	W/Sl	6-11-54	22-11-54
Shorter William	AB	W/Sl	12-11-54	11-12-54
Symes Thomas	AB	W/Sv	18-10-54	7-11-54
Thompson George	AB	W/Sl	18-10-54	7-11-54

H.M.S. FIREBRAND

NAME	RANK	CASUALTY	DATE	LONDON GAZETTE
Moorsom William	Capt.	W/Sl	20-10-54	7-11-54

H.M.S. LEANDER

NAME	RANK	CASUALTY	DATE	LONDON GAZETTE
Albion Daniel	AB	Killed	9-4-55	24-4-55
Bradwell John	LS	Killed	9-4-55	24-4-55
Branchley John	LS	Killed	18-6-55	29-6-55
Butcher Thomas	AB	Killed	14-4-55	1-5-55
Cass George	AB	Killed	18-6-55	29-6-55

NOTES

The Naval Brigade
H.M.S. LEANDER

NAME	RANK	CASUALTY	DATE	LONDON GAZETTE
Grant Samuel	AB	Killed	18-6-55	29-6-55
Green John (Alias Charles)	OS	Killed	16-4-55	1-5-55
Johns John	AB	Killed	14-4-55	1-5-55
Lawson William	AB	Killed	11-4-55	24-4-55
Lellond Elias	AB	Killed	18-6-55	29-6-55
McLean Charles	AB	Killed	10-4-55	24-4-55
Maclin James	LS	Killed	7-6-55	19-6-55
Malone Godfrey	AB	Killed	10-4-55	24-4-55
Nicholls Jesse	LS	Killed	14-4-55	1-5-55
Pawley William	AB	Killed	10-4-55	24-4-55
Wilkey William	AB	Killed	18-6-55	29-6-55
Peel William	Capt.	W/Sv	18-6-55	29-6-55
Dalyell O. W.	Lieut.	W/D	18-6-55	29-6-55
Dupuis Mr	Midshipman	W/Sl	17-6-55	29-6-55
Burrell Sylvester	Qtrmstr.	W/Sl	11-4-55	24-4-55
Burrell Sylvester	Qtrmstr.	W/D	10-7-55	24-7-55
Abbott Joseph	AB	W/Sv	18-6-55	29-6-55
Arnold John	LS	D.O.W.	8-6-55	19-6-55
Austen James	AB	W/M	8-9-55	22-9-55
Bambury William	OS	W/Sl	12-4-55	24-4-55
Bennett James	OS	W/Sl	6-6-55	19-6-55
Booker John	AB	W/Sv	17-4-55	1-5-55
Brickwood John	AB	W/Sl	17-6-55	29-6-55
Buddin William	OS	W/Sv	30-8-55	18-9-55
Bussey Charles	AB	W/Sl	12-4-55	24-4-55
Buxey Peter	AB	W/Sv	12-4-55	24-4-55
Coakes George	LS	W/Sv	18-6-55	29-6-55
Cocker Thomas	AB	W/Sl	11-4-55	24-4-55
Colley Edward	AB	W/Sv	18-6-55	29-6-55
Coxhedge William	OS	W/Sl	18-6-55	29-6-55
Crispin James	Bosun's Mate	W/Sl	17-6-55	29-6-55
Cudlip William	AB	W/Sl	11-4-55	24-4-55
Davis James	AB	W/Sv	18-6-55	29-6-55
Dawkins Francis	OS	W/Sv	11-4-55	24-4-55
Dead Joseph	AB	W/Sv	8-9-55	22-9-55
Doherty James	AB	W/Sl	18-6-55	29-6-55
Flynn Patrick	OS	W/Sv	14-4-55	1-5-55
Gadden William	OS	W/Sl	16-4-55	1-5-55
Gamble George	AB	W/D	17-5-55	29-5-55
Granger Frederick	OS	W/Sv	26-8-55	18-9-55
Gray Charles	OS	W/Sl	9-4-55	24-4-55
Gordon James	OS	W/Sl	7-6-55	19-6-55
Hardy James	—	Missing	18-6-55	29-6-55
Havent Philip	AB	W/Sl	6-6-55	19-6-55
Hawkins Daniel	AB	W/Sl	12-4-55	24-4-55
Hayling William	Capt. Foretop	W/M	17-6-55	29-6-55
Haynes Thomas	LS	W/Sv	6-6-55	19-6-55
Hendon George	LS	W/Sl	16-4-55	1-5-55
Hukins Edward	OS	W/Sl	9-4-55	24-4-55
Hurst Stephen	AB	W/Sv	18-6-55	29-6-55
Jones Henry	AB	W/Sl	13-4-55	24-4-55
Jones Henry	AB	W/Sv	10-6-55	22-6-55
Kennedy Michael	OS	W/Sl	10-4-55	24-4-55
Kennedy Michael	OS	W/Sl	6-6-55	19-6-55
Knowles John	AB	W/Sv	7-6-55	19-6-55
Langley James	LS	W/Sl	10-7-55	24-7-55
Lansen Michael	—	W/Sv	14-4-55	1-5-55
Linnington John	AB	W/Sl	14-4-55	1-5-55
Mable Robert	Capt. Focsle.	W/Sv	11-4-55	24-4-55
Mahoney William	OS	W/Sv	18-6-55	29-6-55
Manning George	AB	W/Sl	18-6-55	29-6-55
Marsh George	OS	W/Sl	6-6-55	19-6-55
Marsh John	LS	W/Sl	17-6-55	29-6-55
Martin Charles	AB	W/Sl	11-4-55	24-4-55

NOTES

The Naval Brigade

H.M.S. LEANDER

NAME	RANK	CASUALTY	DATE	LONDON GAZETTE
Meek William	AB	W/Sl	11-4-55	24-4-55
Merritt George	AB	W/Sl	17-6-55	29-6-55
Muller John	AB	W/M	18-4-55	1-5-55
Murphy Jeremiah	AB	W/Sv	30-8-55	18-9-55
Nayes John	AB	W/Sl	8-9-55	22-9-55
Newby James	OS	W/Sv	9-4-55	24-4-55
Nicholls Henry	AB	W/Sl	18-6-55	29-6-55
Noble Thomas	AB	W/Sv	12-4-55	24-4-55
O'Donoghue Patrick	Capt. Foretop	W/Sl	11-4-55	24-4-55
Pasco Thomas	OS	D.O.W.	7-6-55	19-6-55
Rainsforth William	AB	W/Sv	18-6-55	29-6-55
Reenan John	AB	W/Sv	15-4-55	1-5-55
Regan Robert	OS	W/Sl	12-4-55	24-4-55
Rowe Richard	Gunner	W/Sl	10-4-55	24-4-55
Russell Alexander	LS	W/Sl	17-6-55	29-6-55
Seymour George	AB	W/Sl	10-4-55	24-4-55
Simmons William	AB	W/Sl	7-6-55	19-6-55
Smedley James	Gnrs. Mate	W/Sl	10-4-55	24-4-55
Smith Edward	AB	W/Sl	23-4-55	4-5-55
Smith John	AB	W/Sv	23-5-55	5-6-55
Sobey William	AB	W/Sv	18-6-55	29-6-55
Steer James	OS	W/Sl	18-6-55	29-6-55
Tobin John	AB	W/D	18-6-55	29-6-55
Trace William	OS	W/Sl	18-6-55	29-6-55
Turner William	OS	W/Sl	16-4-55	1-5-55
Wallace Robert	AB	W/Sl	11-4-55	24-4-55
Walsh Herbert	AB	W/Sl	14-4-55	1-5-55
Warner Edward	AB	W/Sl	9-6-55	22-6-55
Wells Robert	AB	W/Sl	10-4-55	24-4-55
Welsh Robert	AB	W/Sl	18-6-55	29-6-55
Williams Samuel	AB	W/Sl	16-4-55	1-5-55
Williams Samuel	AB	W/Sl	9-6-55	22-6-55
Yowson John	AB	W/Sv	13-7-55	27-7-55

H.M.S. LEOPARD

NAME	RANK	CASUALTY	DATE	LONDON GAZETTE
Davis George	AB	W/Sv	13-3-55	23-3-55

H.M.S. LONDON

NAME	RANK	CASUALTY	DATE	LONDON GAZETTE
Twyford Mr	Lieut.	Killed	9-4-55	24-4-55
Anderson John	AB	Killed	22-10-54	7-11-54
Carner John	AB	Killed	17-10-54	7-11-54
Fleming William	AB	Killed	6-9-55	18-9-55
Kenway Thomas	OS	Killed	18-6-55	29-6-55
Spalding J. H.	Act/Mate	Killed	21-1-55	6-2-55
Stacey James	—	Killed	11-4-55	24-4-55
Thomas William	OS	Killed	18-6-55	29-6-55
D'Aeth Mr	Lieut.	W/Sl	13-4-55	24-4-55
Gough	Lieut.	W/Sl	8-6-55	19-6-55
Oldfield R. B.	Lieut.	W/Sl	8-6-55	19-6-55
Ruthven Hon C. B.	Lieut.	W/D	17-10-54	7-11-54
Bailey Richard	Bosun's Mate	W/Sv	7-6-55	19-6-55
Bates William	OS	W/Sl	6-6-55	19-6-55
Beckler Leonard	AB	W/M	10-4-55	24-4-55
Beldan John	OS	W/Sl	10-6-55	22-6-55

NOTES

The Naval Brigade
H.M.S. LONDON

NAME	RANK	CASUALTY	DATE	LONDON GAZETTE
Blae James	OS	W/Sl	12-4-55	24-4-55
Bombey George	OS	W/Sl	7-6-55	19-6-55
Buckley John	OS	W/Sl	7-9-55	22-9-55
Carter William	AB	W/Sl	8-9-55	22-9-55
Cassedy Francis	Capt. Maintop	W/Sl	17-8-55	28-8-55
Conway Peter	OS	W/Sl	10-6-55	22-6-55
Cogger Alfred	AB	W/Sl	8-9-55	22-9-55
Collins John	OS	W/Sl	20-4-55	1-5-55
Cropper Robert	OS	W/M	10-6-55	22-6-55
Daniells Charles	AB	W/Sl	7-6-55	19-6-55
Darby Robert	OS	W/Sl	12-4-55	24-4-55
Evans Griffith	OS	W/Sl	12-4-55	24-4-55
Evans Griffith	OS	W/Sv	10-6-55	22-6-55
Fry John	OS	W/Sv	9-4-55	24-4-55
Gardner Richard	AB	D.O.W.	9-4-55	24-4-55
Gardner Richard	Capt. Foretop	W/Sv	25-7-55	10-8-55
Garrett William	LS	W/Sl	1-11-54	16-11-54
Gillham John	AB	W/Sv	17-10-54	7-11-54
Godding Henry	Capt. Mast.	W/Sl	9-4-55	24-4-55
Gregg John	AB	W/M	17-8-55	28-8-55
Hogan Michael	OS	W/Sl	7-6-55	19-6-55
Hughes Joseph	OS	W/Sv	14-4-55	1-5-55
Johnson Alexander	AB	W/Sl	7-6-55	19-6-55
Leary William	OS	W/Sl	25-7-55	10-8-55
McCarthy John	OS	W/Sv	17-8-55	28-8-55
Mackin Frederick	OS	W/D	5-11-54	22-11-54
Melida John	OS	W/Sl	17-8-55	28-8-55
Mulcahy John	AB	W/D	27-8-55	18-9-55
Murray James	AB	W/Sv	20-10-54	7-11-54
Murray James	AB	W/Sv	6-9-55	18-9-55
Murray John	AB	W/Sl	10-6-55	22-6-55
Nash William	AB	W/Sv	19-8-55	31-8-55
O'Donnell John	AB	W/Sv	10-6-55	22-6-55
Owen William	OS	W/Sl	6-9-55	18-9-55
Pinhorn Samuel	OS	W/Sl	9-4-55	24-4-55
Rawlings John	OS	W/Sv	6-6-55	19-6-55
Sageman Francis	Capt. Maintop	W/Sl	17-6-55	29-6-55
Spalding Mr	Mate	W/Sl	3-11-54	22-11-54
Stevenson Charles	OS	W/Sl	6-9-55	18-9-55
Smith Edward	OS	W/Sl	15-4-55	1-5-55
Smith George	Capt. Foretop	W/Sv	17-8-55	28-8-55
Trace William	OS	W/Sl	17-8-55	28-8-55
Ward James	OS	W/Sv	28-8-55	18-9-55
Watts John	OS	W/Sl	7-9-55	22-9-55
Wildish David	AB	W/Sl	6-9-55	18-9-55
Woodman George	OS	W/Sl	21-7-55	10-8-55

H.M.S. NIGER

NAME	RANK	CASUALTY	DATE	LONDON GAZETTE
Reynolds W. V. E.	Asst./Surg.	W/Sl	8-9-55	22-9-55

H.M.S. QUEEN

NAME	RANK	CASUALTY	DATE	LONDON GAZETTE
Douglas W. K.	Lieut.	Killed	12-4-55	24-4-55
Edy Frank	Qrtr./Mstr.	Killed	19-5-55	5-6-55
Blewitt John	OS	Killed	4-6-55	15-6-55

NOTES

The Naval Brigade
H.M.S. QUEEN

NAME	RANK	CASUALTY	DATE	LONDON GAZETTE
Burcher Alfred	OS	Killed	19-10-54	7-11-54
Burrows Joseph	AB	Killed	9-4-55	24-4-55
Coffin James	OS	Killed	7-6-55	19-6-55
Dudgeon Thomas	AB	Killed	9-4-55	24-4-55
Good Daniel	OS	Killed	9-4-55	24-4-55
Harris William	OS	Killed	10-7-55	24-7-55
Hill Henry	AB	Killed	10-5-55	22-5-55
Jones Robert	OS	Killed	10-6-55	22-6-55
Laverick Robert	AB	Killed	22-3-55	3-4-55
McConchie John	AB	Killed	22-10-54	7-11-54
Mahoney Patrick	OS	Killed	7-6-55	19-6-55
Medlin John	AB	Killed	7-6-55	19-6-55
Soulbrey William	OS	Killed	12-4-55	24-4-55
Taylor Benjamin	AB	Killed	26-4-55	15-5-55
Trino John	AB	Killed	15-4-55	1-5-55
Welsh Stephen	AB	Killed	4-6-55	15-6-55
Whitfield John	AB	Killed	19-7-55	31-7-55
Burnett	Cmdr.	W/Sl	7-11-54	11-12-54
Selby W. D. D.	Lieut.	W/Sl	8-9-55	22-9-55
Urmston W. B.	Lieut.	W/Sl	11-4-55	24-4-55
Urmston W. B.	Lieut.	W/Sv	18-6-55	29-6-55
Wood H. E.	Midshipman	W/Sl	18-6-55	29-6-55
Llewellyn F. R.	2nd Master	W/Sl	17-8-55	28-8-55
Llewellyn F. R.	2nd Master	W/Sl	8-9-55	22-9-55
Aberdeen Charles	AB	W/Sl	23-10-54	12-11-54
Ash William	Capt. Foretop	W/Sl	15-4-55	1-5-55
Ayres Fennesy	OS	W/Sl	17-8-55	28-8-55
Baker Robert	OS	W/D	26-4-55	15-4-55
Beagley Richard	OS	W/Sl	19-8-55	31-8-55
Bevan James	OS	W/Sl	24-10-54	12-11-54
Black Patrick	OS	W/Sv	7-6-55	19-6-55
Boyle George	AB	W/Sl	21-4-55	4-5-55
Bradley William	OS	W/Sl	11-4-55	24-4-55
Brooking Isaac	OS	W/Sl	12-4-55	24-4-55
Broughton Edward	AB	W/Sl	14-4-55	1-5-55
Brown James	LS	W/Sv	4-4-55	20-4-55
Brown John	LS	W/Sv	4-4-55	20-4-55
Bundy Daniel	OS	W/Sl	12-11-54	11-12-54
Bundy Daniel	OS	W/Sl	17-6-55	29-6-55
Bush Thomas	AB	D.O.W.	18-10-54	7-11-54
Butler Durie	AB	W/Sl	4-5-55	18-5-55
Butler Pierce	AB	W/Sl	4-5-55	18-5-55
Carey Alfred	OS	W/Sl	24-7-55	10-8-55
Channon William	OS	W/D	20-10-54	7-11-54
Cheelds Thomas	OS	W/Sl	6-6-55	19-6-55
Cheelds Thomas	OS	W/Sl	28-7-55	10-8-55
Clatworthy Fernando	OS	W/Sl	12-4-55	24-4-55
Clatworthy Fernando	OS	W/Sl	10-7-55	24-7-55
Clarke William	OS	W/Sl	27-4-55	15-5-55
Conway Joseph	OS	W/Sl	12-4-55	24-4-55
Conway Joseph	OS	W/Sl	18-8-55	31-8-55
Corbelly Thomas	AB	W/Sv	12-4-55	24-4-55
Cotter Francis	AB	W/Sl	18-8-55	31-8-55
Crowhurst William	OS	W/Sl	8-9-55	22-9-55
Davey William	OS	W/Sl	28-5-55	12-6-55
Davidson John	AB	W/M	11-4-55	24-4-55
Davis William	OS	W/Sl	15-4-55	1-5-55
Dine Samuel	OS	W/Sv	21-10-54	7-11-54
Egg John	OS	W/Sv	10-11-54	11-12-54
Ellis George	OS	W/Sv	9-4-55	24-4-55
Faithful John	OS	W/Sl	17-10-54	7-11-54
Flynn Michael	OS	W/Sl	17-6-55	29-6-55
Flynn Morris	OS	W/Sl	4-4-55	20-4-55
Garnett Richard	Capt. Foretop	W/Sl	12-4-55	24-4-55

NOTES

The Naval Brigade
H.M.S. QUEEN

NAME	RANK	CASUALTY	DATE	LONDON GAZETTE
Gisby Aaron	OS	W/Sv	10-5-55	22-5-55
Glanville John	OS	W/Sv	12-4-55	24-4-55
Goodyear William	OS	W/Sl	20-4-55	1-5-55
Gordon John	OS	W/Sl	23-4-55	4-5-55
Gordon John	OS	W/Sl	7-9-55	22-9-55
Haley Patrick	OS	W/Sv	22-7-55	10-8-55
Hallet Edward	Carp. Crew	W/D	20-10-54	7-11-54
Hammond Philip Henry	OS	W/Sv	10-5-55	22-5-55
Harris Thomas	OS	W/Sl	7-6-55	19-6-55
Hart Robert	OS	W/Sv	10-5-55	22-5-55
Hill James	AB	W/Sv	7-6-55	19-6-55
Hillier Robert	AB	W/Sv	8-9-55	22-9-55
Holder Henry	AB	W/Sl	17-6-55	29-6-55
Holman Robert	OS	W/Sv	24-7-55	10-8-55
Hooper William	Armourer	W/Sl	15-4-55	1-5-55
Hunter James Edward	Mate	W/Sl	7-6-55	19-6-55
Jackson James	OS	W/Sv	7-6-55	19-6-55
James George	OS	W/Sv	19-10-54	7-11-54
Jones Peter	AB	W/Sl	12-4-55	24-4-55
Jones William	AB	W/Sv	12-4-55	24-4-55
Irving Joseph	OS	W/Sl	8-6-55	22-6-55
Lacey John	OS	W/Sl	12-4-55	24-4-55
Lanahan John	OS	W/D	7-6-55	19-6-55
Lawrence Richard	OS	W/Sl	24-10-54	12-11-54
Lee Edward	OS	W/Sv	17-8-55	28-8-55
Leigh John	OS	W/Sl	30-8-55	18-9-55
Lencock Henry	AB	W/Sv	9-4-55	24-4-55
McCarthy Daniel	AB	W/Sl	16-4-55	1-5-55
McDonald William	AB	W/D	19-8-55	31-8-55
McLellan John	OS	W/D	12-4-55	24-4-55
Mallum Edward	AB	W/Sv	15-4-55	1-5-55
Maslin Joseph	AB	W/Sv	17-10-54	7-11-54
Mason John	OS	W/Sl	13-4-55	24-4-55
Mason John	OS	W/Sl	10-5-55	22-5-55
Matthews John W.	Capt. Maintop	W/Sv	8-9-55	22-9-55
Medlin Nicholas	OS	W/M	11-4-55	24-4-55
Medlin Thomas	AB	W/Sl	8-6-55	19-6-55
Moore George	OS	W/Sl	17-8-55	28-8-55
Murray William	OS	W/Sl	6-6-55	19-6-55
Murray William	OS	W/Sl	6-9-55	18-9-55
O'Brien Robert	AB	W/Sv	8-9-55	22-9-55
O'Brien Roger	AB	W/D	11-4-55	24-4-55
Oliver Richard	OS	W/Sl	12-4-55	24-4-55
Pearce William	AB	W/Sl	7-6-55	19-6-55
Perry Edward	OS	W/Sl	9-6-55	22-6-55
Pierce William	OS	W/Sl	11-4-55	24-4-55
Poliblank Samuel	AB	W/Sl	28-7-55	10-8-55
Reynolds James	OS	W/Sl	10-5-55	22-5-55
Richards William	OS	W/Sl	9-6-55	22-6-55
Rollings William	OS	W/Sl	12-4-55	24-4-55
Rook Richard	OS	W/Sl	19-5-55	5-6-55
Sanctuary William	Mate	W/Sv	17-10-54	7-11-54
Simms Thomas	OS	W/Sl	10-11-54	11-12-54
Simmons James	Carp. Crew	W/M	24-10-54	12-11-54
Skinner William	OS	W/Sv	7-9-55	22-9-55
Smith Edward	AB	W/Sl	12-4-55	24-4-55
Smith Nicholas	OS	W/Sl	21-10-54	7-11-54
Smith Richard	OS	W/Sv	19-10-54	7-11-54
Smith Thomas	AB	W/Sl	18-5-55	5-6-55
Stammers Charles	AB	W/Sv	9-4-55	24-4-55
Stone John	OS	W/Sv	22-7-55	10-8-55
Sture Richard	OS	W/Sl	12-4-55	24-4-55
Sullivan Daniel	OS	W/Sl	8-6-55	19-6-55
Wadham Frank	OS	W/Sl	9-4-55	24-4-55

NOTES

The Naval Brigade

H.M.S. QUEEN

NAME	RANK	CASUALTY	DATE	LONDON GAZETTE
Webber William	OS	W/Sl	7-6-55	19-6-55
White James	Capt. Maintop	W/Sl	12-4-55	24-4-55
Woodgate James	LS	W/Sl	16-4-55	1-5-55

H.M.S. RODNEY

NAME	RANK	CASUALTY	DATE	LONDON GAZETTE
Blyth Richard	LS	Killed	17-8-55	28-8-55
Davidson William	AB	Killed	18-6-55	29-6-55
Gordon Edward	AB	Killed	7-6-55	19-6-55
Hilchey Edward	AB	Killed	6-6-55	19-6-55
Innis James	AB	Killed	18-6-55	29-6-55
Karslake Mr	Mate	Killed	10-11-54	11-12-54
McBurney Andrew	AB	Killed	9-11-54	11-12-54
Meldon George	AB	Killed	31-8-55	18-9-55
Murphy John	Capt. After/Gd	Killed	18-6-55	29-6-55
Quin Edward	AB	Killed	18-6-55	29-6-55
Reid John	AB	Killed	18-6-55	29-6-55
Theylbank William	AB	Killed	7-6-55	19-6-55
Upton James	AB	Killed	15-7-55	27-7-55
Wackerall Henry	OS	Killed	17-8-55	28-8-55
Martin John	Qrtr./Mstr.	W/Sl	18-6-55	29-6-55
Archer James	AB	W/D	22-10-54	7-11-54
Bailey William	AB	W/Sv	24-10-54	12-11-54
Bartlett William	AB	W/Sl	8-9-55	18-9-55
Bluham Matthew	AB	W/Sl	7-6-55	19-6-55
Bogle George	AB	W/Sl	21-4-55	4-5-55
Brien James	AB	W/Sl	5-11-54	22-11-54
Burnes William	AB	W/Sv	18-6-55	29-6-55
Calvo William	AB	W/Sv	17-8-55	28-8-55
Callicott James	AB	W/Sl	8-6-55	19-6-55
Callicott James	AB	W/Sv	18-6-55	29-6-55
Carmichael John	OS	W/Sl	7-9-55	18-9-55
Carmichael John	AB	W/Sl	17-8-55	28-8-55
Carney Daniel	AB	D.O.W.	8-8-55	24-8-55
Childs James	OS	W/D	16-4-55	1-5-55
Clayton George	AB	W/Sv	18-6-55	29-6-55
Coffey John	AB	W/Sv	7-11-54	11-12-54
Coleman James	AB	W/Sl	10-7-55	24-7-55
Collins John	AB	W/Sv	17-8-55	28-8-55
Colvin Henry	AB	W/Sl	23-10-54	12-11-54
Davis Charles Henry	OS	W/Sv	18-6-55	29-6-55
Devnie Michael	OS	W/Sv	18-6-55	29-6-55
Edwards Henry	AB	W/Sv	7-6-55	19-6-55
Elliot Robert	AB	W/Sl	7-6-55	19-6-55
Elliott James	AB	W/Sl	18-6-55	29-6-55
Fallen John	AB	W/Sl	22-10-54	7-11-54
Fennessy William	OS	W/Sv	7-6-55	19-6-55
Fitzgerald Michael	AB	W/Sl	7-6-55	19-6-55
Fitzgerald Michael	AB	W/Sl	8-9-55	18-9-55
Galloway James	AB	W/Sv	5-11-54	22-11-54
Geddis Thomas	AB	W/Sv	18-6-55	29-6-55
Glanville Stephen	AB	W/Sl	18-6-55	29-6-55
Green George	AB	W/Sv	17-4-55	1-5-55
Hadley Alexander	Bosun's Mate	W/Sv	17-6-55	29-6-55
Hayward William	Cox's Cutter	W/Sl	14-4-55	1-5-55
Heath Henry	AB	W/Sv	18-6-55	29-6-55
Holmes James	AB	W/Sv	17-8-55	28-8-55
Holyhonce Robert	AB	W/Sl	23-10-54	12-11-54
Homer John	AB	W/Sl	17-6-55	29-6-55
Hopkins George	AB	W/Sv	6-6-55	19-6-55

NOTES

The Naval Brigade

H.M.S. RODNEY

NAME	RANK	CASUALTY	DATE	LONDON GAZETTE
Hoveden H. F.	A/Mate	W/Sl	19-8-55	31-8-55
Hudsmith Richard	AB	W/Sv	18-8-55	31-8-55
Huntley William	OS	W/Sv	8-6-55	19-6-55
Jaggard John	AB	W/Sl	26-7-55	10-8-55
Keines Michael	AB	W/D	18-6-55	29-6-55
Klast Joseph	AB	W/Sl	7-6-55	19-6-55
Lawrence Thomas	AB	W/Sv	19-8-55	31-8-55
Legg James	AB	W/Sl	29-5-55	12-6-55
Lisk John	AB	W/Sl	17-6-55	29-6-55
Lochrin Thomas	AB	W/Sv	18-6-55	29-6-55
Mahoney Jeremiah	OS	W/Sl	23-4-55	4-5-55
Marlow Thomas	OS	W/Sl	29-10-54	16-11-54
Matthews James	AB	W/Sl	10-7-55	24-7-55
Merewood James	AB	W/Sl	18-6-55	29-6-55
Mullins John	OS	W/Sl	7-6-55	19-6-55
Oats Thomas	Capt. Foretop	W/Sl	8-9-55	18-9-55
Pearce George	Capt. Foretop	W/Sv	18-6-55	29-6-55
Pearson William	AB	W/Sl	18-8-55	31-8-55
Pepper William	AB	W/Sl	13-4-55	24-4-55
Pollard John	AB	W/Sl	7-6-55	19-6-55
Prince Thomas	Capt. Maintop	W/D	18-6-55	29-6-55
Quin Daniel	AB	W/Sl	18-6-55	29-6-55
Remlo John	OS	W/Sl	6-9-55	18-9-55
Richards William	OS	W/Sl	9-6-55	22-8-55
Rommerhill Philip	AB	W/Sv	6-6-55	19-6-55
Ross Alexandder	AB	W/Sv	6-6-55	19-6-55
Shaw James W.	AB	W/Sv	18-6-55	29-6-55
Shawer George	AB	W/Sl	18-8-55	31-8-55
Shepherd William	AB	W/Sl	7-6-55	19-6-55
Sinnot John	AB	W/Sl	17-6-55	29-6-55
Smith James	AB	W/Sv	18-4-55	1-5-55
Stack Thomas	AB	W/Sl	17-8-55	28-8-55
Stanley Michael	AB	W/Sv	18-8-55	31-8-55
Strickland William	AB	W/Sl	7-6-55	19-6-55
Sullivan Michael	AB	W/Sl	10-7-55	24-7-55
Surridge John	AB	W/Sl	18-6-55	29-6-55
Symonds James	AB	W/Sl	8-6-55	19-6-55
Thomas Arthur	AB	W/Sv	6-9-55	18-9-55
Tucker Edward	AB	W/Sv	7-6-55	19-6-55
Turk John	AB	W/Sl	8-9-55	18-9-55
Winnicott John	AB	W/Sl	26-7-55	10-8-55
Wyborn John	AB	W/Sl	19-8-55	31-8-55
Young James	AB	W/Sl	17-8-55	28-8-55

H.M.S. TRAFALGAR

NAME	RANK	CASUALTY	DATE	LONDON GAZETTE
Coleman James	Cox's Barge	Killed	26-10-54	12-11-54
Wilding Charles	AB	Killed	17-10-54	7-11-54
Norman N.	Lieut.	W/Sv	17-10-54	7-11-54
Berry James	AB	W/Sl	6-11-54	22-11-54
Bullock Edward	Mate	W/Sl	17-10-54	7-11-54
Bullock S. T.	Mate	W/Sv	21-10-54	7-11-54
Bullock Thomas	AB	W/Sl	9-11-54	11-12-54
Cock Thomas	OS	W/Sl	21-10-54	7-11-54
Creeds Peter	OS	W/Sl	9-11-54	11-12-54
Day Joseph	AB	W/Sv	26-10-54	12-11-54
Ferguson Norman	AB	W/Sl	21-10-54	7-11-54
Godward Henry	AB	W/Sl	8-11-54	11-12-54
Hards William	AB	W/Sl	9-11-54	11-12-54
Hurds William	OS	W/Sl	17-10-54	7-11-54

NOTES

The Naval Brigade

H.M.S. TRAFALGAR

NAME	RANK	CASUALTY	DATE	LONDON GAZETTE
Nott Thomas	OS	W/Sl	26-10-54	12-11-54
O'Brien Richard	AB	W/Sv	17-10-54	7-11-54
Puddifoot Joseph	OS	W/Sl	21-10-54	7-11-54
Revell William	AB	W/Sl	23-10-54	7-11-54
Webb Richard	OS	W/Sl	2-11-54	22-11-54

H.M.S. VENGEANCE

NAME	RANK	CASUALTY	DATE	LONDON GAZETTE
Lampin Samuel	AB	W/Sl	20-10-54	7-11-54
Lee John	OS	W/Sl	9-11-54	11-12-54
Lemmon Thomas	AB	W/Sl	1-11-54	16-11-54
Lloyd John	AB	W/Sv	4-11-54	22-11-54
Lyons or Leyon George	Mate	W/Sl	18-10-54	7-11-54
Murdock John	Capt. Foretop	W/D	19-10-54	7-11-54
Phillipps Thomas	AB	W/Sl	19-10-54	7-11-54
Roberts George	AB	W/Sv	17-10-54	7-11-54
Tout William	AB	W/D	5-11-54	22-11-54
Wilkinson George	Cox's Pinnace	W/Sl	23-10-54	12-11-54
Wilson Mr	Mate	W/Sl	4-11-54	22-11-54

H.M.S. WASP

NAME	RANK	CASUALTY	DATE	LONDON GAZETTE
Glanville John	Sailmaker	Killed	9-4-55	24-4-55
Logan Daniel	Gunner (RMA)	Killed	6-6-55	19-6-55
Turner Stephen	—	Killed	11-4-55	24-4-55
Woodford John	OS	Killed	16-4-55	1-5-55
Hay Lord John	Capt.	W/Sl	9-4-55	24-4-55
Steele A. C.	Lieut. (RMA)	W/Sl	11-4-55	24-4-55
Ward William	Qrtr./Mstr.	W/Sl	8-11-54	11-12-54
Anderson Charles	AB	W/Sl	11-4-55	24-4-55
Anderson Thomas	AB	W/Sl	18-6-55	29-6-55
Ansell Charles	AB	W/Sv	18-6-55	29-6-55
Branchley William	OS	W/Sl	14-4-55	1-5-55
Bray George	Cap. After/Gd.	W/Sl	9-6-55	22-6-55
Brickwood William	Capt. Maintop	W/Sl	6-6-55	19-6-55
Buckley Robert	OS	W/Sl	6-9-55	18-9-55
Carter George	AB	W/Sl	14-4-55	1-5-55
Colley Edward	OS	W/Sl	10-6-55	22-6-55
Connor Peter	AB	W/Sl	9-6-55	22-6-55
Hargrave Thomas	Gunner (RMA)	W/Sl	11-4-55	24-4-55
Houltram William	OS	W/Sl	10-4-55	24-4-55
Jacobs Charles	OS	W/Sl	25-7-55	10-8-55
Jones John	OS	W/Sl	7-6-55	19-6-55
Jones William	Sailmkr's Mate	W/Sl	9-4-55	24-4-55
Millar John	Gunner's Mate	W/Sl	9-6-55	22-6-55
Pepper William	AB	W/Sl	10-4-55	24-4-55
Pryn Samuel	OS	W/Sv	26-8-55	18-9-55
Sangler Jacob	AB	W/Sl	7-6-55	19-6-55
Sinclair Gordon C.	A/Mate	W/Sv	8-9-55	22-9-55
Sherwood George	OS	W/Sl	11-4-55	24-4-55
Staley Joseph	RMA	W/Sl	12-4-55	24-4-55
Taylor Charles	AB	W/Sl	14-4-55	1-5-55
White William	Surgeon's Mate	W/Sv	13-4-55	24-4-55

NOTES

The Naval Brigade
NO SHIP

NAME	RANK	CASUALTY	DATE	LONDON GAZETTE
Kidd, T. O.	Lieut.	Killed	9-6-55	22-6-55
Kevin A.	Asst./Surg.	W/Sv	10-6-55	22-6-55

NOTES

HER MAJESTY
DISTRIBUTING THE CRIMEAN MEDALS
AT THE HORSE GUARDS.
MAY 18TH 1855.

"Her Majesty in giving the medal to Sir Thomas Trowbridge, who had lost both his feet in action, leant over the chair of the maimed veteran and at the same time bestowed on him the honour of being her Aide-de-Camp."

APPENDICES

APPENDIX I

The accuracy of the following thirteen Returns may be relied upon, as they are, by permission, taken from the Work styled "Despatches and Papers relative to the Campaign in Turkey, Asia Minor, and the Crimea," compiled and arranged by Capt. F. Sayer, Deputy Assistant Quarter-Master-General to the Forces. London: Harrison, 59, Pall Mall.

No. 1.—Return showing the Total Number of Non-commissioned Officers and Men sent to the Crimea from the Commencement of the War to the end of March, 1856.

	Non-commissioned Officers, Trumpeters, Buglers & Drummers.	Farriers and Rank and File.		Men.
Cavalry	479	7,814	equal to	8,293
Artillery	443	10,280	"	10,723
Sappers and Miners	81	1,563	"	1,644
Infantry	4,001	69,298	"	73,299
Total embarked for the East to the end of March, 1856	5,004	88,955	"	93,959

In addition to the above, the following Battalions of the British German Legion and Swiss Legion embarked, and were stationed on the Bosphorus or at Smyrna, namely—

		Non-commissioned Officers, Buglers, and Drummers.	Rank and File.		Men.
British German Legion	1st Jäger Battalion	76	819	equal to	895
	1st Light Infantry	68	870	"	938
	2nd Ditto	73	899	"	972
	3rd Ditto	57	753	"	810
Total British German Legion		274	3,341	"	3,615
British Swiss Legion	1st Regt. Light Infantry	91	1,269	"	1,360
	2nd Ditto, 1st Battalion	48	636	"	684
Total British Swiss Legion		139	1,905	"	2,044

Grand Total embarked from England, the Mediterranean, or India, including Foreign Legions ... 99,618

No. 2.—General Total of Troops *originally* embarked for the East under Lord Raglan.

Officers.	Serjeants.	Buglers, Trumpeters & Drummers.	Rank and File.	Grand Total.
933	1,257	432	23,473	26,095

No. 3.—Total Number of English Troops *present* at the Battle of Alma.

Cavalry	1,100
Artillery and Engineers	3,100
Infantry	22,600
Total	26,800

No. 4.—Return of the Total Number of Officers and Men in the Army who have been *Killed* in the Crimea up to the 1st of June, 1856, distinguishing Cavalry, Infantry, Artillery, Sappers and Miners, as well as Officers, Non-commissioned Officers, and Men.

	Officers.	Non-commissioned Officers.	Men.
Cavalry	8	10	104
Artillery	10	10	111
*Sappers and Miners	9	1	31
Infantry	119	140	2191
Staff	11	...	...
Total	157	161	2437
General Total			2755

No. 5.—Statement showing the Total Strength and the Total Number *Killed* and *Wounded* of each Infantry Division of the British Army.

	Strength of each Division.	Officers, Non-commissioned Officers, and Men.
1st Division	11,011	1,507
2nd Division	12,455	3,258
3rd Division	13,132	1,317
4th Division	12,943	1,450
Highland Division	9,533	639
Light Division	17,211	5,126
Grand Total	76,285	13,297

* Now Royal Engineers.

No. 6.—Statement of Casualties in the 1st Brigade Light Division, the Highland Brigade, and Brigade of Guards.

CASUALTIES IN FIRST BRIGADE LIGHT DIVISION.

REGIMENT.	Total Strength, including Reinforcements.		Number of Officers Killed.	Number of Non-commissioned Officers and Men Killed.	Number of Officers Wounded.	Number of Non-commissioned Officers and Men Wounded.	Total Killed and Wounded.
	Officers.	Men.					
7th	73	1880	5	102	23	402	532
23rd	72	1985	10	118	15	495	638
33rd	68	1604	7	95	21	293	416
	213	5469	22	315	†59	1190	1586

CASUALTIES IN THE HIGHLAND BRIGADE.

42nd	51	1237	1	21	2	119	143
79th	57	1346	...	7	2	55	64
93rd	62	1346	1	8	2	95	106
	170	3929	2	36	‡6	259	303

CASUALTIES IN THE BRIGADE OF GUARDS.

Grenadier Guards	73	2341	5	111	12	410	538
Coldstream Guards	85	2068	8	77	6	202	293
Scots Fusilier Guards	67	2095	2	85	23	336	446
	225	6504	15	273	§41	948	1277

No. 7.—Return of the Killed in Action and Died of Wounds of the British Army in the Crimea, distributed Regimentally, with the date of the Arrival of each Regiment in the East.

CORPS.	Killed in Action.			Died of Wounds.			Date of Arrival in the East.
	Officers.	Non-commissioned Officers.	Trumpeters or Drummers, and Rank and File.	Officers.	Non-commissioned Officers.	Trumpeters or Drummers, and Rank and File.	
1st Dragoon Guards	..	..	..	..	..	..	Aug. 10, 1855
4th Ditto	..	..	1	..	..	1	July 10, 1854
5th Ditto	..	..	2	1	..	..	June 13, "
6th Ditto	..	..	..	..	..	..	Aug. 14, 1855
1st Dragoons	..	..	2	..	..	1	June 24, 1854
2nd Ditto	..	..	2	..	..	6	Aug. 8, "
4th Ditto	2	3	14	..	..	2	Aug. 1, "
6th Ditto	..	..	2	..	1	..	July 7, "
8th Ditto	2	3	16	..	..	7	May 20, " / June 7, "
10th Ditto	..	..	..	..	..	..	April 17, 1855
11th Ditto	..	2	24	1	..	3	June 21, 1854
12th Ditto	..	..	..	..	..	..	May 9, 1855
13th Ditto	3	1	10	..	..	3	June 21, 1854
17th Ditto	2	1	31	2	..	2	May 24, "
Total Cavalry	9	10	104	4	1	25	
Royal Artillery	11	10	111	1	4	48	During May, 1854
Royal Sappers and Miners	9	1	31	6	1	22	April 18 & 24, 1854 / May 9, 1854
Grenadier Guards, 3rd Battalion	5	3	108	1	1	32	April 28, 1854
Coldstream Guards, 1st Battalion	8	3	74	2	..	51	April 29, "
Scots Fusilier Gds., 1st Battalion	2	5	80	2	1	23	April 28, "
Total Foot Gds.	15	11	262	5	2	106	
1st Foot, 1st Batt.	1	..	15	..	..	10	May 5, 1854
Ditto, 2nd Batt.	1	..	19	1	1	14	April 21, 1855
3rd Ditto	..	5	43	3	3	27	April 28, "
4th Ditto	..	..	22	2	..	16	April 15, 1854
7th Ditto	5	8	94	3	8	74	April 22, "
9th Ditto	..	..	14	1	..	6	Nov. 27, "
13th Ditto	..	..	..	..	..	..	June 30, 1855
14th Ditto	..	..	9	..	..	7	Feb. 1, "
17th Ditto	1	1	20	..	..	13	Dec. 15, 1854
18th Ditto	1	1	38	..	2	48	Dec. 26, "
19th Ditto	1	3	70	3	2	62	May 11, "
20th Ditto	1	2	40	2	2	39	Aug. 7, "
21st Ditto	..	1	33	2	1	11	Sept. 14, "
23rd Ditto	10	7	111	6	4	71	April 25, "
28th Ditto	..	1	23	..	..	18	April 16, "
30th Ditto	3	1	104	7	2	47	May 12, "
31st Ditto	2	2	12	..	..	11	May 22, 1855
33rd Ditto	7	6	89	1	1	20	April 14, 1854
34th Ditto	5	1	70	2	2	44	Dec. 9 "
38th Ditto	1	4	18	2	1	20	May 11 & 17, 1854

† Of this number 10 died of wounds.   ‡ Of this number 1 died of wounds.   § Of this number 5 died of wounds.

APPENDIX I

No. 7.—RETURN of the Killed in Action and Died of Wounds of the British Army in the Crimea, distributed Regimentally.—(continued.)

CORPS.	Killed in Action. Officers.	Killed in Action. Non-commissioned Officers.	Killed in Action. Drummers, and Rank and File.	Died of Wounds. Officers.	Died of Wounds. Non-commissioned Officers.	Died of Wounds. Drummers, and Rank and File.	Date of Arrival in the East.
39th Ditto	1	..	3	..	1	6	Jan. 1, 1855
41st Ditto	6	6	104	3	3	32	April 15, 1854
42nd Ditto	1	..	21	..	2	6	June 9, "
44th Ditto	..	..	23	4	3	28	April 10, "
46th Ditto	1	1	19	..	..	12	Nov. 8, "
47th Ditto	..	3	81	2	1	35	April 19, "
48th Ditto	..	..	5	..	..	7	April 21, 1855
49th Ditto	4	5	84	3	5	114	Apr. 19 & 28, 1854
50th Ditto	1	2	34	1	..	20	April 15, 1854
55th Ditto	5	3	84	1	3	55	May 21, "
56th Ditto	..	..	5	..	..	3	Aug. 25, 1855
57th Ditto	3	11	49	5	4	17	Sept. 23, 1854
62nd Ditto	6	5	26	1	..	6	Nov. 12, "
63rd Ditto	4	..	17	..	1	47	Sept. 1, "
68th Ditto	5	..	32	1	..	19	Sept. 3, "
71st Ditto	..	..	..	..	..	..	{ Dec. 22, " / Feb. 3, 1855 }
72nd Ditto	..	..	6	1	..	6	May 29, "
77th Ditto	5	7	68	..	1	333	April 17, 1854
79th Ditto	..	..	7	..	1	4	May 27, "
82nd Ditto	..	..	..	..	..	..	Sept. 2, 1855
88th Ditto	5	8	105	2	3	42	April 19, 1854
89th Ditto	1	..	4	..	..	9	Dec. 13, "
90th Ditto	3	4	40	1	1	47	Dec. 5, "
92nd Ditto	..	..	..	..	..	..	Sept. 15, 1855
93rd Ditto	1	..	8	1	1	10	April 11, 1854
95th Ditto	6	8	72	1	6	98	April 24, "
97th Ditto	7	6	61	1	2	40	Nov. 20, "
Rifle Brigade, 1st Battalion	2	8	44	2	4	42	July 30, "
Ditto, 2nd Batt.	4	9	82	1	5	51	April 30, "
Total Infantry	110	129	1929	68	77	1647	
Staff Officers	3	..	..	2	..	..	
General Total of all Arms	157	161	2437	86	85	1848	

No. 8.—RETURN showing the Total Number of Men of Lord Raglan's Army Sick during each Month, from the landing in Turkey.

MONTHS.	Total Sick or Wounded of all Arms during each Month.
1854.	
April	503
May	1,835
June	3,498
July	6,937
August	11,236
September	11,693
October	11,988
November	16,846
December	19,479
1855.	
January	23,076
To 17 February ....Crimea	9,284
To 25 " ....Scutari	6,725
To 17 " ....Abydos	385
To 25 " ....Gallipoli	70
To 20 " ....Smyrna	500
TOTAL to latest dates in February	16,964

No. 9.—STATEMENT showing the Total Number of Vessels which arrived at Scutari with Sick and Wounded from the Crimea between 18th of September, 1854, and 25th of February, 1855, with the Total Number of Officers and Men conveyed therein, and the Number of each Rank that died on the Passage.

No. of Vessels.	Number Conveyed. Officers.	Number Conveyed. Men.	Died on Passage. Officers.	Died on Passage. Men.
78	316	17,067	6	924

No. 10.—RETURN showing the Number of Officers and Men in Hospital in the Crimea, at Scutari, and elsewhere, at the dates specified below, distinguishing the Sick from the Wounded.

Hospitals.	Last Dates.	Officers.	Men.	Of whom Wounded.
	1855.			
Crimea	February 10	69	4,945	59
Scutari	February 18	76	4,984	Not stated.
Varna	January 20	1	32	"
Abydos	February 10	..	264	"
Gallipoli	February 18	..	54	"
Smyrna	..	..	500	"
	Totals	146	10,779	
Grand Total Officers and Men in Hospitals			10,625	

No. 11.—RETURN showing the Number of Officers and Men who died from Sickness at Varna or elsewhere, from date of landing in Turkey to 6th September (date of Embarkation for Crimea) 903

No. 12.—RETURN showing the following particulars concerning the late ARMY IN THE EAST.

REGIMENTS (by Brigades and Divisions) which composed the ARMY IN THE EAST.	Original Strength on joining the Army in Serjeants, Drummers, and Rank and File.	Number of Officers Killed.	Number of Officers Wounded.	Number of Non-commissioned Officers and Men Killed.	Number of Non-commissioned Officers and Men Wounded.	Total Killed and Wounded.
CAVALRY DIVISION.						
1st (Heavy) Brigade—						
1st Dragoon Guards	353	..	..	..	4	5
4th Ditto	295	..	..	1	4	5
5th Ditto	295	..	3	2	12	17
1st Dragoons	295	..	4	2	7	13
2nd Ditto	299	..	4	2	57	63
6th Ditto	279	..	..	2	14	16
2nd (Light) Brigade—						
6th Dragoon Guards	354	..	..	..	..	..
4th Light Dragoons	299	2	2	17	24	45
12th Lancers	514	..	..	..	..	..
13th Light Dragoons	295	3	3	11	31	48
3rd (Hussar) Brigade—						
8th Hussars	292	2	3	19	21	45
10th Ditto	658	..	..	..	4	4
11th Ditto	297	..	2	26	29	57
17th Lancers	294	2	5	32	34	73
Total Cavalry	4819	9	26	114	237	386
Royal Artillery	7032	11	30	121	632	794
Royal Sappers and Miners	403	9	13	32	86	140
FIRST DIVISION.						
1st Brigade—						
Grenadier Guards, 3rd Bat.	904	5	12	111	410	538
Coldstream " 1st Bat.	919	8	6	77	202	293
Scots Fusilier " 1st Bat.	935	2	23	85	336	446
2nd Brigade—						
9th Foot	586	..	2	14	83	99
13th Ditto	855	..	..	..	11	11
31st Ditto	742	2	1	14	84	101
56th Ditto	846	..	1	5	13	19
SECOND DIVISION.						
1st Brigade—						
3rd Foot	694	..	13	48	259	320
30th Ditto	692	3	19	105	364	491
55th Ditto	966	5	18	87	412	522
95th Ditto	911	6	21	80	361	468
2nd Brigade—						
41st Foot	863	6	13	110	426	555
47th Ditto	682	..	9	84	216	309
49th Ditto	898	4	10	89	325	428
62nd Ditto	574	6	7	31	121	165
82nd Ditto	561	..	..	..	..	..
THIRD DIVISION.						
1st Brigade—						
4th Foot	910	..	5	22	142	169
14th Ditto	689	..	..	9	46	55
39th Ditto	700	1	1	3	46	51
50th Ditto	912	1	4	36	67	108
89th Ditto	691	1	..	4	73	78
2nd Brigade—						
18th Foot	814	1	10	39	267	317
28th Ditto	889	..	9	24	89	122
38th Ditto	909	1	7	22	200	230
44th Ditto	923	..	8	23	156	187
FOURTH DIVISION.						
1st Brigade—						
17th Foot	720	1	5	21	134	161
20th Ditto	955	1	10	42	81	134
21st Ditto	978	..	10	34	100	144
57th Ditto	774	3	11	60	237	311
63rd Ditto	978	4	8	17	127	156
2nd Brigade—						
46th Foot	963	1	2	20	71	94
48th Ditto	851	..	2	5	60	67
68th Ditto	861	5	4	32	71	112
Rifle Brigade, 1st Battalion	975	2	5	52	212	271
HIGHLAND DIVISION.						
1st Brigade—						
42nd Foot	914	1	2	21	119	143
79th Ditto	916	..	2	7	55	64
92nd Ditto	491	..	..	..	..	..
93rd Ditto	911	1	2	8	95	106
2nd Brigade—						
1st Foot, 1st Battalion	911	1	2	15	79	97
Ditto, 2nd Battalion	796	1	8	19	146	174
71st Ditto	891	..	..	..	1	1
72nd Ditto	607	..	..	6	48	54
LIGHT DIVISION.						
1st Brigade—						
7th Foot	911	5	23	102	402	532
23rd Ditto	909	10	15	118	495	638
33rd Ditto	913	7	21	95	293	416
34th Ditto	597	5	18	71	375	469
Rifle Brigade, 2nd Battalion	962	4	15	91	569	679
2nd Brigade—						
19th Foot	912	1	20	73	502	596
77th Ditto	903	5	11	75	606	697
88th Ditto	910	5	16	114	400	535
90th Ditto	813	3	15	44	221	283
97th Ditto	889	7	9	67	198	281
Total Infantry	43,276	125	435	2331	10,406	13,297
Staff Officers	..	3	11	..	..	14
General Total of all Arms	55,530	157	515	2598	11,361	14,631

APPENDIX I

No. 13.—Return showing the state of each Regiment, &c., on its Embarkation for Active Service in the East, its subsequent Increase and Decrease, and Strength on the 1st of April, 1856.

Date of Embarkation of Head Quarters.	CORPS.	Strength on Embarkation.		Reinforcements.		TOTAL.		DECREASE.								TOTAL.		Strength of each Regiment on 1st of April, 1856.	
								Died in the East.		Invalided Home.		Prisoners of War and Deserters.							
		Officers.	Non-commissioned Officers and Men.	Officers.	Non-commissioned Officers and Men.	Officers.	Non-commissioned Officers and Men.	Officers.	Non-commissioned Officers and Men.	Officers.	Non-commissioned Officers and Men.	Officers.	Prisoners of War. Non-commissioned Officers and Men.	Deserters. Non-commissioned Officers and Men.		Officers.	Non-commissioned Officers and Men.	Officers.	Non-commissioned Officers and Men.
July 28, 1855	1st Dragoon Guards	19	358	..	..	19	358	..	47	2	21	..	..	..		2	68	21	286
June 2, 1854	4th Ditto	20	297	10	262	30	559	..	103	6	55	..	3	3		6	164	26	392
May 27, "	5th Ditto	19	295	11	248	30	543	7	81	9	89	..	..	1		16	171	18	371
July 21, 1855	6th Ditto	19	354	4	1	23	355	2	24	9	34	..	..	..		11	58	11	301
May 10, 1854	1st Dragoons	19	294	10	279	29	573	1	89	14	60	..	..	1		15	149	15	416
July 25, "	2nd Ditto	18	299	10	272	28	571	2	89	11	75	..	..	2		13	166	15	404
July 18, "	4th Ditto	20	299	7	345	27	644	3	123	11	74	..	18	1		14	216	14	438
May 29, "	6th Ditto	19	295	12	336	31	631	1	102	11	71	..	..	4		12	177	21	430
May 2, "	8th Ditto	20	294	9	350	29	644	3	105	5	54	1	6	1		9	167	21	463
Jan. 31, 1855	10th Ditto (from Bombay)	26	672	15	223	41	895	2	62	11	85	..	17	1		13	165	28	743
May 15, 1854	11th Ditto	18	295	16	306	34	601	5	109	13	72	..	8	..		18	189	17	419
Feb. 22, 1855	12th Ditto (from Madras)	30	527	11	149	41	676	..	26	13	71	..	..	1		13	98	27	575
May 12, 1854	13th Ditto	20	295	11	288	31	583	6	102	13	89	..	13	..		19	204	14	387
April 25, 1854	17th Ditto	20	294	14	366	34	660	5	110	16	70	1	..	16		22	196	16	464
	Total Cavalry	287	4868	140	3425	427	8293	37	1172	144	920	2	65	31		183	2188	264	6089
From Mar. 19 to Aug. 9, 1854	Royal Artillery	120	3095	268	7628	388	10,723	23	1483	145	2117	..	..	..		168	3600	220	7123
From Feb. to May, 1854	Royal Sappers and Miners	3	403	92	1241	95	1644	20	241	31	157	..	..	4		51	402	44	1242
Feb. 22, 1854	Grenadier Guards, 3rd Bat.	32	946	41	1395	73	2341	8	784	34	430	..	..	3		42	1217	32	1162
Feb. 22, "	Coldstream " 1st Bat	33	920	52	1148	85	2068	13	716	41	271	..	..	4		54	991	33	1088
Feb. 28, "	Scots Fusilier " 1st Bat.	30	932	37	1163	67	2095	5	656	24	332	..	6	1		29	995	38	1113
	Total Guards	95	2798	130	3706	225	6504	26	2156	99	1033	..	6	8		125	3203	103	3363
April 21, 1854	1st Foot 1st Battalion	30	911	28	659	58	1570	2	460	34	183	..	..	8		36	651	27	880
April 14, 1855	Ditto 2nd ditto	25	751	15	204	40	955	4	78	14	169	..	7	1		18	255	25	730
April 14, "	3rd Foot	24	673	34	419	58	1092	3	146	22	106	1	..	2		26	254	32	837
March 9, 1854	4th Ditto	32	911	23	624	55	1535	3	339	21	275	1	2	1		25	617	33	919
April 5, "	7th Ditto	30	911	43	969	73	1880	14	540	23	378	..	25	8		37	951	38	931
Nov. 19, "	9th Ditto	20	549	30	558	50	1107	3	137	18	153	..	..	1		21	291	31	725
June 7, 1855	13th Ditto	30	858	13	192	43	1050	..	87	7	141	..	..	2		7	230	36	865
Jan. 10, "	14th Ditto	22	671	23	506	45	1177	1	77	15	199	..	..	1		16	277	32	878
Dec. 2, 1854	17th Ditto	23	719	31	549	54	1268	3	181	24	192	..	..	2		27	374	31	886
Dec. 8, "	18th Ditto	30	821	30	435	60	1256	1	169	26	209	..	5	5		27	383	37	863
April 20, "	19th Ditto	31	913	32	683	63	1596	6	458	29	312	..	..	4		35	774	29	823
July 17, "	20th Ditto	30	961	41	508	71	1469	6	419	27	201	..	..	13		33	633	35	836
Aug. 15, "	21st Ditto	33	974	25	575	58	1549	2	372	25	224	..	49	3		27	648	33	903
April 4, "	23rd Ditto	31	911	41	1074	72	1985	22	700	21	345	1	46	2		44	1093	31	902
Feb. 22, "	28th Ditto	31	899	32	690	63	1589	1	317	19	232	..	..	8		20	557	41	894
May 1, "	30th Ditto	34	895	46	559	80	1454	16	406	37	300	..	1	5		53	712	27	753
May 15, 1855	31st Ditto	30	740	13	301	43	1041	2	114	13	133	..	..	2		15	249	30	884
March 1, 1854	33rd Ditto	33	915	35	689	68	1604	8	311	17	223	..	..	14		25	548	39	691
Nov. 22, "	34th Ditto	26	793	37	474	63	1267	8	270	25	279	..	..	5		33	554	35	743
April 26, "	38th Ditto	32	910	33	756	65	1666	2	486	23	260	..	9	8		25	763	36	901
Dec. 9, "	39th Ditto	24	660	23	527	47	1187	1	109	17	129	..	..	1		18	239	28	966
April 10, "	41st Ditto	28	869	32	575	60	1444	13	436	21	306	..	..	6		34	748	27	720
May 20, "	42nd Ditto	33	918	18	319	51	1237	2	265	16	136	..	..	2		18	403	32	847
March 10, "	44th Ditto	31	923	32	640	63	1563	6	449	25	250	..	11	1		31	711	33	849
Oct. 12, "	46th Ditto	33	963	26	492	55	1455	3	570	18	196	..	..	3		21	769	35	682
April 10, "	47th Ditto	29	889	26	549	55	1438	3	570	21	288	..	..	8		24	866	34	818
April 13, 1855	48th Ditto	25	802	23	142	48	944	..	73	12	94	..	..	3		12	170	32	827
April 9, 1854	49th Ditto	27	907	39	583	66	1490	9	391	27	256	..	3	4		36	654	33	839
Feb. 24, "	50th Ditto	31	910	32	508	63	1418	4	508	26	172	2	23	3		32	706	34	721
May 10, "	55th Ditto	31	892	33	611	64	1503	12	369	29	313	..	9	2		41	693	26	810
July 30, 1855	56th Ditto	32	861	8	57	40	918	..	38	6	32	..	..	1		6	71	35	841
Sept. 12, 1854	57th Ditto	19	742	35	585	54	1327	10	277	11	209	..	5	8		21	499	34	865
Nov. 3, "	62nd Ditto	20	546	27	533	47	1079	8	246	10	202	1	..	1		19	449	34	638
July 21, "	63rd Ditto	31	977	31	346	62	1323	8	458	26	200	..	4	1		34	663	33	708
Aug. 7, "	68th Ditto	28	841	22	480	50	1321	7	257	16	184	..	24	12		23	477	32	862
Jan. 26, 1855	71st Ditto	32	891	16	178	48	1069	3	94	8	67	..	2	..		11	163	38	900
May 22, "	72nd Ditto	30	607	10	321	40	928	1	100	13	84	..	..	1		14	185	29	763
March 10, 1854	77th Ditto	31	910	37	765	68	1675	15	467	24	321	..	20	..		39	808	32	878
May 4, "	79th Ditto	31	917	26	429	57	1346	6	354	22	171	..	..	11		28	536	33	816
Aug. 26, 1855	82nd Ditto	28	576	9	351	37	927	..	30	4	31	..	..	..		4	61	34	853
April 4, 1854	88th Ditto	32	911	33	1085	65	1996	11	466	22	444	..	8	7		33	925	33	1022
Dec. 2, "	89th Ditto	23	691	24	541	47	1232	4	230	12	199	1	..	5		17	434	29	836
Nov. 19, "	90th Ditto	32	814	23	458	55	1272	5	274	25	204	..	27	4		30	509	27	757
Aug. 29, 1855	92nd Ditto	16	491	9	210	25	701	..	9	2	11	..	..	..		2	20	30	635
Feb. 27, 1854	93rd Ditto	33	911	29	435	62	1346	7	307	22	234	1	1	2		30	544	31	787
April 6, "	95th Ditto	30	911	37	583	67	1494	10	557	30	289	..	..	7		40	853	28	636
Nov. 15, "	97th Ditto	28	889	36	588	64	1477	10	424	19	218	..	..	12		29	654	39	860
July 13, "	Rifle Brigade 1st Battalion	25	975	27	808	52	1783	6	453	14	359	..	..	..		20	812	34	977
Feb. 24, "	Ditto 2nd ditto	32	961	44	831	76	1792	9	498	35	318	..	..	5		44	821	31	967
	Total Infantry of the Line	1402	40,841	1368	25,954	2770	66,795	280	15,146	973	10,131	8	276	204		1261	26,057	1588	40,524
April & May, 1855	Land Transport Corps	28	505	125	6917	153	7422	2	466	15	202	..	1	6		17	675	163	6795
	British German Legion.																		
Oct. 11, 1855	1st Jager Battalion	36	895	6	..	42	895	2	30	..	21	..	..	72		2	123	48	854
Oct. 26, "	1st Light Infantry	36	938	..	..	36	938	..	2	..	..	..	..	2		..	2	39	923
Dec. 22, "	2nd Ditto	31	972	..	..	31	972	..	2	..	..	..	..	4		..	6	36	996
Dec. 24, "	3rd Ditto	29	810	..	..	29	810	..	3	..	20	..	..	3		..	26	35	965
	Total Brit. German Legion	132	3615	6	..	138	3615	2	37	..	41	..	..	79		2	157	158	3738
	British Swiss Legion.																		
Nov. 16, 1855	1st Reg. Light Infantry	52	1360	..	..	52	1360	..	2	..	..	..	..	4		..	4	52	1356
Feb. 9, 1856	2nd Ditto 1st Bat.	25	684	..	..	25	684	..	4	..	..	..	..	..		..	4	25	680
	Total British Swiss Legion	77	2044	..	..	77	2044	..	6	..	..	..	..	2		..	8	77	2036
	General Total of all Arms	2144	58,169	2129	48,871	4273	107,040	390	20,707	1407	14,901	10	348	334		1807	36,290	2617	70,910

R

APPENDIX I

No. 14. — AVERAGE STRENGTH of the several Divisions (before Sebastopol) of the British Army during the months specified below.

	November, 1854.	December, 1854.	January, 1855.	February, 1855.	March, 1855.
1st Division	5511	5692	5909	5197	4550
2nd Ditto	4389	4794	4545	4468	4985
3rd Ditto	1830	4650	5056	5923	6650
4th Ditto	5100	5200	4412	3900	4010
Light Ditto	4385	5174	5196	5090	5688
Siege Train	1022	977	1428	1088	1700
Heavy Cavalry	812	733	1080	1006	1044
Light Cavalry	740	665	657	709	721
Royal Horse Artillery	400	360	350	350	370

No. 15. — RETURN of the Names, Rank, and Regiment (or Corps), of all OFFICERS who remained from the first Landing until they Died or Fell in Action.

(Allies first Landed in the Crimea 14th Sept. 1854.)

NAMES.	Rank.	Regiments or Corps.	Cause and Date of Death.
STAFF.			
Raglan, Lord, G.C.B.	Field Marshal	Royal Horse Gds	Died of disease, 28 June 1855. Commander of the Forces.
Estcourt, J.	Major Gen.	Unattached	Died, 24 June 1855. Adjutant General.
Cathcart, Hon. Sir G., K.C.B.	Lieut. General	ditto	Killed, 5 Nov. 1854. Commanded 4th Division.
Cust, H.	Captain	Coldstream Gds.	Killed, 20 Sept. 1854. Aide-de-camp to Major General Bentinck.
Seymour, C.	Lieut. Colonel	Scots Fusil. Gds.	Killed, 5 Nov. 1854. Assist. Adjt. Gen. 4th Division.
Allix, W.	Captain	1st Royal Reg.	Killed, 5 Nov. 1854. Aide-de-camp to Lieut. General Sir De Lacy Evans.
Turner, H.	ditto	ditto	Died of disease, 1 Mar. 1856.
Yea, L.	Brevet Col.	7th Fusiliers	Killed, 18 June 1855. Commanded 1st Brigade Light Division.
Sharpe, J.	Brevet Major	20th Regiment	Died of wounds, 28 Dec. 1854. Major of Brigade.
Chapman, S.	Captain	ditto	Died, 20 Sept. 1855. Assist. Engineer.
Campbell, W.	ditto	23d R. W. Fusil.	Died of disease at Scutari, 22 Mar. 1855. Dep. Assist. Quartermaster General at Scutari.
Marsh, H. S. St. V.	Lieutenant	33rd Regiment	Killed, 24 June 1855. Assist. Engineer.
Campbell, Sir John, Bart.	Major Gen.	38th Regiment	Killed, 18 June 1855. Commanded 1st Brig. 4th Div.
Layard, A.	Captain	ditto	Died of disease, 7 Aug. 1855. Dep. Assist. Quartermaster General 2nd Division.
Johnstone, W.	ditto	41st Regiment	Died of disease, 10 Oct. 1855. Provost Marshal.
Rooke, W.	ditto	47th Regiment	Died of wounds, 1 Oct. 1855. Major of Brigade.
Adams, H., C.B.	Major Gen.	49th Regiment	Died of wounds, 17 Dec. 1854. Commanded a Brigade 2nd Division.
Glazbrook, C.	Captain	ditto	Died of wounds, 18 Dec. 1854. Dep. Assist. Quartermaster General 2nd Division.
Butler, H.	ditto	55th Regiment	Killed, 5 Nov. 1854. Ditto.
Goldie, T. L.	Brigadier Gen	57th Regiment	Killed, 5 Nov. 1854. Commanded 1st Brig. 4th Div.
Wellesley, E.	Brevet Major	73rd Regiment	Killed, 20 Sept. 1854. Assist. Quartermaster Gen. Head Quarters.
Charteris, Hon. W.	Lieutenant	92d Highlanders	Killed, 25 Oct. 1854. Extra Aide-de-camp to Major General Earl of Lucan.
Strangways, Fox	Brigadier Gen	Royal Artillery	Killed, 5 Nov. 1854. Commanded Royal Artillery.
Tylden, W.	ditto	Royal Engineers	Died of disease, 22 Sept 1854. Commanded Royal Eng.
Nolan, J.	Captain	15th Hussars	Killed, 25 Oct. 1854. Aide-de-camp to Major General Sir R. Airey.
Halkett, J.	Major	4th Lt Dragoons	Killed, 25 Oct. 1854.
Sparke, H.	Lieutenant	ditto	Ditto, ditto.
Longmore, C.	Captain	8th Hussars	Died of disease, 3 Sept. 1855.
Lockwood, G.	ditto	ditto	Killed, 25 Oct. 1854.
FitzGibbon, Visct.	Lieutenant	ditto	Ditto, ditto.
Cresswell, W.	Captain	11th Hussars	Died of disease, 19 Sept. 1854.
Annesley, Hon. R.	Lieutenant	ditto	Ditto, 28 " "
Houghton, G.	ditto	ditto	Ditto, 22 Oct. "
Oldham, J.	Captain	13th Lt Dragoons	Killed, 25 Oct. 1854.
Goad, T.	ditto	ditto	Ditto, ditto.
Irwin, T.	Adjutant	ditto	Died of disease, 26 Sept. 1854.
Montgomery, H.	Cornet	ditto	Killed, 25 Oct. 1854.
Foster, C.	Quartermastr	ditto	Died of disease, 25 Jan. 1855.
Willett, A.	Major	17th Lancers	Died of disease, 22 Oct. 1854.
Winter, J.	Captain	ditto	Killed, 25 Oct. 1854.
Webb, A.	ditto	ditto	Died of wounds, 6 Nov. 1854.
Thomson, J.	Lieutenant	ditto	Killed, 25 Oct. 1854.
Clevland, A.	Cornet	ditto	Died of wounds, 6 Nov. 1854.
Townsend, S.	Major	Royal Artillery	Killed, 5 Nov. 1854.
Swinton, W.	ditto	ditto	Died, 2 Jan. 1855.
Dew, A.	Captain	ditto	Killed, 20 Sept. 1854.
Guille, W.	ditto	ditto	Died, 28 Oct. 1854.
Singer, H.	Lieutenant	ditto	Ditto 2 " "
Walsham, R.	ditto	ditto	Killed, 20 Sept. 1854.
Cockerell, R.	ditto	ditto	Ditto, ditto.

No. 15. — RETURN of the Names, Rank, and Regiment (or Corps), of all OFFICERS who remained from the first Landing until they Died or Fell in Action. — *(continued.)*

NAMES.	Rank.	Regiments or Corps.	Cause and Date of Death.
Alexander, C.	Lieut. Colonel	Royal Engineers	Died, 19 Oct. 1854.
Tylden, R.	Brevet Col.	ditto	Died of wounds, 2 Aug. 1855.
Craigie, A.	Captain	ditto	Killed, 13 March 1855.
Inglis, W.	ditto	ditto	Lost in the *Prince*, 14 Nov. 1854.
Murray, J.	Lieutenant	ditto	Killed, 18 June 1855.
Baynes, C.	ditto	ditto	Died of wounds, 7 May 1855.
Teesdale, H.	ditto	ditto	Ditto, 12 Oct. 1854.
Graves, T.	ditto	ditto	Killed, 18 June 1855.
Hood, Hon. F.	Brevet Col.	Grenadier Gds., 3rd Battalion.	Killed, 18 Oct. 1854.
Cox, A.	Lieut. Colonel	ditto	Died of disease, 26 Sept. 1854.
Pakenham, E.	ditto	ditto	Killed, 5 Nov. 1854.
Rowley, A.	Captain	ditto	Ditto, 16 Oct. "
Neville, Hon. H.	ditto	ditto	Ditto, 5 Nov. "
Newman, Sir R., Bt.	ditto	ditto	Ditto, ditto.
Huthwaite, F.	Surgeon	ditto	Died of wounds, 30 Sept. 1854.
Dawson, Hon. T.	Lieut. Colonel	Coldstream Gds. 1st Battalion.	Killed, 5 Nov. 1854.
Cowell, J.	ditto	ditto	Died of wounds, 6 Nov. 1854.
Elliot, Hon. G.	Captain	ditto	Killed, 5 Nov. 1854.
Bouverie, H.	ditto	ditto	Ditto, ditto.
Ramsden, F.	ditto	ditto	Died of wounds, 5 Nov. 1854.
Drummond, Hon. R.	ditto	ditto	Died of disease, 1 Oct. 1855.
Disbrowe, E.	Lieutenant	ditto	Died of wounds, 6 Nov. 1854.
Greville, C.	ditto	ditto	Killed, 5 Nov. 1854.
Drummond, H.	Major & Adjt.	Scots Fusil. Gds. 1st Battalion.	Ditto, 13 Aug. 1855.
Buckley, D.	Captain	ditto	Ditto, 6 Sept. 1855.
Chewton, Viscount	ditto	ditto	Died of wounds, 8 Oct. 1854.
Cobbe, H.	Brevet Col.	4th (K. O.) Reg.	Ditto, 6 Aug. 1855.
Arnold, W.	Captain	ditto	Ditto, 5 May 1855, while a prisoner of war.
Leahy, J.	Quartermastr	ditto	Died of wounds, 18 Sept. 1855.
Mills, F.	Lieut. Colonel	7th Royal Fusil.	Died of wounds, 18 Aug. 1855.
Monck, Hon. W.	Captain	ditto	Killed, 20 Sept. 1854.
Hare, Hon. C.	ditto	ditto	Died of wounds, 22 Sept. 1854.
Molesworth, J.	Lieutenant	ditto	Died of disease, 5 Oct. 1854.
Hobson, J.	Adjutant	ditto	Killed, 18 June 1855.
Langham, J.	Assist. Surg.	ditto	Died of disease, 4 Feb. 1855.
Unett, T.	Lieut. Colonel	19th Regiment	Died of wounds, 14 Sept. 1855.
Godfrey, P.	Captain	ditto	Ditto, 13 " "
Ker, J.	ditto	ditto	Ditto, 7 Nov. 1854.
Wardlaw, J.	Lieutenant	ditto	Killed, 20 Sept. 1854.
Stockwell, G.	Ensign	ditto	Ditto, ditto.
Lye, R.	Captain	20th Regiment	Died of disease, 10 Dec. 1854.
Dowling, W.	Lieutenant	ditto	Killed, 5 Nov. 1854.
Parr, F.	ditto	ditto	Died of disease, 25 Mar. 1856.
Kekewich, L.	ditto	ditto	Ditto, 16 Feb. 1855.
Ainslie, F.	Lieut. Colonel	21st Fusiliers	Died of wounds, 14 Nov. 1854.
Hurt, W.	Lieutenant	ditto	Ditto, 6 " "
Chester, H.	Lieut. Colonel	23rd R.W. Fusil.	Killed, 20 Sept. 1854.
Evans, F.	Captain	ditto	Ditto, ditto.
Wynn, A.	ditto	ditto	Ditto, ditto.
Hughes, G.	ditto	ditto	Died of disease, 11 Dec. 1854.
Poole, W.	ditto	ditto	Died of wounds, 24 Sept. 1855.
Conolly, J.	ditto	ditto	Killed, 20 Sept. 1854.
Applewhaite, A.	Lieut. & Adjt.	ditto	Died of wounds, 22 Sept. 1854.
Dyneley, D.	Lieutenant	ditto	Ditto, 9 Sept. 1855.
Radcliffe, F.	ditto	ditto	Killed, 20 Sept. 1854.
Young, Sir W. Bart.	ditto	ditto	Ditto, ditto.
Anstruther, H.	ditto	ditto	Ditto, ditto.
Butler, J.	ditto	ditto	Ditto, ditto.
Holford, J.	ditto	28th Regiment	Died of disease, 29 Nov. 1854.
Bell, D.	ditto	ditto	Ditto, 7 Jan. 1855.
Spence, S.	Quartermastr	ditto	Ditto, 7 Nov. 1854.
Hoey, W.	Lieut. Colonel	30th Regiment	Ditto, 29 Sept. 1854.
Patullo, J.	ditto	ditto	Died of wounds, 9 " 1855.
Connolly, A.	Captain	ditto	Ditto, 6 Nov. 1854.
Luxmoore, F.	Lieutenant	ditto	Killed, 20 Sept. 1854.
Gibson, A.	ditto	ditto	Ditto, 5 Nov. "
Ross-Lewin, J.	ditto	ditto	Died of wounds, 7 Nov. 1854.
Johnston, W.	Ensign	ditto	Died of disease, 25 Sept. "
Blake, F.	Lieut. Colonel	33rd Regiment	Ditto, 23 Aug. 1855.
Gough, T.	ditto	ditto	Died of wounds, 18 Sept. "
Burke, H.	Captain	ditto	Died of disease, 18 Jan. "
Montagu, F.	Lieutenant	ditto	Killed, 20 Sept. 1854.
Worthington, W.	ditto	ditto	Ditto, ditto.
Bennett, V.	ditto	ditto	Ditto, 18 June 1855.
Thorold, H.	ditto	ditto	Ditto, 5 Nov. 1854.
M'Grath, P.	Paymaster	ditto	Died of disease, 9 Feb. 1855.
Vaughan, J.	Captain	38th Regiment	Died of wounds, 16 June "
Davies, O.	Lieutenant	ditto	Killed, 18 June 1855.
Eman, J.	Lieut. Colonel	41st Regiment	Died of wounds, 10 Sept. 1855.
Carpenter, G.	ditto	ditto	Ditto, 6 Nov. 1854.
Swaby, J.	Lieutenant	ditto	Killed, 5 Nov. 1854.
Stirling, J.	ditto	ditto	Ditto, ditto.
Harriott, H.	ditto	ditto	Died of wounds, 8 Dec. 1854.
Taylor, A.	ditto	ditto	Killed, 5 Nov. 1854.
Anderson, W.	Surgeon	ditto	Died of disease, 3 Jan. 1855.
Lamont, J.	Assist. Surg.	ditto	Ditto, 5 " "
Cunninghame, R.	Captain	42d Highlanders	Ditto, 5 Sept. "
Fraser, G.	ditto	ditto	Killed, 16 July 1855.
Fenwick, B.	ditto	44th Regiment	Died of wounds, 20 June 1855
Agar, Hon. C.	ditto	ditto	Ditto, 18 " "

APPENDIX I

No. 15.—RETURN of the Names, Rank, and Regiment (or Corps), of all OFFICERS who remained from the first Landing until they Died or Fell in Action.—(continued.)

NAMES.	Rank.	Regiments or Corps.	Cause and Date of Death.
Caulfield, F.	Captain	44th Regiment	Died of wounds, 19 June 1855.
Eyre, R.	Lieutenant	ditto	Died of disease, 15 Oct. 1854.
Thomson, J.	Assist. Surg.	ditto	Ditto, 5 " "
O'Toole, W.	Captain	46th Regiment	Ditto, 21 Sept. "
Woolocombe, T.	Lieutenant	47th Regiment	Died of wounds, 7 Oct "
Powell, C.	Major	49th Regiment	Killed, 28 Oct. 1854.
Dalton, T.	ditto	ditto	Ditto, 5 Nov. "
Rochfort, G.	Captain	ditto	Ditto, 8 Sept. 1855.
Armstrong, A.	Lieut. & Adjt.	ditto	Ditto, 5 Nov. 1854.
Beckwith, H.	Assist. Surg.	ditto	Died of disease, 17 Oct. 1854.
Möller, J.	Major	50th Regiment	Died of wounds, 22 Dec. "
Dashwood, W.	Lieutenant	ditto	Killed, 5 Nov. 1854.
Cuddy, W.	Lieut. Colonel	55th Regiment	Ditto, 8 Sept. 1855.
Rose, J.	Major	ditto	Ditto, 20 Sept. 1854.
Schaw, J.	Captain	ditto	Ditto, ditto.
Warren, J.	Lieutenant	ditto	Died of disease, 22 Dec. 1854.
Birch, L.	ditto	ditto	Ditto, 8 Oct. "
Taylor, W.	ditto	ditto	Ditto, 20 Sept. "
Norris, J.	Assist. Surg.	ditto	Ditto, 22 Nov. "
Swiny, E.	Lieut. Colonel	63rd Regiment	Killed, 5 Nov. 1854.
Harrison, G.	Major	ditto	Ditto, 7 July 1855.
Curtois, G.	Lieutenant	ditto	Ditto, 5 Nov. 1854.
Morgan, T.	ditto	ditto	Died of disease, 11 Nov. 1854.
Mackesy, V.	ditto	ditto	Ditto. 7 Mar. 1856.
Twysden, H.	Ensign	ditto	Died of wounds, 9 Nov. 1854.
Clutterbuck, J.	ditto	ditto	Killed, 5 Nov. 1854.
Smyth, H.	Lieut. Colonel	68th Lt. Infantry	Died of wounds, 28 Nov. 1854.
Wynne, H.	Major	ditto	Killed, 5 Nov. 1854.
Edwards, R.	Captain	ditto	Ditto, 11 May 1855.
Marshall, J.	Lieutenant	ditto	Ditto, 8 June "
Barker, F.	ditto	ditto	Ditto, 5 Nov. 1854.
Smyth, H.	ditto	ditto	Died of disease, 14 Mar. 1855.
O'Leary, J.	Assist. Surg.	ditto	Killed, 17 Oct. 1854.
Egerton, T.	Brevet Col.	77th Regiment	Ditto, 20 Apr. 1855.
Lempriere, A.	Captain	ditto	Ditto, 19 " "
Gilby, B.	Major	ditto	Died of disease, 23 July 1855
Crofton, E.	Captain	ditto	Ditto, 27 Sept. 1854.
Nicholson, J.	ditto	ditto	Killed, 5 Nov. 1854.
Maine, A.	Lieutenant	ditto	Died of disease, 21 Nov. 1854.
Walmesley, R.	ditto	ditto	Ditto, 4 Oct. "
Alder, F.	ditto	ditto	Ditto, 6 " "
Macartney, C.	Surgeon	ditto	Died of wounds, 11 Apr. 1855.
Maitland, A.	Captain	79th Highlandrs	Died of disease, 7 Oct. 1854.
Grant, F.	Lieutenant	ditto	Ditto, 1 " "
Hill, A.	ditto	22nd Regiment Attached to 79th Highldrs.	Died of disease, 21 June 1855.
Norton, E.	Major	88th C. Rangers	Died of disease, 20 May 1855.
Bayley, E.	ditto	ditto	Died of wounds, 8 June "
Wray, J.	Captain	ditto	Killed, 7 June 1855.
Grogan, H.	ditto	ditto	Ditto, 8 Sept. "
Webb, E.	Lieutenant	ditto	Ditto, 7 June "
Maule, A.	Adjutant	ditto	Died of wounds, 14 Nov. 1854.
Banner, R.	Major	93d Highlanders	Died of disease, 6 Oct. 1854.
M'Gowan, J.	ditto	ditto	Died of wounds while a prisoner of war, 14 Aug. 1855.
Abercromby, R.	Lieutenant	ditto	Killed, 20 Sept. 1855.
Wemyss, J.	ditto	ditto	Died of disease, 13 June 1855.
Champion, J.	Major	95th Regiment	Died of wounds, 30 Nov. 1854.
Davis, T.	ditto	ditto	Died of disease, 5 April 1855.
Dowdall, G.	Captain	ditto	} Killed, 20 Sept. 1854.
Eddington, J.	ditto	ditto	
Polhill, R.	Lieutenant	ditto	
Eddington, E.	ditto	ditto	
Kingsley, J.	Adjutant	ditto	
Smith, F.	Assist. Surg.	ditto	Died of disease, 9 Feb. 1855.
Braybrooke, W.	Lieutenant	Ceylon Rifles (attached to 95th Regt.)	Killed, 20 Sept. 1854.
Beckwith, T.	Lieut. Colonel	Rifle Brigade—1st Battalion	Died of disease, 25 Sept. 1854
Rooper, E.	Major	ditto	Died of wounds, 10 Nov. "
Cartwright, A.	Captain	ditto	Killed, 5 Nov. 1854.
Tryon, H.	Lieutenant	ditto	Ditto, 20 " "
Godfrey, A.	ditto	ditto	Died of disease, 27 Nov. 1854.
Shorrock, J.	Assist. Surg.	ditto	Ditto, 21 Sept. "
Hammond, M.	Captain	Rifle Brigade—2nd Battalion	Killed, 8 Sept. 1855.
Forman, E.	ditto	ditto	Ditto, 18 June "
Malcolm, L.	Lieutenant	ditto	Ditto, 5 Nov. 1854.
Gower, Lord F.	Ensign	ditto	Died of disease, 6 Oct. 1854.
Mitchell, J.	Surg., 1st cl.	Staff	Ditto, 24 Sept. "
Pine, C.	ditto ditto	ditto	Ditto, 6 Mar. 1855.
Mackey, P.	ditto 2nd cl.	ditto	Ditto, 5 Oct. 1854.
Browne, W.	Assist. Surg.	ditto	Ditto, 26 Nov. "
Reid, A.	ditto	ditto	Ditto, 5 Oct. "

No. 16.—RETURN shewing the Names, Rank, and Regiment (or Corps) of all OFFICERS who, arriving at any period after the first Landing, Died or Fell in Action, with the Date of their Arrival, and of their Death.

NAME,	Rank.	Regiment or Corps.	Date of Arrival.	Date of Death.	Remarks.
Forbes, John, Adjutant at Varna	Lieut.	30th Foot	Mar. 1855	1 Sept. 1855	Died of wounds } STAFF.
Anderson, C., Assist. Eng.	Captain	31st "	14 Apr. "	5 " "	Killed
Campbell, W.	ditto	5th Drag. Gds.	Oct. 1854	23 Dec. 1854	Disease
Sidebottom, G.	ditto	ditto	ditto	21 July 1855	On board ship
Neville, Hon. G.	Cornet	ditto	ditto	11 Nov. 1854	Wounds
Petre, O.	Lieut.	6th Drag. Gds.	26 May 1855	25 " 1855	Disease
Wight, H.	ditto	ditto	9 July "	23 Sept. "	ditto
Williams, T.	Captain	2nd Dragoons	23 Sept. 1854	23 Nov. 1854	ditto
Boyd, W.	ditto	ditto	ditto	12 Sept. 1855	ditto
Freeman, J.	ditto	ditto	ditto	29 " 1854	ditto
Marshall, J.	ditto	4th Lt. Drag.	6 July 1855	30 " 1855	ditto
Dawson, H.	Lieut.	6th Dragoons	30 Sept. 1854	5 Oct. 1854	ditto
Bowles, C.	Captain	10th Hussars	17 April 1855	25 June 1855	ditto
Siddell, T.	Vet. Surg.	ditto	ditto	30 " "	ditto
Ancell, M.	Asst. Surg.	11th Hussars	7 April "	10 Aug. "	ditto
Hutchinson, Hon. J.	Captain	13th Lt. Drag.	21 May "	2 July "	ditto
Gavin, W.	Vet. Surg.	17th Lancers	20 Feb. "	9 June "	ditto
Harrison, N.	Lieut.-Col.	Royl. Artillery	July "	12 Aug. "	ditto
Oldfield, A.	Captain	ditto	Dec. 1854	17 " "	Killed
Fitzroy, A.	ditto	ditto	July 1855	10 Sept. "	Wounds
Childers, S.	ditto	ditto	Oct. 1854	23 Oct. 1854	Killed
Gordon, A.	ditto	ditto	Mar. 1855	5 July 1855	ditto
Snow, E.	ditto	ditto	May "	6 Sept. "	ditto
Savage, J.	ditto	ditto	ditto	22 June "	Disease
Luce, E.	Lieut.	ditto	Mar. "	11 April "	Killed
Temple, F.	ditto	ditto	June "	June 1856	On board ship
Young, Sir G., Bart.	ditto	ditto	Sept. 1854	22 Oct. 1854	Disease
Maclachlan, D.	ditto	ditto	ditto	29 Nov. "	ditto
Mitchell, R.	ditto	ditto	Mar. 1855	14 April 1855	Killed
Marshall, E.	ditto	ditto	July "	29 Nov. "	Disease
Dawson, J.	ditto	ditto	"	11 Dec. "	Wounds (accidentally)
Yellon, G.	Dep. Asst. Commy	ditto	..	15 Nov. "	Killed (accidentally)
Hayter, W.	ditto	ditto	..	8 Sept. "	Killed
Jesse, W.	Captain	Royl. Enginrs.	June "	18 June 1855	Killed
King, F.	ditto	ditto	Dec. 1854	22 April "	Wounds
Dawson, G.	ditto	ditto	June 1855	7 June "	Killed
Crofton, G.	ditto	ditto	Dec. 1854	15 April "	Wounds
Belson, F.	ditto	ditto	Feb. 1855	14 Aug. "	Disease
Bainbrigge, E.	Lieut.	ditto	Mar. "	4 April "	Killed
Ranken, G.	Major	ditto	Aug. "	28 Feb. 1856	Killed (accidentally)
Carter, J.	Lieut.	ditto	Feb. "	2 May 1855	Killed
Lowry, T.	ditto	ditto	Dec. 1854	7 June "	ditto
Somerville, W.	ditto	ditto	June 1855	3 Sept. "	Disease
Davies, F.	ditto	Grenadier Gds	Nov. 1854	10 Nov. 1854	Wounds
Mackinnon, L.	Captain	Coldstrm Gds.	Oct. "	5 Nov. "	ditto
Jolliffe, H.	ditto	ditto	14 Sept. "	4 Oct. "	Disease
Blair, J.	Lieut. Col.	Scots Fus. Gds	18 Oct. "	6 Nov. "	Wounds
Muller, B.	Captain	1st Royl. Regt. 2nd Batt.	22 April 1855	7 June 1855	Killed
Bellew, W.	Lieut.	ditto	ditto	16 " "	Wounds
Ross, C.	Captain	3rd Buffs	1 May "	31 Aug. "	Missing
Dennis, J.	Lieut.	ditto	ditto	4 Oct. "	Wounds
Hyndman, R.	ditto	ditto	ditto	7 " "	Disease
Stillwell, W.	Quartermaster	ditto	ditto	12 June "	ditto
Browne, Hon. C. Fitzclarence, Hon. E.	Captain	7th Royal Fus.	25 Jan. "	22 Mar. "	Killed
Wright, W.	Lieut.	ditto	20 May "	23 July "	Wounds
Colt, O.	ditto	ditto	ditto	8 Sept. "	Killed
Beauchamp, F.	ditto	ditto	7 July "	2 Oct. "	Wounds
Dent, T.	ditto	9th Regiment	12 " "	5 Jan. "	ditto
Smith, F.	ditto	ditto	27 Nov. 1854	20 June "	Found dead on the road
Le Blanc, E.	Surgeon	ditto	8 Jan. 1855	17 Mar. "	Wounds Shot by a French sentry
Townsend, H.	Captain	14th Regiment	20 Aug. "	29 Nov. "	At Therapia
Renwick, W.	Asst. Surg.	ditto	17 Nov. 1854	2 Mar. "	Disease
Croker, J.	Captain	17th Regiment	17 Dec. "	18 June "	Killed
Seagram, L.	Lieut.	ditto	24 " 1855	11 Mar. 1856	Disease
Simpson, W.	Surgeon	ditto	17 " "	31 May 1855	ditto
Meurant, J.	Lieut.	18th Roy. Irish	20 Feb. 1855	18 June "	Killed
Owen, F.	ditto	23rd R. Welsh Fusiliers	24 " "	30 " "	Wounds
Somerville, R.	ditto	ditto	20 Jan. "	8 Sept. "	Killed
Holden, E.	ditto	ditto	12 July "	9 " "	Wounds
Beck, C.	ditto	ditto	31 Aug. "	29 " "	ditto
Stevenson, J.	Captain	30th Regiment	12 July "	10 " "	ditto
Thompson, J.	Ensign	ditto	Nov. "	10 Nov. 1854	ditto
Kerr, W.	Lieut.	ditto	20 May 1855	23 Sept. 1855	ditto
Fitzpatrick, T.	Ensign	ditto	25 " "	26 June "	Disease
Deane, R.	ditto	ditto	1 Sept. "	8 Sept. "	Killed

APPENDIX I

No. 16.—Return shewing the Names, Rank, and Regiment (or Corps) of all Officers, who, arriving at any period after the first Landing, Died or Fell in action, with the date of their Arrival, and of their Death.—(continued.)

NAME.	Rank.	Regiment or Corps.	Date of Arrival.	Date of Death.	Remarks.
Attree, F.	Captain	31st Regiment	22 May 1855	8 Sept. 1855	Killed
King, T.	ditto	32nd Regiment	...	28 May "	Disease
Heyland, L.	Lieut.	33rd Regiment	2 Dec. 1854	18 June "	Killed
Donovan, H.	ditto	ditto	27 Sept. "	8 Sept. "	ditto
Shiffner, J.	Captain	34th Regiment	9 Dec. "	18 June "	ditto
Robinson, J.	ditto	ditto	ditto	ditto	ditto
Hurt, F.	Lieut.	ditto	ditto	ditto	ditto
Jordan, W.	ditto	ditto	22 Jan. 1855	22 Mar. "	ditto
Lawrence, H.	ditto	ditto	" Feb. "	8 June "	ditto
Clayton, R.	Ensign	ditto	9 Dec. 1854	12 July "	Wounds
Alt, H.	ditto	ditto	22 Jan. 1855	18 June "	ditto
Ramsay, N.	ditto	ditto	24 Feb. "	22 July "	Disease
Maunsell, E.	Captain	39th Regiment	10 Feb. "	10 " "	Killed
Richards, E.	ditto	41st Regiment	Oct. 1854	6 Nov. 1854	Wounds
Every, E.	ditto	ditto	6 Sept. 1855	8 Sept. 1855	Killed
Taylor, A.	Lieut.	ditto	Oct. 1854	5 Nov. 1854	ditto
Lockhart, J.	ditto	ditto	30 May 1855	8 Sept. 1855	ditto
Fitzgerald, L.	Ensign	ditto	16 Nov. "	24 Dec. "	Wounds (promoted from ranks)
Mansfield, W.	Captain	44th Regiment	1 June "	28 June "	Wounds
Curtis, F.	Lieut.	46th Regiment	8 Nov. 1854	2 May "	Killed
Messenger, J.	ditto	ditto	15 Jan. 1855	15 Jan. 1856	Killed (by the explosion of a mine on the road)
Gaynor, J.	ditto	47th Regiment	" "	27 Aug. 1855	Disease (on board ship)
Michell, C.	Ensign	49th Regiment	15 June "	14 Sept. "	Wounds
Platt, A.	ditto	ditto	ditto	11 Aug. "	Disease
Bond, W.	Lieut.	50th Regiment	22 Nov. 1854	8 Dec. 1854	ditto
Stone, R.	ditto	55th Regiment	5 May 1855	7 June 1855	Killed
Evans, C.	ditto	ditto	16 June "	6 Aug. "	Wounds
Shadforth, T.	Brev. Col.	57th Regiment	8 Nov. 1854	18 June "	Killed
Stanley, E.	Captain	ditto	23 Sept. "	5 Nov. 1854	Wounds
Auchmuty, J.	ditto	ditto	ditto	13 " "	Disease
Bland, J.	ditto	ditto	ditto	8 " "	Wounds
Norman, G.	Lieut.	ditto	ditto	30 June 1855	ditto
Hague, G.	ditto	ditto	ditto	11 Nov. 1854	ditto
Ashwin, J.	ditto	ditto	5 Feb. 1855	18 June 1855	Killed
Curwen, D.	ditto	ditto	6 Sept. "	7 Oct. "	Disease
Mitchell, G.	Ensign	ditto	15 Nov. 1854	28 Mar. "	Wounds
Shearman, R.	Lieut. Col.	62nd Regiment	13 " "	8 June "	ditto
Tyler, L.	ditto	ditto	ditto	23 Oct. "	ditto
Forster, J.	Captain	ditto	ditto	8 June "	Killed
Dickson, W.	ditto	ditto	Dec. "	ditto	ditto
Cox, R.	ditto	ditto	22 Aug. 1855	8 Sept. "	ditto
Kilvington, F.	ditto	ditto	13 Nov. 1854	..	Disease
Blakiston, L.	Lieut.	ditto	ditto	8 Sept. 1855	Killed
White, G.	ditto	ditto	22 Jan. 1855	2 May "	Wounds
Fraser, A. W.	Captain	63rd Regiment	8 Nov. 1854	8 Dec. "	Disease
Hunter, R.	Major	71st Highland Lt. Infantry	7 Feb. 1855	30 Oct. "	ditto
Northey, W.	Lieut.	ditto	13 " "	29 May "	ditto
Gilborne, J.	Asst. Surg.	ditto	2 Nov. "	23 Jan. 1856	ditto
Macdonald, J.	Quartermaster	72nd Highlanders	13 June "	16 Sept. 1855	Wounds
Pechell, W.	Captain	77th Regiment	8 Nov. 1854	3 " "	Killed
Parker, W.	ditto	ditto	10 Aug. 1855	8 " "	ditto
Browne, B.	Ensign	ditto	18 Oct. "	15 Dec. "	Disease
Knight, C.	ditto	ditto	29 Nov. 1854	2 Oct. "	ditto
Corbett, E.	Captain	88th Connght Rangers	" "	7 June "	Killed
Preston, H.	Lieut.	ditto	22 Jan. 1855	14 April "	ditto
Grogan, H.	ditto	ditto	17 Oct. 1854	8 Sept. "	ditto
Macdonald, J.	Major	89th Regiment	19 Dec. "	15 Jan. "	Disease
Daly, Hon. C.	ditto	ditto	ditto	29 Dec. 1854	ditto
Hill, A.	Captain	ditto	ditto	31 Mar. 1855	Wounds (prisoner of war)
Darby, C.	ditto	ditto	ditto	..	Died at sea
Longfield, J.	Lieut.	ditto	ditto	20 Oct. "	Disease

No. 16.—Return shewing the Names, Rank, and Regiment (or Corps) of all Officers who, arriving at any period after the first Landing, Died or Fell in Action, with the date of their Arrival, and of their Death.—(continued.)

NAME.	Rank.	Regiment or Corps.	Date of Arrival.	Date of Death.	Remarks.
Crawfurd, R.	Captain	90th Lt. Infty	5 Dec. 1854	24 Feb. 1855	Disease
Vaughan, H.	ditto	ditto	19 May 1855	12 Sept. "	Wounds
Preston, H.	ditto	ditto	5 Dec. 1854	8 " "	Killed
Swift, A.	Lieut.	ditto	10 Aug. 1855	ditto	ditto
Wilmer, H.	ditto	ditto	3 Sept. "	ditto	ditto
Ball, E.	ditto	93rd Highlanders	2 Dec. 1854	9 June "	Disease
Kirby, F.	ditto	ditto	ditto	16 Feb. "	ditto
Fraser, L.	Captain	95th Regiment	22 Aug. 1855	1 Sept. "	ditto
Handcock, Hon. H.	Lieut. Col.	97th Regiment	20 Nov. 1854	9 Sept. "	Wounds
Welsford, A.	Major	ditto	ditto	8 " "	Killed
Hutton, J.	Captain	ditto	ditto	ditto	ditto
Vicars, H.	ditto	ditto	ditto	22 Mar. "	ditto
M'Gregor, D.	Lieut.	ditto	ditto	8 Sept. "	ditto
Rambottom, H.	ditto	ditto	ditto	5 Jan. "	Suffocated in his tent by charcoal
Goodenough R.	ditto	ditto	28 Nov. "	20 Sept. "	Wounds
Preston, G.	ditto	ditto	10 Aug. 1855	31 Aug. "	Killed
Derman, W.	Adjutant	ditto	20 Nov. 1854	18 " "	ditto
Woodford, E.	Lieut.	Rifle Brigade, 2nd Batt.	20 May 1855	30 June "	Wounds
Cary, L.	ditto	ditto	22 April "	..	ditto (at Malta)
Borough, R.	ditto	ditto	5 Sept. "	13 Nov. "	Disease
Dyke, P.	Ensign	ditto	20 Jan. "	19 April "	ditto
Ryder, H.	ditto	ditto	22 April "	8 Sept. "	Killed
Spence, T.	Dep. Insp. Genl. of Hospitals	Staff	11 Nov. 1854	14 Nov. 1854	Lost in the *Prince*
Bassano, C.	Surgeon 1st class	ditto	12 Oct. 1855	1 Feb. 1856	Disease
O'Connor, N.	ditto	ditto	13 " "	7 June "	ditto
Macartney, F.	Asst. Surg.	ditto	8 Nov. 1854	12 Feb. 1855	ditto
Boyle, E.	ditto	ditto	13 " 1855	8 Dec. "	ditto
White, J.	Actg. Asst. Surgeon	ditto	7 Jan. "	3 July "	ditto
Longmore, J.	ditto	ditto	11 July "	21 Aug. "	ditto
Mitchell, T.	ditto	ditto	14 " "	29 Dec. "	ditto
Bayley, H.	Asst. Com. General	ditto	2 June "	24 July "	ditto
Coppinger, W.	Actg. Dep. Asst. Com. General	ditto	Oct. 1854	11 Aug. "	ditto
Tronton, —	ditto	ditto	ditto	2 Nov. 1854	ditto
Nicholls, J.	Deputy Ordnance Storekeeper	ditto	" 1855	3 " 1855	ditto

ROYAL NAVAL BRIGADE.

No. 17.—Return shewing the Names, Rank, and Ship of all Officers of the Royal Naval Brigade Killed at the Siege of Sebastopol.

Rank.	Name.	Ship.	Date of Death.
Commander	L. Hammet	H.M.S. Albion	17 Aug. 1855
Lieutenant	Thomas O. Kidd	ditto	18 June "
Ditto	G. Greathead	H.M.S. Britannia	20 Oct. 1854
Ditto	Hon. C. B. H. Ruthven	" London	22 " "
Ditto	Samuel Twyford	" "	9 Apr. 1855
Mate	H. J. Spalding	" "	21 Jan. "
Lieutenant	W. H. Douglas	" Queen	11 Apr. "
Acting Mate	H. Karslake	" Rodney	12 Nov. 1854

Total Loss of the Royal Naval Brigade, averaging 1200 Men and Officers—
  Officers ...... 8 Killed ... 3 Died of Disease ... 30 Wounded
  Men............ 116 " ... 41 " ... 431 "

[*Note.*]—Returns Nos. 15 and 16 are principally compiled from Returns called for by Mr. William Ewart, M.P., and ordered by the House of Commons to be printed, 17th March, 1857.—Officers who died at Varna, Scutari, &c., or on board ship, but who never landed in the Crimea, are not included in these Returns; nor are those Officers who died of wounds or disease after arriving at home from the Crimea.

APPENDIX II

CHRONOLOGICAL PRECIS OF THE EVENTS OF THE WAR.

Causes of the War, and Preliminary Events.

1808—1820.
 Differences between the various classes of Christians at Jerusalem, and interference of Russia and France
1836.—Visit of the Prince de Joinville to Jerusalem
1847.—The French ambassador at Constantinople complained of the injustice done to Roman Catholics at Jerusalem, and demanded certain concessions to them
1850.—Louis Napoleon (President of the French Republic) authorised the ambassador at the Porte to enforce the demands made in 1847
May 20.—Lord Stratford de Redcliffe expressed his opinion as to the consequences of this dispute
 1851.—Louis Napoleon instructed the French ambassador to demand, peremptorily, certain privileges for the Roman Catholics, alleged to have been granted them in 1740
 1852.—The Russian ambassador protested against those claims
Feb.—Certain privileges offered to the Roman Catholics
Oct.—A Firman granting them published at Jerusalem
 ,, Colonel Rose's opinion of the position of the Sultan
 ,, Russia asserted her right to protect the Greek Christians
1853.
Jan. 7.—The British ambassador at St. Petersburg informed his government that Russia was sending an army to the Danubian Provinces
 ,, 9.—On this day commenced private conversations between the Emperor Nicholas and Sir G. H. Seymour, the British ambassador, in which the former urged the division of the Turkish empire, which he alluded to as the "sick man," and described as unavoidably falling to pieces. These conversations were continued at intervals till the month of April
 ,, 18.—Lord John Russell wrote to Lord Cowley, stating, in effect, that England would not interfere in the dispute between France, Russia, and Turkey
Feb. 28.—Arrival of Prince Mentschikoff at Constantinople, on a special mission from Russia
Mar. & Apr.—The prince laid his demands before the Porte
May 5.—Through the interference of Lord Stratford de Redcliffe, and the French demands being modified, a Firman was issued, which it was thought would have settled the question
 His lordship received the thanks of the Russian ambassador
 Fresh demands made by Prince Mentschikoff
 Those demands disapproved of by the British, French, Austrian, and Prussian ambassadors, and rejected by the Porte
 ,, 21.—Prince Mentschikoff left Constantinople, and the Russian embassy there was closed
 The British and French ambassadors cordially—those of Austria and Prussia less frankly—approved the conduct of the Porte
 ,, 31.—The Emperor Nicholas sent his "*ultimatum*" to the Porte, and allowed eight days for its acceptance
June 4.—By the "hatti-sherif of Gulhany," the Sultan appealed to the sovereigns of Europe on the difficulties of his position
 ,, 16.—The Turkish Divan finally rejected the Russian terms
 ,, 25.—The Russian armies ordered to cross the Pruth
 ,, 29.—The Czar justified this step in a Manifesto addressed to the European Powers
July 2.—The Russian army entered Wallachia and Moldavia
 ,, ,, Negotiations at Vienna, and the adoption of the "Vienna Note," took place during the month
Aug. & Sept.—The negotiations were continued—the Sultan having refused to accept the "Vienna Note" without certain modifications, which the Czar would not agree to

Events of the War.

Oct. 4.—The Sultan declared war against Russia
 ,, 9.—Omar Pasha addressed a note to Prince Gortschakoff, demanding the evacuation of the Principalities in fifteen days
 ,, 14.—The British and French fleets entered the Dardanelles
 ,, 20.—The first hostilities took place in Asia, the Russians being defeated near Orelle
 ,, 23.—Hostilities in Europe commenced in the Dobrudscha
 ,, 24 *to* 28.—Various actions on the river Tchouruksou, and the capture of Shefketil by the Turks
 ,, 26.—The Czar defended his policy and conduct in another Manifesto
Nov. 1, 2, 3.—The Turks crossed the Danube, and took the Quarantine at Oltenitza
 ,, 4.—Battle of Oltenitza, in which the Russians were defeated
 ,, ,, The Turks attacked Giurgevo without success
 ,, 10.—An inflammatory appeal to the people of Greece, published at Athens
 ,, 13.—The Turks recrossed the Danube, retaining possession of Kalafat and the island of Mokan
 ,, 26.—Battle of Akhaltzik, and defeat of the Turks
 ,, 27, 28, & 29.—Repeated attacks on Giurgevo, without any favourable result
 ,, 30.—The Russian Admiral Nachimoff attacked the Turkish fleet in the port of Sinope, with a vastly superior force; destroyed all the vessels except one, and killed about 2,000 Turks

CHRONOLOGICAL PRECIS

1853.
Dec. 2.—The Turks defeated at Baschkady-Lar
,, ,, The Russian fleet returned to Sebastopol
,, 4.—" *Te Deum*" celebrated in the Russian churches for the "victory" at Sinope
,, 12.—The Russians attacked Matschin, and were defeated
Oct., Nov., Dec.—Negotiations were carried on at Vienna during these months, between Great Britain, France, Austria, and Prussia, with a view to adjust the differences between Russia and the Porte

1854.
Jan. 6.—Battle of Csitate, in which the Russians were defeated
,, 8 to 18.—Various encounters took place on the banks of the Danube, generally favourable to the Turks
,, 19.—The Russians defeated in an attempt to retake Shefketil
,, 27.—Count Alexander Orloff arrived at Vienna, as a plenipotentiary from Russia
,, ,, An insurrection, fomented by Russian emissaries, broke out in Greece
,, 29.—Count Orloff proposed terms for the acceptance of Turkey
,, ,, The Emperor Napoleon addressed an Autograph Letter to the Czar
February. The Russian terms were rejected by the plenipotentiaries of the other Powers
,, 2.—England, Austria, France, and Prussia, agreed to maintain the integrity of the Turkish empire
,, 5.—The Russians again defeated in an attempt to retake Shefketil
,, 8.—Count Orloff left Vienna
,, ,, Baron Brunnow, the Russian ambassador, left London, in consequence of the explanations respecting the entrance of the English and French fleets into the Black Sea not being satisfactory
,, 9.—The Czar replied to the letter of the Emperor Napoleon
,, 10.—The Czar received a Deputation from the Society of Friends, to present an Address, urging him to preserve peace
,, 21.—The Czar published a Manifesto, giving a religious character to the war
,, ,, An Address to the inhabitants of the Grecian provinces, calling upon them to revolt against the Turks, was issued at Radobitza
,, 22.—The first detachment of the troops for the East left England
,, ,, The Army and Navy estimates were moved and adopted in February
Mar. 2.—Count Nesselrode, in a Diplomatic Circular, promised the protection of the Czar to the Greek insurgents
,, 4.—Captain Blackwood arrived at St. Petersburg on a mission from England (a French messenger arriving about the same time, for the same purpose), to demand the evacuation of the Danubian Principalities
,, 5.—The French minister of foreign affairs addressed a Circular Note to foreign courts, justifying the course which England and France had adopted
,, 7.—Fuad Effendi issued a conciliatory proclamation to the Greek people
,, 3 to 10.—The Russians abandoned their posts on the Circassian coasts of the Black Sea
,, 10.—Her Majesty inspected the fleet destined for the Baltic
,, 11.—The first division of that fleet sailed from Spithead
,, 12.—A Treaty of Alliance signed at Constantinople between England, France, and Turkey
,, 16.—Admiral Corry sailed from Spithead for the Baltic
,, 19.—The Russian government rejected the terms of which Captain Blackwood was the bearer
,, ,, The Baltic Fleet united at Wingo Sound
,, 20.—Sir Charles Napier visited Copenhagen
,, 21.—British, French, and Turkish vessels of war entered the Piræus, for the purpose of demanding that the King of Greece should remain neutral
,, ,, An English and French army at Malta
,, 23.—The Russians, 35,000 strong, under General Lüders, crossed the Danube, and entered the Dobrudscha
,, 24, 25, 26.—The Russians captured the Turkish fortresses, and established themselves in the Dobrudscha
,, 26.—The Baltic fleet made the passage of the Great Belt
,, ,, Departure of French troops for the East
,, 28.—Prince Danielo, the Vladika of Montenegro, issued a proclamation against the Turks
,, ,, Declaration of war by England against Russia
,, 30.—The Russians defeated with great loss in the neighbourhood of Kalafat
,, 31.—Parliament voted an Address to the Queen, pledging the support of both Houses in carrying on the war
,, ,, French troops landed at Gallipoli
April 1.—In consequence of King Otho's favouring the Greek insurgents, diplomatic relations between Turkey and Greece were broken off, and all Greek subjects were ordered to quit Constantinople within fifteen days
,, ,, Differences arose between the French ambassador and the Porte, on account of this order; and the Porte issued another, permitting those subjects of King Otho who were not implicated in the insurrection, to remain
,, 1 & 3.—The Russians were again defeated in Little Wallachia
,, 4.—The Declaration of War was read on board the English ships in the Baltic
,, ,, Admiral Plumridge dispatched with a Flying Squadron up the Baltic
,, 5.—The first English troops landed at Gallipoli
,, 7.—Sir Charles Napier paid a second visit to Copenhagen, and was received by the King
,, 8.—Prince Paskiewitsch appointed to the command of the Russian troops in the Danubian Principalities
,, ,, The Russians at Odessa fired upon an English flag of truce
,, 9.—Protocol signed by the ministers of England, France, Austria, and Prussia, disapproving of the policy of Russia
,, ,, The Declaration of War received by the Allied Fleets in Baltschik Bay
,, 11.—The Duke of Cambridge and Lord Raglan arrived at Paris on their way to the East
,, 12.—The Czar issued a Manifesto, replying to the Declaration of War by the Allies
,, 12 & 14.—The Baltic Fleet sailed towards the Gulf of Finland

OF THE EVENTS OF THE WAR.

1854.

April 15.—Treaty with reference to the war, concluded between England and France.
,, 16.—The Vladika of Montenegro issued a second proclamation against the Turks
,, 19.—Hostilities commenced between the troops of the Vladika and those of the Sultan
,, 22.—No satisfactory explanation being given by the governor of Odessa, of the firing upon the flag of truce, the city was bombarded by a part of the Allied Squadrons, and considerable damage done
,, 23.—The Russians commenced their retreat from Little Wallachia
,, ,, Battle of Czernavoda
,, 24 & 25.—Sir Charles Napier visited Stockholm, and had interviews with the King
,, 25.—The Greek insurgents defeated at Peta
,, 28.—The Russians defeated at Turnul
,, ,, The outworks of Silistria attacked
,, 29.—The Allied Squadrons in the Black Sea sailed for Sebastopol, with a view to draw out the Russian fleet; but the latter kept close in port

May 5.—Additional war estimates asked for in the British Parliament
,, 9.—The Duke of Cambridge arrived at Gallipoli; Prince Napoleon having arrived on the 29th of April, Lord Raglan on the 2nd, and Marshal de St. Arnaud on the 7th, of May
,, 10, 11, 12.—There was sharp fighting in Wallachia, to the disadvantage of the Russians
About the same time, the Russians obtained successes in the Dobrudscha over the Turks
,, 11.—The siege of Silistria commenced
,, 12.—The *Tiger* English steamer ran on shore near Odessa; she was fired upon by the Russians, and destroyed, and her crew captured
,, 14, 15, 16.—Engagements in Thessaly, in which the Turks were defeated by the Greek insurgents
,, 17.—Libau was taken by the men of the *Amphion* and *Conflict*
,, 17 & 18.—Councils of war were held at Scutari, and on the 19th at Varna; the result being a resolution that the Allies should march to the latter place
,, 20.—Gallant affair at Eckness, in which the *Arrogant* and *Hecla* were engaged
,, 21.—The *Eurydice*, *Miranda*, and *Brisk*, under Commodore Ommanney, sailed for the White Sea
,, 22.—An attack on the Hango Forts in the Baltic took place
,, 23.—The ministers of England, France, Austria, and Prussia signed a Protocol, guaranteeing the integrity of the Turkish empire
,, 25.—The first detachment of the French army left Gallipoli for Varna
,, 26.—Athens occupied by English and French troops, on account of King Otho's complicity in the Greek insurrection
,, 29.—A serious attack of the Russians on the Arab Tabia (one of the forts at Silistria) was defeated
,, ,, The English Light Division left Gallipoli for Varna

June 1.—A blockade of the ports of the Danube established
,, 2.—The governor of Silistria killed
,, 3.—Negotiations (which ended in the assent by England, France, Austria, and Prussia to the "Four Points," that afterwards formed the bases of the treaty of peace) reopened at Vienna
,, 5, and following day.—The Allies established themselves at Varna
,, 6.—Attack on Gamla-Karleby, by the boats of the *Odin* and *Vulture*
,, 9.—The Turks defeated the Russians in an assault on Silistria; Prince Paskiewitsch was wounded, and the command of the district again came into the hands of Prince Gortschakoff
,, 13.—Major Butler, a gallant British officer, who, with Major Nasmyth, greatly contributed to the successful defence of Silistria, was wounded: he died on the 21st
,, ,, The English and French fleets united in the Baltic
,, 14.—Convention between Austria and Turkey signed, under which the troops of the former were to occupy the Danubian Principalities during the war
,, 16.—Defeat of the Turks at Urzughetti
,, 18.—The Greek insurgents defeated at Calabaka, and the insurrection suppressed
,, ,, The Russians defeated in Asia, losing 400 prisoners and six guns
,, 21.—Captain Hall, with the *Hecla*, *Valorous*, and *Odin*, reconnoitred and bombarded the fortress of Bomarsund
,, 22.—The fleets in the Baltic proceeded to Cronstadt
,, ,, The expedition to the White Sea arrived off Cross Island, and soon after declared the ports in that sea in a state of blockade
,, 23.—The siege of Silistria raised; the Russians repeatedly repulsed in assaults, and annoyed by sorties from the garrison, retreating on the night of the 22nd
,, 24 to 29.—Captain Parker, commanding the *Firebrand*, *Vesuvius*, and *Fury*, was employed in destroying the Russian forts at the mouths of the Danube

July 3.—Omar Pasha visited the English and French camps at Devna and Varna
,, 5, 6, 7.—The Turks effected the passage of the Danube, driving the Russians from the island of Radovan, with great loss on both sides; three British officers (Captain Arnold, and Lieutenants Meynell and Burke) were killed
,, 7.—Prince Gortschakoff issued a proclamation to the Dobrudschians, announcing his intention to retire from the province
,, ,, Captain Parker killed in an attack upon the last Russian fort in the Danube
,, 12.—The Emperor of France reviewed, at Boulogne, the troops destined for the Baltic
,, 16.—The French troops sailed from Calais for the Baltic in British transports
,, 18.—The White Sea Squadron attacked the fortified monastery on the island of Solovetskoi, which was partially destroyed the next day
,, ,, The English and French fleets left the Gulf of Finland for the Aland Isles
,, 20.—A reconnoitring squadron left Baltschik Bay for Sebastopol
,, ,, The White Sea Squadron destroyed public property of the Russians at Pushlachta and other places
,, 22.—The squadron attacked and destroyed Kola
,, 25.—A proclamation was posted at Bucharest, announcing the withdrawal of the Russian army to more healthy districts

CHRONOLOGICAL PRECIS

1854.

July 26.—The reconnoitring squadron arrived off Sebastopol, and an interchange of shots took place with little effect
" 28.—A French expedition, under Generals L'Espinasse and Yussuf, started upon an expedition to the Dobrudscha
" 29.—The Turks were defeated at Bayazid
" 30.—The transports with the French troops from Boulogne arrived in Led Sund
" 31.—General Baraguay d'Hilliers arrived, and took the command of the French troops
" "   The French expedition returned to Kostendji from the Dobrudscha, having been attacked by cholera, of which disease 600 men died in one night
Aug. 1.—Prince Gortschakoff took leave of the Wallachian boyards at Bucharest
" 6.—The Turkish troops entered Bucharest
" "   The Turks defeated at Kuruckdere
" 8.—The "Four Points" were agreed to at Vienna, as the bases of a treaty between the belligerents
" "   The Allied Forces landed at Bomarsund
" 10.—A terrible fire broke out at Varna, destroying an immense amount of property
" 9—12.—This time was occupied in landing the guns, and erecting batteries on the island of Bomarsund.
" 13.—The bombardment commenced
" 14.—Fort Tzee (Bomarsund) taken by the French
" 15.—Fort Nottich surrendered to the English
" 16.—The great fortress of Bomarsund surrendered
" 20.—The Austrians occupied Wallachia, under the treaty of June 14
" 25.—Marshal de St. Arnaud issued a proclamation to the army, announcing the expedition to the Crimea
" 28.—Count Nesselrode announced that the Czar would not accept the "Four Points"
" 29.—The embarkation of the troops from Varna commenced
" 31.—Attack on Petropaulovski, by an English and French squadron
Aug. 30 to Sept. 3.—The Allies were engaged in destroying the fortifications at Bomarsund
Sept. 2.—The King of Belgium arrived at Boulogne, on a visit to the Emperor of the French
" 4.—The King of Portugal and his brother paid a visit to Napoleon III.
" 5.—Prince Albert arrived at Boulogne to visit the Emperor
" "   Lord Raglan and Marshal de St. Arnaud embarked on board the *Caradoc* and the *Ville de Paris* for the Crimea
" 6.—The fleets and transports rendezvoused off Baltschik Bay
" "   The Austrian troops, under Count Coronini, entered Bucharest
" "   At a cabinet council held at Vienna, it was resolved, that the rejection of the "Four Points" by Russia, did not amount to a *casus belli*, but Austria declared her continued support of them
" 7.—The expedition sailed for the Crimea
" 8.—The two fleets and the transports rendezvoused off the Isle of Serpents, whilst Lord Raglan, General Canrobert, and their staffs, reconnoitred the coast of the Crimea in the *Caradoc, Agamemnon, Sampson,* and *Primaquet*
" 9.—Prince Albert left France
" 11.—The reconnoitring vessels having returned, a council of war was held, at which it was resolved to land near Old Fort, and to occupy Eupatoria; the expedition then sailed again
" 13.—Eupatoria was occupied without resistance
" 14.—The Allies disembarked at Old Fort
" "   Russian soldiers encamped to the south, about eight miles below Old Fort, were dispersed by the fire from French and English steamers
" 15.—The Allied commanders issued General Orders to their troops
" 15, 16.—The disembarkation continued
" 16.—The Russians finally left the Danubian Principalities
" 18.—The disembarkation of troops and *matériel* at Old Fort was completed
" 19.—The Allies advanced into the interior, and, in the afternoon, the first encounter between the hostile troops took place—a party of Cossacks being dispersed by the British artillery
" "   The French Baltic Squadron sailed for France
" 20.—The Allies advanced to the Alma; and the glorious victory known as that of the Alma, was obtained
" 21.—The English Baltic Squadron arrived off Nargen on its way to England
" "   The cholera prevailed greatly in the army
" "   The Russians sunk a number of vessels across the mouth of the harbour of Sebastopol
" 21 & 22.—The Allies were employed in burying the dead and taking care of the wounded, great attention being paid to the wounded Russians
" 23.—Marshal de St. Arnaud, unable to accompany the troops from ill-health, went on board the *Berthollet*
" "   The Allies marched for the Katcha, leaving Dr. Thomson to take care of the wounded Russians who had not been removed
" "   Prince Stirbey arrived at Bucharest, and resumed his government
" 24.—The Allies advanced to the valley of the Balbek
" 25.—At a council of war, it was resolved, as the Russians had erected strong works on the north of Sebastopol, to make a flank march to the east, and attack the city on the south
" "   St. Arnaud resigned his command to General Canrobert
" "   The flank march commenced, and the English came suddenly upon the Russians, who were marching to Baktchi-Serai; the latter pushed on in great confusion, leaving large quantities of valuable baggage behind them
" "   The troops encamped on the Tchernaya
" 26.—Possession taken of Balaklava
" 27.—Lord Raglan made the first *reconnaissance* of Sebastopol
" 28.—The Allies began to encamp on the south of Sebastopol
" 29.—Marshal de St. Arnaud died; his body was taken to France, where it was interred with great honours

OF THE EVENTS OF THE WAR.

1854.
Sept. 30.—The Russians again invaded the Dobrudscha, and seized the fortresses
Oct. 1.—A small expedition sent from Balaklava to Yalta
,, 2.—A naval brigade was landed to assist the army in the Crimea
,, 5.—The English commenced intrenching a position on the Woronzoff-road
,, 6.—The expedition to Yalta returned
,, 7.—An encounter with the Russians took place upon the Woronzoff-road
,, 10.—The Queen orders the Duke of Newcastle to send her thanks to the army for their heroic exertions at the Alma
,, ,, In the night the trenches were opened before Sebastopol
,, 11.—A gallant little affair occurred at sea, in which the *Beagle* and *Firebrand* rescued an Austrian barque, laden with hay for the English commissariat, from the guns of the Turkish forts
,, 12.—In consequence of accounts which appeared of the privations and sufferings of the troops in the Crimea, Sir Robert Peel addressed a letter to the *Times*, suggesting a subscription for their relief, heading the list with £200
,, 13.—A "Royal Commission" was issued, authorising the raising a "Patriotic Fund," for the relief of the widows and orphans of the army
,, ,, About the same time, the "Crimean Army Fund" was raised... and subscriptions were opened for the families of sailors and marines, for purchasing books, &c.
,, 17.—The first bombardment of Sebastopol took place
,, ,, It was supported by the fleets attacking the forts
,, 21.—Florence Nightingale and her companions sailed from England, on their mission of charity and benevolence, to the hospitals at Scutari
,, 25.—The bombardment of Sebastopol had been kept up, with some intermissions, by the Allies, and returned by the Russians, subsequently to the 17th; and, on this day, the Battle of Balaklava was fought
,, ,, Chivalrous charge of the Light Brigade of the British cavalry
,, ,, Orders were given to clear the harbour of Balaklava
,, 26.—The first Battle of Inkermann was fought, in which the Russians were defeated
,, 27.—Lord Raglan issued a General Order, thanking the troops for their exertions on the 25th and 26th
,, ,, By this time, most of the vessels which had been in the harbour of Balaklava, were removed outside the port, under the impression that the Russians meant to attack the place
,, 30.—Sir De Lacy Evans, hurt by a fall from his horse, resigned his command into the hands of Brigadier-general Pennefather
Nov. 3.—Large reinforcements reached the Russian army, encamped in the rear of the Allies
,, 4.—The Russian grand-dukes arrived at Sebastopol, and a grand religious service was performed
,, 5.—The Battle of Inkermann was fought
,, ,, While that battle was raging, the Russians made a fierce sortie on the French trenches
,, ,, The Dobrudscha was again declared free from the Russian troops
,, 6.—Dervish Pasha arrived at Jassy
,, 14.—A terrible storm visited the Crimea, doing great damage in the camp, and destroying a large number of vessels on the coast, including most of those that had been removed from the harbour of Balaklava
,, 15.—Prince Ghika resumed the government of Wallachia
,, 24.—The Emperor Napoleon addressed a letter to General Canrobert, congratulating him on the successes of the Allies, and heartily thanking the French troops
,, 27.—The Duke of Newcastle again wrote to Lord Raglan, to convey to him her Majesty's thanks to the army. for its "persevering valour, and chivalrous devotion"
,, 28.—Bitter sufferings of the British troops in the Crimea
,, ,, The cholera broke out again in the British army
,, ,, Awful condition of Balaklava, especially of the Turks there
,, ,, The siege of Sebastopol was at a standstill
,, 29.—The Russians made a desperate night sortie; they were driven back by the French
Dec. 2.—A body of Russians attacked the English works, but were repulsed
,, ,, Austria entered into a triple alliance with England and France; by it the latter countries bound themselves to assist Austria, in the event of war between her and Russia; while Austria only bound herself, in the event of peace not being speedily restored, to deliberate how it could be brought about
,, 6.—Her Majesty wrote a letter to Mr. Sidney Herbert, full of tender commiseration for her troops, and desiring that gentleman to let her see the accounts Mrs. Herbert received from Miss Nightingale
,, 12.—Her Majesty opened Parliament. In the Lords, the Earl of Derby upbraided the conduct of the ministry with respect to the war, and questioned the sincerity of Austria. The Duke of Newcastle, then minister of war, admitted that the government had underrated the military resources of Russia
,, ,, Two bills were passed before Parliament separated for the Christmas holidays. The first empowered the Queen to enlist foreigners to serve in her armies, the number being limited to 10,000: the second permitted her Majesty to accept offers from militia regiments of service out of the United Kingdom
,, 15.—Both houses of Parliament decreed a Vote of Thanks to the Army and Navy engaged in the war
,, 22.—Parliament adjourned for the Christmas recess
,, ,, Admiral Dundas retired from the command of the English fleet in the Black Sea, and was succeeded by Sir Edmund Lyons. Admiral Hamelin, also, was replaced by Vice-admiral Bruat
,, ,, General Canrobert, in a despatch to the French government, stated, that although the number of sick had somewhat increased in the French army in consequence of the perpetual wet, yet that its sanitary condition was satisfactory
,, 26.—The Emperor Napoleon opened the French legislative session, and delivered an address, reviewing the state of the war, and pregnant not only with hope, but confidence in the future
,, ,, The Russian Emperor Nicholas, stung by the comments of the press of Europe on the brutal conduct of his soldiers, issued a Ukase, ordaining that whoever, after a battle, committed acts of

CHRONOLOGICAL PRECIS

1854.

cruelty on the wounded or unresisting, should suffer the punishment of death

Nicholas also issued a Manifesto to his people, in which he again disclaimed having entered into the war with any other view than the promotion of the interests of the Greek Christian church; and he ventured to recognise in the loyalty of his people "the pledge and augury of a happier future"

Scarcely a night passed without some part of the lines of the Allies being attacked by the Russians; they were invariably repulsed

1855.

Jan. 2.—The government having accepted an offer from Messrs. Peto and Betts, eminent contractors, for the construction of a railway from Balaklava to the British camp at Sebastopol, an expedition, consisting of seven steam, and two sailing vessels, started from Blackwall with the materials. The vessels carried 500 "navvies" and workmen for the construction of the railway

Negotiations with Russia were renewed, but hostilities were not suspended

Victor Emmanuel, King of Sardinia, gave his adhesion to the Western Powers, and expressed his intention of sending 15,000 men to the theatre of war

„ **5.**—Omar Pasha and his army proceeded to the Crimea, where he concerted measures with the French and English generals. Ten thousand Turks landed at Eupatoria

„ **12.**—The Russians at Sebastopol celebrated their new year with festivities and religious ceremonials. The French opened fire, which the Russians returned; and also made sorties against both the French and English lines, but with loss to themselves

„ **14.**—The Russians issued from Sebastopol and attacked the French trenches, but were repulsed

„ **23.**—The English Parliament reassembled after the Christmas recess

„ „ Mr. Roebuck, the member for Sheffield, stated, that on the following Thursday, he should move for a select committee to inquire into the number and condition of the army before Sebastopol, and into the conduct of those departments of the government whose duty it was to administer to the wants of that army

„ **25.**—Lord John Russell resigned his post as President of the Council. His retirement under such circumstances elicited severe animadversions from the press

„ **26.**—Lord John Russell explained his conduct in the House of Commons. He said he felt he could not resist Mr. Roebuck's motion; admitted that the accounts received of the condition of our army before Sebastopol "were not only painful, but horrible and heartrending;" and added, "there is something, with all the official knowledge to which I have had access, that to me is inexplicable in the state of our army"

„ „ Mr. Roebuck brought forward his motion. He said 54,000 soldiers had been sent from this country to the Crimea, of whom it appeared that not more than 14,000 were then actually in arms before Sebastopol. "I want to know, sir," he asked, "what has become of the 40,000 troops who have disappeared?"

„ „ After a vehement debate, which lasted until past two in the morning, Mr. Roebuck's motion was carried, and the ministry defeated, by a majority of 157

„ „ The Emperor Nicholas issued his last Manifesto

„ **30.**—The Duke of Cambridge, after gallantly performing his duty in the Crimea, returned, after suffering much illness, to England, and landed at Dover

„ **31.**—A Russian spy walked deliberately through some of the English trenches, and counted the guns; he escaped unhurt amidst a fire of musketry

Feb. 1.—The Earl of Aberdeen announced, that the ministry had placed their resignations in the hands of her Majesty

„ „ The Duke of Newcastle defended himself in an earnest and manly manner against the aspersions recently cast upon him by Lord John Russell

„ „ A furious skirmish took place just before daybreak between the Russians and the French; 300 of the latter were killed or wounded before the enemy was driven back

„ „ The blockade of the Black Sea by the Allied Fleets was renewed from this date

„ **2.**—Sir De Lacy Evans, who had returned invalided from the Crimea, received the unanimous thanks of the House of Commons

The Earl of Derby having been sent for by her Majesty, found himself unable to form a ministry which could command a majority in the Commons

The Queen sent for the venerable Lord Lansdowne, who exerted himself for the reconstruction of the government, but without success

„ **2.**—To the astonishment of the nation, Lord John Russell was entrusted by the Queen with the formation of a ministry. His late colleagues refused to take any part in a government of which he was to be the head

Lord Palmerston undertook to form a ministry

„ **5.**—Lord John Russell delivered a speech, in which he retorted upon the Duke of Newcastle, and endeavoured to justify his own conduct

„ **8.**—Cessation of the ministerial interregnum, and announcement of the Palmerston cabinet; Lord Panmure (late Mr. Fox Maule) became minister of war

„ „ Lord John Russell bitterly attacked the "ribald press" for the severe comments it had made on his conduct

„ **8.**—Lord John Russell accepted the position of British plenipotentiary at the Peace Conferences about to open at Vienna

„ „ The cold in the Crimea was so severe, and our troops so unprotected, that men were found frozen in their tents, and many were carried to the hospital, suffering from frost-bite

„ „ Medical mismanagement and improper condition of our military hospitals at Scutari

„ **15.**—Large bodies of Russian troops were seen approaching Eupatoria

„ **16.**—Parliament met for business, and Lord Palmerston explained to the House the circumstances which led him to accept the premiership. He objected to the Roebuck Committee of Inquiry into the state of the British army before Sebastopol

„ „ Mr. Layard commented, with considerable severity, on Lord Palmerston's plans for the rescue of the

OF THE EVENTS OF THE WAR.

1855.

army from the deplorable condition into which it had fallen. He considered Lord Raglan incompetent to the command

Feb. 17.—Battle of Eupatoria, and defeat of the Russians by Omar Pasha and 40,000 Turks. The Russians were permitted to retreat in good order, as the Turks were deficient in cavalry. The enemy left 453 men dead on the field

„ 19.—Mr. Macdonald, the active and philanthropic distributor of the *Times'* fund, having exhausted the sum entrusted to him, returned to England in consequence of ill-health. The *Times* collected another sum (£15,000) by subscription, and sent another agent with it to Scutari, to relieve the wants of our sick soldiers

„ „ An attempted *reconnaissance*, in the neighbourhood of Sebastopol, by Sir Colin Campbell and Generals Bosquet and Villenois, with the object of ascertaining the strength of the enemy, was baffled by the severity of the weather

„ 22.—Mr. Gladstone, Sir James Graham, and Mr. Sidney Herbert, resigned their posts in the new ministry, on account of the objection they entertained to the proposed inquiry, by a select committee of the House, into the state of the army and the causes of the disasters in the Crimea

„ „ The House decided that the inquiry should be a *public* one; and the list of names first proposed by Mr. Roebuck was abandoned, as consisting of men who entertained *ex parte* views

„ 23.—The three retiring members of the government explained their conduct to the House

„ „ A furious night engagement took place between the French and the Russians. The latter were driven from some new works they were erecting; but the French had 100 men killed and 300 wounded. The Russians claimed a victory

„ 24.—During the night the Russians sunk three or four more of their ships in the mouth of the harbour of Sebastopol. On the 3rd of March they were supposed to have sunk more ships to block up the entrance

„ 28.—An alarming earthquake at the city of Broussa in Asiatic Turkey: Constantinople was shaken by a shock on the same day

Mar. 2.—The Russian Emperor Nicholas, after a brief illness, expired in the fifty-ninth year of his age, after a reign of nearly thirty years. His death was produced by pulmonic apoplexy, or congestion of the lungs

In consequence of the death of the Czar Nicholas, the funds rose considerably both at London and Paris

„ „ The new Emperor, Alexander II., issued a warlike Manifesto, in which he promised to tread in the steps of his "illustrious predecessors, Peter, Catherine, Alexander the well-beloved, and of" his "august father"

Dr. Granville wrote a letter to the *Times*, enclosing a remarkable paper sent by him, in confidence, to Lord Palmerston, in 1853, in which, on scientific grounds, he predicted the sudden death of the Czar before the age of sixty

In France and England the Czar's death was the subject of congratulation; but the court of Prussia went into mourning for a month: and at Vienna the information was received with real or pretended sorrow

„ 3.—Alexander II. issued addresses to the Russian army on the death of his father

„ „ The Queen and the royal family visited the wounded soldiers who had returned from the Crimea, and been placed in the military hospitals at Chatham

„ 5.—The committee of the House of Commons appointed to inquire into the state of the British army before Sebastopol, commenced their sittings

„ 7.—Alexander II. addressed the diplomatic corps at St. Petersburg, stated his intention of upholding the principles of the "Holy Alliance," and affirmed that, though the intentions of his father had been misunderstood, God and history would do him justice

The Russians erected works on a mound in advance of the Malakhoff Tower; those new works became famous under the name of the Mamelon

As the spring advanced, the health and spirits of our troops before Sebastopol improved; the merit of having produced this change was claimed by the press as resulting from its exposure of the mismanagement which prevailed in connection with our army

„ 11.—The late Emperor Nicholas was buried in the cathedral of St. Peter and St. Paul

Races were got up in the English camp to beguile the tedium of the siege

„ 15.—A European Congress was opened at Vienna with the object of bringing about a peace on the basis of the "Four Points"

„ 17.—The French were unsuccessful in an attempt to take the rifle-pits the Russians had dug in the neighbourhood of the Mamelon

„ 20.—Lord Lyndhurst, in the imperial house of Parliament, reviewed the proceedings of Prussia, and bitterly reproved the equivocating government of that country

„ 21.—This day was appointed by the government as one of National Humiliation and Prayer

„ 22.—The Russians made a general attack upon the advances of the Allies; a serious engagement took place, the brunt of which was borne by the French, who lost in killed and wounded about 400 men; the loss of the Russians was estimated at over 1,000

„ 24.—An armistice took place between the Allies and the Russians to allow of the burial of the dead

April 4.—The bulk of the Baltic Fleet (consisting of fifty line-of-battle ships and frigates, five floating batteries, eight mortar-vessels, and twenty-eight gun-boats) sailed from Spithead, under the command of Rear-admiral Sir Richard Dundas, Sir Charles Napier having been superseded because he had done comparatively nothing with the enormous means at his disposal in the previous campaign

„ 8.—Establishment in England of a training camp at Aldershott-heath

„ 9.—The Allies opened the second great bombardment on Sebastopol. It commenced shortly after five in the morning, and lasted until seven in the evening. Like that of the 17th of October, in the preceding year, it proved a failure. It was continued with unabated fury during twelve days, and the idea of an assault was then abandoned for the time, as the real strength of the Russian works was considered uninjured

CHRONOLOGICAL PRECIS

1855.

April 15.—The Emperor Napoleon, accompanied by the Empress Eugénie, left the Tuileries to proceed to England on a visit to her Majesty

Omar Pasha and 15,000 of the Turkish troops left Eupatoria for the camp before Sebastopol, and took up their position on the heights above Kamiesch

„ 16.—The Emperor and the Empress of the French landed at Dover, and were received by Prince Albert with anxious courtesy, and by the people with enthusiasm. On arriving at the Bricklayer's Arms, in the southern suburbs of London, the illustrious party proceeded in an open barouche to the Paddington station, and from thence by rail to Windsor, where they were received by the Queen and the great officers of state with much ceremony

„ 17.—The Mayor and Town Council of Windsor presented an address of congratulation to the Emperor Napoleon; similar addresses were presented by deputations from various influential bodies in London

„ „ Through the inattention of some English vessels, the Russian garrison of Petropaulovski embarked on board the *Aurora* and the *Dwina*, and taking with them their stores and four merchantmen, escaped to the Amoor river, where our vessels were unable to approach them. The deserted fortifications were destroyed by the Allies

„ 18.—The Emperor Napoleon was invested by her Majesty with the ensigns of the Order of the Garter

„ 19.—The Emperor and Empress of the French visited the citizens of London at the Guildhall, where an address was presented to Napoleon by the authorities of the city, to which he delivered a remarkable and eloquent reply, containing the memorable observation, that "The eyes of all who suffer instinctively turned towards the West." A sumptuous *déjeuner* terminated the proceedings

„ „ Great excitement was occasioned by the Emperor and Empress, the Queen and Prince Albert, paying a state visit to the Italian Opera. Pit tickets were sold at ten, and even fifteen guineas each

„ „ The Russian rifle-pits, in advance of the English trenches, were carried by assault by a detachment of the 77th, under Colonel Egerton, who lost his life in the execution of his duty

„ 20.—The Emperor and Empress, in company with her Majesty and Prince Albert, visited the Crystal Palace at Sydenham

„ 21.—Napoleon and the Empress Eugénie took leave of her Majesty, and embarked on their return to France

„ „ As the Plenipotentiaries of the other European Powers could not agree with the Russian Plenipotentiary, concerning the basis on which a peace could be negotiated, the Conferences at Vienna were adjourned *sine die*

„ 28.—Pianori, an Italian, fired two pistols at the Emperor Napoleon in the Champs Elysées; the assassin was arrested

„ 29.—Napoleon, on receiving the congratulations of the representatives of the senate on his escape from the attack of Pianori, replied—"I fear nothing from the attempts of assassins; there are existences which are the instruments of the decrees of Providence"

May 2.—A sharp engagement took place during the night between the Russians and the French; all the Russian rifle-pits were taken, together with eight light mortars and 200 prisoners. Many petty actions took place during this month

„ 3.—An Allied Squadron, with 12,000 troops on board, proceeded towards the Straits of Kertch, but was ordered to return just before it reached its destination

„ 5.—First meeting, at the London Tavern, of the Administrative Reform Association—a society for promoting a thorough reform in the various departments of the state

„ 12.—The reserve of French troops at Moslak, in the dominions of the Sultan, consisting of 30,000 men, embarked and proceeded to Kamiesch, thus raising the Allied Forces before Sebastopol to upwards of 200,000 men. Of these, 30,000 consisted of British, 15,000 of Sardinians, 50,000 of Turks, and the remainder of French

„ 14.—Execution of Pianori, the assassin

„ 16.—General Canrobert resigned the command of the French army in the Crimea, in favour of General (since Marshal) Pelissier

„ 18.—Her Majesty distributed medals, in the square of the Horse-guards, to the officers and soldiers who had returned invalided or wounded from the Crimea

„ 22.—The French attacked some formidable works of the Russians in course of erection. A sanguinary engagement ensued; the Russians were driven back, and part of their works taken. The next night the French renewed the attack, and captured the remaining portion of the new works. The Russians left 1,200 dead upon the ground

„ 23.—The expedition started again for the Straits of Kertch, greatly augmented, and carrying altogether about 20,000 troops

„ 24.—The Allied Fleets assembled off the Straits of Kertch, and the troops landed without opposition. The Russian troops blew up their fortifications and magazines on both sides of the Straits, and then rapidly retreated towards Yenikale, a town distant about five miles and a-half

„ „ Kertch fell into the hands of the Allies without a blow. More than a hundred guns were captured, and three steamers, and several other heavily-armed vessels were destroyed by the Russians themselves. Many transport ships were destroyed, and others captured. Four small government steamers and other vessels escaped into the Sea of Azoff. Quantities of corn and other stores were seized by the Allies

„ „ Lord John Russell, having recently returned from the Conferences at Vienna, made a very warlike speech in the House of Commons

„ 25.—The Allies before Sebastopol took a large piece of ground beyond their former position into occupation

„ „ The Allies entered the Sea of Azoff, and sent a squadron to Berdiansk and Arabat. The four war steamers were found run on shore and burnt; enormous quantities of government stores were destroyed. At Berdiansk some coasting vessels, and considerable stores of grain, were burnt

„ „ On the Allied troops reaching Yenikale, the inhabitants took to flight, and the town was taken possession of. It was plundered and fired by the French and English

APPENDIX II

OF THE EVENTS OF THE WAR.

1855.

May 28.—The squadrons arrived off Arabat in the Sea of Azoff; bombarded the fort, and blew up its magazine, but retired on account of the large garrison there rendering landing imprudent. Upwards of one hundred Russian merchantmen, laden with provisions for the army in the Crimea, were destroyed within three days

,, ,, Five Russian vessels, laden with corn, being ignorant that Kertch was in the hands of the Allies, ran into the harbour and were captured

,, ,, Captain Lyons (son of the Admiral) separated from the French squadron at Arabat, and proceeded to Genitchi. The town would not surrender, and Captain Lyons burnt seventy-three ships, and immense quantities of corn

Kertch was plundered, and the museum destroyed. Some shocking outrages were perpetrated by the Turkish soldiery

The Baltic Fleet daily fell in with, and captured, some coasters of the enemy : all the Russian ports in the Baltic were in a state of blockade

,, 30.—The Allied Squadron in the Sea of Azoff sailed to the Gulf of the Don, and from thence to the Taganrog Roads

June 1.—Admiral Dundas was joined near Cronstadt by the French fleet

,, 3.—The Allied Admirals reconnoitred the north side of Cronstadt

,, ,, The Allied Squadron in the Sea of Azoff fired the stores and government buildings of Taganrog, in the face of 3,000 Russian soldiers. A war steamer of the enemy, also, was destroyed

,, 4.—The Allied Squadron in the Sea of Azoff proceeded to Mariopol, where it destroyed extensive grain stores and the public buildings

,, ,, Anapa, the last of the Russian forts on the Circassian coast of the Black Sea, was burnt and abandoned by its garrison. The ruins were visited by Admirals Stewart and Charnier

,, 5.—A General Order announced to the Allied Armies the triumphs of the fleets in the Sea of Azoff

,, ,, The cutter of a British man-of-war, while landing some Russian prisoners at Hango, without notice previously given, and with a flag of truce irregularly displayed, was fired into, and several men killed. The affair was, at first, greatly exaggerated and misrepresented in England, where it occasioned much excitement. A correspondence took place concerning it between Admiral Dundas and the Russian authorities

,, 6.—Several thousand quarters of wheat were burnt by the Allied Squadron at the little town of Gheisk

,, ,, The French and English opened a furious fire against the external works of Sebastopol, and obtained a superiority over that of the enemy on several points

,, 7.—The French assaulted and captured the famous work known as "the Mamelon." In their enthusiasm they assaulted the terrible Malakhoff Tower behind it, but were repulsed with much loss. The English assaulted and took the "Quarries ;" a murderous fight was maintained the whole night

,, 8.—The French established themselves securely in the Mamelon, to which they gave the name of the Brancian Redoubt, in honour of an officer slain there. Among the spoils of the previous night were sixty-two guns and 400 prisoners, fourteen of whom were officers

,, ,, General Pelissier congratulated his troops on their victory

,, 9.—Thirty thousand sacks of flour, stacked on the beach in Kiten Bay, were destroyed ; and the Allied Squadron, having swept the Sea of Azoff, returned in triumph to Kertch

,, ,, The fortress of Cronstadt was again reconnoitred; infernal machines exploded under some of the vessels

,, ,, A truce was held before Sebastopol for the burial of the dead

,, ,, A powerful Russian army encamped near Kars, a fortified city of Asiatic Turkey. Colonel Williams was within the town, associated with the Turkish general as British Commissioner

,, 10.—The inhabitants of Kars desired to aid in its defence, and applied to Colonel Williams for arms

,, 11.—From this date Captain Thomas Baillie re-established a blockade of the Russian coasts in the White Sea. It was maintained until the 9th of October, when the gathering ice rendered it no longer necessary

,, 13.—The French fleet and army left Kertch and returned to Kamiesch. On the following day the English left and returned to Balaklava

,, 14.—A body of Turkish cavalry outside Kars was surprised by the Russians, and many slain

,, 16.—Mr. Stowe, the administrator of the *Times'* fund, was taken ill from the exposure to weather and the severity of camp life ; a few days later he expired

,, ,, The Russians attacked Kars, but were repulsed

,, 17.—The Turkish and Sardinian troops crossed the river Tchernaya, and occupied positions in front of Tchorgoun

,, ,, The English and French generals having agreed that the former should storm the Great Redan, and the latter the Malakhoff Tower, a crushing fire was poured into Sebastopol, and continued throughout the whole day

,, ,, Captain Lyons, who had so recently distinguished himself by his exploits in the Sea of Azoff, was severely wounded during a night attack on the sea defences of Sebastopol. The injury caused his death

,, 18.—At three in the morning the French assaulted the Malakhoff, and the English the Redan ; the latter prematurely, on account of the non-success of their Allies. The Russians being thoroughly prepared, both French and English were repulsed, with enormous slaughter. Some of General Eyre's men, who had been sent to occupy the Cemetery, penetrated into the town, but were glad to retire to escape being burnt to death

,, ,, Mr. Roebuck presented to the House of Commons the Report of the Committee of Inquiry into the state of our Army before Sebastopol

,, 19.—Prince Gortschakoff congratulated the Russian troops upon their victory

,, ,, An armistice took place for the burial of the dead, and some curious interviews occurred between the officers of the contending armies. The bodies of Colonels Yea and Shadforth, and that of Sir John Campbell, were discovered amongst the slain

CHRONOLOGICAL PRECIS

1855.

June 21.—Our fleet in the Baltic commenced sweeping for infernal machines; within three days thirty-three of them were fished up; Admiral Seymour examined one on board the *Exmouth;* it exploded, and injured him and several other persons

„ 23.—In the Baltic, Captain Story discovered and destroyed several small Russian trading vessels; the whole of the shipping of Nysted, amounting to 20,000 tons, was destroyed

„ 25.—Captain Lyons was buried at Therapia

„ 26.—The Turks and Sardinians made a *reconnaissance* into the Valley of Baidar

„ 27.—The Russians seized and destroyed a quantity of provisions intended for the Turkish garrison at Kars

vol. iii.,

„ 28.—Lord Raglan sunk under an attack of dysentery, and expired in his 67th year. General Sir James Simpson succeeded to the command of the army in the Crimea

Sir George Brown, on account of failing health, returned to England; General Codrington succeeded him in the command of the Light Division

Great sickness and mortality prevailed among the Russian troops in Sebastopol

July 2.—The Emperor Napoleon opened the Legislative Assembly at Paris, and reviewed the aspect of Europe in connection with the war

„ „ The Allied Generals in the Crimea received autograph letters from the Sultan, expressing his high admiration of the courage and firmness of their troops

„ 3.—A pension of £1,000 a-year was granted to Lady Raglan; and another, of £2,000 a-year, to the eldest son of the late Lord Raglan for two lives

„ „ The body of Lord Raglan was placed on board the *Caradoc*, which left the Crimea the same evening for England

„ „ Lieutenant Hewett, in the *Beagle*, destroyed the flying bridge between the town of Genitchi and Arabat Spit in the Sea of Azoff

„ 4.—In the Gulf of Finland, Captain Yelverton, of the *Arrogant*, destroyed the fort, barracks, and government stores of Lovisa; the town was afterwards accidentally burnt

„ „ Captain Yelverton drove a body of Cossacks from Kounda Bay

„ 6.—Count Buol, in a diplomatic circular, having stated that the Plenipotentiaries of France and England were adverse to the war, Mr. Gibson asked the ministers, on what ground they were opposed to the peaceable views of their colleague?

„ „ Lord John Russell, in reply, admitted that he had said to Count Buol, that the propositions of Austria ought to be assented to by the Allies, and that he would urge them upon the English government: in fact, that though he was acting with a ministry pledged to carry on the war, he was himself in favour of peace. This declaration was rebuked with much sternness by Mr. Cobden, Mr. Roebuck, and Mr. Disraeli. The latter sarcastically designated Lord John Russell as "a minister of peace and of war"

The *Times*, and other leading journals, visited Lord John Russell with a storm of censure for his inconsistency and want of high principle

Sir E. Bulwer Lytton gave notice of a motion of want of confidence in the government

„ 10.—The Russians opened a heavy fire from the Redan upon the English works

„ 11.—A French soldier was executed on the plain of Balaklava for stabbing his captain

„ 12.—The Russians kept up a tremendous fire, and much mischief was done to the Allies by a storm

„ 13.—Lord John Russell anticipated the result of Sir E. B. Lytton's motion, by resigning. He was succeeded, as colonial minister, by the late Sir William Molesworth

„ 14.—Captain Yelverton engaged a Russian battery at Trangsund, off the town of Wyborg, but was compelled to retire, with some loss

„ 15.—At Sebastopol a body of Russian troops made a fierce attack upon the trenches of the French, but were thrice driven back with slaughter

„ „ Captains Osborn and De Cintré visited Berdiansk in the Sea of Azoff, where they burnt large stores of wheat and forage

„ „ The city of Kars was completely blockaded by the Russian army. The townspeople and Turkish troops suffered severely from hunger

„ 16.—The debate on Sir E. B. Lytton's motion took place; but in consequence of the resignation of Lord John Russell, its effect was neutralised. The latter explained his conduct without clearing his reputation

„ „ Fort Petrovskoi, in the Sea of Azoff, was attacked by an Allied Squadron, and the garrison compelled to retreat. The Allies set fire to the public buildings, corn, and forage stores: many other places were visited, and quantities of government stores destroyed

„ 17.—Mr. Roebuck brought forward a motion for the severe reprehension of every member of the Aberdeen ministry, whose counsel, he considered, led to the sufferings of our army before Sebastopol. The debate was adjourned until the 20th, when it was decided, by a majority of 107, that the motion should not be put to the vote

„ „ The Allied Admirals in the Baltic reconnoitred Sweaborg and Helsingfors; several submarine machines were exploded, but without effect

„ 18.—The Allied Admirals reconnoitred the powerful fortress of Revel

„ „ Another sortie was made from Sebastopol against the batteries of Careening Bay; but the enemy was repulsed

„ 20.—A motion by Lord Palmerston, authorising the Queen to guarantee, in conjunction with the French government, the interest on a loan of five millions sterling to the Turks, met great opposition, and was only carried by a majority of three

„ 21.—Captain Yelverton, of the *Arrogant*, accompanied by the *Magicienne*, the *Cossack*, and the gunboat *Ruby*, attacked the fortress of Frederickshaum, and dismounted many of its guns, but did not follow up the advantage

„ 24.—The *Caradoc* arrived at Bristol with the remains of Lord Raglan

„ 26.—Funeral of Lord Raglan in the ancestral vault of the family at Badminton

„ „ Captain Yelverton, having received a reinforcement, attacked and took the fortified island of Kotka. The public buildings, barracks, magazines, and government stores were destroyed

OF THE EVENTS OF THE WAR.

1855.

    The Duke of Newcastle, late minister of war, arrived at Balaklava.

    The English and French troops worked incessantly in the trenches, and the most active preparations were made, especially by the latter, in preparing for a renewal of the attack. The Turkish army, under Omar Pasha, remained in idleness.

    A Russian deserter informed the Allies that his countrymen were preparing to attack the Tchernaya line in great force

    A French *cantinère* gave birth to an infant in the trenches

    Other Russian deserters brought information of an intended attack on the Tchernaya line

Aug. 2.—Lord Clarendon informed the British ambassador at Constantinople, that Colonel Williams was attached, as British Commissioner, to the head-quarters of the Turkish army in Asia.

,, 6.—The bulk of the Allied Fleets anchored off Sweaborg, or the fortress of the Six Castles

,, 9.—Her Majesty reviewed the Foreign Legion at Shorncliffe

,, ,, The Allies commenced the bombardment of Sweaborg, and continued it for forty-eight hours: the town was destroyed; all the magazines blown up; twenty-three ships burnt, and about 1,000 men killed or wounded; the stone batteries, however, cut out of the solid rock, remained in the hands of the enemy

,, 11.—The inhabitants of Helsingfors fired on a couple of gigs belonging to some French gun-boats; yet the Allies were compassionate or weak enough to spare Helsingfors, which they could have destroyed almost without opposition

,, 13.—The Allied Fleets left the ruins of Sweaborg, and returned to their old anchorage at Nargen

,, 14.—Parliament was prorogued for the session

,, 16.—The Battle of the Tchernaya, or of Traktir-bridge. The Russian attacking force was estimated at from fifty to sixty thousand men, accompanied by 160 pieces of artillery, and commanded by Prince Gortschakoff in person. They were opposed by the French and Sardinian troops. After three impetuous charges *en masse*, the Russians retreated, having suffered a terrible and decisive defeat. The battle lasted from dawn until about half-past nine or ten in the morning. To meet the attacking army the French had but 12,000 men, and the Sardinians 10,000; and of the latter only 4,500 were actually engaged. The French lost 1,542 in killed and wounded; the Sardinians 250; while the loss of the Russians was estimated at 3,000 killed, and 5,000 wounded. General Simpson placed it at "between five and six thousand men"

,, 17.—Generals Pelissier and Marmora congratulated their troops.

,, ,, The Allies opened a fire from their siege batteries upon the Russian works.

,, 18.—Her Majesty, Prince Albert, the Prince of Wales, and the Princess Royal left Osborne for Boulogne, on a return visit to the Emperor Napoleon, who met and escorted them to Paris.

,, 19.—A detachment from the Allied Fleet destroyed seventeen coasters and a Russian steamer at Biorneborg

,, ,, All our mortar-vessels in the Baltic were sent back to England

,, 20.—A series of *fêtes* commenced in Paris for the entertainment of the royal visitors of the Emperor. The Queen visited the Palais des Beaux Arts, La Sainte Chapelle, and the venerable cathedral of Nôtre-Dame

,, ,, The Emperor Napoleon sent his thanks and congratulations to the French army in the Crimea, on account of their victory at the Tchernaya

,, 21.—The Emperor Napoleon accompanied the Queen to Versailles. The attention of her Majesty was chiefly attracted by a painting representing the defeat of the English at Fontenoy. She visited the apartments of the unfortunate Marie Antoinette. In the evening the august party paid a state visit to the Grand Opera

,, 22.—The Queen, the Emperor, and other members of the royal party, visited the Palais de l'Industrie, after which they proceeded, *incognito*, to the Jardin des Plantes.

,, 23.—A grand *fête* was given by the citizens of Paris to the Queen at the Hôtel de Ville. About 8,000 persons were present, and the brilliancy of the entertainment was supposed to surpass anything of the kind ever attempted

,, 24.—Her Majesty, accompanied by the Emperor and Prince Albert, attended a review of 50,000 French soldiers in the Champ de Mars. In the evening the Queen visited the tomb of Napoleon the Great, at the Hospital of the Invalides

,, 25.—The Emperor Napoleon conducted his guests to St. Germain, where they visited the apartments of the banished James II. In the evening they attended a ball of extraordinary beauty and magnificence at Versailles

,, ,, General Simpson informed Lord Panmure that the Russians had nearly completed a bridge across the great harbour of Sebastopol, and that they had large bodies of men employed in erecting earthworks on the north side

,, ,, Lord Stratford de Redcliffe proceeded to the Crimea for the purpose of investing certain officers of the army and navy, by commission under the sign-manual, with the insignia of the Order of the Bath

,, 27.—The Queen, the Prince, and their family returned to England

,, 29.—A shell from the Russian batteries at Sebastopol blew up a French magazine, containing about seven tons of powder. Forty persons were killed on the spot, and nearly three times that number wounded.

,, 30.—A body of Russian infantry approached stealthily and leaped into the advanced trench of the English, where they began to pull down the gabions and to fill up the parallel; they advanced on a second parallel, but were driven back by volleys of musketry, and retired in confusion, leaving many dead behind them

    In consequence of the near approach of the Allies to Sebastopol, they suffered severe losses. The French had about 150 killed or wounded every night; the English usually fifty. One of the French trenches was so fatal to those who entered it, that it obtained the name of the "slaughter-house"

    It was calculated that the Russian mercantile vessels captured, burnt, or sunk, during the summer, in the Gulf of Bothnia alone, amounted to about 80,000 tons of shipping

APPENDIX II

CHRONOLOGICAL PRECIS

1855.

September. Russian deserters or spies frequently entered the Allied camps, saying that the enemy were about to attempt, by an attack on four different points at once, and with a force of 90,000 men, to sweep their assailants from the Crimea.

" 3.—A body of 1,200 Turkish cavalry, besides Bashi-Bazouks, left Kars after nightfall, and cut their way through the Russians . . . . vol. iii.,

" 5.—The final bombardment of Sebastopol commenced at daybreak. The French opened first with a fire from more than 200 pieces of cannon. During the day, the English fired as usual; but at night they employed all their mortars and heavy guns against the whole line of Russian defences. At eight, a Russian two-decker was set on fire, and burnt to a charred wreck. The bombardment was continued during the 6th and 7th; another Russian two-decker was burnt on the latter day.

" 7.—A council of generals decided that the assault should take place on the following morning.

" " The English assaulting columns, amounting to the ridiculously inefficient number of only 3,000 men, entered the trenches, under the command of Sir William Codrington

" 8.—At noon, 30,000 French assaulted the Malakhoff, which was taken; but they were unsuccessful in their attacks upon the Central Bastion and the Little Redan. The English attacked the Great Redan, and entered it, but were repulsed with a loss amounting, in killed, wounded, and missing, to 2,447 men. The loss of the French amounted, in killed, wounded, and missing, to 7,551.

" " About eight in the evening, the Russians commenced their retreat from Sebastopol; about eleven, they began blowing up their magazines; at two, fires broke out in various parts of the city; incessant explosions indicated the blowing up of batteries, &c.; at half-past five in the morning, two of the southern forts were hurled into the air, and the flames from the burning town revealed the Russians in retreat across the harbour, on a bridge of boats, to the north side. Before seven on the morning of the 9th, all the Russian battalions had passed over, and the raft-bridge was disconnected. During the retreat, the Russian men-of-war in the harbour were all abandoned and sunk.

" 9.—The Allied Generals congratulated their troops on the fall of Sebastopol, after a siege of eleven months

" 10.—Soon after midnight a violent storm swept over the burning town of Sebastopol, and stirred the flames into fury; it was followed by a deluge of rain

" 11.—A Russian detachment attacked a Turkish convoy with provisions for Kars; an engagement took place; the Turks were routed and the supplies seized . . . . vol. iii.,

" 12.—Prince Gortschakoff, in a remarkable and dignified address to his troops, recounted the events of the struggle, and cheered his men with the assurance that they had nobly done their duty. He said—"It is painful, it is hard, to leave Sebastopol in the enemy's hands. But remember the sacrifice we made upon the altar of our country in 1812. Moscow was surely as valuable as Sebastopol: we abandoned it after the immortal battle of Borodino. The defence of Sebastopol, during 349 days, is superior to Borodino"

" " Omar Pasha, and a large body of Turkish troops from the Crimea, landed at Batoum

" " Her Majesty and the Emperor Napoleon each addressed congratulations to their troops. The Queen also thanked the French army, and the Emperor thanked the army of England. General Pelissier was made a marshal of France; a circumstance which the English government burlesqued by creating General Simpson a field-marshal

" 16.—A grand religious and military ceremony took place at Paris to celebrate the fall of Sebastopol, and a *Te Deum* was sung at Nôtre-Dame

" 20.—The Allied Armies at Sebastopol celebrated the first anniversary of the Battle of the Alma.

" 21.—A skirmish took place near Yenikale, between a party of English cavalry and some Cossacks

" 23.—The Emperor Alexander issued an address to the Russian troops, thanking them for their courage and perseverance, and appeared still to be animated by a warlike feeling

" " Captain Osborn left Kertch with several vessels, to keep in check the enemy's troops at Temriouk. He burnt a bridge, by which only troops could march to the assistance of Taman.

" 24.—An Allied Squadron left Kertch and proceeded to Fanagoria and Taman, which they took possession of and destroyed. At the latter place, eleven 24-pounders were found buried in the sand

" 27.—An officer and nineteen men were wounded in Sebastopol, by the explosion of a Russian magazine.

" 29.—A body of French and Turkish cavalry, under the command of General d'Allonville and Ahmet Pasha, advanced from Eupatoria on the road to Perekop, with the object of dispersing the Russian troops in that locality. They came upon a considerable Russian force, under the command of General de Korff. The latter were taken by surprise, defeated, and put to flight, leaving fifty of their number dead on the field, and 169 prisoners in the hands of the victors. Six guns, twelve caissons, and 250 horses, were among the spoil. General d'Allonville attempted to drive the enemy from his strong position, and bring him into action, but without effect

" " The Russian army, under General Mouravieff, assaulted Kars. The battle lasted with great fury for nearly seven hours, when the Russians were defeated, and retreated with precipitation, leaving 6,300 of their number dead upon the field, besides carrying away an immense number of wounded. The loss of the Turks amounted only to 362 killed, and 631 wounded. In addition to this, however, 101 of the townspeople were killed

" 30.—The imperial barracks of Sebastopol, which had escaped the conflagration of the 8th, were destroyed by the explosion of a powder-magazine, supposed to have been accidentally fired by an English sailor

" " This day (Sunday) was observed as a Day of Prayer and Thanksgiving, in consequence of the fall of Sebastopol

" " The *Nord*, a paper published at Brussels, but devoted to the interests of Russia, endeavoured to show, that the loss of Sebastopol was an advantage to the government of that country

" " The Emperor Alexander visited Moscow, where, in an address to the governor-general of the city, he says—"Past and present events I accept as the inscrutable will of Providence, who chastens Russia with heavy hours of trial." The Emperor and his brothers then proceeded to Nicholaieff

Oct. 3.—Omar Pasha arrived at Suchum-Kaleh, where he collected an army of 30,000 men.

" " Colonel Windham, on account of his heroic conduct during the assault of the Redan, was made

APPENDIX II

OF THE EVENTS OF THE WAR.

1855.

English governor of Sebastopol, and, at the desire of her Majesty, the rank of major-general was conferred upon him

An Anglo-French commission was appointed to draw up a return of the vast amount of military stores found in Sebastopol, and also to apportion them, according to agreement, between the captors

,, 7.—A portion of the Allied Fleets, with 10,000 French and English troops on board, left Sebastopol and threatened Odessa. The town was spared, the presence of the hostile fleets before it being merely a stratagem to draw off attention from another point

,, 9.—Captain Osborn, in the *Vesuvius*, accompanied by the *Curlew*, *Recruit*, *Weser*, and *Ardent*, commenced a fresh cruise in the Sea of Azoff, where they destroyed an immense number of launches and fisheries

,, 14.—In consequence of a heavy fog, Admirals Lyons and Bruat were detained until this date in the roads of Odessa; but in the evening they arrived off Kinburn

,, 15.—The troops from the Allied Fleets were landed about four miles in the rear of the forts of Kinburn, which was thus cut off from any assistance which might have been sent to relieve it

,, ,, The Emperor of Russia issued a Ukase, ordering a general levy of recruits, consisting of ten in every thousand, throughout the empire

,, ,, Prince Gortschakoff issued an Order of the Day to his soldiers, informing them, that the Emperor had invested him with power to continue or abandon the defence of their positions in the Crimea, according to circumstances

,, 16.—The Allied Forces threw up intrenchments in the neighbourhood of Kinburn

,, 17.—The Allied Squadrons opened a bombardment on the fortifications of Kinburn. The guns were silenced, and after an exhibition of sullen obstinacy, the garrison, consisting of 1,420 men, surrendered; having lost forty-five killed and 130 wounded; eighty-one pieces of cannon were found by the Allies

,, 18.—Fort Nikolaev, at Oczakoff, near Kinburn, was blown up and deserted by the Russians

The Allies reconnoitred the mouths of the rivers Bug and Dnieper.

,, 22.—General Simpson was "relieved" of the command of the army in the Crimea

Nov. 1.—The Emperor Napoleon issued a decree, confirming the promotion of fifty-seven persons, belonging to the French army in the Crimea, to the rank of officer; the nomination of 572 to be knights of the Legion of Honour; as well as the grant of 1,284 military medals, conferred by Marshal Pelissier

,, ,, The advanced guard of Omar Pasha's army in Asia was stationed at about an hour's march from the river Ingour

,, 2.—A body of French and English cavalry made a *reconnaissance* from Eupatoria, and captured 3,000 sheep and nearly 1,500 bullocks, which they found grazing in a valley, under the guard of some Cossacks

,, 4.—Omar Pasha constructed two batteries to command the passage of the river

,, ,, Captain Osborn destroyed an extensive collection of corn, forage, and fuel stacked along the shore at Gheisk-Liman, in the Sea of Azoff. He then visited Glofira, where, also, he destroyed enormous quantities of corn in the teeth of considerable resistance

,, 5.—General Canrobert, who had been recalled from the Crimea, arrived at Stockholm, on a diplomatic mission to the King of Sweden. He returned to Paris on the 2nd of December

,, ,, Government stores at Gheisk were destroyed by Lieutenant Ross

,, 6.—The Turkish army, under Omar Pasha, crossed the river Ingour: the Russians contested the passage, and a battle ensued, in which the latter were defeated. The following day, 347 Russians, including eight officers, were buried by the victors. After the battle, Omar Pasha and his troops reposed at Sugdidi

,, ,, In spite of the resistance offered by Russian troops, Captain Osborn destroyed four miles of corn and hay-stacks, timber-yards, and fish-stores along the coast, to the east of Gheisk

,, 12.—General Simpson left the Crimea for England. Sir William Codrington assumed the command of the army. Major-general Windham was appointed chief of the staff. Sir Colin Campbell obtained leave of absence, and departed for England

The fleets in the Baltic had for some time been slowly returning home. Admiral Dundas remained at Kiel until the middle of November

, 15.—A terrible explosion took place in the French camp at Sebastopol, in consequence of the accidental ignition of a park of artillery, containing 30,000 kilogrammes of powder, 600,000 cartridges, 300 charged shells, and other projectiles. It was attended with fearful loss of life. The French had six officers killed and thirteen wounded; sixty-five men killed and 170 wounded. Of the English who were encamped in the locality, one officer and twenty non-commissioned officers were killed; four officers and 112 non-commissioned officers and soldiers wounded. An English magazine, containing the enormous quantity of 180 tons of powder, narrowly escaped ignition from the falling sparks. It was saved by the heroic conduct of Lieutenant Hope and twenty-five men, who volunteered to mount the roof and cover it with wet blankets

,, ,, Omar Pasha and his army in Asia left Sugdidi, and marched upon Kutais; but, unable to reach it, they went into winter quarters at Choloni

,, ,, The Emperor Napoleon closed the Paris Exhibition. In an admirable review of the political aspect of the war, he stated that—" If Europe once determines on declaring who is right and who is wrong, it will be a great step made towards the solution." * * * " It is definitely public opinion that always gains the last victory."

Colonel Turr, an Hungarian officer in the English service, was arrested in Wallachia by the Austrians, on the false pretence of his being a deserter from their colours. The insulted English government required to be spurred forward by the press before they interfered; and, on their remonstrance, the Emperor of Austria eventually " pardoned" Colonel Turr, and allowed him to be set at liberty

Nov. 19.—Admiral Bruat, the commander of the French fleet in the Black Sea, expired, from the effects of rheumatic gout or cholera

CHRONOLOGICAL PRECIS

1855.

Nov. 20.—Victor Emmanuel, King of Sardinia, left Turin, to proceed to England on a visit to her Majesty

„ 21.—King Oscar of Sweden and Norway entered into a defensive treaty with England and France, with the object of building up in the north a barrier against the encroachments of Russia. It was signed on this day, and the ratifications were exchanged on the 17th of December

„ 23.—Victor Emmanuel arrived at Paris, where he was received with acclamations. He remained there for six days, departing on the evening of the 29th for London

„ 25.—General Williams proceeded with a flag of truce to the Russian camp, and proposed to surrender Kars on honourable terms. He was received with courtesy, and the city capitulated, after the garrison and inhabitants had undergone the most appalling sufferings from famine

„ 27.—General Williams and his staff accepted an invitation to dine with General Mouravieff and his officers

„ 28.—The Russians took possession of Kars

„ 29.—A meeting was held at Willis's rooms, with the Duke of Cambridge in the chair, for the purpose of expressing the national feeling of grateful admiration for the noble services of Miss Nightingale in the hospitals of the East

„ 30.—Victor Emmanuel and suite landed at Dover, where they were received with great honour; an address was presented to his Sardinian Majesty by the Mayor, Aldermen, and Burgesses of the town. On arriving at the Bricklayers' Arms, he was received by Prince Albert, and conducted to Windsor, where he was received by her Majesty at the grand entrance of the castle

Dec. 1.—Victor Emmanuel visited the arsenal at Woolwich, and attended a review of artillery on the common

„ 3.—Victor Emmanuel inspected the dockyard at Portsmouth, and the fleet at Spithead

„ 4.—Victor Emmanuel visited the citizens of London at Guildhall, where an address was presented to him, and an elegant repast prepared

„ 5.—Victor Emmanuel was invested, by her Majesty, with the Order of the Garter

„ 6.—Victor Emmanuel left England for Turin

„ 7.—The Russians surprised the advanced posts of the French in the Valley of Baidar, but after a sharp struggle they were repulsed

„ 16.—Dashing cavalry skirmish near Kertch, between the Russians and the Anglo-Turkish contingent
Severe cases of frost-bite occurred in the Allied camps

„ 22.—The first of the five famous dry docks of Sebastopol was blown up by the French engineers

„ 25.—Christmas-day was spent with due festivity in the British camp in the Crimea. The health of our troops was so good, that the sickness did not exceed seven per cent.

„ 28.—The Austrian government sent Count Valentine Esterhazy to St. Petersburg, with certain propositions for the acceptance of Russia, which it was understood the Allies would accept as a satisfactory basis for the negotiation of peace

„ 29.—The Imperial Guard, having been recalled to France, entered Paris in triumph, where, in the Place de la Bastille, they were met and addressed by the Emperor
A pamphlet, first attributed to the Emperor Napoleon, was published at Paris, entitled *The Necessity of a Congress to Pacify Europe*. It elicited great discussion in the political world

„ 31.—The French and English engineers blew up further portions of the Russian docks

1856.

January.—Theatrical performances, and lectures of an educational character, were got up in the British camp before Sebastopol

„ 10.—A grand Council of War assembled at the Tuileries, under the presidency of the Emperor Napoleon

„ 14.—The Russian government rejected the second and fifth points of the Austrian proposals presented by Count Esterhazy, but accepted the rest of the *ultimatum*. Austria would not submit this conditional acceptance to France and England

„ 15.—The Duke of Cambridge distributed, at Paris, English medals to 15,000 French soldiers

„ 16.—Russia intimated her unconditional acceptance of the Austrian proposals. The news took Europe by surprise

„ 18.—Further progress was made in destroying the Russian docks at Sebastopol

„ 19.—The Russian government, in a circular to its diplomatic agents, announced its acceptance of the Austrian proposals

„ 22.—The Allied Powers demanded certain reforms from the Turkish government with respect to the civil condition of its Christian subjects, as a recompense for the assistance rendered in repulsing the encroachments of Russia. The demand was complied with by the Sultan

„ 23.—Lord Cowley distributed, to a number of the French naval and military officers, the Order of the Bath

„ 24.—News arrived in the Crimea that Russia had accepted the Austrian *ultimatum*, and that a speedy peace might be expected

„ 26.—Still further progress was made in destroying the Russian docks at Sebastopol

„ „ A young soldier, named Day, murdered a wounded artilleryman in an hospital hut for the purpose of robbing him

„ 28.—Sir Edmund Lyons, shortly after his return to England, was *fêted* by the inhabitants of Christchurch, in Hampshire, his native town

„ 29.—The Russians on the north side of Sebastopol opened a heavy fire against the town and its suburbs

„ 31.—The British Parliament reassembled. Her Majesty congratulated the two Houses on the fall of Sebastopol, and stated that she deemed it her duty not to decline any overtures which might reasonably afford a prospect of a safe and honourable peace

„ „ The Sultan attended a ball at the British embassy at Constantinople

„ „ Debates took place in both Houses of Parliament on the Queen's speech, and addresses to her Majesty were agreed upon
General de la Marmora complained to General Codrington, that the agent of some English religious society had been endeavouring to convert the Sardinian soldiers to Protestantism. General Codrington desired him to punish the man if he should be caught repeating the offence

OF THE EVENTS OF THE WAR.

1856.

Feb. 1.—A Protocol was signed at Vienna, setting forth the acceptance, by all parties, of the Austrian proposals as a basis of peace, and deciding that Plenipotentiaries should assemble at Paris

The destruction of the famous Russian docks at Sebastopol was completed after a period of three months' incessant labour.

The ministry published the report of their own commissioners, Sir John M'Neill and Colonel Tulloch, respecting the state of the army in the Crimea during the winter of 1854-'5. Instead of contradicting, it confirmed the statements made concerning the sufferings of our troops and the apathy of superior officers in making attempts to relieve them. The Earls Lucan and Cardigan, General Airey, Colonel Gordon, and Mr. Filder, the commissary-general, were pointed to as not having shown as much energy and foresight as was desirable in men occupying their highly responsible positions

Lords Cardigan and Lucan complained in the House of Lords that their professional characters had been reflected upon in the report. Earl Lucan charged the ministerial report with inaccuracy so far as it referred to him; the Earl of Cardigan wrote a defence of himself to Lord Panmure, which was generally considered to leave the matter just as it found it. The government stated that it was the intention of the Queen to appoint a board of general officers to receive explanations from the officers referred to by Sir John M'Neill and Colonel Tulloch, and to form a report thereon

„ **4.**—The Sultan attended a ball at the French embassy

„ „ The famous Russian fort, Nicholas, at Sebastopol, was utterly destroyed by the French engineers

„ **8.**—Dr. Sandwith, who had returned to England, from Kars, was welcomed and entertained by the gentry of Hull

„ **11.**—Fort Alexander was laid in ruins by the French engineers

„ **14.**—Sir Colin Campbell, who had returned to the Crimea, rejoined the army

„ **18.**—The Sultan granted an imperial Firman, conferring equal rights on all his subjects, without regard to their religion. Great excitement prevailed at Constantinople in consequence

„ **23.**—Day, the murderer of the wounded artilleryman, was hung

„ **24.**—A grand review of 25,000 British infantry took place in the Crimea. Such a number of our troops had not been reviewed at one time for a period of forty years

„ **25.**—General Codrington, in an Order of the Day to his troops, censured the public press on the supposition that it afforded information to the enemy. His order elicited much ridicule in consequence of its not being issued until all active operations of the war were concluded

„ „ The Peace Congress at Paris assembled for the first time. It decided, that an armistice should be concluded between the belligerent armies, and continue in force until the 31st of March. The formal preliminaries of peace were signed, and Prussia was then permitted to send her representatives to the Conference

„ **28.**—Intelligence was received in the Crimea, by electric telegraph, that an armistice had been concluded between the contending states, and arrangements were made for a suspension of hostilities

„ **29.**—Mr. Roebuck moved in the Commons, " That the appointment of a commission of general officers to report upon the report of Sir John M'Neill and Colonel Tulloch, is to substitute an inefficient for a very efficient mode of inquiry; and that the effect of such appointment will be to hide the misconduct of those by whom various departments of our army have been subjected to the command of officers who have been inculpated by the commissioners appointed to inquire into their conduct." The motion was eventually withdrawn

„ „ General Sir De Lacy Evans made a severe and amusing speech in the House, in which he exposed a curious case of army nepotism. Lord Claude Hamilton then charged him with having, on the day after the Battle of Inkermann, advised Lord Raglan to embark the English army, leave their cannon in the trenches at the mercy of the enemy, and abandon the Crimea. General Evans offered an explanation of the matter

Mar. 2.—The Allies and the Russians exchanged civilities across the river Tchernaya

„ „ An order was issued prohibiting the English from approaching the Tchernaya, and holding intercourse with the Russians

„ **3.**—The Emperor Napoleon opened the French Legislative Assembly with a clear summary of the state of events occupying the attention of Europe. " Let us," he said, " await the end of the Conferences with dignity, and let us be equally prepared, if it should be necessary, either again to draw the sword, or to extend the hand to those we have honourably fought"

„ „ Mr. Layard laid before the House of Commons the particulars of Mr. Murray's dispute with the court of Persia

The English army remained in excellent health, but the French troops suffered severely from scurvy and typhus fever.

„ **13.**—Admiral Sir C. Napier, having been returned as one of the representatives of the borough of Southwark, moved, in the House of Commons, for a select committee to inquire into the operations of the British fleet in the Baltic, during the years 1854 and 1855. In doing so he made a violent attack upon Sir James Graham (late First Lord of the Admiralty), who retaliated on him with interest. Admiral Napier withdrew his motion

„ **14.**—At a meeting, near Traktir-bridge, of generals of both the Russian and Allied Armies, the terms of the armistice were definitely agreed upon

„ **16.**—A son was born to the Emperor Napoleon: the imperial infant was denominated the " Child of France"

„ **17.**—A fire broke out at Balaklava during the night, and sixteen men of the army works' corps were burnt to death

„ **23.**—Rejoicing at the Allied camps in the Crimea, on account of the birth of a heir to the imperial throne of France

„ **30.**—A Treaty of Peace was signed by the Plenipotentiaries at Paris. The news was received with great joy in France, but was not hailed with much satisfaction in England. A majority in this country considered a continuance of the war necessary for the vindication of our military glory, and for the attainment of a peace that promised to be permanent

CHRONOLOGICAL PRECIS

1856.

Mar. 31.—The Emperor of Russia, in an imperial Manifesto, announced to his subjects the conclusion of peace

„   „   Peace was proclaimed at Constantinople

The Emperor Alexander visited Moscow, where, in an address to some deputations from the nobles and civil and military authorities, he said, " I prefer the real prosperity of the arts of peace to the vain glory of combats." This speech was followed by the disbanding of the Russian militia

Apr. 2.—Information of the conclusion of peace arrived in the Crimea, and was announced by salutes of 101 guns, fired from each of the three camps

„   3.—A Board of general officers met at Chelsea Hospital, on the authority of a royal warrant, to receive explanations from the officers reflected upon in the Crimean Report of Sir John M'Neill and Colonel Tulloch

„   9.—An Order of the Day, by General Codrington, granted permission to the English army to pass the river Tchernaya—a circumstance which contributed greatly to the growing intimacy between our troops and the Russians

„   13.—The Allied Generals in the Crimea were invited to witness a review of Russian troops. A few days afterwards the Russian general, Lüders, was entertained with a review of both the French and English armies

„   16.—The Peace Congress at Paris held its last sitting. The Protocols of the Conferences were afterwards published

„   „   Sardinia presented a note or protest, on the unhappy state of Italy, to the governments of England and France

„   23.—Her Majesty reviewed at Portsmouth an enormous war fleet, consisting of 240 steam-vessels, including gun-boats, floating batteries, and mortar-vessels

„   27.—The ratifications of the Treaty of Peace were exchanged by the representatives of the Powers engaged in arranging it

„   28.—Commencement of the great debate, in the House of Commons, on the fall of Kars. After three nights' discussion the ministry obtained a majority of 127

„   29.—Peace was formally proclaimed in London

A furious contest took place between the Greek and Armenian Christians in the Church of the Holy Sepulchre, during the distribution of the " holy fire "

The Firman of the Sultan decreeing the equality of his subjects, irrespective of religion, was productive of disturbances

May 4.—This day was appointed as one of general thanksgiving for the peace

„   5.—Debates on the Treaty of Peace occurred in both Houses of Parliament, and addresses to her Majesty were agreed upon

„   7.—General Williams was made a baronet, and, at the suggestion of her Majesty, a pension of £1,000 a-year was conferred upon him

„   8.—Both Houses of Parliament passsed a Vote of Thanks to the Army and Navy

„   9.—Peace celebration at the Crystal Palace

„   13.—England and France entered into a convention with Turkey, binding themselves to withdraw their troops from the Ottoman dominions within six months

„   19.—The inquiry, at Chelsea Hospital, into the accuracy of the Crimean Report by the government commissioners, terminated, after the Board had carried on its investigations during twenty-three sittings

„   „   The freedom of the City of London was presented to Admiral Lyons

„   20.—The Sardinian general and his staff took their departure from the Crimea

„   22.—The Russian emperor visited Warsaw, and issued a sort of amnesty to all Polish exiles. He then proceeded to Berlin, to visit the King of Prussia

„   24.—The anniversary of her Majesty's birthday was observed in the Crimea with great ceremony, and selected for the distribution of French war medals to the English army

„   29.—The great religious ceremony of the Ramazan was observed at Constantinople with more than usual solemnity and splendour, in consequence of the conclusion of peace

„   „   National peace rejoicings; general illuminations and gigantic displays of fireworks took place

„   31.—Terrible inundations occurred in the south of France. Lyons was nearly submerged, and great destruction of life and property ensued

The river Loire also rose, and the inundations extended as far as Orleans

June 2.—The Emperor Alexander left Potsdam to return to St. Petersburg

„   „   The Emperor Napoleon arrived at Lyons for the purpose of alleviating the miseries of the victims of the inundations

„   4.—Lord Gough arrived in the Crimea to perform the ceremony of investiture towards those officers on whom the Order of the Bath had been conferred

„   6.—The ceremony of investiture took place

„   „   The Emperor Napoleon visited Orleans and the valley of the Loire to distribute relief to the sufferers

„   13.—At a meeting held at the Mansion-house, London, to sympathise with the sufferings of the French people, a subscription was opened, and £5,000 contributed on the spot

„   15.—General Williams returned from captivity in Russia, and landed at Dover, where he was received with enthusiasm

„   „   A grand review of the Sardinian troops took place at Turin, when the medals sent them by the Queen of England were distributed by their sovereign, Victor Emmanuel

„   17.—The Turkish contingent departed from Kertch, and the place was restored to the Russians

„   29.—A banquet in honour of General Williams was given at the Army and Navy Club

July 1.—Sir Colin Campbell, having returned to England, visited his native city of Glasgow, where public honours were enthusiastically offered to him

„   8.—Her Majesty reviewed the Guards at Aldershott on their return from the Crimea

„   9.—The Guards marched into London in triumph, and were received with enthusiasm

„   „   A banquet was given to General Williams at the Mansion-house, where the freedom of the City of London, and a sword, of the value of one hundred guineas, were presented to him

OF THE EVENTS OF THE WAR.

1856.
July 12.—The last of the British troops left the Crimea, and the ruins of Sebastopol were abandoned to the Russians.
,, ,, A magnificent dinner to General Williams was given at the Reform Club
,, 15.—The Sultan gave a grand dinner in the throne-room of the imperial palace at Constantinople, in honour of the Allied Generals. In consequence of the opposition of the old Moslem party he did not sit at table with his guests
,, 29.—The last parliamentary war session closed
,, ,, The inhabitants of Sheffield entertained the officers of the 4th Royal Irish Dragoon Guards, to celebrate their return from the Crimea
The Russians endeavoured to reoccupy Serpents' Island, a barren rock in the Black Sea, and would not consent to remove the few men they had sent there until the matter was referred to a meeting of the Peace Plenipotentiaries at Paris
The Board of general officers, assembled at Chelsea Hospital, presented their report to the government, in which they exonerated every officer to whom "want of promptitude or energy" had been imputed, and found out that matters were admirably managed in the Crimea during the winter of 1854-'5
Aug. 1.—Major-general Windham received an enthusiastic ovation from his fellow-townsmen at Norwich
,, 6.—The Russians restored the city of Kars to the Turks
Sept. 7.—The Emperor Alexander II. was crowned at Moscow

INDEX

Index

THE ARMY

Alma, Battle of 1–19
Ambulance Corps 44, 86, 134
Artillery, Royal 1, 22, 43, 68, 85, 103,
127, 215

Balaklava, Action at 34–37
   Prisoners of War at 38

Cavalry
   4th Dragoon Guards 34
   5th Dragoon Guards 34
   1st Dragoons 34
   2nd N.B. Dragoons 35
   6th Dragoons 35
   4th Light Dragoons 35, 38, 42
   8th Hussars 36, 38
   11th Hussars 36, 38, 42
   13th Light Dragoons 37, 38
   17th Lancers 37, 38, 43
Commissariat, Officers of ... 38

Engineers, Royal 2, 69, 85, 132

Field Train Department 215

Guards
   Coldstream Guards,
     1st Bn 3, 24, 46, 86, 136
   Grenadier Guards, 3rd Bn 2, 24, 44, 134
   Scots Fusilier Guards,
     1st Bn 3, 24, 48, 86, 137

Inkermann, Second Battle of 42–65

Land Transport Corps 86, 134

Magazine Explosion, at
   French Siege Train 215–217

Quarries, Assault on 68–84

Redan, First Attack 85–101
   Final Attack 103–125
Regiments of Foot
   1st Regiment, 1st Bn 25, 49, 86, 139
   1st Regiment, 2nd Bn 70, 86, 103, 140
   3rd Regiment 71, 87, 104, 141
   4th Regiment 5, 25, 71, 87, 144
   7th Regiment 5, 25, 49, 71, 87, 105,
145, 216
   9th Regiment 88, 147
   13th Regiment 148
   14th Regiment 73, 88, 149
   17th Regiment 73, 88, 106, 149
   18th Regiment 73, 89, 151
   19th Regiment 7, 25, 50, 73, 91, 106,
153, 216
   20th Regiment 26, 50, 74, 91, 108, 155
   21st Regiment 9, 26, 52, 91, 108, 155,
216
   23rd Regiment 9, 26, 53, 74, 91, 108,
156, 216

Regiments of Foot (contd.)
   28th Regiment 27, 74, 92, 159,
   30th Regiment 10, 27, 53, 74, 92, 110,
160
   31st Regiment 92, 161
   33rd Regiment 11, 27, 54, 74, 92, 111,
163, 216
   34th Regiment 74, 93, 111, 164, 216
   38th Regiment 28, 75, 95, 96, 167
   39th Regiment 76, 96, 168
   41st Regiment 13, 28, 55, 76, 96, 112,
169, 217
   42nd Regiment 13, 28, 96, 114, 172
   44th Regiment 14, 28, 76, 96, 173
   46th Regiment 56, 76, 114, 174
   47th Regiment 14, 29, 56, 76, 98, 114,
175, 217
   48th Regiment 114, 177
   49th Regiment 15, 29, 57, 78, 98, 114,
178, 217
   50th Regiment 30, 58, 79, 98, 181
   55th Regiment 15, 58, 79, 98, 115, 182
   56th Regiment 184
   57th Regiment 30, 59, 80, 98, 116, 185
   62nd Regiment 80, 116, 186
   63rd Regiment 30, 60, 99, 117, 187
   68th Regiment 30, 61, 81, 117, 188
   72nd Regiment 99, 117, 190
   77th Regiment 16, 30, 61, 81, 99, 118,
190, 217
   79th Regiment 16, 31, 118, 194
   88th Regiment 16, 31, 62, 81, 99, 118,
194, 217
   89th Regiment 83, 100, 196
   90th Regiment 83, 100, 120, 198, 217
   93rd Regiment 16, 100, 121, 199
   95th Regiment 17, 31, 63, 83, 121, 200
   96th Regiment 83
   97th Regiment 83, 100, 122, 201,
   Rifle Brigade, 1st Bn 18, 32, 64, 84, 100, 123,
203, 217
   Rifle Brigade, 2nd Bn...... 19, 32, 65, 84, 100, 123,
206, 217

Sappers and Miners, Royal .. 24, 69, 86, 133
Sebastopol, First Bombardment, and
   First Battle of Inkermann
   and
   Minor Actions 22–32
Sebastopol, Second Bombardment of,
   Third Bombardment of,
   Fourth Bombardment of,
   Fifth Bombardment of,
   Final Bombardment of,
   and
   Minor Actions 127–209
Staff. 1, 34, 42, 85

THE ROYAL NAVY AND ROYAL MARINES

THE NAVAL SQUADRON

Sebastopol, Bombardment by
    the Naval Squadron ...221–225

Casualties from H.M. Ships
    Agamemnon 221
    Albion 221
    Arethusa..............222
    Bellerophon 222
    Britannia..............223
    Cyclops...............223
    Firebrand 223
    London...............223
    Niger.................223
    Queen 223
    Retribution...........224
    Rodney...............224
    Sampson 224
    Sanspariel 224
    Sphinx 225
    Spiteful..............225
    Terrible..............225
    Trafalgar 225
    Triton 225
    Vengeance 225

THE NAVAL BRIGADE

Actions, Various,
    1854–1855 228–239

Casualties from H.M. Ships
    Albion 228
    Arethusa..............229
    Beagle................229
    Bellerophon 229
    Britannia..............229
    Dauntless 230
    Diamond..............230
    Firebrand 230
    Leander 230
    Leopard 232
    London...............232
    Niger.................233
    Queen 233
    Rodney...............236
    Trafalgar 237
    Vengeance 238
    Wasp.................238